# Gangway, Lord!

(*The*) **HERE COME THE BRIDES** *Book*

*Gangway, Lord, (The)* Here Come the Brides *Book*
©2010 Jonathan Etter. All Rights Reserved.
No part of this book may be reproduced in any form or by any means, electronic, mechanical, digital, photocopying or recording, except for the inclusion in a review, without permission in writing from the publisher.

 Published in the USA by:
BearManor Media
P O Box 71426
Albany, Georgia 31708
*www.bearmanormedia.com*

ISBN 978-1-59393-506-1

Printed in the United States of America.

Edited by Lon Davis.
Book design by Brian Pearce.

# Gangway, Lord!

## (The) HERE COME THE BRIDES Book

### A Behind-the-Scenes History of (and Episode Guide to) the 1968–70 ABC-TV Series

BY JONATHAN ETTER

# Table of Contents

*To my sister, Sally Jean Etter Christman, who started me on the right path.*

# Acknowledgements

When I began writing the behind-the-scenes history of the TV series, *Here Come the Brides*, I figured I'd be done with it in a year. That was before I started talking to *Brides* leading lady Bridget Hanley. Not only did Bridget provide me with a wealth of information about her fellow cast members, the *Brides* episodes, *Brides* directors, guest stars, etc., but she brought an enormous amount of excitement and enthusiasm to this project. Just as importantly, more than once, when I felt I had conducted my last interview on the subject, Bridget asked me to do more. And just like her *Brides* character Candy Pruitt, Bridget Hanley got her way.

The great enthusiasm and support of the fans from the *Here Come the Brides* Yahoo group was another reason I decided to take this project even further than planned. I am grateful to Teresa – the list owner – for creating the Brides Yahoo group in the first place. Very special thanks are also due to Kim Motteler and Kathy Roberson, and an all-around thank you to the rest of the *Brides* gang on and off the group.

To *Brides* star Robert Brown: Thank you, sir, for taking the time to answer so many questions, provide pictures and write the foreword. Thanks, too, to series semi-regulars Dick Balduzzi and Mitzi Hoag for providing pictures and other materials, and making themselves available for quite a few interviews. A special thank you to both semi-regular Karen Carlson and executive casting director Renee Valente for opening more doors. To series co-star David Soul, the author greatly appreciates your taking the time out from your very busy schedule to discuss your work on the program. And, series regular Susan Tolsky, thank you for being open to so many interviews!

Ditto series semi-regular Robert Biheller, story editor/episode writer William Blinn (truly a great help to this author), wardrobe man Steve Lodge, guest stars Michael Forest, Don Pedro Colley, Marvin Silbersher, and Lynda Day George.

Additional thanks to executive producer Bob Claver, series semi-regulars Eric Chase and Buck Kartalian, Robert Brown stunt double/guest star Dave Cass, guest star/guest director Lou Antonio, guest stars Angel Tompkins, Susan Silo, guest writers Larry Brody, Dorothy C. Fontana, Bridget Hanley's frequent stage co-star, and friend, actress Lee Meriwether, and *Brides* casting director Burt Metcalfe. To the late Henry Beckman's friend, Hillary, I very much appreciate your information concerning the last years of Mr. Beckman's life, and thanks so much for giving me your permission to use Mr. Beckman's remarks to the *Brides* Yahoo group in his chapter. To the International Myeloma Foundation's "Unknown Patient," thank you for allowing me to reprint part of your interview with Ann Lenard for the Mark Lenard chapter. Dewey Webb, how many times have you come through for me, buddy? I was really happy to get that Joan Blondell information. Thanks also to Mercer Girls historian Peri Muhich for her information concerning the Mercer Girls, and for her permission to reprint Asa Mercer's letter to the *New York Times*. Not to mention Bill Endres and his English 102 class/University of Arizona students Nitin Patel, Teresa Gingras, Andrew Thompson, and Kristen Phillips for their superb research on Old Tucson Studios.

Extra special thanks to director Ralph Senensky for allowing me to use a portion of his April 18, 2006 e-mail to *Talking Television* host Dave White for the introductory chapter to this book. This chapter would not have been possible had it not been for the invaluable information provided by the following, additional interviewees: directors Robert Butler, Paul Wendkos, Bruce Kessler, the late Sutton Roley, the late Gerald Mayer, the late stunt coordinator/second assistant director Bill Catching, plus casting director Lynn Stalmaster, and actors Ken Swofford and William Windom. Thanks as well to producers Arthur Gardner and Bruce Lansbury, and actor Peter Mark Richman for their guest commentaries in the *HCTB* episode guide.

To the editors and publishers of the 1968-70 issues of *TV Guide*, I am very much in your debt. Had it not been for your excellent magazine, with its detailed program listings, TV Teletypes, TV Crosswords, and so forth, I could not have constructed so vivid an account of the impact *Here Come the Brides* made during its original primetime run. For providing pictures for the introductory chapter and other sections of the book, I would like to thank Bridget Hanley, Joan Busund, Jerry Ohlinger's Movie Material Store, and Collector's Book Store. Special thanks to my cousin, Amy Kasrprzak, and her husband Robert Kasrprzak for doing the photo scans, (and for them doing so quickly, Bob! Wow!)

To my mother, Ruthanne Etter, sister Betsy Etter, and everyone else in my immediate, and not so immediate family, guys, thanks as always for bearing with me as I once again drove you crazy with another Jon book project!

I'd like to extend an extra special thank you to my editor, Lon Davis, for his advice and constructive criticism, and would be most remiss were I not to thank Brian Pearce for his extraordinary work in designing this book. And, finally, to my publisher, Ben Ohmart, a huge THANK YOU for your tolerance and patience, helpful criticisms, and unwavering enthusiasm and support. Ben, every writer should have a publisher such as you!

"It was a female role in that era, hundreds of years before women's lib, but not women's lib with the angst. It was women's lib with some semblance of a heart, and still a certain vulnerability. I think that if there was anything wrong with women's lib… when it first started, it was so driven that it lost a lot of the humanity."[1]

*Here Come the Brides* leading lady Bridget Hanley

*Bridget Hanley (as Candy Pruitt) at the wheel of the Seamus O'Flynn.* COURTESY
BRIDGET HANLEY

"Today, as I examine my *HCTB's* 'memory file cabinet,' I see clearly Jason, Josh, and Jeremy giving all they had in their hearts and souls fighting to protect all those young women from the east coast [The Brides] who depended on The Bolts to watch over them and keep the bad guys away. It goes without saying, the implication being; all the evils and hardships of everyday life wouldn't happen while they were living with them on Bridal Veil Mountain.

The women were cared for as if each and every one of them were part of a family. Jason Bolt reminded the world how truly valuable the *family* should be nurtured and treated. *'Respect'* is the first word that pops into my mind. It's the story of life as we dreamt it should be from the very beginning of time. Isn't that what all those ancient religious tomes spoke about from all the corners of the planet?"[2]

---

*Here Come the Brides* star Robert Brown

# *Foreword*

As I sit here looking back through the rapid passage of over forty years, my memory-bank has been miraculously refreshed, especially as I think of director E.W. Swackhamer, producer Bob Claver and author William Blinn.

I can vividly see in my "mind's eye" the Columbia Pictures soundstage, located on a backlot in Burbank, California. I was first met at the guarded entrance gate by the former film star, Jackie Cooper, who had become an executive in the film business. At the time, he headed the executive lineup at Screen Gems Productions, which was the name of the company I was about to work for. We drove in together and he gave me a friendly tour of the sound stage and as we walked out through the large sliding doors, he said, "Next, let me show you the best dressing room we have on this lot, bathroom and kitchen included. It was built for Kim Novak, when she worked here years ago, and guess what?... It's yours." He then presented me with a painted metal parking sign with my name on it. I'm embarrassed to admit it remains, to this very day, hidden somewhere under something in my dusty garage store room.

Most of the episodic filming of *HCTB* was created on that twenty-five acre parcel on which a characterful 1860s Seattle set was carefully constructed. It consisted of Lottie's (Joan Blondell) Bar, the brides' living quarters, church and steeple, jail house, Clancey's (Henry Beckman) ship, dock, etc. It also had a small pond hidden behind some tall trees. One scary day after lunch during the second season a fire whipped through the trees and the entire cast and crew heroically fought the flames, and won the day. Another victory for all of us brought the cast and crew even closer together. If the current script we were filming required new and different exteriors, cast and crew would drive for hours to various remote settings. On those many journeys all the passengers got along with each other beautifully. On a daily basis, the warmth and respect we all shared together, on and off camera, richly colored the actors' honest style of performing before the lens. Warmth and respect was the rich fuel that drove all our creative engines as we shot each colorful episode of *Here Come the Brides*.

*HCTB*'s director E.W. Swackhamer was my oldest and dearest friend. We had been drama students together in New York City twenty years earlier. He married lovely Bridget Hanley (Candy) at my home in Brentwood, California, in 1969. While filming the pilot we needed an eighteenth-century New England-type set. So, with producer Bob Claver's gifted help, off we went to MGM's old backlot in Culver City which was just a short thirty minutes drive from Columbia Pictures. That was where Jason Bolt and his brothers, Josh & Jeremiah (David Soul & Bobby Sherman), captured the imagination of Candy Pruitt (Bridget Hanley), Ms. Essie (Mitzi Hoag), and all the other unmarried young women, to find protective, loving, wood-chopping mates. Jason eloquently convinced the women to travel with him on Clancey's three-masted schooner which was headed down around Cape Horn over to the Pacific Ocean, then finally northward bound to Seattle all the way up to the Washington Territory. Later that year I was told that our rented *HCTB* sailing vessel somehow had sunk out there on the high seas. Lucky for us we came home with dry clothes after filming that first episode.

Looking back at yesterday's TV happenings, I realize that they are colored by today's memories. The ones that give me the most pleasure come from fan letters from the viewers who, back in the late 1960s/early 1970s, were still in their teens, dutifully watching *Here Come the Brides* on a weekly basis. Today they have children of their own and, with the aid of the new Sony *HCTB* first year-twenty-six episode disc album, have led the way for their growing family to also enjoy some interesting aspects of each show. I'm told by the many mothers and fathers how their families felt safe and sound sitting there watching the "Brides" confronting the "Bolt brothers" with their problems. While the loggers in town still behaved as they always did. After work, they could always be found at Lottie's, attempting to understand that curious unanswered: "What makes a woman… a woman?" question. They, meaning all the Seattle men, including Jason, Jeremiah, and Joshua, were simply perplexed young men, vainly attempting to fathom life's not-so-clear query; whereas, the "Brides" led the way to understanding that timeless mystery of "MAN vs. WOMAN," etc.

I wonder if those of us from yesterday's world, who are still young at heart, think that today's teenagers might be able to identify with the romantic innocence of all the young women, happily, looking for husbands in the *HCTB* TV series. I hope so.

*Robert Brown*
(Jason Bolt)

1. Bridget Hanley – telephone interview – 2007
2. Robert Brown – by e-mail – 2007

# Introduction

In one of the required history courses I took at Wright State University in Dayton, Ohio, my fellow students and I were asked to read a number of books on one event or historic figure. Following this, we were to present a paper in which we gave examples of the points on which the books agreed, and those on which they differed. When there was disagreement, it was our task to explain why this was so. It was also incumbent upon us to determine what in the books was true, and what was not.

This emphasis on researching a subject (getting as close to the truth as possible), was reinforced by yet another required course. Here, we had to thoroughly research and discuss a subject in the greatest depth imaginable. Every piece of information we could find, every book, every article, had to be read and examined. Then, on the completed paper, each and every source that had been referenced was to be listed.

When I graduated from WSU with a B.A. in history, I began writing and researching books about television and motion pictures. Time and again, I found myself going back to the all-important lessons that I had gleaned during my college studies:

> *Exhaustively research a subject.*
> *Identify what is truth, and what is fiction.*
> *Discuss the subject within the context of its time.*
> *Discuss the subject from as many different points of view as possible.*
> *Compare and contrast — always, always,* always.

These five research tools have been assiduously employed throughout the research and writing of *Gangway Lord, (The) Here Come the Brides Book.* As I stated very clearly to more than one of this book's interviewees, my number-one objective is to provide an accurate and honest account of that classic television series. While some of the revelations contained herein may not please *Here Come the Brides* fans, I would rather run that risk in favor of presenting the truth. For me, a television series as good as *Here Come the Brides* deserves nothing less.

*Jonathan Etter*

"The storybooks all tell us that women are romantic, and men are practical. Well, they're full of shit, I'm sorry. Men are romantic — they're fools, they're fucking fools; women are less romantic. The women are the practical ones — they learn it in child-rearing; the guys aren't all that involved in child-rearing. But the gals…they're the ones who pick up the cleaning and turn on the sprinkler, and all that stuff. They're much more realistic."

---

Robert Butler (Co-creator: *Remington Steele*,
Director: *The Fugitive, The Invaders, Bonanza, The Virginian,
Star Trek, I Spy, Mission: Impossible, Columbo*, etc.)

# Prologue
# *The Real Golden Age of Television*

*The cast, crew, producers, or, as Brides leading lady Bridget Hanley so aptly put it, "EVERY PRECIOUS person that gifted their talents to the series (at least every one there that day").* COURTESY BRIDGET HANLEY

Perhaps no television series better illustrated director Robert Butler's point than the 1968-70 ABC/Screen Gems western/comedy/drama, *Here Come the Brides.* The show featured three strong female regulars: "straw-boss" of the one hundred brides, Candy Pruitt (series leading lady Bridget Hanley); her resourceful, danger-loving friend Biddie Cloom (co-star Susan Tolsky); the show's most frequent voice of reason — saloon owner/businesswoman Lottie Hatfield (veteran actress Joan Blondell); and semi-regular Mitzi Hoag in the role of schoolmarm (and later mayoral candidate) Miss Essie Halliday. *Here Come the Brides* was the perfect conclusion to a decade in which trail-blazing actresses such as Jessica Walter and Melody Patterson were proving young attractive women could be more than decorative objects, and the perfect opening to a decade when a new generation of actresses began enjoying the results of their efforts.

Loosely based on the true story of the Mercer Girls — a group of courageous young women who forsook the comforts of their civilized New England towns and cities to make a new home in the primitive late nineteenth-century Northwest Washington territory — *HCTB* (as its very devoted fans refer to it), with its episode after episode, multi-part storylines, huge ensemble cast (Robert Brown, Bobby Sherman, David Soul, Mark Lenard, Hanley, Blondell, Henry Beckman, Tolsky, et al), high production values, and talented guest stars, writers, and directors, was among those quality television productions of the 1960s and '70s which made these two decades what director Paul Wendkos calls the "Renaissance in American television."[1] Wendkos is not alone in his opinion.

"I have felt for a long time that the 'Golden Age of Television,' usually restricted to those few years of live telecasts from (mainly) New York, actually lasted much longer," stated prolific television series director Ralph Senensky in an April 18, 2006 letter to KSAV 'Talking Television' radio host Dave White. "That the filmed television of the fifties (*Lucy* et al) and the sixties and seventies also were golden.

"Will Geer (Candy Pruitt's grandfather, Benjamin Pruitt in the *HCTB* episode, "A Dream that Glitters") on the set of *The Waltons* one day called me a television pioneer. At the time, I laughed at the idea. With the perspective and objectivity that time provides, I realize that those of us working in television during those years were pioneers. It was a very exciting, creative time."[2]

Enthusiastic people like *HCTB* writer Larry Brody made it so. *Brides* was the very first TV series for which Brody wrote. "I was 23 years old and just off the plane in L.A.," remembers Brody. "But I'd already sold several short stories and a novel while at the University of Iowa, so I had an agent who introduced me to Sylvia Hirsch of the William Morris Agency. Sylvia was the best television agent in the history of the medium. Everyone knew her and everyone trusted her. This made her terrific at getting new talent a break.

"Within 6 weeks of arriving on the scene, I had a feature film deal at MGM, and that seems to have gotten the attention of (*HCTB* director E.W. Swackhamer's assistant) Stan Schwimmer, who brought me into *BRIDES*. Some writers would've thought TV was a step down from what I already was doing, but I loved television and had always wanted to write TV and not films. Go figure."[3]

Brody's fellow writer, and friend, Dorothy C. Fontana, also enjoyed writing for television. Guaranteed television immortality thanks to her work on the much-beloved *Star Trek*, Fontana wrote in quite a few other genres as well, including the westerns *Bonanza, Big Valley, Lancer, High Chaparral,* and *Kung Fu.*

"All those westerns were fun to write," says Fontana. "By the time I left *Star Trek* [before the third season], I had a fair body of credits to my name, and many were westerns. My agent got busy sending me around for interviews and to pitch, and I was lucky in being able to come up with stories that suited the producers. I did three

*Bonanza*s, two for *Big Valley* for producer Lou Morheim, two for *Lancer* for my old boss, Samuel A. Peeples, two *High Chaparral* for producer Don Balluck [writer of the *HCTB* episode, "Wives for Wakando."] On the *Kung Fu,* I only had a story sale. These shows all had a different tone and style, and it was interesting and challenging to be able to write for them. Any freelance writer has to catch each show's style and how the actors work together as a cast, how they project their characters — and then you bring in a guest actor or a strong situation to challenge them. The shows then had very small staffs — usually an executive producer, a producer, perhaps an associate producer and/or story editor. Most often, I worked directly with the producer, who was almost always also a writer and a hands-on producer of the series. Almost all of them were men. I have to say I earned a 'degree' in writing working with these talented people because they all had something about writing to teach me."[4]

Adds Larry Brody: "I watched every episode of *Here Come the Brides* because, dammit, I loved TV. Also, I wanted to learn as much as I could about writing, and by seeing episodes of a series I'd written for I could learn more about tailoring a script for the specific needs of a show."[5]

If Larry Brody was exposed to good writing through series like *Here Come the Brides, Brides* story editor/episode writer William Blinn could see that television was open to good storytelling through early '60s series like *Route 66.* Created by *Naked City's* executive producer Herbert B. Leonard and his associate, Stirling Silliphant, the great difficulties in producing this constantly on-location, across-the-United States series were considerably lessened by the speed with which Silliphant could produce a script. Like *Bonanza,* the stories on *Route 66* ranged from comedy to drama. Incredibly, the majority of the one hundred-plus episodes were written by Silliphant.

Another fast writer was *12 O'Clock High/FBI/Cade's County* producer Charles Larson. "I adored Charles Larson," enthuses *12/FBI* series director Ralph Senensky. "He was just so adaptable and so fast. Many times the script you were handed during your prep period was not the script you ended up shooting. Charlie was very good at character studies; he just rewrote and deepened the interactions between the people. He did so much rewriting, but he would not take partial credit. Some producers did that, that way they could claim a percentage of the residuals."[6]

A guest star on *The FBI,* plus other Quinn Martin series including *Cannon* and *The Streets of San Francisco, Here Come the Brides* co-star David Soul was able to give good performances on those programs thanks to his early television work in series like *Brides.* "What a good way for a young actor to learn," says Soul. "You'd learn from the construction people, from these people who had been around, working for some time. The studios actually carried their crews — a crew got assigned to the show, and the degree to which such things [as *Brides* and other complex, production-heavy pieces including *The FBI, McCloud, The Monkees*] could be done with such alacrity and quality was amazing. The crews were what made the shows. We had some great people"[7]

Among them, *HCTB* star Robert Brown's stunt double Dave Cass, men's costumer Pat McGrath, and director of photography Fred H. Jackman. Other series such as *Star Trek* had creative stuntmen, including the late Bill Catching. Catching doubled for Leonard Nimoy in the first season of *Trek*. Remembers Catching, "Everybody on *Star Trek* didn't know what the hell they were doing. I did about the first eighteen. I said, 'What in the hell is this stuff? What kind of shit is this? How did I get into this? This won't last a year.' And it's still on the air."[8]

Starting his lengthy TV career on syndicated shows such as *The Cisco Kid*, and ZIV-TV's *I Led Three Lives* and *Sea Hunt*, Bill Catching eventually moved into

Route 66's *Todd Stiles (Martin Milner) and Buz Murdock (George Maharis) give their undivided attention to an unknown lovely in a publicity shot for the 1960-64 CBS-TV/ Screen Gems series.*

acting roles in *Bonanza, Kung Fu,* and *McCloud.* On *McCloud,* Catching also served as the program's stunt coordinator. Bill Catching's longevity in the business had much to do with the practical approach he took to his work. "Stuntmen were trying to teach the actor how to move like they do," he explains. "I thought, 'That doesn't seem right to me.' So when I went to double somebody, I would watch them, how they walked; I would pick up something from their movement that I would put in my action for them. I really and honestly think that's why I worked so much. Assistant directors and production managers would say, 'Get Catching. He can double anybody.'"[9]

Among them, *McCloud* guest Jaclyn Smith!

Not too surprisingly, Smith was fond of Catching. *Brides'* Bridget Hanley felt similarly about Dave Cass. Hanley also enjoyed the extras and the crew. She thought very highly of the series' guest casts as well. "We were very proud to have the people that we had on our show," states Hanley. "I think we got the cream of the crop. A lot of good character actors." [10] "A lot of the guys were out of New York," remembers David Soul. "We had people like Daniel J. Travanti and Philip Bruns. Dick Balduzzi, Vic Tayback — real character actors. We had a collection of fine actors and actresses, like Kathleen Widdoes. The people acting in television — there wasn't a lot of positioning and positing. We were real people who just happened to be actors. People who had other interests."[11]

Casting directors such as Lynn Stalmaster and *Brides'* Renee Valente were among the folks responsible for television's fine guest casts. "The business was so much fun in those days," says Stalmaster. "I loved actors who would not play it in the conventional, stereotypical way. I find the word, 'type' abhorrent. That started with me on *Gunsmoke.* I'd always give actors an opportunity to play characters other than what they were identified with."[12]

With a performer like *HCTB* guest star Lynda Day George, typecasting was never a problem. "I never was typecast," declares George. "I never gave anybody that opportunity. If somebody gave me a character that I'd done before, I wouldn't turn it down. I'd just find another character to do. I may have done something similar, but it wouldn't be the same. And I have to say I was very fortunate when I did those characters, because when I did them, I was able to surprise folks. So, those folks were pleased; they expected something different from me each time I worked. They weren't afraid that I was gonna just keep repeating the same character over and over and over. But I never knew what I was gonna come up with until I looked at the script. I had to come up with something fast. You don't have a lot of time when you're working in television."[13]

That was especially true when one was doing a half-hour action series like *The Felony Squad* or a 1950s series such as *The West Point Story.* Recalls *West Point* (and two-time *HCTB*) guest Michael Forest, "They had only two and a half days to do a half-hour show, so they had to really hit it, and hit it hard — they would do two shows in a week. One would finish at noon — they would start the next one at one or two o'clock in the afternoon — sometimes they'd go a whole three days on a half-hour show. Some of those shows had a lot of production value that they had to deal with. They couldn't be wasting time. So you'd better know your lines and get it done, then they could get it in the can. I mean television was kind of rough and tough."[14]

Directors like the late Sutton Roley added to the stress. Known for his extreme close-ups on actors, Roley's 'You Are There' style was perfect for WWII series such as *Combat* and *Rat Patrol*. Having directed more than one war series himself (among them *12 O'Clock High* and *Garrison's Gorillas*), the late Gerald Mayer has nothing but praise for the directors who did such series. "Those were tough shows," states Mayer. "Lots of production. I just remember *Garrison* as a tough show. That series didn't go. It was a good series. Just too expensive. Those [war] shows were damn hard to do. Because you've got guys marching, you've got long lines [of soldiers] to cover, lots of actors to accommodate, and you know, creating reality out of a handful of actors is a real problem. You have to shoot them, and reshoot them, and somehow make it seem like three times as many guys as there really are. It's a real pain in the ass. But a lot of guys were very good at it. The guys who did *The Rat Patrol*, guys like Sutton Roley and John Peyser, were terrific at it."[15]

An episode of a half-hour series (e.g. *Rat Patrol*) was shot in three days or less; as for hour-long shows (e.g. *Combat*), they were made in six or seven days. Without question, working in filmed television could be exhausting. As *Rat Patrol/Immortal* star Christopher George and *O.K. Crackerby/Bracken's World* regular Laraine Stephens made clear to the interviewer chatting with them in a promotional TV spot for their upcoming 1969 big-screen feature, *The Thousand Plane Raid*. "Television, you just go and go and go and you never stop," George said. "Time" Stephens added, was a huge problem. "Time. A schedule to be kept." "When you work," added George, "you lose twenty to twenty-five pounds and your nerves are shot and it's…you never have any time for yourself."[16]

Especially, if, as in the case of *Here Come the Brides* leading lady Bridget Hanley, one was doing a play like *Under the Yum Yum Tree*. Remembered Hanley in a 1975 fan newsletter, "That's kind of grueling. You do your show. It gets over at 11:30 and by the time you unwind it's 1:00 in the morning. Then you get up at 4:00 [a.m.] to do your film."[17]

"The pressure was fierce," adds *Brides* guest star/director Lou Antonio. "I think at one time, and Jud Taylor was president of the Director's Guild at the time, they did an actuary — you know, a life expectancy actuary, and (according to) the actuary of assistant director and directors in episodic television you would live to be forty-nine years old. I got glaucoma from all the pressure."[18]

"I found that as a director, I would get burned out," adds Gerald Mayer "They were doing thirty shows a year. They were grinding schedules. You had three, possibly four days [to prepare]. You reported to the location, ready to shoot at sun-up. The minute there was enough light to shoot, you rolled the camera. You'd do the night-shooting on Friday, if you could contain your night-shooting to one night. Actors had to have a twelve-hour turnaround, the crew a ten-hour turnaround."[19]

Gerald Mayer was very good when dealing with actors. That was not the case with *HCTB* director Nicholas Colasanto. Remembers *Brides* semi-regular Robert Biheller, "Colasanto was from the John Cassavettes school. I don't know where he came off. He kept on telling me that I was like the juvenile delinquents I used to play, embarrassing me in front of this group gathered there. He was an ass! The thing was for me to come in and say, 'Josh, something's going on down at the barn. Better come quick!' You know, a typical Corky scene, and Colasanto — the son of a bitch — made a big friggin' deal out of it. I mean there were people standing around, people who'd come to watch the shoot, and every time I'd come in and do this, he'd go, 'CUT! What the hell is that? What are you doing" What d'ya think, you're a juvenile delinquent like you use'ta be? You're acting like a juvenile delinquent here!' Then I'd do it again. 'CUT!' And he would give me shit. It got to the point where I was pretty pissed. So finally after we got the take, I went to Robert, and I said, 'This guy is giving me trouble, and I don't know why, but it's ridiculous.' Robert said, 'I'll take care of it,' and he did. I don't think the guy ever worked on the show again. So I can't say enough about Robert Brown. Robert Brown was a real gentleman. A real good guy."[20]

Robert Brown did his best to keep a friendly mood on the *Brides* set. "I was aware of other actors coming on stage with us," says Brown, "so I tried to make them feel as though they'd been there all along. That way we kept the sense of camaraderie, I guess. So it had a sweetness to it. Swackhamer helped to do that. He created the tone; I kept it going for him when he wasn't on the set and other people were doing the job."[21]

Accommodating *Brides* guest stars such as "Man of the Family's" Angel Tompkins further eased the strain of production. "In my illusion, my fantasy, or reality, there's courtesy, camaraderie, appreciation," says Tompkins. "An interaction, as if you were on stage and the audience was watching. That's my world that I choose to live in, and I can't always create it. But that's the one I keep working for. So, for me, it is about camaraderie, it is about friendship, it is about meeting people of like interests. Nobody had to agree with anybody else but my concept of when you went to work on a show, you got hired because you were not only qualified, but there was something friendly about you that appealed to the people who were hiring in such a way that you fit in the ensemble of the regular cast."

Showing consideration for the crew was very high on Angel Tompkins' list. "I was taught early on make friends with the crew," says Tompkins, "[to] be gracious and friendly to the crew. And to the cameraman and the gaffers; in terms of the lighting and so forth, they'll all help you out."

Tompkins could also help a show thanks to her ability to work amidst chaos. "Actors that can rehearse in total chaos — those are people that generally do comedy," explains the actress. "They can ad lib a great deal. I can do that. But when you're doing more serious stuff, and you're trying to do difficult moves, it's hard for you to remember everything. If the dialogue is not working well, it's difficult to spew out — you have to work twice as hard. When the production is going great, when the producers and the directors have everybody on the set working with a sense of awe and wonderment, then it's easy, the actors are just fine. But when there's chaos on the set and rancor and disrespect coming from higher up down to the grips and props, when wardrobe is being driven crazy, the actors have to work twice as hard because you don't know where it's coming from, you don't know where the discord is coming from, you don't know if it's an opinion about what you're doing, you don't know what the mumbling and the grumbling behind the lights is all about while you're trying to rehearse. That's why they demand 'Quiet' on the set. Because [noise] does interfere with the acting process." [22]

Like any television series, *Here Come the Brides* had its share of production problems. Women's costumer Betsy Cox definitely had her work cut out for her. As the number of "brides" Jason Bolt and his brothers brought back to Seattle numbered one hundred, there were times Cox had to dress some sixty-seven actresses!

"The wardrobe people really worked hard," praises *Brides* star David Soul. "You had all these loggers and brides. Sometimes, you might have fifteen characters on the set. That's a lot of people on the set. It was a very scaled-up production." [23]

Cox faced other difficulties, too. Remembered Bridget Hanley during an on-line chat with the *HCTB* fans, "when Susan [Tolsky] and I would return from lunch, Betsy Cox would have to put double-sided tape on the bodice V of our dresses because otherwise they would pop up and put someone's eye out. It was mortifying." [24]

While Hanley and *Brides* story editor William Blinn might not have liked it when there were fewer muddy streets during the second season; chances are Cox was not as upset. The mud certainly took its toll on the women's costumes. "We went through more pairs of Mary Janes than you can imagine," laughs Hanley, "and our socks, I'm sure they never got them clean. Or the hems of our dresses, as we came screaming out of the dormitory, or marching out of the dormitory, or crying out of the dormitory, or sneaking out of the dormitory. I don't know how Betsy Cox ever got them clean." [25]

Bridget Hanley's *Brides* co-star Susan Tolsky shared her friend Hanley's admiration of Cox. Tolsky appreciated Cox for a further reason. "Betsy Cox had migraines, like I did," states the actress. "She really got sick. I would get, like, queasy. Migraines are horrible. I got them at a very young age, and it's horrible, there's no relief. There was nothing you could take that would stop it, and I want to tell you there is a high incident of suicide among migraine sufferers. Only within probably the last five or six years did they develop a medication for migraines." [26]

Being very near-sighted as was Bridget Hanley, Susan Tolsky found doing a costume piece like *Here Come the Brides* visually and physically challenging. With the exception of guest Mary Wilcox in the first season's "A Jew Named Sullivan," and Meg Foster in the second season's "Two Worlds," none of the *Brides* women were ever shown wearing glasses. "Susan and I were both very near sighted," laughs Hanley, "and whenever we came on camera, we would over-shoot our mark unless they left big BOULDERS in our path. In fact, I spent a great deal of time falling down. I still do." [27]

Thanks to the Los Angeles smog, Bridget Hanley didn't have the option of wearing hard contact lenses. "At the time," explains the actress, "they only had the hard contact lenses; because of the smog and the heat, I wasn't able to wear my lenses very often. I mean to wear them all day for a shoot, I just couldn't. Susan Tolsky was the same way. She'd take her glasses off; I don't think she ever had contact lenses. Anyway, when I was under contract, when I didn't have my contact lens in or my glasses, because I didn't want to wear my glasses a lot, I would just smile as I walked down the lot so I wouldn't offend anyone."

Since both Hanley and Tolsky went without contacts or glasses, "we were like two blind bats," laughs Hanley. "We would — there was one show ["Wives for Wakando"] when we had to run into a shot from way back in the berm, screaming; I think Susan Howard was in that too, and I have a picture of all of us running and screaming. Anyway, Susan [Tolsky] and I were alone on this one shot, and they kept giving us marks, and we'd overshoot our marks because we could not see. She was counting on me to stop; I was counting on her to stop. Well, finally they put a big boulder there, and we were finally able to see it, but I [still] tripped over it. So we became the laughingstock; they would always kid us if we had long distance stuff to do."[28]

But it wasn't just in action scenes, like "Wives for Wakando," for which the *Here Come the Brides* directors might find it necessary to reshoot the same scene more times than usual. Remembers Tolsky: "we were all in Lottie's [the town saloon run by Joan Blondell's character], late in the day, and this is such an actor's nightmare. There was Bobby, David, Bridget, and me, I think it was the three Bolts and Bridget and me. We were in Lottie's, at a round table, and of course's it's very difficult to shoot a round table, because you shoot a master, and then you've got to do all of your coverage. And it was late in the day. Well, we had to get this scene, of all of us talking about something, the guys had beer, the girls had something called Sarsaparilla — I think it was root beer — because I don't drink and I never have. Well, the worst thing that could happen not only to one actor…is, we got the giggles. We started and each time we heard, 'Okay, okay. Settle down. Speed. Action,' one of us would start laughing. And the guys had beer. So they kept sipping the beer trying to get the scene. Well, the day goes on, and it's getting late in the day, and they're drinking more beer. And we're laughing. It took us so long to get that scene, and me, I'm the worst. I can't help it, but if I start, it was like you hold it in, and you just do a spit take because you can't hold your laughter back. It took — I'm not kidding you — it took close to an hour to get the scene done, so that by the end of that, they [the guys] were so lit. We just, we were sipping root beer, so we didn't have a problem, but they were having just the best old time. We could not stop laughing, and the thing that's so funny, too, is that our director, what was so funny is that directors try everything, they cajole you, [imitating the director laughing], 'Okay now, You got it out of your system,' and when they did that, we'd start laughing. And then they're 'All right. Everybody! You're costing money!' And they start screaming. But it doesn't matter what they do. As soon as we hear, 'Speed. Action,' that's it. We're laughing. So, that beer — those guys were getting it down."[29]

Reality wasn't always fun, however, as evidenced by *Brides* guest and director Lou Antonio's experience on *Naked City*. Recalls Antonio, "Bobby Duvall and I played the sons of Sylvia Sidney and they [the *Naked City* company] didn't always go by the rules apparently. We had to shoot blanks out of two machine guns from a moving car in Harlem. So, we were going along these streets, Bobby and I, without a police escort. They didn't know we were a movie company firing blanks from these two machine guns, because these plainclothesmen kneeled down and came up on us; there'd been a murder the night before. No one had told them we'd be shooting this show. That was pretty spooky. To see guys pulling pistols on you. Thank God we were going fast."[30]

Quite familiar with the methods of Screen Gems, thanks to his work on other Gems series like *Route 66* and *The Monkees*, Lou Antonio was greatly impressed by the way his fellow *Here Come the Brides* directors managed to meet the show's deadline. "That was a heavy show," declares Antonio. "I don't know how the directors did it. With that rain, and all of those…if you had the cast sitting around a table, man, with that many regulars, you had to do something like eight close-ups. And, because of the pressure on that, and so much to do with rain and horses and eight regulars, and no budgets, and only six days, the crew was fast, they had to be fast; the directors had to shoot simply."

Given the tight budgets of Screen Gems, brand-new directors like Antonio would have to "scramble around" when they helmed a series episode. Remembers Antonio, "they only had one zoom camera — zoom lens, and when I directed *The Young Rebels* — with Lou Gossett and David Soul, I had a big battle scene. So I ordered the zoom lens because in those days, you didn't have two cameras, they were just too tight, so I had to reserve one zoom lens. [When] I came in to work to shoot the battle scene, with my preparation of the zoom, the cameraman said, 'They took it away from us. We don't get it. They gave it to another company.'"[31]

That meant Antonio had to come up with something quick. That was when on-screen errors were likely to creep in. To this day, *Brides* fans chuckle about the scene of Jason Bolt and Miss Essie looking down on the people of Seattle from the window of her one-story house in the series' seventh-aired episode, director E.W. Swackhamer's "Lovers and Wanderers." "Just because it's one-story doesn't mean it can't be up on a hill," responds *HCTB* executive producer Bob Claver. "One never knows…people always like to play, 'gotcha.' I don't remember where the exterior was, but if the exterior was up on a hill, then you get that shot. And Swack was a person…it would take a gun to his head to give up a really good shot because he did like pretty pictures. He didn't do distorted angles — not too much, because I hate that. Because, here's the point, you have a job to tell the story. I don't want an audience saying, 'Did you see that shot, that angle? That's interesting.' That's no good — that's not good storytelling, that's distracting. I don't like that stuff. I never use that as a director myself. And I don't like that in my shows. I don't like anything that you notice. I mean it's silly: you've got wonderful actors, allegedly a good script, and even a guy like Scorsese, he does a lot of picture taking that is distracting to me, and I don't know why he does that, cuz he's so good. I mean, if it's part of the storytelling, it's perfect, but all of a sudden you've got a shot, and you've got an audience looking at a shot. That takes the audience out of the story; it has no value."[32]

Director Bruce Kessler saw it differently. "If you're in a set scene, where it's a real set for a long time, it makes it more interesting if you change the angle a little," states Kessler. "It makes the audience kind of blink and pay attention."[33]

"I didn't mind the stuff Swack did," admits Claver. "He didn't do too much camera stuff, he did wide shots, but not tricky, and if he was doing it, it was because he thought it would advance the story. If I saw it, and I didn't like it, we had a talk about it, because that's my job. But I don't remember having any problems with Swack, 'cuz if we ever did start talking about it, there were never two people that would have gotten in a bigger fight than us two. We didn't butt heads, but if we did, it would be a bad head-butting."[34]

Despite the character she portrayed, one wasn't likely to 'butt heads' with *Brides* leading lady Bridget Hanley on the set of the series. "Bridget was the height of ingénue grace and energy and fun," praises *Brides* story editor William Blinn. "She would try anything. She was not protective of the Bridget Hanley image. She was whatever was on the page. Whatever she was called to do, she would do. And if she had a problem, it was always voiced in the most reasonable and straightforward and cooperative way possible.

"Bridget likes the process," continues Blinn. "She likes being on camera. I don't mean in an ego sense. She likes 'What am I doing? What is my character about? How can I make this more interesting?' She's a member of Theater West, as am I, and it's a delight to go in and see her work. And if you tell Bridget, 'I want to have something read next Tuesday, but it's a very small role,' that doesn't matter to Bridget."[35]

The acting bug bit Bridget Hanley quite early in life — in elementary school. Recalls the actress, "The teacher gave us this assignment — I don't remember what the subject was, but we could either write a paper on the subject, or write a play. So I went, 'Ah-hah.' I wrote a play that was later done as the Christmas show for the school, and of course, (laughing) I played the leading role! I went on to do more of those kinds of things in junior high and high school. And my first part in high school — my [older] sister got the lead; she was ahead of me in school — she got the lead in the school play. I was so jealous that I auditioned, and I got the part of the lady ambulance driver. When we did the performances, I got really great laughs. That was what hooked me. It was then when I decided that was what I wanted to do. I not only kept writing skits and things and starring in them, but I did all the school plays and all of that."

Because of her great love for acting, and her excitement concerning her *Brides* character, Candy Pruitt, Hanley always managed to keep the Candy character fresh and alive. "I never got tired of my character," affirms the actress. "Never! Because Candy...there was always something that she could do. Or [she'd come up with] a different way to go about it. I was just gifted with this incredible before-her-time woman, and I was thrilled. I mean to play someone who had such kind of courage and still could have the femininity just because of that era, who could still be a challenger of the male ego, go in for what she felt was right, and not be afraid to confront...and then, you know the romance with Bobby...so wonderful and dear and sweet. I really never felt curtailed in my character at all."[36]

Unfortunately, performers like Bridget Hanley became fewer and fewer as television entered the 1980s. "And it makes you wonder..." says Lynda Day George. "My God! What the hell happened? Because, I look out there today, and it's like a desert. Not because these performers that are out there right now don't have the ability, but because they don't do it! They don't take another step! They do surface work. And that doesn't...it doesn't go anywhere. I mean...'Come on, guys!'"[37]

Adds Susan Tolsky, "Look at those people we had on the show. They were the heart…they were television actors. And whether they came from stage or not, look at the people that we had! They were astounding guest stars. Meg Foster — she had a career! My God, we just had amazing…I mean these are people who had series, and who had credits. So I think it was the tail end of an era that just is not there anymore. Because these people…I don't remember people quibbling about money. We were so thrilled to be working, and that was not just because how young I was. We were thrilled to be working! We were in television. We knew. I don't care how fresh we were in the business. I knew even then that I was now part of television history. I'm not talking about there're gonna be books written about me, that's not what I'm saying. It's just that 'I'm part of television history' — I was very aware of that. And now, it's like 'How much money am I gonna make?'"[38]

"See," explains George, "that was a time when they had real actors on TV, instead of this adorable little thing that just came into town. Can't act her way out of a paper bag, but she's got a real cute backside — she looks great from behind, she caught some guy's eye…she said, 'Okay,' and that was that. 'I want to be a star. I can worry about acting later.' I guess so."[39]

Adds Hanley, "It was less about making money, and more about…it may not have been as devastatingly artistic as it's become, because I think everything grows. But it was before television [was] so big, becoming bigger and better and all of that. I just find it so impersonal now. That's too bad because [then] every studio had their own kind of personality, I don't know how else to put it. I just feel very lucky to have experienced the fact that we were all like families - each studio had its own personality, and people gathered there to do their [the studio's] kind of work; it was not all the same."[40]

"In films at that time, they filmed two different pages a day of script," explains Susan Tolsky. "We did ten to twelve, and we did it in a week. We did it in a five-day schedule, and we did exterior and interior. I mean that's insane."[41]

Gifted writers, producers, directors, talented casts, and crews made that possible. Remembers *Brides* story editor William Blinn: "The reality of the show was that it was collaborative. I think it was probably all a stew of people who came up with various things. It was me with a script, and Claver with a script, and [Paul Junger] Witt with a script. And we had some good directors that had thoughts. Directors like Bill Claxton could have cared less, you know, 'just send me the script and let me know where I show up and I'll shoot it for you.' [But] Swack had a lot of good story ideas and stuff he wanted to do. He'd come in and say, 'You know what you could do with this thing?' and he'd have a twitch, or a contribution to make that would usually make everything better. I don't recall Swack ever saying, 'Okay, fine. I'll shoot it.' He'd always say, 'Well, how about this? Can we do this?' He had a very active and creative mind."[42]

Given the fierce competition in television amongst the three networks, not to mention ABC's need for a hit television series, this was a very good thing. Not having been in the business as long as rivals CBS and NBC, ABC was more willing to gamble with a risky TV series such as *Here Come the Brides*. Noted *Washington*

*Post-TV Channels* television critic Lawrence Laurent, the show "lacked an established, big-name, box-office star," and cast two young singers (David Soul and Bobby Sherman) in straight acting roles." The lead female character was "assigned to the little known Bridget Hanley. Even the important role of saloon-keeper Lottie was changed at the last minute."

According to Laurent, *Here Come the Brides* violated one of the cardinal rules in television: "that a series must have a simple premise; a basic plot that can be summarized in 30 seconds or less." To Laurent, the show's plot line was "terribly involved." Yet, despite such dramatic "flaws," which actually foreshadowed the multi-character, multi-part storylines which came to define such 1980s series as *Hill Street Blues* and *St. Elsewhere*, critic Laurent cited two reasons *Brides* defied the expectations for its failure. "One is the larger-than-life, he-man zest that [Robert] Brown has brought to the role of Jason Bolt. The character appears on TV as a shaggy, cheerful bundle of windy competence that is rare among heroes in the 21-inch world." The other was "the tuneful music that Hugo Montenegro wrote for the series. The plinky strains of 'Seattle' enliven the talk-filled episodes and make bearable the undistinguished writing." [43]

To be sure, Robert Brown's portrayal of Jason Bolt, and the music of Hugo Montenegro were definite assets to *Here Come the Brides*, but anyone who saw first-season shows like "A Jew Named Sullivan," "The Stand-Off," "A Christmas Place," or "Democracy Inaction," would hardly call this undistinguished writing. *HCTB* guest star Angel Tompkins certainly thought highly of *Brides*. Explains the actress, "At that time [in the business], the attitude was, 'women can't be friends.' You know, you have the top five [actresses] who always get called first, who go to all the auditions. Nobody talks to each other, everybody sits outside, looking at each other; nobody can be friends. Well, that's a male myth — women, mothers, and grandmothers and daughters have kept this country running. And the women on that show...*Here Come the Brides* was a promise that a lot of women would actually be working together, that they would have a place to work."[44]

This attitude was reflected on *Brides* not just in Bridget Hanley's take-charge/no-nonsense Candy Pruitt, or through semi-regular Mitzi Hoag's role as schoolmarm Miss Essie, but through one-time characters like Kathleen Widdoes' Dr. Allyn E. Wright, Linda Marsh's Rachel Miller, and Stefani Warren's Lulu Bright. When it came to one-time female characters, *Brides* writers such as Oliver Crawford, Jack Miller, Larry Brody, and Robert Goodwin certainly came up with some rich ones. In fact, the series concluded with a Miller story in which the three Bolt brothers and the rest of the men of Seattle go under contract to a woman who has such grand plans for Seattle that the town can't help but expand.

The series itself expanded the western genre by setting its dramatic situation in the post-Civil War Pacific Northwest — an area of the country where there was considerable precipitation. A western series, with rain, or where it had just rained, was certainly a novelty. The show further displayed originality though the novelty of its concept. Not only did it begin with, and continue to play out an epic theme — the establishment of the town of Seattle — not only did it introduce one of the largest regular (and semi-regular) casts in television history, it frequently ran a number of (continuing) stories in each episode.

*Brides'* uncommon (and risky) approach seemed to work. During its first season it moved from 48th place to 35th place in the Nielsens. In the process it drove Ivan Tors' African adventure *Daktari* off the air. CBS replaced this series with the powerhouse variety show, *The Glen Campbell Goodtime Hour*, as for NBC, it continued to stay with its longtime ratings winner — the quality movie-length western, *The Virginian*.

*Here Come the Brides* also garnered rave reviews very early in its run. "Chalk it up as one of the fresher and entertaining freshman contenders going this fall,"[45] said *Variety's* Pit in his review of the pilot episode, "Here Come the Brides." *TV Guide's* Cleveland Amory was positively glowing in his December 28, 1968-January 3, 1969 review. Describing *Brides* as a "logging-camp saga," "handsomely awash with interesting and even new-fashioned characters," Amory then remarked about the pilot, "This is the kind of comedy that the average show would make so corny that you just couldn't bear it. But in this episode, saints be, you not only bear it, you grin and do so."[46]

Reviews of *Here Come the Brides* were almost as positive the second year. Said *Variety's* Mor of the second-season premiere, "A Far Cry from Yesterday": "Photography and sets were of movie caliber...the acting was first rate throughout."[47] The show also did quite a few ahead-of-their-time stories such as "A Crying Need," "A Jew Named Sullivan," and "Lorenzo Bush."

A definite factor in *Here Come the Brides'* considerable success was story editor William Blinn. Having worked on the excellent *Bonanza* for a year as one of the story consultants, Blinn gained invaluable experience writing in the western genre. Case in point: the lesson taught him by director William Witney during Blinn's scripting of the Wayne Newton episode, "The Unwritten Commandment." "Tell you the kind of thing where you learn, and you just soak up their knowledge," begins Blinn. "Now Billy Witney directed everything in the world. At one time he was the youngest director in Hollywood — I think he was like nineteen when he became a full-fledged director. He started out as a second, the first got injured, and the director quit, and they were on location and so he became a full-fledged director at nineteen. At any rate, we were doing a truly dreadful episode that I had written — Wayne Newton's television debut. Wayne Newton was a big ticket — 'Danke Schoen' and all that, and he had that strange voice and that strange presentation, maybe the best guy in the world. At any rate, as part of the deal, as part of the contract, he had to sing four songs — he had to sing 'Scarlet Ribbons,' 'Danny Boy,' 'Old Joe Clark' and 'Rock of Ages.' It was an Easter story — it was an Easter version of *The Jazz Singer* — he was a saloon singer, and his father didn't want him to be a jazz singer. I hated that script. It was just so corny, so predictable, so everything, and I didn't know you could take your name off the script at that time, or I might have. At any rate, I remember walking into [creator/executive producer] David Dortort's office, and in that office at that time, they were talking about another show that was about to shoot, and Billy Witney — it was Billy Witney's show, and he was in there. David said, 'You look like you got a problem.' I said, 'I don't know how to do this — these songs — they just lay there.' I said, 'He's got to sing this song, he's had supper at the Cartwrights. They come out from the dining room, and you know, and I got this thing, and there's this guitar on the wall [and] 'Do you play guitar, Mr. Cartwright?' 'No, that's my son, Adam. He's in Europe. He plays guitar. Do you play guitar?' 'Yes, I do play guitar.' 'Well, why don't you play something?' — oh, dreadful, awful, terrible.' And Witney, who wasn't directing the episode, said, 'Well, as someone who's done about thirty Gene Autry pictures, about twenty-five Roy Rogers pictures, I'm telling you there's only one way to do that scene.' I said, 'What? I'm listening.' And he said, 'They're at dinner. And they're having dinner, and you have them talking, and they have whatever the last line is that you need to have them say in that scene.' I said, 'Yeah?' He said, 'Then you dissolve, and you open close on the guitar as the first chord is struck. You don't explain it, you don't rationalize it, you don't justify it — you just present it, and the audience watches the song and they're happy.' Now it's very rare that you learn something at that instant. Because a lot of times you learn something and then about three or four weeks later you realize that you've got a new piece of knowledge that you've now incorporated. But I can remember when he said that to me, I'm think-ing, 'That's fucking brilliant. That's exactly correct — I never will forget this piece of knowledge.' And he was the most straightforward, reality-based human being in the world. If ever there was the blue-collar director, it was Billy Witney."

Other dramatic shortcuts William Blinn discovered on his own. "I was learning to write scenes that weren't presenting them [the *Bonanza* directors] with certain problems," remembers the writer. "The first day I went to dailies; it was an episode I had nothing to do with. I was just hired, and we were all going to dailies, I said, 'Okay, fine.' I knew what dailies were, but barely. Well, the scene they had shot was a scene of eight people who had been kidnapped by the bad guys — they were members of a jury, and the bad guys were saying, 'You found my brother guilty, and you're gonna pay,' whatever the hell it was, but they had the eight people, tied hands and feet, in this shack. So you had eight people tied hand and foot, and the first thing you saw was this big wide master shot — eight people, then you saw a raking four-shot, then you saw a two-shot of two of the guys, then another two-shot of two of the guys, then close-up, close-up, close-up, then you went around to the other side and you saw a raking four shot, and you saw two two-shots, and you saw four single close-ups, and I thought I was gonna die, I thought how long will this last? The slowest, dullest thing. So I realized not to saddle the director of photography or the director with something that is that static, because all they can do is just shoot coverage, and then hope somehow the editor will find a miracle."[48]

*Here Come the Brides* received further time-saving help from its regular director of photography: Fred H. Jackman. Praises *Brides* regular Susan Tolsky: "Fred Jackman was the dearest, dearest, dearest man. A lovely gentleman. I can see him to this day sitting in his big director's chair with very little movement. He would say and point, and it was done. He had an amazing camera crew; we did eight to ten pages a day — that's a lot, that's a lot of set-ups, interior and exterior, a huge amount of set-ups. It was just a well-oiled machine, and quiet. I don't remember him raising his voice. Even though he was sitting there and setting up a scene and checking something and doing this or doing that, I could still go up to him and say, 'Fred?' It wasn't like I was interrupting, because he could do his job, and still speak to you. He did not hold his hand up, or say, 'Wait a minute,' or anything like that. He didn't act like he was so busy and like he was MR. DIRECTOR OF PHOTOGRAPHY! He was totally accessible to us, totally accessible, in terms of actor and crew. So I could go up and grab him, and say, 'Freddie, don't shoot me from this side because my eye...' You could say anything to him and he was right there for you. Just an old pro. I could see his arm up, sitting there and he could like point — 'On the light. Do that a little here. And push it over there.' And it was done." [49]

Despite the quality in writing, photography, acting, etc., *Here Come the Brides*, like so many other TV series of the day, just wasn't as good as the motion pictures of the time because it was shot in six or seven days. By contrast, motion pictures were made in three or four months, or longer. Yet, as William Blinn points out, when it came to production values, budget, and shooting schedules, *Brides* and the other television shows of the 1960s and '70s really weren't so different from the movies of the 1930s and '40s. "When you look back on the great directors," says Blinn, "the Henry Hathaways, the John Fords, the William Wellmans, you name them, most of them came out of the studio system, and the studio system...John Ford showed up on Monday, and they said, 'John, this is what you're directing in the next two months. Figure it out.' And that blue-collar, nuts and bolts, put the brick here and put the mortar there, and let's go for it — that takes a lot of discipline to complete and to continue to do. [Richard] Widmark, my favorite actor, once said 'once we started calling them films instead of movies, we lost them.' And I'm right there with him. I mean when we look at [John Ford's] *How Green Was My Valley,* which was shot on the studio lot and all this and that, well, there's no lack of humanity and nuance in there. Or, to go the other way, [Frank Capra's] *Arsenic and Old Lace,* one of the classic comedies of all time, was shot in fourteen days. Now, [in television], "the first thing is, 'How many days do we have to shoot the show? How many pages can we put in the script?' And once you get those things done, it's kind of like a song — it's gonna be fourteen lines, like it or not. It won't do sixteen lines, it won't do twelve lines, it's fourteen lines. Within that framework, you can do some great things."[50]

A perfect example of Blinn's point was the opening (non-stock footage) scene in the *Brides* pilot. Says star Robert Brown, "There's a shot that I have, a photograph, of Swackhamer pointing up — pointing at this real tree. This was the opening shot for the pilot, the one they used, you know, starring Robert Brown. I'd just made an arrangement that the stuntmen were to do all the dirty work — I was not that kind of Hollywood actor [like Brown's co-stars Bobby Sherman and David Soul] that would jump. I didn't want to do that. I said, 'Get the stuntmen.' Well, the tree was maybe five-, six-, eight-stories high, and it was gonna be cut, the top had been cut, with a stunt guy cutting it up there for me. They had to get the close-up of the guy [Brown's character, Jason Bolt] standing, after he had topped it with a saw, the saw kind of swings down, the tree shakes, he waves to everybody, and 'Starring Robert Brown.' That's the shot at the beginning."

Since the shot introduced the Jason Bolt character, director Swackhamer wanted his star Brown at the top of that tree. "I said, 'Swackhamer! What are you talking about?" remembers Brown. "Get the stunt guy.' He says, 'No. I need a close-up of that.' I said, 'Then get me before I climb up the tree.' He says, 'No, no. I gotta have that.' I said, 'Why would I climb that goddamn tree to do that?' He said, 'To get a close-up.' I said, 'Oh. Okay.' So, they wrapped this thing around me, and I had to climb up this huge ladder, and there was a big thing around the tree, so I was safe; I had these spikes in my shoes, but I'm a little fearful of heights. He thought it was necessary to do that — that was his idea. I was at the top of that damn tree just because it was close-up time."[51]

Appearing with Brown in the pilot, and many other first-season episodes was semi-regular Mitzi Hoag. Like most everyone in the *Brides* cast and crew, Hoag very much enjoyed doing the series "[*Brides*] had a lot of exuberance," states the actress. "Exuberance is the word that comes to mind, but you have to remember, I was there in the early beginning. Exuberance, romance. I couldn't call it a comedy, it was a drama, but it had [comedy] in it. I thought of it as set in a period, at a certain time, and the time was very interesting to me. I didn't think of it as a western, because I had worked in a lot of westerns, and in most of the westerns I worked in, they had to do with lawmen and lawlessness, and somebody was being shot. *Here Come the Brides* was more like *Little House on the Prairie*. *Little House* had more of a serious side to it. *Brides* was showing a community — the whole community where you had people doing different things and falling in and out of love and all of the things that happen in communities. The show was an exception."[52]

Making the program an exception from the very beginning was the billing of its principal players. Given the title, one might have expected the top billing to go to a woman, rather than Robert Brown. But once one learned that Brown's Jason Bolt was a fictional version of real-life Seattle pioneer Asa Mercer, once one learned of what Mercer did in post Civil War Seattle, Robert Brown's top billing made perfect sense.

The youngest of fourteen children, born to Aaron and Jane (Dickerson) Mercer, on June 6, 1839 near Princeton, Bureau County, Illinois, Asa Mercer had two older brothers, Thomas (born March 11, 1813) and Aaron, Jr. (born June 23, 1824). Like Asa, both Thomas and Aaron lived in Seattle.

While both Thomas Mercer and Aaron Mercer were to play an important part in the early history of Seattle, it was in the story of Asa Mercer that *Here Come the Brides* found its dramatic situation. Explains 'Mercer Girls' historian Peri Muhich: "The citizens of Seattle deplored the fact that there was a scarcity of women in their town, the proportion being nine men to one woman. Asa, a young, single man, too was concerned at the shortage of 'refined' women. He took it upon himself to discuss the situation with Governor Pickering and the other members of the territorial legislature. Asa had a plan to go back to the New England states where, due to the war, there was an abundance of young, single women. There he would recruit young ladies to come to Washington Territory where they could work as teachers, dressmakers, and milliners. The public treasury did not contain enough funds to sponsor Asa's trip, but private funds were secured from several of Seattle's public minded citizens. So early in 1864 Asa made his first of two trips to New England to recruit ladies to become citizens of Washington Territory."

In New England, continues Muhich, "[Mercer] told how Seattle, in Washington Territory, was a fast-growing town and was in need of teachers and ladies of quality. The city had more than doubled in the years since the first families had landed across the bay at Alki, and the university had been opened just the year before. Mercer explained that as the community grew there were more children of school age but few to teach them. To those willing to go west with him, Mercer made promises of honorable work in the schools and good wages. This was a welcome idea to many in attendance since the war had caused the loss of jobs and left families without men to support them."

As "for the young ladies of marrying age," states Muhich, "prospects of finding a husband in Lowell(Massachusetts)looked very dim," until, that is, Asa Mercer came to Lowell "to invite ladies to go west with him to a place where jobs and men were abundant."[53]

Needless to say, there was plenty of excitement and interest in Mercer's proposal (as was the case with the Bolts' offer in the series). There were also plenty of questions. In *Here Come the Brides*, it was Bridget Hanley's Candy Pruitt who asked most of the questions. Jason Bolt answered them well, but at no time was he as specific and as serious as Asa Mercer.

(With the permission of Mercer Girls historian Muhich, an extract from Mercer's reply letter to the *New York Times* is reprinted here.)

> "In accordance with your request and to satisfy many inquiring minds, I make a statement of the reasons why I have spent so much time and money in the endeavor to introduce a female immigration into Washington Territory.

> "There are many very interesting families in the country but the mass of the population is made up of young men from the Eastern States, who had been well reared and liberally educated. But on arriving at the age of man hood they saw the avenues of trade and successful business forever closed to them; being energetic and ambitious, [they] resolved not to plod on in the beaten path, but to go forth to the Great West, and there carve out a fortune and a home for themselves."

After explaining to the young women of New England and their families what types of men they would find in Northwest Washington, Mercer then told the women how much he needed them: "Churches and school houses there are, but the great elevating, refining, and moralizing element — true women — are wanting. Not that the ladies of Washington Territory are less pure or high minded than those of any other land, but the limited number of them leave the good work greater than they can perform."

Determined to do all in his power to aid in the development of the material of the resources of the territory and the establishment of "right principles in society,"

Mercer appealed "to high-minded women to go into the West to aid in throwing around those who have gone before the restraints of well-regulated society; to cultivate the higher and purer facilities of man by casting about him those refining influences that true women always carry with them; to build up happy homes, and let true sunlight shine round the hearthstone. It is simply a matter of duty on the part of Eastern woman to go to the West, where their presence and influence are so much needed."

At the close of his letter, Mercer made it very clear to the young women and their relatives what to expect once they'd reached Seattle: "Those who accompany me must not expect to occupy a flower garden, or to live upon sweet perfume, but must calculate that they are going into the vineyard to labor, and that their labor will be rewarded."[54]

Jason Bolt spoke almost as eloquently to the ladies of New Bedford. Unlike Asa Mercer, he mentioned nothing about the primitive conditions in Seattle. This was partly because, at this period in the show, Jason was something of a con artist and smooth talker, and partly because at the time he didn't wish to bring up the subject.

But as Jason quickly learned, when it came to dealing with someone as practical and level-headed as Candy Pruitt, honesty was definitely the best policy. In fact, with Candy, that was the one and only way to talk to her. For once Jason admitted he'd tried to find the brides nicer transportation than Captain Clancey's mule boat, once he made it plain to Candy and her friends that the living conditions in Seattle were to be far worse than the six months they would spend on Clancey's ship, the *Seamus O'Flynn* (six months was the amount of time it would take the expedition to reach Seattle), Candy and the other women dropped their objections. Especially when Jason made it clear that he wanted them to take Clancey's filthy boat, clean it up as best they could, and make the living conditions for them, the Bolts, and the other men on board, as comfortable and as pleasant as possible.

Through this sequence, and particularly through the Candy Pruitt character, *Here Come the Brides* firmly established the types of female characters viewers could expect to see on the show. These were to be women in charge, women in control, women who led. These women might be positive or negative characters, comedic or touching. They could be young or old, of different races and religions, married or single. They might be a relative of one of the regular characters, or a career woman; they might be physically handicapped, maybe even a hunter and trapper. The variety of female characters on *HCTB* was extremely impressive.

None was more impressive than Bridget Hanley's Candy Pruitt. In the pilot episode, Candy did all sorts of things. She questioned the Bolt brothers as to their means of transportation, inspired the other unmarried women to accept the Bolts' offer, led a mutiny, got the Bolt brothers to say 'Grace' before every meal, and drew the shy and hesitant Jeremy Bolt out of his shell. And that was just in the first episode!

Bridget Hanley was well cast as the leader of the hundred "brides." According to the actress's Screen Gems biography, at age two-and-a-half, she'd "boldly sat on the back of a swamp alligator!" (The biography was not merely hyperbole; she actually did this!) "Growing up in Edmonds, Washington," continued the biography, Hanley "chopped wood, mowed lawns, raised ducks, buried ducks, played football, baseball, (and) tennis before deciding to become a young lady at 14! The switch of roles from rowdy tomboy to dainty miss came about the day she was asked to join the male track team!" (Once again, the information was accurate.)

Accompanying the Candy Pruitt storyline of a young woman making for herself a new home in the nineteenth-century Pacific Northwest was an even more sweeping storyline: the portrait of, and growth in, the town of Seattle, Washington. As executive producer Bob Claver made very clear, despite its title, *Here Come the Brides* was about the town and people of Seattle. Said the producer in the January 4, 1969 *TV Guide*, "What we are really saying is, wouldn't it be great to live in a small house, be able to walk to the store, and know everyone in a small town? This show represents that simplistic belief. I think people are ready for that."[55]

The strong early ratings which *Here Come the Brides* was soon to enjoy suggested that they were. Perhaps, that is why *Brides* continues to win new fans.

"It is amazing and delightful to be reminded of the impact *HCTB* had and continues to have on its devotees," remarked series regular Henry Beckman to the *HCTB* Yahoo group in the late 1990s. "It is my belief [that] the show proves repeatedly the innate goodness of humankind without being 'preachy.' N. Richard Nash was the one responsible for the whole concept; Columbia Screen Gems had the guts to fashion a series out of such concept when all indications pointed to its potential failure. Name me one other series that has the viewer support accorded *HCTB* by its very nature, THIRTY YEARS after its prime-time run! Ain't no such animal. AND it continues to this day as one of the most constantly viewed TV series of all time."[56]

While fans of other classic TV series would very much dispute Beckman's latter point, there was no question that in putting *Here Come the Brides* on the air in the late 1960s, ABC-TV and Columbia Screen Gems were taking an enormous risk. As Henry Beckman noted, the times just didn't seem right.

1. Paul Wendkos – telephone interview – 2001

2. Ralph Senensky – by e-mail – April 18, 2006

3. Larry Brody – interview – by e-mail – December 19, 2007

4. Dorothy C. Fontana – interview – by e-mail – February 18, 2008

5. Brody – interview – December 19, 2007

6. Senensky – telephone interview – 2002

7. David Soul – telephone interview – 2007

8. Bill Catching – telephone interview – 2004

9. Ibid

10. Bridget Hanley – telephone interview – 2008

11. Soul – interview – 2007

12. Lynn Stalmaster – telephone interview – 2003

13. Lynda Day George – telephone interview – 2003

14. Michael Forest – telephone interview – 2007

15. Gerald Mayer – telephone interview – 2002

16. Christopher George/Laraine Stephens – ABC-TV Interview – 1968 or '69

17. Hanley – *The Brides Activity Fan Club Newsletter* – July/August 1975

18. Lou Antonio – telephone interview – 2008

19. Mayer – interview – 2002

20. Robert Biheller – telephone interview – 2008

21. Robert Brown – telephone interview – 2007

22. Angel Tompkins – telephone interview – 2007

23. Soul – 2007

24. Bridget Hanley – Second Chat: Chatting with Candy – October 26, 2000

25. Hanley – telephone interview – 2008

26. Susan Tolsky – telephone interview – 2007

27. Hanley – First Chat: Chatting with Bridget – October 26, 2000

28. Hanley – interview – 2007

29. Tolsky – interview – 2007

30. Antonio – telephone interview – 2008

31. Ibid

32. Bob Claver – telephone interview – 2007

33. Bruce Kessler – telephone interview – 2007

34. Claver – interview – 2007

35. William Blinn – telephone interview – 2007

36. Hanley – 2007

37. George – interview – 2002

38. Tolsky – interview – 2007

39. George – 2002

40. Hanley – 2007

41. Tolsky – 2007

42. Blinn – interview – 2007

43. Lawrence Laurent -'The Series that Fooled the Handicappers' – *Washington Post* – *TV Channels* – March 2, 1969

44. Tompkins – interview – 2007

45. *Variety* – September 28, 1968

46. Cleveland Amory – Review – *Here Come the Brides* – *TV Guide* – Vol. 16, No. 52 – December 28, 1968, Issue #822

47. *Variety* – October 1, 1969

48. Blinn – interview – 2007

49. Tolsky – interview – 2007

50. Blinn – 2007

51. Brown – interview – 2007

52. Mitzi Hoag – telephone interview – 2007

53. Peri Muhich, Mercer Girls historian – "The Mercer Girls" (webpage) – 1997-2003

54. Asa Mercer – Letter to the *New York Times* – 1864 – Muhich – 1997-2003

55. Dwight Whitney – 'Making Sin Palatable' – *TV Guide* –Volume 17, No. 1, January 4, 1969, Issue #823

56. Henry Beckman – December 1999

"You know, ladies, men are *not* the enemy."[1]

*Here Come the Brides* guest Lynda Day George

Part One

*The Men*
*Who Developed*
Here Come the Brides

"As General Candy comes storming in, she sees her troops are well deployed."

Page 58, Scene 44 – George Sidney Productions
*Here Come the Brides*
Screenplay by N. Richard Nash
THIRD DRAFT REVISED – June 29, 1961

# Chapter 1

# *Created by*
# *N. Richard Nash*

As reprinted by Northwest historian Susan Armitage, the conversation between Eliza Farnham and an Illinois farmer, a conversation which Farnham recalled in her 1846 travel book, *Life in Prairie Land*, began like this:

> "…this bride of yours," queried Farnham, "is the one, I suppose, that you thought of all the while you were making your farm and building your cabin?"

> "No, I never allowed to get a woman till I found my neighbors went ahead of me with 'em," replied the farmer. "And then I should a got one right thar, but there wasn't any stout ones in our settlement…there was a gal I used to know that was stouter and bigger than this one. I should a got her if I could, but she'd got married and gone off over the *Mississippi* somewhat."

> "Did you select this one solely on account of her size?" said I.

> "Why, pretty much," he replied; "I reckon women are some like horses and oxen; the biggest can do the most work, and that's what I want one for."

> "And is that all?" I asked, more disgusted at every word. "Do you care nothing about a pleasant face to meet you when you go home from the field, or a soft voice to speak kind words when you are sick, or a gentle friend to converse with you in your leisure hours?"

> "Why, as to that," he said. "I reckon a woman ain't none the worse for talk because she's stout and able to work. I calculate she'll mind her own business pretty much, and if she does she won't talk a great deal to me; that ain't what I got her for."[2]

Such was the attitude quite a few men had towards women in nineteenth century America. To such men, there were certain things women weren't supposed to do. As Mrs. J.W. Likens discovered when she became a door-to-door book saleswoman in San Francisco's business district in 1871.

"Taking…my…order book in my hand," remembered Likens in *Six Years' Experience as a Book Agent in California*, "I started up Montgomery street, calling on one and all, up stairs and down, in every room. Some [men] looked at me curiously, others with pity, and *some few* with contempt, while I endeavored, in my embarrassment, and in an awkward way, to [sell books]. They would treat me kindly, and were very polite, with the exception of some few ruffians who seemed to have forgotten 'their mother was a woman,' and would hurt my feelings."[3]

*Here Come the Brides* creator N. Richard Nash thought more highly of women. In more than one of his plays, such as *The Young and Fair* (1948) and *Rouge Atomique* (1955), the female characters were the ONLY characters!

Born Nathan Richard Nussbaum in Philadelphia on June 8, 1913, the seventeen-year-old Nash was making ten dollars a fight as a boxer before entering the University of Pennsylvania in 1930. Studying both English and philosophy, Nash published two successful books on philosophy, *The Athenian Spirit* and *The Wounds of Sparta*, before moving into fiction with his first play, *Parting at Imsdorf* in 1940. The play won Nash the Maxwell Anderson Verse Drama Award. (Anderson, whose play *Barefoot in Athens* was one of the many stage credits of *Here Come the Brides* star Robert Brown, was one of the few modern playwrights to make considerable use of blank verse. Blank verse is a form of poetry, with a regular meter, but no rhyme.)

Six years later, Nash, who also taught philosophy and/or drama at Bryn Mawr College, Haverford, Brandeis, and the University of Pennsylvania, penned *The Second Best Bed*. The title came from the famous bequest Shakespeare made in his will, leaving to his wife, Anne Hathaway, nothing but his "second-best bed." Although the National Archives notes that "beds and other pieces of household furniture were often the sole bequest to a wife," and Elizabethan custom had it that the best bed in the house was reserved for guests (the second-best bed being that of husband and wife), the term "second-best" nonetheless carried a derogatory meaning. In fact in James Joyce's *Ulysses*, Stephen Dedalus (the character portrayed by Robert Brown on stage) imagines that Anne had committed adultery. To Dedalus, leaving to his wife the "second-best bed" was Shakespeare's way of punishing her.

Unfortunately, as no description or copy of this Nash play is currently available, one can only guess as to N. Richard Nash's take concerning the great dramatist's bequest. At any rate, the well-received comedy/drama resulted in Nash writing more plays, including 1948's previously mentioned *The Young and Fair*, and 1952's *See the Jaguar*. At some point in his life, Nash also lectured at Yale and Princeton, and won a considerable number of American and international awards, including The American Dramatists Award, The Orbeal Prize, the Wilhelm Gosse Award, the Cannes Prize for Literature and Drama, the Geraldine Dodge Award, and the New American Play Award.

While N. Richard Nash only wrote the pilot episode, "Here Come the Brides," according to *Brides* executive producer Bob Claver, the playwright was used in advisory ways throughout the run of the series. This certainly seems likely given the dramatic situation in *The Young and Fair*. Opening on Broadway on November 22, 1948 at the Fulton Theatre, and closing at the International Theatre on January 8, 1949, with a total of sixty-four performances, *The Young and Fair*, said *Time* in their review: "deals with life at a fashionable junior college for girls. And there's considerable life to deal with, for behind its trim ivied walls Brook Valley harbors more problems than an arithmetic book."

Featuring Lois Wheeler as Lee Barron, "who lacks the courage to admit she is Jewish," and Doe Avedon as Drucilla Eldridge – "like the brat in *The Children's Hour*, she twists and messes up lives," the play also starred the more famous Mercedes McCambridge, Julie Harris, and Rita Gam.

A tale of how people can be "harassed and torn two ways," *The Young and Fair* "has a real sense of how thorny and bewildering life can be," noted the *Time* reviewer, how it could be "an endless emotional seesaw, a constant moral crossroads." Pointing out that "there is so much plot that there is no real plight," and that "the words, like the deeds, smack at times of garish melodrama," the *Time* reviewer nonetheless concluded, "But *The Young and Fair*, though a botch, is by no means a bore. There is always far too much happening, far too much threatening. And an all-female cast acts the play to the hilt — and at moments quite convincingly."[4]

*Here Come the Brides* would present somewhat similar scenarios and characters in the first season's "A Jew Named Sullivan" and the second season's "Two Women." The play's "endless emotional seesaw," and "constant moral crossroads," somewhat described such *HCTB*'s as "A Crying Need" and "Man of the Family," the "brat" who "twists and messes up lives" definitely applied to child actor Stefan Arngrim's Tommy Blake in the latter episode.

Elements of Nash's 1952 play, *See the Jaguar* may also have been present in the second season *HCTB*s "Two Worlds" and "Absalom." In *Jaguar*, the character, Brad — a violent man full of hatred — had a daughter, Janna, who falls in love with the peaceful, loving, gentle Dave Ricks. In the *HCTB* episode, "Two Worlds," Gene Evans, Meg Foster and series regular David Soul enacted a somewhat similar scenario. There was also a point in *Jaguar* where Brad, who owned a small zoo, put an innocent teenaged boy by the name of Wally Winkins in a cage. The second-season episode, "Absalom," starring soon-to-be *Bonanza* regular Mitch Vogel, opened with the teenaged (mute) Vogel in a cage.

While the loss of virginity in Nash's 1958 play *Handful of Fire* may have inspired such *HCTB*s as "After a Dream Comes Mourning," "Mr. and Mrs. J. Bolt," and (arguably) "Wives for Wakando," the five characters in 1956's *Girls of Summer*, with its plethora of misunderstandings, might have resulted in shows like "One to a Customer." One N. Richard Nash play which could definitely be traced to the *Here Come the Brides* series was the one which made Nash a household name. It was of course, 1954's *The Rainmaker*.

Translated into over forty languages, then made into a 1956 film with Katherine Hepburn and Burt Lancaster, and a few years later, a Broadway musical, *The Rainmaker*, cracked the unnamed *Time* magazine critic was "about equal parts sticky romance and lively comedy, crumpled cornflowers and high-grade corn." "Romantic" and "corny" is how more than one talent associated with *Here Come the Brides* has lovingly described the 1968-70 series.

Continued the critic: "The play starts off, like [J.M.] Barrie's *What Every Woman Knows*, with the efforts of a plain girl's father and brothers to find her a husband. Lizzie (Geraldine Page) is all the wrong things: un-coy, intelligent, blunt; failure unnerves her; and she is bleakly staring spinsterhood in the face when a posturing, flamboyant young con man (Darren McGavin) blusters in, swearing that for $100 he can bring rain. With the money in his jeans, he spouts philosophy, poetizes, woos the girl, teaches her to have faith in herself. By the time he rides off to make a new pitch, she is well on her way — with another beau — to the altar."[5]

In the first-season *HCTB* episode, "Lovers and Wanderers," series semi-regular Mitzi Hoag, series star Robert Brown, and series semi-regular Bo Svenson played out part of this storyline. A few episodes later, the Rainmaker's message, "Have faith in yourself," was the lesson taught to co-star Bobby Sherman's Jeremy Bolt by Jack Albertson's rainmaking Merlin in "A Man and His Magic." Like the fictional 'Jeremy Bolt,' N. Richard Nash had stuttered in his younger days. According to the playwright, he wrote *The Rainmaker* as a tribute to his kind-hearted older sister, Mae, who, by always patiently listening to whatever Nash had to say, "saved my life" by curing him of stuttering when he was a child.

Other elements from *The Rainmaker*, such as "when Lizzie herself mimics the wiles of the gals who know how to lasso men," were present in episodes like the previously mentioned "Man of the Family." As for the romantic entanglements of Lizzie's brother, Jim Curry, "a lively young oaf,"[6] they may have inspired such *HCTB*s as "Another Game in Town," and "To the Victor."

Like the play, *The Rainmaker* movie earned positive reviews; *Time* called it "one of the most warmly appealing romantic comedies of the season."[7] That being the case, it was only natural that N. Richard Nash try his hand at making a second movie from another of his plays. By 1960, he'd completed a second temporary yellow shooting script for *The Girls of Summer*. By the end of that year, he'd also written his first Broadway musical, *Wildcat*, starring Lucille Ball.

Describing *Wildcat* to *TV Guide's* Dan Jenkins, Ball called it "a comedy with music, not a musical comedy, but the music is important. I play a (scheming) girl wildcatter in the Southwestern oil fields around the turn of the century."

"We're still looking for a leading man," stated Ball a few lines later. "I want an unknown. He has to be big, husky, around 40. He has to be able to throw me around, and I'm a pretty big girl. (Ball's description of the characters and the situation sounded very much like the *HCTB* episode, "And Jason Makes Five.") He has to be able to sing, at least a little. I have to sing, too. It's pretty bad. When I practice, I hold my hands over my ears."[8]

Interestingly, *Here Come the Brides'* resident comedienne, Susan Tolsky, drew considerable inspiration from Lucille Ball. "She was the best," says Tolsky. "Just to...I don't want to say she influenced me – [but] she gave me a greater appreciation of the sphere of comedy – she could do anything. Working with her and knowing the writers, and talking to her…of course, she scared me to death. She scared me to death. So, having been able to work with her and making her laugh – hearing her laugh [that], was like, 'Who else needs anything in life,' you know. There are many actors and actresses whose work I respected. In terms of drama, and what they contributed long ago, not necessarily now. She was just – you could study her. She was the epitome of comic timing. If you watch somebody that brilliant, to me, it seems that she's just the epitome of that because she did plan every move she made. She was a workhorse – she planned every move, and she had it down pat, and it looked like she never did it before. She was the one that I learned such an enormous appreciation of comedy from."[9]

Kicking off with two previews on December 14, 1960 before its actual opening at the Alvin Theatre on December 16, 1960, *Wildcat* amassed a total of 171 performances before ending its run on June 3, 1961. By that time, N. Richard Nash had two more musicals in development – one, *110 in the Shade*, with lyrics by *The Fantasticks'* Tom Jones and music by his *Fantasticks* collaborator Harvey Schmidt, was a musical adaptation of Nash's extraordinarily successful *The Rainmaker*.

During this time Nash was also working with director George Sidney (*Anchors Aweigh, The Harvey Girls, Show Boat, Kiss Me Kate, The Eddy Duchin Story, Pal Joey*) and the songwriting team of Sammy Cahn (lyrics) and James Van Heusen (music) on the planned film musical, *Here Come the Brides*. Quite a few characters (never seen in the series pilot) appeared in this musical, including the logger Jack, saloonkeeper Mama Damnation, "The Man of the Family's" Reverend Gaddings, bride Rosella, Jason Bolt's love interest Lottie Starr, bride Sarah Carter, seaman Mac Wendell, brides Patricia, Fanny Lou (who couldn't say 'r'), Mabel Ealey, etc. There were scenes of the *Seamus O'Flynn*'s departure from New Bedford, and numerous vignettes related to the departure of the brides – case in point: a 'bride' putting flowers on two graves for the last time. In the Rio de Janeiro sequence, a number of the brides got married, including Candy to Jeremy.

There were other striking differences between this never-filmed musical and the pilot episode of the series. In the pilot, the "Mutiny" sequence (where the disillusioned brides take over the ship and steer it back to New Bedford), was done in comedic fashion. "Comedic" was definitely not the word for the planned film version. During this Mutiny sequence, the women tie up Clancey and fire guns at the sailors. Helping to quell the mutiny is Lottie Starr. At one point, she knocks Candy to the ground, lets "go a sledge-hammer right" at one girl, and kicks another "in the tail." Later in the story, Lottie is the one being hit…by Jason Bolt…*twice!*

Then there was the scene where Clancey throws his mug of beer into Jason's face, and the scene where Candy snatched, out from under Biddie's bed, the tearful girl's reticule. From this, Candy extracts Biddie's wedding dress.

Perhaps the cruelest sequence of all was the 'Hate Jason Bolt' party, thrown and organized by Jason. During this party, the effigy Jason has made of himself is gleefully torn to shreds by the angry brides and sailors. Fans of the 1968-70 series would have been appalled at such scenes.

The dialogue wasn't much better:

Jason *(to lumberjack Big Red)*: "Where the hell are you goin?"
*(To Mama Damnation)*: "Get your tail over here!"
*(To Josh)*: "Shut up!"
*(Upon seeing the improvements the brides have made to Clancey's ship, and the elegantly laid dinner table)*: "I'm a son of a — "

Lottie *(to Candy)*: "Shut up!"
*(To Jeremy)*: "Sally's a giggling idiot, and Mary Ellen's a cow!"
Jeremy *(to Lottie, Jason, and Josh)*: "I dreamed we were on the high seas — and the damn sails were flappin' and the damn ship was pitchin' and the damn spray was comin' up over the sides and I was drippin' wet from head to foot and I was as seasick as a damn dog! Damn, I was seasick."

Candy *(to no one)*: Why did I marry into this idiot family anyway?"

To Aaron Stempel, the women Jason and his brothers planned on bringing back to Seattle would be a "lot of shameless sluts." To Clancey, the women were "scuts."

At one point, Jason gives Mama Damnation a "rousing slap on the butt."

In the song, *All Over the World They're Kissin'*, Jeremy sings about "Girls with round or slanty eyes."

Given the television's industry's strict standards and the moral climate of the time, such dialogue and scenes would have had to go if *Here Come the Brides* were to be brought to the small screen.

When it was, helping N. Richard Nash adapt the concept was the Columbia/Screen Gems house producer who'd immediately expressed interest in the *Brides* project when the studio shopped it around to its' producer talent. His name: Bob Claver, executive producer of the Inger Stevens Screen Gems comedy, *The Farmer's Daughter.*

1. George – 2003
2. Susan Armitage – Foreword to the Second Edition – June 1992 – Roger Conant: Mercer's
    Belles – *The Journal of a Reporter*, edited by Lenna A. Deutsch, Washington State University
    Press, 1993, page x
3. Ibid, page xi
4. 'New Plays in Manhattan' –*Time* – December 6, 1948
5. 'New Plays in Manhattan' – *Time* – November 8, 1954
6. Ibid
7. 'New Picture' – *Time* – December 31, 1956
8. Dan Jenkins – 'A Visit with Lucille Ball' – *TV Guide* – July 16, 1960 – Vol. 8, No. 29, Issue #381
9. Tolsky – interview – 2007

"You can't build a town without women. That was a very pragmatic approach that a lot of towns in the West had at that time. We had good stories — we did stuff that most shows didn't do. I don't remember a lot of westerns doing those kinds of stories or anything else because to this day, women get short shrift in parts. So I think the show gave women opportunities they didn't always have in television. Women were treated respectfully on the show."

*Here Come the Brides* executive producer Bob Claver

# Chapter 2

# *Executive Producer: Bob Claver*

"I thought it was a very valuable show for kids. We didn't talk down to them. All he was really was a grandfather. And now that I am one…it's real easy [because] everybody loves a grandfather. He's not a disciplinarian [and] he usually has some extra money — that combination is gold for kids. So that's what he was, and Bob was wonderful. He had a touch with kids that was just terrific."

"Bob" was Bob Keeshan, and the show *Here Come the Brides'* Bob Claver was talking about was the early morning CBS children's show, *Captain Kangaroo*. Continues Claver: "Jack Miller [not the Jack Miller who wrote second-season episodes of *Brides*] was executive producer of the show. He and Bob put together *Captain Kangaroo*; they invited me into that, and I was in it from the beginning. I was the sole writer for years! We were on six days a week. The Saturday shows we were able to upgrade the age a little bit, cuz kids were out of school. So we brought in ballerinas from the New York City ballet." In so doing, Claver and the other makers of *Captain Kangaroo* were pointing the way towards the first attempt at quality afternoon children's television: the long-running (1963-73) *NBC Children's Theatre*.

Like so many other talents in television, Bob Claver "didn't plan on working in the business. I got drafted after I graduated from college," recalls the producer. "In those days, that's what happened. We were still warlike, but not quite as moronic as it is now. It was Korea; I got drafted and I went into the Service, and I did radio there — live radio. I did a lot of broadcasting, a lot of writing of variety shows and that got me interested. When I got out of the service, I had a cousin who knew a guy who had an agency — a small agency in Chicago. He hired me…I was kind of a runner and whatever."

Beginning his career when television was new (network programming "didn't go across the country" at the time), the young Claver found himself under considerable pressure. "It was such a different time — that era," remembers the director/producer. "The local stations did programs all day. Until the network came [on] — that was at night, and only for a few hours. (Typical nighttime fare included wrestling shows and bowling shows, such as *Make that Spare*).

"You had a chance to really work a lot, and try things out," remembers Claver. "Dennis James had a thing — he could make a sound like bones breaking — it was just awful, incidentally no worse than what they call reality shows today. Nobody was taking it seriously. So that's what was good about it. It was just…you had to fill all this time."

Bob Claver didn't spend too much time in his hometown of Chicago after he'd left the service. "I got with a packaging company which owned *Mr. Wizard* [starring Don Herbert]," states Claver. "That was a big show at the time, and they needed someone who wanted to go to New York. ABC had given them an hour, but nobody who worked in Chicago wanted to go there. So, after one month in [local Chicago] television, I went to New York on my own. I had the job of putting together two half-hour shows and putting them on the air, and that was hard. One of them was a thing called *Time for Fun* which was…I found Bob Keeshan, who had been Clarabelle [on *The Howdy Doody Show*]. That was the beginning of our relationship."

Like many early television shows, says Claver, *Time for Fun* wasn't scripted. "Bob was a clown in that," remembers the producer, "and he was just on the set alone, a half-hour every day. He had a bench and a fountain — and we could make the water go up and down, but it was mostly ad-lib — it was written very much like *Captain Kangaroo*. I wrote blocks [of scenes and actions] — there was an order to them, but not dialogue; then Bob ad-libbed off those blocks. Then I quit — I left that show, and started doing a lot of variety shows for ABC."

Created in 1943 from the former NBC Blue Radio Network, and presenting its first television broadcast on April 19, 1948, ABC didn't really gain any kind of foothold in television until the mid-1950s, thanks to such programs as Walt Disney's *Disneyland* and Warner Bros. hits like *Maverick* and *77 Sunset Strip*. Being the youngest of the three networks, ABC tended to offer its audiences "counter-programming." For example, if one of the other networks was airing a news special, ABC would telecast a variety or dramatic show. Bob Claver recalls one such series.

"I did a show that was two-and-a-half hours a day, five days a week, if you can believe that," chuckles the producer, "all kinds of shows, and I used (puppeteer) Shari Lewis a lot in those days. She had a great career [including a stint as television writer: Lewis co-wrote with second husband Jeremy Tarcher the third-season *Star Trek*, "The Lights of Zetar"]. She was very good, a wonderful technician, and pretty. Her career went very well — she died way too young."

It was Bob Claver who encouraged Lewis to use the puppet that would bring her fame. "She had regular puppets, you know, like Edgar Bergen," remembers the producer. "She brought them in one day, and said, 'What do you think of these?' I went crazy, because she had this one, and this was 'Lambchop,' and I forget the other guys. She never did go back to the other puppets. 'Lambchop' was her primary star."

In doing the two-and-a-half hour (local) variety show, the future director/producer found himself working with other talents who, if not already known, would later go on to national recognition. "Tom Poston ["The Peeper" on *The Bob Newhart Show*, and handyman George on *Newhart*] was the emcee," says Claver, "and they gave me a full orchestra, because in those days, the networks had musicians on staff. I had all-star bands, guys from the history of jazz, from that era, fabulous musicians, wonderful musicians, and musicians are crazy. They're fun to be around because they all belong in institutions."

Continues the producer, "We had [former Tommy/Jimmy Dorsey/Glenn Miller Army Air Force Band drummer] Ray McKinley [famous for such songs as "Celery Stalks at Midnight," "Beat Me, Daddy, Eight to the Bar," "You Came a Long Way from St. Louie," "Red Silk Stockings and Green Perfume"]. He was a great drummer, and he was funny too. [In "Celery Stalks at Midnight," McKinley screams out in a falsetto voice, "Celery stalks along the highway!") We had [Bob Crosby/Artie Shaw trumpeter/cornet player/flugelhornist] Billy Butterfield, and [trumpeter/cornet player/guitarist] Bobby Hackett and [Glenn Miller Army Air Force Band pianist, and later classical music composer] Mel Powell. Mel Powell ended up teaching at Yale from what I understand. We had guests all the time. We broke the show in five half-hour blocks, and it was a lot of fun to do. But the show was really hard — it was just impossible to do."

Then came CBS' *Captain Kangaroo.*

Premiering on October 3, 1955 and airing until December 8, 1984, *Captain Kangaroo* was presented live during its first four seasons. By 1956, Shari Lewis and 'Lambchop' were appearing on the program. Co-starring with Bob Keeshan's 'Captain' were Hugh 'Lumpy' Brannum, and Cosmo 'Gus' Allegretti. "Lumpy had the name, 'Green Jeans' because we gave him the name, 'Mr. Green Jeans,'" states Claver. "And we used literal names. 'Bunny Rabbit' is 'Bunny Rabbit,' and 'Moose' is 'Moose,' and 'Clock' is 'Clock.' [Puppeteer Allegretti played the latter three characters. Allegretti also portrayed "Dancing Bear" and "Uncle Ralph."]

"We used to do it twice a day," remembers Claver. "Once for the East [Coast], and once in the Midwest. The West Coast got them on kinescope. That was an amazing success, that show. People loved that. And the show really worked. The kids loved the show because we really cared — we would not do anything to jeopardize any of the kids.

"The network was wonderful to us," continues Claver. "We weren't making any money, but we were beginning to get ratings, (so the network started bringing them clients). But we were very young, twenty-five, something like that. So we would turn down clients because we thought they were con people. I can't tell you how crazy we were."

During the time Bob Claver worked on *Captain Kangaroo,* his bosses were Louis G. Cowan and Hubbell Robinson. Creator of the radio show, *Quiz Kids,* and the TV game-show hit, *The $64,000 Question,* Louis Cowan's identification with the latter was to cost him his job in the wake of the quiz-show scandals. As for Robinson, who described his efforts to provide high-quality programming to the large television audience as "mass with class," it was he who oversaw the development of such CBS mega-hits as *I Love Lucy* and *Gunsmoke.* Robinson would later executive produce the Boris Karloff-hosted NBC anthology *Thriller,* as well as the 1966 Burt Reynolds/Screen Gems detective drama, *Hawk.* Reynolds' role as full-blooded Iroquois Indian Lt. John Hawk definitely bore the Robinson stamp of opening doors for minorities; in the early '60s, Robinson distributed a memorandum amongst television producers in which he asked them to provide a wider variety of roles for black actors and actresses. Serving as production consultant on *Hawk* was future *Here Come the Brides* casting director Renee Valente.

Bob Claver has nothing but good things to say when it comes to both Hubbell Robinson and Louis G. Cowan. "They were wonderful," enthuses the producer. "They were gentlemen, and certainly liberal in their bent — they would never say, 'Don't have a black person,' or anything like that. They didn't understand *Captain Kangaroo* — particularly Lou. He had taken over the network at the time, and we did a week of try-outs, did it with a crew and everything, but we didn't record anything. We just got into the swing of how we were going to do it everyday. He [Cowan] called me into his office, and he said, 'You know, I don't understand the show at all — it seems slow and draggy and all of that, but everybody seems to like it, the kids like it, so I'm gonna put it to you this way: Do whatever you want, and if you need my help, call me.' And that was it."

Early in *Captain Kangaroo*'s run, a rumor began circulating that the show would be canceled. But Claver had an ace up his sleeve. "It might have been at the end of the first year," says the producer. "Anyway, when I came into my office, because I would go directly to the studio in the morning after we finished the show, there was nowhere to walk — the entire floor was full of mailbags [packed with fan mail concerning *Captain Kangaroo*]. So I called Lou. I said, 'I think you'd better come over.' He came over, and that was the end of taking the show off the air." Backing up Cowan in case it was necessary was the aforementioned CBS exec Hubbell Robinson. "He was a gentleman," praises Claver. "That's a word that is pretty much out of the vocabulary by now. He really was a good guy."

After co-creator Jack Miller, who'd also co-created, and co-produced with Keeshan the New York City WJZ/WABC TV/Channel 7 children's series, *Tinker's Workshop*, left the program, Bob Claver took over. "Jack was with the same production company that I was — the company that sent me to New York," recalls Claver. "We became very good friends for a long time, then we fell apart. When Jack left the show, I became executive producer, and then we got Bob Cleary in as a writer and then I left it.

"When I left it, Bob [Keeshan] was really angry at me," says Claver. "He didn't talk to me for a long time. [Years later] they had a reunion and they didn't even invite me, and I'm a person who goes to…You know what? I've never missed a high-school reunion. I flew across the country for them. So I was very hurt by that. I figured, 'Well, shit. I'm not gonna…' Anyway, about six months before he died, he was here [in Chicago — Claver's home town, to which the director/producer returned after leaving the entertainment business]. He'd written a book [*Good Morning, Captain* — 1995, Fairview Press], and he was signing autographs, near not too far from where I live. I went over and got in line. We went out and had a three-hour lunch. It was very nice. I'm glad we got to do that."

Given the great success of *Captain Kangaroo*, some might have wondered why Bob Claver left. "I knew I had to quit," states the producer. "I couldn't have a career that I wanted to have without credits. That credit was great if you stayed in kid shows but I didn't want to do that. And that show ran twenty-five more years. So I never thought it was a mistake for me. Because I had a wonderful career, and I got to work with a lot of great people. Quitting that show was really smart. And my wife, at that particular period, was very encouraging. That helped a lot."

After Bob Claver left CBS-TV, he did NBC's March-September 1959 *Jimmie Rodgers Show.* "I got canned after thirteen shows for being impossible to work with," remembers Claver. "The agency said that was my problem. I never had trouble with crews or actors. I just had trouble with management, all the time. They just were... they were quite annoying. The network had these people that would show up for stuff — if they were good, it was fine, but they're (that sort of network management) one out of ten."

In the case of *The Jimmie Rodgers Show,* Claver's complaints were more than justified. "Somebody bought the whole show — I forget the name, but it was one of the major tobacco companies," recalls the producer. "They were strange...I can't remember who the woman was, but it was really a valid [performer], a black lady singer — they did not want Jimmie in the same frame with her. None of us were even surprised, because that was still going on. We did raise all kinds of hell, but, we couldn't win. So we didn't bring it up again, we didn't tackle it, we just staged it so that [issue] never came up. I never forgot that — that was a horrible thing to me. Other than that, they didn't bother us.

"Jimmie was a big star," continues Claver. "He had lots of hit records ["Honeycomb," "Kisses Sweeter than Wine," etc.) and he was a nice guy to work with." Co-starring with Rodgers were the musical group, The Kirby Stone Four, singer Connie Francis ["Who's Sorry Now?" "Where the Boys Are," etc.), and the Buddy Morrow Orchestra. "Connie I didn't, I never did understand," states Claver. "She was in another world, and very unattractive." As for the Kirby Stone Four, they were "real hot in those days. That [show] was in the era of summer replacements. All these shows that were on [during the regular season] went off in the summer, so lots of things got to try out there. We took over for *The Eddie Fisher Show* and *The George Gobel Show.* We did that for twenty shows."

Up next for Claver was the 1960-61 NBC detective drama, *Michael Shayne.* Produced by Four Star Productions (the name came from the four Hollywood stars, Dick Powell, Charles Boyer, Ida Lupino, and David Niven, who'd formed the company), *Michael Shayne* starred Richard Denning as the famous Miami Beach detective, Mike Shayne, Patricia Donahue (later, Margie Regan) as Shayne's secretary Lucy Hamilton, Jerry Paris as the detective's friend, Miami news reporter Timothy Rourke, and Herbert Rudley as Shayne's policeman friend, Chief Will Gentry. Missing was Shayne's frequent nemesis, Chief Peter "Petey" Painter. The series kicked off its run with a number of episodes based on previously published Shayne novels. Among these episodes: "Dolls Are Deadly," "One Night with Nora," "Framed in Blood," "Die Like a Dog," "Call for Michael Shayne," "Shoot the Works," "This is It, Michael Shayne," "Murder and the Wanton Bride," and "Blood on Biscayne Bay." Serving as the series' technical consultant was the famous redheaded detective's creator/author, Brett Halliday.

"That was the beginning of my career," remembers Claver. "I was the associate producer. It wasn't a very good show. Richard Denning was a good guy, but not the most exciting actor. Jerry Paris went on to be a very successful director. I used Jerry. He directed the pilot of *The Partridge Family*. Among the directors who got notable, and became names, he was the worst of them. Because he was so overrated. He didn't do his homework. I'd say, 'What are you doing with the scene? [Because] he just forgot stuff. But he had a career with Garry Marshall. Garry Marshall is a wonderful guy." Paris directed episodes of Marshall's *Happy Days, The Odd Couple,* and *Laverne & Shirley*.

Claver's next job at Four Star — associate producing the 1962-63 sitcom, *Ensign O'Toole,* resulted in "my first directing job in film. I directed an episode with Stubby Kaye," remembers the producer ["Operation: Tubby" – April 14, 1963]. "That show had Beau Bridges and Bob Sorrells and Jack Mullaney and Jay C. Flippen. It was a good show, but it didn't make it. Jackie's [Cooper] show was on at that time — *Hennesey,* and that show was much more successful. This show only lasted one season. I thought it was a pretty good show."

Based on the humorous semi-autobiographical novel, *Ensign O'Toole and Me,* and another book, *All the Ships at Sea,* by U.S. Naval Academy graduate and former Chinese River Gunboat Junior Officer William J. Lederer (most famous for the co-authored novel, *The Ugly American,*), *Ensign O'Toole* starred future Disney lead Dean Jones (*That Darn Cat!, The Love Bug, The Million Dollar Duck,* etc.) as the title character. Producing the series was Hy Averback, the one-time narrator, and production supervisor of the amusing and cleverly done 1950's sitcom, *Meet Corliss Archer*. Perhaps best known as the producer of the hit 1965-67 ABC comedy, *F Troop,* Averback's other credits included *The Bob Cummings Show* (a.k.a. *Love that Bob*), *Our Miss Brooks, December Bride, I Love Lucy,* and *The Real McCoys*.

"When I got my job at Four Star," explains, Claver, "he [Averback] was there. They assigned me to him. Nobody asked him [if he wanted Claver], they just sent me. So, it wasn't so good at the beginning. He was kind of stand-offish. Dick Powell was the one who was actually there at Four Star and ran it. Dick was a very smart man, and a good producer. He was a terrific guy to work for. When I came there…I had been making $2,000 a week doing *Captain Kangaroo*. Well, when I got this job as an associate producer, I got $400. They said to me, 'If you work out…' — it was two months to Thanksgiving — 'if you work out by Thanksgiving, we'll adjust this.' And they did. He (Powell) was a man of his word — he was a good man — I went through the death with him, because he was going to the dailies and he was coughing — he had cancer. [Powell died January 2, 1963]. Then Tom McDermott who was his [Powell's] choice, took over. He was also good to work for. It was a very good place. We had great people — Aaron Spelling started there, and [William] Link and [Richard] Levinson — they were good, and they were kids.

"Aaron had a great career," continues Claver. "He was a really good guy. A lot of people are very jealous of him because he had a great career. He didn't do really good shows — they were kind of schlocky. But my attitude was — 'all I know is his shows get a lot of good ratings — that's what the game's about.' Then people got after him because of Tori, and if I had a daughter who was an actress, and I was Aaron Spelling, I would damn well give her parts until the network or somebody complained. Nobody ever did. She wasn't that bad an actor — still isn't. Not very pretty, though."

Still, "Aaron was not in the same place as Quinn Martin," adds Claver. "Quinn Martin's stuff had a lot of quality, and he had a very good reputation. Aaron didn't. He treated actors well — he was the nicest to actors — he was very much there for them. He was a good guy."

Bob Claver's next job at Four Star, which was also his next teaming with Hy Averback, came with the lighthearted 1964-65 NBC comedy-drama, *The Rogues*. Created by Ivan Goff and Ben Roberts (the 1949 Cagney classic *White Heat,* the TV series *Mannix, Charlie's Angels*), *The Rogues* starred Gig Young, David Niven, and Charles Boyer as a family of con-artists whose "marks" generally deserved what they got. What with name guest stars like Walter Matthau and George Sanders, gorgeous women like Raquel Welch, Jill St. John, Camilla Sparv, Danielle DeMetz, and Barbara Bouchet, plus elaborate con games, *The Rogues* was something of a light-hearted *Mission: Impossible.* In fact, *Mission's* future production manager/director/producer Barry Crane and assistant director Bob White worked on the series. "Barry was a serious international bridge player," states Claver. "He was like an assistant manager. Norman S. Powell, the son of Dick Powell, was also there. He was a multi-unit manager. That was a good show. It was very sophisticated and fun to do — we had wonderful actors. That was a wonderful show."

Claver liked his next series even better. That program began his long professional and personal association with Screen Gems exec Jackie Cooper. "Hy and Jackie Cooper were good friends," states Claver, "and thereby hangs my career. My first show as a producer in Hollywood was *The Farmer's Daughter.*"

Based on the 1947 movie of the same name with Loretta Young, and Joseph Cotten, the 1963-66 Screen Gems situation comedy starred Swedish actress Inger Stevens as the title character, Katy Holstrum, and William Windom as Glen Morley, the Washington, D.C. congressman for whom she works. Eventually the two characters fell in love and married. "I had done part of a half-season because [producer] Peter Kortner and Inger went to Sweden," explains Claver. "They did a special [*Inger Stevens in Sweden* — February 26, 1965], and [then] I took over. [Because] I got along great with Inger and everybody else [and] she didn't like Peter, she wanted me to take over the thing. It was okay with Jackie and the network, but I said, 'You're gonna have a terrible time cuz when you tell 'em I did *Captain Kangaroo* — they're gonna be thrilled,' and that's exactly what happened — they just screamed bloody murder. Jackie said, 'Too bad. It's my show, and he's doing it.' Now how many people do you think would defy them like that? Well, from then on, I was never much out of work.

"That whole Screen Gems place was wonderful," continues Claver. "I remember I was in New York — on a (business) trip — I was there to sell a pilot, and I was at the Gotham Hotel, right down the block from Columbia (Pictures). I got a call from Jerry Hyams, who was at that time the president of Screen Gems. He wanted me to come over and see him. He said, 'I have your hotel bill here. I see no calls home. I don't want to see this again. I don't want to see one bill for one night in a hotel where you don't call home.' See, I was inexperienced. I was just a hick. I thought I should be very careful and wary of spending money. So I never forgot that. He was a man... that was an extraordinarily generous thing to do."

As the new producer of *The Farmer's Daughter*, Bob Claver worked with, or brought in, established, and new talents. Some, like Paul Junger Witt, Jerry Bernstein, and Skip Webster would work with him on future Screen Gems television series. Series director William Russell was one who did not. Russell would soon become the main director of the new CBS-TV series, *Family Affair*.

"When I took over the show, there were some assignments already given out," remembers Claver. "Bill Russell was a very nice guy, not a terrific director, but he was one of those guys who got it done fast and he did it nice enough. All of those assistant directors and unit managers — including many of them at Screen Gems — became directors, not very good ones, but they became working directors. I mean, it's not brain surgery. If you can get the job done, and they could, they worked a lot. Bill Russell was a bona-fide worker. He did a lot of *Hazels*. Both Russell and [fellow *Family Affair* director] Charles Barton could be the same person — they were good, hard-working, get-the-job-done people. And if the scripts were good, they didn't hurt 'em, and if the scripts weren't good, they didn't help 'em. They were just there, and the work was good and fast. Then we started going in for guys who might do something interesting. That could get you in some trouble as a producer. Because those guys never knew what they were doing half the time, and the hours started to pile up."

Fortunately for Claver and his associates, *The Farmer's Daughter*'s cast made it easy to deal with such problems. "We all got along fine," says Claver. "Inger and Bill…Inger was okay with him. And Cathleen Nesbitt was wonderful, so the show was really easy to do — they were all pros who wanted to get the job done. And that was an era…because Inger was married to a black man. Now everybody knew that. All the press knew it, all the network people knew it, but nobody printed it. Because they realized that if they printed that, that show was dead. I mean, look at Rock Hudson, maybe the nicest man in this industry. Everybody knew about him, but nobody printed that. Because there was a respect for someone's privacy, and a respect for someone's livelihood. That is now gone."

In between *The Rogues* and *The Farmer's Daughter*, Bob Claver made the first episode of *Gidget* — "Dear Diary – Et Al" [September 15, 1965]. "I did the *Gidget* pilot, and for some reason or other, I didn't want to do it, or they didn't want me to do it," remembers the producer. "I directed Sally's [Field] test out of high school, and I produced that pilot. Billy Sackheim ended up being the executive producer."

After *The Farmer's Daughter* left the air, Bob Claver's next series for Screen Gems was the 1967-68 situation comedy, *The Second Hundred Years*. Featuring future *Here Come the Brides* leading lady Bridget Hanley in the semi-regular role of Nurse Lucille Anderson, *The Second Hundred Years* starred later *Brides* guest Monte Markham as an early twentieth century Alaska gold prospector who had been caught in a glacier slide and somehow preserved alive. Thawed out sixty-seven years later, though chronologically one-hundred-and-one, Markham looks and has the body of a thirty-three-year-old man. That makes him younger than his son — played by veteran actor Arthur O'Connell. Markham also played O'Connell's son. The comedy in the show revolved around the one-hundred-and-one year-old Markham's attempts to adjust to twentieth century life.

"Everybody thought it was gonna be a smash hit because it was such a great idea — NOT!" says Claver. "I hated that show. I didn't like the series idea, and I didn't like the actors. I found that Monte Markham was one of the truly unpleasant people to work with — I hated working with him, and I don't mean as a guy to have dinner with. He was just an annoying whiner. And I said to him many times. 'Look, nobody put a gun to your head to do this thing,' because you're talking about a guy (Markham's character, Luke Carpenter) that was a fucking ice cube for a hundred years."

Nor did Claver care for veteran actor O'Connell. "I thought Arthur O'Connell was a pain in the ass," states the producer. "I found that show a lot of work. It wasn't fun to do. I was the producer and Harry Ackerman was the executive producer, and Harry was a gentleman, gentleman, gentleman. He did tend to over-exaggerate the skill level, but he was a very nice man. I don't remember getting fired from that show. So maybe I moved on to do pilots. I think the first job I had as executive producer was *Here Come the Brides.*"

As noted earlier, the *Brides* project had been a property of the Columbia/Screen Gems studio for quite a few years. The project now being planned as a continuing television series, it was the task of Claver and *Brides* creator N. Richard Nash to revamp the project for TV.

"Steve Blauner was an executive there," remembers Claver. "He was pretty much connected with Bobby Darin. He's the one who assigned me to that. I was thrilled to meet N. Richard Nash, let alone work with him. Nash was a bona-fide Broadway playwright. He'd done a lot of good television in those anthology days, so he was very wary of doing this. He was pretty much out of television cuz he didn't want to do it — he was doing screenplays and stuff, but some way or other, I guess maybe [Jackie] Cooper or [Steve] Blauner managed to talk him into it. Anyway we met, and he was standoffish for a while. And as we went through various drafts, I realized — I don't care if it's N. Richard Nash or Shakespeare, I kept giving him notes, and I thought, He's gonna act on them or I am, but that never came to that. He was wonderfully accepting of my opinion. And he loved the pilot! He didn't like the pilot — he LOVED the pilot! As far as he was concerned, it was the best television experience of his life. So from then on, we used him in advisory ways. So we got a script out, and what a script that was! I wasn't used to reading rich scripts like that. Then we got some good actors. I thought we did a good job. It wasn't easy."

As executive producer of the pilot, Claver "had a hand in a lot of the stuff. He [Nash] had these characters, and you would change them," recalls the producer, "but most of these things I would have to say are ninety percent him. You'd make [just] slight adjustments. I will take credit for the fact that the casting was very good. The actors realized those characters. It all worked for me."

Helping Claver in the casting of the pilot, and later the show's guest casting, was former *Hawk* production consultant Renee Valente. "Renee Valente was a very good casting director, as was Millie Gusse before her," states Claver. "They'd bring in people, and they'd recommend people, but in the end, it's your ass, your name, and your blame. You know, 'Why did you put that person in this part? She stinks.' That you don't need.

So, if you're working that job [producer], and you don't know a good actor from a bad actor, you shouldn't have the job at all. It's an important part of your work."

"All those people we cast — it's a very simple procedure, which you may think is more complicated," continues Claver. "You have a casting director — and you have a script. You give her the script. You say, 'Go get the part of Essie,' and she'll give you a list of ten women. You'll eliminate some that you know and don't want, then you'll say, 'You gotta bring in these people. I don't know them.' Then you have a reading, and you cast the one you choose. And nobody nobody nobody nobody in any television show I've ever heard of has a [final] say, except the producer. That doesn't mean you don't listen to other people. If a director says, 'Well, I've worked with that lady and we don't get along well,' that's enough for me, but in the end, that's how it works."

In casting all of the regular and semi-regular characters on *Here Come the Brides*, Bob Claver had very definite opinions as to whom he wanted in which parts. Topping the list was of course the lead character, Jason Bolt — co-owner and manager of Bolt Brothers Logging with his two younger brothers, Joshua and Jeremy. "I wanted Robert Brown in the show from the start," declares Claver. "I'd seen him in a play at UCLA, and 'Swack' [director E.W. Swackhamer] knew him from New York." ('Swack' and Brown had been friends since their days attending the dramatic workshop at Erwin Piscator's New School of Social Research.)

"Robert Brown was very interesting," praises Claver. "He had a career where a lot of people in the business knew who he was but he really didn't have much of a career as a popular person. (Brown was a highly regarded stage actor whose credits included such Shakespeare plays as *The Tempest*, *Two Gentlemen of Verona*, and *King John*.) He didn't read — we didn't need to test him."

Not being much interested in doing a television series, Robert Brown made it very clear he would neither read nor test. "He could say all that he wants," notes Claver, "that he's not gonna test, but if the network says, 'If he's not gonna test, he's not gonna get the part,' that makes it a tougher decision, but they didn't. And he wasn't all that well known either. So, I'm surprised at them."

Casting singers Bobby Sherman and David Soul as the other two Bolt brothers was another daring move on the part of Claver, et al. Sherman was best known for the musical variety series, *Shindig*, Soul as "The Covered Man" on *The Merv Griffin Show*. Of the two actors, Claver preferred Sherman. "I loved the stuttering," enthuses the producer. "I thought Bobby did a good job with it. He managed to find a balance. The worst thing in the world you can give to an audience is, 'Oh! Is he gonna talk long?' and [have them] be uncomfortable, but he didn't do that. I thought he did a good job. I loved the relationship between him and Bridget. It was nice. It was a love story."

As a result, "we had a lot of Bobby shows," admits Claver. "Those were my favorites because I liked the character and all the rest of it. Bobby had a solid core of people that liked him, as they should have. He was an interesting actor, and a really totally decent human being. A really good human being — still is."

As for David Soul in the role of middle brother Joshua Bolt, "he was all right," says the producer, "a little grouchy, but certainly no problem. David Soul was in a position to cause no trouble, because we could fire him. He wasn't exactly getting tons of fan letters. I don't wish him any harm or anything, but he was just the least interesting of the characters. I mean if there was a show where David was the lead and the only lead, I would probably not want to do the show cuz I think it's hard. There's something about these people — men or women that make it in television or features. I can't say why Elizabeth Montgomery was a giant star in television — she's nice-looking, talented, the whole thing worked. As it did with Barbara Eden, [because] they have something special."

To Claver, there was "nothing very special about David. He's good and nice, but I've never been much of a fan of his work," states the producer. "I just don't think that he's a very interesting actor. He was very competent, but he didn't make you look at the screen. I mean when he did that series with [Paul] Michael Glaser [*Starsky & Hutch*], I thought that Glaser was fascinating. One of the reasons was he had very little competition."

Fortunately for David Soul, *Brides* story editor William Blinn thought differently — thanks to first-season episodes like "A Hard Card to Play," "A Christmas Place," and "Democracy Inaction," Soul was shown to very good effect. Moreover, when the show moved to what some thought a more action-oriented format in its second-season, the more athletic Soul, in Blinn's opinion, was one cast member who benefited from the change.

According to Bob Claver, the biggest casting problem concerned the show's leading lady. "The one we fought for — Swack and I," states Claver, "was Bridget. That was not an easy sell. I don't know why. Everybody was happy once she got the job, and did it, but the network was tough. It was very hard — we had to get very snotty — both of us, to get that done. And obviously, Swack, he must have had a vested interest in that." (When the series began, director Swackhamer, and leading lady Hanley were already in love. Before the second season began, they had married.)

"Everything was perfect for her," adds the producer, "and she was perfect for the part, but she was fairly unknown at the time. I said, to a number of people, 'Why are we even talking about that? Who cares?' Because people tune in to see…they don't tune in to see, unless it's Elizabeth Montgomery or somebody who has a name, they tune in to see the show."

"So, unless it's a one-man show, or a show like *Mork & Mindy*, because you can't replace Robin Williams, you can replace actors." During the course of the *Brides* pilot's production, another casting problem arose. The original plan was to present the now-combined Mama Damnation/Lottie Starr character as a romantic interest for Jason Bolt — something of an *HCTB* version of *Gunsmoke's* Miss Kitty. As a result, two attractive young actresses, Gail Kobe and Joanna Moore, were, at one point, cast in the part.

"Gail Kobe was a wonderful actress, and Joanna Moore was another pretty one," notes Claver, "much prettier actually than Gail Kobe. But it was a bad idea. We just went a whole other way; we wanted a total character actress, not a leading lady." At the suggestion of star Robert Brown, Joan Blondell got the part.

"Joan was perfect," declares Claver. "She was a wonderful lady, with no ego at all. And she was a big star! She was this big, round, ebullient lady — she was great. I loved Joan. She loved doing the show, and she loved working. She was alone pretty much, and she used to lecture me all the time because I was married, but going through the first of my many less than successful shots [at marriage]. She said, 'Don't be alone, don't be alone,' because she was alone and she hated being alone. She'd been married

*Bridget Hanley.*

to Dick Powell, and George Barnes [and Mike Todd] and God knows who else, but I loved her!" The casting of Blondell proved to be a good thing for the show. As well as for one of the first season cast members.

Claver also enjoyed Mark Lenard in the role of the villainous Aaron Stempel. Particularly since, as the series progressed, Stempel's relationship with Jason Bolt changed — from antagonist to friend. "Mark was just wonderful in that part," remembers the producer. "Mark was a very serious actor. He prepared a lot, and he had lots of questions, but again, he was an actor just doing his job."

Another favorite of Claver's was Mitzi Hoag in the role of catalyst Miss Essie; in fact, it was Essie's romantic feelings towards Bo Svenson's Big Swede, and vice versa, which set the series in motion. "That worked very well," praises Claver. "Mitzi Hoag was wonderful. She's a wonderful actress. She never worked as much as I think she should have. She got those parts here and there. She was terrific in that part. Henry Beckman and Susan Tolsky had a good position to play in the story, too. Mostly Henry would just mug and carry on. So we'd use them for comic relief. Doesn't hurt. There were a lot of other girls [and men] who were regulars, too. Some were extras. We used the same people all the time. That didn't happen very often."

Claver also "did all of the guest-casting. I had a casting director," states the director/producer, "but the decision as to who plays in the show, is always the producer's decision. That was my job. I was very hands-on in everything — I was hands-on in wardrobe in all of my shows. That was not exceptional."

Designing the wardrobe for the men — Pat McGrath. Designing it for the women — Betsy Cox. "Betsy Cox would get the things together, and show them to me," remembers Claver. "She was very, very competent. She did very well with Joan Blondell. There was a certain flashiness to Joan's wardrobe; Bridget's was not that way. It shouldn't be. She was a lady."

When it came to the men's costumes, star Robert Brown had the most colorful and vivid outfits; co-stars Bobby Sherman and David Soul generally wore flannel shirts. "Robert was wearing a turtleneck," says Claver. "They didn't have those back then. He did, and who cared?"

Some fans and television critics did. Claver characterizes such folks as "gotcha people. Those are people who have nothing else to do," laughs the producer/director. "It looked good. That's a decision you have to make."

Another decision Claver made concerned location work. "We were pretty much okay with the budget, and, once we'd built that city (of 1860/'70s Seattle) which was on the [Columbia] ranch there, then we really had most of our stuff," explains the producer. "We shot it all out on the ranch, and, when you have a schedule, you can do a lot of work in one day. Nobody gave us trouble."

Nor did the cast and crew mind visits from Claver's young daughter. "When my daughter was little, she loved going to that show," chuckles Claver. "She thought that was a lot of fun. [Of] course all those people, when you're the producer's daughter, everybody sucks around you."

It was also Bob Claver who chose composer Hugo Montenegro to write the series theme. "I did pick Hugo because I thought he was perfect for that show," states

Claver. "And he was. Hugo's a good writer, a very talented musician. And not hip. I thought he did a very good job. We got a song out of that; [Perry] Como recorded that." The song was of course, "Seattle."

Montenegro also wrote themes for the Bolts, for Jeremy, Miss Essie, Big Swede, Clancy, etc. Explains Claver, "The people who do scoring — they write themes for various characters. That's the way they always did it. It helps the audience, it helps with continuity." Montenegro's rollicking, exuberant, and at times, tender, and, at other times, sweeping themes went perfectly with the characters portrayed by Robert Brown, Bobby Sherman, David Soul, Bridget Hanley et al.

"Robert Brown had an ego, but a good ego," states Claver, "Bobby was wonderful and, of course, Bridget, and people like Joan Blondell and Henry — they were all good to work with, and happy to be working, and they liked the show. A lot of people are happy to work — it's not like it's an industry that you don't have your problems in, but Robert was a good guy. He and Swack got along real well — they were old friends from before, and Swack did a fair number of shows. There was no trouble with any of those people. I don't call it trouble when someone says, 'I'm having trouble with this scene,' or 'I don't like this; it doesn't make sense.' They're not idiots — they have a right to do that. I'm very open to that. I just don't like the people who cause Telly Savalas kind of shit, or Peter Falk — that just makes trouble. (Both Falk and Savalas became what quite a few in the business described as "monsters" when they reached television super-stardom with their respective series, *Columbo* and *Kojak*.)

"I don't know about other people, but I've never been hard up enough to work for people like that," says the producer. "I don't wanna be around them. They may be fine if you're having dinner with them, but you want to go to work every day, and wait till somebody explodes? I've never worked with anybody like that — not one person. I mean some people you like better than others, but there were never any troublesome people. I've had a lot of strange people in my career, but they were all fun to work with in their own way. And you know stars always set the tone. So they should set a tone where you should be able to work."

Case in point: Robert Brown. On *Here Come the Brides*, "Big Daddy" Brown watched out for his fellow cast members. "That was kind of a role he thought he had," says Claver, "because he was older than some of the guys." Veteran actress Joan Blondell also helped maintain a happy mood. "She was the spirit of the show," believes Claver (his sentiment is echoed by *Brides* stunt double Dave Cass, wardrobe man Steve Lodge, guest Lynda Day George, et al). "Joan had a great attitude, and she had no conceit. If she had a lousy part that week, she was just terrific. She was just a fun person to be around."

The same was said of *Brides* leading lady Bridget Hanley. It was also somewhat true of Robert Brown. Muses Claver, "I'm sure Robert...there were a couple of weeks when he got short shrift and didn't like it. So any actor in his right mind is gonna say, 'What's going on?' but he didn't roll over anybody."

"They were all very accommodating — the *Brides* people," praises Claver. "I don't remember any trouble with any of them to tell you the truth, though obviously there can be scenes. I remember when I was doing *Partridge Family*, I learned real early on all you had to do with Shirley Jones was tell her the truth. She'd tell you, 'I read next week's script, and I really think it's not very good.' My answer usually was, 'I did too, and we're working on it cuz it's terrible.' Not 'Read it again, Shirley. Maybe you're missing something.' You know, don't ever try that. Just tell the truth and move on, cuz those people, they trust you, and, in a way, they kind of owe you. That's how you get along. [Of] course, working with someone like Shirley is hardly a problem."

Claver had the same feeling concerning *Here Come the Brides.* "It was a good show to do," says Claver. "The people were nice, the sets were pretty good. I liked doing the show. I always thought it was good, and it was shot like a movie, even *Partridge Family* was shot like a movie. That's…the advantage of that is you can make a better-looking show, and you can baby kids through it. But, you don't have an audience. I grew to love audience shows because I loved the feeling of being in a control room, and hearing a joke that you might have come up with — hearing the audience tell you that it worked — that was fun to do, I think. Not very pretty those shows [in a visual sense], but fun to do."

Claver was so busy at the time he made *Here Come the Brides*, he rarely had the time to watch it. "I don't know that I was much of a watcher of television in those days," says the producer. "My wife was an agent — a major agent. We would go out; we'd meet and have dinner at Danny's Hideaway a lot of times — that was the 'in' restaurant. Then we'd go home and collapse because I had to be at work at 4:30 in the morning. We'd get out of there [the Screen Gems studio] early enough, but then we had to do writing. We were making an insane amount of money, which [compared to the salaries of today] is like a joke now. But it was fun to do. The show was getting good recognition, Jackie Cooper liked the show, he and Steve Blauner were fine, but the work was hard."

While Bob Claver had done quite a few series by the time he did *Here Come the Brides*, he'd never done a western. "It wasn't a western in a classic sense," muses the producer, "but it was still a western. I always thought it a western. We didn't have guns, or if we did, very few, and we didn't have violence. It wasn't that kind of a show. We did character studies — we had a lot of good character people."

One thing Claver had to learn very quickly — how to write and produce an hour-long series. "There's a great difference between an hour and a half-hour show," states the producer. "Just the numbers of people, the size of the scenes — it's much different."[1]

Helping Bob Claver quickly become familiar with this sort of production was *Here Come the Brides* story editor William Blinn.

---

1. Claver – interview – 2007

"I don't know that a dictum ever went out, but it was clear we all felt more comfortable when there was a female element in the story telling, and a core female, not just a decorative, 'wasn't she a pretty girl?'"

*Here Come the Brides* story editor/writer William Blinn

# Chapter 3

# *Written by William Blinn*

"'The man runs the house.' Well, we know that's not true. Even in *Father Knows Best*, father *thought* he ran the house, and the children thought he ran the house, but anyone watching from the outside, would…'No, no. He's tolerated, and he's humored, but he does *not* run the house.'"

That was *Here Come the Brides* story editor, and frequent episode writer, William Blinn, giving his view of the popular Robert Young/Jane Wyatt Screen Gems series, *Father Knows Best*. Like many male writers of 1960s and '70s TV, William Blinn enjoyed doing stories where women had strong parts. He was perfectly comfortable working on a television series where women were an important part of the regular storyline. In fact, it was Blinn who wrote the female-friendly *HCTB* story, "Democracy Inaction" — a favorite of both *Brides* leading lady Bridget Hanley and semi-regular Mitzi Hoag.

Though William Blinn was one of television's busiest writers, when he began in the entertainment industry, his original plan was to be an actor. "I started at eighteen," Blinn recalls. "The first year, I was at the Academy [the American Academy of Dramatic Arts in New York — often referred to as the Harvard of acting schools]. I wasn't a bad actor. I could do some stuff that was pretty good, but I wasn't at ease with being an actor and I realized that if everything went really, really well, I would at best be kind of a journeyman actor."

Given some of the graduates turned out by the Academy, Blinn's choosing not to be an actor was probably a good idea. Among the American Academy's graduates: Spencer Tracy, Rosalind Russell, Fredric March, Charles Durning, Jason Robards, Colleen Dewhurst, Lauren Bacall, Kirk Douglas, Robert Redford. "The list goes on and on and on," says Blinn, "They have a [good] track record and a list of graduates — actually, it's the oldest school teaching drama in the western hemisphere. (The Academy was founded in 1884.) It has its ups and downs as any school does. When the Actor's Studio was in full bloom, places like the Academy seemed stuffy."

One of the instructors at the Academy during Blinn's days was *Maude* regular Conrad Bain. Also associated with the school were Bernard Kates and football player-turned actor Bernie Casey. "Robert Redford was in the class after us," remembers Blinn. "I'm probably one of the few people who ever did any stage managing for Rob Redford, and at one point I saw him do Shakespeare, and very well, as a matter of fact. There was no question that he was gonna be a star, apart from his looks, which were you know, drop dead handsome, but he was also a very versatile actor. His looks were a curse for him to some degree, because he's a much better actor than I think some people give him credit for."

During his time at the Academy, Blinn struck up a close friendship with another successful television writer — Michael Gleason. Writer and/or producer of such memorable *McCloud*s as "The Barefoot Stewardess Caper," "This Must Be the Alamo," "The Colorado Cattle Caper," and "Butch Cassidy Rides Again," Michael Gleason would co-create with director Robert Butler the Stephanie Zimbalist/Pierce Brosnan hit, *Remington Steele* in the early 1980s. "Michael was a kid from Brooklyn," says Blinn, "and I was a kid from [Toledo] Ohio. We were both worshippers of Sid Caesar and *Your Show of Shows*. We would take notes on *Your Show of Shows*, [and compare those notes] when we would meet every Monday morning for breakfast."

Like William Blinn, Michael Gleason was working as a stage manager [on Broadway]. About the same time Parke Perrine "who was my associate producer on *The Rookies* and a show called *The New Land*, and did some directing here as well," says Blinn, "he was the old guy when we were at the academy. He was in the Navy, and a man of the world as far as we were concerned, because I was eighteen; Parke was maybe twenty-six or seven."

While both Blinn and Gleason were fans of *Your Show of Shows*, they weren't impressed with too much else on TV. "Like a lot of people who looked at television, we said, 'God, that's awful,'" laughs Blinn. " 'I can do better than that.' So we came back and started writing some speculative scripts, and I came out here trying to find an agent in either '60 or '61. It was the year the Writer's Guild went out on strike, and the first headline (Blinn saw upon reading his first issue of the *Hollywood Reporter*) was 'Writer's Guild out on Strike.' I got some part-time jobs just to keep body and soul together. Mike came out about six or eight months after that.

"We got our stuff read by a couple of agents," continues Blinn. "They didn't want to represent us. But they were very helpful — they didn't shove us out the door. They said, 'There's some intelligence here, there's some craft, lax if you will, but maybe you guys have a future, hang in there.' Then we found an agent, Ivan Green, and Ivan agreed to represent us. Then, in a period…Michael and I have never been able to sort this out, in a period of about two weeks, we did two speculative screenplays, one to *Laramie* (1959-63, NBC, starring Robert Fuller and John Smith), and one to *Rawhide* (1959-66, CBS, starring Eric Fleming, Clint Eastwood, and Paul Brinegar). Neither one of us can nail down which one was the first sale, they literally came within a couple weeks of each other. So we did the rewrites for those. Then we had started a second *Rawhide*, and the first *Rawhide* ("Incident of the Portrait" – October 5, 1962) brought us to the attention of a guy named Peter Tewksbury who was a very…for the time, very gifted and innovative director."

Having a talented director like Tewksbury expressing interest in their work was quite a compliment to Blinn and Gleason. During the first few seasons of the long-running situation comedy, *My Three Sons*, producer/director/writer Tewksbury did some very interesting episodes, including "Countdown" (in which a missile launch, oversleeping, and the end of Daylight Savings Time went into the story mix), and "Organization Woman" (Steve Douglas's sister Harriett believes she can solve the ongoing chaos in the Douglas household by setting up a daily pattern with the help of timelines, charts, and graphs.)

"Tewksbury was doing a show called *It's a Man's World* (starring Glenn Corbett, Ted Bessell, Michael Burns, and Randy Boone), not successful commercially," explains Blinn, "but for its time, very well received critically. The audience that got it really got it. When it went off the air, there was a letter-writing campaign. Those things never work, but it [the show] was very, very helpful to us — both Michael and me. [Because] Peter was much more open than most television producer-directors to having writers as part of the ongoing collaborative team. There was a reading of each script with the cast around the table. They were all great buddies. That was almost unheard of. I don't know how much it helped Michael and me because we were babes in arms at that point. But to be part of the collaborative team was not standard for a television writer."

The episode that William Blinn and Michael Gleason co-wrote, "I Count My Life in Coffee Cups" (November 26, 1962), guest-starred future *Here Come the Brides* semi-regular Diane Sayer ("bride" Sally). Interestingly, when Blinn worked on *Shane* and *Here Come the Brides*, both shows had the cast members, writers, et al, sitting around the table reading the script. *Brides* eventually discontinued this practice.

"Mike and I continued to work together for about a year after that," remembers Blinn. "We did some sitcoms...*My Favorite Martian* ("The Man on the Couch" – November 3, 1963, "A Nose for News" – June 21, 1964) which was not...it paid the bills and that's all I can say. They were all nice guys, but my idea of hell is being in a room with eight other writers trying to punch up a script. I just can't get myself to do that. I can write it, or you can write it, but when I get a whole bunch of people, and we're all gonna contribute, I'm out the door. I'm not part of that."

Continues Blinn: "Following that, Mike and I split up. Very amicably, mainly because, if we split up, and we continued to work, we would automatically double our income, 'cuz we weren't splitting the checks. So I went back to New York, working at the American Academy as a stage manager for a while.

While back in New York, Blinn "wrote a speculative outline for *Bonanza* ("All Ye His Saints") with five-year-old Clint Howard as the star. The kid was just delightful and it was very well directed by my personal manager — a director by the name of Bill Claxton. [Then] I started to write a second spec script for *Bonanza*, and they said I needed to come out here [because] they were not going to accept the rewrite being done in New York. So I came out here and did the rewrite of "All Ye His Saints," followed by a second original [the Tommy Sands/Brooke Bundy episode "The Debt," which served as the series' seventh-season premiere], which was then followed by another rewrite of someone else's script [Yellow Springs, Ohio writer Suzanne

Clauser's "A Natural Wizard" guest-starring Eddie Hodges and future *HCTB* guest Jacqueline Scott.] After that I was offered a job as staff writer on the show, and the guy who was story editor at the time, Denne Petitclerc (he recently passed away), the two of us remained friends and in touch for fifty-plus years. Denne and myself and our wives used to go down to Mexico, deep-sea fishing a lot, and we used to go up to his place in Glen Helen.

"Denne and I were joined at the hip creatively," says Blinn. "We hit it off [immediately]. I was staff writer on the show [but] I got the credit if I did enough rewrite to get a credit on the show, you know, 'Teleplay by William Blinn.' So it was Denne and myself and another guy, Bill Lansford [William Douglas Lansford]. The three of us were the writing staff on *Bonanza* for that particular season. It was an interesting season for *Bonanza* because it was the first season without Pernell Roberts. And I say interesting because even though there had been a lot of negative chemistry between the actors playing the Cartwrights (and Pernell in particular); nevertheless, everyone was a little uncertain as to how the chemistry might have been affected. Would the audience turn away because now there were just three Cartwrights? They didn't know. So, when the episodes started to come on the air, and the audience stuck with the show, and the ratings remained solid, everyone breathed a huge sigh of relief. It was also, I think, just about at that time that Mike Landon started to get interested in becoming a writer himself. [Landon had written the third-season episode, "The Gamble," April 1, 1962.] I don't think Mike wrote anything that particular year. [Landon wrote episodes like "Ballad of the Ponderosa" and "Joe Cartwright, Detective" the following season]. He pitched a couple of things to us. He was very involved when a script was less than perfect, and obviously we had those scripts that were less than perfect; his suggestions and his thoughts were constructive. I liked Mike a lot — I thought he was a good guy from start to finish. [Working on the series] was a great, great, great learning experience for a young writer."

Creator-producer David Dortort had quite a bit to do with that. "David's office was just two or three doors from the writer's office," explains Blinn. "We'd meet every day and he was very encouraging because Denne Petitclerc was essentially brand new to television. Denne had been a novelist and a reporter for, I think, the *Miami Herald* and *San Francisco Chronicle*, but I don't think he'd written anything in terms of television, until, like me, he did a speculative script for *Bonanza*. David not only bought Denne's script, he brought Denne down from San Francisco, and made him story consultant. In that sense, he [Dortort] couldn't have been more encouraging to writers and giving them responsibility and so forth and so on."

Given its longevity and its impact, *Bonanza* was frequently compared to the big one: CBS's long-running *Gunsmoke*. "*Gunsmoke* was the quintessential television western and clearly one of the best television dramas, and series that we ever had," declares Blinn. "I think the longevity of *Gunsmoke* was that Matt Dillon was steady and stolid and straightforward, and he had intelligence, and some little droll kind of humor and all this and that, and the people around him had pace and energy and new stuff that they could do. The guest star parts were all very well written, but at the core was Matt, and right next to him, Miss Kitty and Festus and Doc, and all these people."

The series also boasted a strong team of producers and writers. Among them: John Mantley, Joseph Dackow, Paul Savage, Calvin Clements, Sr., Jack Miller (who wrote three very good, second-season *Brides* episodes), Paul F. Edwards, Jim Byrnes, and Ron Bishop. "*Gunsmoke* was tougher, it was gritty, it was certainly more reality-based than most westerns," states Blinn. "Every once in a while, they did a comedy, but most of the time, they were hard-core action with very well-rounded characters — they didn't do black hats and white hats — they were very fleshed-out characters. Or, they would do a kind of bittersweet love story."

When *Gunsmoke* did do comedies, they did them very reluctantly. "They did this comedy once," remembers Blinn, "and the only reason they did it was they were getting so much pressure about violence that the executive producer of *Gunsmoke* [John Mantley] finally said, 'Oh the hell with it. I'll give 'em something so silly and stupid,' and he did. The premise was a guy came to town, and he went to Matt, and he said, 'You gotta lock me up in the barn. This next Tuesday night, there's a full moon, and the night of the full moon, I turn into an elephant.' This was a guy whose circus had gone out of business, so he was trying to get rid of his elephants. Festus locked him up in the barn, and when he went back in the morning, there was an elephant. You know, the stupidest kind of story, but John Mantley, the executive producer, just said, 'Fine, you want that, I'll give you something stupid and corny.' They put it on Christmas Eve, or sometime when no one was gonna see it.'"

Unlike *Gunsmoke*, *Bonanza* did a number of comedies. "Mike and Dan loved the comedies," chuckles Blinn. "They were cut-ups. Absolutely. Lorne had a good sense of humor, but Lorne was Ben Cartwright. He wasn't serious in a stuffy way, but he was serious. He didn't feel comfortable with the broad-ass, falling down, knock 'em on the nose kind of comedy, whereas Dan and Mike absolutely did. I remember one [story] Michael pitched to us — for the last half of it, Dan was dressed up in a buckskin dress, playing an Indian squaw. If you're doing that, you're doing sketch comedy.

"Dan and Mike loved to play comedy more than anything else," continues Blinn. "They both loved it, and they did it, and they did it very well. We did a number of comedies that particular season. It's referred to as the 'Lost Season' because it doesn't have David Canary [who began in the long-lasting role of the Cartwright's ranch hand 'Candy' in the series' ninth and longest season], it doesn't have Pernell Roberts, and it never flourished much in syndication. We did some very funny comedies — I think they were very funny comedies. We had one with Sally Kellerman and Elisha Cook, Jr., and Hampton Fancher ["A Dollar's Worth of Trouble" – May 15, 1966]. It was delightful. Denne and I had such a good time on that. Fancher was playing a severely nearsighted gunfighter. Everybody thought this cold stare was the gunfighter's 'don't cross me' look, but it was because the guy couldn't see across the room. It was constantly played for laughs. And Elisha Cook, Jr., played a drunken ne'er-do-well. There wasn't an ounce of seriousness to it. It was all just silly. That was the kind of thing that Dan and Mike loved. Lorne had no problems with that. As long as he didn't have to do silly things, as long as he was the guy reacting to all the silliness, he was okay with it. Ultimately, I think it was Chevrolet who said, 'We would like to cut down on the comedies,' because they were the sole sponsor. They didn't think it was good programming for them." Perhaps, but comedies would continue on *Bonanza* until the loss of Dan Blocker.

As both William Blinn and Denne Bart Petitclerc were "relatively new to day-in, day-out television," they understandably had their qualms taking over the writing chores in a series as successful as *Bonanza*. "*Bonanza* was a family western," notes Blinn. "Almost every episode dealt with some kind of family dispute with the pater-familias, with Lorne Greene coming forward to solve the problem or guide his boys into the right way to get to where they needed to get to. But by the time I got to *Bonanza* as a staff writer, there was a little bit of a problem. More times than not, it was number one or two or three in the ratings, and, if you were a young writer, you might not want to jump in because it had been on the air six years, so what kind of credit were you gonna get? You weren't gonna be able to change what they were doing, because what they were doing worked. The only reason I got in there and was able to bring, with the help of Denne Petitclerc, a little bit of fresh spice to the stew was the fact that it was a new deal without Pernell Roberts."

In a way, therefore, the seventh season of *Bonanza* was in some respects a new series. "And because it was the first season without Pernell Roberts," says Blinn, "there was a little bit of insecurity in the office. They were ill at ease with Pernell leaving for commercial purposes, and there was a lot of scar tissue left behind in those two factions. So, those two elements allowed Denne and I to go in and say, 'Hey, I got an idea. Let's do this.' And the powers that be would occasionally, though not always, say, 'Well, okay. Let's try it,' because, they didn't know."

Having played their parts for six straight years, the three stars of *Bonanza* felt it was about time the program depicted a change in the relationship between Ben Cartwright and his (now) two sons. Remembers Blinn: "They were to the point, all of them — Dan and Mike and Lorne, of, 'Wait a minute. These aren't little boys anymore that Papa can order around. These are grown men who can stand up and make their own choices and their own decisions.' So, if there is to be a conflict about what Ben thinks ought to be done, and what Little Joe thinks ought to be done, the conflict is fine, it's just that no one can be ordered to do anything. Because there comes a time when 'Young man, you can't say that,' goes away. That was their reminder, I think, to David Dortort, that 'Time has passed and we [the characters] have changed.'"

Yet it was because of David Dortort that *Bonanza* set itself apart from the other TV westerns of the time thanks to its original form of storytelling. This tradition continued in the seventh season, and through the run of the show. In addition to Blinn's superb "All Ye His Saints," which had little Clint Howard journeying to a snow-covered mountaintop in search of God, other religious episodes presented in the seventh season included "Devil on Her Shoulder" (Ina Balin is accused of witch-craft by her religious fanatic uncle John Doucette), and "Mighty is the Word." The latter, co-written by future *HCTB* writer Robert L. Goodwin (one of television's few black writers) guest-starred Glenn Corbett as an ex-gunfighter turned preacher. "It was a standard-issue *Bonanza* episode," states Blinn. "But it was good, put together well and well presented. Glenn Corbett...I thought he was gonna happen as a star. He was very underrated."

During his one season with *Bonanza*, William Blinn learned things that would prove "invaluable" in his future television career. "*Bonanza* was a winning episode for me," explains the writer, "because, at that time, it was one of the few color shows. It was in color because RCA was one of the sponsors, and they had, at that time, something that very few shows do even now, which is, they would alternate directors of photography. So, when a director came in to shoot a show, he had the director of photography, who was gonna be on the set and on location with him all that next week, by his side when they were looking for locations, [and] when they were talking about sets. He had that director of photography right next door to him, as opposed to having to walk down to the set and grab the DP when he's shooting another episode. Now the reason for that was, RCA wanted to have the best possible color they could have in order to sell their color television sets. So, for a young writer, that made for a very collaborative thing because I could turn to the DP and say, 'Well, why doesn't that work? Why isn't that a good idea?' They were always most eager and willing — most D.P.'s — they tend to be curmudgeons, but when they get asked an honest question, they'll give you an honest answer."

*Bonanza's* best-known directors of photography were Haskell Boggs and Ted Voightlander. "Buzzy Boggs was the one I hung with the most," remembers Blinn. "Everything was much more laid-back then. There was a place across the street from Paramount at the time called Oblatt's, which was a restaurant-bar. Almost every day after work, the *Bonanza* gang would gather over there, and have a drink or a beer for a half-hour or so, and just shoot the breeze. There were very few factions (on the show) — you know, 'You gotta watch out for him because he's on Mike Landon's side,' and so forth and so on, and all that crap."[1]

Maintaining close ties with director William Claxton, Blinn continued to see Landon in the years following *Bonanza's* cancellation. "I knew a little bit about *Highway [to Heaven]*," says the writer, "because they were shooting on the MGM lot when I was executive producing *Fame*. So I would occasionally see Mike and occasionally see Kent McCray and we'd trade stories and laugh. Mike's crew...a lot of Mike's crew had been his crew on *Bonanza* and *Little House* and they...he had a family around him, and he nurtured that. They loved him, and he supported them and protected them in the best sense of the word. I recall Bill Claxton who was directing an episode of *Fame* for me, he directed a number for me, he had gone out to wherever the hell they shot Walnut Creek — the fictional town (in *Little House on the Prairie*), because Mike, in order to make sure it was never gonna be used again, had written a closing episode for the show where the town was destroyed — every building was blown up. Bill Claxton went out there to tape it for his own purposes, and he showed me that tape. The crew was just — male, female, whatever — they were in tears the whole day watching it blow up because it had been home for them for so long."

The cast and crew of *Here Come the Brides* had that same feeling shortly after the wrap on the final produced (and aired) episode, "Two Women" (April 3, 1970). But before William Blinn became the story editor for *Here Come the Brides*, he had one more television show to make: the September 10-December 31, 1966 ABC series, *Shane*.

"Denne was offered the producer-ship of *Shane* by the Herb Brodkin people and ABC, and he took me along," explains Blinn. "He offered me the job of story editor." Executive producer of such critically acclaimed series as *The Defenders, The Nurses,* and *Coronet Blue,* for Her-bert Brodkin, a TV western like *Shane* was quite a change of pace. "When Paramount sold the rights to ABC, they [ABC] went off and got Brodkin. He said, 'Can we change the title?' They said 'CHANGE THE TITLE??? That's what sold the show — the title and the classic movie.' He said, 'Well, if you name your lead character 'Shane,' you can't ever fire him. If you named it *Western Streets*, then you can.'"

Unlike other TV westerns, *Shane* rarely went on location. "I think the reason *Shane* was kind of a minimalist western was largely because the Brodkin organiza-tion would not permit any deficit spending," muses Blinn. "I don't know what ABC was giving them per episode, but that's what Brod-

*Christopher Shea as Joey Starrett in the ABC-TV/Paramount western,* Shane.

kin was willing to spend. Not a penny more. But ABC kept asking for more action, and Brodkin kept saying, 'If you want to increase our fee, fine. If not, we will do our show the way we intend to do our show, which is for the money we're being paid.' Cuz, he's coming off *The Defenders* and a lot of New York shows that were inside four walls. He did great shows."

Like the other Brodkin series, *Shane* bore the Brodkin stamp: in other words, quality production, strong characterizations, and stories that asked the audience to think. Having made a number of films for the Army Signal Corps, Brodkin brought a considerable degree of technical experience to filmed television. He also hired tal-ented directors, like Robert Butler, and skillful writers such as Ernest Kinoy.

"Bob Butler directed the pilot ["The Distant Bell" – September 10, 1966], and he was great fun to work with," enthuses Blinn. "He was a risk taker: he would try stuff that wasn't done. We also had the benefit...now Denne was a terrific western writer, and I had some feeling in that direction myself, but we got some guys through the Brodkin organization who normally didn't do westerns — people like Ernie Kinoy.

Ernie Kinoy was a terrific radio writer; he won a number of Emmys for *The Defenders* and I share an Emmy with him for *Roots*. Anyway, I have satellite radio in my car and I hear Ernie's name all the time on *Lights Out* and various science-fiction shows. Well, when he came in, because he'd never done a western before, he didn't know the stuff you're not supposed to do, and so the stuff you're not supposed to do, it worked. So it was very refreshing. And I used to love to sit and talk with Ernie about movies — he was doing exactly what fate or God (or whomever) had intended him to do. He was a terrific writer for popular mass medium."

Another element that contributed to the quality of *Shane* was the inclusion of its cast in story conferences. "It was very much a team effort," states Blinn, "and there are some shows…I've talked to people who have worked on these shows, where sometimes the producers and writers never sit down with the actors. I worked with one guy who had come off a Quinn Martin show and when the executive producer said, 'Come on, we're going to dailies,' that was a great surprise. He said, 'I'm invited to dailies?' because on the Quinn Martin shows, it was Alan Armer and Quinn who went to dailies, and producers were to sit and work with the writers, and that was it."

Without question, the biggest problem making the television version of *Shane* was the fact that time and again, audiences would compare the TV version to the 1953 Alan Ladd classic. Fortunately, by casting David Carradine as the mysterious gunfighter Shane, this was less of an obstacle. In fact, fans of Carradine's mid-'70s hit, *Kung Fu*, might have been struck by the similarities between Shane and Carradine's fugitive Shaolin priest, Kwai Chang Caine. "David was kind of that character," says Blinn. "He's got his own rhythms, he's got his own stance and attitude and point of view, and that's a good and creative thing to do. So David and Denne, and to a lesser degree myself, we saw each other socially, and Jill Ireland was always fun to work with. At that time, she was just hookin' up with Charlie Bronson and he would come down to the set. It was just pleasant, and again (like *It's a Man's World*), we had a reading on every script."

There was only one occasion during production where William Blinn was particularly anxious. "I think the only time I've had a panic attack in my life was when we had a script that I just thought was dreadful," laughs the writer. "Denne and I tried to rewrite it, and it couldn't get rewritten — it was written by the executive producer [David Shaw – "The Big Fifty" – December 10, 1966. According to information available, *Shane* was David Shaw's first work in television]. I just thought it was awful and we came closer and closer to the cast sitting down to the reading, and I got just a classic panic attack — an impending heart attack, all of that stuff. I just didn't want to be sitting around that table looking at David and Jill and [series regular] Bert Freed, all those nice people, as this dreadful script went on and on and on. But again, my thing with any show that I'm doing, I am more content, at ease, fulfilled, if there's a lot of give and take between the actors and the directors and the writers and a whole bunch of people doing the show."

*Shane* being "one of my favorite movies of all time," Blinn fulfilled other duties on the series. Chuckles the writer, "One of the silly things was when they were casting around for a composer, I don't know how or why, but Buzz Berger, who was

Brodkin's representative out here, terrific guy, terrific producer [*The Nurses, Strange Report, Holocaust*, etc.], he, Denne, David Shaw, almost all the people around, they couldn't remember the theme from *Shane*, because we'd call in composers when we were casting about for the pilot — Jerry Fielding and a bunch of others." Since Blinn knew the theme, "they'd [the producers] say, 'Blinn, go down to the other David's office. We've got another composer for whom you've gotta sing the theme. So, I'd go down and 'Da da da. Da da da da.' They'd [the composers] go, 'Oh, okay. I know that.' Again, the team effort is what it's all about."

Thanks to this team effort, *Shane* quickly established itself as a quality western. "It certainly held its own as a series," states Blinn. "We had some good directors. [English director] David Greene [*The Defenders, The Nurses, Coronet Blue, Ellery Queen, Rich Man, Poor Man, Roots*] directed some episodes ["The Great Invasion" – Parts 1&2 – December 17 & 24, 1966], and we had some other people who weren't normally doing westerns; Brodkin's name and reputation brought them in, so we benefited from all that. My favorite that I recall was the one that Ernie Kinoy wrote — with John Qualen ["The Hant" – September 17, 1966]. Qualen, if you recall the John Ford films (like *The Searchers, The Grapes of Wrath*) was…he showed up, and he showed up on the doorstep in essence saying, 'I'm getting old. I'm getting frail. Shane killed my son. My son should be taking care of me in my old age. He's not there because Shane killed him, and here I am.' Which almost sounds like a *Bonanza* episode, but the psychological burn that Ernie put on it was that Shane did not recall killing the kid. The notion, the fact that he might have killed someone and had become so calloused that it had fallen away from his memory was just eating him up. What kind of a monster had he become? It was a very interesting episode, as the Tom Tully one was interesting (Tully played Ireland's father on the show), and we did one where the family set off to a dance ["High Road to Viator" – November 12, 1966]. *The New Yorker* reviewed it by accident. They were reviewing some very prestigious special that had come on, and the last three or four paragraphs the reviewer in *The New Yorker* said, 'Actually the best show I saw all week was an episode of a western series called *Shane*,' and he went into it, and it was — it was a very evocative, interesting sweet show — very un-western-like. I'm sure ABC hated the hell out of it. Well, that's their problem. So we were doing offbeat things, and towards the end when we were going off the air, we couldn't buy two cups of coffee; the Brodkin organization cut back on everything."

Theorizes Blinn, "I think ultimately what doomed *Shane* was ABC saying, 'We need more action,' and Brodkin saying, 'You pay me more money, you get it. If you don't, you're getting' what I'm givin' you.' And ABC said…and also, the ratings were marginal. So, the last two episodes we shot…My bones ache just to think back on how dreadful they were. We shot one in six days, which for a western was just unheard of. You know, it's back to the days of Red Ryder and Gene Autry if you're shooting on that kind of a schedule. At any rate, it [Blinn's time on the series] was by and large a good educational experience."

Following the demise of *Shane*, William Blinn returned to writing scripts for different TV series, including *Custer, The Big Valley, High Chaparral*, and *The Invaders*.

Having done one season on *Bonanza*, he also watched episodes of that series; this included episodes from the 1967-68 season (the series' ninth), with new series regular David Canary. "I watched some out of curiosity," the writer states. "I also went to a gym in North Hollywood, so I was able to keep up with the gossip. Mike [Landon] and one of the stunt guys went to that gym."

Then came *Here Come the Brides*.

Recalls Blinn: "Somebody called my agent and said, 'Can Bill Blinn come in and talk with Bob Claver about the series?' I thought I was coming in for an episode. I didn't know anything about it. I said, 'Sure. I'll go on over.' My guess is ABC suggested me to Bob Claver. Bob and Paul Witt and Stan Schwimmer interviewed me. We had a pleasant, cordial meeting. Bob and Paul and Stan and I used to go to lunch a lot of times, and Bob's a charming, likable guy with a delightful sense of humor and reality. He was just a neat guy to work with, a terrific guy to work with, and for. I enjoyed our relationship from start to finish. I enjoyed it no end, and recall it as being a very rewarding and creative time as far as putting the scripts and the film together. Bob has a high energy [level], and has a joy about the process. He would take a suggestion from anybody; there was always give and take in a creative, collaborative sense. He was a little bit of a workaholic so I think he probably enjoyed the fact that when he got there at the office at eight O'Clock, I'd been at the typewriter for half an hour; I certainly turned out a lot of pages."

When it came to production of a series, Bob Claver differed considerably from *Bonanza* creator/producer David Dortort. "Bob was a little bit more of a free spirit," says Blinn. "David was a little bit more buttoned up, more organized, more the traditional businessman-producer. David delegated a lot; he had a good organization. Bob was a guy who liked a lot of give and take. As well as being executive producer, he was also a director, and he was more hands-on in terms of putting the film together. Bob was a little bit more out there on the front lines and the actors were very much a part of Bob's deal. They were welcome in his office, and he was often down on the set, and it wasn't just to go down to the set to deal with problems. It was to go down to the set and make sure the lines of communication stayed open. Everything he did, he did with great zest and joy."

That Bob Claver was always open to others' suggestions was proven through an early story conference. Remembers Blinn, "Bob and Paul Witt had both come off half-hours. Neither one of them had ever done an hour [series] before, and I'd done nothing but hours with the exception of a couple of ill-fated episodes for *Martian*. And I can recall one story about rewriting; it had frustrated me sometimes earlier. Bob said, 'Okay, so Jason's up there, and he's talking with so and so, and he says to so and so, 'I'm gonna go see that son of a gun and deal with him.' And we dissolve, and he's walking into the room, and he starts…' and I said, 'No, no, no, no.' He looked over at me [as if to say] 'Excuse me, I'm the executive producer,' and he was never…he never had an ego in front of him, but he was the executive producer. I said, 'No.' He says, 'I'M GONNA GO OVER AND TALK TO THAT SON OF A GUN!' and he WALKS OUT THE DOOR, and then we WALK HIM DOWN THE STAIRS, and he WALKS THROUGH THE BARROOM and people in the barroom look up, and he SLAMS OUT THE BARROOM DOORS, and he WALKS ACROSS THE SQUARE and people in the square look at him, and he's WALKING, WALKING, WALKING, and he WALKS INTO THE OTHER BUILDING and...Bob's eyes widen. He went, 'Yeah! Yeah!' See, for a half-hour sitcom guy, you don't think of that. You think, 'I'm gonna go talk to the man in the market, dissolve, he enters the market,' but in this show, you've got this hour. Well, if you've seen a lot of John Wayne pictures, you know there is a value to how he leaves the room and to everyone saying, 'OH, MY GOD! HERE COMES TROUBLE!' So from that point, and thereon, Bob went, 'Okay, what do you think?' So this [show] really meant getting him out of the sitcommy thing. He was always great fun to work with, and he was a good director. He kept everyone pretty much on an even keel."

These good feelings extended to the set of *Brides*. "In many ways, it was a wonderfully professional cast," praises Blinn. "They were all working hard. Bobby had four schedules at once to keep going, Bridget — because she was the sweetheart of Bobby Sherman — Bobby Sherman was the teenage boy du jour if you will, Bridget's life was very, very hectic. Then her relationship with Swack complicated her life — those were two very, very busy careers with two very, very busy schedules. David was I think struggling to maintain equilibrium as he saw Bobby hit, and David, who was certainly strikingly handsome, wonderfully athletic, David had singing talent of his own which obviously, eventually came to the fore. So it was a very complex juggling act that, to the actors' credit, they never made more difficult than life made it. We never had, as I recall, [anyone] storming off, or throwing pages, or any of that nonsense. We had people complaining, you know, 'I'm not doing anything. Can't I do this? Can't I do that?' But those were adult conversations. Any multiple cast has its own problems, especially if one of the cast hits, and the others don't hit as hard. So within that complicated situation, everybody handled it as well as one could possibly expect."

Much more complicated was writing the show. "It wasn't an action-adventure offering," explains Blinn, "it wasn't a western (at least not a typical western), it wasn't *The Waltons*. It kind of had its own strange niche, so keeping the tonality was always a little bit of a challenge. The pilot was terrific — very well cast, and corny and wonderful. It was meant to be a show where you would get a few laughs, a few sentimental moments that might touch you in a different way."

As the executive producer of *Here Come the Brides*, Bob Claver was of course the one who always had the final say. "Bob always had great intelligence," praises Blinn, "entertainment and pace were in the forefront of what he was trying to get, and again, we were doing a pretty white-bread show. So there was a certain idealized nostalgia that was part of the package, but he tried to stay away from the overtly corny and the tried and tired. Occasionally he would encourage us to come up with a curveball that would make the throw just a little bit different from something similar that had been done on another network. But I don't think we could do a wedding a week (as some expected). I think the idea was mainly to do a show with romance and comedy, and some physical action to it, without necessarily meaning gunplay and life and death. If we had gone another two years, I think it would have been about the building of

Seattle. I think that was part of the osmosis, if you will. As it happened, we didn't have enough time to make it happen. But, had we had another year, we probably would have turned out to be a precursor of *Little House on the Prairie.*"

An ongoing problem for the series had to do with budget. "We were pretty limited in terms of sets, in terms of what Screen Gems could build on the budget," states Blinn. "We were down to the Screen Gems ranch, where the town was located, the town square — it was really quite small, and the illusion of this ship being docked there, the ship was parked, literally, in the parking lot. And surrounding the ship were all the cars for the crew and what not. So you went down there and would think, 'How're we gonna do this?' But the directors and the DP (director of photography) were able to make you believe that that ship was pulling up to a dock, so here we were in Seattle, and the town was behind the ship. It was, in many ways, quite an illusion to continue to bring off week after week."

Ditto convincing the series viewers that it had recently rained. Remembers Blinn, "In most of the episodes, not all of the episodes, we tried to wet down the town square all the time, so there was a lot of mud, and a lot of slush — it wasn't the kind of dusty dry western street that we're using to seeing on television. And also, Seattle being Seattle, obviously, rain had to be part of the process."

Still, with the exception of a few episodes, most notably the first season's "A Man and His Magic" (December 4, 1968), viewers never saw it raining. "Frankly, it's easier to get the sense that the rain just passed before the camera started rolling than to see the rain," explains Blinn. (According to wardrobe man Steve Lodge, director of photography Fred H. Jackman had somebody on the set whose specific duty was to keep the streets wet.) "I was all for that," replies Blinn. "I think that was a different look, a good look, and it gave a little bit of reality to a show that had a lot of cotton candy. If you had the pretty girl walking across the square and the street of the square is just dry and level, that's one thing, but if you have the pretty girl from New Bedford walking across the street, and the street's muddy and sloppy, then you've got the fish out of water. That maybe gets you to the next episode."

While other shows like *Star Trek* and *Judd, for the Defense* were open to tackling controversial themes like homosexuality, racial prejudice, and alcoholism, *Here Come the Brides* generally avoided those areas during its first season. But when *Brides* took over the canceled *Judd*'s time slot the following season, it became a more serious and dramatic program. Many associated with the series, including executive producer Claver, saw this as a good thing. William Blinn had a different view. "I've nothing against shows that do relevant topics," states the writer, "but clearly *Brides* was not that venue. It wasn't designed for it — it was a sentimental comedy. If we got specifically into a message-y tone, we were in the wrong place. We were doing rap while in the choir loft, and that doesn't go together."

Trying to produce a show with so many regular and semi-regular characters, and thus so many different story areas were among the creative problems of the first season. "It was a collaborative thing," says Blinn, "Bob, myself and Paul Witt, and obviously the network had their say, so it was a balancing act. When I came in, there were writers that Bob had worked with before — Skip Webster being one of them, and Screen Gems had their people whom they trusted, and I was trained to bring in some new writers. At the same time Screen Gems had their menu (of do's and don'ts) that we also dealt with. Which was fine. I don't think anyone came in with a script — that would be just too much work. Because if someone says no, you've just wasted a month. Every once in a great while, someone will come in with a speculative script. That's how I got my job on *Bonanza*. But that's very much the change, not the rule."

As was often the case with a TV series, *Brides* writers were introduced to the series and its characters, through a viewing of the pilot. "So the writers were familiar with the show," explains Blinn. "You have screenings for writers who have some credits; you get eight or ten or twelve writers into a room, you tell them what you're gonna try to do. You show them the pilot, you say, 'If you've got any questions, give me a call. If you have any story ideas, give me a call as well.' Well, out of that ten or twelve writers, maybe five will walk out of the room and say, 'I hate that show,' [and] maybe five or six will call you back and say, 'I have some thoughts, or some questions.' So you set up an interview. The writer goes in, you sit down with the story editor and the producers, and you have four or five or six ideas. You sit there with the producer and story editor and kick it around. You kind of get a sense of what kind of stories they're looking for, so you come in with, 'Well, suppose somebody comes to town and wins Clancey's boat in a gambling thing?' You kick that around, you see what comes out the other end. They (the writers) come in with story ideas that get generated into an outline. If that outline seems to work, then that gets generated into a script. That's less prevalent now, that mode of operation has largely changed, I think, only because so many of the shows are staff written. An hour show will have eight or ten or twelve writers on staff which I can't quite conceive of, but they do, and they have six or eight producers on each and every episode."

Given *Here Come the Brides'* large cast, Blinn, Claver, et al, were kept very busy making sure everyone in the cast felt they were not being short-changed when it came to scenes and dialogue. Says Blinn, "You know you're in trouble when you have the cast sitting around the table, and you've got one cast member going through the script, turning the page, turning the page, turning the page, turning the page. What they're doing is counting their lines; you know you're gonna hear from them after the reading. And Robert would get frustrated; he would be okay if the chemistry worked out to be a trio, but if it was a duo with him bringing up the rear, he was not a happy guy. That's not uncommon in any kind of ensemble. I saw a little bit of it in *Bonanza*. When the episode would tilt heavily toward Little Joe, you could see Lorne start to count the lines and turn the pages, that went on in *Fame,* and when I was doing *The Interns*. When we first put that show together, and it was my fault, no one called me on it at the time, we had too many actors, we had too many leads, and we ended up, as the season went on, trying to pare them down, because we just — we could not deliver what we had to deliver. Now it's something that's done with great facility in terms of shows that have eight and ten running cast characters."

But, thanks to Bob Claver's "open-door" policy, and other wise practices, the *Here Come the Brides* cast was one of television's happier ensemble series. "Anytime you have an ensemble cast, obviously there are going to be some episodes where people are not going to be center-stage," notes Blinn. "We always had conversations with the actors about what was going on. What they could expect, what they wanted to do. If they know that, they accept that. If they understand that that's the process, they're going to be very happy human beings. Robert was always…clearly interested in the show. His main interest was in making sure the character of Jason Bolt remained heroic and stalwart, and in the center. Bobby was fine. David was probably the most frustrated of the actors because he was the third guy through the door a lot of times. He was a good actor, and also at that time, a very good singer, and strikingly handsome, but for whatever reason at that time, Bobby had that androgynous thing that twelve year old girls absolutely eat up alive. So I think David was frustrated, and we tried to address his frustrations. I think we gave him some episodes, and he was always good. When we gave him something to do, he was always good. That's why he ended up doing *Starsky and Hutch* because I remember saying to Aaron Spelling, 'This is a guy you oughta look at.' David was maybe a little bit miscast in *Brides*, but he certainly could be an action hero."

In the case of Bridget Hanley, there were no problems whatsoever. "She's a wonderful comedienne," praises Blinn, "a wonderful, dramatic actress. She did a very serious guest-star part for me in *The Interns* ['Sookie Post' in the October 23, 1970 episode, "Miss Knock-A-Bout"], played in theory, a girl whose problem is being homely, which of course Bridget was not, and is not. So we had to kind of dress her down for that. Bridget is just a consummate professional; if she had a problem, it was a major problem. Otherwise, she'd be, 'Oh, I can do this. I don't want to bother anybody. I don't want to bother you.'"

As for *Brides'* two comedians, Henry Beckman and Susan Tolsky, to Blinn, Beckman seemed to have more opportunities. "Henry could be in the bar with Joan, and also he had that kind of vague romance with Joan," notes Blinn. "Susan [as bride 'Biddie'] was a little bit trapped in the girl's dormitory. Her comedy tended to be the same kind of comedy, and there was a lack of Susan for those moments of…you know, Bridget had those moments where she could get you to cry a little bit, but those moments were few and far between for Susan." When they did come, however such as in "A Jew Named Sullivan" (November 20, 1968) and "Loggerheads" (March 26, 1969), Susan Tolsky was simply superb. She most definitely got viewers to cry. (This one anyway.)

Susan Tolsky also had a few 'put 'em in their place' moments with *Brides'* male characters, including Seattle leader Jason Bolt. Still, most of the time, it was Candy Pruitt who went head to head with Jason. "Candy was not going to be pushed around," says Blinn, "and Robert…the character of Jason certainly cared deeply for the ladies, and was delighted to have the ladies there, and all this and that, but, there's no question he was a male chauvinist. Bridget's character would call him on that time after time after time."

Faring not nearly as well when it came to their characters were semi-regulars Cynthia Hull (Ann) and Carole Shelyne (Franny). "This is supposition on my part," explains Blinn, "because we never had the conversation, but I think Bob (Claver) was trying to get Cynthia and Carole in there more. Every time you can get a new face in there, hopefully you can get a new color in as well, coming out of that face or that character. Cynthia was very bright, energetic, and pretty in a non-actressy way. I think maybe had we gone another year, we would have found a lot more for Cynthia to do. She was quite versatile."

Given that executive producer Claver generally enjoyed working with women far more than men, Blinn's hypothesis might well have been true. "Bob was open to female characters," states Blinn, "and one of the things we found out was that there are some things an audience will just plain watch, and one of the things they will just plain watch is a wedding. You know, you've got the groom, you've got the bride, you've got the mothers, you've got the fathers, you've got the suitor, you've got a thousand things to cut to, you don't have to hurry it along, and it can be very touching. Now years later, a lady who is no longer with us, a production executive at CBS…I'd done two or three pilots for her, she said, 'Well, you've got your formula.' I said, 'I don't think I've got a formula. I would resent that if I had a formula.' She said, 'Well, the last three pilots you've done for me had a birth, a death, a wedding, and a funeral.' I said initially, 'No. That's not true.' Then I thought about it, and she was right. It wasn't a formula, but there are some things, some experiences that we share that I'd say are universal, and one of them I think, how do I phrase it…? The female experience is so profound and, I think, closer to nature than a lot of the male experience, and the more valuable in the sense that they do not get swept up in the competition of who's gonna get to first base first. They can, but it's more our bag than theirs. And I think Bob would agree with that. Bob felt good with that, and also, dealing with Inger Stevens, she was such a good actress, and such a versatile actress. I think he wanted to take advantage of that in our cast as he had with *Farmer's Daughter.*"

"So Bob would like shows where the women were spotlighted more than shows where the guest cast was all-male. The whole male/female thing was integral to [the show], and obviously when we got the adventure [aspect], we lost a lot of the male/female thing. So there was an ongoing kind of dialogue that was never finished, but always going on. Probably more in the second season, than in the first season because once we got into more action-adventure and less sentimental comedy, we were moving away from the strength of our performers — with the exception of David and Bridget. Bridget was always wonderful, and she was able to shift gears. But it was really hard for Robert. I think David probably could have done it, and probably did do it to the best of his will, but he was not a happy guy, and I think that showed in terms of his commitment. But working for Bridget was always, always fun. She did her homework, she never showed up unprepared, or had a silly problem. If she had a problem, it went to a germane issue within the script. She was always the height of professionalism, and fun to work with. And of course she loved working with Swack for any number of reasons on any number of levels, and that just made for a happier set. I mean she was such a good soul that when you had her with Susan Tolsky, or Joan Blondell, or Clancey, she just brought great stature and commitment to those kinds of scenes."

Like everyone else in the series, William Blinn greatly enjoyed his nearly two seasons on *Here Come the Brides*. "It was one of the happier shows I worked on," says the writer. "I had more pleasant experiences. Particularly in the first season. Because Bobby and David were new to it. Not that they hadn't performed, but they hadn't done a series before. And Robert was fun. As for Bridget, well, Bridget's main ingredient is enthusiasm."[2]

There was a lot about *Here Come the Brides* that Bridget Hanley loved. Unlike her character, Candy Pruitt, Bridget Hanley would soon become a bride. The bridegroom was series star Robert Brown's longtime friend, pilot director E.W. Swackhamer.

1. Blinn – interview – 2007
2. Ibid

## "Hello, Candy."

*Here Come The Brides* pilot director E.W. Swackhamer
telling his soon to be-wife Bridget Hanley that she
has won the all-important HCTB role of Candy Pruitt

# Chapter 4

# *Directed by E.W. Swackhamer*

"Erwin Piscator is the man who invented 'epic theater.' There was nothing like that before. They put everything together: acting, dance, music, narration, choruses, chanting, back-screen projection, process photography. Even the news broadcasts now — when you see something (or someone) in the foreground, the screen behind them — what's happening in Iraq, whatever, that's 'epic theater.'"[1]

That was how *Here Come the Brides* guest Marvin Silbersher described the theatrical movement begun by German director Erwin Piscator and his associate: German playwright Bertolt Brecht in the 1920s. Erwin Piscator played an important part in the lives of Marvin Silbersher and his friends, Robert Brown and E.W. Swackhamer. Piscator was one of the trio's instructors at the New School of Social Research's Dramatic Workshop; Piscator founded that workshop.

Given the sweep and scope of such Swackhamer-directed *Here Come the Brides* as the pilot episode, "After a Dream Comes Mourning" and "Two Women," the production and location-heavy *McClouds* ("Sharks!" "Our Man in the Harem," etc.), and the on-location shooting of the 1976 WWI/WWII miniseries, *Once an Eagle*, it's more than likely that E.W. Swackhamer absorbed the elements of 'epic theater' and worked this into his directing style. 'Epic' was a very good way to describe the premiere episode of *Here Come the Brides*.

"Swack created the tone and feel of the thing," declares *Brides* star Robert Brown. "Absolutely. Those other people [the other series directors], I don't know if they were chosen if they had a similar point of view, but Swack was doing quite a few of them. When he was directing, he was doing lots of pilots that found their way on the air. He would do many of them because it would establish the thing."[2]

In addition to the physical look of a show, E.W. Swackhamer almost always extracted fine performances from his actors. "Many of the directors — they're just part of the machine," notes Brown. "They're not bringing the human...they're not freeing the set up with openness, and it shows in the final analysis. So it would seem that the Swackhamer shows [in *Brides*] were the more human of the bunch, the more organized, and maybe the more relaxed."[3]

That was due in part to E.W. Swackhamer's education at the New School of Social Research's Dramatic Workshop in New York City. Along with friends Brown and Silbersher, Swackhamer had studied acting at the workshop. "Swack and Robert go back to when they were eighteen," states the director's widow, *HCTB* leading lady Bridget Hanley. "They had just gotten out of the Navy, and they went to school together at the New School for Social Research; Swack started out as an actor."[4]

*Shooting a scene, observed by, left to right: Robert Brown, E.W. Swackhamer, Bob Claver, LeRoy Kinzle; crewmembers in background.* COURTESY BRIDGET HANLEY

"We became very good friends," says Brown. "As close as any two guys could be. Without falling in love — we weren't homosexuals — just guys that respected each other from the very beginning."[5] "We were very close buddies in drama school," adds Marvin Silbersher. "We did four years together at the Dramatic Workshop."[6] During that time, the three men started their own theater.

"We had this teacher at the school whom Swack and Bob Brown — they tried to help him, but he cheated them terribly," says Silbersher. "He turned out to be a terrible person behind the cash register. He was like a thief — he did terrible things to Swack and Bob Brown. The outcome of this was we had a revolution. The boys came to me. They said, 'What can we do, Marvin? We can't stand this guy. He's a darling at school, he's a great teacher, but behind the cash register, he's a monster.' I said, 'Well, I have a theater where we can go. So they all…Walter Matthau was with us, too; they all followed me to upstate New York and we started our own theater."[7]

Like so many beginning talents in the performing arts, E.W. Swackhamer experienced very difficult times financially. "He'd been set to go to Harvard, or Princeton, cuz he'd grown up in New Jersey," relates Hanley, "but his dad went through the Depression, so, all bets were off. So he was broke in New York, the shoes wearing out, living in a little tiny one-room that he had to lock tying his one tie around the doorknob. Robert Brown would take him to his mom and dad's house to fatten him up and get him to eat. And he went to the Actor's Fund and got new shoes because he had run holes in the bottom of his shoes — it was the real actor's story."

"Swack worked as an actor on Broadway a couple of times," continues Hanley. "He and Bill Windom did two French waiters in 'Remains to be Seen.' They were brought down to the front of the stage by the director who said, 'GENTLEMEN! This is NOT a play about two French waiters!' Robert Brown's brother, Harold, told Swack he was one of the best actors he had ever seen. Swack told that story for years. Robert stood up for him in class and everything."[8]

"He had a couple of acting jobs," remembers Brown. "He was very good in the summer stock company that I was with — I got going before anybody. I was in a summer stock company while I was still in dramatic school. I got a professional job and became a member of the union. When I played in *Our Town*, Swack played in *Dark of the Moon*. He had the leading actor part in that. He was excellent in that."[9]

During their work in summer stock, Brown and Swackhamer did things other than acting. "I was hired to be the stage manager," explains Brown, "Swack shared that role, and he got to be assistant director."[10] Since this particular summer stock company was a professional one, Brown received his Actors Equity card. Swackhamer being more in need of money than Brown. "I gave him half the salary," says the actor. "That's how he got to be a member of Equity."[11]

While Brown's acting career was moving along very well — such was not the case with E.W. Swackhamer. "Swack was still in there fiddling," says Brown, "he wasn't in anything, and he did lots of jobs to make a living. That's how he got to be a stage manager — an assistant stage manager on Broadway, that's how he met Jackie [Cooper].

"His job in the evening was understudying," continues Brown, "and, if he had to understudy somebody, it would be Jackie. Well, through that contact, Swack kept going. Jackie kept using him for other things, then Swack started directing plays — on, and off Broadway. He worked with [Elia] Kazan [on stage] — 'Gadge' was what they called Kazan."[12]

It was while working with Kazan that E.W. Swackhamer discovered his true calling. "Swack was a professional stage manager in New York," explains Hanley. "He worked with Elia Kazan on *Cat on a Hot Tin Roof.* Then Kazan, as Swack always called him, asked him to direct the road company. He said, 'Oh, okay, okay,' and for a week he was just as happy as he could be, and he didn't figure out why until he really sat down and thought about it. He said, 'You know I was in charge but I just never had to think about myself.' I mean he loved the pressure being off him — of having to be centered on his own being, which you have to be as an actor. That was kind of his turning point. Because once he did the *Cat on a Hot Tin Roof,* he found that directing was just his *métier.*"[13]

If E.W. Swackhamer's work with Elia Kazan led him into directing, his association with Jackie Cooper kicked off his lengthy television career. "Jackie came out to Los Angeles," recalls Hanley, "and he's the one that asked him to come out. Swack sent him a letter, cuz it meant moving the family, and all of that. He [Swackhamer] said, 'I won't be a go-fer.'"[14] After Cooper made it plain to E.W. Swackhamer that he did not want him as a 'go-fer,' the director accepted his offer. "They worked at Universal for a long time," [on Cooper's series, *Hennesey*], remembers Hanley. "Then I think Jackie moved over to Screen Gems and Swack (associate producer/director/writer on *Hennesey*) kind of came along with the team."

"Jackie was really an incredible mentor," continues the actress, "He wanted Swack out here because of his talent, and Swack learned film, he was an avid, avid…he wanted to know everything he could about it. So he went to work to add to his repertoire: directing in the theatre, acting, he even took dance lessons from Martha Grahame. He loved film, he loved the possibilities, and he really, really, he was mentored well, observed well, and Jackie Cooper made sure he really knew his stuff, and he did. Swack was always experimenting with shots and moves, and things — that was just part of the fun of it."[15]

"Working with Swack was like a dream," enthuses Marvin Silbersher. "He was a really marvelous director, a very gifted man. He was a very well-prepared colleague. He'd been through all the existence of theater — dance, he'd studied piano, he was a joy to work with. And so much fun. He was a very close connection to the actor. He would talk to you about his thoughts, and ask for your thoughts. He got you to collaborate — to get exactly what he wanted to do. If you had a suggestion, he would accept the thing. He would say, 'Yeah, try that.' He was a very helpful director. He wanted it to come from you. Not something that was somewhere else. So going to work with Swack is like a holiday. Really. You never felt pressure. We felt the pleasure of the full event."[16]

"Swack was a good women's director," adds *Brides* semi-regular Mitzi Hoag. "I thought he was a great director. Swack just gave you…he appreciated actors, and he would give you such confidence and reassurance. Actors often feel unsure and frightened and nervous, you know, 'Am I doing the right thing?' because you're out there and committed to doing something, but you're not watching yourself, you don't know if you're doing right or wrong or anything, and the director's your eye. Swack was great at that. He would see what you were gonna do, and in the case of Miss Essie, he left it up to me. He let me create the character; there's not time for a lot of discussion. I'm sure Swack molded [Hoag's performance], but it was so un-intrusive that you didn't feel like you were pushed one way or the other — he let you do your work. He was so experienced — he directed all different kinds of shows. I can't think what he couldn't do. He was a funny man, had a great sense of humor."[17]

"Swack was just extraordinary," glows *HCTB* regular Susan Tolsky. "What a sweetheart, what a dear. He was an extraordinary man, delightful, and I wish there were more of him in the industry now — we'd probably have better television. Dear God, Dear God! I think the coldest thing in my house now is the TV. He was wonderful, and the pilot was my first experience with him. Talk about accessible, talk about easygoing, talk about prepared, talk about listening to actors. I don't ever remember him coming up and saying, 'You know, that's not really how it needs to be.' He gave free range. I think...something that I will always remember about Swack — he loved actors. He trusted actors — I worked with one director on *Love American Style* — it was on a Monday — they shot those things in one day — I remember him coming in yawning. 'Oh, I was in Vegas all weekend. What show are we doing today?' And

*E.W. Swackhamer directing the pilot episode with, l to r, Bridget Hanley, Karen Carlson, Susan Tolsky.* COURTESY BRIDGET HANLEY

we came to blows. The producer came down and overrode the director in my favor, cuz he was not prepared — he can not tell me what to do when he's not prepared. That's another story, but Swack was prepared. He loved actors, he didn't crack the whip. If he directed, to an actor, in my recollection, it was more of a suggestion than 'DO IT!' He was a puppeteer — he put you in the right place, and he was joyous — he loved his job, he enjoyed his job, so how could we not enjoy working for him? We wanted to do the best we could for Swack. He was a wonderful, wonderful gentleman. He was a lovely man." [18]

"Swack and I — we were like brothers," says *Brides* semi-regular Dick Balduzzi. "About eighty percent of my shows were from Swack. I met him at an audition — I was up for the part of 'Angie' in the pilot, *Marty,* and he had about a hundred guys to see. He kept asking me weird questions. He said, 'Do you like theatre?' I said, 'Of course. I love theatre.' He asked all about — nothing about the role. He wanted to find the inside of my character. He always worked that way. He could bring out the quality in someone, and we all knew...We worked like theater, because he would rehearse, which was pleasant to do. We would rehearse, rehearse, and then shoot because he liked the development of character. I did so many shows with him — he was like my own brother. Bob Brown had a good relationship with him."[19]

As did Bobby Sherman and David Soul. "They were young — David and Bobby," says Balduzzi, "and they listened, because they liked him, and because he was a theater

*Brides leading lady Bridget Hanley, and her new husband, E.W. Swackhamer, on their wedding day.* COURTESY BRIDGET HANLEY

actor and director. He gave them a lot of good advice and they loved that, especially Bobby. Bobby was more of a musician than an actor. Swack helped them with guidance and experience."[20]

"As an actor, Swack was a very supportive director," agrees Soul. "Swack taught us all. He'd say, 'Who do you think I'm gonna cut to? When we do this cut-away, what would your reaction be to that scene? When he delivers this sentence, what would be your reaction? Do you think we should do a cut-away here? Yes? Good.'"[21]

"Oh, I just…I miss him," says Soul's former wife, *HCTB* semi-regular Karen Carlson. "He was just…he was very intense when he was working in terms of — he knew what he wanted but he had a way of doing it that didn't make you nervous or… and I was young and still relatively inexperienced, but I just remember his smile — wonderful, jolly, happy smile, and then of course he just welcomed us into his home. When he and Bridget married, we were there probably every other weekend. It was special — it was really a special time."[22]

"I never heard a negative," adds *HCTB* story editor/episode writer William Blinn. "I have a feeling that Robert Brown might get impatient with Swack, because he [Swackhamer] did like to move the camera. There'd be times, I know, when I was doing *The Rookies* and Swack was directing episodes, I'd be in the office at eight O'Clock or so, and around 9:30, I would stick my head out the door, and say, 'How we doing on the set? How much film do we have?' They'd say, 'We don't have any film yet. Nothing's been printed.' and I'd like, 'Well, okay, fine,' and then, at 10:00, 'It still hasn't been printed.' I'm, 'Well, it's ten O'Clock. The day's already half gone.' And then ten-thirty, 'Anything printed yet? Yes, you got one take.' JEEZUS CHRIST! ONE TAKE! How much film? 'Uh, it's three minutes' worth of film.' 'WHAT???' So you had one shot, obviously very complicated, but by the time he got the shot staged and rehearsed, and then got a print, that shot was worth three minutes of finished film. That same skill is what relates to the shot in the pilot [that shot being The Brides and the Bolts on Clancey's ship, the *Seamus O'Flynn*, as it nears Seattle] I mean, he loved to move the camera. He did it with great facility, but those things take a lot of time to set up."

Continues Blinn: "the panning over the brides — that's Swack. You know [Fred] Jackman was a good guy, and a good DP, but he was a technician. He would not have had the…that was Swack. Shooting the scene through the eyeglasses [the second season's "The Eyes of London Bob"], the long-lens rack focus [the same season's "Two Women"] — all that stuff would be Swack. Swack directed a lot of the best episodes, and because he had directed the pilot, he was in many ways a creative touchstone for the cast. He was the one that set the mold as far as they were concerned."[23]

Not only did E.W. Swackhamer 'set the mold,' elements of his former teacher Erwin Piscator's 'epic theater' were present in many of his *Brides* episodes. For example, in the first season's "Lovers and Wanderers," semi-regular Mitzi Hoag performs a musical number in voice-over — that wasn't the sort of thing one would expect from a comedy-drama. But, it was one of the things one would find in Bertolt Brecht and Erwin Piscator's epic theater. In the early first season comedy, "And Jason Makes Five," Swackhamer presented viewers with two Busby Berkeley-type 'numbers'; in the following episode, "Man of the Family," he literally drew viewers into the town church at show's beginning and right up to the sky in its finale.

In the second season's "The Eyes of London Bob," the audience got an idea of what it might be like to start losing one's sight, thanks to Swackhamer's frequent telling of the story from 'Bob's' perspective. The later "The Fetching of Jenny" (written by *The Wild Wild West*'s artist turned story consultant Henry Sharp) featured musical numbers — one spotlighting Bridget Hanley, plus Hanley and Joan Blondell masquerading as charwomen, there was also Robert Brown, Mark Lenard, and guest star Alan Hale going through exactly the same motions in the same spot. As for the series' finale, "Two Women," Bridget Hanley couldn't be blamed for thinking her late husband a genius when he made this episode. Like the pilot, this episode was chock-full of striking visuals and flowing camera work. Dramatically, and stylistically, "Two Women" was a great departure for *Here Come the Brides* and series co-star David Soul.

"Swack had great ideas," says Hanley. "He had a great visual sense, and he loved telling a story through a shot. But he didn't want it to be static. He didn't want it to be just cutting back and forth, back and forth, back and forth, so he tried to do as many traveling shots as he could. He loved traveling shots, and then he would go in and cover what he thought was the most important if there was time, or sometimes he'd just leave it alone. He loved to keep the camera on the move — that was so exciting because that felt more like theater, I guess. He loved film, he loved theater, and he loved film because of all the possibilities. There were certain things he loved to make all one shot and he would go in and cover it if he needed to. He did love to have shots on the move — that was very exciting for him and the cameraman, and the crew got excited too because it was fun. It wasn't just a sedentary camera shooting everybody and everything from only one angle. So he did long dolly shots, and he wanted to always stretch and see, not what he could get away with, but where he could go with it. He believed in telling the story. However it needed to be told, in his opinion, that's how he chose to do it."[24]

This caused problems more than once. Recalls *McCloud* stunt coordinator Bill Catching, "Swack was...we used to call Swack 'Hitler,' — he was German [actually, Swackhamer is a Dutch name], and we called him 'Hitler,' because, BY GOD, there was only one way to do something and that was his way. Swack and I didn't see eye to eye at first, so the first one or two *McClouds*, we didn't get along too good. Because he had certain ways that he wanted to do something, and I said, 'Well, wait a minute. I've done about fifteen of these shows, and they're not in keeping with what McCloud has done.' 'Well, I don't care,' he said. 'WE'RE GONNA DO THIS!' So, after doing a couple of shows with him, I learned how to get around him — agree with him. So I would, 'Yep. Yes, Swack. Yes, Swack.' 'Well, wait a minute,' he'd say. 'You don't like it?' I said, 'No, Swack. But you said you want to do it. Let's do it.' 'Well, wait a minute,' he'd say."[25]

"He wanted his way," admits Hanley. "He was the baby of his family, and he was very strong about his vision. He had a lot of buddies, but he wasn't always popular with everyone he worked with. I don't think they thought he was petulant or anything, but he wanted to supersede what they wanted, and that didn't always work. But that's what makes…if everybody is just too kind and kind of backs away from each other, not the best product gets done. And, as in any marriage or in any relationship, compromise is mandatory — not to compromise your ideals or anything, but sometimes in relationships you have to compromise to allow the other person to have their life as well. So with people that he trusted and respected, he was a great team player, but he did like to be boss on the set, not in a bad way, but he was kind of…that's who you went to first, rather than going to the camera operator, whom we all loved."[26]

"Swack was great to work with," adds Dick Balduzzi. "He worked like a theater man too. He'd try all kinds of work that pleased him creatively. I think that's the great thing about being in that position where you can try things like that. I think that's how a director directs — he's gotta know the camera, every angle, be a good cinematographer. He was a guy that did his homework — he knew every shot that he wanted to do. He knew every scene — how it should be played."[27]

"He had a photographic memory," explains Hanley. "He had such a warehouse in that brain of his. You never saw him really write much down — his scripts were kind of pages folded over. I don't recall him making notes. It was all in his head. He could read a script once, put it down, and never have to look at it again. He knew the actor's lines better than they did. He just had that capacity — I think his daughter Elizabeth has the same thing. I mean it was amazing — he would run lines with me sometimes, and say, 'Oh, Bridgie, you don't know 'em yet.' And he would be off-hook. He was amazing, but he would then — a lot of times if he was on location and stuff, he would take a script with him to dinner, and go over what he had done that day, and just refresh himself, then look through whatever — the twelve pages or whatever they were planning to do the next day, just to refresh himself, but that was it."

Continues Hanley, "He used to, when there was the time to do it, he would spend quite a long time rehearsing the scene, which is really lovely because you get just extra stuff. A lot of time when you're rehearsing on your own, you make up the other person, then, when you're with the real person, you gotta be free enough just to go with what they're giving you. Swack was an actor and he loved to rehearse, and the actors of course love to rehearse. He was just an actor-lover. He knew the process and that was so refreshing because not everyone did. He was excited about it and he passed that excitement along. He was intrigued by people's choices. He would encourage, and say, 'Ooh! What about this?' and 'Let's try this.' He was always on the side of the actor."[28]

"He was a remarkable guy," praises Robert Brown. "A great human being, honest as the day is long, and talented. Never superficial, just a leader as an individual — a man of character and professional respect. He was one of the good people." [29] "He always watched," says Hanley. "He was like the best audience anyone could ever have."[30] "He was the consummate pro," adds David Soul. "He understood what the show was all about; whatever was happening [in the story], he was in on it. He was sweet, gentle, positive, very supportive, and very positive about what you were doing." [31] "He wouldn't tell you how to read a line," remembers Dick Balduzzi, "but he would work it so that he'd get the results he wanted. And he loved low-angle shots. He would take the crane way up and shoot down from different angles. In the beginning of *Love on a Rooftop*, I think he went up in a helicopter and did the opening shots. He would do things like that. He loved to do angle shots."[32]

"Swack was just a neat guy," enthuses William Blinn. "He was such a master at encompassing a large amount with one camera move. And he loved to use the boom. He loved to use the whole thing. All his films have a certain visual movement that's part and parcel of the opera. He had all the moves, all the gait you need to get around the track. He had that in ample supply."[33] "He was a very stylish director," agrees Soul. "Very stylish in his use of the Chapman crane. He used the camera in the old John Ford way — there was a lot of flow in his work, but the shots were always simple. He gave television a great look; he made a set or a location look bigger than it really was. And he did cutaways, and tracking shots, and long lens rack focus, and he could cover so much in a single shot. You'd have a well-conceived crane shot widening into a master. So he spent a lot of time looking for things that could be shot at wide angles. And he was very impatient. He would stand by the camera, rocking on his heels, 'Okay, Okay. Let's do it! Cut! Print it! FUCKING GREAT! Let's move to the next shot."[34] "He was extraordinarily energetic," laughs Mitzi Hoag. "Things were fast. You got what you wanted, and he got what he wanted, and you moved on."[35]

As the years passed, E.W. Swackhamer never lost that energy and speed. Remembers Robert Brown's stunt double Dave Cass, "I worked on a pilot with Swackhamer for Paramount — *Force*-something. It was with Wings Hauser. And Universal did a series of two hour movies of the week called *Desperado,* based on the 'Eagles' song, with Alex MacArthur. I was doing those for Charlie Sellier, Jr., who had founded Sunn Classics, did *Grizzly Adams* and all that, and Swackhamer was doing these *Desperado* two hour movies of the week. E.W. came in and directed two of them back to back. Well, years later, I was off doing *North and South, Book Three,* and the producer I worked for — Larry Levinson, he was doing three two-hour movies of the week in Las Vegas — *MacShayne* with Kenny Rogers. I came in on the second one, and E.W. was directing the second one. Course it was fine, because we knew each other all those years, and had a lot of water under the bridge, and then they wanted to go right away with the next one. There wasn't time to bring in another director to produce it so they asked E.W. He said, 'Ah nah, I can't do that. I can't do two back to back.' I looked at him and I said, 'E.W., why don't you save this for someone who doesn't know you?' 'Well, don't tell em, Dave.' Cuz he'd just done two with me back to back four years ago. He did two [*MacShaynes*] back to back and they came out well. He cut the film when he shot it. He was a very lean director. Then he'd go in and just take a little of the air and the fat out, and walk away from it. Virgil [Vogel] was like that, too."[36]

"Swack was a little like Virgil," laughs William Blinn, "and he was like Bill Claxton, although Swack was more free-form than Bill. There were more camera moves, a lot more things that lent a certain flow to the film. He was an energy bucket, and very pragmatic, because he could shoot all the action, he could do all that stuff. Once you gave him more time to do it, he got to the nuances and the soft edges, a little more quickly than some of the other guys did. I mean, he could find those moments, those grace notes where the symphony's more eloquent because the orchestra isn't playing. He was always wonderful to work with; actors loved him and that showed on the set. My experience with Swack was always a good, collaborative, and pleasant set to go to."[37]

Thanks to E.W. Swackhamer's direction of the *Here Come the Brides* pilot, the show got off to a very good start. "*Brides* was a show that was very foreign to the networks," explains executive producer Bob Claver. "Sweeping shots were kind of standard, but we did do that more, and I remember the show looked pretty good. When it looks good, you want to get wide shots and show it. I think Swack did a really good job with the pilot. He did a terrific job, and it made a big difference. When you have a good script, and the director comes through, you're in good shape."[38]

Muses William Blinn, "I think in terms of directors, *Brides* had Swack, Paul Witt, and Bob Claver. The other guys — they were kind of in and out. They worked hard and did well. But in terms of setting the tone and the look of the show, it was Swack and Paul and Bob Claver. Freddie [Jackman — *Brides* regular director of photography] was more comfortable with Swack, because Swack had directed before. Paul was not a first-time director, but I don't think he'd ever directed a single-camera show. Bob had done a lot of directing, but most of it had been in half-hour sitcoms, so I think Freddie was probably more at ease with Swack. Not that the others were unpleasant. It was just that he and Swack came closer to talking the same language."[39]

"Swack and Jackman were kind of a team," agrees Robert Brown. "Swack had a good visual sense, and Jackman had all of the technical aspects. Swack knew what he wanted, and Jackman taught him how to do it so that it would move to the next shot. He showed him how to do it technically. He was just a great man — Jackman, and his crew, it was like a family. Whatever it was, Jackman was willing and friendly, so they had a good relationship. Their egos were not threatening to one another. Swack would come up with the panning shots; he would come up with the long lens rack focus. Absolutely. He'd call for lens number, lens number — he would get the softer lens, and Jackman would make little improvements, whisper to him, and teach him how to do it carefully, and Swack would nod, and we'd have the next camera angle for the next setup. But Swack was in charge — he was absolutely in charge. By that time, he had a history of successful pilots, many pilots that sold — *The Flying Nun*, for example. He would be the one that was respected — he was like a producer/director — a really creative producer/director, but their egos were not threatening one another — that sometimes happens with creative people." [40]

"They were really a good team," says Bridget Hanley. "Freddie loved Swack and he loved him. Freddie didn't have to teach Swack — some directors you really have to teach, but Swack, I mean Swack loved to do dolly shots, and tracking and all of that, he loved that, and Freddie did, too. Freddie with other directors might do more, maybe I'm just being precious about Swack, but they really...I am sure that Freddie would say, 'Hey, Swackhamer! Why don't you tweak this here by doing...?,' you know, because they really were a team."[41]

The two men's friendship continued off the set. "He and Dottie, his wife, we would go and see them," explains Hanley. "We would stop at their house every anniversary after we'd been out for dinner. And we would wake them up, and we'd laugh and yell for an hour, then we'd go home. They were very, very dear, dear friends. Really close friends."[42]

Also close with the couple were Screen Gems executive Jackie Cooper and his wife, Barbara. "Jackie and Barbara were really, really, really close friends," states Hanley. "When Swack passed away, later on there was a big gathering, I gave a big [remembrance] party at our house, with family, and friends, and Jackie and Barbara were there." [43]

"When Swack died, it was like…he was like the center of a lot of our lives — with a lot of people in the industry," says Dick Balduzzi. "He got us all together, at least once or twice a year. It was like family — we knew we'd see these people every year."[44]

"Over the years, with special events, like people getting married at their house, or the 4th of July parties at their house, they kept us all connected," adds Mitzi Hoag. "And Swack was great about using actors he loved. So I worked for him a lot and knew their kids. It was a continuous, extended family — that started with the [*Brides*] show."[45]

"We palled around," says Balduzzi. "We saw each other a lot. His daughter studied with my wife, who was teaching dance and ballet, and Swack used to come to the dance recitals. He was a nice man — I enjoyed working with him. His work was concentration, and producers loved him because he would get his work in on time, and below budget, sometimes way before time."[46]

So, if producers were invited to the annual 4th of July party at the Swackhamers, it was a good bet they would go. "He'd invite anywhere from a hundred to a hundred and fifty people," remembers Balduzzi. "A lot of people that worked with him — producers, the guy that did…Stephen Bochco used to come with his wife. James Cromwell came. He had all his cameramen — Fred Jackman used to come with his wife, and Marvin Miller [associate producer on the *Brides* pilot], he came with his family. Stan Schwimmer [line producer on *Brides*] used to come, and course Bernie Slade and his wife and the kids. All the kids — our kids grew up together. David used to come. I think Bobby came. Bob Brown always came. I think Glen Larson came. There were so many because Swack would invite people from different shows — the producer from *McMillan & Wife* — a lot of people from the industry. Dick Baer — he wrote the pilot for *Marty* — he and his family would all come to Swack's place. Swack kept in very good touch with all his writers and producers. Bernie Slade, Dick Baer, all of them. They were all at the 4th of July party. Course the St. Paddy's Day party…Swack liked to drink, but he never drank while he was working. While he was working, he never touched a drop."

"Swack was the center of a lot of people," continues Balduzzi. "There were a lot of people from New York that he would bring into a production. James Earl Jones, and Yaphet Kotto — New York stage actors like that. He worked with Peter Falk a lot. And J.D. Cannon and Dennis Weaver and Julie Cobb. I can't tell you how many people he helped in the business — young actors like Sally Field and David and Bobby. Sally was in our group." [47]

"Swack was cool," agrees Balduzzi's fellow 'logger,' Robert Biheller. "When I moved up here to Washington, he came up here to film *The Perfect Family* with Bruce Boxleitner and Jennifer O'Neill. When he heard that I was here, Swack gave me a part. Someone had been cast, but he recast it with me. He was a cool guy and a good director. He was a consummate director; he was always prepared."[48]

"Swack's one of the best directors I ever worked for," adds *HCTB* guest and director Lou Antonio. "Back when I started guest-starring you had six days to shoot an hour show, now you have eight, and unlike a lot of TV directors, who were mechanics because of the rush and the time, he not only knew the mechanics backwards and forwards, he knew what the relationships were. He knew how to help an actor. He was quite unusual and quite special as a director. He didn't inspire me [to become a director], but when I had a question, I would go to him and say, 'Hey, how do you do this, Swack?' He was very helpful." [49]

Like *Brides'* Virgil Vogel, E.W. Swackhamer encouraged the directing career of future director Dave Cass. "I met E.W. on *Here Come the Brides*," says Cass, "and to my knowledge, I was the only person that E.W. would ever let shoot second-unit for him. He always liked to do everything himself. He was just this big blustery guy — you know, 'All right, pal. Let's go! Let's get this done.'"[50]

That E.W. Swackhamer felt very warmly towards Dave Cass was evident when he told the stuntman what the initials E.W. stood for. Those initials were a closely guarded secret. Given what Dave Cass had done, it was understandable why Swackhamer took Cass into such confidence. "E.W. always said I saved Bridget's life," chuckles Cass. "She was driving a buggy on the backlot of Screen Gems and the horse went nuts. She fell out of it between the traces — the area between — where you hitch the horse to the wagon. I was doubling Robert at the time. I was just standing there watching the shot, and I got in there between her and the horse, until she could get out. So whenever E.W. was directing, (and Cass was working with him), he swore all those years I worked with him that I saved her life. I said, 'E.W., I didn't save her.' 'Yes, you did,' he'd say. 'You saved my new bride's life.' He was twittipated over her probably till the day he died. Swack was a good guy. I used to tease him because he had a Cougar he bought new in the '60s, and he still drove it. He said, 'It still runs.' I'll tell ya, they broke the mold when they made E.W. Swackhamer."[51]

"He had a wonderful memorial," remembers Dick Balduzzi. "Bridget taped the thing. It was beautiful. There were a lot of people that spoke — it was great. Swack knew how to handle people. There were a couple of people he liked to bat around, but he was very cool — a cool guy. He used most of the people that he knew as actors — he more or less put us all into *Brides*. Sometimes a director has a say of who goes where. He was pretty much left alone at Screen Gems because he had that knack for picking the right people."[52]

As for guest-starring roles, "those were done through the studio," reveals Balduzzi. "Swack would definitely have a part in that — he was directing most of them, so he would read them. Bob Claver was good, too. He knew exactly who was right for the parts. I think Bob and Swack and Renee Valente would have been the ones to do that. Tony Thomas and his partner — they were there at Screen Gems, too. And

Burt Metcalfe and Ernie Losso. There were tons of casting people that were always good as far as Screen Gems was concerned."

"Swack set the style for *Here Come the Brides*," states the actor. "I think he and Claver worked well together. Then of course all the guys that Swack used they also got to direct some of the segments. Bob Rosenbaum — he was one of Swack's people, he got to direct some of 'em." [53] [The first season's "Democracy Inaction."]

*Bridget Hanley and E.W. Swackhamer on their wedding day.* COURTESY BRIDGET HANLEY

"Swack ended up doing a ton of pilots and setting the style," says Hanley. "He truly believed in a vision, and he had a right as the director to choose his own style. But then other directors would come in and change the style, and sometimes that displeased him, but he also knew that he did exactly the same thing. I mean he started *Law and Order*, then the style changed, and he went back to do it again, and it was fine, because he loved the actors, but he did not have that great a time. He was changeable — if something didn't work, he would say, 'You know what? Let's try this,' but he liked to be in charge. Because he knew what he was doing, everybody could relax, and do their work. Everybody could contribute. Certainly the actors he was desperate to have contribute, and anyone else, too. He always was aware of what was going on; he was very intelligent and very up on all the new things, and he would take bits from what he thought was appropriate and add them on to his style — it could implement but never conquer. The crew loved him, mostly. He was better with the crew and the actors than he was with the bosses. They were all buddies. They all worked to make the best product."[54]

"He and Bob Claver had different directing styles," adds William Blinn. "With Swack, there might have been another way to shoot it. He would start with a wide shot, and go in for a close-up — that was one of the things he liked to get to."[55]

"He missed doing theater," says Hanley. "We went to the theater all the time — that was part of our life, and he directed a friend of mine's play out here when he had some time. That was fun for him, and, he loved it when I was in the theater and doing things."[56] Like the *Columbo* movie, *Columbo Goes to College*. "[*Columbo* star Peter] Falk knew Swack from New York," remembers Dick Balduzzi. "I was on that show, and Bridget was on that show, and Swack's daughter Elizabeth was on that show. That was one of the last ones he did. The last show I did. After Swack died, I just lost everything. We were very, very close." [57]

"Not everybody liked him," admits Hanley, "but I certainly did. And Susan Tolsky did. Swack adored her. He loved Dennis Weaver, too, and Dennis loved him — Swack directed a lot of *McClouds*." As did Lou Antonio. "Lou Antonio and Swack...they really adored each other,"[58] remembers Hanley.

In fact, the only people director Swackhamer really clashed with were series producers and studio bosses. "He loved being the boss and setting the [series] style in the pilot," states Hanley, "then it didn't always continue. That was hard for him. He felt so strongly about that. That happened on a couple of things, but he was fired only one time. And it was for those reasons — he wasn't a great sort to bend to the powers that be."[59]

Directing over twenty-five pilots, eighteen of which were to become successful series (among them, *The Flying Nun, Quincy, Eight is Enough, Nancy Drew*,) nominated for an Emmy for his work on the 1978 six-hour miniseries, *The Dain Curse* (based on the Dashiell Hammett novel of the same name), E.W. Swackhamer died of a ruptured aortic aneurysm on December 5, 1994, in Berlin, Germany. At the time he was scouting locations for his next production.

Reflects the director's widow, Bridget Hanley: "There were times when, after Swack died, there were crews and people that I talked to, and they said, and it had been several years after Swack passed away, they said, 'Well, we haven't been SWACKED yet.' Which meant they hadn't met anyone quite like him yet. That to me was such a kudo to him. He loved the crew. And they loved him."[60]

1. Marvin Silbersher – telephone interview – 2008
2. Brown – interview – 2007
3. Ibid
4. Hanley – interview – 2007
5. Brown – interview – 2007
6. Silbersher – interview – 2008
7. Ibid
8. Hanley – 2007
9. Brown – 2007
10. Ibid
11. Ibid
12. Ibid
13. Hanley – 2008
14. Ibid
15. Ibid
16. Silbersher – 2007
17. Hoag – interview – 2007
18. Tolsky – interview – 2007
19. Dick Balduzzi –interview – 2007
20. Ibid
21. Soul – interview – 2007
22. Karen Carlson – interview – 2007
23. Blinn – interview – 2007
24. Hanley – 2007
25. Catching – interview – 2007
26. Hanley – 2007
27. Balduzzi – 2007
28. Hanley – 2007
29. Brown – 2007
30. Hanley – 2007
31. Soul – 2007
32. Balduzzi – 2007
33. Blinn – interview – 2007
34. Soul – 2007
35. Hoag – 2007
36. Dave Cass – telephone interview – 2007
37. Blinn – 2007
38. Claver – 2007
39. Blinn – 2007
40. Brown – 2007
41. Hanley – 2008
42. Ibid
43. Ibid

44. Balduzzi – 2007
45. Hoag – 2007
46. Balduzzi – 2007
47. Balduzzi – 2007
48. Biheller – 2007
49. Antonio – interview – 2008
50. Cass – interview – 2007
51. Ibid
52. Balduzzi – 2007
53. Ibid
54. Hanley – 2007
55. Blinn – 2007
56. Hanley – 2007
57. Balduzzi – 2007
58. Hanley – 2008
59. Ibid
60. Ibid

"That cast, in all its diversity, truly had an ensemble feel on the set. When people sat down to eat, nobody was treated as an outsider, people didn't scatter to their trailers, or ignore you when it came time for them to walk into the scene and take the stand-in's place, they didn't have somebody off-camera doing their lines when it came time for your close-up. Robert Brown was standing right there with me, acting opposite me, no different than the scene itself. They gave to each other, and there was a warmth and a friendship there which I expected would carry on for the rest of my life when I would run into them again. I ran into Robert Brown and David, I ran into Bobby and Bridget later on, and even E.W. Swackhamer. Whenever I called or sent a note, when I found out we'd be doing another show, there was always a response, there was never a dismissal."[1]

*Here Come the Brides* guest star Angel Tompkins

Part Two

# *Perfect Casting from Top to Bottom*

*Author's note: My original intention was to provide full chapters on each member of the regular cast. With* Brides *co-star David Soul, this simply wasn't possible, given how active Mr. Soul is as director, actor, etc. The unexpected death of Henry Beckman, and not wishing to impose on Mr. Beckman's very close friend, Hillary, during this difficult time, kept me from going into any extensive detail concerning Mr. Beckman's work, pre- and post-*Brides*. As for series star Bobby Sherman, and veteran actress Joan Blondell, because Mr. Sherman co-wrote his autobiography, and a biography was recently written on the late Miss Blondell, I decided it was best to devote their respective chapters solely to their time on* Here Come the Brides. *I hope this book's greater degree of focus on the careers of the* Brides *semi-regulars will compensate for these shorter chapters.*

"Yessir, ladies, we've got everything in Seattle. Everything! But, we haven't got you, and, if we haven't got you, we haven't got anything."

Jason Bolt, to the marriageable young ladies of New Bedford in the pilot episode, "Here Come the Brides"

# Chapter 5

# *Starring Robert Brown*

Sir Laurence Olivier, General Douglas MacArthur, General George Washington, Albert Einstein, Tyrone Power, jazz great Ethel Waters, President of the United States Theodore Roosevelt, *The Night Before Christmas* author Clement Clark Moore, director Elia Kazan, Republican Senator Jacob Javits, Dame Judith Anderson, Cardinal Cushing, Charles Laughton, violinist Jascha Heifetz, dancer/actor Fred Astaire. There was one thing all of these people shared in common — they were all part and parcel in the life history of *Here Come the Brides* lead Robert Brown. To *Brides* executive producer Bob Claver, Brown was the one and only actor who could play the lead part of Jason Bolt. Since the character was assigned a larger-than-life task in the show (a task based in historical truth, as previously noted), it was vital that a larger-than-life sort of actor be cast in the role. To Claver, Robert Brown fit this description.

Brown's background certainly equipped him to play such a character. "My father, [William Brown] my dear father was born in Kent, England" reveals the actor. "In the 1880s. His father was a military man, in the Boer War. He was wounded and blinded, and he had to come home. My father had to leave his private school because somehow my grandfather, something happened to him, he died, and something happened to the money. I don't know what. He [Brown's father] was a man who never spoke much about his history. He finished public school — public school was what they called the private schools. He then went to London to get a job [as a butler], and the job he found was at the wonderful Hotel Grille. Where the royals spent their time. The Savoy Grille. He was invited to work in these various castles and stately homes. To do parties and things. After a couple of years, he and his brother decided to head across the "pond," — as he used to call it) — to America. He came via Canada, they came across the border. [Then] in New York, somebody got him letters and took them somewhere and he became Teddy Roosevelt's butler" [at Sagamore Hill, the "summer White House," from 1902 to 1908].

It was at Sagamore Hill that William Brown met his future wife, Margaret MacKenzie. "A very attractive, sweet Scottish woman, born in the Isle of Skye, in Scotland, she met my father at Teddy Roosevelt's," the actor explains. "She was a traveling companion, traveling with Lady Somebody or Other, and Lady Somebody or Other was staying out there at Teddy's house, and had to quickly return home. My mother was hired to stay on and work at the Roosevelt home. She may have been a maid. It was something in the domestic life."

Two or three years after William Brown became the butler for Theodore Roosevelt, World War I began. "Our president in Washington [Woodrow Wilson] didn't want

*Robert Brown and Fred Astaire.* COURTESY ROBERT BROWN

anything to do with it," says Brown. "Oh no, no, no, no, no, no, and Teddy was saying, 'Get those Huns.' My father was with him every day, he was his 'first man,' bringing him his clothes out, and my father became his emissary; he went to Canada. He [Brown's father] wouldn't take any money, just a bottle of cognac, to pay for the train, and four years later he was on the first ship going across to the war, and the last ship coming back. He was in the trenches; he was wounded, then on the hospital ship. He was in the British Army, then he came back home."

Continues Brown, "The Roosevelts were so enamored with this young fellow, that Sara Delano Roosevelt, Franklin's mother [Franklin was Sara's only child]…she had these two old estate buildings. These four-story, stone buildings, with a garden in the back, and, on the second floor, there was a door that slid open, opening up this one large...it could be made into a large dining room for special events, and there were quite a few of them. FDR and his family had a black staff. Sara Delano had a continental, a German cook, and an Irish...and my father was the butler. For those special occasions, he ran the whole show, told the cooks what to bring out. Then, that period, I don't know how many years he stayed there, anyway something happened, and he went off and worked elsewhere. Then he was working in New Jersey, at this hundred-room house, for Lucy Keane. Before she died, she gave my father the Blue House which is outside of Elizabeth, New Jersey, on the road to Trenton." According to Robert Brown, the Blue House always had to be blue — nobody could change the color.

"It had been Washington's headquarters in the battle of Trenton," says the actor. "I was born in that house, and we lived there until I was five or so. My brother was a couple of years older — he had been going to school in the Bronx in town. My father didn't like the idea of that kind of life. He decided to come back to New York into butling."

Upon returning to butling, Brown's father "worked for Clement Clark Moore's family — the American aristocrats really. Famous names — from 'The Four Hundred' I guess they were called," reflects the actor. Following his work for Clement Clark Moore's descendants, William Brown moved his family to the Bronx. "He got on a subway [the Lexington Ave. Subway] and worked his way uptown," Brown states. "He got off at 170th Street in the Bronx, and headed for 'The Grand Concourse'. My father found a school, a public school, right next door to this building, where the apartments were up on the third floor, maybe the fourth floor, and he just took it, and in we went. He found this building so we wouldn't have to cross the streets. He didn't want us to live on the estates. He wanted us to have a life."

Even though, as Brown points out, the people for whom his father worked, were not the sort to advertise their wealth. "It wasn't new money," states the actor. "It was the people who had it for a century or more. They were the children of these super-wealthy people, and were just so pleasant — they would each wear hand-me-down clothes. They weren't showing their money, as our world does today. When somebody today makes some money, they get the big fancy whatever, and they publicize it. But these wealthy people were simple people, and they passed their millions on to people who needed it."

Once the Browns moved into their new home, they were exposed to a different culture.

"It was a nice section of town," says the star, "upper middle class, and I grew up in this English home where everything was proper, but we were living in an entirely Jewish neighborhood. There was a mezuzah* on our door when we came in. I was told by the janitor when I came back from the war [World War II], he said, 'Oh, you

---

*A mezuzah is a piece of parchment (usually contained in a decorative case) inscribed with specified Hebrew verses from the Torah *(Deuteronomy 6:4-9 and 11:13-21)*. These verses comprise the Jewish prayer 'Shema Yisrael.' They begin with the phrase, "Hear, O Israel, the Lord your God, the Lord is One.' A mezuzah is affixed to the doorpost of Jewish homes to fulfill the mitzvah (Biblical commandment) to inscribe the words of the Shema "on the doorposts of your house." *(Deuteronomy 6:9)*

know, Robbie. Your mother wouldn't let me take that down. I was taking it down one day when you first came to live here. Your mother heard my screwdriver against the door jamb. She opened the door, 'Why yes, Mr. Verhort, (he was a German), what are you doing, Mr. Verhort?' I said, 'Oh, I'm taking this down.' What is it?' she asked. 'It's Jewish prayers.' She said, 'Put them back up right now. Don't take it down.' I said, 'Oh, I didn't know you were Jewish, Mrs. Brown.' She said 'I'm not. But put it back. Christ was a Jew.'"

Nor did Margaret Brown let her son Robert accept money from their Jewish neighbors for doing them a favor. Explains the actor, "Our neighbors across the hall, the Goldbergs, their children had grown and gone to college; they became lawyers and moved downtown, so the parents were alone in this apartment. They [the parents] asked me one day if I would, on Shabbat, that's the Sabbath — that's Friday night though Saturday sundown — they asked me to turn on the lights, and light the stove, and turn it off. I said, 'Sure.' And they gave me a nickel. I came back home. I said, 'Oh, Mama. Look what I've got. I got paid. First money I ever made.' She said, 'Oh, wonderful, Robbie, what is it?' I told her. She said, 'Come with me.' She walked across the hall, rang the bell, and told the Goldbergs, 'My son would like to give you that nickel back.' I just looked at my mother. She nodded, and I gave the nickel back. 'But he did this for us,' they told her. She said, 'No, no. We're neighbors. Neighbors never receive anything other than maybe a friendship. That's how we live.'"

Since William Brown had worked, and was continuing to work for the aristocracy, Margaret Brown saw to it that neither of her children said anything which might make the neighbors uncomfortable. "She said, 'Robbie, don't tell the neighbors what your father does for a living'" remembers the actor. "I said, 'Why, Mama.' She said, 'They wouldn't understand.' So I never did.

Having seen one of English comedian Arthur Treacher's motion pictures, Margaret Brown thought anyone who heard what her husband did for a living might think he behaved like Treacher. Robert Brown related this to the actor when the two of them performed in the 1965 W. Somerset Maugham play, *The Circle*. "We used to go out together," states Brown, "he and his wife and I, and I told him the story of my father being a butler. I said, 'You ruined my life.' He said, 'What d'you mean. What d'you mean?' I said, 'You absolutely destroyed my childhood.' He says, 'I don't understand. I didn't know your mother. Did I know your mother? I don't think so.' I said, 'You ruined my life when you played in that comedy — *My Man Godfrey*, or something like that.' Because he was this fussy, funny, goofy guy. And as I came home from the movie that day, that Saturday, my mother, who had seen the matinee showing with me, said, 'Robbie, I wouldn't tell your friends what your father does for a living. They wouldn't understand.' Treacher said, 'Your father was a butler? I said, 'Yes.' He said, 'My father was a hoofer. A hoofer. And in those days — you couldn't…If I had a girl I wanted to see, I couldn't bring them home because hoofers were the lowest. Your father was a butler — oh, my God! All the butlers that I wished I befriended because they were so important!'"

Since he wanted to be accepted by his new Jewish friends, Robert Brown "used to tell people I was half-Jewish. So I was acting, trying to fit in, trying to be just the opposite of what people who come to this country did," explains Brown. "They tried to be like the Anglo-Saxons. The Anglo-Saxons [WASPs — White Anglo-Saxon Protestants] were the people that everybody wanted to be like. I was trying to be like the Jewish people. I learned more about them than I did about my father's group, the English and Scottish people."

Robert Brown also explored his environs. "I loved to travel in the city when I was a young man," the actor says. "The German neighborhood was on East 86th Street, there was the Hungarian neighborhood in the '70s, and the Jewish neighborhood down on Delancey Street, and the Oriental Chinatown in various places. And I would go down and spend time in these sections, on the days after I'd finished school, not telling my parents where I was. They thought I was out playing stickball with the other kids."

Despite developing an open-mindedness from such travels, Brown's bearing and manner were greatly influenced by his father. Recalls the actor, "I was well, well, well dressed with the clothes from a thrift shop my father took me to — Miss Islins. Miss Islins only opened a couple of days a week, they knew my father, and they would wait for the great clothes in my size and they'd send me down to a place in the village that for a couple of dollars, whatever that was wrong with it, they'd fix and sew it back. So I had clothes from Saville Row, in London, and the shirts and the shoes. So I was dressed — I was really something and I got so used to it, and I sounded different. I didn't sound like I was from New York. My brother Harold sounds like he's from New York. He sounds like a real Bronx kid, and I didn't. Because when I came out of the service, I was listening to my father and people who were in the upper group. So I, boy, I must have picked up his accent, because everybody thought I was [from the aristocracy]. I was not conscious of that. It was so deeply ingrained that I didn't even think of it."

Brown certainly had known wealthy people before he and his family moved to the Bronx. Recalls the actor: "We used to go to Bar Harbor, Maine, every summer, and we lived over the garage — the chauffeur with the ten-car garage, and my father had this whole place for the summer. So I knew what spoons to use, and I knew the children, and in those days, the kids were not the middle class, or the upper middle, they were the aristocracy. But they dressed so simply — each had hand-me-down clothes from their brothers, or whatever, they were taught not to show their wealth, they didn't, and that's how I lived and dressed."

As a result, when Brown later played Jason Bolt on *Here Come the Brides,* he was able to bring a common man/aristocratic air to the character. And, when the series moved into a harsher, more realistic tone in its second season, Brown adapted to the change quite easily. "So," notes the actor, "while I kept my father's way of speaking, and was able to play classical parts in the theater and so on: characters like James Joyce and Thomas Chatterton, [affecting a Brooklyn accent] I coulda played dese kinda guys if I had to play dose kinda guys. You know, you do whatcha gotta do. I think I did play those kinds of characters once."

When war broke out between the United States and Japan, Robert Brown, like so many other young men of the time, enlisted in the armed services. In the Navy. "I was very pro-American," states the actor, "you know, 'Fight! Kill the Japs!' And I was at Iwo Jima, the landing there. I wasn't there at the time, but we were in that area. We left Saipan with the same Marine division that was on Iwo Jima. We left Saipan with this convoy, we didn't know where we were heading, we were going to Japan to land in Japan when the bomb was dropped, and when the bomb dropped, we didn't know that, we just started going in a circle, for a couple days circling, circling, waiting to see what was gonna be, and we killed lots of time. Then we landed on the southernmost island chain of Japan, like the Annapolis of Japan, and that was not far from where one of the bombs dropped. The people had all left this island, and had gone up in the hills. We stayed there for a while and left Marines there, and we went back to Saipan to get the Army and brought the Army back to relieve the Marines and that was about three weeks later when we got back. So I saw what war was, and the end of war, and I was then, I never knew any Japanese people, but I was sorry that we had been at war. After having suffered all of that, we achieved nothing, and war is nothing, it didn't change anybody. I'm against war. So was Jason, I think."

It was while he was in the Navy that Robert Brown decided to become an actor. "I remember sitting on the decks at night," says Brown, "looking at the stars, and I am coming from the movie theater — the screen, it wasn't a movie theater, below, and I began to dream of the life that I was watching with Fred Astaire and all these people. To me, Fred Astaire was the epitome. I later got to meet him. Anyway, when I came back from the war, I didn't tell my mother and father that I was going to be an actor. They wouldn't understand, especially my father. He had come from a line of whatever it was; he was in that upper life.

"When I became an actor, I went to the Dramatic Workshop — the New School of Social Research," continues Brown. "It was a great school — Harry Belafonte was our classmate, and Walter Matthau, Rod Steiger, and Bernie Schwartz (who was Tony Curtis). [Founders of the school] Erwin Piscator and Bertolt Brecht were active in doing creative things that were not standard. It was a liberal place. But I was never aware of politics. One of my teachers, an acting teacher, was a Communist. I hated him. Bret Warren — later on I hated him."[2]

Explains *Brides* guest Marvin Silbersher, "Swack and Bob Brown and myself — we had a Summer Theater, and the teacher Bret Warren, who was a teacher of ours in school turned out to be a terrible person. Swack and Bob Brown went out to help him start a summer series on Long Island. They gave him money. He raked them over the coals, took advantage of them. He was like a thief. I fell into the same trap the next year. They warned me, warned me." As a result the three men (and Walter Matthau) "started our own theater. From that, we did a production of *The Glass Menagerie*."[3]

By that time, or perhaps a little bit later, Robert Brown had appeared in his first Broadway play, *Skipper Next to God*, written by Jan de Hartog and directed by Lee Strasberg. "Lee Strasberg taught two classes at my school," remembers Brown, "this was before the Actors' Studio. This was 1947. Kazan [and Robert Lewis and Cheryl Crawford] started that school — Elia Kazan who was called 'Gadget,' or 'Gadge.' Strasberg had been one of the three leaders of the Group Theatre [the other two were theater director and drama critic Harold Clurman and American theatre producer and director Cheryl Crawford]. That was the theater that existed in the '30s and '40s, the most adventurous group, and all the great stars came from that place." Among them, the aforementioned Elia Kazan, Harry Morgan [whose son, Christopher, became an assistant director on *Brides*], John Garfield, Franchot Tone, Ruth Nelson [*Brides* guest] Will Geer, Howard DaSilva, John Randolph, Clifford Odets, Lee J. Cobb.

"I was in a directing class of Strasberg's, just watching," continues Brown. "I didn't do any directing — it was the history of acting — 'History of the Theatre,' it was called. Strasberg said at the end of a class, 'Anyone here a member of the Actor's Equity Association?' which was the union, and that summer, I had gotten my equity card in a summer stock company. So I raised my hand. He said, 'Wait until after the class breaks up.' He hired me to be in a play on Broadway that John Garfield was starring in — *Skipper Next to God*, and there I was, in an improvisation group backstage that worked behind the scrim, the screen where you can see other people, that is, their images. I was one of the Jewish passengers. There were eight of us, or twelve of us: [*HCTB* guest] John Marley and a group of others. We were acting in scenes that we created ourselves. I was one of the offstage voices. The play was about a ship with Jews who travel all over the world, because nobody would let them stop anywhere. It's a factual story. There was one little cabin where the people lived — that's where the little scenes were played, and on the deck, all the big things were happening. The people who came into the cabin onstage came from us, because we had been doing these various improvisations with them to get them ready to play the scenes. That was 1947-48. That's where I met my first wife, who was a friend of an usherette who worked there. And I fell in love with this wonderful lady. We got married, and had a child."

Opening on January 4, 1948 at the Maxine Elliott's Theatre and playing till January 30 of that year, *Skipper* then opened at the Playhouse Theatre that same January 30. By the time the play closed on March 27, 1948, a total of ninety-three performances were given. Also appearing with Robert Brown and John Marley in *Skipper* was future *HCTB* guest Joseph Bernard. "Joe Bernard knew how to do political stuff," says Brown. "He became buddies with John Garfield, [a.k.a. Julie Garfield]. Julie Garfield took us all to the opening, or a special showing of his movie, *Body and Soul*. We all went and sat in this special room. He was a sweet guy. Si Oakland was in *Skipper Next to God*, too. He was one of the major characters in that."

Lee Strasberg was impressed enough with Brown to use him again. "Years later," recalls the actor, "I did a play that Strasberg directed with his daughter [Susan]. The name of the play was [George Bernard Shaw's] *Caesar and Cleopatra*. She was Cleopatra, and Franchot Tone, who had been at the group theater years before — [he had a] wonderful, wonderful voice [he was also in it]. I was Apollodorus — the golden Apollo [a patrician amateur of the arts]. We were playing — we toured the country and we were coming to New York, and the theater wasn't available to us, they were supposed to have closed the play that was in there, but they had stayed open. We went out to Connecticut, to the Westport Theater — a country playhouse that had been owned by the Theater Guild which was the major production company on Broadway."

"One of the first weeks, Susan came to my dressing room," continues the actor. "She says, 'Robert, are you free for supper tonight?' They called it supper; dinner was at four. I said, 'Sure.' She said, 'Well, come on.' And I had a little car, and I drove her home. Her mother, Paula Strasberg, and father had rented a house in Westport, and as we were driving there. I said, 'Gee, that was very nice. Why did your mom think of me?' Because her mom had told Susan to invite me. She said, 'Oh, Marilyn's coming.' I said, 'Marilyn who?' She says, 'Don't give me that crap! *Marilyn who?*' I said, 'You don't mean Marilyn Monroe.' She said, 'Of course I mean Marilyn Monroe.' I said, 'Well, well, well,' I was stuttering. I said 'W-w-w-why?' She said, 'Well, she saw the play. She was there opening night. She thought you were cute.' I said, 'Gee.' She said, 'She likes you rich guys.' I said, 'WHAT?' She said, 'Don't give me that! What do you mean '*what?*' Everybody knows about you.' I said 'What do they know?' She says, 'What do you mean, '*what do they know?*' Everybody knows about your family.' I said, '*MY FAMILY?* Tell me what you know.' And she's, 'Well, come on, your parents, and Brown Brothers Harriman...' Well, Brown Brothers Harriman was one of the biggest stock firms and Averell Harriman, and also, Little Brown & Company, the publishers. That's who...they thought I came from these families because I seemed so...[born to the good life]. So all these years, in school and afterward, everybody thought I was [related to such famous Browns]. That's why Vincent Sardi's gave me a special ticket, and I got special tables, and they put me on...they gave me an account to use. So I had this strange life as a young actor."

In 1950, Brown appeared with jazz great/actress Ethel Waters in *A Member of the Wedding*. Brown laughingly recalls: "She walked through my dressing room to another outside back door, and I turned. I was sitting almost bare-assed, and then she stopped and looked at me. She said, 'I ain't too old to cut the mustard!' She was a truly special human being; she sang when we weren't working. And every performance that she did, early (before the curtain rose) when she was in half-costume, she'd go out on stage and sweep the stage, and the back door, with a big broom and dustpan. I was so impressed with this great artist. That's what she did to keep her concentration keen."

Not long after that, Robert Brown "got a job in Maxwell Anderson's [1951] play, *Barefoot in Athens* [in which Brown played Lamprocles, eldest son of Socrates and Xanthippe] and Lotte Lenya, who was Bertolt Brecht's wife, played my mother," recalls the actor. "It was quite an event. We toured with that. That's where I met Albert Einstein. I met him at Princeton. Max Anderson wanted to open the play in Princeton, New Jersey. That was the first place we played before we went on the main tour to Philadelphia and Boston, [and] those theaters. When you tour a play for Broadway — you get the big theaters. But this was the McCarter Theatre in Princeton.

"Princeton was where Einstein was with his Institute of Advanced Studies," reveals Brown, "you know, the think tank, the great thing that was started at Princeton. It's a separate building there — huge, wonderful-looking, eighteenth century. Anyway, one day, the day of opening, we rehearsed little scenes and did curtain calls, you know, that's what you do before the opening and Max Anderson came out on stage. He says, 'Listen, ladies and gentlemen: A very important friend is coming to the play tonight — Dr. Einstein. And I want you to not go up [stairs, after the performance], stay down here on stage, and wait for him to come back. We don't want him climbing stairs; it's a rickety [staircase]'– the dressing rooms were up above. So we all waited and I was standing somehow, with dear Max, I don't know why, I just happened to be, and his son, Alan Anderson directed it, and we were kind of hanging around, and hanging around, and Max said to the stage manager, 'For God's sake, go out and see where the hell he [Einstein] is. Maybe he doesn't like it or something'. Sure enough, the stage manager ran back and said, 'We just saw him drive away.' He [Maxwell Anderson] said, 'Oh, Christ, he hated it. Oh, Christ, he hated it.' So they gave out [the next day's scenes] who was coming to rehearsal tomorrow, we were told what scene would we do. I wasn't needed; my guess is that Lotte wasn't needed either. My scenes were with the family."

Maxwell Anderson had hoped Albert Einstein would see the play. Like many other learned Jewish men living in Germany, Einstein had been forced to leave his native country when Adolf Hitler became chancellor of Germany. Intelligent men like Einstein being a threat to Hitler's ambitions, the scientist could have identified with the situation in Anderson's play. The play had the brilliant Greek philosopher Socrates being put on trial for corrupting the youth of Athens with liberal thoughts. "Barry Jones was Socrates," remembers Brown, "and John McLiam was in it. McLiam was in dramatic school with me. He was gonna be a writer. He married Roberta Roberts. He did very well with his career."

The day after Albert Einstein had seen the play, Robert Brown encountered the scientist. "Many of the actors that I knew were older guys who had played at the McCarter," says Brown. "They toured with plays and stuff, and they knew this hotel that was inexpensive. So I went back to the hotel [the night Einstein saw the play]. When I woke up the next day, the night before had been drizzly; so my hair was curled. I started to wander around, looking for a restaurant cuz the hotel didn't have any place to eat — it was out of the way kind of, and I found myself near the edge of the campus, and I thought I might find something cheap right near by."

Continues Brown, "A car pulled up, and they rolled the window down, and somebody was saying…I said, 'I'm sorry. I'm new here. I don't know the directions.' That's what I thought they were asking. Well, the back door opened, and there was Albert Einstein, with his hat on. He closed the door, and the woman [sitting] next to the driver, said, 'You get him home on time.' And they drove away."

To Brown's surprise, "Einstein grabbed my arm, and in we walked into the campus, and into this little place, facing the Institute of Advanced Study. There were a couple of pine trees that were still green because it was the winter, and we sat on a bench, on a little hill, under the trees. He said, 'This is where I sit sometimes, and nobody bothers me.' He had a wonderful German accent. He then told me, he spotted me because [he thought] I was the only Athenian walking down the street [because Brown's hair had been curled from the rain]."

Having seen the play, Einstein recognized Brown as one of the actors. "He wanted me to tell his friend [Maxwell Anderson] what he thought of the play," Brown explains. "He had to leave, didn't come backstage through the theater — somebody didn't tell him or something [to do that], so he went out the stage door. There was a line [at the theater entrance], they wanted his autograph, and he hated that, so he fled because of the autographs. He gave me some thoughts and opinions [concerning the play], then asked about me and my child."

Absorbed in conversation, the two men suddenly realized a good bit of time had passed. "He patted his wrist," remembers Brown, "and he said, 'What watch? (What time?)' I said, 'We're late. We're late!' I ran down to get a cab, and was putting him in the cab. He said, 'No, no.' He pushed me in first, then I was holding the door, and he got in after me, and I grabbed the door and shut it," and the cab pulled away.

On the way to his home, Einstein asked Brown, "'Do you know your telephone number. I said, 'Yes. I'll be happy to give it to you.' He said, 'No, no, no. Do you remember it?' I said, 'Yes, I do.' He says, 'You know. I don't know mine. I don't remember mine.' I said, 'Oh, really.' He said, 'Yes, because there's always someone there to dial it for me at home.' 'Oh,' I said. Then there was another long pause. He said, 'Bob, do you know your address?' The driver turns around and says, 'Dr. Einstein. Everybody knows where you live.' He says, 'I don't remember the number of the house.'"

A short time later, at the end of January 1952, audiences saw Robert Brown appearing opposite Dame Judith Anderson at Manhattan's Civic Center, in the revival of Clemence Dane's 1934 play, *Come of Age*. Judith Anderson had appeared in the 1934 original. Brown was cast as real-life, seventeen-year-old English poet Thomas Chatterton (November 20, 1752-August 24, 1770). The play had Chatterton, who has taken his life with arsenic, asking Death, who's come to take him, to allow him to "come of age" among the living. Centuries pass before Death agrees; Chatterton is then returned to the present day. He falls in love with a woman (Anderson), then is betrayed by her when she learns he has signed a contract to write for Hollywood. Realizing that Death has granted him his request to live, as he has experienced both joy and despair, Chatterton accepts the second coming of Death with no regrets.

"It was a very dramatic play," states Brown, and "Sir Richard Addinsell [*Fire Over England, Goodbye, Mr. Chips, Gaslight, Blithe Spirit, Scrooge*] wrote the score. Sir Richard Addinsell had written the 'Warsaw Concerto' [for the 1941 film, *Dangerous Moonlight*, a.k.a. *Suicide Squadron*, starring Anton Wallbrook and Sally Gray]. He had a twenty-eight piece orchestra, or an eighteen-piece orchestra backstage, and they had a tenor and a soprano. It was poetry and music, in rhyme, we played our stuff that way — Judith Anderson and myself, we would do our scene, and behind us, the music would start."

Among those to take in the play was Judith Anderson's friend, Laurence Olivier. "I met him with Judith Anderson, whom he knew and cared for," remembers Brown. "Olivier told this story...he was very impressed with Ralph Richardson — who played the character roles. He says, 'Well, Rafe' — he called him 'Rafe' — he says, 'Rafe was being interviewed by the press, and we were all standing there, and one of the fellows from the press said, 'Tell me about your acting profession.' Rafe says, 'What d'you mean, acting profession?' 'That's what I wanted to talk to you about,' the man from the press says. Rafe says, 'There's no such thing as an acting profession.' The man from the press says, 'Of course there is.' 'No, no, no,' Rafe tells him. 'It's an acting addiction.'"

Chuckles Brown: "Well, I wasn't addicted. I loved it, when it was real and true, but Hollywood didn't do it for me because I never worked in that creative way that some people are lucky enough to do, when they make films. Most of it was show-biz, done for profit, rather than because it was an important tale."

Having worked for the great stage actress Katharine Cornell and her husband Guthrie McClintic in *Come of Age*, Robert Brown was then hired as a standby for Christopher Plummer (playing the role of Count Zichy — a Hungarian in the Austrian government) in the 1955 Christopher Fry comedy, *The Dark is Light Enough*. Katharine Cornell's leading man was Tyrone Power.

"I had a dressing room and a costume and everything, ready to go," remembers Brown, "and thank God that nobody was ill. Because I had a little baby. So I was given the job; Cornell and McClintic wanted to help me. I got various great jobs that way. The ingénue in the play — she and Tyrone Power were friends, and something happened. He sent her a bouquet of flowers to celebrate something — some mistake she'd made on stage, and she kept it in a box. He did something else, and she gave a flower back to him. It was some kind of a salute, some kind of joke between them. Well, I would often wait in the wings or backstage, and there was an inner set — it was a set within a set, in an ancient barn, with hay to store. And one night — moonlit night — it was the end of an act, there were these big barn doors up stage center, and I was there [waiting], just listening, nobody else was near me. I was right there at the doors, and something happened on stage. Miss Cornell made an offstage exit, leaving the young woman and Tyrone Power, and the stage manager was there with his cue-book, going to the other side because it was right about before the curtain came down. She said to the stage manager, 'Send Mr. Power to my dressing room immediately!' and then she went to her dressing room which was near the stage. Power was on the other side of the stage — in a little corner, not as big a room. Well, Power came out, and closed the door quietly and smiled at me, and the stage manager said, 'Miss Cornell would like to see you in her dressing room.' He says, 'All right,' and in he went."

At which point, everyone in the production, including production manager/actor Keene Curtis, and actor turned director Sydney Pollack, went about their business. "The backstage lights came up and everybody had their fifteen/twenty minutes," explains Brown. "The crew went into their little room to play some cards or drink a glass of beer, or whatever, and the actors [including Brown's friend, Donald Harron] were up in their room, and I was there waiting. I didn't have any place to go, and I was kind of interested — because of the way she'd moved toward her dressing room. The door opened after a while, Power backed out and closed it, and he stood staring at it. Then he turned and I was the only one there. He came to me and he said, 'My God, she fired me!' I said, 'I beg your pardon.' He said, 'She fired me; I had to beg for the job back.'"

Power then explained why the practical joke he'd played had gotten him into trouble with Cornell. Reveals Brown, "He said, 'You know this thing about the flower,' I said, 'Oh, I think I heard that.' 'He said, 'That flower — I gave her [the ingénue] a flower, and she gave it back to me, and I put it,' and he opened his costume, and there was the flower. [In the play] he'd been shot, or something, and she [the ingénue] was fixing him up on the bale of hay or something like that, and [when she saw where Power put the flower], she didn't break up — it was so amazing; he thought she'd laugh or something. Well, Cornell was witness to this. She told Power, 'Actors can not do that to one another. We're in the theater — this is a place of responsibility — you should know that. Your father was an actor. I knew him.' He [Tyrone Power, Jr.] said, 'She was magnificent. Of course she was right, but I've been getting away with murder since I've been a star in Hollywood.' And he was so famous. He was the one who probably filled the theaters every night. And that was it. Just a great story about the difference between Hollywood and the theater. They [theater actors] came to it as if they were priests of the church — these were the rules that could not be broken."

As Brown himself learned during the run of *The Dark is Light Enough*.

"I was coming down the stairway to my dressing room," recalls the actor, "and somebody was coming up. They backed away and back down the stairs again. This was one of the principal actors — an older actor, famous. So I came down, and later on in the day, I said to that actor, 'I'm sorry.' He says, 'Don't be. The rule is, when any actor is coming down the stairs, whether it's an intermission or not, you train yourself to make room for them properly in case they're heading for an entrance. You can't delay them or in any way inhibit them."

In addition to performing in plays based on historical figures such as Socrates and Thomas Chatterton, Robert Brown did autobiographical pieces like James Joyce's *Portrait of the Artist as a Young Man* and Emlyn Williams' *The Corn is Green*. "That [*Corn*] was kind of a lovely play," recalls Brown. "It was done with a famous film actress [Ann Harding, who co-starred with *Brides'* Joan Blondell in the 1947 film, *Christmas Eve*]. I played her student [illiterate Welshman] Morgan Evans [based on Williams himself]."

*Portrait of the Artist as a Young Man* had Brown portraying author James Joyce. "The Joyce estate liked what I did [in the earlier, *Ulysses in Nigh Town*]," states Brown, "and you couldn't play Joyce unless the estate gave you the rights." *Ulysses in Nigh Town* featured Brown as Stephen Dedalus. "Burgess Meredith directed it," says Brown. "I co-starred with Zero Mostel, [playing Leopold Bloom], Carroll O'Connor played [Dedalus' friend] Buck Mulligan. He played three or four other characters, too. (The play had a cast of sixteen playing a total of sixty-two characters!); Anne Meara was also in it. This was in 1957. It was a highly regarded play."

Also 'highly regarded' was American theatrical producer/director Joseph Papp. Wanting to make Shakespeare's works accessible to the general public, Papp had founded the New York Shakespeare Festival in 1954. "I knew him very well," says Brown. "I met him at the Actor's Lab — he was the stage manager there. I helped him get his first Ford Foundation, which got him going at the Park — Central Park."

(In 1957 Joseph Papp was granted the use of Central Park where he would produce free presentations of Shakespeare's plays.)

"The first thing I did for Joe Papp was a production of [Shakespeare's] *Two Gentlemen of Verona*," remembers Brown. "I did another play at a theater on Fifth Avenue. About the Irish Republican Army. The name of the play was *Mountjoy Prison*. It was about the killing of one of the convicts in this big prison. I was one of the Black and Tans. The Black and Tans were Irish who worked with the British. My character had to block the stairway with a rifle so that people couldn't come up. We rehearsed the play for about three weeks." During one performance, the production had a powerful effect on the IRA members who attended. "Everybody stood up and started stamping their feet on this wooden floor and yelling, 'Idiwaddy, idiwaddy. Yup, yup, yup,'" remembers Brown. "To see these old gray-haired men doing that. It was chilling."

One play which never took off was *Head of the House* with Lee Remick. "She and I were boyfriend/girlfriend," says Brown. "This was after she had been going with the son of a well-known actor. The boy's father was into art. So, we became an item, and then she went to stardom. She was lovely, sweet, simple, and came from kind of an interesting family. They had some money, and lived on East End Avenue and 57th Street. I would run into her from time to time [after Remick became a star]. We'd smile and wink and remember."

Other plays included Shakespeare's *The Tempest* with Sam Jaffe, and *King John*, in which Brown played The Dauphin. One play of which Robert Brown was particularly proud was 1963's *The Deputy*, written by German author and playwright Rolf Hochhuth. The play presented Pope Pius XII (Leader of the Catholic Church during World War II and the Holocaust) as a Nazi sympathizer. Despite the numerous atrocities committed against the Jewish peoples, Pius had tried to stay neutral. "He didn't do his job as a loving leader," states Brown. "The play was about this young man [Count Riccardo Fontana, SJ] a young special Roman Italian whose father was Count Fontana, a nobleman who ran the bank of the church. This young, talented priest, whose job was in Berlin, discovers that the Jews are being annihilated [during *Kristallnacht* –'The Night of Broken Glass']." On *Kristallnacht*, November 9 and 10, 1938, 8,000 Jewish shops were ransacked and destroyed all over Germany and parts of Austria. Jews were beaten to death, 30,000 Jewish men were taken to concentration camps, 1,668 synagogues were ransacked, and 267 synagogues were set on fire.

In the play, sickened by what he has seen, the young priest comes back to Rome to tell the pope. "And when you go to the pope," says Brown, "apparently this is how it goes. You have to go through the various hierarchies — one up, one up, and then you get to the pope. He [the young priest] couldn't just drop in — even though his father was in the place with the pope. The pope's reaction was not helpful. This is a true story — this aspect of it, then the priest goes to die with the Jews because he has lost his faith."

The touring company of *The Deputy* often met with protests. "We played in Cincinnati and Cleveland," remembers Brown, "and in Cincinnati, they were picketing us and shouting at us — their cardinal was down on the play. San Francisco was okay. We did a major, major tour with that play."

One theatergoer who was very impressed with the play was Boston's Cardinal Cushing. Cushing, who officiated at the marriage of future U.S. President John F. Kennedy, and who baptized many of the Kennedy children, played a major role in drafting the *Nostro Aetate* — in Latin, "In Our Time" [The *Nostro Aetate* was the Declaration on the Relation of the Church with non-Christian Religions. The document was voted on by the Second Vatican Council and promulgated on October 28, 1965 by Pope Paul VI. It officially absolved the Jews of deicide — the killing of a God.)

"Cardinal Cushing was the most famous Cardinal in the country," states Brown. "If there were a pope needed, he would be taken. He was a special guy, Well, Cardinal Cushing said to me, and, to the papers, that, 'Every thinking man should see this play. Everyone should see this play and decide for himself.'" Robert Brown was himself greatly affected by the play. "I was the only actor that played the eight performances a week," says Brown, "and you would start to sense the audience's reaction from the sounds they made. One night, I heard people crying, and when I did things that would get into the heart, I softened it up by moving from that place, or turning upstage, so the pain [of hearing the crying]

*Brown in* The Deputy.
COURTESY ROBERT BROWN

wouldn't be as great cuz I couldn't handle it." One night the content of the play, and the emotions it required from Brown, really got to the actor.

"At the end of this one scene, I was center stage," remembers Brown, "they were setting it up with my father — the Count Fontana. I was sitting in the chair, or he was sitting in the chair, and I couldn't...I just was overwhelmed and I walked off-stage and collapsed in the wings. The emotional...it was so great that it finally got to me, and I'd been playing it for a long time. Well, this wonderful actor — English actor [Alan Napier] who was in movies looked out at the audience and said, 'Oh, my son. My poor son.' Then he walked off, and the curtain came down. Then the stage manager walked out and said, 'Is there a doctor in the house?' Two or three doctors came running back. They gave me bananas and oranges and stuff. About ten minutes later, I went on with the play. So, it became physical — I was needing something — some food. But I finished the play. Then I walked out, and there was this wonderful applause. It was terrific. But that reaction was because of the stress and strain of that remarkable play. It was just amazing. It's something that just chills me — playing that character, what that play was about."

By the time Robert Brown finished his run in *The Deputy* (in 1965), he'd done quite a bit of work in television (*Perry Mason, Bonanza, Wagon Train, The Lawless Years*), and more than one motion picture, including 1962's *Tower of London.* The actor might have received more film work had he not been blacklisted. "My mother-in-law, she was a famous advertising woman, or department-store woman," states Brown. "She was the president of Saks, or Lord and Taylor, or she was at a big advertising agency. She called me into her office one day, and she says, 'Is there anyone, are there other actors in your union named Robert Brown?' I said, 'No. I'm the only one.' I'd kept my name, because I wanted to do it as a tribute to my family. I didn't want to change it. I'd been advised to change it."

As Brown learned, it might have been wise to change his last name. "She slid these two books over at me," he recalled. "One was *Red Channels* ('The Report of Communist Influence in Radio and Television,' issued by the right-wing journal, 'Counterattack on June 22, 1950), and one was *Aware.*"[4] (AWARE was also the name of a private anti-Communist group made up of lawyers, professors, businessmen and actors whose declared objective was "to combat the Communist conspiracy in entertainment communications."[5]) "Anybody whose names were in these big journals were blacklisted," states Brown. Those names included bandleader Artie Shaw, *Laura* novelist Vera Caspary, *HCTB* guest star Will Geer, entertainer Gypsy Rose Lee, even voice actor Bill Scott (Bullwinkle, Dudley Do-Right, Peabody, etc. on *The Adventures of Rocky and Bullwinkle*).

Reveals Brown, "The reason I got mentioned was that I was seen around town a lot of places with noted and fancy people, and I looked like a movie actor, I had that kind of look. There was a May Day parade one year; Harry Belafonte said to me, 'Come on, let's march.' I said, 'Sure.' So I marched with Harry. I was still in dramatic school at that time. So I was photographed apparently, and from there, they did some searches, and all the conventions and places I went to to picket for this or that, I was recorded. They didn't get me as a Communist, they got me as a 'Pinko,' or Fellow Traveler. So I was a Fellow Traveler, and when I was in the plays, all these wonderful things, all these wonderful roles, I was brought into the agents' offices, and to the studios, to test for a movie, and I never got them. I didn't think anything about it because I got lots of parts that good actors didn't get, in New York. So I never thought of it, until my mother-in-law showed me these things in the mid-fifties. It was then that I learned that all those years that I had been struggling and missing so many was because I was not kosher. It was a case of guilt by association. And I've gotten to know many, many of the people whose fathers... the Hollywood Ten — they went to jail because they wouldn't name names, but everybody knew I was too imaginative, fanciful, I guess, to be a member of the Communist Party."

Fortunately for Robert Brown, once he started working in television, and once the "Red Scare" was over, he found a good bit of work. Still he wasn't as active as he might have been. That was due to his own choice. "Fame wasn't in the cards for me,"

Brown states. "I didn't like the Hollywood life. You go to these parties, and when you drop in, you're — unless you're trying to sell yourself, well, some people like going to parties, but I would always have to drink a lot. I had a couple of belts of whiskey to get so that I would feel that I wouldn't be the way I really am — I'd drink so as to get into a 'Hey! How are ya?' mood, that kind of stuff."

Going to parties was part of the business, it helped actors and other talents get work. "There's a lot of desperation in the business," states Brown, "a lot of desperate people. That doesn't mean that they're bad people, they just want fame more than anything, and they focus on their careers. So they go to these parties. They join the Actor's Studio. I didn't do any of that. I was ambitious, but not like that."

Nor did Brown attend conventions. (Until recently, that is — and that was done as something of a lark.) "I did the *Star Trek* ("The Alternative Factor")," Brown says, "and some company sent me a lot of money to sign little trading cards, and asked me would I come to the thing cuz I'd make thousands and thousands of dollars. Every year I've said, 'No thanks, no thanks, no thanks.' Not that I was against the money, it's

*Robert Brown with Lorne Greene in the Paramount* Bonanza *episode, "Blessed Are They."*
COURTESY ROBERT BROWN

always nice to have a chunk of money, but I don't feel like I need to show off. It's not for me."

Nor was Brown all that fond of doing guest shots. "The *Bonanza* ("Blessed Are They") was all right," admits the actor. "They [Lorne Greene, Pernell Roberts, Dan Blocker, Michael Landon] got along. They pretty much stuck together which was kind of wonderful, but the way the crew and the directors...it was punched out...it didn't seem like...I had a pleasant role, in that beautiful little church — but it was like coming into somebody's family. And unless you were ambitious to join that family, I just came to do the job I was hired to do. It was always uncomfortable when they were so closely related to one another. That's how it is when you have to be acting, with the people that you're talking to, but off the set, I found that that wasn't the life for me."

During the production of the October 12, 1960 *Wagon Train* episode, "The Albert Farnsworth Story," Brown picked up an invaluable piece of advice from actor Charles Laughton. "It was one of the last performances played by this great English actor,

Laughton," remembers Brown, "and he and I were waiting and talking and he said, 'It sounds like you're a stage actor.' So I reminded him of something that we had done years and years before — this was at the time when I was doing the play with Jack Garfield (*Skipper Next to God*). Laughton had come to our classroom to do this one-person play. He did it sitting on the stage floor, we were just sitting around him. He was so impressive in that play. He said, 'Oh, God, that was wonderful!' We got to be real buddies on this *Wagon Train*. He then asked me how I made the transition to film from the theater. I said, 'I don't know. I didn't make it — I just kept doing it the same way.' He said, 'Oh, my. Listen, I'm gonna tell you something that I've never told anybody. So you can't tell anybody. "

Whereupon Laughton explained the importance to Brown of adjusting one's level and degree of performance to where one was in the shot. "The master shot [the shot that encompasses everything in the scene] is the first thing most directors do," explains Brown. "When they do the master — a lot of times you don't plan on what you do. They have people on the set who watch you and write down what you did at that time, but it's up to you to kind of think of that. So when they say, 'Cut,' you kind of think about what line you did what on. [That way, the action in the master will match the action in the two-shot, or the over the shoulder shot, etc.] Then you get the medium shot, the close-up, the over the shoulder..."

Needless to say, while broad and showy actions might work in a master, if the actor kept those actions the same in a two-shot, it would come across as too strong and obvious. As Laughton pointed out to Brown. "He said, 'how you moved, your eyes...depending on how close you were gonna be [to the viewer], all of this can be controlled," says Brown. "It can be with the same intensity, but not as 'loud.' He said, 'Here's what I do,' and he showed me as if he had a knob in his solar plexus. So we were working there, more than an hour, him showing me how he worked this 'knob.'"

That Robert Brown benefited from Laughton's advice was evidenced by the fact that he was soon starring in television series pilots, including the infamous *Yellow Bird*. Produced by Selig Seligman (*Combat, Garrison's Gorillas*), "the same people," notes Brown, "that did *Alexander the Great* [with Brown's *Colossus* co-star William Shatner]," *Yellow Bird* "was confusion. I got my friend Carroll O'Connor in it and (*HCTB* guest) Pat Harrington, Jr. was in that as well. It was directed by Richard Donner, and we were shooting for months — in Nassau, it was one of the most expensive pilots, cost millions, over a million or something. For a pilot, that was unheard of at the time. Had it gone, Carroll wouldn't have been Archie Bunker. It was an adventure series, which should have had Humphrey Bogart, or somebody like that in it, about a couple of guys who were brought in to be spies, they were corralled into it. Carroll would play different characters; he would wear different costumes and stuff. It was a comedy as well — a comedic adventure."

(The *Yellow Bird* concept certainly wasn't a bad idea. On January 9, 1968, Robert Wagner, in his first television series, began a two-and-a-half season stint as Alexander Mundy: a professional thief forced into stealing for the U.S. government in the tongue-in-cheek ABC adventure, *It Takes a Thief*. "Al" frequently resorted to a variety of disguises during the course of an assignment.)

"Carroll wanted the script changed," remembers Brown. "Since they wouldn't do that, he gave his notice. He said, 'Of course, I'll do the pilot, but I won't do the series. You'll have to find a replacement. So a lot of things were going on there. And it flopped. Well, that all reflected back on me. Because I was the star."

Soon, Robert Brown had another shot at a television series when he was considered for the role of Napoleon Solo in *The Man from U.N.C.L.E.* ("That was a real toss-up between me and Bobby Vaughn," recalls Brown. "I knew him when he was still in college.") Then came the even bigger and what proved to be more successful *Hawaii Five-O.* "Orson Welles was supposed to be in it, too," remembers Brown, "playing the other character (Five-O chief Steve McGarrett's arch-nemesis, Wo Fat) I signed a contract to do it, and this was right before *Here Come the Brides.* The director [Paul Wendkos] hadn't been hired at that time. Wendkos did lots of hot shows.

Continues Brown: "I said to the producer [Leonard Freeman], 'Will you please, when you go to Hawaii, look for a school that my daughter [Laurie] can attend? I raised my daughter after my wife had died, so I was the mother-father. He said he would. Then, on the day they were going, we had a breakfast-lunch on their way to the airport, and we were there chatting. He [Freeman] said, 'Do you have any thoughts about character?' and I said, 'Yes, I do. There's one thing I would really like if possible.' I was rather slender then and looked sort of like — I wanted to find…I said 'Whoever JFK's tailor is, I want to be in those kinds of clothes exactly. I want to get the look of that, because I want to have that kind of character.' I didn't want to have a lot of guns around; I wanted to use the thing of negotiation and charm and wit to negotiate things and put things right. If I had to use a gun, I was gonna get other people to help me, and maybe do something with that — it was something to do with the brain running the show rather than just guns, if that was possible. 'Oh, that's interesting, that's interesting,' they said, and they went off, and they were gonna come back in a week's time. Well, a week went by, two weeks, and I was getting anxious, because it was close to departure time (when shooting would begin in Hawaii.) My agent called once or twice, then she got back to me. She said, 'Robert, I don't know what happened. What the hell did you say?' I said, 'What do you mean?' She said, 'Well, the network called today. They said they'd been very busy. They said they were buying you out — your contract.' I said, 'Great. Now I've got no job. What happened?' 'I don't know,' she says, 'They didn't say. They're just paying you whatever it was — maybe $25,000 not to come to work.' It was a lot of money — to me — a lot. So I could not find out what the hell I'd said. I had her try a couple of times, and when she called back, she said, 'No, they're not available. They're busy with this or that.' And that was the end of it. Then something else [another part] came up."

By pure coincidence, Robert Brown finally got to the truth of the matter. "I had a Rolls Royce," says the actor, "and I lived in Malibu, and at the corner of Sunset Blvd., where Sunset hits the ocean, there was a gas station — a Texaco, I think it was. I pulled in, and the young fella ran around the car and looked at it, that was when the people at the gas station filled up your car, and we were talking, and he said, 'You know, I'm an actor, too.' I said, 'Oh, my gosh, that's great.' He said, 'In fact, I'm gonna…I don't know if you know,' and he named the name of this producer. He said, 'I'm going to his house tonight. I'm going with his daughter.' I said, 'Oh, say hello for me. My name's Robert Brown.' He says, 'Okay.'

"Well, the next day I was back in L.A. driving somewhere," remembers Brown. "And I got a couple of calls. They said, 'Call so and so right away.' I did. Then they sent an agent, and he said, 'Get over to the studio, blah, blah, blah, right now, to see so and so.' Which I did. So I was there, and waiting for this man to come in, he was in his office, sitting on this big couch — in this non-office-looking office, and in he comes, 'Hello, there.' He says, 'Long time no see.' I said, 'Yeah. Probably about a million dollars worth, huh?' He says, 'What do you mean?' I said, 'That's what the guy [Jack Lord] doing it has probably made since then.' He said, 'Oh much more than that.' I said, 'You're kidding.' He said, 'No, no, I'm not kidding. I'll tell you because you were involved,' and this was the second year or so, maybe the third year of *Hawaii Five-O.*

"He said, 'We had a budget of so much per episode. But we bought some property — built a studio in Hawaii, a real soundstage, but Jack Lord had bought the land that we were to build the studio on for a good low price, so we pay him every month, a rental, to lease the land, and a percentage of this and that so we don't have to raise his salary for the [show's] budget; it won't affect the weekly budget. Oh, he's got twenty-five million or more now.' I said, 'JEEZUS, THAT'S WHAT YOU DID TO ME! WHAT THE HELL!' He said, 'Well, they told you, didn't they?' I said, 'No. What the…just because I wanted to look like JFK?' He says, 'What are you talking about? Oh I forgot about that. No, you were in it.' See, we were coming to get you, but when we came back, CBS said, 'We're gonna replace the actor you've chosen.' We said, 'WHAT DO YOU MEAN, REPLACE HIM? THIS IS THE GUY WE WANT!' They said, 'No, no, no, no, you can't. Because Jack Lord's buyout is $100,000.' Well, my buyout (at $25,000) was less than his. So they said, 'We're gonna save some money by giving the show to Lord.' And that's how it went."

"I've had so many things like that in my life," laughs Brown. "I was just overwhelmed with these disasters, so eventually I just said, 'SCREW IT, BROWN! YOU DON'T NEED THIS! Just do voice-overs, and make a nice buck. Sure, it's not the same thing. But since you're not in love with the fame game…' Because I never played the game the way you're supposed to in order to get the jobs and stay famous. Fame wasn't in the cards for me, so I never played it. And there we are — that's one of the many.…the story of a happy but sad, lucky actor who had lots and lots of opportunities and in some ways I did okay, in other ways, I didn't do as well as somebody else might have done. But I was lucky — I had lots of opportunities. Life just takes you the way it takes you."

In the case of Robert Brown, life was about to take him to the lead role in the new ABC-TV series, *Here Come the Brides.* Thanks to an executive producer at Screen Gems by the name of Bob Claver, and an unsold pilot made by *Brides* co-star Joan Blondell's one-time husband, Dick Powell. The name of the pilot was *Colossus,* a.k.a. *The Infernal Season.*

Directed by the meticulous Don Medford, and written and produced by Richard Alan Simmons, *Colossus* co-starred Brown as Irish stuntman/actor John Michael

Reardon (one of the first stuntmen to do a new kind of entertainment known as 'moving pictures') and William Shatner as Reardon's Swedish, land-buying friend, Eric Tegman. "Dick Powell was the executive producer," remembers Brown. "He was one of the owners (of Four Star). He was gonna bring the pilot to New York and put it together, but when he died, it was shelved, people forgot about it, they were so busy with the funeral, and so on. So, all the contracts that he [Powell] had, expired; Shatner got something else, and I got something else, but when it played on the air [on March 12, 1963, as an episode of *The Dick Powell Show*], it got terrific reviews.

"Shatner was a very sweet guy," continues Brown. "I'd met him in New York years earlier. At Christopher Plummer's house. Shatner was a good friend of Plummer's, and he came to Plummer's house with some Canadian actor — Plummer was from Canada. [as was William Shatner.] Shatner was an easygoing, non-ego fellow. Easy to work with. He wasn't vain, preoccupied with his intelligence, just an open, solid actor. A good actor with a range that he never showed off. He was not a show-off, the best actors aren't. When one finds oneself doing that kind of acting, you're doing it wrong. You get stuck on your own press — that's not the way, but it's human — these dumb things happen. Shatner was a real good guy. I thought he was a fine man. He was the same when he was doing *Star Trek*. He was serious, but he had a sense of humor. He was a good, non-phony-baloney actor. And he's now poking fun at himself. He's a good fellow. I respect him as an actor, and as a man. The actors that I respect the most are the ones that didn't feel they were special. They might have felt that way, but they didn't brag."

Thanks to the camaraderie between Robert Brown and William Shatner, *Colossus* made for a very good pilot. "It was about these two immigrants — coming to California, to America, our adventures in the beginning," says Brown. "We had lots of vignettes of little stories. It was a terrific thing. And I think it was the thing that won me to Bob's [Claver's] heart. So they came to me with this series [*Brides*], and they wanted me to test. 'I said, 'No, no, I don't do tests anymore. I'll read the stuff, and if they want me, I'll do it. That's it.' I wasn't a big, powerful, fame guy. I was no longer interested in Hollywood cuz I'd been around. And I was just kind of dry on television. But they didn't want me to read. They said, 'We need you to do a test.' I said, 'No, no. If you want a test, you'll have to pay me for the test.'"

At which point, talks began with Brown's agent.

Remembers Brown: "The agent called and said, 'We came to a deal. You're gonna do it. And they want you to go to…they're having a party on the set there. They've been testing all the people, and at the end of the day, they want you to come to the party and meet them, and see what you think.' I said, 'Oh, that'd be fine.' So I wind up on the stage at Screen Gems — they were having a wrap party for the finishing of all of the tests, and there was Bobby Sherman and David Soul, and I knew Bridget.

Continues Brown: "Swack said, 'C'mon sit here with the guys. On the stage.' So I went up and sat around the table, they sat me alongside Bobby Sherman and David Soul. They had champagne and wine and food, and we were all laughing and talking, and congratulating each other that we were going to be working together. And Swackhamer was filming all of this! I guess the studio had said, 'We gotta see how they all look together,' and Swackhamer told Claver he knew how to get the film. I guess he told Claver it would be kind of a joke. If they hadn't chosen me, I never would have known how they'd gotten this film on me, because Swackhamer told me afterwards what he had done. At first, I was pretty pissed off. Anyway, that's how it all began."

For Robert Brown, that beginning almost ended during production of the pilot. "We were shooting something on the set," remembers the actor, "had all these cables going, and all this and that, and somebody was shouting, 'Robert, Robert, they need you on the phone here! It's one of the big magazines.' I said, 'Well, I'm kinda busy.' They said, 'No, no, it's important. You've got an interview here.' So, I ran to the phone without watching, and I tripped over the goddamn cable, and I couldn't get up. My foot was badly twisted — it had gotten caught in this cable. So they took me to the hospital and the doctor nearby. We were out there shooting at the backlot, in the Valley, near Warner Bros. — we did a lot of the major stuff there — they had two studios there where we did the work. Anyway, the doctor taped it up. He said, 'You can't move on it.' And we were three-quarters of the way through the pilot! So, I thought, 'Well, this is it. Wow! What a way to end it!' Because I knew they'd have to replace me — I knew I couldn't do it. So it was really sad, and I think they stopped filming."

Fortunately for Brown and the *Brides* company, the pilot's assistant director (or maybe its second assistant director) came up with a solution. "He was a young guy just out of college," recalls Brown. "I think it might have been Michael Dmytryk — the son of the blacklisted director [Edward Dmytryk]. He drove me home, and as we were driving home, he said, 'Listen, I was at UCLA, and I was on the football team. There's a great doctor...(The doctor had a Japanese name, I think it was Watanabe), would you mind stopping at his office on the way? We'll go right by it.' I said, 'I've been to the doctors — a couple of them.' He said, 'This guy is a doctor who treats athletes.' I said, 'Oh, Christ! Well, okay.' So in we go, and the doctor took the bandages off, and put my foot in a hot steam thing — circular water thing, and did this and that. The opposite of what they were doing [to Brown's foot] with ice. Then he taped it in a special way. He said, 'Now you walk on it. Go ahead. Walk, and balance the weight. Walk through the pain.' I did — I walked back and forth to the office, back and forth in the hallway. He said, 'The thing you gotta do is walk on it.' I said, 'They said not to.' He said, 'No, no. This is not a broken bone; it's a torn ligament. In order for it to heal properly, you've got to walk on it. So every day you come here at the end of your job, and I'll rewrap it, do whatever I have to do.' So, every day I went back to this doctor. And I called the studio and said, 'I'm walking. I'll be in tomorrow morning just as usual. But I've got to get a zipper — have a zipper put in my boots so I can zip up the boot, and bend it a certain way.' Because I couldn't get my foot into those big boots that they had. So they put a zipper in behind the fur, whatever it was, they put it in at the back so it couldn't be seen. Then I was all set to go, and I continued the pilot. And it was a big, big hit.

"It was an unusual show," continues the actor. "It wasn't just an ordinary comedy about girls and guys, it was about other things. It told a heroic story about the goodness of man. It was a show about relationships; the brothers, how they behaved with one another, how they backed each other up, how the older one was like a father who took care of things, he was able to get around problems and difficulties and tough moments with humor. That's just part of life. I do things in the same way. And it was a highly developed, romantic, kind of yesterdays drama, with love and romance involved, the romance of the country at the time, the romance of the West — [the brides] coming from the East to live in the West. It was about the building of a new world, one in which every man should be respected and cared for, a show about opening up sensitivity and being respectful of others. My character would convince his brothers to respect things. And they saw that.

"The church was the center of town, and why shouldn't it be?" points out Brown. "That's the way it was structured at the time, but it wasn't rightwing, Christian, it was more…every man was in there. God was not just a Christian god, but the god of mankind. Then there was the beauty of the dialogue and the point of view of the stories. I really feel privileged to have been part of that time. In its funny way, in its odd way, now that I look back on it, *Here Come the Brides* had a sense of truth to it, and a goodness that…I was proud to be connected with it."[6]

As a result, Robert Brown did not 'cut up' on the set like so many of his fellow cast members. Remembers *Brides* semi-regular Dick Balduzzi: "He used to get angered when we were horsing around and made things light. We wouldn't do that when it was time to shoot. When it was time to shoot, we shot, we didn't fool around and waste any time or anything. But, we had our fun. So he'd get annoyed, and we used to laugh at him. Then he'd really get pissed off at us. He'll deny it now, but he did. Because he was very serious. He wasn't as loose as a lot of actors were. Some of those guys can go with the flow and it runs smoother, but Robert Brown wasn't like that. He wasn't a typical Hollywood actor."[7]

Brown's view of acting certainly was serious. "It was more like a religion," says the star. "You learned the rules; you admired it, and had a great humility for it — that's how I felt about acting and the theater. It was a job. It was what I did for a living, and I took it seriously — I was there on time."[8]

"I think he was nervous about the situation of carrying the show, of the responsibility of that," muses Balduzzi. "I think he felt that responsibility because he had the major role, so he didn't like a lot of that playing around and fooling around. I remember there was one time where I was having trouble. I wasn't feeling well, and I had this scene with him, and I didn't know my line. He was looking at me like I was flubbing purposefully. Knowing him afterwards, and I've known him for years, I can't understand why he was uptight, because he was, is, such a pleasant guy, very quiet and very knowledgeable. A very bright guy. "[9]

"Robert Brown was the sage of the group," agrees *Brides* casting director Renee Valente. "He was the elegant one. His background — he had that theatre background, and he was like 'Big Dad,' and kind of there. In many respects, he had that 'Come to me with your problem' manner. He was lovely." [10]

"I kind of ran the set," says Brown. "I would always watch to see if an actor was mistreated, and I would complain to somebody up above. That kept the sense of camaraderie, I guess, and the crew liked me because I wouldn't let any of them get into trouble. I always respected the crew. You absolutely don't treat the gaffer like they're the gaffer. That became the thing that everybody followed me on, I think. The feeling that you have about the crew, including the crew in whatever things you can, that's a good thing because they're your audience. They're the ones who are right around you, and they'll tell you, the guy holding the boom, the microphone, the guy pushing the dolly, you're playing with them and to them, and they'll tell you if they think you blew the director's cut. You'll ask, 'How did I do?' They'll say, 'Well, geez. I think he liked the first take better.' So I might say to the director, 'Can we run it again. I'd like to give it another shot.'"

Brown has nothing but praise for the crew who made *Here Come the Brides*. "For the pilot," remembers the star, "Perc Westmore was the makeup man. He spent time with me in the beginning — he liked Joan Blondell, too. He was the head guy of the Westmore family, and talked about Bette Davis a lot. He had this special mirror — silver mirror given him by one of the great stars. Westmore created the look [of Jason, et al], and that was a very important factor. He was a wonderful guy."

The look E.W. Swackhamer, director of photography Fred H. Jackman, and their associates brought to the series also impressed Brown. "It was on the Columbia backlot," states the actor, "and nobody was doing that kind of film anymore, so we had — that part of the backlot had a lot of pine trees, and the little pond, and you could cut in other places that we filmed. There was a place in the San Fernando Valley where we went to — a water-storage place, it was a lake, it wasn't far to get to; when we did the lake shots, we'd do the pond for close-ups on the lot, then we'd go over to, and it was a half-hour drive or less, the water-storage area on 405 — the San Diego freeway, which was in the hills there. There were two or three other places we'd go to on occasion, one had the big trees, and they would cut to Mt. Hood, which was a little further away, that served as…whatever our mountain was, the mountain in Seattle. They did a good job because many people thought we were filming on location all the time. Well, we were on location, but it was right there. We had a soundstage for the interiors, where most of the stuff was done. The church had an interior, and it was on the soundstage. They could just whip it up, but it was as if you were shooting on location. We weren't — we were right there in Burbank, minutes away from the old Warner Bros. studio."

Complementing Brown's off-camera role as 'Big Daddy' was his on-camera role as 'Big Daddy.' "I played it as if all these kids were his kid sisters, rather than girls he wanted to screw," laughs Brown. "If I find one, then I'm out of it, then I'm involved with my own family, a new family. So I was there as a parent to all the girls, to protect them. To see that we would find them husbands, or take care of them."[11]

"Robert really took over the father role," notes series regular Susan Tolsky. "And Robert, in that role, was the wrangler. He had to keep everything…in terms of the show, he was like the big guy. That was something, in my opinion, that he chose to be — the head wrangler in this situation of the show. And he made some good choices. I did not know Robert. I came out here in July of '67, and I had the pilot in December of '67. I was just out of college. There were people that I knew — of course, Joan Blondell, and Henry Beckman I recognized, but I did not know Robert. I did not know much of his work or his background until we worked together. He was just like, very tall. His character was dramatic, his presence was dramatic. His presence was very dominating. Until I saw him fall off a horse. No, I didn't see him fall off a horse. But his presence was very…there was that theatrical thing that you could see — that thing that Mark had, but it was different — he carried himself dif-

*Brown's 'Jason Bolt' escorts guest star Heidi Hunt's 'Becky Hobbes' down the aisle in the sixth-aired* Brides *episode, "Letter of the Law."*

ferently than Mark. So, at the time I really didn't feel — this is just to me, that Robert was that approachable, and I don't mean that in a bad sense. You have to understand I was in my twenties, and I hung more with Bobby and Bridget. I just didn't feel an imminent warmth from Robert that I did from a lot of the other people. But again, that may have been just me, and I don't mean it in a negative sense."[12]

"Robert was an aristocratic gentleman," states series semi-regular Karen Carlson. "If you went to dinner at Robert's house, which David and I did many times after we were married, he lived in this great big wonderful old Spanish hacienda, and everything was just so perfect, perfect, perfect. The table was perfectly set with the correct... you used the correct...it was just beautiful, lovely, lovely, and he was, and still is, I understand, bigger than life. Just bigger than life — that's a great way of putting it."[13] "Robert was almost Shakespearean in his presentation," adds William Blinn. "Not only was he handsome, and large, in terms of acting style, he was a presence. When he walked into the room, he FILLED THE ROOM! With an actor like Robert, who has a larger than life presentation, you kind of want to use that."[14]

As a result, a certain storyline began to emerge.

Laughs co-star David Soul: "We started calling Robert SUPER-LOGGER because, during the course of a show, there'd be this problem that would develop. It would get worse and worse. Everybody's thinking, 'What do we do? How do we...?' 'Don't worry. Here Comes SUPER-LOGGER to SAVE THE DAY! SUPER-LOGGER will take care of it! SUPER-LOGGER will solve the problem!'"[15]

The makers of *Here Come the Brides* certainly treated Robert Brown like SUPER-LOGGER. "Claver wanted me as the star," states Brown, "and I guess they figured that I was gonna hit it, or the show was gonna hit it, or something, because I had this special treatment. I didn't ask for it. They gave me this special house, with a bathroom and a living room and a kitchen. It had been built for that beautiful girl, Kim Novak (whom Columbia Pictures expected to be the next Marilyn Monroe). They furnished it for me with antiques and stuff because I'm a collector of antiques. It was lovely, remarkable, and I had my own private parking. I still have the parking sign in my garage. I'm not kidding. They took it down and gave it to me — this metal plate, saying 'Private Parking.'"[16]

Not too surprisingly, the special treatment, plus all the praise he was receiving from critics, columnists, and the Screen Gems bosses went to Robert Brown's head. As Brown himself would later admit. "I couldn't find a hat to fit, my head was so large,"[17] the star told *Brides* fans during an on-line chat. "He thought he was a big piece of shit," says men's wardrobe man Steve Lodge. "He started thinking it was his show. Even more his show than Joan Blondell's."[18] "Robert's ego did get a bit big," agrees William Blinn. "When so many people are telling you how wonderful you are, it's hard not to get caught up in that. But he was never unpleasant, never unpleasant."[19] "There was no question barrel-chested Robert Brown was the STAR of the show," chuckles David Soul. "But he was very generous and kind. He gave me a lot of support."[20] "He was a friendly guy," admits Lodge, "but he had this bad habit — he'd come up and lean on your shoulder, and put his whole weight on it, and I wasn't the only one he ever did that to. But because he was a star, you had to just kind of stand there and take it."[21]

So, when Steve Lodge saw what *Brides* editors had done with the 'Christmas Reel,' he very much enjoyed it. Laughs the wardrobe man: "Robert had this habit, like David Janssen and most of 'em, by the middle of the season, he had gained about fifteen or twenty pounds. These guys used to start off real trim, then they'd be going to these dinners and everything. When they got too heavy, they slimmed down, and by the end of the season, they'd be back in shape again. Well, Robert was kind of heavy in this scene where he had to go mount a horse. He put his foot in the stirrup and got halfway up. That was the farthest he could go. He couldn't get up in that saddle. So, when they did the Christmas Reel, they took that shot of him trying to get up on that horse, and they cut it so that, you can do it easier now with tape, but back then with film, you had to get prints made up, well, it looked like he tried to get up and couldn't get up, tried to get up and couldn't get up, tried to get up and couldn't get up. They made fun of him like that, and the crew at the Christmas Party just went nuts watching that. He didn't like that at all. They gave him some shit about that, but he never found out who put the film together that way."[22] "Robert didn't like too much physical work," states Dick Balduzzi. "We had jokes about Robert because he wasn't very athletic, but never maliciously."[23]

Most of Brown's action scenes were handled by his stunt double Dave Cass. "Robert Brown was great to work with," enthuses Cass. "Robert knew his limitations. He wouldn't push the envelope for himself."[24] If a scene required that one of the Bolt brothers perform some stunt-work, Brown was more than happy to relinquish such tasks to co-star David Soul. "And," states William Blinn, "if David was being spotlighted as a result of that, Robert would be frustrated, but he also understood that if we need someone to run up a hill and jump over a wall, David was a better candidate than anybody else. That was just a reality."

As was writing stories around the show's teen heartthrob, Bobby Sherman. "When you've got a kid who's got twelve-year-old girls lining up down the block," says Blinn, "you have to serve that. Robert was cool with that."[25] "The kids loved Bobby Sherman," agrees Brown, "so Bridget would get more to do. Which was fine with me; Bridget's a sweetheart." Nor did Brown seem to have a problem with Soul and Sherman singing. "I was happy to see both David and Bobby singing," states the actor. "I didn't have a sense that they were gonna steal my business. I wasn't competitive that way. I remember, I used to get — they used to measure the number of bags that would go to the studio, and I got more bags than anybody by ten times. I went to most of the television stations, too, so the press was fair for me. But I never had my own fan club like Bobby. Today his fan club is big. I just got sort of sucked into the fan club."

It was understandable why Brown didn't feel threatened. After all, throughout the run of *Brides*, he retained top billing, and he did receive certain honors. "The press club up there [in Seattle] arranged with the governor to make me honorary mayor or something like that," recalls the star. "And they voted, in the women's press club, or the Hollywood press club, they voted for me as the 'Most Promising Actor,' and I received the Golden Apple award."[26]

Nor did it hurt that *Brides* story editor William Blinn saw Brown as a colorful character. "I don't know as I can speak for N. Richard Nash," states Blinn, "but I think the Jason character was just another version of Starbuck from *The Rainmaker*, a very compelling and charming and delightful rogue. Robert could play that to the max. He proved that in the pilot. The Jason character was a fun character to write dialogue for."

As a result, Blinn frequently gave Brown a great amount of dialogue. "He wasn't fond of sitting down and learning all that," remembers Blinn. "That was a lot of words to memorize, and, more times than not when I would give him one of these humongous speeches, I would hear, not ever impolite, or in a disrespectful way, 'Can't we cut this down? This seems like a lot of words. Can't we trim this?' So, I'm not sure how much time he devoted toward being letter-perfect on the lines. I mean, you'd write something that we all thought was gonna be good, and when you'd look at dailies, you heard about maybe sixty percent of what you thought was really gonna be good. I know Bob would try to impress on Robert, 'the script's pretty good, and we need you to step up to the mark and give full measure' which Robert later on acknowledged that he hadn't and felt bad about it, because Robert's a thoroughly decent human being, a very, very nice man."[27]

Indeed, Robert Brown is the first to admit he didn't know his script and lines as thoroughly as Blinn and the others might have wished. "I was playing it day by day, script by script," states the actor. "You don't want to get too much information about the script because you want to discover that in front of the camera when you're playing the scene. So I tried to keep it as fresh as I could, and not do too much. In the makeup chair, I would do the final polish. I had trained myself to do that, to do what I was being paid to do, to do the work that was handed to us in the morning. Sometimes, the day before you got some pages of the script, you'd break down when you were gonna be working, what scenes you were gonna be doing, who was in them with you. So you had the pages, and I would work on them, but not hard."[28]

"There were times when you wanted things just to come spurting out at a hundred miles an hour," says Blinn, "and, because he wasn't sure of the lines, there were pauses in there and 'Wells,' and 'ers,' and 'ums,' and stuff like that. When you just do that once or twice, it's not a big thing, but when it becomes part of the fabric of the speech, the speech loses its focus. So, there were times when that was a little frustrating."[29]

It wasn't just on *Here Come the Brides* where Robert Brown employed such methods. "We did this show called *Visions*, [a CBS movie of the week]" says Steve Lodge, "and Robert Brown was cast in the lead [as Professor Mark Lowell — a professor who has visions of the future]. Lee Katzin was the director. We went to Colorado, to Denver, got out on location, and the script has Robert talking on the phone [doing dialogue onscreen and off]. All Robert learned was what was onscreen. Katzin said, 'No, Robert, I want you to do the whole thing in front of the whole crew and everything. I'm gonna shoot the whole conversation on your end.' That's the way they did it — that's the way it's always done. You know, you shoot your side of the conversation, then you shoot the other person's side of the conversation, then you cut it in the editing room. Well, Robert had only memorized the part that said he was onscreen. We went over and over that. And that was the first day of shooting! I'd gone and wardrobed him, and taken him locally to get stuff, and all that crap. That night Katzin said, 'Fuck him!' And they fired him. Because he was too difficult. He wasn't gonna admit he was wrong. I mean, if Robert had said, 'God, I'm sorry. I really blew it,' but he wouldn't do that. He was...'It says here in the fucking script that I'm here!' So they replaced him with Monte Markham, who was a real sweetheart."[30]

It wasn't that Robert Brown was being intentionally difficult. He was simply following the advice of Marlon Brando, who'd suggested he approach dialogue in that way. But Brando was a film and stage actor; there was time for that sort of approach in those media. In television, where constraints in both time and budget were a reality, such an approach might slow things down. Had Robert Brown told William Blinn, Lee Katzin, et al, why he was not working that hard on his dialogue, he might not have earned a reputation as being a difficult, uncaring actor. Brown had a valid and intelligent reason for choosing not to explain his behavior.

"I didn't tell anybody why I was doing it that way," admits the star. "You don't talk about what you're gonna do. When you do that, you're giving it away, and it becomes self-conscious. Then the freedom that you want to achieve doesn't happen because you're reacting, instead of acting. So that was a private thing, one of the methods that I used to keep it as open as I could."[31]

"When he was on his game," states Blinn, "we were in great shape. But when he wasn't hard on himself, when he didn't demand a hundred percent of Robert Brown, and thought that seventy-five percent was enough, it probably was okay, but those of us in the dailies, in the business, knew we could have had a better impact had we had more from Robert. That's why a lot of times I gave Ed Asner or someone like that a lot of the exposition. Well that does take the onus off Robert in terms of memorization, but it also takes the emphasis off Robert, so he was caught in a little bit of his own Catch-22."[32]

Brown's take on Jason Bolt resulted in another 'Catch-22.' Unlike Blinn, *TV Guide*'s Fritz Goodwin, Dwight Whitney, and others, Brown didn't see Jason Bolt as a 'Super-Logger' able to talk and charm his way out of whatever problems surfaced. Nor did he see Jason as an Errol Flynn-type swashbuckler, much less a hunk of man. "Joan [Blondell] was the one who told the press she knew Flynn and that I reminded her of him," remembers Brown. "So that upped my status, and my jaw dropped. I didn't see myself that way. I saw Jason a little differently. I'd look at the script, and I'd think, How the hell am I gonna stick Jason into this? And I'd find some actor to think about that would help ease me into that episode, and then, once it got going, that [new] part of the character showed up. I was just playing it on a day to day basis, with a let's smile when you can, let's be warm and respectful of each other attitude. That's what I still admire and adhere to as best as I can. Be that way with life and yourself certainly and all others around you, and maybe the idiots on the outside might catch on and try to be something of that thing you admire."

These new parts of the character, these layers and levels of performance were already on display as early as the pilot episode. For example, Brown showed Jason to be a man willing to listen to another person's point of view — in this case, his younger brother Jeremy, who told Jason and Josh that the brothers Bolt weren't asking the young ladies of New Bedford to "go upstairs for an hour." They were asking them to give up the security and stability they'd had in New Bedford to make a new life in a new world. In the episode that followed: "A Crying Need," it was Jason who first accepted the idea of a woman doctor. As a result, a new story area was opening for the series — a female character in charge. This character reappeared in the next episode: Holly Houston ("And Jason

Makes Five"), Rachel Miller ("A Jew Named Sullivan"), Lulu Bright ("The Firemaker"), Emma Peake ("Two Women"), etc. Jason's attitude towards Holly Houston in "And Jason Makes Five" opened up yet another story area — forgiving one's enemy, seeing their point of view. That theme was used again in episode #5 ("A Hard Card to Play"), then in "Letter of the Law," then in "A Jew Named Sullivan," with the excellent Linda Marsh's Rachel Miller forgiving her bigoted enemy, Amanda (Kristina Holland).

*Brown as 'Jason Bolt' with guest star Michael Ansara as 'Chief Wakando' in the fifteenth-aired episode, "Wives for Wakando."*

Jason's relationship with Stefan Arngrim's Tommy Blake, his talking to Tommy man to man, rather than man to child in episode #4 ("Man of the Family") helped set the stage for Ox's unforgettable relationship with Charlie Bates in episode #9 ("The Stand-Off"); thanks to such relationships, when Candy Pruitt's little brother and sister were introduced in the second season, they rarely came across as 'cutesy' — certainly not in the early second-season episode, "Hosanna's Way."

By continually bringing forth these new traits in Jason Bolt, both Robert Brown, and the writers, slowly changed *Here Come the Brides'* focus from a romantic comedy-drama to an adult western. Thus, being quite proud of his work in *The Deputy*, having grown up in an environment where he'd been exposed to so many different peoples and cultures, it was not surprising that Brown prove quite amenable to the series' more adult and serious tone.

"I played the character with humor and principle," states the actor. "I tried to get that going rather than just playing a con man who wants to keep his mountain and money and wealth and power. It was a sweet human tale, and Claver must have had a lot of principle because he was trying to communicate that aspect of humanity and current events that we sometimes squeezed in."

Brown also opened the door for co-stars Bobby Sherman and David Soul, not to mention the other series regulars (and semi-regulars) through the way he viewed Jason's relationship with all of the series' characters. "If you look at the beginning stuff," notes the actor, "my character was the one that everything bounced off of, but there were a lot of people, a lot of girls, a lot of characters in town. So, as the show continued, a lot of times, I was just one of the fellows standing around."[33] Unlike some series stars, when it came to seasons, episodes and guest stars, Brown did not play favorites. "I didn't talk about it outside," says the star. "That's part of the rules, you just don't betray that. If I had another point of view, I just didn't contribute that to the press, or to the gossip people. There were some things, I'm sure there were, that I wasn't nuts about at the time, but they were little things. We hired certain people [like guest stars William Schallert, Peter Whitney, former models-turned-actresses Lynda Day George and Angel Tompkins] and they knew how they faced the camera, and what came off of that, but a lot of the performers were not all that trained. They didn't have a lot of experience; they were new, and the character actors [John Anderson, R.G. Armstrong, Eddie Firestone, Ken Swofford, Steve Gravers, etc.] joined in as best they could."

Having been a struggling actor himself, Brown had no problems when a *Brides* episode focused more on a series co-star like newcomer David Soul (episode #5 — "A Hard Card to Play") or an untrained, new guest star (Meg Foster in the second season's "Two Worlds.") "Most of us have to make a living," notes Brown, "and this is a tough profession. I remember this one time, I was on the unemployment line, and it was a long line. Well, the door opened behind me, and the wind blew in; I turned to look and there was this chauffeur holding the door open for a famous actress — stage actress. She walks in behind me, and she had a big mink coat on; I just looked at her, and said her name. She says, 'What are you staring at me for? You're wondering why I should be here? Well, I paid my unemployment insurance. I need this money as much as anyone else. I'm gonna buy a lunch today.' LUNCH? This money which we're standing in this line for is for a month's rent. Some of us actors need this money to live. Most actors do. If you don't, then you've been in Hollywood too long."

Typical of Robert Brown's generosity was his behavior towards his friend E.W. Swackhamer. "I had a house in Malibu Colony, that Swack rented once when I did a picture in Europe," remembers the star. "When I came back, he was still in it, so I stayed in the guest house outside." Brown also lent a helping hand to his friend, screenwriter Alan Marcus. "He'd written this story [which was similar to *Brides*]. They didn't have his name on it until I talked to him. He still had rights to the story — they then had to see him, and they had to pay him money every time it [*Brides*] played."[34]

As *Here Come the Brides* continued, in order to keep the entire cast happy, it was inevitable that there be a Candy Pruitt episode or a Captain Clancey episode or an Aaron Stempel episode. This emphasis on devoting most of an episode to a particular cast member, with the other cast members generally lending support, had long been the procedure on such ensemble westerns as *Bonanza, Gunsmoke, The Virginian, The Big Valley.* That sort of approach generally guaranteed a series a good long run — thanks to the behavior of its star, Robert Brown, *Here Come the Brides* began moving to this point perhaps more quickly than anyone anticipated.

Yet in moving the show to such a point, Robert Brown began undermining the importance of his own character. As Brown is first to admit, he was none too good about keeping himself out front. "There are people who find ways to move their careers along," states the actor. "I never knew — I was an idiot about that, so I would say the wrong things, and I was not over-fond of the bosses. I was overly candid. In fact, it was a problem. I was trying to prove that they weren't running my life. I did do the PR stuff, but I just never played the game. I know I didn't. I was never an intimate of the people who ran the show, and that's unusual for the people on top. They go out and do things, and they talk.

"I have a high regard and respect for the work we did yesterday," states the actor, "but at the time I don't think I was too caring or conscious because I made trouble. I guess I was looking for an exit. There were so many wonderful things that I could have gotten and just didn't. And there were so many things to do with my life, that, as an actor, I became less interested in the profession of it, and in the business of being well known. Being a celebrity, that was not my interest."

So when Brown received his next television series as leading man — the syndicated Ivan Tors series, *Primus*, he didn't push himself very far. "God, I hated that," groans the actor. "Ivan Tors (*Flipper, Daktari, Gentle Ben, Cowboy in Africa*) was a sweetheart. He was a very nice man, and he was sorry that I wasn't more involved with fish; he was a real addict for the swimming creatures. I just liked to eat them. I mean I was a city kid –raised in New York. What do we know about life under the ocean? I had a swimming pool at home, a big one, but I didn't go in much.

"Ricou Browning [co-creator and producer of *Flipper*, among other things] was great underwater" praises Brown, "he was the head of the underwater [photography unit]. And we had the best crew. I had a great double, too. Plus they gave me an apartment at the Jockey Club in North Miami Beach, and a Corvette stingray and a motorcycle, and a gold watch — $10,000 or something, and we shot in Nassau and Florida. It would have been, if they could have found the right...because somebody would have been great in that role, and I'm sorry that I was not the right guy. I'm terrified of sharks and all that; I had to go in with those things. That was sort of the end of the career. I didn't want to play the fame game, power and money, it just wasn't fun."

But Brown did a few more guest shots, including *Mannix* ("The Girl in the Polka Dot Dress") and two excellent episodes of *Police Story* (the first, "Little Boy Lost," also guest-starred *Brides* alum Joan Blondell; the second, "To Steal a Million," featured *Brides'* regular Henry Beckman). "Then I started doing narration and voice-overs," relates Brown. "I would drive in from Ojai — I came up here to escape the famous life. I did one more job (the 1994 *In the Heat of the Night* episode, "Poor Relations") when Carroll O'Connor (who'd had Brown on his series, *Archie Bunker's Place*, in the

1979 episode, "Man of the Year") called and said, 'Brown, I've put you in as a guest star in *Heat of the Night*. I said, 'O'Connor, I told you. I don't play heroes anymore.' He says, 'No, you don't. I'm playing the hero. You're playing the scoundrel.' I played a con-man. It was a comedy — one of that show's few comedies, and I think I won some award, or somebody gave me something, or said something nice. So I went down and did my last job. I went to Georgia."

*In the Heat of the Night* ("Poor Relations") made for a nice end to Robert Brown's television career. The episode reunited him with Anne Meara. "She had been with me in *Ulysses in Nigh Town*, explains the actor, "and she was with [*Brides* guest] John Marley's group when we did improvisations, at his home, at his apartment. Anyway, I hadn't worked for a couple of years, had just been doing voice-overs, and she said, 'How you feeling? You look great, Bob.' I said, 'I feel terrible.' She said, 'What do you mean?' I said, 'I got here and I haven't found the character yet.' She said, 'What do you mean you haven't found the character?' 'Well, I haven't researched yet,' I said. 'I haven't opened up things.' She said, 'You don't have to research. You *are* the character.' Well, I was in the first shot — it was a close-up of me — they did the master later. There was this close-up of me talking to the guy at the desk in the police station. And I was trying to steal a painting — I played this thief. So, the camera was backed up against the corner of the wall on the set and there was a door behind the camera and Annie Meara was standing in the doorway out of the way of the crew, and just as they were getting ready to say, 'Action,' she raised her dress over her head all the way up over her head to show her bare breasts, and they're 'Action,' and that…I looked amazed, and I started to kind of smile, and that was what the character did. She helped me through that tough moment when I didn't know what the hell to — it was just there. I was in the moment, so that was a performance that I played in the moment."

"After that," says Brown, "I retired because I had done well. I had a big house, and a butler, and nine servants, and I lived well. I walked away happily with some loot and mostly good memories. I flopped plenty, by the way, because I didn't try to succeed, and that was my mistake. If I loved it — it's like a marriage — if you really love someone, you go through everything; if you don't really love it, you take the thing and get the hell out. I get those questions sometimes, 'Whatever happened to Robert Brown?' I'm not kidding. So I say, 'I don't know quite who he was. That was this character I played years ago.'"

At eighty-four, Robert Brown has no desire to re-enact that character. "I am married to a wonderful, wonderful artist, and we've been together for twenty-nine years, and people say I look swell," laughs Brown. "'You don't look your age,' they tell me. I guess I don't. I have all my hair, and a beard, a little, trimmed, elegant beard, and famous friends, who are envying my life."

Part of which has been spent learning more concerning his parents' history. "They didn't speak much about themselves," admits Brown, "and I learned as I grew older something about my father's life. Then my mother — I went back to Scotland with her, she took me to the Isle of Skye and the Hebrides — she had been away for fifty, sixty years."

Always one to enjoy travel, since his retirement from acting, Robert Brown has made quite a few trips to Europe. "In Italy," states Brown, "the people never left the area. They'd been living there for centuries. So I really got to love the sense of yesterday, because if you know what yesterday was like, you might understand what today is like. Just interest in today, if you're interested in current events, that's not rich enough, that just flies by. But if you know what motivated that, or what was lost that had been there, or what good new stuff comes through, or bad — the slaves, stopping slavery and so on — that wasn't done in the proper way; there's more anger and hate in the world because they haven't been included properly. And what is the western world today? You see Europe and how it's changing because people from these other countries are coming into them, they're bringing their culture with them, they're wrecking the culture from yesterday with their own glib life. Rather than keeping the structures the way they had been, they've put the neon around. So yes, I'm interested in life.

"'To know what you are today,'" quotes Brown, "that's what Socrates said, when he spoke during his trial of the four hundred, when he was tried for corrupting the youth of Athens. He said, 'Before you get to know me, you have to know how I became the sort of fellow that I am.'

"That's how you got to be who you are. That comes from history."[35]

1. Tompkins – interview – 2007
2. Brown – interview – 2007
3. Silbersher – interview – 2007
4. Brown – 2007
5. *Time* – Seven-Year Justice – Friday, July 6, 1962
6. Brown – 2007
7. Dick Balduzzi – interview – 2007
8. Brown – 2007
9. Balduzzi – 2007
10. Renee Valente – interview – 2007
11. Brown – 2007
12. Susan Tolsky – interview – 2007
13. Karen Carlson – interview – 2007
14. Blinn – 2007
15. David Soul – interview – 2007
16. Brown – 2007
17. Seattle Town Meeting Chat – June 3, 2000
18. Lodge – interview – 2007
19. Blinn – 2007
20. Soul – 2007
21. Lodge – 2007
22. Lodge – 2007
23. Balduzzi – 2007
24. Dave Cass – interview – 2007
25. Blinn – 2007
26. Brown – 2007

27. Blinn – 2007
28. Brown – 2007
29. Blinn – 2007
30. Lodge – 2007
31. Brown – 2007
32. Blinn – 2007
33. Brown – 2007
34. Ibid
35. Ibid

"You're not askin' them to go upstairs for an hour. You're askin' them to go clear across the country to be away from their homes and families for the rest of their lives."

Jeremy Bolt to his brothers Jason and Joshua
in Episode #1 ("Here Come the Brides")

# Chapter 6

# *Co-starring Bobby Sherman*

"Bobby is the sweetheart of all time. He was very concerned and knowledgeable. He had agent, manager, publicist — he was really building a career."[1]

*Here Come the Brides* semi-regular Mitzi Hoag's brief assessment of *HCTB*'s second-billed star Bobby Sherman pretty much summed up the personality and performing career of the singer-actor. *Here Come the Brides* was the second time Bobby Sherman made it big. The first time had been on the 1964-66 ABC variety series, *Shindig*.

Thanks to his friendship with actor Sal Mineo, Sherman came to the attention of an agent by the name of Dick Clayton. This resulted in his auditioning for the people who were to make *Shindig*. Producer of the series was Jack Good; owner of the production company was Selig Seligman. That was the Selig Seligman who'd done series pilots with Robert Brown and Bridget Hanley, the Selig Seligman who executive produced the critically acclaimed 1962-67 ABC/WWII drama, *Combat*, and the tongue-in-cheek 1967-68 ABC/WWII adventure, *Garrison's Gorillas*, the Selig Seligman who made the motion pictures, *Charly*, *The High Commissioner*, *Diamonds for Breakfast*, etc. Auditioning for such a successful producer was a lucky break for Bobby Sherman.

Based on this audition, which had Sherman singing along with a recording of the Freddy Cannon hit, 'Palisades Park,' the future co-star of *Brides* was hired as the "house singer" on *Shindig* for a total of twenty-six episodes, at $750 per show. While producer Good's original plan was to appeal to a wider audience than teenagers, the enthusiastic response of Lucille Ball's children, Lucie and Desi Arnaz, Jr., to the first aired episode on September 16, 1964 caused him to drop this idea. Lucie Arnaz's great liking for Sherman was soon reflected by teenagers across the nation.

Performing hit songs when the original group or singer was unavailable, Sherman then began receiving bags of fan mail, requests for interviews from fan magazines, and so on. Instead of letting all the adulation and attention go to his head, he concentrated on doing his job. He also noticed how performers with negative feelings didn't last long in the industry. So even when he performed a song he didn't care for, he kept his feelings to himself. Unlike quite a few performers older than him, Bobby Sherman had the common sense to realize how lucky he was. Rather than becoming jealous and envious of people like *Shindig* guests the Righteous Brothers, who suddenly hit it big, Sherman analyzed why they'd become a success. In doing so, Bobby Sherman began laying the groundwork for his own successful career.

For example, when he performed other people's songs, he put his own personal touch on the songs. He also made contacts with artists like Ray Charles, learned how the camera operated, and how to perform in front of an audience, and, most importantly, realized that nothing — from success to the run of a series — could last forever. As a result, when *Shindig* was canceled, Sherman was not as upset as the other regulars. In fact, by the time *Shindig* aired its last episode, on January 8, 1966, Bobby Sherman was ready to move on.

To acting!

After a concert tour in South America, a series of performances at a dinner theatre in Canada, and another series of performances in bars across the U.S., Sherman, who'd dated a couple of *Shindig* dancers and series fans, then made a few appearances on *The Dating Game*. This resulted in a TV commercial for the hair tonic product Vitalis; after this break came guest shots on such lighthearted series as *Honey West* and *The Monkees*. Sherman's familiarity with all the lines of his script made a favorable impression on *The Monkees* producer, Ward Sylvester, as did the way the singer-turned-actor treated the series DP, Irving 'Lippy' Lippman. By showing genuine interest in Lippman's off-set life (i.e. asking him questions about his children), Bobby Sherman established a good rapport with someone who could make him look very good on screen. Irving Lippman would later work with the singer-actor on *Here Come the Brides*.

Shortly after he guest-starred on *The Monkees*, Bobby Sherman encountered Steve Blauner, the head of development for Screen Gems. Finding Sherman's style reminiscent of his longtime client, Bobby Darin (famous for such hits as "Splish Splash" and "Mack the Knife"), Blauner took to Sherman immediately. Sherman also scored with Renee Valente, who oversaw and cast the main (and guest) roles in *Here Come the Brides*.

"Bobby is a very, very sweet guy, [was] a very sweet young man and I liked him very much," says Valente. "Steve Blauner was very close to Jackie Cooper at Screen Gems, and he pushed Bobby Sherman like crazy. I tested Bobby, and he was very good. It was kind of a different role for the kind of person that Bobby was. He worked very, very hard at it."[2]

Flown to New York for a screen test directed by E.W. Swackhamer, once he returned to California, Sherman learned he'd won the part of Jeremy Bolt. Like the show's leading lady Bridget Hanley, Sherman felt a very close connection to his character. As was the case with Hanley, Sherman went into his screen test with considerable enthusiasm and confidence. Upon learning he'd won the part of Jeremy Bolt, the singer-actor celebrated this accomplishment by purchasing a 1962 midnight-blue Rolls Royce — the sort of automobile he'd long desired.

Laughs Robert Brown's stunt double Dave Cass: "I remember Bobby driving his Rolls Royce into the gate. He looked like this little teenager driving this huge Rolls Royce, and these little teenage girls…there'd be hundreds of 'em waiting outside the gate. The guards used to have to crowd them away so he could pull onto the lot."[3]

Adds *Brides* regular Susan Tolsky, "When Bobby got his Rolls Royce, he took each one of us to lunch. He took Bridget, and he took me. He wanted each person

*Bobby Sherman as Jeremy Bolt.*

to enjoy their time. So I had my little ride. I can remember I was the first up [on the set] after lunch, or the second one after lunch, so I had to get in his Rolls Royce in my wardrobe and go to lunch with him. You saw all kinds of people at lunch. You'd see the 'gorilla' walking around..." [4]

Having developed a great deal of maturity and confidence since his days on *Shindig*, Bobby Sherman quickly realized the great opportunity *Brides* was giving him to build a singing career. "He took advantage of that particular brand of Bobby Sherman and sold a lot of records," states co-star David Soul. "He played that card pretty much for all it was worth. But Bobby was always very personable and nice. We got on very well. We had a very cordial relationship." [5] "Bobby was career-driven," adds Robert Brown. "Very professional in his music. The kids were the ones most addicted to his music because he was a rock and roll musician, and performed pop music. Bobby had somebody who worked for him, and kept his fan clubs going. He was doing a lot of PR for himself." [6]

"Bobby and David were terrific," enthuses *Brides* semi-regular Dick Balduzzi. "Especially Bobby. He wasn't quite then the big rock star. A lot of the young people went for Bobby Sherman. I think that's why he got a majority of the exposure." [7]

But Bobby Sherman never received top billing on *Here Come the Brides*. Either in the first season, or, even in the second season. Says *Brides* story editor William Blinn: "The thing that was the biggest problem for Robert, and I don't know if he knew this consciously, I don't think he ever used it consciously, was the fact that Bobby was the star. It got to the point where clearly we had a teenage audience, largely a teenage audience, and they were crawling over Bridget's back fence to see what she was all about, and Bobby had to have bodyguards everywhere he went. He would finish shooting on a Friday night, and be whisked to the airport, and he'd fly to Seattle and Salt Lake and Boise and other cities, and play the stadiums filled with forty thousand screaming teenagers, get back Monday morning exhausted, and the pages...we usually tried to give him an easy day on Monday for that very reason. Well, Robert tumbled to that. He realized that he, Robert, was gonna work harder on Mondays because Bobby needed time to catch his breath. I think that ruffled his feathers a bit, but again, Robert was, and is, a terrific guy." [8]

Being Candy Pruitt, the sweetheart of Bobby Sherman's character on *Here Come the Brides,* Bridget Hanley started getting a lot of attention from the fan magazines herself. More than once, Hanley and Sherman made joint appearances at concerts. Remembers the actress: "Bobby and I were asked to come up to the Campfire Girl's gathering in Seattle, Washington. He of course, because he was the teenage heartthrob; I was asked because I grew up there. So they were claiming me now. Seattle and the environs have always been user friendly for me. So we were invited to go up to the Campfire Girls' State Convention, and I was going to sing the theme song, 'Seattle.' We got up there. We brought our [*HCTB*] clothes to change into, and there was only one dressing room. It was just surrounded by curtains. Bobby and I both looked at each other, and we're, 'This is not gonna work, gang.' He was stunned because he was going out on concert dates and everything, and treated like royalty, so it was very funny.

"Well," continues Hanley, "we were able to figure out how to cut the curtained dressing room in half so we could each have our privacy. Then Bobby went out [on stage] and, of course, the place almost came down — all these teenage girls, even less than teen. Then he called me out, and I had my little dress on that I normally wear, and I had my 'Candy' hair, and I went out and I sang the theme song probably lower than any of the male people have ever sung it, and while I was singing it, my pastiche, on the top of my head, fell off, right in the middle of the song, or right towards the end. I was MORTIFIED! So, while I was singing, I picked it up, and when I was through, I figured...I just flung it out into the audience, and I got almost as BIG A SCREAM as Bobby had. That was a great time for me because I had a chance to visit my family."[9]

Having encountered screaming teenage fans during his days on *Shindig*, Sherman handled the screaming teen bit very well during his two seasons on *Here Come the Brides*. Nonetheless, doing both the show and weekend concert dates took its toll. Explains Susan Tolsky: "He would do concerts on the weekend, and on Monday, Bobby would come in about four feet shorter than he was when he left, and I would go, 'Hi, Bobby. Good morning,' and he would go, 'Susan, Stop Screaming!' Because he had just performed in front of thirty-five thousand screaming girls. But Bobby would...He had a thing with me, where Bobby would, when he was so tired, and half the time, when he was, he would come up to me, he wouldn't say a word, he'd just turn his back to me and stand there and I had to scratch his back. Just run my fingers — cuz I had nails, and I just had to run my fingers up and down, and what that was from is when he was very young, he had broken his collarbone and the only... you can't put a cast on it, and you're very uncomfortable because it's not a thing you can hitch up. His mother used to just scratch his back to relax him. So the way that Bobby relaxed was, and there'd be times I'd be doing interviews, and there'd be photographers and he'd come up and just put his back in front of me, and I would just continue what I was doing and I'd scratch his back. Or he'd have somebody come to my dressing room and say, 'Have Susan come and scratch my back.' So whenever he came up and turned his back to me, I knew what it meant. So I had kind of a fun thing with him. You liked Bobby immediately. As soon as you see him, you want to hug him and grab him. So anything he did was fine. His character was more defined than David's."[10]

Laughs Karen Carlson: "Bobby, even though he was older than David, I always thought of him as like a younger brother, a little brother, and, of course, then when David and I divorced, he and [Sherman's ex-wife] Patty got married not too long after that. That really blew the studio out of the water. When Patty and David got married, I think Bobby and I talked a couple of times. We haven't talked probably in fifteen, twenty years. Bobby was just kind of like a little brother. We didn't spend very much time socially with him."[11]

"Bobby and I were very, very close and good, good friends," adds Bridget Hanley. "He came to the house a couple of times and signed some pictures for charity, but he's a very private person. He never asked me anything personal, and I never asked him anything personal. When we were working, he would do a scene and then go off and do something else or play a guitar. David and I knew each other better because we'd been under contract together. David and Karen and Swack and I would go out to dinner together, or they'd come over, or whatever. Everybody has a different relationship."[12]

According to Susan Tolsky, Sherman, Robert Brown and David Soul "were very close. Robert kind of was just Robert," says Tolsky. "There was not a lot of segregation. They were always laughing and goofing."[13] "I was friendly with Bobby and David," agrees Brown, "but not big, big friendly. I visited Bobby once or twice at his home, met his mother."[14] "Bobby Sherman was kind of more relaxed than David Soul," adds *Brides* semi-regular Buck Kartalian. "Soul was a little more serious. They were kind of opposites — Soul was very serious and somber; Sherman was more relaxed and fun. He was more fun to work with than Soul."[15]

"Bobby and David were the nicest guys in the world," adds *HCTB* wardrobe man Steve Lodge. "They'd sit around and play guitars between shots and sing, and have a ball. David was kinda shy, but he still was a singer. He'd play his guitar — he always had his guitar with him. Bobby was very busy doing weekend shows — concerts. He would leave on a Friday afternoon and come back Monday morning, and he was just tired as hell. His whole…This is a quote from him. Somebody said, 'Bobby, why are you doing this? You're wearing yourself out.' He said, 'Look, I got a chance to be big on a show called *Shindig*. And this is my second chance. Not many people get a second chance. So, I just want to make the hay while the sun shines cuz it ain't gonna last forever.' There's a smart guy. Most of them don't know that — Robert Brown didn't know that. Bobby Sherman didn't hang around on the set. He was always in his dressing room, or with Ward Sylvester, or something."[16]

"He was always gentle," notes Mitzi Hoag, "very much his character actually. A gentle person himself in the context of the show. And he was well known as a singer, particularly among younger girls. Some of that occupied some of his time."[17]

Especially during the show's second season. States William Blinn: "Bobby Sherman was the teenage boy *du jour* if you will, and he had four schedules at once to keep going. So, during the second season we tended to focus more on individual characters. Part of that was due to Bobby's success as a teenage idol, part of that was ABC saying, 'Look, he's on the cover of *Tiger Beat*, he's filling up stadiums, you gotta service the Bobby Sherman fans.' So David was…you know, I cast David in *Starsky and Hutch*, so I'm not knockin' David for an instant, but he was not happy playing second fiddle to Bobby Sherman. They got along personally. I don't think it ever boiled over."[18]

Ironically, while Bobby Sherman did move from a co-starring billing to a starring billing (after Robert Brown) with the beginning of the second season, as a result of his seven-day schedule, the other characters on the show began getting more to do. Sherman having become a star during the show's more comedic first season, he often seemed out of place in the show's more grim and realistic second-season episodes. Not so Robert Brown — after all Brown had done many serious plays on the stage, including *The Deputy*, as well as Post *Brides* guest shots such as *Police Story* ("Little Boy Lost"). Brown was excellent in downbeat dramas.

As for third-billed David Soul, despite being moved to fourth billing during the second season, he was the one member of the *Here Come the Brides* regular cast to enjoy the greatest success following the series' cancellation. The approach David Soul took from the very beginning of *Here Come the Brides* had much to do with that.

1. Hoag – 2007
2. Valente – 2007
3. Cass – 2007
4. Tolsky – 2007
5. Soul – 2007
6. Brown – 2007
7. Balduzzi-2007
8. Blinn – 2007
9. Hanley- 2008
10. Tolsky- 2007
11. Carlson – 2007
12. Hanley – 2007
13. Tolsky – 2007
14. Brown – 2008
15. Buck Kartalian – telephone interview – 2008
16. Lodge – 2007
17. Hoag – 2007
18. Blinn – 2007

"There're a hundred girls on this boat. You could be havin' the time of your life."

# Chapter 7
# *Co-starring David Soul*

"He was always reliable. He was always there. He always did his job." Such was the opinion of *Here Come the Brides* regular Susan Tolsky concerning the third male star in the series — David Soul. "Truthfully," continues Tolsky, "I think David probably had one of the hardest roles. I have to be honest. It was a hard role. I mean you've got very flamboyant characters in this thing, and he could have been a nice back-board for all of that — that could have been done that way, but it wasn't, so I think he had a difficult role. I don't know if there was more he could bring, or more they could write, or if that was the essence of the role. David just had a harder job — he was around a lot of other, wilder, more flamboyant characters, and because they kept it open — it was a harder role to play. He did a good job with what he had. I think everybody did, but his role was the harder one."[1]

"David was the in-between brother," adds *Brides* star Robert Brown. "In life, the in-between brother somehow gets lost, and maybe that's what happened with his character. I felt that he wasn't given enough to do. He didn't know, he didn't have any growth much, but he had a steady job, a little bit of money, and he met the girls. He didn't have a background that I really knew much about — I knew he was a solo performer, a singer. And he rode horses beautifully; he was an athletic kind of guy. But his personality didn't just come jumping out at you. He wasn't a very good actor at the time. I think he got better as he went along. Maybe it was the role — because it didn't tell him what to do. I don't think David had a sense of acting. I don't think he had a desire to be an actor necessarily."[2]

Robert Brown was absolutely correct. Like so many successful stars in the business, David Soul hadn't planned on becoming an actor. "He'd actually had a contract offer with the White Sox," explains Soul's former wife, Karen Carlson. "He turned it down to pursue his career. David was very athletic. He was a skier, and played baseball, but not football, and definitely not golf. Golfing with him was agony. He swung the golf club like a baseball bat. So, the ball ended up four holes over to the left."[3]

As a performer, David Soul began his professional life as a singer, playing on the guitar he'd been given during his stay in Mexico. At the time, Soul was hoping to enter the diplomatic corps, following in the footsteps of his father. Interested in Latin American studies, the future *Brides* co-star learned as much as he could about Mexico — from the political party, the PRI (*Partido Revolucionario Institucional*) to the music of the country. "It seemed kind of strange to these Mexicans," recalls Soul, "this blue-eyed blond Norwegian expressing such an interest in their country. But they befriended me, and someone gave me a guitar. That got me interested in folk music."[4]

This interest in folk music took David Soul back to the States and eventually to New York City and *The Merv Griffin Show*. There he was billed as "The Covered

*Bobby Sherman, David Soul, and Robert Brown as Jeremy, Joshua, and Jason Bolt.*

Man." Remembers *Brides* executive casting director Renee Valente: "Merv Griffin introduced a singer who had a paper bag over his head and a guitar. He performed, I watched, I thought, 'He's gotta be an actor. Who else would come up with a paper bag on his face?' I called Merv Griffin. He told me who it was. I said, 'I'd like to see him. Have him call me.' And he did. That's how I found David. So I read David and auditioned him, and he had that wonderful quality that women were gonna go crazy about. He was also a political [science] major, and…his father was a worldwide minister. So David was very well educated, well traveled, and still very simple. Very involved with being…doing good with people. He just had a lovely quality of giving. And graciousness. And I thought his acting was pretty good."[5]

As Renee Valente already knew, and *Here Come the Brides* viewers were to discover, David Soul was a very good singer. According to Karen Carlson, Soul came by this talent naturally. "David's family…there's not a single one of them who's not musically talented," says Carlson. "He's got a sister that can sing close to opera, he's got one who plays the guitar and sings; he's got a brother who…they just all… They're all musically talented, but none of them had sought that as a career. So Christmas was always…they had lived in Germany, and so the Christmas songs were always sung in German around the traditional Swedish Norwegian ceremony. There's a candle-lighting…this was of course when we would all be together at Christmas. We'd do these wonderful ceremonies. Just all of them singing together were amazing, just amazing."[6]

Brought into Renee Valente's New Talent Program at Screen Gems following an audition piece for Valente and casting director Eddie Foy III (who would later cast for such series as David Janssen's *Harry O*), Soul was offered a contract. Under its terms, he'd be making $250 a week. "In the New Talent Program, I was nurtured and supported and trained," explains Soul. "As part of the process, I was loaned out to various shows that were made on the lot — shows like *Bewitched, I Dream of Jeannie*…" (plus other series like *Star Trek* and *Flipper*, which were made at other studios), and "happening at the time."[7]

Through the New Talent Program, Soul met longtime friend and *Brides* leading lady, Bridget Hanley, as well as future *HCTB* semi-regulars Christopher Stone, and guest stars, like Susan Howard. Recalls Carlson: "When David was under contract to Screen Gems, it was Susan Howard and Michael Margotta, there were a whole group of us, Chris Stone, they all were in the New Talent program. I wasn't, but they all were, and because we were married, we just kind of all were in that group. I remember Susan being a part of that group. I remember Susan as being kind of quiet."

So was David Soul. The actor was also shy. "Oh yes, he was shy," laughs Carlson. "So was I. We were both very shy and he doesn't — I don't think people would think of him as shy, but he still is. He still is!"[8] "He was very shy," agrees Valente. "That's why he had a paper bag over his head. That's what I liked about that, and that's why I wanted to meet him. I knew it had to be an actor."[9]

In Renee Valente's opinion, David Soul was quite different from his co-stars. "I'd go with them on the publicity junkets," remembers Valente, "and we'd have great fun together. Robert Brown would be the mainstay that all the reporters wanted, and

David would be the shy, unassuming guy, and Bobby Sherman would be the kid who wanted music, it was just…they were lovely people."[10]

In contrast to star Brown and the second-billed Sherman, Soul didn't get as much build-up or promotion. "*Brides,* rather than hire another freelancer, as was the case with Robert Brown and Bobby Sherman, went to the New Talent Program and hired me to play the third brother," explains Soul. "I made $350, or $450 a week."[11]

*Bobby Sherman, Robert Brown, and David Soul as the Brothers Bolt.*

Even though David Soul's casting helped keep production costs down, there was still a problem. Recalls Valente: "I was casting that out of my New York office at the time, and I had my talent program on the coast. Bob Claver did not want to use anybody who was in the talent program. He said, 'No, no. I'm not gonna use them, and pay for the talent program.' He was one of those early-on, anti-establishment directors. Very bright, but really wanted to do everything his way. But Bob Claver had to get an okay. From the network. From Jackie Cooper, who was head of the studio. You still have to get okays, so nothing's changed. And, I started with wanting David Soul to be the co-star. Bob Claver didn't want him. He read David [and] he said, 'No, No, No!' But I wanted David desperately. Well, Bob Claver was leaving town, so I called David because Bob and I were gonna have coffee at a coffee shop. I said, 'Listen, at 5:00, or whatever time it was, I want you to come into the coffee shop and apologize for interrupting our coffee, and say you really had to talk to me, because you've decided you just don't want to be in the talent program. You want to stay in New York and do theater, because that's what acting is all about.'"

Soul did exactly as Valente wished. Laughs Valente: "I said, 'I'm not gonna discuss this with you now! Why don't you go to my office, and I'll meet you there?' When he left, Bob Claver said, 'Now! You see? That's what I'd like.' And that's how David Soul got in *Here Come the Brides*."[12]

Despite this opportunity, the Joshua Bolt character left much to be desired. "I was sort of the middle brother," says Soul. "The middle brother usually gets short shrift. I'd get dialogue like, 'Hi, Jeremy! Where's Jason?' or 'Anybody seen Jason?' So, I wanted more to do."[13] "It wasn't that he was overlooked," states Susan Tolsky. "When they did the Bolt Brothers, he was never excluded, but when you're the middle brother... I mean you have the father image of Robert, and you have the young brother Bobby, and you have David stuck in the middle. Look at any middle sibling, just look at any middle sibling, you can pretty much see the same thing happening. That's the way things are in real life."[14]

"He was the typical middle kid in the series," adds Bridget Hanley. "On *Brides*, I don't know whether his character was as well developed as the others."[15] "David's character was not as well written as far as definition goes," notes Mitzi Hoag. "He was just the middle brother, while Robert was the con artist and the sort of magical storyteller. But sometimes that doesn't matter — sometimes an actor can bring something specific to it."[16]

While Soul certainly wanted to bring more to his character than was there, he still "didn't have a problem," says Renee Valente. "This was his first series, he was so happy to be working regularly. He and Robert Brown became good friends. He and Bobby Sherman had music in common, and he loved Bridget and everybody. He was just a happy kid. Like he was in a playground."[17]

"He certainly wasn't used to the degree that he should have been used," believes story editor William Blinn. "He was always there, and a great-looking guy, and terrific. Had the network been fonder of David, he was the guy who could do the action-adventure. He was very athletic, he was in terrific shape, and looked great, which is why he ended up two or three years later on *Starsky and Hutch*."[18]

While some might have felt David Soul made a mistake when he chose the part of Joshua Bolt over that of younger brother Jeremy, as the years following *Brides* made clear, the actor was laying down the groundwork for what turned out to be a very successful career in the industry. "I had some fun and some frustrations playing the character," says Soul. "There was a lot to learn. But there were no boundaries for me as there were with Robert and Bobby. With Robert, it was 'SUPER-LOGGER solves the problem. And Bobby played J-J-J-J-Jeremy."[19]

As a result, unlike Robert Brown's Jason or Bobby Sherman's Jeremy, Soul's Joshua Bolt could fit into any situation — be it dramatic or comedic. Josh could also separate himself from his brothers — keeping the family together wasn't as high on Josh's list of priorities as it was Jeremy's. In fact, of all the characters, Joshua Bolt offered the most freedom for the show's writers. "As a character, David would be a lot more fun to work with because you're kind of defining him," states William Blinn. "We didn't get the chance to work with him as much as we would have liked to. But even when he was frustrated by what he was being offered on the *Brides* set, he was always pleasant and open and fun to be around."[20]

"With his music, he had skills, he had a base," adds Bridget Hanley. "He sang well — he was very musical. He was creative in that arena, which then led into the acting. The character just didn't happen. It was…it all kind of becomes one — the one feeds the other. So, when someone can take one art form and meld it with many others to become a whole, that's amazing. Maybe that is a natural. Because there are kids — you know kids are so free, but a lot of adults…it's freeing up — it's going back to your child — not your childhood necessarily but having the same eyes as those of a child, bringing a lot more in to your process than trying to plot and plan. David was just a very interesting guy — he wasn't just good looking. He was very smart. Karen is too. Absolutely."[21]

"He was a very interesting actor," says Renee Valente. "He had interesting quali- ties — he wasn't just an eight by ten glossy. There was a tremendous vulnerability about David; he was one of the subtler performers on *Here Come the Brides*. And I remember both David and Bobby wanted to do their own stunts, and when Aaron Spelling was gonna do *Starsky and Hutch,* he called me. He said, 'Renee, I can't get anybody for this show. Can you help me?' It was just gratuitous because we were friends. I said to Aaron, 'I tell you the two people that I'd go for, and that would be David Soul and Paul Michael Glaser.' He read them both, and called me, and he said, 'My God, Renee!' And of course, the rest is history."[22]

"I think *Starsky and Hutch* was better for him," muses Mitzi Hoag. "Because David was a tumbler and physically active. This [*Brides*] was his first real role, and he had been on some baseball team. Everybody in the beginning of the show was exuberant, and the guys were also trying to stake out their territory as their charac- ters because there's competition among guys. Well, one way of David's competing was to tumble — he'd do back flips and front flips, in his costume, and there were a lot of men, and a lot of women, so there was a sort of heightened tension there with attractions."[23]

Laughs Susan Tolsky: "David was…because we had so many pretty girls, David was busy 'dating.' I didn't step in the way of that. I teased and played with him. We were not enemies, we'd laugh and have a good time, we hung and we talked and we played, but I just left him alone when I saw him hone in. He always had a guitar and he would strum around the set and everything — I think he had a tremendous love for music."[24]

In time Joshua Bolt displayed a musical talent; that added another dimension to his character. Still, Soul wanted more growth in the character. Says Bridget Hanley: "I think maybe part of David's frustration came from what he wished could have hap- pened. He always was prepared. He always dug way deep for his character. I thought it was a pleasure to work with somebody like that. He was kind of a firebrand in his own way, and I mean that in the kindest way. But I think he did everything that he could do. And sometimes he would over-think it. I don't mean that in a bad way, but he would come in with so much there was no way to do it all. He had so much back-story he could give in the moment. It wasn't always possible to do all of that in a given scene. He just prepared everything."[25]

"I think David is an amazing actor," adds Carlson. "At that time we were just fledglings, and that was the beginning of David developing his style of working. His style of working is real research. He's a hard worker, A HARD WORKER. David is just a real perfectionist — he's incredibly thorough. When he did *Starsky and Hutch*, he went down to Venice [Beach], went out on patrols with the police, rented an apartment so he could do that, and he had such…I can just imagine when the writers came into the first session, and David had probably, oh, PAGES — legal-sized pages he had written on the character development of Hutch: What He Ate, Where He Slept, Who Did This, Da, Da, Da, PAGES AND PAGES OF IT! I can just imagine! It takes some pretty exceptional writers to know how to take all that and digest it and use it, [especially] when you're under a real time frame, and pressure, and the network."[26]

Like Bobby Sherman, David Soul had definite thoughts about his wardrobe. "I remember the clothes," says Carlson. "I still have one of David's shirts from *Here Come the Brides* that Betsy [Cox] had made. David liked the big kind of fluffy shirt-sleeve things — he had this sense of how he wanted it to look. I remember Betsy finding this material that was very old-looking and I loved it. I wore it through all my pregnancies actually."[27]

"He wanted what he wanted," adds Robert Brown. "Both he and Bobby Sherman were dreaming of careers and the fame game. But they didn't seem to…they didn't strut their stuff. And rightly so, because, they were talented."[28]

David Soul's perfectionism extended off the set. Laughs William Blinn: "He was always…the odd thing was that Saturdays, David, myself, and Paul Witt, and eight or ten other guys, would go out to Rancho Park and play touch football Saturday morning until we realized that there was only one play for whatever team had David. Which is, with David, you go long, cuz no one could run as fast as David. No one could cover him. No one could keep up, and it just got to be pretty boring after a while, you know, another long pass to David."[29]

Never losing his interest in politics, David Soul was, like so many other performers in the industry, very concerned about what was happening in the late '60s. "We were both politically motivated," states Carlson, "we were very politically involved. Naively, because we just…we had this passion, and yet, I don't think we did too much research and knew what we were doing. We were very anti-Vietnam. I remember going up to San Francisco, the two of us; I think Bridget was with us. And Susan Oliver — Susan had talked me into going to Canada to paint baby seals red, to help save the seals.

"I remember us flying to San Francisco. She was still getting her license at that time, so we were all on this little private plane, flying up to San Francisco to go into the hospital with the soldiers that had returned. I remember David playing and singing for them, reading to them and talking. We went up several times to do that. Then we went East to campaign for Humphrey. I remember Susan and I on a plane flying to help Senator Humphrey with his campaign."

For both David Soul and Karen Carlson, the assassination of Robert Kennedy was something of a turning point politically. "It was the beginning of the end of everything for us politically when all of that was happening," says the actress. "We'd all taken everything to heart, and were so actively involved in not understanding. Actually, I can't say it was the beginning of the end because it was after that David and I moved. When we got married we [soon] moved to Benedict Canyon, and that was actually when I remember going up to San Francisco with the vets and all that. Maybe that was the beginning when we started getting so involved.

"I remember that night," continues Carlson. "We were sitting…David had worked late. He got home late and so we missed being able to go to the Ambassador where Bobby Kennedy was speaking, so we were watching it on television. I remember Michael [Margotta] and Susan [Howard] were next door. We were living in an apartment at that time off Beachwood. We watched Bobby Kennedy come out. He had given his speech, and then we had kind of turned the sound down. David and Michael and I know there were four or five of us all sitting in the room together, they started debating this and that, but I happened to be looking at the television and suddenly I realized there was something happening, something was not…and then I remember hearing people outside yelling, and I said, DAVID. Turn it up! TURN IT UP!'"[30]

So, when *Here Come the Brides* began reflecting the turbulent times with a more realistic and downbeat approach — one that presented a more historically accurate view of post-Civil War Seattle, David Soul was in favor of that. "We dealt with some fairly interesting relationships," recalls the actor, "showed respect for indigenous peoples. When you're doing a show about the survival of a settlement, it's a natural progression to move into stories about the social and economic upheavals that will occur as the town continues to grow. As any television show develops, you have to expand and explore."[31]

That was certainly happening with Soul's Joshua Bolt character. To *Brides* semi-regular Dick Balduzzi, Soul did a very good job with what he was given. "David was down to earth, a good actor," praises Balduzzi. "It was the beginning of his career, and he became very, very strong in his characters, like *Starsky and Hutch*, but his career went up and down the scale. He should have gone on big from *Starsky and Hutch*; he had a good start. I thought he was really good in that part on *Brides*. He tried real hard to do his best. He wanted more work, wanted stronger roles, which he never got. But there were a couple episodes that he was featured in, and he was excellent. He was good in that show about the gambler ["A Hard Card to Play"]. He had a knack for good acting. He studied hard. Went on to do some good things."[32]

"David Soul was just a real cool guy," adds *Brides* wardrobe man Steve Lodge. "He wanted to do something with himself. I remember Bobby Sherman and Robert Brown shared a bungalow building. It was like a duplex. Bobby's dressing room was on the one side, and Robert's was on the other, but David, they just kinda figured he was a nobody and put him in just a regular dressing room — you know, one of those on wheels. And then David started getting hot. He went on *Starsky and Hutch,* and next thing you know he's directing, and all that kind of stuff. I just used to chuckle to myself about that because of the way they treated him over there."[33]

Despite this treatment, David Soul exhibits no bitter feelings about his days on *Brides*. "They were all happy shows," says the actor. "I have very, very fond memories of the people, starting with Bridget and Joan Blondell. Robert Brown was a dear, dear friend, and Bobby was fine. Bill Blinn was a lovely friend, too, and I'm still close with Renee Valente." Soul also keeps in touch with his former wife, Karen Carlson.

Following the cancellation of *Here Come the Brides*, David Soul guest-starred on a number of series — from *All in the Family* to the Quinn Martin series, *Dan August*, *The FBI*, *Cannon*, and *The Streets of San Francisco*. "And once you got on the roster with Quinn Martin," says Soul, "you'd come back and rotate from show to show."

After reaching superstardom with *Starsky and Hutch*, Soul did quite a few TV-movies: among them *Salem's Lot*. There were other series as regular too, including *The Yellow Rose* and *Casablanca*. In the latter, executive produced by *Roots'* David L. Wolper and co-produced by *Judd, for the Defense's* Harold Gast, Soul played the Humphrey Bogart character of Rick Blaine. "It was the greatest thing in the world," says Soul. "David Wolper used the actual sets from *Casablanca* [both the classic motion picture, and the series were produced at Warner Bros] and our director of photography was Joe Biroc. Joe Biroc had done the Jimmy Stewart films, like *It's a Wonderful Life*. He made the show look really rich."

David Soul continued to work in television through the '90s, "then I got tired of L.A.," says the star. "I didn't like it there anymore. It's like the end of the world. So I moved to England and started working here."[34]

"And now he's doing theater, and I'm so proud of him," states Bridget Hanley. "He's getting these incredible reviews."[35]

Bridget Hanley also did much work on stage. Some years after *Here Come the Brides*.

1. Tolsky – 2007
2. Brown – 2007
3. Carlson – 2007
4. Soul – 2007
5. Valente – 2007
6. Carlson – 2007
7. Soul – 2007
8. Carlson – 2007
9. Valente – 2007
10. Ibid
11. Soul – 2007
12. Valente – 2007
13. Soul – 2007
14. Tolsky – 2007
15. Hanley – 2007
16. Hoag – 2007
17. Valente – 2007
18. Blinn – 2007
19. Soul – 2007

20. Blinn – 2007
21. Hanley – 2007
22. Valente – 2007
23. Hoag – 2007
24. Tolsky – 2007
25. Hanley – 2007
26. Carlson – 2007
27. Ibid
28. Brown – 2007
29. Blinn – 2007
30. Carlson – 2007
31. Soul – 2007
32. Balduzzi – 2007
33. Lodge – 2007
34. Soul – 2007
35. Hanley – 2007

"Well, you sure had me fooled. I thought you meant it. Every word on that handbill. That line of fast talk you gave those girls. You're nothin' but razzle-dazzlers. When I go to that meetin' tonight, you better be prepared to answer a whole lot of questions."

# Chapter 8

# *Co-starring Bridget Hanley*

"It will probably always be, work-wise, one of the most extraordinary experiences of my life. It really launched my professional life, even though I had done other things before."

Such is leading lady Bridget Hanley's opinion concerning her two-season stint as Candy Pruitt on the 1968-70 series, *Here Come the Brides*. Of all the talents connected with *Brides*, none is more enthusiastic about the show, none has done more to keep its memory alive than Bridget Hanley.

*Here Come the Brides* wasn't just a television series to Bridget Hanley. It was the beginning of her marriage to series director E.W. Swackhamer. It was about a town in which she grew up. It featured a regular character — Candy Pruitt's little sister, Molly, whose character name was provided by Hanley; Molly was the name of Bridget Hanley's baby sister, who was twelve years younger than the actress. The star of *Brides* — Robert Brown — was a longtime friend of Hanley's husband, E.W. Swackhamer, and of course, Hanley herself. The actress already knew *Brides'* third male lead, David Soul as the both of them were in Screen Gems' New Talent Program. Soul and his wife, Karen Carlson, often saw Hanley and her husband, E.W. Swackhamer, in the years during and after *Brides*. Hanley also began her longtime friendship with Susan Tolsky during the run of the series.

While other actresses may have been considered for the role of Candy Pruitt, it's doubtful that any of them would have brought the same degree of enthusiasm to the part. Not to mention same believability. Playing a tough, strong-willed woman wasn't much of a stretch for Bridget Hanley. She'd been that way from day one.

Placed in an isolation ward in a Minneapolis hospital when she and seven other newborn babies contracted viral pneumonia, Hanley had been the only one to survive. "I don't know exactly what happened because I wasn't too alert," laughs the actress, "but I remember my mother telling me she had to sit on the edge of her bed, and they told me that she had to decide whether she would go see me or not see me before she was released from the hospital. And she obviously had seen me, but my mother...I was the only one that survived. I guess it was kind of a mess in the hospital because it was kind of a first time, one-time only situation. I think that it was a very scary time."

About as scary was another life-threatening incident a few years later. That one involved an alligator. "My dad was in the Marine Corps and we lived in Cherry Point, North Carolina," recalls Hanley. "It was during the war. Mary Jo [Hanley's older sister] and I wandered off one day, and it was very swampy in Cherry Point,

*Bridget Hanley as Candy Pruitt.* COURTESY BRIDGET HANLEY

North Carolina. And I guess, I mean I don't really recall it, but I guess I sat down, I got kind of tired, and I sat on what I thought was a mossy log, and it started to take off. And Mary Jo pulled me off, I think, and raced me home, screaming, 'BRIDGET, BRIDGET SAT ON AN OLLIGATOR!' and my mom and dad didn't know what to think, but they did send a force out, and they found the olligator and shot it. I don't really recall, but I guess I was very lucky. I must have a guardian angel. ABSOLUTELY!"

*Patti Cohoon as Molly Pruitt.*
COURTESY BRIDGET HANLEY

Bridget Hanley's "olligator" ride occurred when she was about three years old. "There are a lot of memories I have of when I was three," says the actress. "I think it was because it was wartime, and everything was kind of dramatic. I think that people were so emotionally in tune with everything that was going on that, even at that age, I remembered a lot of things, and I remembered Christmases — you know things were not available so we decorated our tree with yarn, and made things for it. I remember all of that — getting a doll buggy that was made out of Marine canvas and plaster of Paris wheels. We've got dolls — Mary Jo got one named Cherry, and I got one that I named Molly, and later on, I had my real baby sister, Molly."

Molly was the third child of Doris and Leland Hanley. Doris was born Doris Linea Nihlroos; Leland was Leland Francis Patrick Hanley. "They called her 'Dorie' instead of Doris," laughs the actress, and "they always called her 'Nosy Nalrosy.'"

When Bridget Hanley's mother and father married, "the Swedish and the Irish got together," says the actress. "My dad was born in Spokane, and he played football at Northwestern, where my uncle Dick Hanley coached for years. And my Uncle Pat was a backfield coach, and my Uncle Mike coached in Boston, and Daddy was — I think — an All-American. He originally was gonna go to Notre Dame to play with Knute Rockne. And he was there, and my Uncle Dick called Mr. Rockne. He said, 'I need Lee here.' So Daddy gave up Notre Dame and went to Northwestern."

Shortly after their daughter Bridget's birth, Doris and Leland Hanley moved to "Cherry Point, North Carolina, when my dad joined the Marine Corps at the request of his older brother," states the actress. "He [Leland Hanley's older brother] talked all of them [his younger brothers] into joining. And then, we moved to Malibu,

California, just briefly, and then to Klamath Falls, Oregon, at the time when I was, like, four. I had pretend friends then, and, I just remembered 'THE THREE BEARS!' The Three Bears came with me from Cherry Point, North Carolina. They drove in little cars all the way to Klamath Falls, and when they arrived, I remember running in and saying to my mom, THEY GOT HERE! THEY GOT HERE! She said, 'WHO? WHO?' And I said, 'THE BEARS!' And my mom came running out and welcomed them and, of course, there was nobody there. But the three bears were my buddies."

"We lived in Klamath Falls, Oregon, for a while because my dad was still in the Marine Corps," continues Hanley. "Actually he was due to be sent off to the war the next day when the truce was called. I remember my mother had us stand up — she gave us a Coca Cola, and had us sing 'The Star-Spangled Banner' — I think I was five or four or something like that."

There was a great deal of singing in the Hanley household. "My dad sang beautifully," says the actress. "He used to sing to us every night when he was home; he traveled a lot, and my mom played the piano. She was just brilliant — she was really on the verge of becoming a concert pianist when she married my dad, so we took piano lessons. I could hear her in the kitchen sometimes, when she was preparing dinner, when I was playing, saying, 'No, no,' when I hit the wrong note. My sister, Mary Jo, was a really good piano player. I remember one time we were playing a duet at the recital. I kept goofing, and my mother finally yelled from the audience, 'START OVER!' So I never did a recital again, nor did I play the piano really much. But I can read music. That's one great gift that was given to me by the piano lessons, but piano just was not my instrument. I went on to play the flute, which I loved, and I played in the band and the orchestra. And I sang in the choir. So I really owe my mom and dad…music was a part of our household. And we put on plays — Mary Jo and I — so there were a lot of the arts going on in our household. It was not forced — it was just part of it, it really became a part of us."

The family moved to Seattle, Washington, and a short time later they moved to the Washington city of Edmonds. There, Bridget and her older sister, Mary Jo, frequently took in the Saturday matinee. "Downtown Edmonds had one little movie theater," recalls the actress, "and we would usually go to the matinees. We just begged to be able to go, and we just loved it. It was amazing. And I loved musicals, and they also had serials on; there was *Nyoka, Queen of the Jungle*, and that just knocked me out — it was just so fun. And about a year and a half ago, or two years ago, Bill Blinn found *Nyoka, Queen of the Jungle* online, or in a store or something, and gave me the whole set. I was so excited!"

Football being so much a part of the Hanley girls' lives, it was inevitable that the two (and later, three) sisters start playing football. "We all grew up not only watching, first of all, listening to football, we played it with all the boys in the neighborhood," laughs the actress. "We played flag football — it was just Hurry, Scurry, and Cheat. We loved football as adults, too, and my husband was thrilled because that was his kind of way to relax. He loved football."

Football wasn't the only sport the Hanley girls played. "We had a tennis court on our property," remembers the actress. "The frost had cracked the tennis court, and we learned how to hit the cracks and make the ball bounce vividly. We wouldn't do that when we played with each other, but when we played with any of the guys or any other friends, we would hit the cracks and we'd always win. My dad one time… We were playing with a couple of guys from the neighborhood or from school or something. I remember my dad coming out and saying, 'You girls can play better than that! What are you doing?' That ruined our whole career.

"My dad ruined a couple of my careers: tennis and track," laughs Hanley. "When I was in junior high school, I beat the fastest guy on the track team. They called my mom and dad to see if I could join the male track team. My dad said, 'ABSO-LUTELY NOT!' So that was the end of my track career."

By junior high, Bridget Hanley had pretty much figured out what sort of career she wanted. Writing a play in the sixth grade, in which she played the leading role, the actress "went on to do more of those kinds of things as I got into high school. When I was in the band, the orchestra, the choir, and a small group called the 'Mellow-aires,' this wonderful man named Ed Aliverti, — he's still a dear, dear friend — he was like just such a mentor, he encouraged us and all of that. [Acting] just became a real kind of thrust for me. It was where I felt really better — I just felt kind of homely, as a gawky teenager — I grew six inches in one year, and even the teachers said to me, 'Don't your parents feed you?' Then I got pudgy, the teenaged times were rather awkward, and the music and the drama, and all of it — that pretty much was where I felt the most at ease, and the most creative, obviously. But I wasn't a bad student. I also grew up in a great town that had a great school system. A lot of friends that I had from the age of five and six when I first started school are still friends, and I see them every time I'm home. We're all…and you know you can't lie to somebody you've known since you were six. So we all keep each other honest, and we have a great time together. We just laugh. And it's just — it's really fun. It's kind of an idyllic way to grow up."

Complementing Bridget Hanley's interest in drama were her dance classes. "I took what I call now, because it makes everybody laugh, a triple-threat dance class," chuckles the actress. "It was tap, acrobatic, and ballet, all in an hour and a half. I could do back-bends and splits — I mean, I was really good. And I loved to tap dance. Ballet…well, I have a couple of pictures, and you can just tell from the pictures that it was not my forte, but I thought I was fabulous. And my friend Dana and I were in the dance classes together. Dana was one of my best, best friends in pre-first grade, and she lives on the east coast, but we're still in touch. I spent my fifteenth summer with her family — the whole summer in Hawaii, and oh, we just had the best time, because that's where her mother had been born, then they moved back there. They asked my parents if I could come for two weeks. (Hanley wound up staying the whole summer because) they called every two weeks, and said, 'Can she stay longer?' It was great."

The same year Bridget Hanley got her first TV set. "The first television I ever had was when I was fifteen and I was in high school," says the actress. "I remember watching *American Bandstand* and racing home so I could see the whole thing because it was people my age — dancing and having a great time." Being a dancer, Hanley loved the MGM musicals. "Fred Astaire, Gene Kelly, Ann Miller, Ruby Keeler — watching anybody tap dance," glows the actress. "I wanted to be Ann Miller. Later when I saw her hair-dos, I kind of changed my mind. But the way she danced, I just wanted to be that. Not Eleanor Powell, and, or, oh, Leslie Caron, I knew I could never be like them. But I figured the other ladies had kinda chubby legs, so I could have been big in the forties or whenever that was. And then when *The Jackie Gleason Show* was on — remember the June Taylor Dancers? I wanted to be a June Taylor dancer, and that never happened. Then I met Dick Van Patten's wife, Pat, and they're good friends of mine, too. She was a June Taylor dancer, so I got filled in on all of that. So it was great. And my husband studied with Martha Grahame, cuz he started out as an actor, with movement and all of that stuff. He had kind of a magical way with him. He would explain what he wanted, and then trust, and I think that for an actor, when a director trusts you, you're the freest. He was great at movement and moving the camera, and he backed — that was one of his favorite things to do, not just shoot and cut. He loved to do long masters, and he was really, really good at it. But I'm sure that his training — training becomes a part of you, and you forget which you're using when. I think a lot of us had had some kind of dance training at some point. I think now it's required, but then it was just part of childhood if you were lucky."

Having decided to become an actress, Bridget Hanley "started college at the San Francisco College for Women. There was only one drama professor," she remembers. "It was a girl's school, and the boy's school — the University of San Francisco — was across the street, but they wouldn't let us be in each other's shows. So they were playing girl's parts, and I got all the men's roles at the San Francisco College for Women because I had the lowest voice. I remember still tap-dancing, and walking on my hands down the hallways, and doing my back-bends, doing all of that stuff, to show off for whatever reason, I just kept doing that, so it kind of stayed with me into…and I can't do it anymore. But I can still tap dance. In fact I just did a long run of *Nunsense* with Betty Garrett and Lee Meriwether, and Barbara Mallory, and a couple of other ladies. We sang and danced and it was really, really fun. And then we've done it again on a couple little mini-tours, and they're trying to book us for some more places."

"I left San Francisco College for Women because I realized I was going nowhere in my career," continues the actress. "I already had decided that that's what I wanted — I wanted to major in drama, and they just didn't have enough of that. I have still dear, dear, wonderful close friends from there, but I couldn't decide whether I would quit school and join the San Francisco Mime Troupe, or go back to the University of Washington, which had, at that time, aside from Northwestern, one of the finest drama schools in the country. They had three theaters that ran simultaneously all year long. So I decided I'd just go home and get my degree there. And I did. And all I had to do, except for oceanography, which I got a 'D' in, all I had to take were drama courses and costume classes — it was a wonderful program. I took that for two years, and I was rehearsing in a play all the time. So it was really like doing summer stock, but really good summer stock. I actually stopped doing musicals after I graduated. I did a couple of musicals at the University of

Washington, but after I graduated with a B.A. in drama from the University of Washington. I left immediately for San Francisco, because it was familiar, to start my career in the theater."

"I got a job selling coats at a department store on Market Street, and roomed with one of my ex-roommates from San Francisco College for Women," continues Hanley. "She kept saying 'When are you going to get a job in the theater?' because I had been there a couple of months. I said, 'After Christmas, after Christmas.' She finally said, 'Bridget, it's after Christmas.' So I went out and got a job in the theater that day. I got a part in a play, and then I heard that Marian Healy, who'd also graduated from the University of Washington, was doing *Private Lives* at the Little Fox Theater in San Francisco, so I went down and saw it. I said to the director, 'I want to audition for you,' and being so young and brave and everything, and I loved the show — it was so fun, I said, 'I want to audition for you in case you do something else or whatever,' and that…I went home and at two-thirty in the morning the phone rang! It was this director. He said, 'Are you available to take over as the bronchial French maid?' and I had to go in the next day — go into the part. I said, 'You bet I am!' and so I called the other theater and told them I was not available. I went down, had one rehearsal, and played it. I also understudied Marian, and when Marian left — I got to go in and play Sybil."

While that was going on, Bridget Hanley got another acting job going. "They were doing *Under the Yum Yum Tree* up the street," remembers the actress, "and they had me understudy for that, and when…Stefanie Powers started that run up there — she wasn't there anymore — it was another young woman, and when she left, I got to go into the part, and I got my equity card. Then I did *Under the Yum Yum Tree* again down in San Diego with Howard Duff, Jack Ging, and Barbara Stuart. This man named Hal Geske, who was Barbara's agent, was down there, and he told me, and I had already met him once, because I'd been flown down to Los Angeles with an actor who auditioned for Monique James [the head of the casting department] at Universal [TV]. We'd met Hal Geske on that trip. He'd told me then that "If you ever move to L.A., call me.' I thought, 'Yeah, yeah, sure.' And then he told me that again in San Diego."

After Bridget Hanley moved to Los Angeles, she found herself working in an Elvis Presley movie. "I got to be standing next to Elvis in a couple of places, and they kept me coming back every day," recalls the actress. "All his henchmen and everything. They invited me to a party, and it was a little too vile for my taste, so I left, in my little black dress and pearls. Anyway, Joan (Blackman, or Freeman) starred with Elvis in that movie, and we just — we didn't meet like in any great way, we were roommates for a while, and the first play I got out of the newspaper was *Under the Yum Yum Tree*. Because they were casting here for *Under the Yum Yum Tree*, I called up the producer. I got his name out of the phone book. I said, 'You need look no further.' He had me come over that day. I got the part. I played it with Del Moore, Jimmy Best, and Chanin Hale. Richard Erdman directed it, and then I did *Private Lives* again at the Ivar Theatre. It was those two plays that Eddie Foy (from Screen Gems) came to see, and it was those two pieces that made them interested in putting me under contract.

I'd already been asked to go under contract at NBC by Ethel Winant — to go into their New Talent Program, and I had accepted that. Then I got the Screen Gems one, and they were paying more money than I was getting at NBC, so I called Ethel…I never worked for Ethel again. Then, I met Swack."

While in San Diego, Hanley also heard from "Jane Dreyfuss from William Morris. She came down, saw me, and said she would really, really be interested and to call her if I moved to Los Angeles," remembers the actress. "So I called her, too. We went and had a big meeting. She said, 'Bridget, I would be thrilled to represent you for theater, but I can't seem to jog the television and film guys.' She said, 'You would be absolutely lost to be here without that [television and film].'"

Not long after her arrival in Hollywood, Bridget Hanley appeared in her first series pilot as a regular. "The show was called *The Pirates of Flounder Bay*," remembers Hanley. "It was at MGM, and the producer was the producer of *Combat* — Selig Seligman. They had tested everybody in town, had seen every blonde in town, and finally they decided to see me. I was totally reverse color hair. I was more of a comedienne, I was just so against type, but they brought me in. They called me back after my first reading, they said, 'Can you be available this afternoon?' I said, 'Yes, I can.' And then I remember walking down a street outside the studio. There was a Catholic church right across the street from MGM. I thought, 'Maybe I should go in and say a prayer.' Then I thought, 'Don't make a deal with God! I'll never know if I got this on my own.' So I didn't do that. Then I went back and they had me read with somebody. Then they called me back a third time and had me read with somebody else. And I got it. I got the part. I was absolutely in heaven."

Continues Hanley: "Alan Rafkin was directing it, and I was just star-struck, awe-struck, sun-struck, you name it, I was struck, and getting to work with Keenan Wynn and Basil Rathbone, and Jack Soo…And the producer, Selig Seligman, said, 'YOU ARE MY NEW STAR!' He kept taking me around and introducing me as his 'NEW STAR!' I just thought Selig was the be-all and the end-all. He introduced me to everybody."

"Everybody" included *Combat* stars Vic Morrow and Dick Peabody. "I was so in awe of all those guys," says Hanley. "They were crawling around on a cement floor with brush on it. It was just so fun, cuz here I was at MGM, all these movies and things, all the stars, and going up to wardrobe, and going into wardrobe, and being taken on different sets…They put me in a dress, that I think was from Glinda the Good Witch, or somebody from *The Wizard of Oz*, and it had what's her name in it: Billie Burke; it had her name in it. And every time I'd go to MGM on anything, I'd look in the costume to see if I was wearing something that somebody else like that had worn. But now there are no wardrobe departments. Now they just buy stuff and sell 'em at resell places or whatever. I think that they still build costumes for films and stuff, but not like they used to. Anyway, it was such a thrill and they…I had to come in and show the director. They went, 'Uh-huh, turn around, turn around,' and they suggested some more padding in the bra area. I went back in and came out. 'Uh-huh. Turn around. Turn around.' They suggested some more. I came back. 'Turn around. Uh-huh. Uh-huh.' The director looked at me. He said, 'You know, Bridget.

If I had known this, I would have hired Ronnie Schell for the part.' He and Ronnie Schell were very good friends; I knew Ronnie. It was hysterical — we just had the best time."

That Bridget Hanley was held in high regard by both Seligman and Rafkin was evidenced by the name actors who were working with her in *Pirates*. As already noted, one was Keenan Wynn; the other was Basil Rathbone. "And Hal Peary was on it, and Jim Begg, and Peter Bonerz," remembers Hanley. "And it was also with an actor named Bill Cort who was just…we grew to be such fast friends, and we adored each other. Bill Cort and I were the young leads in it. After we shot it, we called each other every day for three months to see if it had been sold, 'What'd you hear? What'd you hear?' Cuz that's when it took three months to find out if it had been sold. We were so young and wanted it to happen so badly, and it didn't. And when we shot…I have a picture of me sitting next to Basil Rathbone, we were at a banquet within the script, and I was all dressed up and it was so fun, and he was there, and in the middle of a sentence, he belched. We all fell over, laughing. I thought, 'How would I…first of all, how could I ever sit, be with Basil Rathbone, and then also be privy to his belch? It was just amazing."

Though Keenan Wynn was known to be a heavy drinker, Hanley didn't remember him "being into the bottle, but there was a bottle in our scene," laughs the actress. "I had to break it over his head because he was a pirate. He was really fun. I don't recall him being untoward, or boozed up, but then I never knew when people were smoking crack. I never attributed any behavior to that because it was so foreign to me. Well, I had to practice with a breakaway bottle, so they took me off in the corner of the set, and they were helping me practice with the bottle…I was perfect every time. I practiced and practiced for about forty-five minutes. Then they said, 'You're fine. Go! Just do it!' So we got into the scene. I cracked Keenan Wynn on the head with a breakaway bottle; I drew blood. But he forgave me.

"We all had such a hysterically funny time," continues Hanley. "We shot it on the backlot, on stages at MGM. I was just in heaven. Charlie Dierkop, great actor, I have a picture of him picking me up, and it's just my behind, in this long dress, and when actors used to put together their book, that was the end of my book. I put 'THE END' across my butt. Charlie keeps saying, (for years) 'You promised me that picture!' Anyway, when I talked to Alan Rafkin years later about why *Pirates* didn't sell, he said, 'Listen, the thing was there was so much action and no story.' I mean, it was all action and no substance and no story."

As Bridget Hanley soon discovered, there was a very great difference between working on stage and working in television. "My first television job I was turned away at the gate," laughs the actress. "They sent me to the extras' gate. I went around to the extras' gate; they wouldn't let me in! I finally said…I started to scream — 'THIS IS MY FIRST TELEVISION JOB! AND I'VE GOT THIS PART, AND HERE'S MY SCRIPT! CALL SOMEBODY!' They finally did. And got me on. Oh, it was so…it was an awful way to start."

Things weren't much better once Hanley made it to the set. "So, it's my first television job," she continues, "and they said, 'MOVE THAT BABY OVER HERE!'

and I thought they were talking about me, so I started to move cuz I didn't know. The director, very dear, came up. He said, 'They're talkin' about the light.' And I didn't want anybody to know this is my first job!"

According to Hanley, one advantage she had when she began working, a characteristic that made her feel comfortable on set, was very poor eyesight. "One eye tests 20/150, and the other 20/375," laughs the actress. "I think I made that number up, anyway now they have soft lenses, so I can see again, so it's just heaven. But it was really kind of wonderful in a way because it takes the pressure off all of that that's going on around you; it only leaves you with the inner sanctum of what you're doing, and who you're doing it with. It was really quite wonderful, kind of a wonderful way to begin, because my concentration was just so pleasant, and not distracted by anything that was going on in the crew or the whatever. Now of course, I wear my lenses all the time and I think of all that I missed — all those years. Soon as soft lenses came out, I was able to wear contacts."

One thing Bridget Hanley didn't miss, after she began wearing soft lenses, was tripping. Laughs the actress, "On *Brides*, the guys sometimes…Susan and I would be coming in to make a proclamation, and the three of them would drop down on their hands and knees, and I'd open the door and start to do my march, and we'd fall right over. They were down just to make us fall — it was probably on a rehearsal, and we tripped."

In addition to having a great sense of humor about herself, Hanley developed a very good work ethic. Muses the actress, "We all talk about…I used to eat lettuce and potato chips, and turn in pop bottles to get that, and then because the potato chips were really yummy, and the lettuce made them expand, you felt really full. I mean comparing poverty was kind of a lot of what we did when we were between scenes for a long time. But it was possible then. The world has changed so much — just the rents and things — I don't know how young people make it these days. I mean we were able to, in a safe neighborhood, get a really terrific okay place, you had a roommate, and if you made a little more money, you didn't worry. You were able to survive and be safe. I had to plan how many times a week I drove my car, but that was a beginning, and it's lovely to remember those times, because they were happy times. Because I was on the road doing what I really had longed to do probably my whole life. I was in the range of the comediennes at that time, not necessarily the beautiful leading lady, and I think there was a big distinction. So, one of my first television jobs was a *Hank*, my next one at Screen Gems was *Gidget*; I did all of those comedy shows — *Farmer's Daughter* and *Love, American Style*. I did about four or five of those, and Arnold Margolin was one of the producers at one point, and we still laugh. I just had a ball — it was so fun, the women were fun."

It was through her agent, Hal Geske, that Hanley met her future husband, E.W. Swackhamer. "I was just thrilled," enthuses the actress. "I was with Hal for a very long time. He was the one who said to me after I signed, 'You've got to meet this director named E.W. Swackhamer.' And it wasn't romantically. It was like business because he just felt that he was one of the best directors around. But every time I would go to read for something that Swack was directing, like *Hazel*, he was off scouting locations, so I never got to meet him. The first time I did was when they wanted to test me to go under contract at Screen Gems. Swack was going to be directing all the tests. So I put on my one dress, the little double dress, and blue coat, and went in. I'd already done my first television show and I'd done a *Gidget* and a *Farmer's Daughter*, but this was really a big deal, and I was very excited. I was so nervous to meet him, and I guess I was about five minutes late, so I decided to do one of those 'slide into first base,'

*Newlyweds Bridget Hanley and E.W. Swackhamer toast one another on their wedding day.* COURTESY BRIDGET HANLEY

things. I opened the door, slid over towards the desk, said 'SAFE!' and pulled his... Stan Schwimmer, who was Swack's associate producer, pulled Stan Schwimmer's tie. I don't know what got into me. I think Swack was so stunned he didn't know what to think. Anyway, we then got into a very nice conversation. And we talked a lot and everything, and then I was excused. And then they let me know who I was gonna be testing with, and what the scene was. So, when I heard that I was testing with... there were only six pairs, I think, or something, and everybody else was testing...all the other women were testing with men. I was the only one that was testing with another woman. And she was voluptuous and blonde, and like really...I was so...I felt untypical Hollywood, and she was just like buxom and gorgeous. I called Hal up and I said, 'You can kiss this contract goodbye! This wonderful Mr. Swackhamer who you told me so much about. He put me...the only one...that he put with another girl. So I just figure it's over,' and I explained how beautiful she was and all of that, and I said, 'And guess who has to wear the slip in the scene,' — it was *me*. Well, little did I know, dummy me. It was for *My Sister Eileen*, and it was the funny part. I ended up getting the contract, and the woman that I tested with ended up being a very dear friend, and later, one of my agents. She now lives in Seattle — Sharon DuBord. She was with the McKell Jennings agency, and then took over when Walter McKell was not well and now has quit agenting — obviously."

One of the complaints that was often lodged against Hanley's studio, Screen Gems, was that it was cheap. "It seemed like a lot of money to me at that point," states Hanley. "Yeah, it was minimal, but, to me, GOD, it was sure better than unemployment. The rewards to me, in those years, were more artistic than financial, and I would never trade the two ever. EVER! When I went under contract, WOW! It looked pretty good to me!"

At Screen Gems Bridget Hanley met David Soul. "David and I did scenes in the attic at Columbia Pictures," she remembers, "and we were under contract to Screen Gems. [Screen Gems was the television division of Columbia Pictures.] There were quite a few people who were under contract to Columbia, and Walter McKell — who was an incredible acting teacher, acting coach — theater person — he later became my agent. He was running it [the acting class which Hanley and Soul took], and Charles Strasberg, the son of Lee Strasberg, taught there for a while. Anyway we usually picked theater scenes. We wouldn't go to class, if we were shooting a show or something, and I remember David and I did a play by Elaine May — *Not Enough Rope*. We worked together quite often up in the attic, and talk about ghosts. It was so special to be there. Cuz there were those ghosts in the attic — all the stars that had been at that studio — it was the most magical time. You could just feel the energy of those stars. At MGM, you felt the same way, but it was more tangible things. It was the costume department and the makeup department, and the costumers were so skilled, and the backlot was so magical."

Next to Robert Brown, David Soul was the other *Brides* male star to whom Bridget Hanley was the closest. "He and Karen would come over," recalls the actress, "and they would bring Jahn, who was a month younger than Bronwyn — she was born March third, and he was April third, and they would sit and stare at each other. We saw David probably more than Karen; Karen and I have been friends for a long, long time — she's a really extraordinary...we had good times together. And I met David's son Christopher when we were on *Brides*. We were asked to go to Minneapolis, where I was born, and where David was from. We were asked to come to this parade. We rode in the back of a convertible — we just had the best time, and I met his son, and he was in little velvet rompers — he is now a marvelous actor."

Having met E.W. Swackhamer, Bridget Hanley "absolutely fell in love with him professionally when we were rehearsing for the test scene. He was...I had never...I mean, it was just amazing. And I just...I wrote him a thank you note. And he wrote me a thank you note. And after we started under contract, we had classes every day, and we got tapped doing the episodic stuff. We did *I Dream of Jeannie, Farmer's Daughter*, but Swack was doing *Love on a Rooftop* at that time, and he invited all of us. At the end, there were three people chosen from New York, and three people chosen from the west coast, so there were six of us, and we were all put under contract.

Later David Soul joined, and Hilarie Thompson, but at first there were just the six of us, and Swack was shooting on the stage — on the Gower lot right next door to where we had classes. He invited all six of us to come to the set anytime we wanted to observe or whatever, and he would answer any questions that any of us might have and everything. He was just so great. He would take people out to dinner and to the theater — and there were two little blond kids running around the lot, around him, and I just obviously assumed that he was married, and he came in and gave us not only on the set classes, but he would talk to us and ask if we had questions and all of that stuff.

"Well, one day I went home and took a nap and I had a dream and it was about him, and he was saying, 'Don't do westerns!' I said, 'Why?' And he said, 'You know all about that. You know all about that.' I must have been in an editing session. Well, the phone rang and it was him, asking me if I'd like to go out to dinner and to the theater. I figured it was my turn because he had taken everybody else out, the guys and the ladies. So I said 'Well, sure.' So we went out and saw [the Kaufman-Hart play] *You Can't Take it with You*. We met at the Brown Derby restaurant. I was just like in heaven. When I got out of the car, I spent a lot of time getting ready, and the parking lot attendant said to me, 'You must be meeting someone very special.' And I said 'Yeah, I am.' But I didn't, and again, it was not in a romantic way. Anyway, dissolve to...I later found out he was not married. We started to date, and we never went out with anybody else. And we got married, as my friend Dick Bare the writer, said, 'In a whirlwind courtship of three-and-a-half years.' It was just a magical, magical — we got married in Robert Brown's backyard in Brentwood, just immediate family because it was between the first and second season of *Brides*. And it was very popular. And everybody...we gave one magazine the rights to do pictures, and Gene Trindel the rights to photograph it. This was a photographer that often worked with us for other things, and he would be at events, he worked for the studios and everything and he was just great and he agreed to do it if we would give him an exclusive — he would be the only one that would have wedding pictures. So this wonderful photographer took all of our wedding shots — he had an exclusive because *Brides* was right at its height, and so we got them and they were wonderful, but, we never put them in an album — we had them in an envelope, then suddenly, I don't know, it's like years later we couldn't find them, and I looked everywhere. I went through everything in the house — we had three floors in our house — one was kind of a rumpus room and laundry room and everything — below ground and then two stories above. I looked everywhere, everywhere, and all through the years I was so sad, and I couldn't reach the photographer. Well, several years later, after Swack passed away, I was cleaning out to pack up and move. It was three years after he had passed away, and I was gonna move. So I was packing up things — and there they were. They were not — I know it sounds airy-fairy, but we had a couple of things like that happen at that house, but that one was the most extraordinary because I had searched every nook and cranny of that house, and there they were! They were on top of — I mean they were in cupboards that I had gone through!"

Like the series they were both doing, the marriage of Bridget Hanley and E.W. Swackhamer was filled with some comic moments. "There was a helicopter circling during the wedding," remembers the actress, "and a humming bird circling my head. Everybody was afraid that the humming bird was going to lose it on my veil." There were dramatic situations, too. "I could not get married in the Catholic Church," explains Hanley, "because Swack had been married before. The blond children were

his children, and so, my step-children. They're now grown and have their own children — we're all very, very close. And they have their own really neat mom."

Trying to help Bridget Hanley resolve her problem was Nancy O'Connor — wife of Robert Brown's very good friend, Carroll O'Connor. "Because Swack had been married before, Nancy O'Connor helped me write practically every order of priests all over the world," says Hanley. "No one would marry us because they wanted me to prove that the first marriage was invalid. I said, 'I can't do that. It was valid.' I said, 'In other words, what you're saying to me is I could get married in the Catholic Church if I were to go and try to unsettle things and prove that his two glorious children, who have their own mom

*New bride Bridget Hanley.*
COURTESY BRIDGET HANLEY

and dad, if I go and prove that they're bastard children, then I can get married in the Catholic Church? Nuh-uh. So long.'

"They kept trying to talk me out of it," continues Hanley. "They said, 'Pray. Pray to forget this man.' And all of this stuff. I said, 'No thanks.' So we got a judge, Rob Wyman, who married us. And he said in the ceremony, I think he had kind of a little stage fright. He said, instead of 'Whomever God joins together, let not man put asunder,' he said, 'Whomever God puts asunder, let not man join together.' And he never went back and straightened it out. And then after the brunch and everything, we took off with the kids and Swack and I — we went back to a little house where we ended up living — had our reception there, and all of that."

That both Bridget Hanley and E.W. Swackhamer had a great sense of humor was evidenced by their behavior during their first Christmas. "Our first married Christmas we lived in this little house on Haskell and Encino Avenue, and it was a HUNDRED AND TEN DEGREES on Christmas!" laughs the actress. "So, we closed all the curtains in the house, turned on the air conditioning, built a fire in the fireplace, and pretended it was snowing outside."

One thing Bridget Hanley did not (and does not) like about living in Southern California was (and is) the absence of cold weather. "We have no weather here," laughs the actress, "so, when it rains, we all go out and do dances in the street. I grew up right outside of Seattle, in Edmonds, and we had rain, and we had snow — the

*Hanley and her wedding cake.* COURTESY BRIDGET HANLEY

silence of snow, and magical Christmases and everything. So when I moved down here, I lived sitting right next to the air conditioner, because it was just too hot."

Being from Seattle, when Hanley learned there were plans to do a new television series called *Here Come the Brides*, which was based in Seattle, she knew she had to be in that series. "When I was put under contract at Screen Gems, they were testing for the show, and they didn't test me," she recalls. "I said, 'Wait a minute, you guys,' and I started banging on everybody's door. I said, 'You don't…Hey, you guys, I'm from Seattle, and I bite my nails! And I know who the Mercer Girls are!' I didn't remember much about them. I remembered there was a book about the Mercer Girls, and I remembered kind of knowing about it because it was part of Washington State history. But it didn't go into depth — it was kind of an exciting story, and that's about as much as I recall thinking about it then. I had to fight and scratch and yell and scream and holler to get that part. They had tested everybody in town. Finally, they got so tired of me banging on their doors they said, 'GOD! TEST HER!' and Bobby came in to test, and Bob Claver directed the test because Swack and I were already dating, and we did not feel it was right to have…so Bob did the test, and ABC chose me! And I was screaming…I remember I was sitting — I had this little one-bedroom house in Morro Canyon with four sticks of furniture in it. I remember sitting by — I had a wall phone. I remember sitting by the phone cuz I knew that they were gonna make the decision that day or something. The phone rang, and I think my heart went out the window, and somebody said, 'Hi, Candy!' and I just shrieked — it was so great! It was my husband-to-be that called. They said that he should be the one to call."

Once Bridget Hanley was cast, she then began creating Candy Pruitt. "There were a lot of questions I just didn't ask because I was so busy preparing my…trying to bring their pages to life and my character to life that I didn't spend a lot of time asking questions," explains the actress. "Most people think *Here Come the Brides* was an off-shoot of *Seven Brides for Seven Brothers*; it was very reminiscent, but I think that probably both of them were based on a similar idea. It may have come from the same idea about the Mercer Girls or whatever, but *Brides* was not a spin-off of *Seven Brides for Seven Brothers* — it was written by N. Richard Nash. It was its own story. Alan Marcus was also involved, but the Jeremy character came from Nash. I was just thrilled that it was about Seattle, and about the Mercer Girls which I had to study in school. I thought, 'Oooh, what an adventure, and how fun.' And not realizing that they were all without their men because of the wars. I learned a lot through the show, and a lot more through [Mercer Girls historian] Peri Muhich because of what she's done. The thing is I understood how lucky I was to get to play such a before…. it was just really…it was really a fun time, and then of course we also got a chance to do some of the dramatic stuff."

In contrast to Eleanor of Aquitaine, whom Hanley portrayed years later on stage in the play, *The Lion in Winter*, the Candy character required very little research. "With Eleanor of Aquitaine, in *Lion in Winter*, I did a lot of research," states the actress. "With Eleanor, I wanted to know more about the times, about what history said about her, so that I could become a part of that era. I tried to create for myself what was on the paper. With Candy, aside from the little book on the Mercer Girls, I wanted to create who I wanted to create from that script. I thought of myself as a young girl coming to Seattle on an adventure, but my own different adventure. There was a lot that I could draw from. But aside from saying, 'It is,' instead of 'It's,' and didn't swear, which I didn't anyway, there were certain things, getting certain attitudes, certain ways of behavior. The costumes did a lot, the costumes really helped us

*Hanley having fun with the wedding cake.* COURTESY BRIDGET HANLEY

give our character, and the mop caps, and the funny nightgowns. We didn't have to do a lot of heavy historical research. I thought there was so much available from the picking that was right in front of us that I could use, and then my own heart, and my own feelings about Candy. If I had thought it was to be made historically accurate, I would have done all my homework. I would have done research, but I was never led to believe it was like 'based on,' so, therefore it was like open territory. Except you have to be hopefully true to the writer's concept of words."

According to Hanley, "a lot of things were improvised and never done again. No one ever expects to do just one take. Everybody has their own way of working. I learned my lines, but I [also] knew my cue lines. Robert [Brown] may have liked to have left things up to chance. But it isn't until you get in there with the real people, and then you hope that you haven't gotten yourself so stale by over-learning it that you're not able to roll with whatever's going immediately. That's the fun of acting — to respond. If you know everything, for me, if I know it well enough, then I'm much freer to be spontaneous.

"The best thing an actor can do is to truly be able to listen," continues Hanley. "That is a huge, I mean, it's HUGE! Because, if you don't really listen, then you can't be affected. And that's really very, very important. Shelley Winters used to come in and run sessions and stuff [at Hanley's acting classes]. One time, somebody asked her what was the difference in acting for the stage and acting for film. And she said, 'For acting on stage, you talk out loud. For acting on film, you think out loud.' Isn't that a wonderful description? You don't have to do as much. But thinking means listening, too. And that's the key to acting — to really listen. Because many times you can, if you're responding to someone and listening to them, it can really change your whole performance in a proper way, or in a very interesting way, or just give you another possibility. It's a never-ending, learning process."

In the pilot episode, viewers saw Bridget Hanley "thinking out loud" in her expression following her triumph — which was getting the Bolt Brothers to admit that Clancey and his vulgar crew needed to learn some manners. Giving further ground to Candy, Jason Bolt put the young woman and her fellow brides in charge of cleaning up Clancey's ship. As Hanley made clear through her reactions in the pilot, while Candy was excellent about standing her ground, "she doesn't know how to retreat," states the actress. "Giving up the leadership didn't work for her."

Getting Candy out of such situations (and doing it in a way which allowed her to save face) was the task of Bobby Sherman's Jeremy Bolt. "I was able to be vulnerable with Jeremy," says the actress. Hanley's reaction to Sherman's stuttering scenes added further dimension to her character. "I would watch him like I would never know how long he was gonna stutter, whether Candy was sympathetic or frustrated by that I don't know," admits the actress. "A lot of it just comes naturally with the part, if you really dig deep. When you're doing a series, you have to dig deeper, because you're trying to come up with new facets to the character, to the character's personality, and the character's relationship to other people. That's what makes it fascinating. And to be able to — oh GOD — go to work and be able to do what you want to do is just the most sublime feeling in the world."

While Bridget Hanley felt comfortable working with David Soul and Bobby Sherman, she had her qualms when it came to working with as skilled and talented a performer as Mark Lenard. "Oh, wasn't he a wonderful actor?" exclaims the actress. "They all were buddies from New York, and I remember when I first met Robert, I was intimidated to meet him, and I was really intimidated to meet Mark when I first met him. To be acting with him, I was like, 'Am I up to it? Can I possibly hold up my end of the bargain here?' It was great because he just had that snarly...and Candy wasn't afraid of him. We all became good friends, and I remember when I called him about Swack passing away, he was just very sad. Then I remember when he passed away, I was very sad."

In time Hanley became so confident about her role on the show, "I think I got a little haughty," she laughs. "I think there were like two shows in a row that I wasn't doing much. I just felt like, 'Why?' you know, 'What am I doing?' So I was being selfish — you know, you get kind of used to...so I kind of went on the warpath. Made me feel great but it didn't change anything. And it wasn't wanting to be number one. It was watching everybody else; you want to get in there and do your thing, too. It's not about competition — it wasn't competitive. It was just longing because it was a great story, and I just wanted to have something. So I went knocking on Bob Claver's door. I said, 'WHAT'S HAPPENING TO MY CANDY CHARACTER?' He said, 'Well, come on. Sit down and we'll talk.' And we talked a bit. I just had to get it off my chest. Then I was fine. Yeah, the profession isn't all about being able to perform — there's a lot of insecurity that's behind all that performing. That was the only time, I think, that — I don't know — that I just wasn't happy as a clam. I was selfish and wanted to be in every single one, and I was. But sometimes it was just kind of like show up and go home."

Of the fifty-two *HCTB* episodes produced, there was only one which she did not like. It aired during the first season. "I think I tried to fix those things," laughs the actress, "you can only do so much with attitude, because you have to kind of go... 'Well, they've approved the story,' but I must say that on the whole, I couldn't have been more thrilled with what I got to do, and the various circumstances that they came up with. We had a lot of fun."

"We enjoyed the fact that it was what it was," she continues. "I think we were lucky because there was an incredible chemistry. With all of us, and I'm not sure, and I've guested on enough series to know that it doesn't happen everywhere, you can kind of feel it. Also, a lot of it, it's what you allow to come in and put out, too. It was an old-fashioned show, but I think there was something kind of lovely about that. There was this wonderful group of people from everybody from the top on down to the stand-ins, Joanie Blondell had her original stand-in, Irene, and Dottie Hayes was our body makeup person, and she had worked with Joan for a long, long time, and Dottie gave me — when Swack and I got married — she gave me an antique tablecloth and napkins that had been a wedding gift to her, and we just, these people were just charming, and I know it sounds really silly, but there wasn't a sour apple in the barrel.

"It just felt like being part of old history," reflects the actress, "and I'm sure it doesn't feel so much like that anymore. I know that none of the studios now really feel that way. But then, just the history and the pomp. The wardrobe ladies…you stood on these kind of velvet raised circles and three-quarter…all these mirrors, and they just took such pains with fittings and things, everybody was an artist. Not that they aren't now. Boy, I think that the makeup people and wardrobe, all of those people are like THE HEROES, and still to this day, I mean, they're the ones you see first thing in the morning and the last thing at night, and they can make or break you. And I would say I have never felt so blessed as to have been surrounded with really, really…I mean they are artists, and my makeup man, Carl Silvera, and Perc Westmore was teaching me how to bead my eyelashes, like they did in the old-fashioned days, and I mean, all of these makeup people, the Westmores, and they go on and on. Those were the ones that were teaching me! And I was just… and they were so skilled, and so willing to share. And wardrobe — Betsy Cox, I know that there are probably a lot of people like Betsy Cox, but she was MY Betsy Cox. Betsy Cox was just the best. She did a lot of my husband's shows too; he just adored her. It was all part of Screen Gems, and I'm sure he was thrilled and delighted —

she probably wanted to do the show, and he really wanted her. She was living on a boat for a long time, and now she's moved to Florida. And we kept saying, 'We must get together.' I mean, all of us have our own memories, and our own special people. I just feel blessed, really lucky, and I cherish the times. I cherish all the memories that I can still remember, even the ones I don't."

Like many, Bridget Hanley enjoyed the *Brides* music. "Hugo Montenegro was so fabulous!" raves the actress. "I think I met him only once. His music — it added so much — I had a recording of some of the music, just playing it, when I was learning lines, it just added so much to the preparation time. I didn't have a tape of the theme song, and there was something called 'Candy's Theme' and I never had a chance to meet him and ask him if that was Candy's, but I chose to believe that it was. Perry Como made the theme song a smash hit."

During the run of the series, "they added to the set," remembers Hanley. "The church was part of the ranch, so they decided to shoot there, the bar was also there, but the dormitory was new. They left that until the show was sold, and when it sold, they built the dormitory. And now it's not there anymore."

As was the case with other series of the time, *Brides* was a collaborative effort, as noted earlier. "We had a lot of great writers," praises Hanley. "Then we had a reading at the table. We used to do that for a lot of the first season. We had a chance to talk about what we felt about each show, our take on it, and that changed some of the episodes. So we all worked together. Until I don't know if it was Bob Claver who said, 'No more table readings!' because everybody was saying, 'Well, I would like…' and 'What about?…' By then we pretty much knew who our characters were so we'd just come in with it."

*Bridget Hanley as Candy Pruitt in two separate* Brides *outfits.*

PHOTOS COURTESY BRIDGET HANLEY

When it came to which season she preferred, Bridget Hanley liked both. "The first season was rain and mud, and everybody went by foot except for the occasional horse, or the occasional wagon," notes the actress. "It just looked like tough sledding, so to speak. Living conditions weren't the finest, and we were trying our best to be dainty and fabulous in the mud. It was great fun. Bringing the kids in the next year — I liked that part of the second season. And I got to name Patti Cohoon 'Molly.' The only thing I missed was they didn't muddy the streets as much — they went more to horses, and a couple of guns. And every time I was put on a horse, it pooped. It was an absolute embarrassment; Freddie Jackman would always make comments. There was more use of the Angeles Forest too, and we went up to the top of Coldwater Canyon. The third season we were actually gonna go to Seattle and shoot the exteriors — a lot of exteriors but we never got a chance. So Angeles National Forest was our location. Plus they used a lot of the berm and the lagoon and the ranch. They were so good about creating that illusion."

Because it was a Screen Gems series, the cast of *Here Come the Brides* found themselves involved in the studio's press tour in Mexico (marking the 1968 Olympic Games), prior to the series' September 25, 1968 premiere. "It was our first press tour," explains Hanley. "It may have been a Screen Gems tour for all the series. We had the best time — it was really fun. It was more like play than work — but we worked hard with all the press. I remember a lot of us from all the different series all having a great time. I think there were people from elsewhere, too; I don't know if it was typical. We went to Mexico City and we met with the press and did all kinds of gatherings and dinners and things like that."

During the tour, the group attended bullfights, and at one point, Bridget Hanley decided to get in the ring. "I probably volunteered," she laughs. "I'm sure, if it was Candy, she volunteered. Bridget may have been a little reticent. So I was in this kind of knicker pants and a shirt and everything, and they put me out in the middle of the ring, and then they let in a baby bull. The baby bull looked just like a big one. Well, I tried to be brave for about three minutes, then I turned around and ran like hell. And I outran the baby bull. I leaped…I was kind of suspended on the fence. They took a picture of that; I think the picture shows me beginning my run. And everybody…I don't know if they were proud of me, or embarrassed."

The Mexico trip was just the beginning for Bridget Hanley when it came to publicity for *Here Come the Brides*. "I went around the country," says the actress. "I remember when I went on the first promotional tour for *Here Come the Brides,* they had me throw footballs with 'Crazylegs' Hirsh, who played for my uncle. He was excited about it, and so was I. He was pretty damn impressed with how I threw the football."

The men on *Brides* were very impressed when Hanley kicked the football. She kicked it so hard it landed on the stage roof. "I think we just…the football came out and the guys were playing, and I said, 'Lemme join,'" she remembers. "I think they were so surprised when I did that, they didn't say much. I remember I had a pink dress on, too. We used to throw the football back and forth, every once in a while. It wasn't a regular event, as far as I recall, or I probably would still have bruises."

Being a lover of sports and very athletic, Bridget Hanley enjoyed doing her own stunts. "One time, they had me drive a double-team wagon," recalls the actress. "They forgot to bring in my stunt double that day, so I said, 'I can do this.' So they, you know, cuz I was not a scrawny little wimp. They let me do it, and the horses, in this particular path we had to go around, would kind of see the camera, and would kind of freak. So, we had to do it several times, and on, I think about the third or fourth time around, they started to freak again, and I tried to put on — there was a brake in the wagon, and I put the brake on as hard as I could, but they…the horses took off, and I tried to rein them in and couldn't, and the reins snapped. I was thrown right out of the wagon onto my head, and Dave Cass, who was Robert Brown's stunt double, pulled me away from the wagon before the back wheel went over me. I always say, aside from Dave Cass, all the second-year hairpieces that were piled on top of my hair saved my life. And, of course, they called my husband who was in the Screen Gems studio on Gower. He came out; there was a knock on my dressing room door and I opened it. He was standing there. He said, 'DON'T YOU EVER DO THAT AGAIN! YOU WAIT FOR YOUR STUNT DOUBLE TO GET THERE!' I said, 'Yes, sir.' So, they never asked me to do that again because I probably would have. You know, some people are really trained and capable. I just figured — I was strong — I mean, I could ride a horse. I didn't know why I couldn't drive the wagon — I just didn't realize that the horses would spook and take off like that."

Since Bridget Hanley was from Seattle, there were times she participated in Seattle-based events. "I was brought up to throw out the first pitch for the Seattle Pilots baseball team," she remembers. "There was a big story about me being on the plane with all the guys; a lot of the wives weren't pleased that I was on the plane with their guys, and they didn't laugh very long either. But it was so exciting to be asked to come home to do that. The Seattle Pilots were…their future was not sunny."

*Leading lady Hanley at an autograph session for WUSN-TV.* COURTESY BRIDGET HANLEY

'Sunny' was a good way to describe the reaction and press given *Here Come the Brides.* Recalls Hanley, "Once *Brides* hit and we were doing well, our press people — Betty Goodey was one of them, and Harry Flynn — oh, God, they were wonderful — they were just the best press people, and just like best friends, because they treated us so nicely, well, they were called a lot. Especially by the teen magazines; Candy and Jeremy were like the new kids on the block."

The teen magazine, *Tiger Beat*, was very active in covering *Brides.* "A lot of times they would contact the studio," says the actress, "and then, I'm sure…I never spent much time…Betty Goodey or Harry Flynn, one of them was usually around until we kind of got to know a lot of the people at *Tiger Beat*, so we were not left in the mouth of the 'Tiger.' I guess we were really hot with the younger crowd. I mean, Bobby was a heartthrob, and I guess I was half a throb. So there was a lot of jealousy from the young ladies, but then there were a lot of young men, too, and I am hearing from a lot of them now. They are in their forties and beyond, and talk about how they just loved Candy. It's just very sweet. Not the power one feels, but the joy, the absolute joy that I feel — that a show that I loved so much, that we were not just alone in that. That, and when the fans started to riot on street corners across the country when we were canceled. That was before most people had color TVs."

Because *Here Come the Brides* brought her into contact with so many young people, and because she so loved working in the series, Bridget Hanley was more than happy to do publicity for the show. "There weren't that many talk shows, and it was really kind of new territory, publicity-wise," states the actress. "So a lot of it was through magazines and in-person press junkets. It was fun for us, and it was kind of a more level playing ground, so to speak. We were all having a good time and were relaxed. We weren't rushing on a lunch hour or something. It was quite a wonderful happening, and I was just so pleased to be part of it. It wasn't such a huge community. It was more one on one meetings, rather than, like now, the Internet and the computer; it's just much more streamlined now, and less personal."

Among the questions often asked of Hanley — how did she do her hair? "It was a big deal with my hair," she laughs. "All the girls — they all wanted to have a 'Candy-do.' The guys liked the hair, too. I did a photo layout of the hair." Hanley definitely had her male admirers. "There was this kid that wrote," remembers the actress, "and he told me they used to play 'Horse,' the basketball game. Whoever won, whoever spelled 'Horse' first would get to kiss Candy. They got to pretend that they kissed Candy. Then there was a litter of pigs named after me...there were one or two high points like that."

Like Robert Brown, Joan Blondell and *Brides* co-stars Mark Lenard and Susan Tolsky, Hanley was profiled in *TV Guide* during the run of the series. "I was very excited," she remembers, "because I had just moved into a new apartment. Earlier, in the time between the pilot and when we sold it, I'd found this wonderful place in Beverly Hills. It was like a two-story...it was a duplex. I spent all my time and money fixing this place up, and then I found out why they let me have it for $200 a month because they were gonna sell it. So they sold it, and I found this other place — great little apartment, but I had not been in there any too long, and I had hardly any furniture. Well, I decided that I would cook dinner and that we would have a nice homey time with the *TV Guide* for my interview. The fella came, and he was so sweet and everything and very nice, and asking me questions. I thought, 'He's gonna ask me how old I am,' because that had happened other times. So, I planned to take two years off my age. And, when he asked, 'What year were you born?' instead of taking off two years, I gave him two years on. And I didn't realize until we were almost through — we had this long, long, long interview, and he said, 'Well now that you're X years old...' I went, 'WHAT?' He said, 'Well you were born in nineteen-whatever, whatever. I said, 'I lied. I was trying to take two years off, and I put two years on. Please print it.' But he never did. See, at that time, people were particularly age conscious. So, adding two more years to my actual age, I thought it would be hysterical. Anyway, I cooked dinner. I got my recipe for this chicken dish from my hairdresser, Joyce, I got my salad recipe from my makeup guy, Carl, and I built a fire, which I had never done before, and the smoke was coming out into my room. So it was a memorable evening; it christened my new place."

By the time the 'TV Guide' article was published, "Swack and I were living in a house on Haskell Avenue and Encino," says Hanley. "We walked up to the market to get some groceries, and he discovered that the issue was out. So he bought like fifteen copies, and he said, really loud, 'HEY!' and I had no makeup on, and my hair was a mess. He said, 'HEY! YOU KNOW WHO'S RIGHT HERE! SHE'S RIGHT IN HERE!' I mean, there was no way I could get out of that market fast enough! It was just mortifying! But he did buy fifteen copies."

*Two slightly different 'Candy-dos.'*

PHOTOS COURTESY BRIDGET HANLEY

While *Here Come the Brides* only lasted two seasons, Bridget Hanley continued (and continues) to encounter situations where it's clear people remember the show. "Years later, I was living in Encino," says the actress, "and I went down to the tea shop to get some birthday cards or some gift or something. This woman kept looking at me and I thought... I didn't say anything. She says, 'Excuse me. Aren't you an actress?' I said, 'Oh. On better days!' Because my hair was all bushy; I had a baseball cap on; I had no makeup on, I was just in my neighborhood, and I was trying to get in, get out, and go. Then she came up to me when I was at the checkout and she was right behind me. She said, 'You know. I know I've seen you on a lot of different shows and I think a series, but I don't think I ever saw you on *Better Days*.' She thought it was a soap opera. I told that on several talk shows. She just was so riddled — the whole time. I said, 'No, no, no. I'm talking about the way I look. I am mortified about the way I look.' Then, she was mortified."

"But it's very sweet," says Hanley. "People are very sweet. They will come up to me in the supermarket and start talking to me as if they knew me. Although now people come up and say that they just saw something that I did in the theater. That thrills me! But it thrills me if people have seen something that I was really proud of. Like *Here Come the Brides*. Still, a lot of times, there would be the thing about, 'How much money do you make?' And that's usually from younger kids. And now it's like,

'Didn't you used to be somebody?' I remember Susan Tolsky said to me one day [in a perfect imitation of Tolsky], 'Oh, Candy! It's just exhausting being a has-been!'"

"But we still get fan mail saying how much it meant to everybody growing up," notes Hanley, "and how much it has helped them with their children. And now I get e-mails from their kids."

Forty years after *Brides'* original run, Bridget Hanley continues to be invited to Seattle and Washington state functions. "Seattle was just thrilled when the show came out," remembers the actress. "They just really love the fact that there was a series about Seattle. And in 2007, I was the Grand Marshal for the Fourth of July parade [in nearby Edmonds, Washington]."

Like other series of the 1960s, there is a great deal of innocence one can find in *Here Come the Brides.* "I was never brought into the court of Standards and Practices," says Hanley. "I never wore anything suggestive. Usually you were brought in if you said bad words, and we didn't. We weren't allowed to, so, they didn't visit us that much." Following *Brides'* cancellation, Hanley did take on earthier roles — like a sex-education teacher on *Love, American Style.*

Yet once she became pregnant with her first daughter, Bronwyn, Hanley temporarily retired from acting. "I didn't get pregnant, even though heaven knows I tried the whole second year of *Brides,*" states the actress. "My doctor said, 'Will you just stop worrying about it? When it's the right time, you'll be pregnant.' And it was the right time. My agent didn't think so. He said, 'There goes your career.' I said, 'You know what? The career can always go, but this…' I patted my stomach, 'this child will always be here, and part of my heart. And that's the truth, and now I have two. So I didn't really care. And, yes, it did impact my career. But, SO WHAT! Life has to go on, too. Listen, there were disappointments, but then I look…right next to me were my two little girls who needed something, and the disappointments…you didn't have time to spend drowning in sorrows about losing a part. I mean, I've been very fortunate — I don't feel deprived. I feel enlarged, actually, because of the life I've had, other than just being on a set from 5 a.m. till ten. That's a lot of fun. No dishes and laundry there."

The birth of Bridget Hanley's first daughter was about as dramatic as the actress's own birth. "I went to Arizona, when Swack was shooting *Man and Boy,* which was Bill Cosby's first feature," remembers Hanley. "I was there for quite a while, doing my deep-breathing, my natural childbirth exercises, and getting as big as a house. Then the doctor insisted that I get home by a certain date — it ended up being the very night before the big earthquake. One of the crew people…Bob Rosenbaum's wife had called the set, or motel, or wherever they were staying, she ended up getting through, which was very unusual, and then Swack was actually able to get through to me. I didn't know who it was; I was such a wreck. I said, 'Who's calling?' 'Bridget!' Swack says, 'This is your husband!' It was just an absolutely frightening experience — I thought Bronwyn was gonna come right out my nostril."

Doing around one television guest shot a year until her two daughters Bronwyn and Megan were much older, Bridget Hanley returned to series television in the 1981-82 situation comedy, *Harper Valley, P.T.A.* Following the cancellation of that series, the actress did a few guest shots on *Simon & Simon*. "I did three *Simon & Simon*s," states Hanley. "I was one of the first women to get my lights punched out; I slid down a wall…I had great roles every time — it was so fun." Hanley also auditioned for the mid-80s series, *Trial by Jury*, and its producer, *American Bandstand* host Dick Clark, "I was, 'Want to see me dance?'" laughs the actress. "But I didn't. Raymond Burr hosted it, and Joe Campanella, and a bunch of us were lawyers, we'd learn a new face every day. I did that show because my daddy had just passed away with Alzheimer's and I wanted to prove that I wasn't getting it. Talk about mind work, instead of leg work, that was unbelievable, but it was fun; we all had a good time."

Like other family members who've dealt with Alzheimer's, Bridget Hanley was shocked by the suddenly bizarre behavior of her father. "It was very odd behavior," remembers the actress, "Very scary. I never knew whether my dad was locked in. Or we were locked out. Then I went through the same thing with my mom. Hers was stroke-induced dementia. I was with her when she passed away: I sang to her at that time. That was an amazing thing — to have that with both parents."

Though her husband was a very active television director, Bridget Hanley "never ever worked for Swack unless I could read for the part. I remember there was a pilot that I did; I didn't want anybody to know that I was married to the director. And this one guy was hitting on me in the airplane going up there, then somebody, when we got up there, told him that I was married to the director. That ended that. Well, I went in for wardrobe. The lady said, 'Boy, you're lucky to get this part.' I said, 'Oh, yeah?' She says, 'Yeah. A lot of other people were up for the part. I'm so glad you got it.' I said, 'Like who?' She said, 'Well, the director wanted his wife…' And I drew myself up to my full height in my high heels, and I said, 'I AM THE DIRECTOR'S WIFE!' She just melted like the Wicked Witch of the West. And, during the whole shoot, there wasn't anything she wouldn't do, you know, she'd say, 'Do you want coffee? Do you…' I said, 'Oh, please. Just stop!' But I remember when I first walked on the set, Freddie Jackman from *Brides* was the cinematographer. He said, 'Well, I see Mrs. Swackhamer is late on the set.' So, by then, my whole cover was blown."

Depressed (like so many others in her profession) by what was happening in television in the early '90s, Bridget Hanley then turned her attention to stage work. As a result, she frequently ran into actors with whom she'd worked on television. Like Anthony Zerbe. "I loved Anthony Zerbe!" glows Hanley. "He's a completely skilled actor. Every time I see him, he's good. He was just terrific. When I was doing my James Dickey stuff, we'd show up at the same time — he and Roscoe Lee Browne. And Anthony Zerbe hit me on camera. We were doing a scene where we were married, and he just hauled off and belted me. I knew he had to do it in the long shot, but I didn't think he was gonna slug me in the close-up. I think it was probably one of my better scenes."

It was when she began working in theater that Hanley formed her close friendship with Lee Meriwether. That friendship continues to this day. "We have a great time together," says Hanley, "but I didn't meet her right away. Cuz Lee was off with the circus. She joined a circus and was gone for quite awhile. Then I was gonna read for a female version of *The Odd Couple* to be done with her, but I didn't want to do the part that they offered." Eventually the two got together for *Play it Again, Sam* with Frank Gorshin in Long Island. "Oh, [Lee] is just amazing," raves Hanley. "And she sings. She's terrific. She did one of the national tours of *Nunsense* with Kaye Ballard and Mimi Hines, Georgia Engel, and Darla Love. Lee and I are very close friends."[1]

"We have a lot of good times together," agrees Meriwether. "I love working with Bridget. It's a wonderful experience — it really is, and always stimulating and fun. Bridget is so enthusiastic. Her energy is amazing. She is an instinctive actress, and just brings to the table so much wonderful insight. She does a lot of homework, and is always prepared. It's really wonderful, just terrific. She works very hard and comes up with marvelous ideas."[2]

Besides Lee Meriwether, longtime friend Robert Brown and guest stars Marvin Silbersher and Kristina Holland, Bridget Hanley frequently sees *Brides* series regular Susan Tolsky and story editor William Blinn. "When you do a series, you always say, 'We'll never lose touch,'" notes the actress, "but then you get on to another round of guest things, or plays, and you're into your next family. All of us have so many damn families, there's no way in the world that one could have enough time to spend with everyone that you'd really like to. But I knew Robert before *Brides* and Susan is always really honest. When she's your friend, you know she's your friend. She calls my daughters her 'babies.' Mark Lenard the girls knew when they were little, and Bill and Annalie Blinn…I remember Bill and Annalie walking onto the set of *Brides* and they had [their son] Christopher in one of the little carriers. Bill is one of the funniest, driest…he is just fabulous. And Patti Cohoon…well, now, she and her husband make movies."

"I thought all the children that did our show were just very talented," continues the actress. "It was fun. They were sweet kids and they loved to be part of it — everybody seemed to have a good time. Guest stars always loved to do our show. It was an old-fashioned show, and I'm sure it was kind of different for them. A lot of the guest stars were just so excited to do it because, one, we had so much fun and, two, we were shooting out at the ranch. So it was just like being on holiday. It was great. There was only one guest star who shall remain nameless, who said that they never felt tended to or appreciated, and we were in absolute shock. Because we always…a lot of times we'd all have lunch together, some people we felt were more approachable than others, and sometimes I was in awe of the guest stars. Mostly we all got together and had a great time. But this guest star — he said he never had had a worse time, that nobody was friendly, and this and that and the other thing, and I was just mortified, because we were all having a great time and thought he was, too."

Like her friend Robert Brown, Hanley wasn't always on the set. "A lot of times when the guest women were in, I wasn't there," says the actress. "I don't remember having problems with any of them or any of our male guest stars. I would remember if I had not liked them. There were a couple of people here and there — directors, that I walked around. But we had a great time. If we had done one more year, I think we would have been on for quite a few years. Maybe like *Bonanza*, but I don't know if we would have focused on the guest characters as much. After a while you do that because the regulars probably want a rest. We never wanted a rest. We just wanted to be in there doing it."[3]

1. Hanley – 2007, 2008
2. Lee Meriwether – telephone interview – 2008
3. Hanley – 2007

"What this town needs is women. Help the town grow. Be good for business."

Aaron Stempel to the people of Seattle
in Episode #1 ("Here Come the Brides")

# Chapter 9

# *Co-starring Mark Lenard*

"Somebody once asked me, how do you play the role?" related *Planet of the Apes* 'heavy' Mark Lenard to writer Chris Claremont in a 1974 issue of the *Planet of the Apes* magazine. "And I said — and it's what I feel about this role too — that I look at it from the point of the character, that nobody does evil just for the sake of doing evil, or very few rational, sane people do. They do it because they need something, they want something, he's rough and so forth, depending on what stories they come up with, but he believes he is right.

"Nobody does evil for the sake of doing evil, they do it because they need something, they want something, they believe in something.

"Urko is the same."[1]

'Urko' was the 'ape' character Mark Lenard portrayed on the September 13 — December 27, 1974 CBS series, *Planet of the Apes*. But Lenard could just as easily have been talking about the many villains he'd played on such series as *Mission: Impossible, The Wild Wild West, It Takes a Thief, The Felony Squad, Hawaii Five-O*. He could have been talking about every episode of executive producer Quinn Martin's two biggest hits, *The F.B.I.* (1965-74) and *Barnaby Jones* (1973-80). On both of those series, the criminal characters were regularly presented in a very sympathetic, compassionate light.

Lenard could also have been talking about recurring TV villains like Barry Morse's Lt. Philip Gerard on QM's 1963-67 series, *The Fugitive* and Eric Braeden's Captain Hauptmann Dietrich on the 1966-68 WWII drama, *The Rat Patrol*. While there was certainly dimension and depth in Gerard and Dietrich, the admirable and likable qualities of these two villains was something that evolved over the course of both series.

In *Here Come the Brides*, these qualities were in the Aaron Stempel character from the very beginning. After all, had it not been for Lenard's Stempel, the Bolt brothers never could have made the trip to New Bedford, where they found the one hundred "marriageable" brides. Even more importantly, since Aaron Stempel owned the sawmill, and the brothers Bolt ran a logging operation, since all four men lived in the same community, the Bolts worked together with their nemesis quite frequently, and often reached a compromise. Lenard's view of his *Brides* character fit perfectly within the series narrative. "I never considered myself a heavy," the actor told *TV Guide's* Leslie Raddatz. "I consider myself a lead in a series, and I try to give the character dimension."[2]

Says *Brides* story editor/episode writer William Blinn, "Mark understood that he was the 'villain' or 'antagonist' in the piece, but he never had any complaints. He was very well served, because there were times where he had a lot to do; in a lot of episodes, he wasn't just the villain. I think Mark realized, 'Well, okay, I've got more colors here than I might have,' [because] there were times when he said, 'I like this.' He was very aware of the fact that the Stempel character had more colors than a lot of characters like that sometimes did."[3]

"Mark was just wonderful in that part," adds *Brides* executive producer Bob Claver. "He did ultimately use that [the colors]. Mark was a very serious actor. He prepared a lot, and he had lots of questions, but he was just an actor doing his job."[4] "Mark made mar-

*Mark Lenard looking properly villainous.*

velous choices," enthuses "After a Dream Comes Mourning" guest Marvin Silbersher. "He and Swack combined to make a wonderful character out of Aaron Stempel."[5]

Yet, like *Brides* series star David Soul, Mark Lenard hadn't planned on becoming an actor. Born Leonard Rosenson in Chicago, Illinois on October 15, 1924, Lenard's original goal was to be a writer. Ann Lenard, the actor's widow, recalled in a June 1, 1997 interview in *Myeloma Today*, the bi-monthly magazine published by the International Myeloma Foundation: "Mark's parents ran a resort and had sent him to school at the tender age of four. He graduated from high school at age sixteen and wanted to enter the Foreign Service. Mark wound up going off to fight World War II. When he came back, he wanted to be an author and moved to New York to write. Oddly enough, a friend was producing a play about James Joyce [*The Exiles*] and wanted a writer to play the lead. Mark gave it a try and found his calling."[6]

Written by Joyce in 1914, following the completion of his *A Portrait of the Artist as a Young Man* and just before he began writing *Ulysses*, *The Exiles* took place in the Dublin of 1912. The plot revolved around the character Richard Rowan (based on

Joyce himself), and whether he should stay in Ireland and try to Europeanize Ireland by teaching Romance Languages, or leave the country, as Joyce himself did. Throughout the play, Rowan voices his fears that if he stays in Ireland, he will become paralyzed and bitter. The ending of the play never answers the question concerning the character's final decision.

Following *The Exiles*, Mark Lenard did multi-character plays like *The Hasty Heart* and multi-character, multi-story plays like *My Mother, My Father and Me*. The former (written by John Patrick, and based on his WWII experiences as an American Field Service volunteer serving with Montgomery's Eighth Army in Egypt) told the story of four wounded soldiers — one American, another British, a third an Australian, a fourth African, who rally around a less-than-pleasant Scotsman when they learn the man is dying. As for Lillian Hellman's *My Mother, My Father and Me*, cracked *Time* magazine in their review, "in this emetic comedy, Playwright Hellman retches over psychoanalysts, alcoholics, beatniks, sentimental Negrophiles, romanticizers of the American Indian, epicene writers, slick shysters who run homes for the aged, the eel-spined younger generation, the middle-aged materialistic middle class, the hot-and-cold war-babied economy, the affluent society, and — horror of horrors — store-bought bread. This catalogue of latter-day evils presumably calls for the wrath of Jeremiah."[7]

"Catalogue" was a good description for the many characters regularly seen throughout the run of *Here Come the Brides*. Not to mention the many storylines that ran in so many episodes. Given director Robert Butler's point that a television series' writers always move towards the strengths of their leads and regular characters, Mark Lenard fans could well have made a case that when it came to the show's plotlines, the background of the series' antagonist was as much as a key factor in determining the plotlines as was that of the series' star, Robert Brown.

Particularly when one considered such Mark Lenard stage credits as Henry Denker's *A Far Country* concerning Sigmund Freud's first critical case of psychoanalysis, (the play, in which Lenard played Freud in the touring company, was one of the actor's personal favorites), Carson McCullers' bittersweet *The Square Root of Wonderful*, Henrik Ibsen's *Little Eyolf, Rosmersholm*, and *Hedda Gabler*, plus Herman Melville's ambiguous *Benito Cereno*, Paddy Chayefsky's serio-comedy, *Gideon*, Anton Chekhov's comedy, *Country Scandal*, John Whiting's *The Devils* (based on the nonfiction book *The Devils of Loudun* by Aldous Huxley), even William Shakespeare's *Measure for Measure*.

The latter, according to critic Frederick S. Boas, was one of William Shakespeare's "problem plays." A problem play (a term coined by Boas in his 1896 work, *Shakespeare and his Predecessors*) was a type of drama frequently associated with Henrik Ibsen. The "problem plays," stated Boas, "introduce us into highly artificial societies whose civilization is ripe unto rottenness. At the close our feeling is neither simple joy nor pain; we are excited, fascinated, perplexed, for the issues raised preclude a completely satisfactory outcome."

Mark Lenard having done a good bit of work in the problem play arena, it should have come as no surprise that when *Brides* moved into a more serious (and at times, ambiguous) tone in its second season, the Aaron Stempel character became far more prominent in the stories. Of course, Lenard's work relationship (and friendship) with series star Robert Brown had something to do with the character's greater exposure. "We're both stage people," Brown told *TV Guide*, "we've even played some of the same roles."[8]

"Mark Lenard was a good man," Brown says. "He was just a nice gentleman, not a show business guy, quiet, not fame-bent. He wasn't glib. I could communicate with him a little more easily than I could with others. He was about the same age, and had a dry wit. I saw him after [the series' cancellation] socially. We went to see each other. Which most of us didn't do.

"We'd see each other from time to time in the evening," continues Brown. "He lived not far from Carroll O'Connor's house — the top of Sunset before you go down to the ocean — the Palisades; I would see Mark there, and I would see him in New York. I used to do narration and voice-overs for years [the IAMS commercials], and he did that, too. We made a living doing that, a good living."[9] "Mark became the spokesman for SAAB," Ann Lenard told *Myeloma Today*, "and most of those commercials were taped in New York. So, we got to spend several months a year in New York. Mark never wanted to leave New York. He wanted to be a Broadway actor."[10]

"Mark Lenard was one of my actors at CBS," explains Marvin Silbersher. "He must have worked for me thirty times before I went to do *Brides* with Swack. He was a wonderful actor, a marvelous actor who never got the occasion to show all the sides that he could do. I mean, he could play anything."[11] "Mark Lenard was a wonderful actor," agrees *HCTB* semi-regular Dick Balduzzi. "His preference was stage — he was a New York actor, so he brought a lot to the show. He didn't play a 'heavy' like some people play a 'heavy,' [case in point, Eddie Firestone, and his fellow trappers in the second season's "Hosanna's Way"] so there was more of a challenge, of wit, of words, with the two of them [Lenard and Brown]. They both being professional stage actors — that added to the characters."[12]

Especially when it came to the "talk-overs." The talk-overs, which quickly became an *HCTB* tradition, (Bridget Hanley and Henry Beckman were excellent at those) were those scenes where two or more characters were talking (usually very loudly) at the same time. Two of the best Jason Bolt-Aaron Stempel talk-overs came in "Democracy Inaction," and the episode that followed — "One Good Lie Deserves Another."

"I think there was a challenge there, too," muses Balduzzi. "When stage actors work in that direction, there's always a challenge. They know how to work against each other, which was good. Talking at the same time as the other person — I think that's stage experience. You learn that on stage."[13]

"Subtext," which Constantin Stanislavski, developer of the "Acting Method," saw in the works of playwright Anton Chekov, was another thing an actor learned on stage. "Chekhov often expressed his thought not in speeches," wrote Stanislavski, "but in pauses or between the lines or in replies consisting of a single word...the characters often feel and think things not expressed in the lines they speak"[14] "It was Chekhov who first deliberately wrote dialogue in which the mainstream of emotional action ran underneath the surface," wrote Martin Esslin. "It was he who articulated the notion that human beings hardly ever speak in explicit terms among each other about their deepest emotions, that the great, tragic, climactic moments are often happening beneath outwardly trivial conversation."[15] Since Lenard had done plays by Anton Chekov, and had studied the Stanislavski method (as did all actors), he was quite skilled in communicating unspoken information to the audience.

Maybe because, as *TV Guide's* Leslie Raddatz pointed out, Lenard was an "introvert who buries himself in the part he plays."[16] "You watched him because he did very little," says *Brides* regular Susan Tolsky. "He stood out when he was on camera — he was deliberate. What he did was meaningful and you could learn from him. He never flailed — his acting was never all over the screen — it was very quiet; that's why you watched him. He had that dimension — it's Stempel, you know."[17]

"Mark Lenard was never remote or cold," adds William Blinn. "He was a very accomplished stage actor, I recall seeing him off Broadway when I was a student in New York, and he was…he stayed within himself. He had a good time, he was always pleasant to work with and flexible at a whole bunch of things, but he was one of those guys who showed up, knew the words, [and then] went to his dressing room… He chatted amiably with everybody, he was certainly nice to be around, but he did not wear his heart on his sleeve. Robert was more that way."[18]

"Mark did a lot of theater and he was a very good actor," agrees *Brides'* executive casting director Renee Valente. "I think he did his job. He did whatever he had to, and he did it very well. He was very happy to be a part of *Here Come the Brides*, but he didn't become one of the group."[19] Mark was a nice guy," remembers *Brides* wardrobe man Steve Lodge. "He always played nasty, sleazy guys, but in real life, he was a real nice gentleman. I remember one time [*Brides* semi-regular] Hoke Howell and I and [*Brides* guest star] Rance Howard, and two or three other people, decided we were gonna put together a movie company and make a movie. Mark came to our first meeting — he was very interested in that, so we got to know him a little better. He called me one time, said, 'Could I meet him in Beverly Hills?' I met him. We had lunch together and chit-chatted a little bit about whether this was really gonna happen, or whether it wasn't. All I could tell him was I wanted it to happen. Never did. But, now that you think of it, it was kind of like Stempel. He was like, 'Sounds to me like you got a deal goin' there. Maybe I should get in on this.'"[20]

"Mark Lenard was great," chuckles Robert Brown's stunt-double (and *Brides* guest), Dave Cass. "He was easy to work with. He was the perfect guy to play the nemesis of the Bolt brothers. But he came in, did his job, and left."[21] "I don't think he was so much of a joiner," muses Valente. "He was more established in the acting field at that time. As was Robert. He and Robert — their backgrounds were similar — they both came from the theater. And, out of that came the change in the show. So, I think the kids [Bobby Sherman, Bridget Hanley, David Soul, Susan Tolsky] were over there, Joan Blondell was there, and Mark and Robert were over there."[22]

Yet despite the age and career differences between Lenard and the "kids," Susan Tolsky found the introverted Lenard very accessible. "Mark was more sedate," says the actress. "He wasn't officious. He wasn't standoffish. He was very welcoming. I mean, you would look at him, and at first, you might be a little intimidated, then he would say something and you'd just be on the floor. So Mark I always felt I could play around with, he hung with the guys too, but he wasn't like a goofball. He wasn't like Henry, because Henry was a goofball. Mark wasn't the type you'd go up to and say, 'Hey, let's go bowling on our lunch hour.' With Mark, I just wanted to sit with him and talk about a crossword puzzle. He was a kind of quiet

*Mark Lenard as Aaron Stempel.*

intellectual that you would sit and chat with. He was extremely bright, an extraordinarily bright man."[23]

Educated as a child in a one-room country school house in South Haven, Michigan, to which his family moved from his native Chicago, Mark Lenard certainly was bright. In his Pacific Palisades home, he converted the garage into a study. There he read Shakespeare, archeology and anthropology, and wrote and painted. According to Lenard, the turning point in his education came in the sixth grade. "We got a new teacher," the actor told *TV Guide's* Raddatz. "She became interested in me and got me interested in reading. I read Shakespeare and *The Book of Knowledge* from cover to cover. I changed. From then on, I opened up — I felt I had something." [24]

Written by 9th Century Islamic scholar Ali ibn al-Madini, *The Book of Knowledge* (about the Companions) concerned Ilm ar-Rijal, "the science of people." Because this science was first applied to the prophet Muhammad, Muslims were quite insistent on accurate biographies. Character biographies and 'life-stories' being crucial tools for an actor when creating a character, through his reading of *The Book of Knowledge*, Mark Lenard was very well equipped to bring great dimension, depth, and introspection to the parts he played. Making him an even more interesting performer was the way he used humility and pride. "'When I'm in the city, I think of myself as a small-town boy,'" he told Raddatz. "'When I'm in a small town, I think of myself as a city boy.'"[25]

His fellow performer Susan Tolsky sensed that. "He was the epitome of old-school gentleman," notes the actress. "He had a very regal appearance, projected that old-time gentleman so well, but he was such a dear, dear man. There's not a bad thing I could say about Mark."[26] Adds Steve Lodge: "All the clothes that he wore, those 'Prince Albert' suits — they were all Dale Robertson's from that train show he had done [the 1966-68 Screen Gem series, *Iron Horse*]. They just re-fitted 'em on Mark."[27]

Mark Lenard was quite flexible when it came to the parts he played in movies and television. Besides portraying a Romulan and a Vulcan on the original 1966-69 series *Star Trek*, the actor was seen as assistant district attorneys on the critically acclaimed Herbert Brodkin series, *The Defenders* and *The Nurses*; a casino operator in the Farrah Fawcett *Girl with Something Extra* guest shot, "How Green Was Las Vegas"; Yoshio Nagata in the 1969 *Hawaii Five-O* episode, "To Hell with Babe Ruth"; the Magi, Balthazar in George Stevens' 1965 epic, *The Greatest Story Ever Told*; prideful, "accept-no-help-from-anyone" rancher Ira Stonecipher in the 1968 *Gunsmoke* "Nowhere to Run"; the (literally, and figuratively) iron-fisted Count Draja in the 1967 *Wild Wild West* "The Night of the Iron Fist"; Sheriff Mike Galvez in the same year's *Judd, for the Defense* episode, "Firebrand"; and Jim Plummer, the former partner of Peter Duel's charming outlaw, Hannibal Heyes, in the 1971 *Alias Smith and Jones* episode, "Exit from Wickenburg." Added to these roles were four *Mission: Impossible* guest shots, and big-screen features like Clint Eastwood's *Hang Em High*, and a stint as narrator on the 1974 TV feature, *QB VII*.

Then came the CBS series, *Planet of the Apes*. In that series, Lenard portrayed the military gorilla, 'Urko.' Once the actor overcame his reservations about playing such a character and quickly adapted to his uncomfortable makeup and costume, he learned how to create and maintain the posture of a gorilla; in addition he developed appropriate gestures and expressions. Lenard further enhanced the reality of the series by pointing out to the producers, et al, things that were ridiculous — among these, humans beating up gorillas. Just as was the case with *Brides* Stempel, Lenard saw *Planet of the Apes'* Urko as being an important mover of the plots.

Having done "maybe thirty shows" with Lenard, *Brides* guest Marvin Silbersher probably would not have been surprised that Lenard brought so much dimension and reality to the Urko character. "Mark did some great stuff," enthuses Silbersher. "We used to talk over all the things that we did at CBS. We just had a grand time. I thought he was great on *Star Trek.* In fact, I'm instrumental in sending him out to the coast, because one night in the apartment on 86th Street and Riverside Drive, we're talking. He looked kind of downhearted. I said, 'Mark, what's the matter?' He said, 'Well, Marvin, I just can't seem to get anywhere here in New York. I work for you and I do this and I do that. I have no major plays, I have no major TV.' I said, 'Why don't you go to the coast?' He said, 'What?' Hollywood?' I said, 'Why don't you think about doing a series where you can play the Indian marshal — an Indian who becomes a marshal cuz he could look like that.' He says, 'Well, that's an idea.' Next thing you know, he's on the coast. So when we were doing *Here Come the Brides*, he said, 'I took your advice.'"[28]

Following the cancellation of *Planet of the Apes*, Mark Lenard returned to doing guest shots, including *Little House on the Prairie* ("Journey in the Spring," Part 1, in which he portrayed Peter Ingalls, the father of Charles Ingalls (series star/producer/writer/director Michael Landon), *The Bob Newhart Show, Hawaii Five-O* and the 1978 anthology, *Greatest Heroes of the Bible*. Then came Lenard's last television series, the February 27-May 1, 1979, *Cliffhangers*.

Produced by Universal Studios, and airing on NBC, *Cliffhangers* turned the rotating series concept on its head by taking three separate series, actually serials, and airing all three (*Stop Susan Williams, The Curse of Dracula*, and *The Secret Empire*) under the same title in the same hour. Lenard played the evil dictator Thorval (ruler of the underground city of Chimera) in *Empire*. Part science-fiction, part western, the western portion of *Empire* was filmed in black-and-white; the science-fiction scenes that took place in Chimera were shot in color.

Despite the innovative concept, *Cliffhangers* was doomed to a short run. Following that, the bulk of Lenard's television and film work continued to be in the science-fiction genre, the highlight was of course his reprisal of Ambassador Sarek in the *Star Trek* films and new *Trek* TV series.

According to the **actor's** widow, Ann Lenard, the *Star Trek* episode "Balance of Terror" which featured Lenard as a Romulan Commander, was a role offered to the actor about one month after he and his wife moved from New York to Los Angeles. The Lenards had met quite a few years earlier in an acting class. "I was working as a fashion model," Ann Lenard recalled in *Myeloma Today*, "Mark as an actor. We were not immediately drawn together. I thought, 'Here's a typical conceited actor.' At the same time, Mark was thinking, 'Here's a typical vapid model.' But, we quickly got over our first impressions."

As Ann Lenard revealed in this same interview, she was neither model nor actress. "I dipped one toe into the theater for about two years, but modeling helped pay tuition bills while I was studying to be an art historian," she told *Myeloma Today's* Unknown Patient. "I eventually worked in this field for several museums, specializing in 19th Century French art."

Mark Lenard's love of classic theater may have been the reason he could bring so much dignity and class to parts like Aaron Stempel and Urko. "He always kept his hand in the theater," Ann Lenard stated. "He and Walter Koenig [Chekhov of *Star Trek* fame] often worked together in *Actors* and *The Boys of Autumn*. Mark would play Huck Finn and Walter would play Tom Sawyer.'"[29]

Had multiple myeloma — the form of cancer which ultimately cost Mark Lenard his life, not developed in the actor towards the end of 1995, Lenard probably would have continued to do films and television.

With the kind permission of the International Myeloma Foundation's Unknown Patient, (who conducted the following interview with Ann Lenard,) the remainder of his article, "Mark Lenard: A Class Act," is reprinted in its entirety below ("UP" is the Unknown Patient, "AL" is Ann Lenard):

*UP:* How and when did multiple myeloma enter into your lives?

*AL:* It was October, 1995. Mark came home from a massage and thought the therapist had broken his rib. He went to his doctor and had an X-ray and it looked fine. So, he went about his business. And then, at the beginning of December, he had been running around taping commercials and he came home very tired and complaining of severe back pain. The doctor admitted him to the hospital to find out what was wrong. They did all sorts of tests over a four day period. One test showed that he was anemic. So, they called in a hematologist. The hematologist did a bone marrow biopsy and discovered multiple myeloma.

*UP:* It sounds like you found out what was going on very quickly. Many people who present with serious symptoms go for months without getting an accurate diagnosis. In my case, it was the better part of eight months from first symptom to diagnosis. Mark, however, was anemic, fatigued and had bone pain at diagnosis.

*AL:* Yes. I remember what the doctor said after the diagnosis. He said that the prognosis was excellent. He said they would give Mark plasmapheresis and chemotherapy and he should be fine for several years. It seems like such a contradiction now, given that Mark was Stage III at that point.

*UP:* Well, not necessarily, I've been Stage III for years now. It really depends on how well you respond to treatment and how much your body chemistry is disrupted by the disease. Did he have any kidney problems when he was diagnosed?

*AL:* No. They found that it had not affected any of the other organs at that time.

*UP:* It sounds as if he was what is called Stage III A, which has a better prognosis than Stage III B, which is when people are in Stage III and also have kidney problems. So, what did they recommend?

*AL:* They put him on melphalan and prednisone, which he seemed to tolerate just fine with the first treatment. The second cycle, though, he had a very bad reaction. It seemed to affect his stomach and he lost weight. Because Mark had diabetes, they kept him in the hospital for each cycle to monitor the dosages very closely and also manage his insulin and blood sugar levels. After the second cycle, he came home and seemed to feel somewhat better, although the back pain was still severe. But then, it seemed to get into the nervous system and affected his ability to swallow. And, from that point on, the struggle wasn't only against the myeloma. It was also against the aspiration pneumonia that developed because he was swallowing into his lungs.

*UP:* He had a neuropathy that affected the swallowing mechanism?

*AL:* Yes. We were told that it was very rare. Whatever the reason, he continued to swallow into his lungs. So, he kept getting these pneumonias. They kept pulling him out of one pneumonia after another. He was in the hospital and tested often to see what bacteria were present and what antibiotic they could give him. It was like this virtually from March 1996 until November, when he died.

*UP:* That's more severe and faster than almost any experience I've heard about.

*AL:* It was this constant problem with pneumonia. The myeloma went into partial remission after three more cycles of chemotherapy, this time with Vincristine and Adriamycin (VAD).

*UP:* When Mark was diagnosed, what did you do, other than what you had to do immediately to deal with the disease?

*AL:* Well, because of the pain, he felt exhausted. So, we just tried to conserve his energy. He didn't really want to talk to a lot of people. He just wanted to block everything out and save his energy. One of my daughters was very interested in alternative approaches. She sent me all of these books about alternative therapies— not that we would have considered that as a substitute for traditional therapy, but really in addition to the other things we were doing. We started massaging him every day, doing physical therapy and playing tapes, trying to keep him entertained. But, basically, he wanted to close out the world and concentrate on fighting the illness.

*UP:* How did you deal with it?

*AL:* I just tried to think of ways to keep his morale up. For the first two cycles of chemotherapy, his morale was excellent. But after he went back into the hospital for the third time and started with the continual pneumonias, he got very tired. I would go to the hospital every day to play tapes for him and to massage him. He couldn't deal with physical therapy at that point. So, they taught me how to do parts of the physical therapy.

*UP:* How did Mark handle the situation?

*AL:* Mark was a very intelligent man and he had a tremendous amount of pride. I think that whatever he felt about it, he didn't want other people to know, including me. Occasionally, I was aware that he was scared, but he'd try not to show that.

*UP:* How did you deal with it?

*AL:* I tried to stay positive because I felt it was the only thing that I could do to help Mark. The doctors started giving a poor prognosis at the end of March 1996. I really just tried to do everything I could to keep both of us positive. I wanted to feel that if Mark died, he would at least have lived in hope. Many of our family and friends were very supportive. What I found the most supportive were notes they would send. I was spending each day with Mark in the hospital. And, when I came home, I found that I was tired and needed time to recharge my own energy. I didn't want to talk on the phone. So, everyone kept sending Mark such nice cards and personal notes.

*UP:* How widely known was it that Mark had myeloma?

*AL:* We didn't tell any of Mark's professional friends that he had myeloma. When he was diagnosed, we got the impression that it would be like the diabetes — that it could be controlled via medications and that he would be able to go on working. In March, when he had to be hospitalized for pneumonia and the outlook changed, I decided not to go public because I felt it would be too hard for me to keep everyone updated and I wanted to focus on Mark. So, we didn't tell anyone, except for a few members of our family, anything until the last month. *UP:* As "The Unknown Patient," I certainly respect that point of view. So, eventually, Mark succumbed to the infections?

*AL:* Eventually, the stress on his liver from the infections and the effects of malnutrition became too much for him. Throughout it all, Mark was determined to hold on. And, until his kidneys began to fail, he could hold on. His doctors would tell me that they couldn't believe how strong he was. My daughter wanted him to be seen by a faith healer. So, we had him seen in the hospital by a woman who was a faith healer. After she saw Mark, she told me that he was holding on for me and that I needed to let him know that he had a choice. Mark died shortly thereafter from kidney failure. *UP:* How did Mark's fans react to the news of his death?

*AL:* They sent thousands of cards and really wonderful letters. People said such nice things about Mark. Some even said that the character of Sarek had inspired them to change their lives.

*UP:* When I learned that Mark had died of complications of myeloma, I went into our database and found that you contacted the IMF last April. How did you come to find out about the IMF?

*AL:* I had questions that I didn't think it was reasonable to take up the doctor's time with. So, I called the National Cancer Institute (NCI) and the NCI gave me information about how to reach the IMF. I called the IMF several times. I wanted to fill in the gaps in what the doctors had told me and I relied heavily on the NCI and the IMF for this information. I had questions about chemotherapy options. I also wanted to find out whether anything could be done about the neuropathy. So, I called organizations dealing with other conditions that affect the nerves. I called organizations dealing with AIDS, Alzheimer's, strokes, Parkinson's Disease, hoping to find out something that we could do. *UP:* If you were to give advice to people who were newly diagnosed, or had a loved one who was recently diagnosed, what would you say to them?

*AL:* I think I'd emphasize something that Dr. Thompson said in *Myeloma Today*, which is that you don't only want to be an informed patient, you also want to be included in the decisions. If they tell you they want to give Alkeran instead of Vincristine, you are in on the decision. And, be sure you understand why it's necessary to do something before you do it. I would also advise people to call the IMF and write to the IMF, as well as the NCI, and their local cancer center to get as much information as possible. *UP:* Well, thank you. We appreciate your taking the time to tell your story. I'm pleased that the IMF was able to be of help. And, as one of Mark's many fans, I'd like to thank you for sharing him with us. He was a class act![30]

1. Chris Claremont – *Planet of the Apes* magazine, 1974
2. Leslie Raddatz – 'When is a Villain Not a Villain?' – pg. 35 – *TV Guide* – Vol. 18, No. 11, March 14, 1970 – Issue #885
3. Blinn – 2007
4. Claver – 2007
5. Silbersher – 2007
6. "The Unknown Patient – Mark Lenard: A Class Act" – *Myeloma Today* – June 1, 1997, Summer 1997, Volume 2, Issue 7
7. "Gathering Toadstools" – *Time* – April 5, 1963
8. Raddatz – "When is a Villain Not a Villain?" – pg. 36
9. Brown – 2007
10. Ann Lenard – *Myeloma Today* – June 1997
11. Silbersher – 2007
12. Balduzzi
13. Ibid
14. Reynolds, Elizabeth (ed.), *Stanislavski's Legacy*, Theatre Arts Books, 1987
15. Esslin, Martin, *Text and Subtext in Shavian Drama*, in *1922: Shaw and the last Hundred Years*, ed. Bernard F. Dukore, Penn State Press, 1994, pg. 200.
16. Raddatz – "When is a Villain Not a Villain?" – pg. 36
17 Tolsky – 2007
18. Blinn – 2007
19. Valente – 2007
20. Lodge – 2007
21. Cass – 2007
22. Valente – 2007
23. Tolsky – 2007
24. Raddatz – "When is a Villain Not a Villain?" – pg. 36
25. Ibid
26. Tolsky – 2007
27. Lodge – 2007
28. Silbersher – 2007
29. Unknown Patient – "Mark Lenard: A Class Act" – *Myeloma Today*
30. Ibid

"Real men want real women. Not floozies."

Lottie Hatfield to Jason and his brothers
in Episode #1 ("Here Come the Brides")

# Chapter 10

# *And Joan Blondell as Lottie*

"Joan Blondell was kind of the matriarch of the show," said Robert Brown's stunt double, Dave Cass. "She was the spirit. Even in her later years, she was just a kick in the pants. She was always funny, she was always up. She was the matriarch of that show — you were drawn to her — around her. She knew everyone's name: their first name, knew what you did. She was happy to be there, and we were all happy to be around her."[1]

It is often said that actors on a show — particularly the lead actors — establish the mood on the set. That was certainly the case with *Here Come the Brides* co-star Joan Blondell. Unlike the other regulars on the show, Blondell's Lottie Hatfield had not been in the original pilot. Remembers *Brides* leading lady Bridget Hanley, "we had to re-shoot because we had three different 'Lotties.' Joanna Moore was the first one, and I don't know what happened there. We weren't really privy to a lot of that stuff. It didn't work for whatever reason, and then they hired Gail Kobe. I worked with her more because they kind of changed the ending a little bit, and then they decided that — it may have been the same reason, as with Joanna Moore, because Gail and Joanna were young, and blonde; it was too easy for Jason to fall for Lottie on an ongoing basis. I mean Gail Kobe was wonderful, but they were worried that it would be too much of an instant romance for Robert — it would be like 'Another brother bites the dust.' They wanted to leave all the guys free and just tempt everybody with Jeremy and Candy, I think. I'm not sure how, or who, thought of Joan. But we were so fantastically fortunate that she was free and available, and wanted to do it."[2]

It was *Brides* star Robert Brown who suggested Blondell. "There were two other actresses that played the part — younger actresses," says the star, "and I remember somebody higher up asked me what I thought since I was on the set a lot. I said, 'Well...' because I understood what they meant. They thought there was too much sex going on. They didn't want to make it [the relationship between Jason and Lottie] like a sexual thing. Rather than having a [regular] pretty girl to flirt with, and make it seem like he was sleeping with, they wanted to keep that open because some-where along the line, Jason might fall in love with one of the girls. So I suggested two actors, and one was Joan Blondell. The other was a famous English actress who was in town — character actress, in her fifties, a leading actress. I think she wasn't interested. I think she considered television beneath her."[3]

That was *not* the case with Joan Blondell. "She had no problem," states *Brides* regular Susan Tolsky. "She just dropped in, and she was a champ. I don't think it mattered whether it was this show or another show — it was something she wanted to do. She

*Some of the regular cast of* Here Come the Brides, *clockwise, from left: Bobby Sherman, Bridget Hanley, David Soul, Robert Brown, Joan Blondell.* COURTESY BRIDGET HANLEY

just took joy in it. And she came onto a show…look what she came onto? Who had a name? I mean, it was such a gamble; she just got dropped down into this group of nobodies really. Nobodies in terms of a television track record."[4]

"She was wonderful," says *Brides* semi-regular Mitzi Hoag. "She was a movie star, very down to earth, had a lot of stories to tell about doing films. [She was] charming, fun to be around. We were a bit in awe, and pleased that she was there, and that we were working with a movie star."[5] "Everybody perked up when Joan came on," agrees wardrobe man Steve Lodge. "Now there's a movie star! Robert Brown was not a movie star!"[6] "She was just Mother Earth," elaborates *Brides* executive casting director Renee Valente. "She was great with her lines, no trouble whatsoever. She had a wonderful little mobile home, planted a garden. She was just Mother Earth and everybody adored her. When you get a group of young actors, and they're working with an established film star, it means a great deal to them. They respect that. They give someone like that [respect], or they used to anyway; they loved to hear her stories, and just be with her."[7]

"She was just the best!" raves Bridget Hanley. "Susan and I would sit at her feet, and she would just regale us with stories; she knew everybody and everything. She and Jimmy Cagney — she would be reading letters, when she was in her little makeup room and we were in ours, and we'd hear her laugh, and we'd say, 'What's so funny?' And she'd say, 'Oh, it's just a letter from Jimmy,' and we'd say, 'Jimmy who?' and she'd say, 'Jimmy Cagney.' And we'd just faint — we'd all just faint. She knew everybody! But she never trashed anybody. She would, every once in a while, she'd come to dinner with Swack and myself after we were married, between the first and second year of *Brides*; she'd come to dinner, and tell us some really good stories, which I always kept private, which I still will. She wasn't one to gossip, but she sure had a lot of great stories. She just had a ball — we just had more fun."[8]

Adds Tolsky, "Joanie was a movie star…['30s], '40s and '50s, and we just sat at her feet and prayed she'd tell us stories. Joan was amazing. Of course, Joanie had her own dressing room; my dressing room and Bridget's dressing room looked like outhouses. They were these wooden things that you walked in and you had to be careful not to break your nose on the back wall. The other people, as they should have, had trailers, you know trailer trailers. Well, Joanie had her trailer, and her makeup artist usually did her stuff in her trailer, and then she'd [Blondell] come to hair and makeup and get her hair, cuz they did a whole bunch of stuff to her, so she'd come in and be with us. Joan came (to hair and makeup) later. She didn't need two hours — [like Tolsky, Hanley, et al] we all had those cascade curls in the back. Carl Silvera I think was Joan's makeup artist. She didn't have a whole lot [of makeup] — you know she's so beautiful; they put on the base, did her eyes, [so] I don't think she came in for two hours, I don't think she did that. After Carl did Joanie, he would come and do Bridget, Larry Abbott did me.

Continues Tolsky: "We were in the makeup and hair trailer one morning; we started our day at six, which meant I was up at four. We were in makeup and hair from six to eight, because we had all the hairpieces and all that crap. Anyway, I remember Joanie was sitting in the chair in the makeup trailer one morning and I'm pretty sure

Bridget was there. I remember coming in and getting touched up and getting my hair done. And to this day I can remember…Joanie was to my left. She was sitting in her chair, and she had a letter she was opening and she was reading it. All of a sudden she would go, 'Ah, ha, ha, ha.' And then she'd be quiet. And then she'd go, 'Ah hah hah, that Jimmy. That Jimmy!' And of course, knowing her, and the way she played with us, it was like she was baiting us. So I wanted to know, 'Jimmy? Jimmy Stewart? What Jimmy is she talking about?' Because if she talked about a Jimmy in front of us, we gotta know, that it's not Jimmy Jordan. So finally, I said, 'Um, Joanie. Who's Jimmy?' And she went, 'That Jimmy?' I said, 'Well, Jimmy who? She said 'My neighbor, Jimmy Cagney.' And of course, you could hear the jaw drop — the real Jimmy Cagney! She's lying to me. 'Really Jimmy Cagney?' She said, 'Yes, Jimmy. He's my neighbor in Martha's Vineyard.' I said, 'Is that really a letter that he wrote, is that his handwriting? Is that your letter from Jimmy Cagney?' It was like we were so insane. She's talking like 'That's Jimmy Cagney.' 'You mean James? *Yankee Doodle Dandy* -- all these things go through your head. We were like, you know, 'Who are you talking about?' You could tell, she was not doing this…it had nothing to do with ego; she was playing with us. She knew that we were pups, that we respected her. I don't think she would have done that if she didn't respect us and know how much we respected her. It was done totally with love and with such respect from an era that you don't find now. It was just something else that you don't see in the business now."[9]

Being a friend of Carroll O'Connor's, Robert Brown already knew James Cagney. "He was friendly with Carroll," explains Brown. "And Carroll was one of my closest friends; he would have me around a lot. I remember going over to Jimmy's house once. I was waiting for my car to be brought up, and I didn't know what to say. I said, 'Jimmy. You know, Joanie Blondell — she spoke of you all the time,' He said, 'She did?' He looked at me. I said, 'Yes, yes, she did.' He said, 'If I were you, Robert, I'd give whatever Joan Blondell said about me a wide berth.' 'A wide berth,' that's what he said. I guess he was talking about sex. I figured it out that's what [he thought] I was suggesting. Which I wasn't. Because his wife was inside…Bill." [10]

Given Joan Blondell's sensitivity, it was understandable why Cagney was surprised that she would gossip, which of course she had not done. Says *Brides* semi-regular Karen Carlson, "I remember we had to do a big promo thing for *Brides,* where they picked you up in a limo and you went and did this big dinner thing and met all the affiliates. That night, David and I…the limo that picked us up, we lived not too far from Agnes Moorehead, and so they picked up Agnes, and that was an amazing ride. When we got there, we were all sitting at the *Brides* table. Joan said to me, 'How did you all get here?' I said, 'Well, we were in a limo with Agnes Moorehead…' and she said, 'Heavens! You'll ride home with me.' So we did. We drove back with Joan and we were there until the sun came up the next morning, sitting on the floor talking. That was the day Judy Garland died. Joan had been one of Judy's best friends, and she had many times been the one that got the call and raced to save Judy from too many pills or whatever. That one time she hadn't."[11]

On that particular evening, Blondell told Carlson and Soul stories about her former husband Dick Powell — the man, muses Carlson, "I think she never really got over. The studio had a lot to do with their breaking up."[12] Therefore, Blondell was very concerned about what was happening with newlyweds Carlson and Soul.

Explains Carlson, "When David and I decided we were gonna get married, which was like four months after we met, the network was very...whether it was the network or the studio, I don't remember, but whoever was in charge of doing all the publicity, they were very upset, because their whole publicity gimmick was around the fact

*Robert Brown as Jason Bolt and Joan Blondell as Lottie Hatfield at the entrance to the Seattle church.* COURTESY ROBERT BROWN

that they had these three handsome, eligible bachelors playing this show. This was gonna help build an audience. So suddenly David was getting married. Well, they had Renee Valente come out from New York to meet me and dissuade us from getting married. But to David that was just not gonna happen. So, the only thing that they could do, and I say 'they,' because I don't know if it was actually the studio or the network, but whoever, they decided that the only way they could punish us was for me to no longer be a bride. So I only did four or five shows. Well, Joan Blondell saw this happening and said, we were just a young newly married couple, very much in love, and she sort of took me under her wing. She decided that this was not healthy for this young marriage — for us to be apart [especially] with David surrounded by women every day. So she hired me as her personal assistant. That way I would be on the lot and on the set every day. I could be in her 'honey-wagon.' I did everything, took care of her two dogs — she had two little pug-nosed dogs. I typed — she was writing a story book on them, so I was typing out the drafts for her. I was running errands, any personal errands, whatever. That kept me with David. I would go in with him every day, and leave with him at night. Joan recognized that David and I needed to have more time together as a newly married couple; she shared a lot of her secrets with me. She was truly amazing."[13]

"She was a treasure," adds Soul. "A guardian angel and a mother who loved us and looked after us."[14] "I thought she was a great spirit," agrees Robert Brown. "I remember she helped get this great dog for me. She knew Bob Hope, someone of that top ilk, who had this wonderful dog — this was the first time this little puppy was [taken] out. She brought it to me, and I bought it — the dog came with me every day to the set. Joan was so happy. And they got her a special trailer, a bigger one than anyone else's. Good old Joan — we all miss her."[15]

"She was just a dear," adds Susan Tolsky. "She was a sweetheart, a total professional. Exquisite. Even then. She was absolutely gorgeous. And the one thing that I remember more than anything else about Joanie, and again, I can see it, and it brings such a sense of love and warmth and days missed to my heart. Her eyes always sparkled. I never saw Joanie without her eyes sparkling. And sometimes I would just stare at her. Because no matter what, her eyes sparkled. She was just exquisite."

"I think there was a certain spirit that she brought to the show," continues Tolsky, "just from the fact [from] who she was — her years, her experience, her openness, her total accessibility. Which is also something that I was totally in awe of — she made herself totally accessible. And [she was] honorable. And loyal. She had a stand-in that I bet was with her for four hundred years. But she — I never heard her say a bad thing about anybody except one person. And to say that she was the heart... You know, you can say 'Mark,' and you can say 'Henry,' and you can say, 'Robert,' but they still — altogether, did not have her whole experience. She was so special, and she was the third 'Lottie!' [So] to have her drop down into that — that neophyte grouping — in terms of all of us in television — she was like another category that we were all aware of. It didn't seem to faze her — it wasn't that she walked in and said, 'Remember who I am?' It was never ego about her — she certainly melded with us beautifully. But she was in a different category."[16]

Despite this different category, Blondell was very down to earth. "She drove herself to work and back," remembers stuntman Dave Cass, "and she got herself an inflatable man. The wardrobe department gave her a hat and a coat for it; that way she'd have 'somebody' in the car riding with her."[17] "It wouldn't surprise me if she did have the inflatable doll," says Karen Carlson. "She did not like the dark, and I'm sure that had something to do with some of the things that happened in the early Hollywood days. I remember we always left at the same time, or they would make an effort to wrap her earlier so that she could be through and out of there before it was dark. And she had her dogs."[18] Adds Bridget Hanley: "I remember her driving in with her dogs every morning, and me thinking, 'this is so cute.'"[19]

Joan Blondell absolutely loved her two pugs, Bridey and Fresh. Karen Carlson still has Blondell's original draft on the storybook she wrote concerning the two. Blondell did other writing, too. "She would just start writing things she remembered," says Carlson. "I have that [material] in a box somewhere. I remember thinking, 'I need to do something with this.'"[20]

Like others who knew her, Bridget Hanley has continued to be a great fan of Joan Blondell. "She was just unbelievable," praises Hanley. "So kind and dear. Bawdy. And funny. And so talented. And when she really liked somebody, another woman, she would say, in her voice, as only she could do it, 'NOW, THERE'S A DISHY DAME!'

"I always thought she was the DISHIEST DAME OF ALL!'"[21]

1. Cass – 2007
2. Hanley – 2007
3. Brown – 2007
4. Tolsky – 2007
5. Hoag – 2007
6. Lodge – 2007
7. Valente – 2007
8. Hanley – 2007
9. Tolsky – 2007
10. Brown – 2007
11. Carlson – 2007
12. Ibid
13. Ibid
14. Soul – 2007
15. Brown – 2007
16. Tolsky – 2007
17. Cass – 2007
18. Carlson – 2007
19. Hanley – 2007
20. Carlson – 2007
21. Hanley – 2007

"The female of the human species ain't worth a good spit."

Captain Roland Francis Clancey
in Episode #1 ("Here Come the Brides")

# Chapter 11

# *With Henry Beckman (and the* HCTB *Fans)*

"Here's a thought. Perhaps the producers really din't [*sic*] expect the show to take off like that? In that event, they'd have to recruit a lot of new writers who mayn't have had time to REALLY study the shows [*sic*] 'bible'; an hour long show is not a piece of fluff, yaknow. I've written 'em and they are blood, sweat and tears with a lotta frustration thrown in just to make the writer writhe in agony. And, too, I always had a soft spot in me head for the guest stars since they would be stepping onto new ground, and facing new people, etc. Unless guest stars had been watching the show, they may not have had an inkling until show time. Been there and done that, one too." [1]

That was *Here Come the Brides* regular Henry Beckman giving the actors/directors/producers (et al) point of view during his time as a member of the *Here Come the Brides* Yahoo group. A regular member of this group from 1999 to 2000, by the time Beckman began exchanging e-mails with various *Brides* group members, he'd done close to forty years worth of television, not to mention quite a few movies — among these: the 1953 Marilyn Monroe drama, *Niagara*; the 1956 Alfred Hitchcock feature, *The Wrong Man*; 1963's *Twilight of Honor*; 1968's *Madigan*; the John Wayne western, *The Undefeated*; and 1976's *Silver Streak*. Television guest shots included westerns: *Bonanza, The Virginian, Gunsmoke;* doctor shows: *Ben Casey, Marcus Welby, M.D.*; science-fiction and horror: *The Immortal, Kolchak, the Night Stalker, Night Gallery;* drama: *Route 66, The Fugitive;* animal-based: *The Littlest Hobo*; crime-dramas and mysteries: *Police Story, Columbo, Shaft, Mannix, Tenafly, Cannon;* courtroom dramas: *Perry Mason, Owen Marshall, Counselor at Law.* There were also comedies: *I Dream of Jeannie, The Monkees, Love, American Style;* even religious dramas like *Insight.* Beckman did series as a regular, too, such as *McHale's Navy,* and *Peyton Place.*

Despite this overwhelming body of work, Henry Beckman didn't spend his few months on the *Brides* group dropping names or exaggerating his importance, in spite of the fact that he was perhaps the only Canadian actor to have won two Canadian Academy Awards. This same sense of modesty applied to his time in WWII; his first taste of combat was on D-Day!

Explained Beckman's friend Hillary in a September 2007 e-mail, "Henry is going through some problems with his legs (and arms) — haunting injuries from both being injured in Normandy during D-Day (w/Canadian Intel.), he volunteered for this mission — 93% of the Canadians were killed that day as they had no support from the Allies but for a few Polish Squads. Can you IMAGINE a 17-year old today doin' this, seeing the red water ahead and still getting off the boat? He is so humble, all he will say is, 'We did our job that day.' The atrocities he saw that day — the wife of one of his war friends (unwillingly) told me a bit of what they saw/did before we revisited Normandy and Juno Beach 5 years ago." [2]

"It is important to know, as it was so important to him, that he lied about his age to join the Canadian military," Hillary disclosed in a July 2008 e-mail. "The Canadians were the first to enter Caen in Normandy, and the last to leave. He was with 'Intelligence.' The poor guys who were at D-Day, 6, June, never stood a chance. They heard that ALL was quiet and tranquil. For Henry, he KNEW (what) laid ahead of him, and he STILL got off that boat, swam through red waters and crossed the sands red with the blood of his fallen fellow men. There was NO stretcher support, NO air support, there was no help from the allies on Juno Beach." [3]

A Knight of Malta, Beckman, explains Hillary, "has ALWAYS been a very private person, partially due to his ability to avoid the 'Hollywood' scene, but due to his humility. He RARELY speaks of his time at Normandy, only with the same, 'I only did my job that day' answer. At the Holocaust Museum in France (Caen/Normandy), there were a group of Belgium tourists who saw him pass by with his Canadian medals — they *literally* were at his feet weeping in thanks, begging for just ONE photo with him and this (was a) group of about 75 people! He was terribly embarrassed, but accommodating to each and every one of them." [4]

Henry Beckman was equally accommodating when it came to answering the questions of the *Brides* group. More than once he emphasized the importance of collaboration. "It's always a group effort," he told *Brides* fan Nan. "If writers give a particular character good lines, the character should use them to advantage as long as it forwards the scene (and the play!) No one actor can carry a scene in my belief." [5]

Nor did Beckman play favorites when it came to guest shots. "During my years of t.v. appearances, I don't remember one episode in any one series that was anything but serene and cool," he told *HCTB* fan Pat. "I hope I had something to do with that, but I rather think it was those series stars who had the good sense to realize how fortunate indeed they were, because the fickle finger could as easily have passed them by or upset the applecart. I firmly believe that those who went on to obscurity played a large part in their own demise. I've been so lucky to be remembered thus fondly thirty years [plus] after the fact and I attri-bute [*sic*] much of that to the wonderful people with whom I've worked and cemented friendships, which still hold, in large part, to this day." [6]

Crew members who worked with Henry Beckman on *Here Come the Brides* have fond memories of the actor. "Henry felt more comfortable with the crew than with the actors," says wardrobe man Steve Lodge. "There was always a poker game going behind the set, and Henry was the king of that. Of any of the actors, I'd say Henry would have been the prankster. He was the heart of that whole thing; he enjoyed his Schnapps. And he was playing a part where it didn't matter if he was half in the tank doing the part or not."[7]

"Henry could drink," laughs Robert Brown's stunt-double Dave Cass. "Oh, yeah, yeah. He was perfect in that part. He was the biggest comic. I directed…four, five years ago a miniseries for the Hallmark Channel called *Johnson County War*. And they needed this part of an old governor — I used Henry Beckman. And Henry remembered me from *Here Come the Brides*. We sat and talked about *Here Come the Brides* all day long."[8]

According to more than one e-mail from Beckman however, he was always sober when playing the part of Clancey. "Adult beverages are strictly forbidden on a motion picture sound stage," he explained, "although I'm sure you've heard a lot of stories about actors who've violated this rule. Usually the prop man makes up cold tea and ginger-ale is used for beer, but I've been on a few sets that used real beer. Just sipping, mind you. In fifty-three years in this business, I've never taken a drink before or during work, and I WILL confront ANY actor, anywhere in the world, who does drink during working hours. It's patently unfair to ones fellow performers."[9]

Beckman enjoyed poking fun at his *HCTB* screen image as a boozer. "I think the only difference between me 'n' Clancey is that he drinks like a fish," he joked to fan Kim. "I gave up drinking some time ago (and haven't felt right since)."[10] "No, dearie," he began in a more serious e-mail to *Brides* fan Pat, "I never had the good luck to have Mike Connors (or anyone else) sub-stitute [*sic*] whiskey for coffee. Bad ass as some people might have thought me, I had an iron-clad rule — no messing with the props and no booze on the set in any form. I would not have reported any culprit, but he would know he'd been hauled over the coals when I got through with him. Raising hell does not jibe with professionalism on the set, no exceptions. If one needed medicinal whiskey it would not be at the expense of the other performers. I had rather people think of me as a prick who brooked no nonsense than as a horse's ass who risked the success of the show by tolerating outrageously unprofessional behavior. We had our fun at all times, but not at the expense of the show or other players."[11]

When it came to discussing background, Beckman was straight and to the point. "Ok, I give up!" he cracked during the group's 'Where We're From' conversational thread. "Born Halifax, Nova Scotia. Moved Boston, Mass at age 3. Primary Education New England. Returned N.S. '37. Joined Cdn army in Yarmouth, N.S., moved to Halifax, Transferred to Cdn Intelligence, then to Shelburne, N.S., then Ottawa, Ontario, then to Jasper, Alberta; then Prince George, B.C. back to Halifax, to London, England; to Normandy, wounded, back to England, back to Halifax, back to Yarmouth, to New York City (Amer. Academy Dramatic Arts), 2 years, fifteen more years in NYC, to LA, (Hollywood) thirty years, and finally to Deming, WA. Still sitting here wondering what it's all about."[12]

Two days later, Beckman added a bit more to the bio. "Oh, yeah! forgot Toronto," he said. "Six months or so, 'cause I was working there so much hotel rooms were more expensive than having an apartment. And I forgot Royal Military College in Kingston, Ontario. Intelligence course there where Pierre Burton was my captain and almost my undoing."[13]

What Henry Beckman never told the *Brides* group was that he'd been a regular on: the 1962-63 John Astin/Marty Ingels sitcom, *I'm Dickens, He's Fenster*; the 1963-64 Gary Lockwood drama, *The Lieutenant*; the 1962-66 Ernest Borgnine/Tim Conway sitcom, *McHale's Navy* (final season); the first season of the 1964-69 prime-time soap, *Peyton Place*; the Sep.-Dec. 1971 Sandy Duncan sitcom, *Funny Face*; the 1975-76 Jack Palance crime-drama, *Bronk*; and, the first season of the 1985-88 Don Adams sitcom, *Check It Out*. He didn't tell them about winning two Canadian Academy Awards either.

Nor did the actor blow the *Brides* series and his role on the show out of proportion. "I fell in love with the show the moment I signed the contract to play Clancey," he joked. "It became an obsession with me the first time I got a paycheck for same. I still drool over the show, mostly because I meet such wonderful people on the HCTB fanclub [*sic*]."[14] Beckman was just as gracious when responding to the members' speculation concerning his *Brides* character. "Dear Kim & All," he told them, "You're right on the money! A large part of me and my background went into the shaping of Clancey. I grew up with sea-farin' people in Nova Scotia. They lived at the top of their lungs to be heard over the roar of the tides (forty feet in places) and the whine of the lobster boat engines and capstans."[15] After another member talked about how much she enjoyed the actor's Irish accent, because it reminded her of her great-uncles, (all of whom had Irish accents); she then explained how she and her cousins would deliberately anger the uncles, just so they could hear the accents. Replied Beckman, "Shame on yez, tormenin' yer elders!!! Yez otta be horse-whipp and if I had a horse I'd whip yez wid'em! I hope I came by the dialect honestly. Grew up to some extent in Tidnish and Amherst, Nova Scotia."[16] That Henry Beckman had fun with the 'Clancey' accent was undeniable. Case in point: the anecdote he told member Trish, the one concerning a compliment paid him by a woman in a supermarket; the woman told Beckman how much she loved his Scottish accent. "I had a great laugh over that one, 'though not in the presence of the deluded lady in question," the actor related. "I shoulda got a Emmy jist fer dat, dearie — e.g., pretendin' to be a Irishman through the twists and turns of a Scottish Burr. To my mind, that's one helluvan acting chore!"[17]

"Henry was just a goofball," laughs Susan Tolsky. "He was so wonderful because he loved being scruffy. He loved that old boat — that half a boat — docked on cement! He just had a ball playing that role. I think it was one of the most fun things that he did. When guys can be scruffy, they love that crap. They don't have to shave. They don't get powdered down. We had a lot of fun. He was always fun to be around."[18]

"He was just wonderful," agrees Renee Valente. "He was just a grand character, everybody was crazy about him. I think they all just would hug him, and that was that."[19] "Henry Beckman loved going to parties," adds Robert Brown. "He was always cutting up and having fun, you know — performing off camera. I enjoyed Henry — I enjoyed his spirit. He was a good fellow."[20] "I thought he was just great," laughs Karen Carlson. "He was just a gruff old fart. I just loved Henry."[21]

As would probably most anyone given the self-deprecating qualities the actor displayed on the Yahoo group. After that group had talked about how Kathleen Widdoes' Dr. Allyn E. Wright would be a great romantic catch for Captain Clancey, Beckman responded with: "Nice try, girls, but, at the time, my life was too full to

*Henry Beckman as Captain Roland Francis Clancey.* COURTESY HILLARY

even fantasize. In retrospect, though, Lottie woulda filled the bill. Feisty, independent, dance-hall queen with a heart-o-gold, lotsa booze and lotsa money, a spare room at the saloon and could shake a mean leg when the occasion arose. What more could a man ask?"[22]

Nor could Beckman — who was disgusted with the treatment the Vietnam vets received when they'd returned home to the U.S. — resist a political joke. "Usually the wardrobe wrangler has one, maybe two 'double' costumes, just for such emergencies," he replied when answering a fan's question about wardrobe. "Ten? Not likely. And by them by the Yard, from Molly of the Natl Org for Women (the NOW gang) Yuk, yuk, yuk."[23]

When different fans spoke of how much they enjoyed writing fan-fiction, Beckman encouraged their efforts with the following. "Dear Bluebird: (and anyone else who wants to write)," he began, "The time, the place, the occa-sion [*sic*] doesn't matter — what matters is the message. <Once upon a time W. Somerset Maugham was invited to lecture, a journalism class, for a substantial fee. (at Oxford? Cambridge? Who knows?) The class was seated, auditors in place, pro-fessors [*sic*] beaming at such a 'catch'. Mr.

*Brides regulars Bridget Hanley and Henry Beckman with a sponsor.*
COURTESY BRIDGET HANLEY

Maugham walked in, laid his thick burden of papers, notes, references on the lectern. Clearing his throat, he asked 'How many of you here wish to write?' EVERYone [*sic*] raised his/her/its hand. Mr. Maugham again cleared his throat, and said: 'Well then, go home and WRITE'.> Message con-cluded. [*sic*] Love and such, Henry (CapClancey)"[24]

# Hillary's memories of Henry Beckman

*Author's note: In the last decade of his life, shortly after losing his son, Stuart, Henry Beckman became very close with a young woman named Hillary, who took care of the actor in the last years of his life. Below her thoughts on her good friend.*

He was always such a private person. There really is no way to define what we had. He and his dear wife of forty-three years, Cheryl, was his "soul mate," she was a wonderful woman, larger than life, so beautiful and graceful...you could write a whole chapter just on their meeting, his writings and stories about [her] were so charming and touching — oh how well he knew as soon as he saw her — told her "not to think too hard about it or she might say no [to his marriage proposal]."[25]

He was SUCH a good man. His quiet humility and dignity were a lesson to all that knew him.[26] There was SUCH A HUGE BODY OF WORK THAT HE DID. IT WOULD HAVE BEEN IMPOSSIBLE TO PICK JUST ONE [role he played]!! He wrote a book called 'Hollywood with its pants down,' where he wrote a paragraph on each actor he had worked with, from Marilyn Monroe, to River Phoenix, there were just too many to list."[27] He was very detailed in his writings, his vocabulary quite extensive and [he] liked to use more obscure words rather than everyday words.[28]

He had a nurse due to his injuries from the military [and] he fell off an 'ice cutter' in the Antarctic, while filming a movie, breaking his leg again! He had a few stints, like falling off of cameras — he always did his own stunts. He was not accident prone.[29]

*On Henry Beckman's dedication to the 'Brides' series and the fans:*

The year they had it [the annual fan get-together] in Seattle for the first time, was FOUR months after we moved to Maui, after he had lived just above Seattle for over ten years!! After that, we were on the wrong side of the planet, although I know prior to that he was one of the few actors and the *ONLY* primary cast member who took the time to fly across the country attending as many of these as he could just to give something back, because that is the sort of man he was… always giving back.[30]

*Hillary on her years with Henry Beckman:*

In the last nine years, I probably knew him better than anyone as often we would talk until the sun came up, laughing about how odd life can be, that we would end up traveling the world together — who would have thought![31]

Henry was my *whole* life. He was my best friend, my "life partner," MY ANGEL. We traveled the world together, living in France, Hawaii, Mallorca, and had just begun our lives here in the beaches just south of Barcelona (but still within the same "zone" of Cataluna, about twelve-fifteen minutes from Barcelona) where he had a view of his beloved ocean from most of the rooms in the house.

Sure there are lots of men who like the way I look, but how many take the time to want to know the person inside? My last boyfriend was still carrying around modeling shots of me from ten years earlier, rather than current shots, that's the English for you, appearances, appearances, appearances, all that is important.

People never could figure us out in public. Was I a daughter? A trophy wife? A high class call girl? Oh what fun we had playing with the nosy people, especially in France. On a flight from Paris to Nice, a woman in front kept glaring back at us. In perfect French I finally stood up and said [to Henry], "Monsieur! If you do not pay me the 500,000 euros for last night, I will *leave* this plane *right now*, and you can go play on your yacht in Cannes alone!' Well, that put her in her place! She finally turned around. As we were eating pistachio nuts, towards the end of the flight the cup of shells fell over, we laughed and kicked them all under HER seat and listened and smiled sweetly at her as the stewardess reprimanded her."[32]

*Hillary on Henry Beckman's passing:*

He was taken quite ill and hospitalized from a diagnosis of "Hypothyroidism," that had been left undiagnosed for goodness only knows how many years. The doctors just wanted to chalk things up to his age on paper. The man never looked a day over sixty-five. And I always begged them to dig just a bit deeper as nothing ever happened slowly as it would were it just a sign of "old age."[33] [Henry Beckman died on June 17, 2008, in Barcelona, Catalonia, Spain.]

*Hillary on the actor's legacy:*

His work lives on through his films and through all the people from all over the world who still write. I know he turned my life upside down. The years I had with him were the HAPPIEST years of my life! I have no regrets, none! He was the best of the best, a true gentleman, the last of a dying breed. What a great, great man!!![34]

1. Henry Beckman – message #1268 – Tue Aug 3, 1999 3:18 am
2. Hillary – e-mail – September 21, 2007
3. Hillary – e-mail – July 10, 2008 – 4:07 p.m.
4. Hillary – e-mail – February 16, 2008
5. Henry Beckman – message #2883 – Fri, Sep 10, 1999, 1:46 p.m.

6. Beckman – message 4516 – Sun Dec 19, 1999 – 1:31 a.m.

7. Lodge – 2007

8. Cass – 2007

9. Beckman – Message #1563 – Fri, Aug 13, 1999, 11:35 p.m.

10. Ibid – message #1076 – Tue, Jul 27, 1999 – 5:39 p.m.

11. Ibid – message #4531 – Sun., Dec 19, 1999 – 4:43 p.m.

12. Ibid – message #2504 – Sun, Sep 5, 1999 – 11:55 a.m.

13. Ibid – message #2716 – Tue, Sep 7, 1999 – 11:26 p.m.

14. Ibid – message #3567 – Wed, Oct 27, 1999 – 2:43 a.m.

15. Ibid – message #1037 – Mon, Jul 26, 1999 – 7:34 p.m.

16. Ibid – message #2783 – Wed, Sep 8, 1999 – 9:39 p.m.

17. Ibid – message #1941 – Thu, Aug 26, 1999 – 1:04 p.m.

18. Tolsky – 2007

19. Valente – 2007

20. Brown – 2007

21. Carlson – 2007

22. Beckman – message #2119 – Mon, Aug 30, 1999 – 12:41 a.m.

23. Ibid – message #1565 – Fri, Aug 13, 1999 – 11:40 p.m.

24. Ibid – message #1884 – Wed, Aug 25, 1999 – 6:04 p.m.

25. Hillary 'Beckman' – e-mail – July 12, 2008, 5:11 a.m.

26. Ibid – July 10, 2008, 4:07 p.m.

27. Ibid – July 10, 2008, 4:50 p.m.

28. Ibid – July 10, 2008, 4:07 p.m.

29. Ibid – July 10, 2008, 4:50 p.m.

30. Ibid – July 12, 2008, 5:11 a.m.

31. Ibid – July 10, 2008, 1:06 p.m.

32. Ibid – July 10, 2008, 4:07 p.m.

33. Ibid – July 10, 2008 1:06 p.m.

34. Ibid- July 10, 2008, 4:50 p.m.

"And I can make corn fritters too…And I can make butter popovers, an' strawberry-rhubarb pie."

# Chapter 12
# *With Susan Tolsky*

"A character actor is usually considered somebody that plays comedy, but not necessarily. A character actor is Ted Knight on *Mary Tyler Moore*. At another time, he would have been a leading man — because of the way he looks. But, because of the role, he's a character actor. Morey Amsterdam and Rose Marie — those were character actors. You don't consider character actors as stars — they're just a secondary group. Character is always like supporting."

That was *Here Come the Brides* regular Susan Tolsky's definition of a character actor — a definition which she applies to herself. While one might wish to argue with Tolsky about this definition, one would be wise not to do so. Susan Tolsky is adamant about this definition; she will not budge from her position. "When I see Robert Redford, whether I see him in *Out of Africa* or *The Electric Cowboy*, Robert Redford is always Robert Redford," states Tolsky. "[But] there are actors who take roles, who can play different roles where you don't just go, 'There's Robert Redford.' Alec Guiness plays characters, Peter Sellers plays characters. But DeNiro is just DeNiro, Pacino is Pacino. They don't consider leading actors as character actors."

The same applied, and applies to actresses. "You can sit in a casting session, and I can tell you there's only two categories," declares Tolsky. "There's leading, there's ingénue, in the sub-group, there's character actors. If you're beautiful, you can play Indian, Lithuanian, Eskimo. Amanda Blake [Kitty on *Gunsmoke*] played an ex-hooker. She wasn't a character actress. Those were considered leading lady parts. There were very few women character roles."

Especially young women character roles. Most had been in comedies. So, when Susan Tolsky played a character role in the western-comedy-drama, *Here Come the Brides*, what she was doing was groundbreaking. Unfortunately, as is often the case with pioneers, Tolsky received scant attention for this achievement. Though, to its editors' credit, *TV Guide* did profile the actress during the run of *Brides*.

The lack of attention didn't bother Tolsky. And she was quite candid about what she did on the series whenever she was interviewed. Laughs the actress, "You know when you do these interviews, you remember all those magazines, [such as] *Tiger Beat*? We did a gazillion of those, they would go, 'Your character?' and I said, 'She doesn't have a boyfriend. What more do you want to know?' I mean, this is the best friend to the pretty girl, this is the homely friend of the pretty girl. There were moments and I have said this, and I will still say it, I did fifty out of fifty-two episodes. I'm happy not just at the level where I know I'm doing my job, I'm happy with approximately three to four minutes worth of work — there were two scenes to me that stood out, and those two [were] worth two years of my work. Because, for me, it's not a matter of catharsis, it's not a matter of trying to be somebody that I'm not. I, this is just, I'm honest about who I am. So I'm honest about the character it was just... She's not the pretty one. She's the funny one. She's the one who looks to all the others with her boyfriends. She knows she doesn't have one. It's hard to get one. And everything pretty much that she does she does because she's funny. But that's who she is. It's not like I sit and write four hundred reams of paper on this character."

Brides *regular Susan Tolsky with Roddy McDowall in the Roger Vadim–directed MGM black comedy,* Pretty Maids All in a Row.

But as early as the second-aired episode, "A Crying Need," it was clear that Susan Tolsky was quite capable of being very dramatic — in fact that was already present in the actress's view of comedy. "I had two loves," she states. "I loved medicine and I loved drama. I was working in hospitals when I was fifteen. I started out in medicine for two years, then I switched to drama. It was a very difficult decision. [Particularly since] a lot of girls in those days didn't have an aim, except maybe to get married and have babies. I don't regret my choice or anything, but I did start [comedy] at a very young age. I found out that I was one of those girls who had a good personality, which meant that I really wasn't what you'd call 'beautiful,' so I think comedy comes out of not necessarily funny things, but a lot of very serious and romantic things in one's life. I realized quite young that if I made people laugh, I could go anywhere. And be accepted anywhere, and that was fine because it did made me feel good; laughter always made me feel good. Comedy was something that I got into when I was extremely young. I was doing... it was probably known as stand-up. I had some imaginary friend, and talked to them — it was worked up into a whole comedy routine. When I started working in theater, the main thing that influenced me was my drama teacher in high school — Cecil Pickett. He was extraordinary in that he recognized what one did best and [he] nurtured that instead of trying to make me sound wonderful in Shakespeare. He knew that second banana was what really I did, and those are the roles he cast me in. And also we did speech and drama tournaments, he let me direct the one-act play, which was incredible — out of nowhere he let me do that. We had something called 'duet acting,' and we also had something called 'after-dinner speaking,' which again was stand-up. I had a bracelet with medals on it because I won a lot of after-dinner... your finals — if you made it to the finals — you performed in front of the entire — at the banquet that night, and then the judges judged you. That was the best influence I had — Mr. Pickett — because he encouraged the proper thing. Then, I went to college."

College was the University of Texas. "Eddie Foy III [son of the famous vaudeville performer, Eddie Foy] truly discovered me at the University of Texas," states Tolsky. "There was a program there [at Screen Gems] called the New Talent Program — he was at Screen Gems; he was the casting director. He went on a talent tour of several colleges, he came to the University of Texas; I did a scene for him, still knowing that I was coming out to L.A. Most of the people who graduated from the school of drama were going to New York to do theater. I was coming out here. Eddie Foy saw my scene and gave me his card, and encouraged me to come out. [But] I had the feeling I was not the type they were looking for. I was not stupid — I knew they were looking for pretty people. I was aware of that, but he gave me his card, and he said to call him when I came out. Well, I packed the car after I graduated and I drove out [to L.A.] and I landed on the July 4th weekend. When I called him a few days later, he said, 'You've been here since the weekend! Why haven't you called me?' I don't know how he even knew. I don't know. It was very creepy. He said he wanted me to come by. He said I could join the New Talent Program even though they wouldn't put me under contract. He said, 'You can take the classes and you can do everything that we do,' but, of course, David Soul was in it, you know, all the pretty people. [But Foy] let me be in the program without being under contract. So we got to see the [new] scripts that were coming in. When the *Brides* script came in, I implored him [Foy] to let me read for it. He said, no, my Southern accent was too heavy, and that it's [the accent] New England. I said, 'Please just let me do it.'" Foy agreed.

Though Tolsky won the part of Biddie, it "was not a regular role," explains the actress. "I had like three lines, or four lines. [But] they had something called ASI, which [is an abbreviation of] Audience Survey Institute. They tested the pilot, and apparently, my character rated very well. That's when they came and asked me to go under contract as a contract player at Screen Gems. I said, 'NO!' I said, 'I want a contract just to do the show,' because I knew they could have done that when I first came out. They didn't do it, so I said, 'No.' [So] they said they would not hire me to do just the show. I said, 'Okay.' My agent at that time said, 'Who do you think you are? Are you out of your freakin' mind?' I said, 'Are you gonna back me in this?' He said, 'No. You take the job.' I said, 'You're fired.' And that's when I got a manager. I told her what was going on [and] she approved of what I was doing. I said, 'I know they want me for this part. And I'm not going under contract now.' Sure enough, a couple of weeks went by; they came back and asked me to be in the show. I had done a — I got my SAG card on a show called *Second Hundred Years* — [starring] Monte Markham [and] Arthur O'Connell — that was the first show I did; the second show I did was a *Bewitched,* and then I did the pilot of *Here Come the Brides.*"

At the time Tolsky did the *Brides* pilot, she already knew Bridget Hanley and David Soul. And, "as soon as the *Brides* cast was together, it was a family," notes the actress, "cast and crew, it was an extraordinary experience. We were very close — we were all very close. A bunch of us — all of us were just like… just really fell off the cabbage truck, except for Joanie and Henry Beckman, who had been around. But the rest of the cast, we were pups. We didn't care — we just were having such a wonderful time because we were working. Bridget and I got along famously; David was wonderful, Robert really took over the father role, Joanie was an entirely different category. The pilot had a big cast of girls that never showed up again, but when the show sold and it got to the regulars, we were very tight, extremely tight."

One of the things that distinguished *Here Come the Brides* was the number of young people in both cast and writing staff. "These were a lot of young, young people," states Tolsky. "And that was part of the joy — the writers were young, so it was interesting to see how the writers started writing for the characters. My character was very specific — I'm the homely second-banana to the pretty girl [and] at first there would be lines that I didn't feel my character would actually say. I would either have to bring that up, or change them for my comfort, and then once you did that, they would write [that] — it wasn't like [I] had to go in and have a conference, [or] start screaming, 'I WANT MORE MONEY!' and all that crap. It was just that they dropped in a line and wrote for you."

Chief among the writers was story editor William Blinn. "Bill was so wonderful," enthuses Tolsky. "What a wonderful, not only writer and editor and human being, he was just a joy to be around. Everyone loved Bill. What a delight, a hard worker, he was just right in there in the arena with us. Bill was the head writer, he was the overseer. I think Bill was concerned with all the characters. When you're head writer, it's like admiral, you're the five-star general, everybody's gonna look to you to blame if something doesn't go well. He had to be concerned about the core of the show and those characters, and then you infuse your story and your depth. I never felt neglected or left behind, or anything. I did fifty out of fifty-two — I exceeded my contract, and again, I wasn't even to be a regular, so I did okay. I'm not complaining. I worked. They didn't have to put me in all of them. I exceeded my contract."

In addition to speaking with William Blinn, Susan Tolsky, like the rest of the cast, could also talk to the show's executive producer, Bob Claver. "Bob Claver would show up and it was like, 'Oh, he's the producer,'" remembers Tolsky. "He was very hands-on, but we would call Bob at the office. If something went wrong, there was no problem. Just go to the phone and call Bob. He was very hands-on, a very nice man." As was line producer Stan Schwimmer. "He stood out because you would have said, 'Oh, is he the banker? Is he the accountant?'" notes the actress. "He was very nice, a little bit more quiet. You looked at him, and he was always thinking. You looked at the guy — his mind was always…you picture him very involved, intellectual — which was probably a good twosome with Bob Claver. Bob was more out there — more social."

By contrast, the show's other line producer, Paul Junger Witt, "was a go-getter," recalls Tolsky. "The other two were more laidback, but he always had the wheels turning, [that] go-getter energy. He always interacted with us; I can remember him laughing and joking. He was a mover and a shaker, [and that was] exciting because it was for us, it was for the show. [His] energetic, participating, active, positive, go-getter attitude did not offend in any way because it was for the show — he was working the show, and [he] was quite positive, very optimistic, available, laughing, and 'how are you?'"

As a result, Witt's breaking off contact with the tightly knit *Brides* cast and crew in the years following the series' cancellation came as a considerable shock. "Something that was very disappointing after we did *Brides* — Paul Witt never hired me again," states Tolsky. "I never read for any show of his, and as I am recalling this, I remember talking to several other cast members who had the same experience. He went from *Brides* and continued to work, and I'm not condemning the man — this is not a business where you're an entity — this is a business where you're working with hundreds of people to produce one product. Once you work, they're done with you. 'Thank you so much. That's a wrap,' and 'Farrah Who?' That's the mean-spirited nature of the business. That's fine, and that's the way it is. But that [the years after *Brides*] was a different era. You're talking forty years ago. And this is a very close group of people. We were aware of each other's talent, we all respected one another, we all worked together. I was so angry…[and wondered] 'Why can't I talk to this man at home?' There was no reason for that. It was a very self-absorbed career move. For him, there was a sense of ambition, and that was not a bad thing. But a producer can call in anybody they want! I never auditioned for him again!"

Nor apparently did Witt show up at any *Brides* reunions. "We had a reunion — twenty years, or twenty-five [years ago]," says the actress. "I don't even remember if he was there. I'm pretty sure Bob Claver was there. We did have a reunion of cast and crew."

One thing Susan Tolsky greatly enjoyed about *Here Come the Brides* was being around so many men. In the case of the series' second season-assistant director David Hawks, "I was just in awe of the fact that he had a Hawks name," remembers Tolsky. [Hawks is the son of noted director Howard Hawks.] "Bridget and Swack socialized with a lot of other couples, and I know they were very close with Fred Jackman. I have such enormous love for Freddie." The camera operator was another favorite. "I worked with the man on many commercials," states Tolsky. "He was a marvelous, marvelous man, and the best boy, or somebody, was a huge, huge man, so light on his feet — he was like kind of prancing — he would kind of float across the sound stage. It was like this three-hundred-and-fifty pound guy — this huge man, and the sweetest man. I like big men — I would always go up and hug…you just feel so safe in the arms of a bear."

Tolsky also has fond memories of stuntman Dave Cass. "He was a sweetheart," praises Tolsky. "I worked with Dave later on — he was wonderful. I remember him being very present and a fun guy to talk to — he was a beautiful man, a handsome guy. Dave did a lot of horseback riding, so I was always talking to Dave. I loved horses, and he was a wonderful horseman. See, we had something called 'falling horses'— the 'falling horses' are very skittish if they fall, [so] they have mounds that they create with hay and grass; they don't fall on hard ground." Tolsky frequently asked Cass questions about working with "falling horses" and performing other stunts. "I was always enjoying him," laughs the actress, "and driving him crazy about stunts. I wanted to know everything. I don't remember him as being at all stand-offish, or unavailable. He was just one of the group. Dave very much was part of the family."

"The guy for Bobby…the stunt people would just take my breath away," the actress continues. "I've always been just in awe of stunt folk. I don't remember if David had one. I don't remember doing a lot of [her own] stunts [although Tolsky did stunts in other shows]. I remember rolling down a hill. We didn't have a lot of stuff like that. We really didn't. I know that Jean Allion was my stand-in; the stand-ins were also extras on the show. I don't remember if Jean stunted. I did my own stunts in a Disney film. I did my own falls — if there were little tumbles. When I did stunts on the Disney shows, they had a stuntwoman there to do them in case I couldn't do them. I remember I went up to them and I said, 'She is going to get paid, isn't she, whether she does them or not?'"

Assistant director Jim Hogan who later became the series' unit production manager was another crew member Tolsky liked. "Jim Hogan was immensely efficient," praises the actress. "Efficiency was probably his middle name. He — this is just recall — the job came first — he was extremely efficient. I don't remember him ever raising his voice. It was like, 'Ten minutes, Susan. We need you in ten minutes.' But maybe they're still messing with your hair. So they'd come back and say, 'We need you in five minutes.' But Jim Hogan would not come and go, 'GET ON THE SET NOW!' I've heard of people who have done that. He'd stand by your door and wait for you to escort you. He was a gentleman about that."

Jim Hogan's behavior was par for the course on *Here Come the Brides*. "Women were always treated with respect," says Tolsky. "Until they played jokes on the fact that I couldn't see without my glasses. Bob Claver was part of that. They were all part of that. They thought it was very funny. We would block a scene, an interior scene, and then they'd call out, 'Oh, Susan, we need you in makeup,' (and while Tolsky was otherwise occupied), they'd move a door, and then (when the actress returned to the set), I'd try to find the door to walk through, and I'd hit the wall. OH! They did things like that, and it was HYSTERICAL! And the exteriors — they'd say, 'Oh, Susan. Don't forget. Hit your mark!' And it [the mark] was a pebble buried in the dirt! HOW AM I GONNA SEE THAT? I mean, it was so funny. But it was all done with such love. They just thought it was so funny because to this day I can't see without my glasses. I actually started the show with contacts, but the days were so long, and the lights were so bright, and my migraines, there was no way I could control those!"

As noted earlier, women's costumer Betsy Cox suffered from migraines. "I could look at her, and she could look at me, and we both knew when the migraine hit," says Tolsky. "She was wonderful. She was wonderfully competent, just a joy — she was my first costumer, the one that I really got to know — to work with more than five seconds. I think she really enjoyed the period, and I don't know how long she'd been in the business. But a lot of period [costuming] was done."

Due to her status in the industry, special attention was given to Joan Blondell's wardrobe. "They built Joanie's wardrobe," remembers Tolsky, "but they pulled our stuff [from storage]. Bridget had five dresses and I had four, and those were all from (the) 'Western Costume' [company]. Every once in a while I'll see one of those dresses, and I'll go, 'My God! They're still using them!' We just kept wearing the same dresses over and over, so when we had to do other things, in terms of wardrobe, it was a hoot and a half. Like the barmaid [dress] — I had four or five sets of falsies in, but some of my skin showed. It was always fun to get out of those [regular dresses]. When we had our female guest stars on, Betsy enjoyed that too. Oh, absolutely. Absolutely. And she had dressers. The dressers a lot of times would be the ones that would get us in the stuff — those things were all done down the back, so the dressers would come. They had the clothes ready for us, and helped us into the stuff, but Betsy was the wardrobe mistress, the head costumer — she was the head gal."

Since the wardrobe was period wardrobe, it was important for Tolsky, Bridget Hanley, et al to take care of it while in costume. "If we were up on the first shot after lunch, we would stay in 'em," explains Tolsky. "I always put a robe on anytime there was food. I put a robe over a wardrobe. If we were not in the first shot after lunch, sometimes we'd get out of them (because) I may not have worked again until four O'Clock. They go by the set-up. It doesn't matter who's in them [the set-ups] unless they're working with Joanie and decide to do all her stuff and not keep her around. To keep the wardrobe fresh, you [would] always get out of it. If we left the studio for lunch, we usually just stayed in wardrobe, because there were a million studios around there."

Like leading lady Bridget Hanley, Susan Tolsky dealt with the problem of hair-pieces. "We had so many hairpieces," she laughs, "even though they were — those rods and curls and all of that, once they placed them on, they had to redo them. I had three hairpieces on, and Joyce Marsden was my hairdresser. This top piece that we had on, the only thing that was my hair was those little curls at the ear, and the top piece... my head hurt so bad, she tried to fit the bobby pins in the holes in my head where they'd been for two years, she tried to fit em in the same groove, so all of that took quite some time."

Another discomfort concerned the trailers. "We had the guest trailers," remembers Tolsky. "Bridget and I and Mitzi and Henry — I believe there was a three-person trailer where the boys were, and I believe Joanie had her own. But truly [for] the rest of us they were like wooden — they were like outhouses. I don't remember if they had trailers for the guests — I don't think they put them in our outhouses. They [the trailers] were very cold, they just had little heaters in there, they were not insulated, they were horrible. So I'm pretty sure that they gave the guests different accommo-dations, but not us."

Despite the less than lady-like trailers, and the problems with hair and ward-robe, Susan Tolsky loved doing *Brides* thanks to her co-stars, the semi-regulars, etc. "I remember Cynthia Hull [who played Ann] being a sweet gal, really nice gal," says the actress. "Nice and friendly and into the role. We were all…we were so thrilled to be working. I don't remember amongst the girls one moment of jealousy. I don't remember, 'YOU HAVE MORE LINES THAN ME!' I'm talking about crap down the line in my career when I ran into that later on. I don't remember one moment of that — we were all young. We were all working. There was no conflict with the girls. We were so thrilled to be working, and it was a big show, we had a big group."

*Bridget Hanley as 'Candy Pruitt,' and Susan Tolsky as Biddie Cloom.* COURTESY
BRIDGET HANLEY

The friendship Tolsky formed with Bridget Hanley continues to this day. "She's just the epitome of lady," praises Tolsky. "Bridget is always dressed to the nines. She always looks beautiful. I was so thrilled when Bridget and I had scenes together, always loved having scenes together. I knew what I was there for, she knew what she was there for, and we were thrilled to be working. I just remember her being open and free and playing with everybody, that's how we felt, so sometimes I'd have to go, 'BRIDGET! PULL YOUR SKIRT DOWN!' I think that was more the feeling we had with the crew that we could just do that. We would all goof. I can remember her goofing around, and I can remember myself goofing around, but there was no 'Should we do this?' It was part of what that series was, what the group was."

One thing often said about the *Brides* characters was how much these parts were like the people who played them. To Susan Tolsky, that certainly applied to first-season semi-regular Mitzi Hoag. "Mitzi had to fall in the mud hole," remembers the actress, "and I don't remember anybody, any of the actors saying, 'I'm not gonna do that!' So, yes, she would try that — I remember Mitzi falling down. She's a dear, what a sweetheart. She's just the dearest little thing in the world. I adore Mitzi. That character [Miss Essie] was very easy for her because that's very much who she is. Just an open and loving and available and sweet and dear, that's Mitzi, totally, totally Mitzi Hoag."

Unlike her *Brides* character Biddie Cloom, Susan Tolsky fared quite well romantically during the run of *Here Come the Brides*. "I met Christopher [Stone]," says the actress. "He was with the New Talent Program. We started dating on *Brides*, dated for about five years. He did one of our shows, he also did [the Bob Claver-produced] *The Young Interns*. Then we parted ways. I think Christopher was so busy [dating] he didn't give as much attention to his career as he could have. I think he did later on. I think he and Dee [actress Dee Wallace Stone] did. I think it [the dating] was a fun thing for him. The guy was an ex-Marine. He was a handsome guy, and he played [around]. He was just having a good time — he was a guy."

There were a lot of "guys" on *Here Come the Brides*, including first-season semi-regular Bo Svenson. "Bo Svenson was a wonderfully tall, good-looking guy," says Tolsky. "We had a lot of guys and a lot of gals. And a lot of the guys hung, and a lot of the gals hung. I mean here were these loggers — these guys are walking around with hatchets and big boots, and they don't want to sit down and have tea with us, because here we are with eighty-seven lacey petticoats and nine pounds of hair. So even though we interacted, I remember Bo being around the guys a lot — they tended to hang together and shoot the breeze. And we tended to…you know, it's like a teenage dance — the guys on one side, the girls on the other.

"Those guys were just a hoot and a half," continues Tolsky. "They loved getting dirty and having scraggly beards, scratchin'— they were just the most wonderful guys, and that's not to say they weren't all gentlemen. Because if they were in regular clothes, they'd just be 'Hello, Susan. How are you?' But these guys loved being in those costumes and getting dirty and walking through dirt. Even those saloon scenes — they all just kind of swaggered around — it was just a hoot to watch them. Buck Kartalian [who played Sam]…they had me hooked up with Buck a lot. Buck was the short… he was in *Planet of the Apes* — for some reason, they had me dancing with him, or doing something with him. Vic Tayback was a hoot. I later did *Alice* and it was just a joy to see him again and work with him. I did several of the *Alice*'s, and he was just a pleasure to work with. Bobby Biheller [who played Corky] I remember. He had such a wonderful name, and he was such a cute guy. Barry Cahill [who played McGee] seemed to be a little more mature. He was like one of the more mature gentlemen. [Because] some of them were just silly and rowdy and we had fun with them. Vic was just in on anything. Jim Almanzar [who played Canada], OH, MY GOD! He did a lot of stuff because Screen Gems and Columbia were doing a lot of stuff, and I remember him driving up on other Columbia Screen Gems shows. I remember seeing some of those guys work at that studio again, which also made me feel very good that the studio was using them. James did a lot of stuff after that."

As for Dick Balduzzi [who played Billy Sawdust], "Oh, Dick!" exclaims Tolsky. "Oh Dear God, he's at every wedding of Bridget's daughters. Dick and Phyllis, MY

GOD. Seeing them is just a joy. Dick and Phyllis were also involved with the Special Olympics. I was at the Special Olympics for fifteen or twenty years. At least fifteen, and then it got to be very money-oriented, and I stopped participating because it got to be not about the kids anymore. But Dick and Phyllis were always there. Dick was involved with them for years and years and years. He's a super guy. I love Dick. Seeing him is just a joy."

One of Susan Tolsky's most enjoyable Post *Brides* experiences was her time as a regular on *Madame's Place*. The name of the series was based on the hand puppet played by ventriloquist Wayland Flowers. "We had a fabulous crew on that," states Tolsky. "We had to have a fabulous crew because we did seventy-five shows in fifteen weeks. We did a show a day, so we did have a close crew; we had a party at the end of the show."

Though Tolsky has played and continues to play other parts (many in voice-over), the role of Biddie on *Here Come the Brides* is the part for which she is most likely to be remembered. "I know I saw some of the shows," remembers the actress. "I truly have never been one to watch my work. It's quite frightening for me. I'm still in shock that people remember the show. Every week, there's fan mail. They still come up to me — I find that astonishing. It's shocking that people still remember that show, and remember it fondly. They come up and they go, 'You're Biddie.' I'm honored that people remember things like that. I'm very fortunate, actually. When I got into the industry, if I'm not mistaken, it was approximately thirty to thirty-four men's roles to one woman's role. Having gotten in as quickly as I did and being able to maintain a career all these years, is incredible in itself. Worth some sort of award they should give me. They were not doing a lot of female-oriented shows [at the time], a lot of women were not working. So I was very fortunate in the way I got in and in the kinds of roles I played because I became reliable — they knew what they were buying. It was a commodity — they knew what they were getting. There were very, very few women playing those second banana roles on television."

"[Biddie] was fun to play," laughs Tolsky, "she really was. She tippled a little bit. She only had one boyfriend, and he was a shyster lawyer so you can understand... poor Biddie — she never quite got it together. To this day, I can still see her walking across...I can still see her in those stupid costumes, WITH ALL THAT HAIR walking across to Lottie's, walking from the dorm to Lottie's, and that silly music playing because the second year they introduced 'Biddie's Theme,' and she's totally oblivious, to anything except getting where she's going. I look at her, and I go, 'You poor dear! You poor dear!'"

In addition to 'Biddie's Theme,' the second season introduced Patti Cohoon and Eric Chase as Candy Pruitt's younger sister and brother, Molly and Christopher Pruitt. "They only did a few episodes," remembers Tolsky. "Eric was a little hellion at the time. He was a little boy — he wanted to run and play and do. Eric was younger (than Patti Cohoon). He was a kid. He was there on the screen, but you had to catch him. Patti was a little lady, but they were kids. A little rambunctious."

Though some, like story editor William Blinn felt the second season was more action-oriented than the first, Susan Tolsky saw little difference between the first and second seasons. "For me it all rolls into one," states the actress. "The second year they gave me a little more latitude — the dimension of my character...they composed 'Biddie's Theme.' When you see Biddie walking, she has her own theme, and I was enormously honored by that because I was not in the regular cast — I came in on a fluke. [So] the second year they gave Biddie a little bit more attention. I have no problem with a little bit more drama coming in. I had no problem with that because it's always a compliment. Comedians can do drama [whereas] people that do drama are not necessarily comedians. So for them to give me a little bit more depth to my character, I was honored by that, and I really wasn't aware that there was a big controversy as to what the show was — it was a western. When you have horses and you have a saloon, that's a western. I didn't have a problem with that. I didn't see any enormous changes. I just saw more of a tightening and definitive characters."

An actress who is one "to tell the truth. I will always tell you the truth," Susan Tolsky thus has no qualms in pointing out that "ONE OF THE GREAT MOMENTS OF MY CAREER!" occurred after *Brides*. Thanks to Lucille Ball (whom Tolsky calls "Big Lucy") and her daughter, Lucie Arnaz ("Little Lucy"). "Big Lucy had something like four hundred shows," explains the actress, "remember she had those shows called *Here's Lucy* and *There's Lucy* and *Where's Lucy* — she had like a million of 'em, and there was, at that time, her daughter, Little Lucy, was on one of those shows, and what Big Lucy was wanting to do they were gonna have a spinoff of a Big Lucy show for Little Lucy, and have Little Lucy's own show.

"They had the part narrowed down to three finalists to be Lucie's pal in the spinoff that was gonna be done on Lucy's show," continues Tolsky. "The three girls, of [whom] I was one, the final audition was in front of Big Lucy — we had to go to her home. It was a Friday; I was the last one — I think there were three girls, there may have been more — it could have been five — either three or five, anyway we had to go to Big Lucy's house to audition in front of Big Lucy, and talk about nervous! This is Friday, and I was the LAST ONE scheduled. So my time there was like at 4:30 in the afternoon. I remember going into the house and her husband [Gary Morton] met me at the door and put me in a little room because apparently there was somebody there who was just leaving. And then Little Lucy came out and brought me into the room, and Big Lucy wasn't there. Well, I was a wreck. Because I'm now gonna be the Sibyl and I felt like four eunuchs were gonna bring her in on a board or something. She came in the room and she was extremely gracious. She said, 'Is everything okay?' I said, 'I...I...I'm very nervous. I'm very nervous!' She said, 'Just relax. And you'll do the scene with Little Lucy. And everything will be fine.' 'And whatever, whatever.' We did the scene and I heard her laugh, and that's all I remember! — hearing her laugh. KNOWING THAT I MADE BIG LUCY LAUGH! Afterwards, there was a tray of tea and coffee on the table. She said, 'Please let me. Just relax. And calm down and have a cup of tea or coffee or whatever.' And she handed me the cup and it was rattling. It was, like, rattling. She said, 'You're such a wreck. It's over. Don't worry about it.' And I said, 'Well, I have to tell you something, Mrs. Lucy — I called her Mrs. Lucy. Today is Friday, and it's after five, and Monday's a holiday,' and I said, 'So, whoever gets it is not gonna find out until Tuesday, if then.'

So I said, 'It's gonna be a long weekend, and I'm very nervous because I'm sitting in your home and I just auditioned for you and I heard you laugh…and I'm babbling like an idiot,' and she says, 'Don't worry. Everything will be fine.' And she chatted and finally I left. I went over to a friend's house and I called my agent, my manager, I believe I was with William Morris at the time. So I called my manager, and I called my answering service, and there was like, eighty-five calls from my manager, one-hundred-and-fifty calls from my agent. I'm thinking, 'Oh, my God! I did something terrible! I'm gonna be reported! They're after me!' I was, like, a wreck. So I called my manger and I said, 'What is going on? What is going on?' She said, 'Well, I just wanta tell you that the president of William Morris company just called me and said, that some woman called the switchboard and said she was Lucille Ball, and asked to speak to the president of William Morris. So they put the call through and here was the message — she said, 'Lucille Ball wanted me to give you this message directly.' I'm sorry I get very…[tearful] cuz I can remember it. She [Ball] said, 'Tell Susan she got the part. And to have a nice weekend.' I…still to this day, remember that. She went out of her way! She made the call! And because it was a three-day holiday I can still hear in my head her saying, 'Tell her she got the part. And to have a nice weekend.' And, it was a magnificent moment in my life. To have not only gotten the part, but to have had such a gracious, gracious woman treat me that way. And there were other, many other moments with her that were very dear. But she used to call me and pretend — she knew everything that I did. There's a million stories about her — she was just marvelous to me, and having the opportunity to work with someone whose career you just can't comprehend. To have been in her presence, to have such a gracious and warm reaction from her was quite extraordinary."

Another pleasant experience: Tolsky's guest shot on *Barney Miller*. "This was at the end of the run [of that 1975-82 comedy series]," recalls the actress, "and there was no script. We went there, and they would bring down like two pages and then they'd be 'Okay, everybody have a break and we'll come down with some more pages.' But the cast was fabulous and the execs were wonderful and the crew…we all just sat around until the next pages came down. The people, OH GOD! THOSE PEOPLE WERE WONDERFUL! That was joyous because of the people, even though we were waiting for work."

Moments like that became less and less common by the 1980s. "The fifties and sixties and seventies — that was a wonderful era," reflects Tolsky. [This was due in part to people in the industry like Troy Donahue.] "I was involved with the Special Olympics for almost twenty years," says Tolsky. "I know Troy came one year, and… I'm always shocked when somebody comes up to me and says, 'Oh, Hi, Susan. It's so nice to meet you. I'm a fan of your work,' and… 'BUT YOU'RE TROY DONA-HUE!' He was a nice man."

Tolsky also speaks highly of the actresses from the fifties, sixties, and seventies. "Connie Stevens is just a hoot and a half," laughs the actress. "A really nice lady. Diane McBain, Diane Baker. OH MY GOD! She was beautiful! I met her…[at] forgive me, I call them 'the has-beens convention.' And Carol Lynley. They took your breath away! Lovely, lovely ladies. Stefanie Powers was a strong lady. I don't think I ever met

Stefanie. The image I get from her — the aura and wavelength that comes across is, 'Don't mess with me!' Suzie Pleshette [was] like that, too. Oh what a beautiful lady. And what a dear, dear wonderful person."

So Tolsky always enjoyed the wide variety of guest stars appearing on *Here Come the Brides*. "They just fit right in," says the actress. "We were welcoming. We had a fun group. There's a feeling…if you've ever been on a bad set, you'd know the difference. I can remember people saying, 'Oh, you all have so much fun,' and of course we'd been up for twelve months — we haven't slept, but we're still working. "THIS IS JUST A WONDERFUL GROUP!' That comment was quite frequent. We were all just a family. Loving each other, and it sounds crazy, but that truly [was] the way it was. We really, really enjoyed coming to work. We all hung around. All stayed together. There just never was another feeling like that."[1]

1. Tolsky – 2007

"We weren't separated on *Brides*. There were so many of us. I think the show was an exception — just a lot of really nice people, people who had fun."[1]

First season semi-regular/second-season guest star Mitzi Hoag

Part Three

*The Semi-Regular Cast of*

Here Come the Brides

"No, I certainly won't kiss a man who doesn't believe in religion."

Mary Ellen to storekeeper Frank
in Episode #1 ("Here Come the Brides")

# Chapter 13

# *Brides*

## *Mitzi Hoag: A spirit of adventure*

"At the time I was raised, women didn't have a lot of choices," explains *Here Come the Brides* first season semi-regular/second season guest Mitzi Hoag. "We were living in the same house with my grandparents, and my grandfather was my very favorite person. He had been a cabin boy on a sailing ship when he was twelve years old and then he worked all his life on the water. He was a captain of ore freighters; he had a fishing fleet at one time, and there was even the time the hull split on a ship and he managed to save everyone. So, he was a hero to me. He had an adventurous life, and I wanted to have an adventurous life. In those days, there were not a lot of ways for women to do that; acting seemed like one of them."

Brought up by a mother who worked in a bomber plant ("She wanted to do that"), it was easy to understand why Mitzi Hoag wished for adventure. "I think what attracted me to acting was the adventure of it," muses Hoag. "You do get a lot of adventures acting. They're not dangerous, usually." Although in one show, Hoag had to stop a stagecoach, "and come in quickly, riding a wagon with two horses. You get a lot of help with that, but it was a little uneasy making. "

Ditto the low-budget 1967 Roger Corman-produced *Devil's Angels*. "I remember when I auditioned for [director] Daniel Haller for that," laughs Hoag. "You go in like a character, and I remember I had high boots and I was putting my boots on, just acting like the character. Now it seems like, 'What were you doing?' but you have to convince them that you can play this character. So I did. I didn't feel embarrassed at the time. I was being tough. You have to be a little bit like a kid in the sense that you jump into something and do it with energy and passion. [If] you can't stand outside yourself, you can't do the work. You have to be in it. There's a lot of play involved in it."

Playing Hoag's boyfriend in the movie was her fellow *Here Come the Brides* semi-regular, Buck Kartalian. "I was playing Bucky Kartalian's love interest," remembers the actress. "Buck had been a professional wrestler — a very short man, he had powerful arms. Wrestling was mostly acting; Buck played this character named 'Mighty Mouse.' Now, actors lie about their skills in order to get work, and all these actors, besides John Cassavettes, were kind of I think there were maybe four or five of us in this group around him. There were like three or four men who were his [Cas-savettes'] buddies. They all said, 'Ride a motorcycle? Sure. Of course I can.' And then they went out and took lessons.

"Our very first shot was taking off in gravel," remembers Hoag. "We were near Patagonia, Arizona, which is just a one-street town, close to the Mexican border. So we are taking off in gravel and [were] meant to [take a] curve. Well, the fellow in front of us, who was on his bike alone, panicked, and went straight for the sound truck. You just saw these people getting out of the way really quickly. Then Bucky put his head down and said, 'Mitz, I'm gonna have to confess.' He went to the direc-tor and said, 'I can't handle this.' The director [Haller] was probably used to such things — he was one of Roger Corman's regular directors. He took the actor on the bike in front of us, and Bucky and I — he put us in the back of this troupe of extras [real bikers] hired from off the street. They were meant to go no faster than thirty-five miles per hour. Well, we were practicing and the camera was panning them, and we couldn't keep up with them. There were a whole lot of scenes where we were not on the bikes, but the actors did learn. John Cassavettes, of course, had a double, but nobody else did. It was fun. Roger Corman was very nice, and one thing that was interesting — he loved to have people around him, like his directors and staff and stuff, who had gotten their PhD's, so you had a lot of brainy, intellectual people around. The movies were low-budget and fast; I just worked on two." [The other was 1967's *The Trip*, concerning a man trying LSD for the first time].

Hoag began her performing career as a dancer. "I had danced in summer stock when I was a kid," she explains, "and my mom had been a Highland dancer — the family was of Scottish descent. My grandparents came from Nova Scotia, and before that, Scotland, and Scottish games were a big part of it [the family heritage]. People would gather and play soccer and bagpipes; there'd be dance competitions, and my mom did that. So when she was growing up, what her mother did was take her to lessons, performing, that kind of thing. My mom did the same thing with me. But I was not meant to be a dancer! I got inter-ested in acting since performing was what was expected of you in the family." "Aside from summer stock, I did a whole lot of theater," continues Hoag. "I remem-ber when I was working in summer stock, the star was wearing…this was before contact lenses were common; she was wearing contacts that covered her entire eye, and it looked extremely painful. She had to wear them because she had to climb up high stairs. She was so determined. She was quite a trouper. She went through a lot of pain and anxiety."

Mitzi Hoag was rather determined herself. "I went to a college in Mountjoy, Illi-nois, [for] two years," she remembers, "they had a University of Chicago plan so I got my B.A. Then I went back to Cleveland [the actress's hometown], and I worked in a theater there. Then I worked in the graduate department at Western Reserve University, and did a whole lot of theater — really good plays, and got to do good difficult roles. I was there two years, and then went to New York City. I did a play off Broadway called *Eloise* — I played Eloise, and that was the story of Eloise and Abelard. [The play was based on the poem, "Eloise to Abelard," by eighteenth-century poet Alexander Pope. Eloise and Abelard were two tragic real-life lovers in medieval France.] That ran for nine months off Broadway. In the meantime, you know, you study all the time in workshops, and that fit my way of learning. You read something, and then you try it out, and experiment — you go to workshop, read a little more and that's the way I garden. You use the same process in gardening and growing food."

Mitzi Hoag's reason for moving to California was personal, rather than professional. "I'd been going with a young man who went to California first," explains the actress. "Then he called and asked me to marry him. I hadn't planned on going to California, but I wanted to marry him, and I did. I came to California, and then I started doing theater out here. I did a whole lot of really good theater. I played *The Miracle Worker* on Santa Monica Blvd. — I did Annie Sullivan [the teacher of the blind and deaf Helen Keller], and it was a very successful production, and from that, Ross Hunter was there on opening night, and he got me an agent, and also a part in a movie called *Tammy and the Doctor* [produced by Ross Hunter Productions and starring Sandra Dee and Peter Fonda]. But I kept on doing theater. I went from that to *Call Me by My Rightful Name* [Michael Shurtleff's 1961 play dealing with a racial triangle of a white man, a black man, and a white woman] — I was doing really good parts in all of these, and then I worked with a theater group at UCLA. I did Ellie Dunn in *Heartbreak House* [George Bernard Shaw's complex play dealing with the indifference and ignorance of the upper classes towards WWI and its after-effects], and [the anti-war WWI satire] *Oh, What a Lovely War*. Carroll O'Connor played Captain Shotover in *Heartbreak House*, and Marsha Hunt was [also] in it. Oh, she's a lovely, lovely lady — she's wonderful. That was a very successful production. Carroll O'Connor and I had a wonderful scene together that the *New York Times* critic...he was doing a tour of the country talking about theater, and he described that scene between the two of us as 'magical.' That's a very nice compliment. We worked well together. I was also three months pregnant with my daughter and having a lot of sickness, so I was running off stage and getting to a wastebasket. But we did very good work in it. I started getting TV things from that. Later on I did *Joe Egg* [a.k.a. *A Day in the Death of Joe Egg*, about a British couple struggling to save their marriage while raising their only child — a ten-year-old girl suffering from cerebral palsy) but that was after I had been working in television for quite some time. I also did Masha in [Anton Chekhov's] *The Seagull*."

Hoag's work on stage brought her to the attention of Quinn Martin Productions' casting exec, John Conwell. As can best be determined, the QM/20th Century Fox series, *12 O'Clock High* marked the actress's television debut. She played an English girl, Dorothy Hall, who has just married Hawaiian gunner Pineapple in the October 23, 1964 episode, "The Climate of Doubt." "John Conwell did do a lot of recruiting from the Broadway stage," remembers the actress. "And I also...you know, you're always working in theater workshop, and I worked at Theater West, and the Actor's Studio, and in a couple of really good parts at Theater West, I got more work from that. There were directors in both places, and you got to know a lot of people. If they saw you doing theater, they often hired you for other things."

One director who hired Hoag was John Erman (*Stoney Burke, The Fugitive, The Outer Limits, Ben Casey, Star Trek, Marcus Welby, M.D.*). "He was in Theater West also," states Hoag, "so I did a couple of *That Girl*s. Theater was always…you rehearsed a certain length of time — sometimes three weeks, sometimes a month, but then you performed. Seven, eight, nine, performances a week. It was a really an in-depth acting experience."

Having stage-trained actresses like Mitzi Hoag doing television made things much easier for TV producers and directors. "Television is so fast," states the actress. "You go in, you work, you hope it's all right, and you're out. It's very different from theater where you had time to rehearse and a character would evolve. When you work in the theater, it's a co-op, kind of an evolution with the director. The director has a vision of what he wants the play to be, so you're working with him, and it evolves slowly, maybe [over] three weeks, four weeks, if you're lucky, five days a week, eight hours a day. You have a lot of time to talk about it, and you yourself make a decision about what this character wants and how does he go about getting it, the obstacles in getting it, and the director is part of all that. In television, the director is working as fast as you are. You create the character. He doesn't mold it as a theater director might. A director, besides working with the actors, is possibly working on rewrites of the script. He's got this whole crew lighting, so he's got a whole lot of other responsibilities. The theater director — it's true that he sits in on the lighting and stuff — but that happens towards the end of rehearsals, the same way as the sets. Yeah, the actor does have more responsibility [for his character] in television. If you give a bad performance in TV, you can't blame anybody but yourself. You see it afterwards, and you go 'Ohhhh.'"

Such was Hoag's feeling concerning Winifred Bowers, the character she portrayed on the March 11, 1971 *Alias Smith and Jones* episode, "Stagecoach Seven." "I seldom watched anything," admits the actress. "That was foolish in a lot of ways. The reason I say that is because if I had taken the time to watch it…my focus was more on [daughter] Abby and earning a living, but you learn things watching — each show has a tone to it. I did a terrible job in *Alias Smith and Jones*. There was this one scene where I was supposed to tell off this weak husband of mine, Dana Elcar, and I overdid it. I played it realistically, well, that show had a kind of tongue-in-cheek quality to it. So [series star] Pete Duel said to me, 'That wasn't right, Mitzi. It was too realistic. You overdid it.' It was all wrong for the show. Had I had the time to watch, I could have learned things. When you go into a show, and maybe you haven't seen it, that's pretty foolish. You want to learn as much as you can, often you learn it from the actors themselves, but you're wiser if you saw the show ahead of time."

Despite Hoag's feeling about her character, "Stagecoach Seven" was an enjoyable episode, thanks to series stars Duel and Ben Murphy, and guest stars Hoag, Elcar, Steve Ihnat, Keenan Wynn, et al. "It depends on the cast, really," notes the actress. "I worked with Elizabeth Montgomery on some sort of TV film [*Second Sight: A Love Story* — 1984], and she was just so gracious and welcoming. When you get a star, they can kind of set the tone for the whole week and the whole show. And when one is friendly and gracious, it makes a difference — you feel welcomed to the set. Elizabeth, because she was a longtime star, had a kind of old Hollywood feel. She had all those years on *Bewitched*. [Samantha Stevens] was a very successful character."

The same was true of the characters played by James Arness and Amanda Blake on *Gunsmoke*, and Michael Landon and Dan Blocker on *Bonanza*. Hoag guest-starred on both series, at least twice. "It was nice to see Miss Kitty and James Arness," remembers the actress. "When you go on a set, most often the stars, the regulars, are very pleasant and welcoming. It's rare to have any kind of bad experience. It was just the way things were."

Hoag's first *Bonanza* episode, "Three Brides for Hoss," (produced during *HCTB* story editor William Blinn's season with the program), was in some ways a try-out for the role of Miss Essie. Not only was the actress's Libby Spencerfield a meek, quiet sort who fell hard for a big galoot (Dan Blocker's Hoss Cartwright), she hailed from New England. "It was fun," remembers the actress, "but it was three actresses [the other two were Danielle Aubry and future *HCTB* guest Majel Barrett] all vying for Hoss. I think I worked only two days. Dan Blocker was a big, friendly guy. When you're not there very long, you don't get to see them more."

Guest-starring for Michael Landon on his three later series, *Little House on the Prairie, Father Murphy* and *Highway to Heaven*, the actress's memory of Landon is much stronger. "I loved working with Michael Landon," enthuses Hoag. "Michael Landon was wonderful to work for. I did the very last *Bonanza* — "Stallion." I don't remember that it ever showed. Clu Gulager and I starred in it. [E.W. Swackhamer directed.] Swack and Clu and I went to see a screening of it. While we were there, the producers came in and announced to Michael Landon that the show was canceled. Well, it was right before Christmas, and it was like the end of November. He was appalled they did it at that time, and no one was to work up until Christmas. That mattered to the crew. Michael Landon paid their salaries through the end of the contract."

"Michael Landon was wonderful," continues the actress. "He was fun, had funny stories to tell, [and] made things easy. Some stars would do that; others would be kind of distant. He was pretty much of a powerhouse...As an actor to work with, he was very giving. He was the same way as a director, encouraging and giving, and just a great storyteller."

Other pleasant talents were James Garner, with whom Hoag worked on *The Rockford Files*, and Shirley Jones — from the Bob Claver executive produced *The Partridge Family*. "James Garner was a charming man," remembers Hoag. "Some stars make a habit of just kind of introducing themselves and speaking to the people who come on the set. [And] *The Partridge Family* was fun. The kids were fun, and Shirley was wonderful. I [played] an entertainment reporter. I had praised one of the kids excessively in an article, and it went to Danny's head — he thought it was about himself. I think the only time you saw me in the show was when I was watching a concert, then at the end of the show, I come in and apologize to the youngest boy [Chris], saying that I had put the wrong name down, that I really meant *him*. Shirley was a professional, she was certainly beautiful, and a musical comedy star. I saw her on Broadway in *The Music Man*, so I was impressed. She was really nice, very down to earth, not behaving like a star. A nice lady. She didn't feel like TV was beneath her.'"

Hoag's role as Sheila Faber in the above-mentioned *Partridge Family* ("Star Quality") was the first of four guest shots on the series. As noted earlier, *Brides/Partridge* executive producer Bob Claver really liked the actress's work. So much so, he wanted her to be a regular on *Here Come the Brides.* But there was a problem. Explains Hoag: "When I did the *Brides* pilot, I also did the pilot for *Hawaii Five-O* [the two-hour Paul Wendkos-directed "Cocoon," which included Steve McGarrett's first encounter with recurring villain Wo Fat]. Bob Claver called me up after the *Brides* pilot and, after a lot of people had seen the pilot, asked me if I wanted a contract. Well, it was the mistake of my life that I said, 'No.' It truly was. For a lot of reasons. I was supposed to be going to Hawaii to be a regular in that show — to be his [McGarrett's] secretary, really, but then in the writing of it, they found that they're not gonna use the secretary much because that was all office scenes, and he had all these other people. Now my agent knew this, but I didn't know it — not good communication there. So I said, 'No' to Bob Claver. I didn't know, until I talked to my agent, that I was not going to be under contract to *Hawaii Five-O.* I wanted to go to Hawaii and do that. I wish I had stayed with *Brides,* because I've just had longer friendships with many of those people, and I loved the character, too. So I wasn't thinking. If I had been thinking, I would have said something like, 'Let me get back to you,' and talk to my agent. My agent was horrified that I said, 'No.' It was foolish. I was not good at building a career."

Hoag had much more to do in the *Brides* pilot than in the "Cocoon" episode of *Hawaii Five-O.* "The only thing I remember [about *Hawaii Five-O*]," says the actress, "it was a brief scene in the pilot: Jack Lord came up and was introduced to me and we were talking; he said, 'You know what? You have an Irish mug!' And, of course, he had an Irish mug, too."

By contrast, for the *Brides* pilot, "I had to audition, had to read, and I think they had somebody else in mind until I read," remembers Hoag. "There was this character lady from *The Brady Bunch* — Ann B. Davis, I believe…I'm not sure, I believe she read for the part, too. All I did was read for Swack and the producers. I was not tested on film. I don't know if [Screen Gems executive] Jackie Cooper had anything to do with the casting. Swack did a lot of the casting. Swack is the one I can see at the reading. I remember Swack laughing. They went with the take I had on the character in the reading; that was what they liked."

Pointing out that Miss Essie was based on Lizzie in N. Richard Nash's *The Rainmaker,* Hoag is surprised to learn that Katharine Hepburn had played the character in the 1956 motion picture. "I associate it with Geraldine Page," states Hoag. "Geraldine Page played it on Broadway. She was such a marvelous actress. I'd seen her do *Sweet Bird of Youth* on Broadway with Paul Newman. I really liked that character. I liked that she was a schoolteacher, and that she was shy and unsure of herself, but nevertheless did what needed to be done. I liked the fight scene in 'Lovers and Wanderers'; I liked the chance that she got to be feisty and yell at the guys. It was not a one-dimensional character at all. She had the courage to say that women could vote — she looked it up; she was encouraged to run for mayor."

Miss Essie was not the only reason Mitzi Hoag so loved her time on *Here Come the Brides.* "I just love filming outdoors," exclaims the actress. "That's one reason I like westerns so well. I love the Northwest and Seattle, and Oregon, and Washington. We went to the local mountains. That was fun. We'd all be on a bus, in our costumes, and go up and film up there. I remember there was kind of a biographical novel about a family in Wyoming, the woman was a schoolteacher. She graduated

*Mitzi Hoag as Miss Essie Halliday.* PHOTO COURTESY MITZI HOAG

from Wellesley College, took the stagecoach out; there was this incredible journey in bitter, bitter cold in one of the western states. She ended up marrying [naturalist/ founder of The Sierra Club] John Muir's nephew. But the thing that interested me was that she was a schoolteacher. She reminded me of Miss Essie. Being a schoolteacher was one of the few ways women could support themselves if they didn't have a mate."

Playing "a whole lot of mothers of murdered children, [or of] drug addicts," it was ironic that Mitzi Hoag did not continue in the role of Miss Essie when the series became grimmer in its second season. But the disappearance of Miss Essie, the actress reveals, had nothing to do with the career goals of co-star Bo Svenson. [Svenson played Miss Essie's boyfriend, and eventually, husband, Oleg 'Big Swede' Gustafson, on *Brides*.] "Bo was a little…there were all these men," explains Hoag, "all these stars, and after a while, certain people start staking out their territory. It's a natural thing to do. You hear other actors say, 'Well, I wouldn't do that,' but, as soon as you get in that position, you always do. Well, Bo wanted to become a star. He wasn't planning to do that character too long. He was not happy there — there was a lot of competition between the men — a lot of it was done through humor, but Bo was more stark somehow. Not as a character. But he wanted to be elsewhere, and to be playing the lead. He was ready to leave. I know sometime after he did, he said to me…he saw me somewhere, and we were chatting, and he said, 'You know, I didn't realize how that would affect your character — my leaving.' But they could have worked around that. It wasn't his character that caused me not to continue. It was that I refused the [*Brides*] contract."

Like so many semi-regulars and guest stars to appear on *Here Come the Brides,* Mitzi Hoag treasures her association with the series. "It was one of the happiest sets I worked on," notes the actress. "There was such a pleasant energy. In the pilot, there were so many people. Often in shows, you may, when you go in and you're doing something, unless you're doing the lead, you may be there for two days. One day possibly, so you don't really get to know people, and sometimes people will react — not to you, but to the character you're playing. But, on *Brides,* there was just so much vitality, partly because of the number of people — there were a whole lot of men and a whole lot of women. Bridget and I used to have such fun because it [was] still the days when the studios had lots of antiques, and we were fascinated with those. So, just working on the set, looking at what was in Miss Essie's house…And I don't know, that time really interested me, too, historically."

With *Here Come the Brides,* Mitzi Hoag began a long-lasting friendship with leading lady Hanley. "Bridget and I quickly became fast friends," says the actress. "We often went out together after working — there's a place on Riverside Drive — a Japanese restaurant we would go to. Everybody loved Bridget. She is lovable and funny. And you know, she's a beautiful woman and that combination — a beautiful woman who's very funny — is really appealing to people. And she has just lots of energy. And so dear. Everybody loves Bridget and to have that kind of personality as a star of a show is a great gift, really. And, of course, she and Swack, they were not married at the time, but they were sweethearts. There must have been over a hundred people at their Fourth of July parties. Fred Jackman was there, everybody in the crew was there, and it was a very special event — done more to, I think, keep people together. Even though it was once a year, it was really special. I remember during the run of *Brides* and after, for years, there was always a ping-pong contest at the pool, and lots of food and camaraderie. And Swack was great about using actors he loved. I worked for him a lot and knew their kids."

Being a great fan of Bridget Hanley, Hoag was glad when Hanley received parts where her talent for physical comedy was displayed. "She's just terrific at physical comedy," states the actress. "When we'd have these Fourth of July parties, with swimming and all that kind of thing, Bridget would do these incredible dives — she'd do a flip-over, off the diving board into the pool. Everybody would bring their kids, and she would lead the kids — she would lead them in different jumps off the diving board. I saw her once on a *Simon and Simon,* and she was playing a villainess. The older Simon had to knock her out, and she's up against a wall, and he hits her, on the side of her face. She did a complete body collapse as if she had been knocked out. Her whole body just collapsed, and kind of in pieces, so it had a comedy element to it. That show had comic overtones. I have never seen an actress doing anything like that in my life. I was just astonished. She was so physical, and could do such comic physical things. If you ever see that *Simon and Simon,* look for that. It's really great."

Hoag also thought highly of the series' director of photography, Fred H. Jackman. "I liked him so much," enthuses the actress. "He was really nice. He liked the character of Miss Essie, so he was good to me as far as the lighting and all that kind of thing — he really liked the character. He worked fast. From my point of view, he did. I don't know if a director would say the same thing, but from my point of view, he would get the work done quickly, and we all looked pretty good. It was a lot of complex work; plus, it was a period piece."

One off-set talent who made things a lot easier was executive producer, Bob Claver. "I worked for Bob Claver a lot," says Hoag. "He had me read for a pilot for an Italian lady which I didn't handle well, and when Bo left, at the time, I was in a play which I did in L.A. and Toronto — *Joe Egg* — with Noel Harrison. I spoke to Bob Claver and I said, 'I'd like to do this play. It'll be on in both cities. Is that a problem?' He said, 'No. It's okay. Go do the play.'

"I liked what I had to do in all three [*Brides*] shows," states the actress, "the pilot, and the two other [episodes featuring]'Miss Essies' about running for mayor [William Blinn's "Democracy Inaction"] and marrying [William Wood's "Lovers and Wanderers"]. The people who were doing the writing were wonderful. We had wonderful writers, and wonderful directors. You seemed to have more time with Swack. It makes a big difference when you have a personal relationship with the director."

Hoag found that creating the physical appearance of her character was quite easy. "The glasses were already in the script," remembers the actress, "and [women's costumer] Betsy Cox was great — just finding things for us to wear. By the time I was cast, though, everybody had their hair pieces. They had so many people — they used up a lot of the Screen Gems wigs. So the only thing left for me was an Apache wig to match my dark hair; they made it look just fine.

252 Gangway, Lord, (The) Here Come the Brides Book

Continues the actress: "One thing that was nice about *Brides*, or any show where you have a large cast, and I don't know if other actors would feel differently about this, but…somehow the responsibility is spread, and, in a lot of ways, that's a relief, because you're still carrying on your life with your family, and all that sort of thing. It's a lot of hours. So I liked that the work was kind of spread around. Stardom and who gets top billing — that's something the agents work out. It also has to do with past experience, and who bargains best."

Unlike Susan Tolsky and Bridget Hanley, Mitzi Hoag had future professional contacts with *Brides* line producer Paul Junger Witt. "I read for Paul Witt for *SOAP*," remembers Hoag. "I didn't know him well. He was kind of in and out. You didn't have the same relationship with him as you did with Bill Blinn and Bob Claver. But Witt had me in to read for other things after *Brides*, and so did Bob Claver. But I didn't get *SOAP*."

Yet thanks to her experience as a dramatic actress, Hoag found plenty of work after her *Brides* stint with Quinn Martin, and powerhouse producers Aaron Spelling and Leonard Goldberg. "I worked for Spelling/Goldberg a few times," remembers the actress. "They were gracious, but they were not around all that much when you were working. The director was in charge. [Since] they were still working on new scripts, in those cases I was having to do my internal work for the character."

Interestingly, the role of Miss Essie got Mitzi Hoag work in series like Bill Bixby's *The Incredible Hulk*. "Bill Bixby was getting ready to do a new show," she remembers.

"He and the producer wanted to meet me because they had seen the pilot. They just liked the performance so they wanted to meet me. My agent didn't say if they were considering me for a part — he just said they wanted to meet me. That particular character had an impact — there were a couple of instances of that where people wanted to meet me."

Hoag was also considered for a regular role on the Lorimar Productions hit, *The Waltons*. "I wasn't right for the show," states the actress. "I read for the mom — [the Olivia Walton character that was ultimately played by Michael Learned]. We had to do a lot of readings for things. That was kind of hard. You usually didn't get the script ahead of time. That had that wonderful old character actress, Ellen Corby, and we wore those extreme hats. Mary Jackson, who was Miss Mamie or Miss Emily, was charming. She was fun. She liked that job. I remember she had a beautiful house she bought in the Hills, and I remember her giving me advice when I bought my first house about paying my mortgage."

"I did a lot of police things, too," adds Hoag. "In a lot of those I was playing mothers who had something tragic occur — raped daughters, murdered sons — all that stuff. I loved Angie Dickinson and Earl Holliman on *Policewoman*. I loved my conversations with Earl Holliman — for years we were going to the same pet store, and I would see him and talk. I talked to him more than to Angie. She was not around when I was working. Earl Holliman was a wonderful actor, very active in Actors and Others for Animals. I remember having a long talk with him in the pet store about how his mother came to live with him when she got older, how much he liked that."

When Mitzi Hoag did the first-season *Harry O* [episode] "Second Sight," she played the secretary of blind author Stefanie Powers. "Stefanie took me out to dinner," remembers the actress. "She's an extraordinarily intelligent, interesting lady. I liked her enormously. We had a mutual friend in Noel Harrison — she worked with him in a series [*The Girl from U.N.C.L.E.*]."

Hoag's aforementioned guest shot on *Alias Smith and Jones* "Stagecoach Seven" was one television production the actress was unlikely to forget. But it had nothing to do with her performance. "It was the day of an earthquake," says Hoag. "I was living in West Hollywood — a single mom at the time, and my daughter was very little. I remember moving down the hallway and kind of being thrown from one wall to another and grabbing my girl. Our dog went under the dining room table, and Abby, my daughter, had these records of Bobby Sherman's, which he had given her — they started playing at the wrong speed — you know, that kind of cartoon sound they make. Bobby, afterwards, said, 'Well, I hope it was some help to you.' Anyway, I got to the set of *Alias Smith and Jones* — we're out in Thousand Oaks, and I was just shocked because everybody got there in time. They all had a story to tell of people in the valley. They'd left their wives at home with every dish in the kitchen on the floor, battered house and everything, but everybody got there! Everybody got there on time. And I thought…'THIS IS THE RIGHT PRIORITY? That we all must not be late for the shoot?'

Continues the actress: "I had to get my girl off to school and got to the set very early in the morning — we were way out there in Thousand Oaks, which is quite a long drive. When I got on the set, I met Pete Duel and Dana Elcar, and Pete talked a lot about his father. He seemed depressed. I remember riding on the stagecoach — I had a great time riding on the stagecoach, and that show was kind of tongue-in-cheek. Pete Duel…he did that kind of thing really well."

Mitzi Hoag was herself skilled at comedy. Among her other TV guest shots were the situation comedies, *The Jeffersons*, *The Facts of Life*, and the comedy-drama *The Love Boat*. "*Love Boat!*" exclaims Hoag. "Oh, my God! I worked with Larry Storch. He was a comic. And comics are not actors. So he was sort of doing his comic shtick. And I was playing an Italian — which was not too convincing, either. See, I did a lot of Irish plays, so I always had an Irish dialect and a British dialect right to hand, and if you can do British dialects, you can do a convincing American Southern dialect. There's a similarity in it, but, on *Facts of Life*, I should have been doing a slightly New York dialect more like Mindy [Cohn]. I didn't do it because I was cast right away, and BAM! I went right into rehearsal. I didn't get it down. In *The Jeffersons*, I remember overhearing a conversation between two of the women stars, one of them saying I was a good actress, the other saying, 'Yeah, but they haven't given her much to do.' That was often the case on sitcoms where you had five or six people doing the leads. You just kind of come in and be the fill. Because they had their stars under contract and had to give each of them something to do."

In 1975, Hoag starred in her own situation comedy, *We'll Get By*. Unlike writer/producer Alan Alda's hit series, *M*A*S*H*, *We'll Get By* "was not political at all," states Hoag. "It was a really solid sitcom, kind of like *The Bob Newhart Show*, about a family with three kids — Paul Sorvino and myself [as the parents] and Devon Scott (George C. Scott's daughter), Willie Aames, and Jerry Hauser [as their children]. Alan was still working on *M\*A\*S\*H* — he was such a workhorse. We'd start rehearsing on Thursday, he'd come to us on Friday, he'd written some scripts ahead of time, and he'd adjust scripts and stuff over the weekend. We'd film on Sunday with a live audience. That was fast for me. Sitcoms are fast, and I really enjoyed working with Alan and Paul Sorvino and the kids. The shows were funny and good, and Alan wrote most of them, so I was very impressed with him. Very impressed. We were all disappointed when the show was not picked up — we went to New York to meet the high mucky-mucks at CBS — they assured us that they were behind the show, blah, blah, blah, but, they weren't. I was really sorry CBS decided not to continue it, because we were just getting in the groove. We did thirteen and one of them, Alan said, it was funny, and aside from funny, it was well done."

Two years later, Mitzi Hoag had another series chance with the Andy Griffith TV-movies, *The Girl in the Empty Grave* and its sequel, *Deadly Game*. "I was a regular on that," remembers Hoag. "We shot it up in Big Bear. Lou Antonio directed *Girl in the Empty Grave*. Andy was the star. It was a mystery, but there was comedy in the writing — it just came out of the dialogue. That was fun. We all wished that that series had gone. We made two movies of the week, the first one was meant to be a pilot, but it was not picked up as a series. Everybody, not myself, cuz I'm more cynical, was looking at property up there, because we would have shot in Big Bear. That would have been fun. I love working up North. But I had this agent who was stabbing me in the back. I didn't find out until later that he was angry that I got that part [Gloria] and that there was somebody else he wanted to get that part." Hoag learned this because "an ex-agent of mine went into the agency. He let me know that this other agent was working against me, and I didn't...I just kind of let it go. I did go to another agency, though."

Hoag went on to do twenty-two commercials with the same director, Leslie Decter. "They were really good commercials," insists Hoag, "and he was such a wonderful director to work with, very creative, and he liked my work, so, he kept having me in."

Continuing to work in television throughout the 1980s, Mitzi Hoag retired from acting in the early '90s. "I met another man," explains Hoag. "I remarried, and I was seeing my girl through college, all that kind of stuff — there were other things going on in my life. I don't even have a television now. I haven't had for a long time. But my grandson is nine and he loves to see things I've done."

Like so many other performers of her generation, Hoag is glad she worked when she did. Reflects the actress: "You know, they talk about the '50s being the Golden Age of Television, but as far as actors were concerned, I think the '60s and '70s were. There was just lots of opportunity, lots of product, lots of energy. That was a good time for television. The people working in it were really wonderful — we had wonderful writers and musicians. It was just so different when we working — there were a lot of dramatic shows, but now there are all these reality shows and sitcoms — it's a different world. In the '60s and '70s, we were able to make a living going from show to show. We had all these hour shows."

In addition to retiring from television acting, Hoag retired from stage acting. She describes stage acting as being "kind of like an airline pilot — with hours of boredom and a few moments of terror — when you have to come up with something. I loved a lot of the acting. I really loved it. But I've done it, so I no longer want to do it."

Television-wise, "I liked the period stuff I did," states the actress. "Being outdoors with horses and things like that, but it's the past. I'm older now — there's different interests, different responsibilities, you do a lot of different things. You don't have a whole lot of life left, so I'm just much more interested in other things. I was always interested in nature. I had a lot of that growing up in Ohio — you know, deciduous trees and berry bushes, and creeks and rivers — that was an important part of my life as a young woman, as a kid. As a kid — the adults were all off — my mom was working in a bomber plant, my dad was working, so I had an awful lot of time alone and an awful lot of places to explore: fallow farm fields with creeks around the side and then we lived near this wonderful river — a rocky river that had been made by a glacier, and there was a hole 'round the city of Cleveland — I had that to explore, and I was just fascinated, walking around there by myself, and coming, going up a little rise, and finding a field of wildflowers and the birds. I always had collies — one was born the [same] year I was, and then my parents moved further out into a rural area and I had that, too. We were in a little house and there was this eighteen-hole golf course behind it, and across the highway, you'd go down into the rocky river area and that was just fascinating to me, you know, seeing birds and small animals and the raccoons. I loved that — I always had that deep connection and then when I went to New York; of course, I didn't have that at all. But then I did a lot of camping in the National Parks and backpacked down the Grand Canyon, and all the…I went cross-country, stopping at Yellowstone and the Grand Tetons and Bryce and Zion, and OHHH, JUST INCREDIBLE! I've belonged to Sierra Club for years, so that's always been a just really important and life-giving thing to me. Even now in this city — this…urban suburb, I have squirrels and possums and lots of birds and that connection. I just had a possum eat a native huckleberry bush I planted. He just ate it down to the roots. And one of my nephews — he lives in a suburb where they cut down a whole lot of forest; the deer have nowhere to go — the deer are eating all the plants.

"You know, I learned a long time ago.…I'd seen *Candide* on Broadway, and I forget the character's name, but the old man who has that wonderful song about 'Make your garden grow,' well, that's what interests me now."[2]

# *Karen Carlson: "I Wanted to be a Susan Tolsky"*

"When I was fourteen," remembers *Brides* first-season semi-regular Karen Carlson, "my parents had…we had taken one vacation ever in my life, and we took two weeks and camped out — all the way up to Oregon, then down the coast, and coming back to [her hometown of] Louisiana. When we went though Los Angeles; I remember we went to Grauman's Chinese Theatre. I was just in awe of everything. I remember as we were driving out Sunset, I was looking out the back window. My dad said, 'You liked it, didn't you?' I said, 'I think so.' He said, 'You'll be back!'

The words of Karen Carlson's late father proved to be prophetic. A few years later, Carlson returned to California. When she did, she found herself working with Bob Hope (that was her first job) then Gene Kelly. Then, she replaced sixties sex goddess Raquel Welch on a television variety series. Performing was not the career Karen Carlson had envisioned for herself when she was in her teens.

"I had planned my life a whole other direction," states the actress. "Originally, I had wanted to study languages, and possibly be a linguist. I studied German in college, can't say I was good at it, although I can probably recognize some of it." When that didn't work out, Carlson hoped to "work at the U.N., and get politically involved diplomatically. I look back and think, 'I'd have been pitiful,'" she laughs. "The things that I believe in would probably not go very far in the diplomatic world today. Well, those doors — especially with the pageant, all those doors closed."

The 'pageant' was the 'Miss America Beauty Pageant.' Carlson was first runner up to the Miss America of 1965 — Vonda Kay Van Dyke. Carlson's talent was singing. "I sang 'As Long as He Needs Me' from *Oliver*," remembers the actress, "and, thank the Lord, that I was not Miss America! Because I was able to walk away and shed that, and not have that follow me for the rest of my life, and affect everything I did. Vonda had to carry that forever. I've lost touch with Vonda, so I don't even know where she is, but I know that we would talk and that's how she would be remembered. I am not a fan of beauty pageants. Although I think it's different today than when I was in, because now I think girls go into it to use it as a vehicle for what they want to do with a career, whether it's broadcasting, or even being a teacher — they use the scholarship money toward that. So I think women approach it differently, especially the Miss America [Pageant]. The Miss USA and the Miss Universe, and all of those [other pageants] — I think those are more about the beauty and the look and the title. I think the girls who go for Miss America are pretty much career-minded, and want to use it as a vehicle. So, more power to 'em!

"I had no desire to be in the pageant," continues Carlson, "it was kind of a fluky thing. I found myself sort of being coerced into doing this. It started at the University of Arkansas. My sorority put me up to run for Miss USA while I was gone one weekend, knowing that I didn't want to do it. They gave me the old, 'For the sorority and your this and your that,' so I said, 'Okay. Fine. What am I gonna do?' 'You'll sing.' I said, 'Okay. Great. I'll sing.' I had planned to sing…I was working on a song — Nina Simone's — I think it was called 'The Other Woman,' or 'You Can Have Him,' or something like that. That week before we were to do this thing, the pageant officials said my song was too risqué. I just recently found the song on a CD and played it. I thought, 'My Goodness! How the times have changed!' But anyway, suddenly I was pushed against the wall, so I had to come up with… I just grabbed for that song ('As Long as He Needs Me'); I had absolutely no intention of winning, I was just doing this to please my sorority sisters, and no one had told me that if you did win, you had to go on to the Miss Arkansas so it just became…it snowballed, and I truly never… I'm not a fan of beauty pageants — I have never watched one since. After I won, I found that it took all to go forward with my plans. I spent a year traveling. Vonda went off to Japan; Miss America then actually went international, so I took over for her for a short period. After that year, I just had so much road experience that trying to go back to school — I knew my life had changed. My dad had passed away — he'd passed away a week before the pageant, so I think I was numb because we were very close. It just sort of…that was it. So when I finished this year [as the first runner up], I really didn't know where I was going, or what I was gonna do. I wanted to go to New York. That was really where I wanted to go, but, at the time, I think there were young girls who were coming in, and living at the 'Y,' or somewhere. Anyway, there was like a series of rapes and murders, and so to ease my mother's mind, I decided I would go to Los Angeles. I had gotten advice from a fellow who made computers for NASA — he made 'the eye,' the little camera that would go up in the space. He was just this brilliant man, and my mother said, 'Go to somebody who is totally objective.' I couldn't think of anybody else I knew who didn't have a clue [as to] who I was, or what I did, nor cared. So I went to him, and just kinda laid out my problem — you know, 'What do I do? Where do I go?' He said, 'Well, it seems to me that YOU are the product. You are your best product, so you need to invest in yourself. Take whatever money you have, and do that.' So, I headed toward California, I think because it was such a wonderful memory with my family — that kind of pulled me there."

Carlson's first night in Hollywood, California, turned out to be a very memorable one. "I got there through [one-time Governor of Arkansas] Winthrop Rockefeller, but that is a long, involved story," states the actress. "He had his little private jet fly me. They dropped me off…I arrived the night of the Watts Riot [beginning on August 11, and continuing until August 15, 1965] not knowing a thing, didn't even know…I was staying at the Hollywood Roosevelt Hotel. A cop at the front door said, especially with my [Southern Louisiana] accent, 'You're not going anywhere. Don't you know what's going on? Go up and turn the television on.' I did. And I barricaded myself in the bathroom for the night. That's my first night in Hollywood — I spent it barricaded in the Hollywood Roosevelt bathroom — brought the chest of drawers over, and I had my escape plan out the window with a fire escape — that was my actual beginning. I think I arrived on a Tuesday. A Monday or a Tuesday. I had my first job the following Saturday, and that's a whole other long story. With Bob Hope."

Thanks to an unexpected encounter with Hope's agent, Louis Shurr. Nicknamed "The Bloodhound," Shurr had an impressive list of clients, including Betty Grable, Bert Lahr, and Carole Landis. "I literally ran over…bumped into on the sidewalk and knocked over Louis Shurr," remembers Carlson. "I was walking down the street, not looking where I was going, and knocked him over. I helped him up. He was about four-foot-eight. I just was in awe. He said, 'Come in to my agency.' I went in, not knowing what an agent was. He said, 'Tell me your story,' and I told him. He said, 'Okay, kid. You wanta be in show business.' I said, 'Yeah, I guess.' That was like on a Wednesday or Thursday. On Saturday, I had my first job. It just was…a Cinderella story — those things just don't really ever happen — that's just rare. It was with Bob Hope, James Garner, and a cow. The one thing that Louis used was the 'Miss America' — just to get the introduction, just to give me some validity. That was the only time that anyone knew or used it because after that show, about six months after I'd been with Louis…and that show led me really…I went from that onto just doing all the variety shows — Phyllis Diller was starting a show, Red Skelton, just all these different variety shows. That Miss America got me the introduction to Bob, but then past that point, when Louis passed away, he was the only one who knew about the Miss America thing."

Good advice from former Miss America Lee Meriwether was the reason Carlson's association with the pageant stayed a secret. "Lee Ann Meriwether and I had lunch when I first went out," explains the actress. "She took me to lunch and said to me, 'If you're serious about being an actress, then don't let anyone know. Don't use it! It'll just kill you in the water. Either that or turn around and go home.' So really, only in this last year, I guess with the Internet, my kids told me that there was this site you could go to, and they found out all this, and they said, 'Geez, Mom!' So I finally went on and saw the site. I said, 'Oh. Great!' This is the first time, in this year, that anyone has ever in all these years, has known, or questioned or asked me about that ever!"

Knowing of Meriwether's talent, Carlson would have liked to see her get even better roles than she did. "Lee never got the opportunity to do the level of material that she wanted to do because she just…she was not taken real seriously," states the actress. "Her name had value because of what she did do. Her name had a lot of value, but I think the depth of what she wanted to do — she never got to go for that. Cuz you get — you really get categorized, and put…in L.A. anyway, I know you do, women, especially, I think."

Another Miss America who turned to acting was Mary Ann Mobley. "I think Mary Ann was very happy," believes Carlson. "She and Gary [Collins] had a lovely lifestyle and a really solid marriage. I think she was very happy with things as they turned out. I don't think she had any great serious desire to be a really serious actress."

Such was not the case with Carlson. "I took over for Raquel Welch on *Hollywood Palace*," remembers the actress. "She went off to do *One Million Years, B.C.*, and I took over the calendar girl thing. It was like a dinosaur. It was like the last of the variety shows. They had a different host every week, and I remember I worked with Gene Kelly. Rich Little and I met on that show, and we dated for a little while. He said, to me, 'This is a dying era.' I said, 'Yeah.' I looked around and I saw all these gorgeous girls. I thought, 'Wow,' cuz on top of the variety show thing really getting ready to take a dive — it was a dead-end if you were counting on looks or anything. I think I went from that to *Laugh-In*. I did two or three *Laugh-In*s as one of the go-go dancers, and it was just like one big free-for-all."

Making the best of her opportunity, Carlson had created a comic character on *Hollywood Palace* which she then took to *Laugh-In*. "I'd kind of tried to…I didn't just want to be the pretty girl that walked out holding the calendar," explains the actress, "so I tried to create this kind of really dingbat character, somewhere between Gracie Allen and Lucy. I hoped to carry that over into *Laugh-In*, but Goldie [Hawn] was already established and gaining momentum [thanks to Hawn's previous series — the 1967-68 sitcom, *Good Morning, World*], and she had that, and physically, I didn't. Goldie had all the physicality going for her that I didn't have. I just became a go-go dancer, I was perfectly happy to do that, and wait to move on to something better."

During Carlson's time on *Laugh-In*, she became friends with two of that series' talented comediennes — Jo Anne Worley and Ruth Buzzi. "The three of us lived in a big old Spanish hacienda house up in the Hollywood Hills," recalls Carlson. "We were kind of roomies for a while. We all roomed in that for a very brief time because then I met David and went off to get married. Seth Riggs owned the house."

By this point very serious about acting, Carlson went to New York to begin learning her new craft. "I had been trying to take a course with Strasberg at UCLA and I didn't understand a word," admits the actress. "I didn't have a clue what he was talking about, so I went off to New York. I studied with Sanford Meisner; I started studying with him, but he...you had to make a commitment, where you only took the class; you couldn't work. I couldn't afford to just study and not work — I had to continue to support myself. Meisner had a protégé named Jack Walther, who had a class that was Sanford's class, but he taught everything, so in that class, oh my gosh, there was Jon Voight, Teri Garr... Jack then brought the class out to Los Angeles. That class was just incredible — there were lots and lots of people: Eva Marie Saint, Cindy Williams; I studied with David Craig who was married to Nancy Walker. He would teach an actor who's not really a singer how to perform a song for musicals. Then I studied with Uta Hagen; I studied privately with her. And Stella Adler. I started with her in New York, and then she came out to L.A. and I would study with her when she was in L.A. She would usually come out just for the summer. So my studying was pretty intensive. I was always studying. I was always somewhere studying with someone through that whole period. David actually is the one who introduced me to Uta Hagen. She I think was the one person that I... that just sort of... suddenly the whole key unlocked for me, and I began to understand what the whole process was about. It was when I came back from New York that I actually started to get very small parts. I started getting roles. That was when *Here Come the Brides* came in."

It was series star Robert Brown who got Carlson on *Brides*. "I was working for Johnny Mathis at the time," remembers the actress, "and, one morning, going up to work, which was at Sunset and Gower, this fellow got on the elevator, with just this wonderful, open smile, and sort of a little bit of a very distinguished accent, and he said, 'Hello, I'm Robert Brown. And you are...' And I remember thinking, 'Uh-huhhh,' but he was so...He said, 'I am just...I am headed on...I have a meeting,' and he had just gotten *Here Come the Brides*, and he was soooo enthusiastic, and pleased and happy and open. It was kinda lovely. I don't even remember if we exchanged numbers — I have no idea. I don't even remember. All I know is I started dating Robert and he was very kind of, fatherly to me, I think that was — I kind of thought of him as comforting — he was a total gentleman, and I didn't feel like I was going to have to do anything in order to see this person — I just felt very comfortable with him, and so, I guess it really wasn't that long. He said to me, 'I've put your name in to play one of the brides.' I said, 'Oh, okay,' and I went in and had my meeting, I guess. I don't remember the meeting, but all I know is suddenly I was gonna be playing one of the brides and that first day on the set I just was so excited and I didn't want to be a… I never was late — I always was too early. I got there so far ahead of everybody else that they got me into makeup and they were trying to get a shot of all the guys on the dock as the boat's coming in. And so they said, 'Would you mind if we used you? Put you up in this huge boom thing? Would you mind if we used you as focal point so they've got somebody to react to?' I said, 'No, that'd be great.' So I was sitting up there when I…suddenly the three brothers come walking out onto the dock in the scene, and I looked down and saw David, and I think my heart just went *KEW* right then! That was the day that we actually met, and Robert Brown told me later, because he actually was our best man in the wedding, he told me later, that he took one look at me, he took one look at David and he knew I was smitten, and went, 'Oh boy! What a mistake that was.' Anyway, it was very nice."

By that time, Carlson had dated other men in Hollywood. Such as *Man from U.N.C.L.E.* star Robert Vaughn. Remembers the actress, "I was the first… where they had three — you had a guest, and three mystery people, and you listened to them — *The Dating Game* — the first nighttime *Dating Game.* I guess the show was on in the afternoon, and then they went to nighttime. For the first nighttime show, Sally Field and myself were the two people who had to choose someone. I remember Sally — whoever she chose, they took her by helicopter downtown to a restaurant for dinner or something, landed on top of a hotel and then flew her back. That was her thing. Mine was that the bachelor that I chose, and I thought when they — just before he came around the curtain, they said starring in *Man from U.N.C.L.E.*, I was really hoping it would be David McCallum, although I guess he's like five-foot-four, but I was hoping it would be him. Instead Robert Vaughn came around the thing and I went, 'Oh. Yeah. Okay.' Well, our trip was a trip to London and I think the reason being…well, Robert's a smart businessman — the way they got him on the show was because he was getting ready to speak at the Geneva Peace Conference. So this was gonna pay for his trip to London. So we actually flew to London and I remember him working the whole time in first class — he was working on his speech. We got there — we had dinner or something, and then he left the next morning, and I got to spend three or four days with this really fun chaperone. We just rode bikes all over and laughed and Robert came back. We had a couple days there dating and going to a nightclub, seeing a play and whatever, so they could, of course, photograph it and do all that sort of stuff, and then we came back and as a result when we came back, we had one or two dates in L.A. and he had, I guess, had them call me in to do *Man from U.N.C.L.E.* After that we were just friends. We were from two different worlds. I'm from the country but my life is not necessarily simple. I wasn't into things — I don't care about things, but he was well known, and a star. I was just a fledgling, building my way up, trying to stay out of everybody's bed."

The sixties, being what *Brides* guest Lynda Day George describes as a "very ballsy time" in the business, ("That's a really good way to put it," notes Carlson), Karen Carlson ran into some very unpleasant situations. Recalls the actress, "You would go…I can remember going to an interview — the higher you went up at Universal, the higher the offices, the higher the floor numbers, the more you were going up to people of importance. I just remember going to an office way up on one of those floors, for what I thought was a reading, and when I got inside the office, the person was on the phone with his wife. So I sat down and he then got off the phone with her, punched the thing to his secretary telling her to hold all calls, and then I heard this little click thing, but it didn't register. Then, supposedly, we were gonna do this reading, and he said, 'Why don't we just sit over here on the sofa where we can really be comfortable,' and proceeded to, I mean, put himself on me. I got up to try and get out the door and it was locked, and that was not the only time that something like that happened in terms of where I would find the door was locked. These guys would have these little... like a security button that was under their desk, and they'd just hit this thing, and the door would lock. And it only took maybe once or twice, and I was wise to that. It was...I look back at all of that, and I'm so amazed that I survived intact."

Carlson devised a pretty good escape plan for such situations. "I would have a date with somebody," she explains, "and I would always have a reason or an excuse why I had to leave. I would meet them somewhere so that I could drive my own car so that I could escape. And did. So many times I can't even tell ya."

Not that there still weren't incidents which took the actress completely by surprise. Says Carlson: "I remember going with a producer to a club on Sunset Blvd. and him flipping something into my hand...his daughter was with us. We went to a Diana Ross concert at Universal, and then we went to this place to have dinner. His daughter, who was like twenty-something, and her girlfriend, were with us, having dinner, then they went off to the bathroom. He slipped something in my hand and said, 'Why don't you go join them and have a good time,' and I looked at this thing. I knew that what I had in my hand was not something that I had any idea what to do with — I was SCARED! I literally went out the BATHROOM EXIT! You walked down this hall...I just remember this big door that said, 'EXIT,' and I WENT OUT THAT EXIT and hitched back to the Beverly Hills hotel so I could get my car. I went home and DIDN'T ANSWER THE PHONE FOR A WEEK! I was terrible. I just would leave. I didn't have social skills in those areas. I was greener than green. I just didn't know anything in those areas, and when my little internal alarm would go off, I would RUN cuz I didn't know what else to do."

News traveling fast in Hollywood, situations like the above grew fewer and fewer. "I think I probably pretty much had a reputation," believes Carlson. "I had the same reputation in high school — you know, if you wanted to have a really good time, pick Carlson, but if you want to fool around or do anything, forget it! Go somewhere else."

Early in *Brides* run, 'bride' Carlson married series co-star David Soul. "He was Norwegian, and I was Swedish," she says. "I have always been told you can't put the two in the same boat together. Well, we did. And, in my book, I came from that fairy land where you only get involved if you're really in love. I was smitten with David, I think when I looked down and I saw him that first day — my heart went *BING!* Later in the day I was walking from my dressing room, going somewhere, and I heard somebody singing and playing this song, so I sat down on the steps of the trailer. I didn't know his name — I saw the name up there — David Soul — but I didn't know who that was. I just heard this person singing and I sat there, listening. He stopped and I was waiting for him to start again, and suddenly the door opened, and it was David! I was so startled, and he was startled, because I was sitting there. I said, 'Oh, my Gosh! Was that you singing?' He said, 'Yeah.' I said, 'Wow! That was wonderful!' He said, 'Would you like to come in?' and I think I went in. That's really the thing that…I just remember… it was a Charles Aznavour song, so David was my introduction to Charles Aznavour music and [musician/actor] Jacques Brel. Then [years later] he went on and took some of [*Adventures in Paradise* star] Gardner McKay's poetry and put it to music, which was kind of in the same flavor. We became very dear, close friends [with McKay] through [*Rebel Without a Cause/The Outsider/Sybil* writer] Stewart Stern. Stewart was one of our son's godfathers, and so, we all became really good friends, and Gardner wrote poetry, and David…this was years after *Brides*, but David would take the poetry and kind of put it to music. There are several of them on his album he put out. The music was the thing that really…because I just had never heard anything like that. Now that David lives in London, he's actually worked with Aznavour. They've done several shows together, I think."

Carlson has fond memories of her acting days on *Here Come the Brides*. And semi-regulars like Buck Kartalian. "Oh, God, I loved Buck!" enthuses the actress. "Buck was so huggable. I just remember him being…I think everyone had a pretty good sense of humor. We did the work, but I just remember them also loving to fool around and kid around, which was very good for me, because everything I had done up to that point was pretty serious. At one point, I felt like the only reason I got a job was because I could cry. So it was just wonderful with people who had this great sense of humor, and truly, once you entered the studio, and you went onto the sets, it was kind of like going back in time. It was truly like stepping back in time to that era. It was really like a big dream. And I was in love."

As was Carlson's friend, Susan Tolsky. "I loved working with Susan Tolsky," says the actress. "I haven't talked to her in a long time, but one of my dear friends here [in Tennessee] is one of her close friends. We just discovered it one day by accident, and picked up the phone and called her. And Susan's incredibly psychic. She picked up the phone immediately. I remember her being just so much fun and wanting to be pretty. Then I remember her falling so much in love with Chris [Christopher Stone] and just everything about her softened, and by that point, our lives had all gone different directions. She was just fun and funny, and I wanted to be a Susan Tolsky. I just thought she was great. When I first started, I wanted to be Carol Burnett. I wanted to be the next Carol Burnett. I didn't want to be a leading lady, or care about looks, that kind of thing. I wanted to do, really, character stuff and, of course, maybe I could do it now, but back then I certainly couldn't get those roles."

The actress also enjoyed semi-regular Mitzi Hoag. "I loved Mitzi!" she exclaims. "What a wonderful spirit! I remember her very fondly, and beautiful…I thought she had beautiful eyes. William Blinn, of course, I went on to do a series for; I did a series called *American Dream*, which was Bill Blinn's show, and by the time the pilot aired and we got picked up and we were shooting it in Chicago, they put us all over the place — nobody could find it. Nobody could find it! And it was really a wonderful show. So we got canceled and were hoping that NBC, whoever had had *Hill Street Blues* — they had canceled it. We were up against *Hill Street Blues* for Emmys and we won two of them, but we were gone, we were already canceled, and we were hoping NBC would pick us up [in place of *Hill Street*], but it didn't happen. There were political problems there. At that point, I was on to having a baby."

While Karen Carlson cannot remember fellow "brides" Cynthia Hull (Ann), and Diane Sayer (Sally), she certainly does recall leading lady Bridget Hanley. "Oh, my God! I love Bridget!" says the actress. "I loved her then. She was just sunshine and energy and was the mother — she was really kind of the mother of all of us. She just kinda kept us... like all her little chickens around her and mothered us all. Bridget was like a tomboy — very fun. So much fun, spirited, and fiery. Bridget would be out there with the guys when we played football. I'd just be the goal. 'I'll be the goal. Run this way.' Yes, she was like Maureen O'Hara — Exactly. Exactly right. The ones I remember the best were Susan and Bridget because we were friends. We spent a lot of time together outside of the studio."

Brides' *Karen Carlson in the 1972 Warner Brothers drama,* The Candidate.

Like Susan Tolsky, Karen Carlson stayed on the *Brides* set even when she wasn't working. "When I had small parts...you would find me on the set, very quietly in a corner, watching, because that was a great learning feeling for me," she explains. "To watch the directors, the lighting, the camera, the angles, all kinds of thing. I just was absorbing anything and everything that I could — I was really kind of a sponge, just working and observing and learning."

As a result, Carlson found a good bit of work as guest star on *The FBI, Ironside, The Incredible Hulk,* and in motion pictures such as the Robert Redford/Michael Ritchie drama, *The Candidate.* Remembers the actress: "When I did *The Candidate,* Redford said to me, 'Don't do television! Because you have the potential to be a film actress, and to be fine. You keep studying, you keep working at it. Television will end your film career.' I really had hoped to follow that advice. But after David and I separated, I had to survive. I had to support my kids. So I really didn't have a choice — I couldn't hold out and just wait for the film. I was fortunate, though, because I did get to go back and forth a bit, between, and got to do it all. Except theater. I couldn't really afford to do theater. It just didn't pay the bills."

So Carlson did all manner of television. One of her earliest post *Brides* guest shots came on the long-running anthology, *Death Valley Days*. "That was an amazing show," states the actress. "Oh, my goodness. That was where you went in in the morning. You read for it. If you got it, you were on a plane by noon, arriving in Kanab, Utah, by 12:30 or 1:00 p.m. On the set by three, shooting by four in the afternoon. And good luck if you hadn't had a chance to read the script. I mean that was an amazing show to do, and at the end, on the last day of shooting that, I remember the producer coming to me and saying, 'You know, we'd like to use you for a second show. Would you mind just staying on?' I said, 'Yeah, but aren't they gonna know?' He said, 'Oh, they won't be shown back to back.' So I did two [episodes], back to back."

The actress also assured herself a place in *FBI* TV-series history when she became one of the few female guest stars on the series to portray an FBI agent — the fifth season's "Boomerang." Carlson's other QM guest shots included *Banyon* (co-starring *Brides'* Joan Blondell), *Barnaby Jones,* and *The Streets of San Francisco*. Producer of the latter was former actor, John Wilder. "The way I met Quinn was through John Wilder," explains the actress. "John is probably one of my very closest friends; he was married to Carolyn, and to this day he is like a brother. My children and John's children were all going to the same school at that point, so through John, it seems to me that's when Quinn brought me in. I remember doing a *Streets of San Francisco* ("Legion of the Lost"). Joan probably recommended me for *Banyon* — I don't remember. I remember shooting that in downtown L.A., in the Bradbury building. I know that part of that second year [of *Brides*], I think I had started getting other jobs, and Joan...our agreement was that if I got another acting job, I could go do that and come back which is what I did. So I was blessed because I had the same arrangement with Johnny [Mathis] and I don't remember what shows I did, because *Brides* was the first time I was really given to have a specific character. Part of that [period] I was mainly doing just kind of day things. Sometime then my own career started to happen. I remember doing a show with Henry Fonda (*The Smith Family* –"Rumpus Room") — he taught me how to do needlepoint."

In 1970, audiences saw Carlson on the big screen in the low-budget Roger Corman feature, *The Student Nurses* (written, directed, and produced by Stephanie Rothman); the same year TV audiences saw her in the David Janssen thriller, *Night Chase*. The latter "was an interesting experience because I had a nude scene in it," remembers Carlson, "and, again, I know that must have been because I was so young and inexperienced. That was supposed to be a closed set, and it wasn't a lovemaking scene — it was just me lying on a bed. I can't remember if that was when he (Janssen) kills me, or if he kills the guy [Carlson's lover in the story.] I can't remember the story. Anyway, I had my robe on, and I went to lie down on the bed and looked up and the rafters were just full of people. OH, MY GOD! I was horrified! I jumped up and grabbed my robe and ran off the set, and called my agent. I said, 'I can't do this! I can't do this.' So he came to the set and the producer came. Well, long story short, that changed one of the SAG rules, because when I agreed to do the show, that scene wasn't in the script. It was just a scene where she and supposedly this guy have made love, and they're lying...he's asleep, and she's just lying there, kind of with her eyes open, and then Janssen walks in on them or something. It wasn't written that I was supposed to be lying there, nude. Somehow they had changed that, for European release, they were gonna do a European release, but that was never something I was aware of or agreed to; I was so green, I was afraid to say anything to anybody for fear that I'd lose the job. So, I didn't want to say anything, and we'd already shot for several days, so I'm already in stuff. So they came on the set, and, as a result, it literally changed the SAG ruling in terms of disclosure. For any actor, any type of nudity that's gonna be asked of [you], that has to be disclosed up front before you ever sign a contract. And when it says, 'Closed Set,' it literally means 'Closed Set.' That defines it — it wasn't at that point. So I feel like, 'Well, that's good. I helped changed the rules of SAG,' and yet they kept me on. I got to finish that job. I mean, here I was, not trying to make waves, and I was...I just made the ocean."

Two years later, Karen Carlson assured herself a place in *Bonanza* series history when she played U.S. Marshal Theodora Duffy in the fourteenth-season episode, "The Marriage of Theodora Duffy" — the last *Bonanza* episode filmed (according to the actress), the second-to-last *Bonanza* episode to air. "That was gonna be my big, huge break," states Carlson. "They had just cast Tim Matheson [as the Cartwright's new ranch hand, Griff King], and I was gonna come in and be the new female addition to the show. I remember that was [originally] called "The Marriage of Duffy McBride." That was my introduction to the show. My contract was to be this new character in the show."

The ratings for the series having gone down due to the loss of Dan Blocker, Carlson only got to play the role of *Bonanza*'s first-ever female regular a total of one time. "We were shooting the last show of *Bonanza*," remembers the actress, "with no forewarning. They'd been on...for years, and they never...not a word had been said to them, and the NBC officials took them to lunch. They came back... Michael [Landon] was too emotional, and couldn't speak. Everybody's going, 'OH, MY GOD! WHAT HAS HAPPENED NOW?' Then the producer's standing there, and very emotionally, saying, 'Well. We just went to lunch with the NBC officials who announced that THIS IS OUR LAST SHOW!' Took 'em to lunch, fourteen years, and 'Guess what, guys? You're shooting your last show!' THAT WAS IT! Just gave 'em the axe, and I remember everyone in absolute, just stunned silence, then Michael trying to speak, and it was decided that we would take a thirty-minute break or whatever until everybody could pull [themselves] back together, and I remember people lined up at the phones cuz it was like two weeks before Christmas, and hearing crew members say, 'Honey, take the such and such back. We don't...we're not gonna have income...' I just remember it being unbelievable. I went back to my dressing room, bawled my eyes out... I just remember thinking, 'Well, okay, there goes my big shot!' And it was so wonderful working with those guys. Michael was just so...he was directing the show. He said, 'Okay, all these years...' because we were supposed to have a shot where two guys come through the door. They throw the door open; I blast them with a shotgun. Well, of course, in *Bonanza* days, they would get shot, and there would be no blood, no anything. Michael said, 'Okay, we're gonna save this scene until the last day, and we're gonna shoot two versions. We're gonna shoot the network version and we're gonna shoot the…the *real* version, and then we're gonna give em that one, but we'll have a back-up.' So we shot, and when we shot that scene we shot the first one with no blood, no anything, then we shot the second one, and I mean there was blood everywhere, and people went flying through — they didn't just fall dead — they pulled them by ropes — blasted them through the door. I've always wondered — I've never seen the show, which one…obviously the other one made it to air. I would have loved to have been there when they watched that [the more violent, bloody version] in dailies. OH, MY GOD!"

Being a fan of Michael Landon, Karen Carlson thoroughly enjoyed working with him. "I loved working with him as a director," says the actress. "I wouldn't use the term 'genius' to describe him. Not a lot of people meet that. He had incredible insight and foresight, both in terms of the business and people. And a great sense of humor. I thought he was a terrific person. *Genius?* I don't even know exactly what that means. I was just a fan of his as a person."

For a brief time, Carlson had also played the role of Ellen Meredith, daughter of Ingrid Bergman's Libby Meredith, in the 1970 Columbia Pictures feature, *A Walk in the Spring Rain.* The movie reunited Bergman with her 1964 *The Visit* co-star, Anthony Quinn. "Guy Green was going to direct," remembers Carlson. "I just…was so, so excited. I got the role and our first read-through…Tony Quinn wasn't there for the reading, and I was just so in awe of Miss Bergman. Then Guy had to tell me like three days later that he was having to replace me because Anthony Quinn had never heard of me. He didn't want to work with somebody that he hadn't worked with, somebody whom he'd never heard of, or whom he couldn't watch. He didn't want to have to do anything more than in one take. And Guy, because Guy was from England, and was still trying to get his foot in the door in this country, he couldn't afford to buck Anthony Quinn and the studio, and money and all the powers that be. At that point I was too young and naïve and too green to understand what any of that meant. Now I completely understand. I probably would have to do the same thing. Anyway, after that, Guy and his wife and his daughter — we were all…Gardner again, this is where we all had dinner together, and we became very good friends. We were neighbors."

Carlson has fond memories of working with series stars Robert Wagner and Stefanie Powers on the November 11, 1980 *Hart to Hart* second season premiere, "Murder, Murder on the Wall." "Stefanie and I were neighbors," she explains, "and she said they were getting ready to do this show, and how did I feel about doing it? I went in and read, and got it. We shot that in New York, and that was great! Then, years later, [when Carlson moved to Tennessee], I got a call, and was asked to drive over to Wilmington, North Carolina. They were gonna do a spin-off from *Matlock,* they wanted to do that with a couple, and they wanted Robert and me to be this couple. So I drove over there, and this was pre-cell-phone days. I got there, only to be told that the network decided to can the idea because the ratings were dropping on *Matlock,* and they decided they should put more energies into getting the ratings back up rather than trying to do a spin-off. They canceled Robert's flight, but we had dinner. I had a lovely walk on the beach, then turned around and drove back to

Tennessee. Working with Robert Wagner was fun — just fun. He was a hard worker, but fun. And Stefanie and I were good friends for a while. At one point I was doing a project, and when I finished it, I was gonna go to Africa with her. This was after Bill [Holden] had died. She was headed back to put things together, and I was gonna go with her, but I didn't finish shooting in time, so I couldn't make it. I could very easily have gotten sidetracked into that [working for the William Holden Wildlife Foundation in Africa], and just stayed there, and done that. I just lost touch with all those people when I left L.A."

Those with whom she did *not* lose contact were former husband, David Soul, and casting executive/television producer, Renee Valente. "I met Renee before David and I were married," says Carlson. "When we got married, she and her husband Burr [Smidt] came to the wedding in Shreveport. She also is my family. The weekends — even after David and I separated — that was where I took my boys. We just lived a block from each other."

When it came to whether it was Karen Carlson or David Soul who ended their marriage, "I really think *I'm* the one who separated us," believes the actress. "Another person had entered the scene, and I was hoping he'd come to his senses and realize what he was losing, but you know, [that] didn't happen. I finally decided that I would give him the complete, total ultimatum: I would get a divorce, and surely he would come flying into the courtroom and end it. And say, 'NO, NO, NO!' But he didn't do that either. So we ended up divorced, and I was devastated.

"But," reflects Carlson, "life just happens, and we all make choices. I have a deep respect for David and love for him that will always be. I'm his family. His mother and father had been my mother and dad. They said, 'You didn't divorce us. You just divorced David.' So they have remained my mom and dad for all these years. And one of David's sisters is a professor at the college where my last two sons chose to go. And she just calls them, though they have a completely different father, her nephews. It's kind of an unusual family. We don't accept those terms 'stepbrothers,' 'stepfather,' all of that. We just don't. David is just...he and I are not married. Nor do we live together. Nor would we ever again. We have a love and respect. He's family — he's just family."

In fact, Carlson and Soul were on such good terms, they worked together again in his mid-eighties series, *The Yellow Rose*. "My scenes were all with David and Edward Albert, who was just such a sweet guy," remembers Carlson, "and Cybill Shepherd and Sam Elliott. I had been warned that Cybill and I would have a problem, [but] she and I got along just great. She's a hoot. She's basically a free spirit — kind of always has been."

Carlson also had a semi-regular role as Nancy Scotfield on the 1986-87 season (the 10th season) of *Dallas*. "I did like the last four or five shows," recalls Carlson. "I brought the Ewing clan down. The offices close up, the FBI comes in, and that sort of thing. I worked with Victoria and Patrick and Larry, and the fella who played my brother, can't remember his name — I got him to steal files; he worked for the FBI."

Moving on to become a producer, director and writer, Karen Carlson has no regrets as to where she is at this point in her life. "My hat's off to the actresses who are hanging in there out in L.A. because it takes a lot of courage to grow old before the camera, I think," states Carlson. "It just takes a lot of courage. But I believe that everything happens as it's supposed to happen. I really do. The greatest challenge in life I believe is to find something that you absolutely love and that you're passionate about. Then just follow it. Have the courage to follow it. So many people don't.

"I can't imagine living any other way."[3]

1. Hoag – 2007
2. Hoag – 2007
3. Carlson

"Strawberry rhubarb pie! Miss Cloom, will you marry me?"

---

Logger Sam to Biddie Cloom
in Episode #1 ("Here Come the Brides")

# Chapter 14
# *Loggers*

## *Robert Biheller: Playing Poker with Clark Gable, David Janssen, and Fred MacMurray*

"Acting," *Here Come the Brides* semi-regular Robert Biheller will candidly admit, was "something I always wanted to do. I was born in L.A. — I couldn't avoid it. I must have been needy! I started out on the stage, in high school theater, then college, majored in theatre arts, the whole bit, then I was doing plays around L.A., got an agent while I was there. I had a friend whose father was a producer, so I did a pilot. Jan Clayton was the star. Sam Marx was the producer. They asked me if I could chew gum and walk at the same time. I didn't study in New York. I took classes from people in L.A. Started doing that when I was young. [Director/producer/writer] Sherman Marks was one of my teachers, and when I was really young — I think it was high school, there was a group…Ben Bard, who was a silent screen actor…now he was reduced to having a class, he put on plays and things."[1]

Robert Biheller is being a bit minimizing of his former acting teacher. According to actor Ben Bard's son (journalist Bartley Bard), Ben Bard Drama [the school the actor founded in the 1930s], was "one of the largest and most respected acting schools in Hollywood."[2] Noted graduates of the school included Alan Ladd, Jack Carson, Shirley Temple, Gower Champion, Angie Dickinson, Cliff Robertson, and Gig Young. The bosses at 20th Century Fox certainly thought highly of Bard — in the 1950s, he headed the New Talent Department at the studio.

Like most television actors of the time, Robert Biheller did "lots of plays: *Rashomon*, *Blood Wedding*, *Waiting for Godot*, *Hamlet*, but I didn't play Hamlet. I did Shakespeare in college — never anything big. I did *Oedipus Rex*, James Joyce plays, did *Becket,* the play, *Winterset*. Lots of work in college."

It was while he was in college that "I got up for a part in [*The*] *Young Savages* with Burt Lancaster," remembers Biheller. "John Frankenheimer was the director, and it was really exciting for me because it was a major part — they acted like they had discovered something, but what happened was…it ended up that

Frankenheimer cast it in New York, so I was kind of out, but then they hired me to do a part in it. I was on it for a couple weeks."

Biheller has good things to say about working with Burt Lancaster. "He was a very nice man, very pleasant to work with, a good experience for kind of a first time almost. And Dina Merrill was in it. Dina Merrill was very down to earth, very nice. She played Lancaster's wife. I had one scene…we were gonna rape her in an elevator — but at the last moment he appears, so we have to break for it. Dina Merrill was very, very pleasant to work with. Nice woman, good actress. But Frankenheimer… had a mouth on him. He did *Turn of the Screw* with Ingrid Bergman on *Playhouse 90* or one of their shows, and his mouth was so foul that Ingrid Bergman called him aside and said, 'If you keep it up, if you say one more thing, I'm walking.' He was great, and Shelley Winters…she's interesting, too."

But not in a positive way. "I did a *Batman* with her ["The Greatest Mother of Them All/Ma Parker," October 5 & 6, 1966, ABC]," laughs Biheller, "[I] played her son, 'Pretty Boy.' She was such a pain. At one point, it was so funny — the director, Oscar Rudolph…we had Batman and Robin in the electric chair; we were gonna kill them, and the clock is ticking. Well, the Parker family — we're standing there waiting, but the clock was inanimate — it was not working, and Shelley had to stop the proceedings because SHE was a METHOD ACTRESS! SHE NEEDED THE CLOCK TO BE TICKING! Oscar says, 'QUIT WITH THE FUCKIN' ACTOR'S STUDIO BULLSHIT! LET'S GO!' Then, at one point, we'd gone out for lunch, came back to the set, we're all standing around the set…we hear a scream - it's Shelley, crying, 'Help, Help. I've fallen!' Oscar says, 'LEAVE HER!' I mean she was a PAIN! She wanted me to wear lifts, and have a gap in my teeth — she had all these ideas for me. I didn't take any of her suggestions."

Biheller has good things to say about *Batman* star Adam West, however. "Adam West was terrific, he was fun, but [co-star] Burt Ward's a schmuck. He just thought he was…He was a putz." As for [the episode's] sexy henchgirl, Tisha Sterling (in the role of "Legs" Parker), "she was HOT and bubbly and out there," remembers Biheller. "I liked her. I LIKED HER. YEAH! DEFINITELY! She was the daughter of [actress] Anne Jeffreys and [actor] Robert Sterling, so I had to tell her the story — 'Hi, I'm Robert Sterling.' 'Hi, I'm Fred MacMurray.'"

Biheller was referencing the parties of his friends, the Langs. It was while attending these star-studded affairs that he met the likes of MacMurray and his actress-wife June Haver, Clifton Webb, Clark Gable, Cesar Romero, et al. The Langs were director Walter Lang (*Tin Pan Alley, State Fair, Sitting Pretty, Cheaper by the Dozen, With a Song in My Heart, There's No Business Like Show Business, The King and I, But Not for Me, Can Can*), his actress wife, Madalynne Field — a.k.a. "Fieldsie" (friend and secretary to Carole Lombard); she also appeared in Mack Sennett shorts, and, future TV director Richard Lang (*Kung Fu* — multiples; *Harry O* — multiples; *Charlie's Angels* — first season — multiples; *The Streets of San Francisco* — multiples; *Quinn Martin's Tales of the Unexpected* — multiples; *Fantasy Island* — pilot film; the David Janssen TV-movie, *Nowhere to Run*; and the excellent eight-hour Janssen miniseries, *The Word*.)

"When I was a kid," explains Biheller, "one of my best friends in high school was Richard Lang. Richard was Walter and Fieldsie's only child, and the house that they lived in was the house that Nixon used to live in. Walter Lang had such an eye — there was a tree in the backyard — he had it moved two inches just for the aesthetics of it. The Langs were all very big. They were big people. Richard was a big guy. And jovial. And the bar in the house was big and the glasses were big, and the drinks were big. So I'd be there, getting crazy with these people."

Being a "very close friend of" Richard Lang, "I was always over at his house," says Biheller. "I would be invited to parties. I'd be at a party at their house, surrounded by these movie stars — you just never knew who you were gonna meet over there. One party…all of a sudden I'd turn around and they'd say, 'Bob. We'd like you to meet the KING,' and it'd be Clark Gable and his wife. Then Clifton Webb would come leaping in, and on and on and on. In the meantime, David Janssen was a close friend of Walter and Fieldsie, and Walter had a real liking for David. So David became kind of a friend of mine. We [everyone at the party] used to play cards, and we'd drink a lot, and I was younger than all of 'em. I was sixteen, and I would be invited to these poker parties, I'd be playing poker with Fred MacMurray and June Haver."

Thanks to his longtime friendship with Richard Lang, Biheller heard some amazing stories. "We were in his bedroom one day," remembers the actor, "and I noticed the Academy Award — it was Gable's Academy Award for *It Happened One Night*, and it was all banged up. Richard said when he was a little kid, he'd been at Gable's with his parents. He went to the door of the bedroom [where Gable had slept with wife, Carole Lombard], and he wanted to go in the room [because] when she died in the plane crash, Gable locked up that room just the way it was." Naturally curious, Richard Lang kept begging Gable to let him in the room. "In order to quiet him down," explains Biheller, "Gable gave him the Oscar. He [Lang] proceeded to use it as a hammer." When Clark Gable died, his *It Happened One Night* Oscar went back into the Gable family.

During his high school years, Robert Biheller was also close with Noel Blanc — son of the great cartoon voice artist, Mel Blanc, "Man of a Thousand Voices." "I kind of had known Mel since I was a kid in high school," says the actor. "I used to go to breakfast at his house, and he'd tell jokes. Noel was kind of my best friend in high school, and they opened up, along the way, a production company. Did a thing called *Superfun* — I worked on that, and there were a bunch of restaurants opened up called Looney Tunes, and I wrote for that [when Biheller turned to writing later in his career] — they did 'Looney Tunes' kind of shows."

Biheller's mother also knew some famous folk. "My mother was a dress designer — custom knits" explains the actor, "She'd sell to Neiman-Marcus; she had her own store, and she catered to high end [customers]. She had people like Julie Andrews, and Marilyn Monroe and Eartha Kitt for customers."

Besides getting parts in movies like *The Young Savages* while still in college, Robert Biheller guest-starred on shows such as *The Many Loves of Dobie Gillis*. "I think I was still in college when I did that," believes Biheller. "Bob Denver was a good guy. [Star] Dwayne Hickman was a pain in the ass. I saw him berate an extra. I think he thought he was really something. His brother, Darryl, was the better actor [and, now] Dwayne Hickman has kind of disappeared. Rod Amateau directed *Dobie*. Working with Amateau was great. He knows what he's doing, moves fast. I wish I had worked with Tuesday Weld [who played Hickman's dream girl, Thalia Menninger on the first season of the show]. She was a hell of an actress, very underrated. I sold a screenplay to a man named Marshall Backlaur, who produced *Pretty Poison* with Tuesday."

Once he graduated, Robert Biheller began guest-starring on series such as *The Richard Boone Show, Jesse James, 87th Precinct, Eleventh Hour, Sam Benedict, The Great Adventure, Combat,* and *Malibu Run*. "Scott Marlowe was in *Malibu Run*," remembers Biheller. "He was an up-and-coming, guest star-ish, moody. Moody and broody. I think he did some QM [Quinn Martin series]. I did quite a few QMs."

Including the third-season two-part *Fugitive* ("Landscape with Running Figures"). "Landscape" reunited Biheller with his old drinking buddy, David Janssen. "David drank!" laughs Biheller. "He took me out to lunch several times, and one time, the last day of the show, we went out. I didn't have any more dialogue — all I had was a scene where I try to rape [guest star] Barbara Rush — she screams. He comes running down the street, and I come running out of this building. I get into a little quick fight with him, then I leap into this truck [with fellow juvenile delinquents] Robert Doyle and Judee Morton. So David and I went out to lunch, and we drank. We had the proverbial three-martini lunch, and [when they did the fight after lunch] I accidentally decked him. Knocked the wind out of him. That was a fun show to do. Barbara Rush was cool. She was a good actress. I worked well with her. It was a nice scene — that particular one. [Director] Wally [Grauman] got into it. I remember one time, because I was [playing] kind of a stupid person, he had me drool. 'Beavo' was the character's name. And Robert Doyle! Boy! Was he a good actor! Kind of looked like Robert Walker, a little bit. I liked Doyle a lot."

Director Grauman thought pretty highly of Biheller. "I was in quite a few shows with Wally directing," remembers Biheller. "There was a point where he kind of mentored me. On *Blue Light*, (a 1966 ABC adventure starring actor/singer Robert Goulet as double agent David March), I was just on as kind of an assistant director. Wally was just kind of teaching me the ropes. Then I got busy acting again. Wish I'd stuck with it [directing]."

Not that Biheller was doing badly as an actor, especially when he was working with directors like Robert Altman on shows such as *Combat*. "[*Combat* star] Vic Morrow was kind of moody," remembers Biheller. "A loner. One of the shows that I did was called "The First Day." Jack Hogan was one of the running parts on that. We have a moment in the show...I'm this big-mouth punk, and the show is about the first day for these soldiers to join up with their new unit. I'm a loud mouth, and I say things...I'm a coward really, and Hogan's character has got my number. Well, in the show, we're supposed to lock eyes. We turn around. He sees me reacting to someone. We turned around and we lock eyes, and it's very intense, or supposed to be, because we would just crack up. We laughed so hard, we'd stop, get hold of ourselves...I don't know how many times we did this until they got pissed. You know, time is money."

Another war series on which Biheller guest-starred was the Quinn Martin/20th Century Fox drama, *12 O'Clock High;* Biheller guest-starred in the second-season's "Big Brother." [The title referred to the older brother of Colonel Joe Gallagher (series star Paul Burke)]; the character was played by Jack Lord. "Paul Burke was a nice man," praises Biheller. "Jack Lord was aloof. I didn't get around him. Robert Dornan was the co-pilot [Captain Fowler]. WHAT A PERSON! He was conservative even then, and just really out there. [Series regular] Chris Robinson [Tech Sgt. Sandy Komansky] was a good guy. Chris I worked with on *Young Savages*. He was the one who got the part that I was supposed to get."

Then there was *Dennis the Menace:* "Jay North [the child actor who played Dennis] was a nice kid. I ended up in a baby crib — was something to do with paternity. It was fun." And *Twilight Zone*. "Donald Pleasence was the star of that one," states Biheller. "He was a good guy. I met Rod Serling [the show's creator/announcer] and that was neat. He was a nice man, smoking cigarettes. Died of lung cancer. It was neat to have done that show."

What made the ninety-minute Ben Gazzara/Chuck Connors drama, *Arrest and Trial*, memorable was Connors' behavior. "He was a big guy," says Biheller, "and one day he left the set! He got furious because somebody wrote something on his chair. He just walked off the set. It was pretty funny. They were just teasing him — somebody had written something kind of strange on his chair."

Another "big guy" was James Arness — star of the long-running CBS western, *Gunsmoke*. "I had this big scene that I did with Arness," remembers Biheller. "I come into town to kill him. He yanks me off the horse...Now I'm like 5'5" and he's like SEVEN FEET TALL or whatever, and the show had gone for...it was going over to the seventh day, and it was getting close to five O'Clock. So we're working on the scene, rehearsing it and everything, the next thing I know he goes away from the set, and then, 'All right! We're shutting down. Mr. Arness has taken off his sideburns.' Which meant another day. Another four or five hundred bucks. So everybody's happy — 'Mr. Arness is taking off his sideburns.'"

One guest shot Biheller wasn't about to forget was the January 13, 1964 *Wagon Train* episode, "The Jed Whitmore Story." "My whole part in *Wagon Train* had nothing to do with the regulars," says Biheller. "It was pre-Neville Brand. I played Neville Brand as a young man and I played him as a bad guy — they do this whole thing with me, and then [in the story], it's years later. Neville Brand was a wild guy — he was a character. HE WAS A CHARACTER! I was having lunch one day with him, and it was so funny. We're in the Universal commissary, we're in conversation or whatever, and this hot blonde, or whatever she was, walks in, and walks by, and, my eyes go directly to HER! Neville reaches out and grabs me and says, [imitating Brand], 'YOU DON'T LOOK AT THAT! YOU'RE WORKIN'!' You don't look at that kind of stuff!' He was so funny. 'GET YOUR MIND ON THE PART!'"

Early in his television acting career, Robert Biheller had two shots at making it to series regular status. "I did this pilot, *Diamond Jim*," he says. "It didn't go. That was with [MGM musical star] Howard Keel. On that one I would have been a regular — played a hotel page — kind of a character who was gonna be his boy. I did *Diamond Jim* at the time they were making [the American International/Roger Corman feature] *The Raven* [starring Vincent Price, Boris Karloff, and Peter Lorre]. Karloff was so dapper. I saw him one time at a market in Hollywood, and he was just a dapper gentleman. Then I went to the set of *The Raven*, went on the set and watched them shoot a couple of scenes with Karloff and Lorre." Being a fan of Howard Keel, Biheller enjoyed working with him on *Diamond Jim*. "Howard Keel was terrific in those musicals," says Biheller. "A lot of people say that *Here Come the Brides* was based on *Seven Brides for Seven Brothers*. It kind of was the same story as *Seven Brides for Seven Brothers*."

Biheller fared a little better with the James Franciscus series, *Mr. Novak*. "That was supposed to be a running part," states the actor, "story about a high school and this teacher, Mr. Novak [Franciscus]. After the pilot was filmed, and it sold, they decided that my character was too tough — I was supposed to be a delinquent. They didn't want to go that way." So, as far as Biheller was concerned, that was the end of his association with the series. Then, later, "someone comes up to me and says, 'I saw you in *Mr. Novak*.' I said, 'I don't think so. I had a nice part in the pilot, but...' 'No,' he says, 'I see you every week.' So, I turn on to watch the show, and, in the titles, there's this shot of me walking down the hall. Then, in the show itself, they'd have an assembly, and they'd use the same footage, and I was singled out, because I had a part in the pilot. So there I was. I called the Screen Actor's Guild, and said, 'Hey! I'm in the show every week.' Well, they had to pay me for those first thirteen weeks. They had to pay me for the titles and for every show I was in."

When not doing television series guest shots, Robert Biheller was working in motion pictures, like 1963's *Captain Newman, M.D.*, starring Gregory Peck. "I was on that for eight weeks," remembers Biheller. "Peck was kind of aloof. I think he's a great man, and a great actor. He's a liberal, so I have nothing but good things to say about him. The movie was about a psych unit, and there were something like twenty actors — kind of working actors who ended up getting absolutely nothing in the movie — we wore pajamas and got in bed. We had Vito Scotti, Michael Pataki... Pataki and I go all the way back to college. He was the lead in *Rashomon*. I did lots of work with him — on the college level — on stage. I went to college with Pataki, Paul Comi...I knew John Ritter quite well because my brother-in-law was very good friends with him and in the same class at USC."

A year or so after *Captain Newman, M.D.*, Biheller did the comedy, *Never Too Late*, starring Paul Ford, Maureen O'Sullivan, Connie Stevens, and Jim Hutton. "I didn't have too much to do in that," admits Biheller. "The producer was Norman Lear, and I had a scene with Paul Ford and Maureen O'Sullivan in the department store. They must have been out shopping for baby clothes [Biheller played a young husband]. I remember laughing at Paul Ford. He was funny."

Around the same time, Biheller did *Dear Brigitte*, starring James Stewart and future *Here Come the Brides* guest, Billy Mumy. "I was cast in the picture," recalls the actor, "and I think I had like three days on it — played this gambler who overhears Billy Mumy, who's got his way with numbers, and we get into this thing — I've got this plan to make money at the race-track. So I did two days, and then they were gonna pick me up whenever. Well, there's a contractual…there are laws, with the Screen Actor's Guild, you can do that, but if you go to work in a certain period of time, they have to pay you for the whole time. So I worked the two days, then suddenly — my agent called me and told me that I needed to go for an interview with *The Fugitive*. So I went to an interview with *The Fugitive*. They cast me, and so now I am getting into costume for *The Fugitive*, then the phone call comes into the costume department saying that I'm not in the show any longer. I call my agent up and say, 'WHAT THE HELL IS GOING ON? I have a really nice part in *The Fugitive*. I want to do that part!' She said, 'Well 20th Century Fox has a thing — they work with QM (on *12 O'Clock High*)…' They [both companies] ended up having to pay me for all the time. They had to pay me for *The Fugitive*, and then they had to pay me for all the days in-between the time, the two days I did [on *Dear Brigitte*] to the [third] day because the deal was that Mr. Stewart had another commitment. So, I'm telling my agent, 'Mr. Stewart has another commitment, and poor me — I lose a good role.' Well, they [the producers of *Dear Brigitte*] never got around to me anyway until three weeks later so they had to pay me for three weeks plus [for] *The Fugitive* thing so I really made out. Anyway, Jimmy Stewart was a nice man. And Mumy and I were kind of friendly."

The same year as *Dear Brigitte*, Biheller appeared in the western, *Young Fury*, starring Rory Calhoun and Virginia Mayo. "Virginia Mayo was okay," says Biheller. "She was no longer in her element, cuz this was kind of a B-movie in a way. She was kind of a star. She did lots of stuff with Cagney and this one and that one. She still looked pretty good, [of] course she [had] aged. Rory Calhoun was a good guy, happy-go-lucky, always knew what he was doing." Also in the picture was William Bendix. "He only had one big scene," remembers Biheller. "He was the blacksmith in town; we ride in and burn his place down. He came in and did it, but he was sickly, he did the movie as a favor for [the film's producer] A.C. Lyles, then he went home and died. A.C. Lyles made a bunch of little westerns, fillers. A.C. Lyles is still around. He's got to be a hundred. A.C. was in PR, and he just knew everybody. I mean in *Young Fury*, we had Richard Arlen [best known for the 1927 Oscar winner, *Wings*], and Lon Chaney, Jr. [star of Universal's *Wolfman* thrillers]. And Lon Chaney, Jr. was a drinker. He always had a towel, cuz he'd sweat like a pig, he'd put stuff on the towel — smelled minty. Christian Nyby is the one that directed *Young Fury*. He directed the original *The Thing* [*From Another World*, 1951]. He was a good guy. I liked him. A good, solid, no-nonsense director. He got it done on time. He did a good job, knew what he was doing."

Nyby worked again with Biheller on *Bonanza* in his second guest shot, the eighth season's "Napoleon's Children." Two seasons earlier, Biheller had the good fortune to appear in one of the *Bonanza* classics, the William Witney-directed, November 15, 1964 episode, "Between Heaven and Earth." Also guest-starring in that episode was Richard Jaeckel. "Richard Jaeckel was a good guy," praises Biheller. "He had kind of a niche. He was very underrated — some of the war movies he did were terrific." Like many others in the business, Biheller enjoyed working with Michael Landon. "I had met Landon a couple times before I did the show," remembers the actor. I liked Michael a lot. We became kind of friends. He was always quite nice to me. One time he said to me, just jokingly, if I would marry his wife, he would give me $50,000 because she was a customer of my mother's. We had a lot of fun when we were doing "Napoleon's Children." There was a character who came out to the set. I don't know how he got on the set, but he was kind of funny looking, and we couldn't stop laughing. Well, we had this dramatic scene where he [Joe Cartwright] captures me…he's holding me behind the neck — but all we were doing was laughing. We couldn't stop — one of those things where we lost concentration."

Not long after the *Bonanza* episode "Napoleon's Children" (which originally aired on April 16, 1967), Robert Biheller became a semi-regular, playing the role of logger Corky, on the new ABC/Screen Gems series, *Here Come the Brides*. "I forget how that whole thing happened," admits Biheller. "I really had no idea whether I'd be in it or not. They did some kind of preview of the pilot, and I got some good reviews. They would run the show for an audience, and the audience would say [imitating a breathy teenage girl fan], 'He's cute!' or whatever. So I got to be in it, and it became a recurring part. I wasn't told that it was gonna be a running part."

Even though Biheller had a running part, "there was a lot going on in that show," notes the actor. "A lot of people, so you were thrilled if you got something to do. Because there was a lot of 'THE FOREST IS ON FIRE! Better come quick!' 'Okay, Corky. We'll be right there' dialogue." Biheller preferred the episodes in which he was given more to do, including "One to a Customer," "The Log Jam," "A Kiss Just for So," and "The Crimpers."

"There were a lot of fun, crazy things that happened on that set," remembers the actor. "With all the guys and loggers. Buck [Kartalian] was always carrying on. He would just do anything for attention — drop his pants or whatever — they'd egg him on and he'd do it; he was a funny dude." That sort of absurdity bothered Robert Brown. "Oh yes, oh yes," agrees Biheller. "Robert wasn't aloof, but he had his place. He wasn't like the jokesters. He was kind of like a parent, telling us to behave. We probably deserved it. He'd 'Ssssh' us. He'd say, 'Be quiet! Concentrate! We're doing a scene here.'" Co-star David Soul was very similar to Brown. "I got along very well with David," says Biheller. "We wrote a song together. Never went anywhere with it. David was more intense, more to himself, more on a serious level." And shy: "I remember when he used the bag over his head," continues the actor. "He'd go on the talk shows with a bag over his head, and I remember kinda being a go-between [with Soul and Karen Carlson]. I ended up at their wedding. I knew that they both liked each other, and I kinda pushed cuz I liked her. She's a neat woman."

As for second-billed Bobby Sherman, "we did a lot of stuff together, Bobby and I," remembers Biheller. "I was kind of like the tag-a-long in a lot of stuff, like the bear one, [the second season's "The Solider"] and a bunch of them. What did they consider me on the show — the foreman or something?"

Biheller has fond memories of leading lady Bridget Hanley. "I liked Bridget a lot," says the actor. "I saw Bridget at the twenty-year reunion. Bobby was there, [and so were] Bo, David, Robert, Henry. Lot of people. It was at some restaurant in Beverly

Hills. A very nice get-together party. That was the last time I saw any of the *Brides* people. I talked to Bridget about the cabin [the one owned by Hanley's grandparents]. Gave her a recipe or something." (To help save her grandparents' cabin, Bridget Hanley wrote a cookbook, to which both *Brides* cast members and series fans contributed recipes. The proceeds helped raise enough money to keep the cabin in the Hanley family.)

Besides the show's leading lady and leading men, Biheller enjoyed the series' other stars, too. "I liked Mark Lenard a lot," states the actor. "He was a good guy. You'd think he'd be more stodgy or whatever, but he was just a good guy. And Henry Beckman was a fun guy, good actor, always knew what he was doing. Scene stealer. Yeah, he was really into Clancey." As for Susan Tolsky, "she was just fun. Out there, bubbly. She's a character. She was a good one — my romantic interest. That just happened that way. I'd get a script, and that was it — Corky and Susan."

Having worked with, and known quite a few veteran stars, Biheller found *Brides'* Joan Blondell very pleasant. "She was a nice woman," states the actor. "I found her to be pretty genuine, unlike Shelley Winters. She'd talk about old Hollywood, and she had her little dogs. She had a basket for them, they always seemed to be around."

In addition to Mitzi Hoag and Bo Svenson, two other favorite semi-regulars of Biheller's were Cynthia Hull (Ann). "I could have liked her if I wasn't married," laughs the actor, and Hoke Howell [The general store owner, Ben Perkins]. "I knew Hoke for a long time," says Biheller. "He was a good friend of Dal's [second-season guest Dal Jenkins — Biheller's longtime writing partner]. Hoke was a character. He was outgoing. Pretty much did his job."

Like the other *Brides* cast members, Biheller thinks very highly of the series' executive producer, Bob Claver. "He was nice," praises the actor. "Very pleasant to work with. Knew what he was doing. Knew what he wanted. Good producer, too. Pretty much knew where the show was headed and what was going on. He never yelled at me. And [William] Blinn had quite a career. He wrote [the teleplay for Alex Haley's] *Roots*."

Biheller has nothing but praise for the series' director of photography, Fred H. Jackman. "I liked him a lot," states the actor. "He was a good guy — really knew his stuff. He had a real creative collaboration, a good rapport with all the directors, and Swack was a good director." Biheller also got on well with the show's assistant directors. "Jim Hogan [later unit manager on *Brides*] was a good guy. He kept things going, kept things tight, and then Henry [Harry] Morgan's kid, Christopher Morgan, was kind of a character. Had a just kind of dry sense of humor. David Hawks...I almost didn't even know that he was Howard Hawks' son."

During his two seasons with *Here Come the Brides*, Robert Biheller did other TV shows. "I was freelance," explains the actor. "I'd get a job, wait, get another job, wait, go out for parts. I was not signed to any one studio. I wasn't signed to *Brides*, so there was no security. When the *Lancer* [episode, "The Escape"] came up, they got into a little problem with *Brides*, because *Brides* had a show [with Corky] and they wrote me out of the show, then I didn't work for a couple of shows." That same year, audiences saw Biheller, *Brides* regular Henry Beckman, and *Brides* guests Sheree

North and Steve Ihnat in the Richard Widmark detective drama, *Madigan.* "The stuff I did was with [director] Don Siegel," recalls Biheller. "Don Stroud is the one I worked with. He was kind of moody. He was up and coming. I don't know what happened to him. They were grooming him for something, but I don't think it ever happened."

In 1970, Robert Biheller appeared in two offbeat motion pictures. One was *Myra Breckinridge.* "That was a wild picture," chuckles the actor. "The casting director, Michael McLean, was a friend of mine — I'd known him for years, and he'd been a friend of John Barrymore, Jr.'s (a.k.a. John Drew Barrymore). John had long, flowing, gray, white hair. He looked good — he looked like an old Christ. He was a very handsome guy. Anyway we formed a little friendship, but he'd been something of a troublemaker. About two days into the picture he disappeared."

Which, given what was happening on *Myra Breckinridge,* was probably not a bad thing. "That was a wild thing," laughs Biheller. "That got way out of hand. [Charles] Manson was on that picture, dealing out drugs, and I heard stories about that movie. The director, Michael somebody [Michael Sarne] had just done a big movie with Donald Sutherland [1968's *Joanna*]. The first scene he shot of *Myra Breckinridge* was a stagecoach on a set, with a bunch of little people fornicating. And I guess Richard Zanuck [at 20th Century Fox — the studio that made the picture] seized the film and burned it. There was a lot of action on that movie, I'll tell you."

Something of a send-up of Hollywood, with Raquel Welch as the title character, Mae West, John Huston, and Rex Reed, *Myra Breckinridge* also featured a young up-and-coming actress by the name of Farrah Fawcett. "I thought Farrah Fawcett was kind of uppity," says Biheller. "Maybe she was scared. And Rex Reed, what a character. Mae West was tiny — four foot or something — wore big platform shoes. They'd clear the set when she was working; everybody had to stay away from her. But my stuff was with John Huston; we had this scene where I did an imitation of Brando. Huston seemed to be jovial. Knew what he was doing. Obviously."

Which also held true for Otto Preminger — director of Biheller's other 1970 feature, *Tell Me That You Love Me, Junie Moon.* Remembers the actor: "I went out for this movie, and I met Otto. I was taken into his office, sat down, and Otto looked at me. And I looked at him. He started laughing at me. And I started laughing at him. We're just both laughing. He said, 'Fine. You're in. The part is yours.' Now I had a scene — one scene…and my second wife was Nicola Trumbo — her father was [blacklisted writer] Dalton Trumbo. Well, Otto Preminger was one of the people who helped break the blacklist. He gave credit to Dalton — on-screen, for *Exodus.* Both he and Kirk Douglas [*Spartacus*] put Dalton's name on screen. Well, years later, I'd married Nicki, and Dalton had this thing where he would write in the bathtub. He had this board across this big tub, and he'd have a typewriter on that thing, cigarette hanging out of his mouth."

This habit of Trumbo's was worked into *Junie Moon.* "There were three of us in this story," says Biheller, "and one [of the three] was a gay character, played by Leonard Frey and there was one other person, and myself. We were artists — one was an artist (painter), one was a writer…and we lived in this house on the beach. We shot the movie in San Diego. And what happens is, this woman moves into the house, and she's impregnated. She has a baby, and she delivers it to the three of these guys. Liza Minnelli turned out to be the baby, and the father — Leonard Frey — the gay character, turns out to be the father. He takes the baby.

"Anyway," continues Biheller, "the point is that when they do the scene where we get romantic, I'm in the bathtub, and the scene is really from — Otto took it from his knowledge of Dalton; Dalton was his friend, so here I was, all these years later, kind of playing Trumbo. Otto was really the authoritarian. Cuz at one point the woman comes into the bathroom, and I'm in the bathtub, and you hear him yelling, 'Mrs. (whatever her name was — Angela) 'I DO NOT VANT TO SEE YOUR NIPPLES!' Cuz this camera is coming into the bathroom as she gets in the tub with me. Oh, God! It was FUNNY! Anyway, I thought Leonard Frey was a terrific actor. Dal and I did a pilot called *Leonard* [with Frey as the star]. Half-hour situation comedy."

'Dal' was Dal Jenkins, Biheller's longtime friend and writing partner, and guest star in the second-season *Here Come the Brides* episode, "The Road to the Cradle." As previously noted, he and Biheller had first worked together — as actors — in 1965's *Young Fury*. Like Biheller, Jenkins wanted to write. "I'd always been interested in writing," says Biheller, "in the whole process, and I ended up, actually started writing some spec scripts. I wrote one spec script for *My Favorite Martian* and he [producer Jack Chertok] liked my writing, but for some reason I never got hired. Anyway, one day I got a call from [ventriloquist] Paul Winchell, and Winchell hired me to write his television show — a kid's show — [*Winchell and Mahoney Time*, 1965-68]. I wrote three hundred episodes! When I was doing *Brides* I was writing the show. [The association with Winchell had nothing to do with Biheller's not doing more *Brides* episodes.] Paul was a perfectionist. He had been a major star back when television first came in, and he had a deal with Metromedia. He owned half of the show, and Metromedia owned the other half, and it was a syndicated show. I would write three shows a week. They were kind of full, almost like situation comedy, with three acts — a beginning, a middle, and an end. And we did all kinds of special effects; we did all kinds of stuff. It was a real good learning situation.

"I'd write shows, turn them in, and in two days, we'd shoot five shows," laughs Biheller. "I'd come to the set, sometimes I'd be walking onto the set, and there was a clubhouse — that's the main set, and it's in a barn. Knucklehead [Smiff] and Jerry [Mahoney] sit at this desk and inside this desk kind of situation, Paul would be controlling their heads. He would have two guys that would control — he'd put one arm into Jerry so he could knock the gavel, that left another hand free to let Snitchy the Snail come out of the cheese on the desk — he played various characters. I got fired after three weeks on the show, cuz part of the deal was you had to learn the mechanics of it."

As far as Winchell was concerned, Biheller hadn't. Explains the actor, "If Jerry was gonna be making a pie, Paul needed both hands to work with — you couldn't' have the mouse come up or whatever. And, a lot of times, Paul would be playing characters like Count Drink-a-Lot, and W.C. Cornfield, these various characters who would come and push the story forward. So I got shit-canned. A week later, they hired someone else. But I guess I was better than that someone else cuz they hired me two weeks later. Then I worked for three years straight."

But Winchell wasn't about to pass up the opportunity to let Biheller know how he felt about the scripts he had, and was, writing for the show. Chuckles the actor, "I'd come down to the set, and all of a sudden, you'd see Jerry and Knucklehead at the desk, and I hear across the room, [imitating Jerry Mahoney's voice] 'Well. Here comes that son of a bitch!' And Knucklehead would say, [imitating Knucklehead's voice] 'What are you talking about?' And Jerry would go, 'Did you read the script about the gypsy? It sucked!' Then Knucklehead would go, 'Well, I didn't think it was that bad.' 'Not that bad?' Jerry says, 'You…' So Paul was doing a number on me."

(Unfortunately, any opportunity to check out the quality of Robert Biheller's scripts for *Winchell and Mahoney Time* is forever gone. According to IMDB, Winchell and Metromedia got into a dispute over syndication rights to the series. This resulted in the company destroying all of the series' tapes. Winchell later received $17 million in damages.)

By the time Robert Biheller finished with *Winchell and Mahoney Time*, "I was writing screenplays, and optioning some of those on a small level," states the actor. "I've had three significant writing partners. Dal is the one I ended up writing the most with. Before that I wrote with a fella named Charles Kuenstle, and then Lawrence Grusin who was some relationship to [jazz artist/TV and movie composer] Dave Grusin. I had worked with Charlie Kuenstle on [the CBS 1963-64 American history anthology] *The Great Adventure*, then I later met Charlie outside of [the] William Morris [offices]. He came out of the entrance when I was going in or whatever, and we started talking. He said he had written some things, and they were getting produced. We started talking about a screenplay, then eventually got together on that screenplay, wrote it together, and immediately, when it came out, we optioned it for pretty good money. Unfortunately, it was optioned by Aaron Rosenberg and Ira Steiner. They had done *Valdez is Coming* (with Burt Lancaster), and a few things, and Ira was the president of ICM (?) or one of the big things, and Aaron was a big producer. He did a lot of Sinatra's movies (1967's *Tony* Rome; its sequel, 1968s' *Lady in Cement*; and the 1968 crime drama, *The Detective*), *Mutiny on the Bounty* with Brando…so the screenplay went nowhere. Then Charlie and I wrote [the 1972 TV-movie] *The Astronaut* [starring Jackie Cooper and Monte Markham]."

"Jackie Cooper was a good guy," praises Biheller. "I worked with him in *The Great Adventure* and that was about a [Confederate] submarine during the Civil War. John Houseman produced the show. I remember walking through the sky — because we all died." The episode to which Biheller was referring, "The Hunley" (September 27, 1963, CBS) was the premiere episode of *The Great Adventure*. (The Hunley was the name of an experimental submarine, built by engineer James McClintock, with which the Confederacy hoped to destroy the Union blockade of Confederate ports.)

Prior to *The Astronaut*, Biheller and Kuenstle wrote the thirteenth-season *Bonanza* episode, "Warbonnet" (December 26, 1971). "The story was done with Chief Dan George," remembers the actor. "It was a good story, and we had done a good job on the thing, but we didn't go on to do the screenplay. They tossed the screenplay to someone else, which we thought was not right. That just kind of pissed me off." Biheller showed his disapproval by going with the pseudonym, 'Robert Blood' for his onscreen credit.

Teaming again for a *Bearcats* (Rod Taylor and Dennis Cole), Biheller and Kuenstle then "split up, and I started writing with Grusin," says the actor. "We just wrote screenplays and optioned them, then I started writing with Dal. We'd get hired. We'd write the story, then we'd write the screenplay. I met Dal in 1964. He was in *Young Fury*. We became very friendly, good friends, and there was always something that he wanted to do. We started working on this script together — this idea we kind of started formulating. We had written this script, this screenplay called 'Rattlesnake Vic and the Prophet's Daughter,' and this has been all over Hollywood, We have had so many people…We have been close to going…that's one that Chartoff/Winkler optioned. They made *Raging Bull*, *Rocky*…that script has been around and around and around. It was optioned by Tony Curtis and Rod Amateau. Martin Sheen was involved. We had so much going on with that. So we got a reputation. People would call us and we could go pitch our ideas and that kind of thing. Hell of a way to make a living. It's a great script, but nobody's going to know it now. It comes back to haunt us now and then."

Among the television series for which the two men wrote were *Charlie's Angels* and *Chips*. "We had a good relationship with Aaron Spelling's producer, Ed…somebody," notes Biheller. "And we would meet with the story editor. What you would do is, you go in, you have an idea, you go in with two or three ideas for *Chips* or whatever show. You sit down, you go over the ideas; they say, 'Oh. I like that one.' Then they assign you to go to story, then you do a twenty-page story or outline, then they make whatever changes they want to make. Then you'd go to screenplay, or you wouldn't, or whatever.

"We didn't do a lot," continues the actor. "Kind of because we were more into the screenplay area, and of course, you didn't work if you were over thirty. It's idiotic, but it was kind of a known fact, especially in television, that they were interested in young people because the young people knew what was going on; the old farts didn't know anything. Old, like if you were in your late thirties or early forties. GOD! So we wrote a lot of screenplays that were optioned and, unfortunately, not made. That's the business! We optioned to Chartoff/Winkler, Henry Jaffe, Ray Stark Productions, Stephen Friedman, Last Picture Show, etc., etc. We'd go in and do a pitch, write a deal, and get a screenplay. And the jerks couldn't put it together. That's the way it goes."

Though Robert Biheller still remains in touch with Jenkins (they call one another frequently), he later went back to solo writing. "I wrote for Heatter/Quigley," says the actor, "The *Hollywood Squares* people. Then I wrote a show called *Namedroppers*. I was one of the writers on *Namedroppers* with Lohman and Barkley — they were a team in L.A. Quite well known. They did this quiz show, kind of a *To Tell the Truth* type show. We'd come up with the questions. You'd guess, 'Who is this person?' You'd write jokes for celebrities, write their responses. You kind of directed the gist of the questioning and the responses that could lead to it. It was kind of like *Hollywood Squares*. I hated it. You got your credit though. I did all kinds of writing. Wrote a script for [Steven] Bochco — *Griff* [an early-seventies detective series starring Lorne Greene and Ben Murphy). I ended up walking with Bochco on the picket line during a Writer's Guild strike. I came up with an idea for *Griff;* he hired me to write a script."

In the late eighties, Robert Biheller moved to the state of Washington. Around that time he got an acting job in *The Last Innocent Man*. "Ed Harris," remembers Biheller. "HBO movie. I played a detective/investigator. That part I got when I came up to Washington. Then I did a thing called *Fire in the Sky* [also for HBO]. That was with [director] Rob Lieberman, who is an old friend of mine and someone that I kind of helped. He had already cast the part, then he recast me into the part. I was on the picture for like three weeks. Then I did another thing called *The Favor*, then *The Perfect Family* with Swack."

Other than those roles, Robert Biheller has pretty much retired from acting. "The acting I don't know," reflects Biheller. "Not so much into that anymore. You get called out for a part, and it's some stupid part. I remember I went for one that was for some USA television movie. I entered the room, the director's there, the producer's there, the casting director's there, several other people are there, and I'm looking at them, they're looking at me. They say, 'Well, are you ready?' I said, 'Yeah, I'm ready.' Then the guy [the other actor] says, 'Is there a public phone around here?' 'Yeah,' I say, 'down over there on the dock.' That's my line. And I'm standing there looking, and…stupid, so stupid. They could just cast from a photograph. So there was a point in L.A when I'd been sent out — it was for a commercial, and the treatment was so horrible, I got sick to my stomach. I thought, I'm not doing this anymore, this is not good. So, when I moved up here [to Vancouver, WA], I went into business and opened up a video production company. We would do promotional videos, all kinds of things. We did a major project — *English is a Second Language* for a Japanese production company. We did historical documentaries, (1998's *Let 'Er Buck* — a history of the Pendleton Rodeo), commercials, local kind of stuff. That lasted for about five years. During this time, we made *Great River of the West* [*The Columbia River*, 1993]. We wrote it, produced it, I narrated it. We were just in business — we got paid by the city. That gave me an insight into where I lived."

As of this date, Robert Biheller is still working as a writer. "I still work on screenplays," he admits. "have a few things going on, but nothing concrete. I'm kind of semi-retired, but I keep my finger in it. And I still get messages from fans. There's the *Here Come the Brides* fan club; somebody, out of the blue, will want a picture, and ask, 'how'm I'm doing?' I would have done more of the *Brides* shows had I been available."

Married to his third wife for twenty-four years, Robert Biheller left Hollywood in 1984. Like so many other actors and actresses to do television in the 1960s and '70s, he has positive memories of those years. "They're doing good stuff today, but that was a Golden Age," states the actor. "There were so many great shows. It was the REAL Golden Age."[3]

# Dick Balduzzi: Man of many parts, man of many accents, man with many credits

"I did thirty-three of those, played all kinds of roles."

That was thirty-three episodes of the 1952-59 hour-long CBS variety series, *The Jackie Gleason Show*. The Gleason show that introduced Jackie Gleason's unforgettable Ralph Kramden and the rest of the *Honeymooners* stars; the Gleason show that featured the actor who played "all kinds of roles" — *Here Come the Brides* semiregular Dick Balduzzi. Being a New York actor, Dick Balduzzi got along well with Jackie Gleason; Gleason was born in New York City — Brooklyn, to be specific. "I knew Jackie because I worked in Toots Shor's [restaurant]," explains Balduzzi. "That's how I got a lot of my jobs. That's where all the sports and all the theatrical people [went]." As well as other notable figures, like "Prime Minister of the Underworld" Frank Costello, head of the Luciano crime family. "I met Frank Costello in Toots Shor's," remembers Balduzzi. "He was like a gentleman mobster — dressed to the T. He was well liked, even though he was the heavy end of the mob. It's incredible how many people came into that restaurant.

"Gleason hung out there," continues Balduzzi. "That was his second home, and I met all the producers [of the Gleason shows] — Jack Philbin and the directors — they all went to Toots Shor's. So I did quite a few shows. And the Gleason show was done at CBS, live. Always a packed audience, in a big theater on Broadway there — it was quite an experience. I wasn't that old at the time. I had to turn down a lot of theater jobs because I was dedicated to that. In fact, I was signed to do some plays in Washington [state]; I turned that down because I was still working on the Gleason show. You never know how your career's gonna go. You gotta go with the flow.

"Jackie was terrific," praises Balduzzi. "He'd come in at the last minute. He never rehearsed during the week. He'd only come in Saturday morning — the show was Saturday night, and sometimes, if he didn't know his lines, they would paste them around. They would have lines written all over the set. One time he was stuck underneath something, and right up on the furnace at the top they had the lines written. They would put 'em — plaster 'em all around."

While doing a stage play in Pennsylvania, Dick Balduzzi ran into another such actor. "The old guy who was a director," remembers Balduzzi, "he was about eighty-five years old. He wanted to still act. He directed the show, played a grandfather, and I'm playing the young husband. He's sitting there reading the paper, and I'm talking to him and we're having a scene…He's not looking at me. I grabbed the paper. He went…he had all his lines written on the paper. I broke up laughing. Then I handed him the paper back. I mean, I didn't know what he was doing, why he wasn't focusing when I was talking to him."

Dick Balduzzi thoroughly enjoyed working on *The Jackie Gleason Show*. "Jackie had all these characters [Ralph Kramden, The Poor Soul, Joe the Bartender, The Loudmouth, Reginald Van Gleason III, Rudy the Repairman, Fenwick Babbitt]," remembers Balduzzi, "and every segment was like a musical. They traveled all over

the world. They won a trip to Europe. We did things like in Italy, Germany, different countries — they would present sketches and dress in costumes. It was fun, it
was really great. Actually, June Taylor [choreographer of The June Taylor Dancers]
incorporated all of us actors into her work," says Balduzzi. "If they [the dancers]
had a scene in the railroad station, we'd play guys on the train, or we'd play guys in
the depot moving luggage, moving within the dance rhythm. Whatever we did, she
incorporated us — bellhops and waiters and small pros. We were like a company
and they would use us whenever they needed us, or doing anything on the show. It
was a great experience because I got to meet all of 'em."

An actor since his high school days, Dick Balduzzi did "a lot of plays. When I
went into the Navy, I did Special Services; when I decided to go into acting school,
that's when I went to the Goodman Theatre in Chicago. I studied there for three
years, got my degree, worked a lot in theater and summer stock. I directed a lot, too.
I did a play that was called *End as a Man* [Calder Willingham's brutal portrait of
life in a Southern military academy] with Sal Mineo. That was in the summer theater. It got tremendous reviews. But Mineo wasn't up to par in doing something like
that. I also did plays with [actress/dancer/writer/theater director] June Havoc. I did
a lot of summer stock in Chicago. Worked for the Park district in Chicago, where I
directed *The Miracle Worker* and [Agatha Christie's] *Mouse Trap*, and *Texas Trilogy*
by Horton Foote [author of *Baby the Rain Must Fall, The Chase*].

New York and Broadway being the goal for aspiring stage actors, Dick Balduzzi
moved there a short time later. "I studied at the Berghof Studio (a.k.a. HB Studio)
with Uta Hagen and Herbert Berghof," says Balduzzi. "I did several off-Broadway
productions, never did get on the big macho stage, though. I was up for many things,
but it seemed like Bill Hickey always beat me out. Off-Broadway I did *The Servant
of Two Masters* [an eighteenth-century comedy written by Italian playwright Carlo
Goldoni], a show, *The Storekeeper*, a musical about the Barber of Fleet Street, and
there were several other small productions. Off-Broadway, you try to do as much as
you can, get in as much as you can."

One play Balduzzi did proved quite helpful when it came to getting television
work on the West Coast. Remembers the actor: "A friend of mine came in from
Chicago, and he's looking for a room and we — all of us actors — had a rooming
house on 71st Street in Central Park West. I said, 'There's a room available. You'll
have to talk to the landlord.' I think we were paying eight bucks a week. This was the
early days — early fifties, so he came in, and right away, lucky guy, he gets a script.
He reads it over. He says, 'I don't want to do this show.' I said, 'Are you kidding? It's
pre-Broadway, and then it's Broadway.' He said, 'I don't like it.' It was called *Noah*. It
was about Noah and the ark and all his family. He said, 'Would you do me a favor?
Just drop it off for me down on 69th Street.' I said, 'Sure, I'll do that.' But, before
I did that, I read it. And the part that he was up for, I was right for. It was Japheth,
the young blond, light-haired, he was the very fair one of the sons. So, I went in, and
knocked on the door. The stage manager answered. He said, 'Shhh, Shhh, they're
rehearsing, come on in.' So, after they stopped, I looked in the middle, and there's
[Sam] Jaffe, with the rest of the actors. And my heart fell because first of all, I didn't

know he was playing the lead role. Secondly, he was one of my idols all these years. The stage manager said, 'What's wrong?' I said, 'This Don Friedman does not want to do this show. He asked me to return this script.' He says, 'He doesn't WANT to do the show?' I said, 'No.' I said, 'I think I'm right for this part. Do you mind if I read for it?' He said, 'Just a minute.' So he walks over to the director, and Sam, in the middle of it, Sam's looking at me. He walks over and he says, 'What is your name?' I said, 'Dick Balduzzi.' He says, 'Ah! I-tal-i-an?' I said, 'Yes.' He said, 'Are you studying. Are you working?' I said, 'Yeah, I'm studying with Uta Hagen.' He said, 'Ah! Uta! Good actress. Good teacher.' He says, 'I understand you want to read for this part?' I said, 'I'd like to, Mr. Jaffe.' He says, 'Well, look it over. And then come over and we'll run the first scene.' I looked it over, and I'd already read it. But I really worked on it. Because there was a part where you really have to use all the facets of acting — a lot of it's pantomime cuz he's [Japheth] the first one that comes out of the boat. So you gotta relate to…the eyes and everything. It's shocking. Well, everything worked. It worked beautifully. And we read and finished. They applauded. And, MY HEART…I never was so excited in my life. They said, 'Mr. Balduzzi, you have the part.' I thought, 'Oh my — How great!' Then we had a pre-trial right up in the White Barn Theatre in [Norwalk] Connecticut. That's where they did all the tryouts."

(Founded by actress, producer, and theater impresario Lucille Lortel on the property of her 18.4 acre estate in Norwalk, 'The White Barn Theatre' got its name from an old horse barn on the estate. Lortel's purpose in establishing the theater was to present unusual and experimental plays, promote new playwrights, composers, actors, directors and designers, and help established artists develop new directions that commercial theater might not have allowed. Lortel more than succeeded in her purpose. Many of the plays that opened at the White Barn went on to successful Broadway, and Off-Broadway runs.)

So, by making it to the White Barn, Dick Balduzzi definitely seemed to be on his way. "Well," recalls the actor, "the night of the performance, the place was packed with producers, directors, all over from New York. After the first scene, second scene in the first act, Sam collapsed, had a stroke. So I grabbed ahold of him and I yelled, 'CLOSE THE CURTAIN!' They closed the curtain, and they announced it. And we lost the show. We went back and did it three months later as a reading; it never did go to Broadway. That's the breaks. But that's how I met Sam Jaffe."

Impressed with Balduzzi, Jaffe told the actor to call him when he went out to the West Coast. Balduzzi did. This resulted in a guest shot on the March 4, 1964 *Ben Casey* episode, "The Lonely Ones." Jaffe played the regular role of Dr. David Zorba on the series. "Sam introduced me to [executive producer] Matthew Rapf, and a couple other people, and the director was Leo Penn," explains Balduzzi. "Leo knew me from New York. He said, 'Dick, sit down. You have a small part, but it's a nice part. It's with Jill Ireland. Your character is a bartender, and it's a nice scene, because she's hooked on drugs and booze, and you really get to sympathize with her.' I said, 'Good. I'll come do it.' That's how I got that part — through Sam Jaffe. And then we became friends. I saw him — he lived in Beverly Hills, too, so I used to see him now and then. That's how you get parts sometimes."

"[The movie] *Dear Heart* was one of my first shows out here," remembers Balduzzi. "I had met some people who were related to [the producer] Martin Manulis, and I'd gotten fabulous reviews in the *Chicago Tribune*. So they called Martin. I think it was his sister — she called him, said, 'You've got to use this young man…he's coming out to the coast.' Martin said, 'Well, have him call me.' And at that point, he was doing *Dear Heart* with Angela Lansbury and Glenn Ford and Geraldine Page. I had worked with Gerry [Page], was very close to her as a friend. Anyway I called Martin. He said, 'Come over to the studio,' and Del Mann was there — the director. He was just wonderful. Del Mann was one of the New York directors. He said, 'You know, Dick, I heard so much about you.' He said, 'The show's all cast, but there is a small part of a bellhop who brings up Angela Lansbury and Glenn Ford's luggage.' I said, 'Look, I'm new out here.' They said, 'Well, you got it.' I got two days out of it! I couldn't believe it because I was doing theater for two hundred a week, and I was getting almost two hundred a day on this picture. That was something new to me — this film business. So I got to talk to Del Mann. I said, 'I know you did the original *Marty* [the Academy Award-winning 1955 film starring Ernest Borgnine]; I just wanted you to know that I did the pilot for the series. I played Angie. He said, 'Oh, you would make a good Angie.' I said, 'Well, I don't know. I don't know whether it sold or not.' I mean some people like Del Mann were wonderful. And Angela was wonderful. I used to sit on the set just to hear her stories. And when I did [Lansbury's hit CBS series] *Murder, She Wrote*, [guest star] Marie Windsor was wonderful. She was the head of our crooked scheme. Marie had some great stories."

By the time Dick Balduzzi moved out to California, he was already something of a television veteran, particularly in live television. "I did [*Robert*] *Montgomery Presents*, did about three of those and different shows in *U.S. Steel Hour*, *Philco* [*Playhouse*], *American Heritage* — did about three of those, *Mr. Citizen…The Blue and the Gray* was a series, *The Valiant Lady* was a soap opera — I did a lot of that stuff in New York while I was there."

The early days of [live] TV presented its casts and crews with plenty of problems. "We did this play, *The Cook for Mr. General*, recalls the actor, "they made it into a movie of the week. Had this wonderful actor from England, who played in a movie called *Wee Geordie*. He was a big, muscular guy. I played the general's aide. We had to go down the line, and check out all the soldiers, and this one guy had long hair — he was playing the Greek immigrant who got in the United States Army. The general says, 'Get that hair cut there, soldier!' and he [the soldier] doesn't respond. I touch him on the shoulder. I say, 'He means you,' and he turns around and whacks me. It was a thing with him [the character] that anyone who touched him he would react to that and sock him. Well, he socked me in rehearsal, and I took the fall. But when we did it for real, he grabbed my arm to protect me, to keep me from hitting the floor; he didn't know that I knew how to fall. So, when he grabbed my arm, my spine hit the floor and I really hurt it. I really should have reported it then but in those days, any job was a job. But I had a lot of trouble with that spine. I'd be painting and it hurt."

On another occasion, "I remember doing a live show where they froze, and couldn't get their lines out," says Balduzzi. "You know, you can't do that in live television. So whoever was doing the scene had to come in and improvise and take over. Then there was the scene on [*Robert*] *Montgomery Presents*. That show starred Jackie Cooper. It was about a bus driver who went through a stop sign or something, and so many children get injured. I played an ambulance driver who picked up the kids, and had a little dialogue. We had to bring them to the hospital, and everything was really moving. Well, dress rehearsal was fine until the scene with the head nurse. The head nurse was supposed to appear then, this girl [playing the nurse] never showed up! This was a dress rehearsal in front of cameras and everything — Thank God it wasn't on the air! Because we couldn't find the girl. Finally someone…the security guard found her — she was inebriated. Went out to lunch; she had too much to drink. And she had a major part in this thing, so the director's going BANANAS! He's going wild! So he calls up his girlfriend, who was an actress, and a quick study. She came in, did the part; the security took this other girl out so fast! It was a scary moment, but Montgomery knew nothing about it. Everything was done so fast, and it was so well done. I think I had some lines with that girl. But I couldn't understand what the hell happened to her. Either she got panic-stricken, or…But why she would go out and drink? Anyway, most of the actors were prepared, and it was exciting doing live television. We had people like Julie Harris, Jack Lemmon, Charlton Heston."

Even though the majority of the dramatic presentations in the 1950s were done live, there were some exceptions. "I did this show in New York," remembers Balduzzi, "a movie of the week they called *Sacco and Vanzetti* [based on the true story of the two early twentieth century anarchists executed for the armed robbery and murder of two payroll clerks in South Braintree, Massachusetts]. Sidney Lumet directed it. I had a very small part. We had Marty Balsam, and the one who's on *Law and Order* — Steven Hill. Marty Balsam and Steven Hill played Sacco and Vanzetti and then the convict from Venezuela was Peter Falk — they had quite a cast on that show — that was the early days of television, but this they filmed — they didn't shoot this one live."

If 1964's *Ben Casey* ("The Lonely Ones") marked the beginning of Dick Balduzzi's Hollywood TV career; 1965's *Marty* was the television pilot that established him. "I think the pilot of *Marty* started me off," feels Balduzzi. "It really built me a little name there at Screen Gems. They started using me for different shows. I had to do the audition [for *Marty*] with Tom Bosley, in front of Jackie Cooper, Harry Ackerman, and Harold Hecht, cuz he had the property; [Paddy] Chayefsky [the writer of *Marty*] wouldn't release that for ten years. After he died, or something, I don't know what the deal was. But Chayefsky didn't want that to be made into a series, I don't think. Anyway, all these people, [including future Paramount casting director] Millie Gusse, they were all sittin' around in this room and Tom and I did this one particular scene. There were two other guys up for the part — Bernie Kopell and somebody else. Anyway, Jackie came out and grabbed my hand and said, 'Congratulations. You got the part.' Well, things like that, you know. That's what's part of the business, that's what the excitement is."

Particularly excited about the opportunity handed to Balduzzi was Mildred Gusse. "Millie Gusse called me into her office," remembers Balduzzi. "She said, 'BOY! This is gonna do it for you! You're so good in this!' Well, wouldn't you know that NBC [the network that was considering *Marty*] picked three shows. They picked *I Dream of Jeannie*, they passed on *Marty*, they picked *Camp Runamuck*, which lasted, I don't know, nine segments, and there was another one. But we got left out, and I think a lot of it was because it was an ethnic thing. The only ethnic show that was on was *Molly Goldberg*, and I don't know, *Marty* was a good pilot. Swack directed the pilot, but, that's part of the game."

Fortunately for Dick Balduzzi, Screen Gems soon gave him work. In 1965 he appeared on three Screen Gems comedies: *I Dream of Jeannie* ("The Moving Finger"), *Gidget* ("All the Best Diseases Are Taken"), and *Bewitched* ("Illegal Separation," "The Very Informal Dress," "A Strange Little Visitor"). "Elizabeth [Montgomery] and I were very close on the set," says Balduzzi, "and I knew her husband [William Asher] very well. I did about four *Bewitched*s. Elizabeth was terrific, and Dick Sargent [Montgomery's co-star] and I were also very close, because Dick and I did Special Olympics for many years. Elizabeth was very prominent at his memorial. That was a big thing that we had — she spoke, and she was terrific. I went to her memorial, too. Now there're only about two or three [*Bewitched* stars] left. Bernard Fox [who played the recurring character, Dr. Bombay] is still around. They had a great cast on that show, but Elizabeth was the power on the set. Cuz one time Bill said something to me. She said, 'He's doing it all right. I like the way he's doing it.' He just shook his shoulders and we went on with it."

Things didn't go as smoothly with frequent *Bewitched* co-star Paul Lynde (Uncle Arthur) when Balduzzi guest-starred on Lynde's 1972-73 sitcom, *The Paul Lynde Show*. "I really, really had a bad time with Paul Lynde," states the actor. "For some reason he took a disliking to me, and kept…well, first thing when you're doing a three-camera show, in rehearsal, you don't have to blast everything out — you're rehearsing — there's a boom up there, right? So, I made an entrance, and I did some shtick, and I had a funny character. He said, 'Is that the way you're gonna read it?' I said, 'Why?' He said, 'They're not gonna hear you out there.' I said, 'Well, isn't there a boom up above me?' And he looked at me like I was dead! He gave me such a dirty look. From then on, he never spoke to me on the set. Even during the show, he tried to upstage me and everything. I thought it was very rude. Anne Meara and Jerry Stiller — they were recurring on the show [as Grace and Barney Dickerson], I went out to dinner with them the night after we shot. They said, 'Don't pay any attention to him. He's a very nervous wreck and this is his big show. He gets so nervous.' I said, 'Well, it's not necessary to be rude.' I mean, I can understand that, but I've gone with some big heavyweights that don't treat you like that."

Such as Anne Bancroft and Angela Lansbury. "Two women I really loved," enthuses Balduzzi. "They were wonderful. Just wonderful ladies. Just great." As was Donna Reed. "These women were wonderful," states the actor. "All the women I worked with — Shirley Jones and all of them. They treated the cast with respect. When you're a small character man, and they respect you, that's all that counts for me."

Respect for others was something *Police Woman*'s Angie Dickinson had in abundant supply. "Angie was just great!" raves Balduzzi. "When we did the scene, it was so nice; she and Earl [Holliman] were so cooperative. Years later, I went back and saw them in the commissary. She said, 'Hi, Dick.' She remembered the show I did. It's amazing how some people are so astute and remember what you did as an actor. That really impressed me about her."

Another actress about whom good things were said was *The Farmer's Daughter* star Inger Stevens. "*Farmer's Daughter* was one of my first jobs at Screen Gems," remembers Balduzzi. "I played a newsman who ran the news stand. I worked for [*Farmer's Daughter* executive producer] Bob Claver a lot. Bob was good, very professional, always tried to incorporate good characters. I did a crazy thing on *The Girl with Something Extra* [starring Sally Field and John Davidson]. There was a wedding…I came in with this hippie character. I played this minister like a real hippie with long hair. Bob fell over on the floor — he loved it. That went over big with him.

"Sally Field I worked with several times," continues Balduzzi. "I did a *Flying Nun* with Dick Wilson ("Young Man with a Cornette," November 23, 1967.) We were on a boat, with beards. We're old, and dying and cold. We see this nun flying over, and we think we're in heaven. They were very funny scenes, cuz we're praying, telling all our sins. Sally sees us down there, goes and gets help. Sally was young and she was just beginning. She did *Gidget* — she was quite a little actress. That led to bigger and better and more dramatic roles for her. She had that quality of innocence, that quality that Patty Duke had when playing the young kid [*The Patty Duke Show*]. That was a natural quality; Sally was very good."

Balduzzi also appeared in the series pilot, "The Flying Nun" (September 7, 1967). "That was a funny show," laughs the actor. "I played a Jewish sailor. I'm on top deck, and I see this thing flying around, so I run down, down the hatch, and I grab the skipper, Dabney Coleman. He says, 'What's wrong with you?' and I say, 'You won't believe this! You've got to see it, Captain. Come. Come. You've gotta see!' He says, 'What? What?' I said, 'There's a nun flying around up there.' So we go up there, and she's gone. He looks at me — very carefully. He says, 'Fisher. Are you a bewildered… are you a religious man?' I said, 'Well, sir. I'm Jewish.' He says, 'And you saw the vision of a nun?' I say, 'Yeah.' 'How do you explain that?' he asks. I said, 'Well, sir. If it was a religious thing, wouldn't I be seeing a rabbi?' On [*The Tonight Show Starring*] *Johnny Carson*, one of the comedians, Joey Bishop, mentioned that. He says, 'This is a funny scene.'"

In the previous season, Balduzzi worked with up-and-coming young actor Peter Duel in Screen Gem's *Love on a Rooftop* ("Dave's Night Out," November 29, 1966). "There was a scene where Pete wanted a night out with the boys," remembers the actor. "Pete wanted a night out, so he gets a card game up with the boys, and there are about four or five of us playing cards — it was a very funny scene." A few years later, when Duel starred in the hour-long comedy-western, *Alias Smith and Jones,* Balduzzi paid a visit to the set to see the star. "He took me to lunch, and it was very nice," says the actor. "I was just thrown overboard when he died. I can't believe he did something like that [Duel was rumored to have committed suicide]. It's incredible. You never know. And look at Albert Salmi. That was horrible. Also Gig Young. Taking his wife to New York, and shooting [her, then turning the gun on himself]. These people killing themselves in a hotel. And Ed Flanders…he was a very good friend of mine. I just couldn't believe it when these guys did themselves in. I guess they get to a point where they're suffering so much. I guess he had cancer. And Brian Keith…You know, it's amazing what happens to these people like Pete Duel. Their careers are going so well, then they destroy themselves. It's unbelievable. I never was in that position. I never was that successful to have to do anything."

Balduzzi was hardly what one would call a failure. For in September 1968, he began a two-season run, playing the semi-regular role of logger Billy Sawdust on *Here Come the Brides*. Also playing loggers were Robert Biheller (Corky), Buck Kartalian (Sam), James Almanzar (Canada), Barry Cahill (McGee), Andy Romano (Pebbles), and Vic Tayback (Jason's man). The group came to be known as "The Magnificent Seven."

"Swack called us 'The Magnificent Seven,' because we were always an ensemble," explains Balduzzi, "but, as the series went [on], we had our little spot. I think I did eight shows, and I think I only had maybe two or three of 'em that I had some nice work in — maybe two or three scenes. There were so many people they had to share all the things so The Magnificent Seven got maybe one or two days in the sun. But it was fun because when you have a group like that, you're so united together, it's such a pleasant…you love going to work. We had a lot of laughs. We had a lot of fun — every day someone would cut up. We knew our limitations, what we could get away with, what we shouldn't do. Because they [the actors] were all professional. All these guys went on to do other shows. I think after *Brides*, Cahill got bigger roles. Vic died young. Almazar was a very quiet man — always laughed a lot, but he wasn't such a jokester, like some of the others. Biheller was a 'pepperpot' — that was our nickname for him. And Buck was a character. He had red shorts on; he'd drop his pants all the time to break up the tension. Robert [Brown] didn't like that — he'd really get pissed off at us. We made things light, but when it was time to shoot, we shot. We didn't fool around and waste any time or anything. And when the loggers got to work with the principals, it was fun. We all mixed in together. I don't think too many of us [loggers] worked together — if we did, it was as an ensemble. When we had separate scenes, it was with one of the principals, or one of the cast members — with Bobby or David or Bridget. I didn't have too much to do in the pilot. They established our characters as we went on but I really didn't do a lot of planning, because the characters were pretty well defined. If I had been on the show every week, I probably would have developed something substantial for my character — mannerisms, habits — but it was sporadic. It was never anything that we knew in advance — maybe a week or so — that was it. But if I wasn't involved in the scene, I watched the others work. And they had some good people on as guest stars."

Not to mention a good leading man in Robert Brown. "Robert Brown wasn't a typical Hollywood actor," reflects Balduzzi. "I guess his first series was a thing called *Piranha* or something; he did a lot of work all around, and played mostly professional men — doctors and lawyers. Then he started going into voice-overs, did very well in commercials, and he settled for that. We've been friends for years — we were at both [Swackhamer] girls' weddings, we were at the parties Swack always had — always at the house. Bobby and David were terrific, especially Bobby. He wasn't quite then the big rock star. David was good. David was down to earth, a good actor. I had a great rapport with both of them. We'd kid a lot. And I worked with Bobby when he had that show, *Getting Together*. [I] played a secret-service man who dresses in drag, trying to capture some information. It was hysterical, being in drag, especially with my nose. And then, of course…well, Susan and I, after *Brides*, we worked together on Special Olympics. I've been doing it for thirty-five years. We used to do it at UCLA. Now we do it at Long Beach State. Been there for nine years. It's more family oriented now. It's great. I love working with those kids. I get to know them. There's about seven or eight of us that are still with them. All these years."

Like Bridget Hanley, Susan Tolsky and the other *Brides* cast members, Balduzzi thinks very highly of the show's regular director of photography, Fred H. Jackman. "I thought Jackman was great," states the actor. "This guy did things way in the past. I wish I had known that then, because I'm a collector of film. I go way back to the twenties and thirties, and forties. I loved the people in that era. They were so good. They were so natural. You didn't consider them as actors. But there were some that were great character actors like Paul Muni. Spencer Tracy was a natural actor, probably the best out of all of them. Jackman worked with so many of them."

Balduzzi also liked the pilot's associate producer, Marvin Miller "Marvin Miller was a kick," he says. "We got along real well, had a lot of laughs. He and Swack and I just kidded a lot. He did casting and production for Bill Cosby's show. I did four episodes of that. I was a schoolteacher called Mr. Green. Cosby directed some of those shows.

I would have enjoyed working with him in New York. He was directing some of the segments, and he would do it by numbers. I had never experienced anything like that. There were scenes where all of us were together, and we were all supposed to look at something at the same time. He would count. 'One two, three, four,' and then we'd turn. I thought it was hysterical because I don't do things by precision."

During the second season of *Here Come the Brides*, Dick Balduzzi was on location in Yugoslavia, playing the role of Pvt. Fisher in the ensemble World War II comedy, *Kelly's Heroes*. "I didn't get to be in many *Brides* in the second season because of that job, in Yugoslavia," explains the actor. "I left in July and I didn't get back until after Christmas. I was in Yugoslavia for almost five months. We had so many problems on that show. It was like a movie within a movie. We were in those half-tracks and they were blowing everything up around us. When the live bullets hit the ground, they do it electronically by pushing buttons. One time the special effects guy said to us, 'Anyone who doesn't want to be in the danger of this scene can get out.' So, a lot of us did. That was scary on the half-track because the buildings were going down, and this guy — they called him "Boom-Boom" — supposedly, he was a munitions expert for the Germans in the Second World War. He did all our special effects. He blew up everything. Where they blew up the barn in the scene that we all had in the barn, we had to run like hell cuz the thing flew about five-hundred…it was really scary."

Among the stars of *Kelly's Heroes*: Clint Eastwood, Telly Savalas, Donald Sutherland, Don Rickles, and Carroll O'Connor. "O'Connor was very serious," remembers Balduzzi. "I didn't realize he was such a comedian because he always played heavies. In Yugoslavia, he and Nancy (his wife), and I used to go to Mass every Sunday. He was very down to earth. Sometimes he wouldn't mingle with the guys in the hotel dining room, in the bar section. But he liked to gamble. And they had a casino so he

*Left to right: Clint Eastwood, Donald Sutherland, Dick Balduzzi, and Telly Savalas in the 1970 MGM WWII adventure,* Kelly's Heroes. COURTESY DICK BALDUZZI

would go there with a couple of the guys. But he wouldn't mix in a lot, like Telly did and Sutherland. Eastwood was more quiet. He was by himself a lot. Had his own little group. But Carroll wouldn't mix with us — he was more with his family. He got the best deal of all of us. He got the beginning of the show, and the ending of the show, and they paid him all that way for nine months, so he traveled all over. And he spoke fluent Italian. When he did that picture, *Cleopatra*, he was in Rome for many months, made tons of money on that. They had a hiatus for I don't know how long. That picture made a lot of people wealthy, but it almost destroyed Fox."

Serving as a production assistant on *Kelly's Heroes* was an eighteen-year-old American by the name of John Landis. Remembers Balduzzi: "There was a young man who was a gofer on *Kelly's Heroes*, and Brian Hutton [the director] gave him a job, like running errands, and doing things (like a fifth assistant) just to give him some work while he was in Yugoslavia. He played a nun because the producer's wife [who was to play the part]...her driver lost his way; she didn't make it on the set. So John Landis, this young kid who was broke, they dressed him up as one of the nuns walking by. He did all of these parts. All of us felt sorry for him, we'd take him out to dinner one night. After he got started [as a director], he did *Animal House*, then he did *Into the Night*, and [in the latter] there was a whole [round-table] scene with a lot of nuclear scientists. He hired a lot of directors to play small parts; I played a nuclear scientist."

During the production of *Kelly's Heroes,* Balduzzi became friends with Telly Savalas. When Savalas later hit it big with *Kojak*, he told Balduzzi he could guest. "But I would never go to him for a job," says Balduzzi. "I'd always go and read for it. He'd get very pissed off. He'd say, 'Why don't you just tell me?' I said, 'What's the difference? I got it. I'm here.' Well, I went in and read for this one particular part [the bartender in the March 9, 1975 *Kojak*, "I Want to Report a Dream"], real nice part. I played a bartender who gives him information about a certain guy. The director I read for didn't seem like he was interested in my reading. I told [casting director] Milton Hamerman, I said, 'You know, I don't think I'm gonna get this part.' He said, "You read real well, Dick.' I said, 'Yeah, but did you see his reaction? He didn't even pay attention.' He said, 'Well, don't worry about it.' And I got the part.

Continues Balduzzi: "I went in early to rehearse myself cuz I'm playing a bartender behind the scenes. Then Telly's trailer pulls up so I run over there. He said, 'What are you doing here?' I said, 'I'm playing Angie.' He said, 'Wh--...didn't you...? How come I didn't know?' 'Well,' I said, 'I read for the part; I got it' I said, 'You want to run the scene?' He said, 'Yeah. Let's run it.' So while he's dressing, getting ready, we're running, running, running. We get on the set, and the director's there. He didn't say 'Hello' to me or anything. I'm thinking, 'This guy has it in for me.' I thought the worst, but it wasn't that way. The director said, 'Let's run one.' We ran it and, [of] course, it went smooth. He said, 'That was pretty good.' Telly said, 'What do you think? You're fooling around with New York actors! We don't...this guy's an actor from New York!' So the director said, 'Well, let's shoot one.' And we shot it. And it was good. Then, because it was good, and they liked it, they wrote in another scene for me. So that was nice. Every time I worked with Telly, he treated me like I was one of the top...even though I had smaller roles. But he was that way. Telly was a good person — he died way too young."

A year before he did *Kelly's Heroes,* Dick Balduzzi worked in the John Cassavettes motion picture, *Faces.* "I worked with Cassavettes for about three months," says the actor, "then I had to leave, because they shot night for night, and I had a family. I couldn't start at midnight and work till five or six in the morning; I had to leave. Well, John was so gracious that anyone that worked on his shows, he gave them a small percentage of the residual. So I'm still getting money from that show that was done, in the 1960s. I mean, a pittance, like $25 or $15 or $20, but I get something every year. He saw to it that the actor and the people working with him were taken care of."

That wasn't always the case. "I did this remake of *Postman Always Rings Twice,*" remembers Balduzzi. "My friend John Furlong and I played two guys who bring in the sign, when the guy takes over the restaurant. The owner starts dressing up the restaurant and he wants to put in a neon sign, so John and I were the two guys that brought in the sign. We had very little dialogue but we were still stuck for a whole week, because it was raining [at the location]. They built a whole beautiful 1930s set in Santa Barbara, on this woman's vacant field. You should have seen the labor and the wood and everything [as] the gas station and the café were built. It was a beautiful set. Anyway, we were in our trailers for a whole week because it was raining so hard. I said, 'You know what we should do, John? Let's just write some dialogue — write some ad-libbing while we're bringing in this sign.' He said, 'Okay. Good.' We did about two pages, not knowing whether we were gonna use it or not. Finally after a week went by, [director Bob] Rafelson came in, he said, 'Guys. Looks like it's not gonna let up. We're gonna have to shoot this. We'll put raincoats on you and we'll bring in the equipment and all that.' And Sven Nyquist, Bergman's right-hand man, was our cinematographer. So I got to meet him, and that was a thrill. Anyway, I told Rafelson, I said, 'You know, Bob. We wrote a little dialogue for the scene maybe to help you move it along.' He said, 'Let me hear it.' So we went and did our little shtick. He said, 'I love it. Let's do it.' So we went on in the rain. We did our little shtick. They shot it, put it on a Moviola [a viewing device for editors] so they could see the thing, and the crew was laughing, and one guy playing one of the lead characters — John Colicos — he said, 'Thank God, this is a very funny scene. Thank God that we've got something that lightens up this production.' Well, lo and behold, who's standing on the side watching all this but [star Jack] Nicholson. He's got a scowl on his face. So, just as Bob is talking to the two of us about doing it again, Nicholson walks over and looks at my friend and me. He says, 'I want you two guys to know that you're now in a major motion picture!' and he walked away. I said to Rafelson, 'What the hell?' Rafelson said, 'Don't say anything. I'll take care of it.' I don't know why Nicholson did that, but the scene got cut out of the picture. I think it was because he [Nicholson] wanted a heavy-handed film. Well, the picture's awful, I thought it was terrible, never even matched half of what [John] Garfield and Lana Turner did [in the 1946 original]."

Balduzzi also had trouble with Michael Parks. In that case, the problem was Parks' acting style. "The director was Brian Hutton, who also directed me in *Kelly's Heroes*," says Balduzzi. "I didn't know Michael Parks. I couldn't understand a damn word he was saying because he was one of those method actors. I told Brian, 'Would you tell him to speak up a little bit cuz I can't understand him. I don't know when the hell to come in on my cue.' Brian told Parks. Parks got a big kick out of it. He wasn't being difficult. He was just doing his thing."

In 1983's *Cocaine and Blue Eyes*, the problem was star O.J. Simpson's difficulty in remembering his lines. "I played a bartender," says Balduzzi. "He was sort of a private detective. It was a projected pilot. He had a lot of questions to ask me, but he couldn't remember his lines. Swack directed that, and Swack was hysterical — he was laughing on the side, because he knew I was getting frustrated as hell; we had to start over every time. But O.J. was very gracious. When I arrived in my dressing room, there was a big basket of fruit and a nice card, welcoming me on the set. That was a nice scene, but it took a long time to shoot."

Almost a year before that, Dick Balduzzi did one of his favorite shows — the January 8, 1982 *Darkroom* episode, "Guillotine" (a remake of the September 26, 1961

*Thriller* episode of the same title.) French actress Danielle De Metz played the part of Babette Lamont in the original; Patti D'Arbanville was Babette in the remake. "I enjoyed working with Patti," says Balduzzi. "And it was a good part. I played this French guard who was very sadistic. He was going to execute her boyfriend. So I got to use my French accent. I have a book of accents, phonetics, and things. When I did *Zorro*, I worked with the Spanish accent, trying to get the right flavor. Toughest accent for me was always German. Italian I could do. French I could do, and Spanish, but German. That was always tough for me.

"I didn't care for the director on *Darkroom*," continues the actor. "He was a younger director. I think it was his first or second show. And I had this big scene with Patti, but he waited till the last minute to do that. Then he was really obnoxious. He kept pushing me. He said, 'Come on, come on, come on. We gotta go. We gotta get this done!' I got furious. Patti pulled me aside and said, 'Don't let him get to you. Take your damn time. Screw him!'"

Balduzzi's guest shot on the 1971 Larry Hagman/Donna Mills sitcom, *The Good Life* was a much more pleasant experience. "I had a very funny scene," remembers the actor. "My friend Jay Sandrich directed me in that segment. I was this guy who comes in to take care of these dogs; they get away from him. And he's got them on a leash so they drag him, literally, pull him all over the place. They were worried about that scene, They wanted to get a stunt double to do it. I did it myself. It worked out beautifully. It was a very funny scene."

Another pleasant experience came on *Barney Miller*. "My whole scene was with Steve Landesberg," recalls Balduzzi. "He was a wonderful guy to work with, and everyone came up to say 'Hi' and welcome me to the set. The only one who didn't come up was Hal Linden. I was surprised because he was in the scene. [Co-star] Ron Carey, I knew. Ron and I were very, very good friends, but we never saw one another socially. Which was very weird. I knew him all the time, because I used to work the Actor's Blood Bank, and Ron and his wife would come in and give blood every year. I had a very funny part in that show. I was a priest, in the confessional, and this guy pulls a gun on me. They had me hang around because they didn't know if they were gonna write me more scenes. They wrote the show as they went along."

Star Anne Bancroft's 1980 comedy, *Fatso*, which she also wrote and directed, was another production which kept Balduzzi "around." "She was just a super lady," praises the actor. "I played Uncle Phil; there were a lot of Italian people on that show. We were on the show for weeks because they just kept us around. I remember there was a woman. She was a character actress. She and I would cook in the kitchen. [Star] Dom DeLuise would come in and he'd cook, too. We always ate on the set. We always had pasta, sauce. Anne loved it. It was great."

Another actor who was good to his friends was Michael Keaton. When Keaton did the 1984 comedy, *Johnny Dangerously*, Balduzzi was cast as one of the prisoners. "We were friends," explains the actor, "and he had all these small parts in the prison scene played by actors that he knew. He got about five guys — friends of his, to play parts. There was one scene in the prison where they talk about his mother; it [the talk] goes down the line before he goes berserk like Cagney [in the famous scene from 1949's *White Heat*].

Besides *Here Come the Brides'* E.W. Swackhamer, one director with whom Dick Balduzzi particularly enjoyed working was actor-turned-director Jerry Paris. "I worked with Jerry Paris a lot," states Balduzzi. "I worked with Jerry in a movie called *Two on a Bench*, which we shot in Boston. That was with Patty Duke, Ted Bessell, Alice Ghostley, and John Astin. That's where he first met Patty Duke. She had her baby with her — Sean. He was a little tot, only like a few months old. John adopted the little boy. We shot for about ten days in Boston, and while we were shooting in the Commons, Ted Bessell had a late call. Jerry says, 'I'm gonna play a trick on him. I want everybody in on it. Don't let on what's happening. Okay?' 'Okay,' we all agreed. So we got this beautiful, beautiful girl. She wasn't even on the show. She was just in the audience. Jerry says, 'I want you to do this.' When he comes on the set, you go up to him and slap his face, then give him his key, and say, 'I don't ever want to come to your place again.' Then walk away.' Now, the place is filled with spectators. All around, cuz we're shooting in the Commons. Finally Ted comes in. He says, 'I'm here. Hello, everybody.' Paris gave this girl the cue. The moment Bessell was on center stage, she went up to him and slapped him in the face. He says, 'WHAT? WHAT? WHAT?' And she handed him the key and walked away. He says, 'Wait! Wait! Wait a minute! I don't even know you!' He's telling the people, 'I don't even know this girl. I don't know her. What's going on? What?' And everyone's hysterical. Finally, it dawns on him. He says, 'JERRY PARIS! YOU SON OF A BITCH!' We all laughed. Jerry did things like that all the time. That was fun. Patty Duke, Ted Bessell, John Astin, Alice Ghostley, Robert Cornthwaite, Andrew Duggan. And Duggan was a big Irish guy. He was great. He and Alice Ghostley flew up together. They kept drinking Bloody Marys because they both hated flying. And all of us went out to a different restaurant every night. It was nice; it was a great company."

As was the cast of the hit sitcom, *Happy Days*. "We had a great time on that show," remembers the actor. "I played a tattoo artist. I knew [Tom] Bosley from doing the pilot with him — *Marty*. I didn't get to work with him and Marion Ross. I worked with all the kids. The kids were great. Ron Howard was just a wonderful kid. And Henry [Winkler] and I knew each other. We took a class together. Dick Schaal, who used to be married to Valerie Harper, he had a group that he picked. We all worked together doing scenes and doing projects. It was like a workshop."

In 1973 Dick Balduzzi guest starred on the Jerry Paris-directed sitcom, *Thicker than Water* ("The Piano Teacher," June 27, 1973). The short-lived show (only nine episodes were broadcast, according to IMDb) starred Richard Long and Julie Harris as Ernie and Nellie Paine, a constantly-at-odds brother and sister. In the episode Balduzzi did, "someone was courting Long's sister — Dick Van Patten was the guy," says Balduzzi. "I played a private detective whom Long hires so as to find out what this guy was like who was courting his sister. I don't know how they got Richard Long and Julie Harris for the show. Anyway, Long hires me as a private detective, and, I have a lot of my own wardrobe: shoes, hats, and things I like to wear when I play different characters. Well, Long asks me a lot of questions, about fifteen to twenty questions in this scene that we had, so I brought in this long coat. It was like salt and pepper — those old-fashioned coats in the thirties. Inside, I had my neighbor, who was a seamstress, make pockets — ten pockets on each side of the coat. I put these notes in it, so when Long would ask me a question, I'd open up the coat and pull out a slip that had the answer. Well, they went wild — Jerry Paris, all of them. The costume designer said, "I wouldn't have thought of that. That's fantastic!" I used that in the whole scene. It was a big hit. The next day, I worked another day on pick-ups or something, and I went in…I brought in all this memorabilia — Broadway shows, playbills, and scripts."

Balduzzi also took Ken Howard by surprise when he guest starred on Howard's short-lived 1974-75 QM crime drama, *The Manhunter*. "Played his cellmate," remembers Balduzzi. "I'm known for drunk guys, and I played this guy that way. Howard couldn't keep a straight face. He would break up every time I spoke to him. Finally the director, they took the camera off Howard and put it on me. I had to say the lines with his back towards me cuz he was laughing so hard through the whole damn scene. Then I think he…I saw him out at dinner one night, and [when Howard saw Balduzzi] he said, 'This is the guy. This is the guy that had that scene that I couldn't get through.' He blamed me for causing him not to be able to do the scene. But we finally got it and he settled down. He was a nice guy." Balduzzi's *Police Woman* guest shot had him playing another alcoholic. "I went in and read for this guy. It was a nice little scene, about an alcoholic who ran this hotel; he was always drinking and fell asleep. Then someone got murdered at one of the cottages. He gets very upset and breaks down. I read the scene, and it went so well, the director said, 'Cut and print,' I said, 'What?' He said, 'You got it. That's what I wanted.' I thought, Wow! How easy! If they were all easy like that…"

In "Santa '85," Balduzzi's December 15, 1985 guest shot on *Amazing Stories,* the actor was 'Drunk #1' in a story about a "bunch of drunken Santa Clauses who get arrested," says Balduzzi. "They put us all in jail. The real one — he was a wonderful actor; it was an *Amazing Story* about Santa living at the South Pole." In another episode, "I played a bartender, had a scene with Dom DeLuise. Burt Reynolds directed that. He only did a few shows."

In 1973, Balduzzi played Philly — an alcoholic friend of Lou Grant's in two episodes of *The Mary Tyler Moore Show*. Balduzzi had done the series in 1971 as well. "The first one I did, I played a strikebreaker," explains Balduzzi, "then I went in and read for Philly — this alcoholic friend of Lou's — [a] character that comes in the office. Lou always gives him a handout, and gives him a drink. That was a great group [the cast of *The Mary Tyler Moore Show*], they had great camaraderie, and we got to know each other — cuz I did two musicals with Gavin [MacLeod] — *A Funny Thing Happened on the Way to the Forum*, and *High Button Shoes* — we played partners. Well, when the whole cast came to see us in the show, Mary was still married to Grant Tinker. They all came. All the writers, everybody came. I think that's how I got on the show — that was the first year of the show. And Gavin and I had worked together in Yugoslavia [on *Kelly's Heroes*]. Anyway, when Grant came on, he said, 'You two guys oughta do a show together.' I said, 'Would you produce it?' And

Mary started laughing — they all laughed. But they came and saw the show, and they never got over it. We really were good — Gavin and I were good in that, got a lot of recognition, and, as a matter of fact, Grant even called the producer. He said 'There's a guy you've got to see to play Hysterium [in *Forum*]. He's just fantastic and natural for the part. The producer said, 'Well, I can't do that because Larry Blyden is co-producing the show, and he's playing Hysterium. It was with Phil Silvers and Larry Blyden playing the two leads; they went over big in New York. Both won Tonys. But I was so grateful to Grant recommending me for that part."

Besides hiring Dick Balduzzi for three *Mary Tyler Moore Show* episodes, Tinker then called him in for *The Bob Crane Show*. "They had an actor who couldn't cut it," explains Balduzzi. "So, at twelve noon, I get a call from Grant. He said, 'I need your help.' I said, 'What's the matter?' He says, 'We've got this character who's a friend of Bob Crane's. He has a scene with him; they're both plastered. This guy can't cut it. Can you come in and do it for us?' I said, 'When are you shooting?' He said, 'Tonight. You've got enough time to rehearse, then we're gonna have a dress rehearsal. If you can do it, come in now.' I said, 'All right.' I did it and got the script right away. Then they gave me a dressing room. I changed. I worked from around one O'Clock till three O'Clock trying to memorize the lines and get the blocking. Then, at three O'Clock, they had a dress rehearsal where they used the cameras, and they had a little audience. Well, whatever happened, God was with me. Went over real big. Got a standing ovation. At night, Grant introduced me. He said, 'This man came in here today and did this role.' Which was very nice. Then there was a bigger part that came on with a wonderful actor, Ronnie Graham. Ronnie Graham was a character on *The Bob Crane Show* — Mr. Ernest Busso [Crane's landlord, and an inventor]. They brought me in as his associate — he was a manufacturer of toys." (Balduzzi played the role of Petri in the April 24, 1975 episode, "Acute Bussophobia.") "We had a good time," the actor recalls. "Ronnie was just great to work with. He was a New York actor — lot of preparation, timing, and everything. [In the other episode, the actor Balduzzi replaced] was a young actor, like a leading man type. I don't think he was a running part on the show. He was a friend in the series of the Bob Crane character. He had worked a lot. He was a working, but not a recognized actor. Handsome guy. Real tall. I'm the complete opposite. But they wanted someone to capture that part."

When not playing a drunk, Dick Balduzzi often played a bartender. One such opportunity was in the 1972 TV-movie, *Playmates*. "With [Alan] Alda and [Doug] McClure," remembers the actor. "Weird thing happened to me on that set — God saved my life. I went in prepared and there was no one on the set. So I went behind the bar, and looked at stuff I was gonna do. I think we shot it at Twentieth [Century Fox]. Anyway, I'm standing at the bar and I'm walking back and forth. Then I just moved to my left, and the goddamn pipe came down and hit the bar where I was standing. And the (set construction) guy was there. I said, 'HOLY...WHAT THE HELL?' He said, 'Oh, I'm sorry. It didn't hit you, did it? It slipped.' I said, 'JESUS CHRIST! I WOULD HAVE BEEN DEAD!' I mean God saved my life! I couldn't believe it — it was a matter of seconds. It was break time — lunch-time. He shouldn't have been there. That was scary, I tell you. I was very nervous. Ted Flicker directed that show — I don't think I told him."

In the 1975 TV-movie, *A Shadow in the Streets*, Balduzzi's performance was so real that others came forward to help him. "That was with Tony Lo Bianco and Sheree North," recalls the actor. "The director was Dick [Richard] Donner. We shot down in Skid Row, and it was a time when the slasher was cutting throats, and it was scary as hell because we were shooting night for night. It was really dreary down there, and we had to shoot in this old hotel. What I played was a private detective [Bense] who follows Tony Lo Bianco, who just got out of prison. He's released because they want to find out...he had this big heist from a bank and they wanted to tail him and find out where the money was hidden. Well, lo and behold, he knows someone is on his tail. So I'm down there, looking through the window of the hotel — he's inside, and I'm watching from in front of the building. He sees me, but I don't know he's seen me. He goes out the back way and comes around and grabs me by the hair, pulls me back and says, 'You son of a...Why do you keep tailing me like this?' Well, in this scene, I was yelling like crazy, and all of a sudden when we took the first shot, three of these guys came in to help me: three bums, right in the middle of the shot. So we stopped, 'Cut!' Donner says. 'Cut!' He says, 'What are you guys doing?' They said, 'This guy was being harassed. We were gonna help him.' The producer, producer-writer John D.F. Black, was there. He said, 'You should have left it in! You should have left that in — that was a great shot!' Anyway, Donner was very loose on this set. I think this was before he went into the big features."

Not the sort of actor who enjoyed doing his own stunts, Dick Balduzzi lost some parts because of that. "I was turned down in a helicopter thing, because I wouldn't go up in that to do a show," admits the actor. "They had a scene up there; if the guy wants to do it himself, he's placing himself in jeopardy. They have to offer hazard pay most of the time."

Television and motion pictures weren't the only productions that could endanger an actor. "I did a commercial once for this shoe company, and sometimes people lie," says Balduzzi. "They had three of us hardhats dancing on a plank, and they raised it to about two or three feet, and that was fine. I said to the director, 'That's as far as you're going, isn't it?' He said, 'Yeah, that's as far.' Well, when we shot the damn thing they put mattresses at the bottom so we knew we were gonna go up. They went about six or eight feet up with this plank and we're dancing...[of] course every one of us fell off at one time. And we had these heavy boots on — doing this dance. A guy came up to me. He said, 'You know you guys deserve hazard pay for this.' I didn't know what the hell hazard pay was. But I made a lot of money on that commercial."

In the 1981 George Hamilton comedy, *Zorro the Gay Blade*, dysentery was the problem for Balduzzi and his fellow cast members. "We shot in Cuernavaca, which was a fantastic place," raves Balduzzi, "but everyone was getting dysentery, getting sick down in Mexico. I did eat some salad, and I think that's what did me in. We had to shoot way up in the mountains. They built this little hut, my scene was up there, and it was like the Angeles National Forest. It was a two-hour trip to get there. Well, I was sicker than a dog one day. But George was very gracious because I had a six

O'Clock call. I was just throwing up and doing both sides, you know, loose bowels. George said, 'Dick. Go into my trailer and just lie down until you feel a little better. Then we'll shoot the scene.' I did, and fell asleep. Then they got some ice cubes for me, and just wet my mouth because my fever was up to 104! So we ran the scene and I forgot to take my socks off. I had my socks on under my sandals — Mexican sandals, because the character was barefooted — he was an old peasant. It didn't look bad because they didn't shoot down low."

During the course of production, 20th Century Fox studio head Sherry Lansing paid a visit to cast and crew. "She came down," remembers Balduzzi, "and was very pleasant. And Helen Hayes was living in Cuernavaca at the time. And Maurice Evans was living there. So I got to meet 'em all. They all came on the set. There were a lot of artists, and a lot of Americans — writers, living down there at the time. I'm sure there still are. That was a long shoot, but I enjoyed it because I had my own place. And I cooked one night. The housekeeper for me made these tortillas, so one night I had the whole crew come for dinner. Had one night with all the actors and producers, and I made Italian food. They loved that. I did that to get away from the regular Mexican food."

Directing the picture was Hungarian-born Peter Medak. "He did a wonderful film with Peter O'Toole that got a lot of notoriety," recalls Balduzzi, "a well-known film. [The movie was 1972's *The Ruling Class*.] Anyway, there was this scene…I'm playing an old peasant guy, who gets robbed by the Alcalde, and I'm talking to Zorro. He goes to my door and makes a 'Z.' He says, 'You know what that is, don't you?' I said, 'Yes, it's a number 2.' They showed that scene to promote the film. George Hamilton was on about ten talk shows, and they showed my scene with him on every talk show. He never mentioned me. *Ten times* you can not mention my name? But he was all right."

Not so Hamilton's leading lady Lauren Hutton. "Lauren Hutton was a pain in the ass," states Balduzzi. "She would never want to rehearse. 'No. No. Do it on the set.' But we had great masters teaching us the manual arts — had this great, great teacher — his name was Phil Romano. He worked a lot with Basil Rathbone. He was good with swordplay. He had special times where he would show everyone the art of sword-fighting, the movements, how to handle the sword. She didn't want to do it. She just did it on the set. So, when they reshot her scene, she just went along with what she could do. So they didn't cover her with the camera that much."

Thanks to his problems with a very well-known comedy actor, Balduzzi had to turn down an opportunity to work with one of his favorite directors, Jerry Paris. "It was *The Odd Couple*," explains Balduzzi. "Jerry just wanted me as maître d in the restaurant. I think I only had one line in the show. Klugman was terrific, but the guy I couldn't stand was Tony Randall. Randall started picking on me. 'Why won't you do this?' he says. 'What's wrong with it?' and he's interrupting my conversation with Jerry. Randall got me so pissed, I got nervous."

As a result, Balduzzi started a cigarette. "He went, 'Ah, ah, ah! We don't do that!'" remembers Balduzzi. "'We don't smoke on this set!' I said, 'Okay.' And the more I talked to Jerry about it, Randall would say something and interrupt, and Jack would say, 'Leave him alone! For Christ's sake, shut up! Let him say what's he got to say!' I took Jerry aside. I said, 'Look. I'm not making a lot of money, but they've established me now. I can't work for this. It's only one line, so they're offering me the minimum wage — it's $500.' I said, 'I've built my salary up to...if I'm gonna work a day job, I get $1,000 or more.' He said, 'Dick, I understand. Don't let him bother you. He does things like that. He's like an old man, but he comes through in performance.' I was so annoyed with Randall. I felt bad I had to turn Jerry down."

Balduzzi turned down other work too because of that $1,000 rule. "That happened a couple times," recalls the actor. "They called me in on this big soap. I turned it down because I was not going to make $1,000 a day doing the show. If you're gonna stick to your guns, you lose things. And, if you get another job [at a lower salary], they report it. [So when the actor/actress goes out for a new role], they'll say, 'Well, last week, you worked for $500.' This is the rotten part of the business. I never liked to deal with that, and I never had a damn good agent who would fight for me. I went through fifteen of 'em. I couldn't find one that believed in my work. So I got most of my jobs on my own. [*Brides* guest] Ken Swofford recommended me for a job. Directors recommend you, too."

Consequently, maintaining a good reputation in the business, particularly a reputation as a talent who was easy to work with, was a very smart thing to do. "If you're working with someone on the set," notes Balduzzi, "they'll say, 'I worked on this show, and blah, blah, blah.' I used to listen a lot to that. There are certain things I never liked talking about, but there are people, like Paul Lynde. He offended me terribly, and I didn't mind telling anyone. I didn't enjoy working that show. That's probably one of the few shows in my whole career that I never enjoyed working."

One show Dick Balduzzi very definitely enjoyed was William Conrad's 1971-76 series, *Cannon*. The actor guest starred on the show twice — the first time in 1973's "Arena of Fear," the second — 1975's "The Conspirators." "Bill Conrad was great!" enthuses Balduzzi. I loved working with him. The thing that amazed me about him — when he did his close-ups, he never wanted the other actor to read lines. He would use cards. He had an assistant who would write out all the dialogue and he would read from that. He didn't want the other actor there. He was a good artist, did about three hundred radio shows. And he had that great voice!"

"There were three or four of us on that show ("The Conspirators") who were theater-minded," continues Balduzzi, "Martine Bartlett and Tom Skerritt, and another actor who did theater. So Bill took us into his dressing room once. He did this thing — a Chekov thing, classic Russian play, *The Boar*. He made this tape of it, invited us in his dressing room and did this reading. It was FANTASTIC! I said, 'Bill, you should have that published. This is brilliant. You did a great job with that!'"

Shot on location in Twin Falls, Idaho, "The Conspirators" also guest-starred Hilly Hicks, "who quit acting to become a preacher," reveals Balduzzi. Another co-star was veteran character actor Dabbs Greer. "Bill loved his fish," says Balduzzi, "and he was a great fisherman, so he talked the studio into going up to Twin Falls, Idaho, cuz they have great trout up there. We shot that the week after Evel Knievel made his famous jump over the Snake River. They'd had all these hippies and yippies that followed

Knievel all around; all these bikers took over the city. Well, this was a small community and very gentle people, so when they found a body in the falls, it was shocking. That shocked the town. They didn't know what the hell was coming."

Given what had recently happened, the QM company's initial reception by the townspeople of Twin Falls was rather cool. "They were very leery of movie companies," explains Balduzzi, "but once they got to know all of us, we had a wonderful time. We were there almost a week — about ten days. They got to know us so well we became part of their family. Balduzzi kept in touch with both William Conrad and Tom Skerritt following that particular production, "Tom Skerritt came to our house for one of our Christmas parties," remembers the actor, "and I worked with Bill again on (the 1980s series) *Jake and the Fatman*. He got even heavier when he did that. Bill Conrad was a good eater. He loved his fishing and his eating. So that was a fun show. We recollected our moments in Twin Falls, Idaho."

Though there is no indication Dick Balduzzi ever guest starred on Karl Malden's Quinn Martin series, *The Streets of San Francisco*, to this day, the actor remains close friends with Malden. "Karl has signed a lot of my work, and he's gotten up there, but he's holding his own," says Balduzzi. "You know, you play it as it goes, because one week you feel great, the next week something's wrong. Karl's funny as hell. He's got a marvelous sense of humor." *

Of course Balduzzi has stayed in touch with *Here Come the Brides* Bridget Hanley through the years; from time to time, he has seen his fellow *Brides* cast members. "We had a reunion at Carroll O'Connor's place, The Ginger Man, a bar that he had, and we all got there, except Swack, because he was shooting something else," remembers Balduzzi. "And Mark couldn't get there. He was doing something in New York. But Biheller came. Clancey [Beckman] came. David Soul came. Bobby Sherman...And Brown was there. It was a wonderful party. We got to invite our wives to it.

It was really nice to see all those people after all those years."[4]

## *Buck Kartalian: An actor who loves to work*

"I don't mind. As an actor, when I'm acting, I don't feel like this is more important, and this is less important. There is no such thing. I just do what I do."

That is *Here Come the Brides* semi-regular Buck Kartalian's response when asked whether he regrets making a B-picture such as the early 1970s cult hit, *Please Don't Eat My Mother*. Though there are some actors who would never do anything like *Mother*, or an Aaron Spelling series like *Love Boat* or *Fantasy Island*, or ANY television, Buck Kartalian professes to no such snobbery. "I love to work," he says matter-of-factly. "I'm eighty-five years old, but I feel like a teenager. I've done I don't know how many TV shows. I lost count after one hundred and fifty to two hundred. I worked with Brando, Newman, Yul Brynner, Lloyd Nolan...I worked with everybody. Did a lot of plays. Even done musicals."

---

*This interview was conducted a year or so before Malden's death.

Like many in the business, Buck Kartalian drifted into acting. "I was in World War II, in the Navy, and I didn't know what the hell I was gonna do," he admits. "I ended up in a gymnasium on Times Square called George Marker's Gymnasium. He was an old, old, retired wrestler. He had a marvelous place. Anyway, I got out of the service and found this gym. I said, 'Hey, this is great here!' This is 1946 — kind of near the end of vaudeville. And I learned to do some flip-flops, and they had this thing that they called a harness — you can learn flips on it, and I got to be a good flipper, and in the corner there were some weights, and I got interested in weights, then I'd fool around with the wrestlers. I learned just a little bit about everything, so in about six or eight months, I had a build you wouldn't believe. But I never weighed more than one hundred and fifty pounds, and I'm not tall; I'm about five-foot-three. Then people were saying, 'Buck, there's a contest. You should enter it.' I said, 'Nah, I don't want to enter it.' But I did — and I won 'Mr. New York City.' Then I was in [the] Mr. America [competition] — I came close. I was runner up, but I was just fooling around, hanging around the gym."

Kartalian's "fooling around" with other wrestlers attracted the attention of a professional wrestling manager. "He grabbed me," remembers Kartalian. "He said, 'You're coming along with me. You're gonna be one of my wrestlers. We'll go on a little tour every week.' I said, 'Hey, I only weigh one hundred and fifty pounds. These guys weigh three hundred pounds!' He said, 'Hey, I want a showman. You're funny. You slide under the guy's legs. You jump over his shoulder. You're in the air more than…' So I wrestled [professionally] for about five, six months. And people would invite me to their homes. They thought the wrestling was real."

In fact, it looked so real that a clever gimmick between Kartalian and another wrestler resulted in that wrestler being badly hurt. "You'd get a new wrestler every once in a while," explains Kartalian, "and one time, this guy says, 'I've got a great ending. I lift you up and I kick you right in the balls.' I said, 'Oh, shit!' He said, 'They'll get angry, right. That's the idea. Get 'em peaked.' I said, 'Yeah. Okay. We'll practice it in the gym.' So, as soon as we get to the locker, the arena, this guy says, 'C'mere, I'll show you what I do.' He lifted me up and WOW! WOW, it was so beautiful! But it looked vicious. I said, 'Oh, wow. That's terrific!' Well, just before we go on, I said, 'I don't know if we should do that or not. The audience — I've been here four or five times and they really like me. They might get so angry…' He said, 'Isn't that the idea?' So, we're wrestling, and he says, 'I'm gonna do my kicking you in the balls,' I said, 'Go ahead.' So, he does it, and I go, 'Ohhhh!' I really sell it, and the audience is screaming and yelling. Then I finally get up and I look up. There's a commotion in the ring; they're beating the hell out of him. They're yelling, 'FOUL! FOUL!' They beat him up, knocked his teeth out, broke his arm. I went to see him in the hospital. I said, 'Gee, I'm sorry.'"

That Buck Kartalian had developed a convincing acting style while wrestling soon became evident. "I knew a couple of these actors," explains Kartalian, "and one day at the gym, they were going out for a reading. They said, 'Hey, Buck. You wanna keep us company?' I said, 'Where are you going?' They said, 'Oh, two blocks down. The theater. We have an audition.' I said, 'Okay.' So I go down with them. We sit down on the side of the theater, and this lady comes over and hands me a book, hands the other two guys a book. I said, 'No, no, no. I'm not an actor. I just came with my friends.' She just looks at me, doesn't take the book back. So I'm holding it, and the guys are laughing. Then the two guys go in [for the audition] and come out [when finished]. So we get ready to go. I get up. I'm walking out with them. The lady says, 'Just a minute! Where are you going?' I said, 'What do you mean, *Where am I going*? I'm going to the gym. I just came with my friends. I'm not an actor.' She says, 'Get on it! Get in there!' I said, 'All right. I'll play your game.' I walk on stage. I don't know what the hell I'm doing. There's this bright light, and out in the audience, it's pitch black. Can't see a thing. I hear an English voice say, 'Are you ready?' I said, 'I don't even know what I'm doing here. I came with my friends. I'm not an actor. I just came with my friends. The lady hands me this book, and she told me to come over here on stage.' There was a long silence. He says, 'Turn to page eight.' I said, 'WHAT?' So, I turn to page eight, and somebody comes on stage. He says, 'Read the part of Samson.' So, I read this thing for a couple of minutes. He says, 'Thank you very much.' So, I'm laughing. I'm leaving the stage, the other guys are howling, and, as we go, the lady says, 'Just a minute! Just a minute! Let me get your number.' I said, 'Oh, for heaven's sake. All right. I'm at this gym all the time.' So, I give them the gym number. Three weeks later, I get a call. The lady says, "We would like to see you at the theater.' I said, 'What theater? What are you talking about?' I couldn't figure out what she meant. She finally says, 'Listen. You're the guy who came in with several actors, and you said, you weren't an actor. I made you go in and read.' I said, 'Oh, yeah. So, what do you want me for?' She says, 'I don't want you. The director wants you. You're hired.'"

The director was Peter Glenville. The theater — the Broadhurst Theatre on Broadway. The play — William Shakespeare's *Romeo and Juliet*. "It was an all English cast," notes Kartalian. "Except for Olivia De Havilland."

Kartalian's role of Sampson in *Romeo and Juliet* soon led to bigger things. "So I'm doing the show," says Kartalian, "the show's almost over, and Jack Hawkins [a member of the cast] says, 'Well, Buck. What are you gonna do now? You're not going back to wrestling?' I said, 'No, no. I like this acting stuff.' He says, 'You know, Buck. I want to tell you something. Don't ever, EVER take an acting lesson in your life. You are such a natural. You just open your mouth, and you're there.' He says, 'What they're doing is they're replacing Harvey Lembeck in *Mister Roberts*. You even look like him. Go down there and see the guy.' So I went down to the theater and read for the Ensign. The play was, is, wonderful. Much, much better than the movie. The movie stayed with the officers and just neglected the crew. But the play is really about Mister Roberts and his great love and loyalty for the crew, and the crew vice versa with Mister Roberts. The crew — each crew member had an individuality. One was a scaredy cat. One was a tough bully. In the movie, they took away their characters. They became just like a bunch."

"John Ford directed it and used his own people, old friends," continues the actor. "Then Ford got sick, and Mervyn LeRoy took over, and LeRoy invited Josh Logan to come in and see the movie. [Logan had directed the Broadway play.] He said, 'I'd like to do some additional scenes.' [LeRoy agreed.] Well, my agent had told me, someone was coming into town to direct [the movie version of] *Roberts*. He said, 'I don't know who it is, but it's some big shot. Maybe you want to go down?' I said, 'Yeah.' So I went down. There were maybe fifty or sixty people there, and I look and I see Josh Logan. I go, 'Oh, my God. Oh, my God.' Because he used to come every month and see the play. [During which time] I got to know his wife. They really liked me. Well, she saw me. She comes running over, grabbed me, hugged me, yanked me out of the line, and the next thing I know Josh is saying, 'I'm gonna write a scene for you, Buck' — the soap scene. So I was in the movie, and in the play for two years on the road. Everybody wanted me to do it in summer stock."

Thanks to his willingness to try new things, Buck Kartalian soon found himself a very busy actor. "Before you knew it, I was working all over the summer stock," says Kartalian. "I did every show imaginable. I had so much fun. I loved it. We'd rehearse one show, then run it a week or two. In the meantime, we would be rehearsing another show. We ended up doing six, eight shows a summer. And one time, this guy throws me a script. I said, 'You made a mistake. You got me singing. I don't sing.' He says, 'Buck, I spoke to the piano player. Don't worry about it.' The show was *Kiss Me, Kate*. I played one of the three gangsters. So, the guy says, 'Go see the piano player.' So, I see the piano player. He says, 'All right,' (then began playing the piano, cueing Kartalian with) 'The girls...' So I...'The girls...' I got up there and did the number. I sang — like you won't believe — it was a funny, funny thing. I went up and down, and they howled. When I came out, Patrice Munsel, big opera star, she played the lead in it; she was up the aisle there. I looked at her — tears were coming down her eyes. She said, 'Oh, Buck! I never heard anyone sing so badly and be so good. You're amazing!'"

"Amazing" was a good description for Kartalian. "I'd be in a play, play two different parts," recalls Kartalian, "and people didn't know I did those two different parts. Many times I did that. I did *Threepenny Opera* down in the village, and when I came to California with my wife, we met a guy. He ran a little theater — he's the one that did *Please Don't Eat My Mother* — Carl Munson. He had a little theater, and then there was another guy — a director of plays...I ended up doing two, three, four plays, one after the other. Every kind of play imaginable. I got reviews you won't believe. And at that time, when people saw you, I got five, six movies from the plays I did — feature pictures here and there."

Among them, the John Cassavettes/Roger Corman movie, *Devil's Angels*. "We had such a good time on that," remembers Kartalian. "We had a ball. I got along good with John Cassavettes. We had dinner together and we talked and gabbed. But when we went to Mexico, they wouldn't let us back. We said we were making a movie. They said, 'Sure.' They didn't believe us. They arrested us, then John made a call. I learned to ride a motorcycle for that. They asked me if I could ride a motorcycle. I said, 'Oh, no. Forget it.' The agent says, 'Buck! Buck! Tell 'em you can.' So they asked me. I said, 'Well...' The guy says, 'You'll learn out there,' and I sure did. I crashed a few times, hurt my arm. But I learned — before you knew it, I was giving people who lived in the town rides on my back seat."

In the mid 1950s, Kartalian was introduced to a new experience: automobile driving, in the movie, *Cell 2455*, featuring Vince Edwards. "I got the movie," says Kartalian, "and had to drive a car. I said, 'I never drove a car in my life.' Vince says, 'You're kidding.' I said, 'No. I came from New York City. I don't have any car. Why do I need a car in New York City?' He says, 'Well, Buck, don't worry about it.' So we get in the car and it was a big, big set. When I say, 'set,' it's a huge road. They said, 'All right, Vince, get in. Buck, you're the chauffeur for the mob. You drive.' I said, 'I don't drive.' They said, 'Come on. Don't fool around. Get in the car.' I said, 'I'm serious. I don't drive. I came from New York. I don't know how to drive.' The guy says, 'All right. You got ten minutes to learn. And it's a shift car; you got the clutch.' I said, 'Okay.' He says, 'Take Buck down there. Teach him how to drive.' Ten minutes later, he says, 'You're ready?' I said, 'Yeah.' Then, we're rolling. Well, they're scared as shit; they're way the hell out in the end — a quarter of a mile away. The guy says, 'When I say, 'Action,' you speed up. I want you to come as fast as the car will go, and stop right in front here.' And he made a mark. I said, 'That's nice. He made a mark.' So, 'okay.' And the guys — they relay [the action] to each other. I'm sitting there and they're scared, they're frightened to death. The one guy says to the other guy, 'Action,' and he says to me 'Action,' and I push the thing. The car went *poop, poop, poop*. They said, 'Okay let's do it again. Buck, it's gotta come up slowly — the clutch and the brake.' I said, 'I got it now.' And this time I get it perfect. The car just shot — I went as fast as that car would go, and I jammed the brake on. I was so…it was just damn luck. And the thing screeched and stopped exactly in the spot where I was supposed to stop. I got out; everybody [in the car] falls out. Everybody was white as a sheet. Anyway, the next day, I went out and bought a car."

Like his fellow *Here Come the Brides* semi-regular Robert Biheller, Kartalian worked in *Myra Breckinridge*. "The director was a young guy," remembers the actor, "and there was a guy from New York who was casting it. I read. The director thought I was good, but this guy from New York, I never liked him. I'd done *Studio One, Armstrong, Danger*, so this guy thought I could only play Italian gangsters. He said to the director, 'He's a little too short, isn't he? He's supposed to be an acting teacher. How tall is an acting teacher?' I mean stupid, stupid."

Director Stuart Rosenberg's method for casting Kartalian, *Brides* guest Lou Antonio and other good actors in Paul Newman's *Cool Hand Luke* made about as much sense. "Stu told us how he cast it," laughs Kartalian. "He said, 'I know so many good actors. Who am I gonna use?' Well, the last week, he put about six pictures under each character. He said, 'On Monday, I came down, took one picture, and threw it in the wastebasket, took another and threw it in the wastebasket, took another…just at random, wherever my eye went, whatever pictures were left, at the end of the week, they got the parts.' I said, 'You son of a bitch! That's the way you cast?'…We got to know Newman pretty good. And Conrad Hall was a wonderful cameraman."

Another highly respected director with whom Kartalian worked was Franklin J. Schaffner (*Patton, Nicholas and Alexandra*). "He was a very good director," praises Kartalian. "There are directors that concentrate on the camera, and directors that work with the actor. Schaffner was with the camera." So it was up to Kartalian to develop his character, Julius, in 1968's *Planet of the Apes*. Remembers the actor," Schaffner says. 'The camera opens up on the gate, and you're sitting here.' I said, 'I'm sitting here? Well, what am I doing? Just sitting here?' I said, 'Mr. Schaffner, why don't I be smoking a cigar? I smoke cigars anyway.' He gave me a look — if looks could kill…I said, 'Well, it's a good idea. If I'm not doing anything, I might as well be smoking a cigar. We're human right? The apes are human.' He looked at me — he didn't have much of a sense of humor.'"

But Kartalian's idea made it into the movie. "It's a funny, funny moment," states the actor. "Soon as that thing opens up, you see him puffing away at a cigar. It's so amusing. There's always a little laughter. It's a nice touch — people remember it. I was really lucky cuz all my stuff was inside the cage, inside the jail, and it was cool, air-conditioned. But it was difficult eating. We just drank malts and stuff through a straw. I had my own makeup man. The same guy took care of me."

*Planet of the Apes* offered a vivid example of the strong impact Buck Kartalian's acting style had on other people. "A funny thing happened," remembers the actor. "Some pretty girl was a stand-in for Kim Hunter [the chimpanzee, Zira]. We worked on the thing for two weeks. I'd come on the set, and she'd come over, she'd see me. I said, 'How did you recognize me?' She said, 'From your eyes.' I said, 'Oh.' So, she'd sit and talk to me, and I to her. One day, she's talking to me and talking to me, she reached over and grabbed my paw and started fondling it. I said to myself, 'Oh, my God! She's falling in love with an ape!' It was funny. She was caressing my hand, holding it, squeezing it. She didn't know what I looked like [without makeup]. She was falling in love with a gorilla. Actually falling for me as a gorilla!"

Later, while signing autographs for *Planet of the Apes*, "I did this show in Philadelphia," says Kartalian, "and this old guy came in. He says to his wife, 'That's him! That's him! That's him!' I did a show there forty years ago. Philadelphia, in the Park. He says, 'I remember you in it. I never forgot you.' I said, 'You're right I was in that play. My God! That's forty years ago, and you remember me?' He said, 'You don't know what you did to us. That was such a great role that you did!' You know, it's amazing the influence you have on people. And I remember the producer didn't want me in the play. The director wanted me, but the producer thought I was too short. Well, when I did the play, the producer apologized to me. I played a sergeant in that, a Communist."

Kartalian's work with actor-director Clint Eastwood in 1976's *The Outlaw Josey Wales* showed him to be a quick study. "We went to Arizona," remembers Kartalian. "There was a cowboy street there, and I had a scene with Clint Eastwood. He never told me anything, not a word. He was directing, and very serious, didn't say too much. When he said, 'Are you ready to do a scene?' I said, 'Yeah.' 'Okay,' he says, 'Let's do it.' And we did it. Then I looked at him, and he gave me a tiny smile. That was it. Fastest I ever shot a scene. Usually they do it ten to fifteen times to cover themselves. We just shot the thing ONCE. Boom! That was it. I had it down. I knew what I was gonna do, and he was very pleased. Then he moved on to his next scene. I did that in one day. Went out there the first day. Shot the thing the second day. Went home the third day."

The same year audiences saw Buck Kartalian as Julius in *Planet of the Apes*, they saw him, and Joan Blondell, in the Elvis Presley feature, *Stay Away, Joe*. "Elvis had about three or four of his friends," recalls Kartalian, "they would light his little cigarillos, they would wait on him hand and foot. He was very, very nice, a very easy guy and open to suggestions. I remember I said to him at one point, 'This scene — this is supposed to be a real fun moment. You gotta make it light.' He wasn't upset that I told him that. He said, 'Oh, sure. Thanks, Buck.'"

Working with producer/writer Andrew J. Fenady on 1980's *The Man With Bogart's Face* was another pleasant experience. "I played a Greek," remembers Kartalian, "and my girlfriend's a big, tall…I'm hiding from her because she always wants sex. Won't give me a rest. I did that with a Greek accent. I do accents — all kinds of accents. I learned that from the stage. I picked up a lot of stuff from the stage, and summer stock. I really enjoyed working with Andy Fenady. He's a funny, nice man."

Working with E. W. Swackhamer was one of the things Kartalian liked about playing the semi-regular role of Sam on *Here Come the Brides*. "I worked with Swackhamer several times," says the actor, "and the men who were in it, he'd worked with them before. He liked to use the same people. Swack was a very nice man to work with; you could talk to him. And Bridget was a lovely, lovely girl. I didn't meet Bridget until *Brides*. Robert Brown was very nice, very serious guy, not too much humor. I remember one time I had a scene with him. Just he and I were standing, and I'm watching what he's doing. He's making a little pile of dirt, we're standing together, and he made this pile of dirt, four or five, six inches, and he stood on top of the pile, just before we started our scene. I look at him. I said, 'What the hell are you doing?' He says, 'What do you mean?' I said, 'You're six-foot-four. I'm five-foot-three. What do you want to be taller for? What is the point? The camera's gotta get in both of our faces somehow, cuz we're talking to each other.' I said, 'If you want to get high, why don't you get on a ladder and talk to me?' He looked at me. He didn't think that was very funny. He was a nice man, but very serious about his work."

There was quite a bit of humor that did not make it into the show. "The men could be raunchy," states the actor, "and we always fooled around. The guys always fooled around, you know, like *this is my girl*. We did all kinds of crazy things, a lot of fun things. And we did stuff — Balduzzi and I — that you couldn't put in the show. We did that just to entertain the other guys."

Buck Kartalian's view of the series' first and second seasons might come as a shock to *Brides* fans. "The first year they kind of concentrated on the guys, and the brides coming," states the actor. "The second year, they focused more on the women. It's kind of hard for women to do comedy — at that time anyway. The second year, they used mostly the women."

Next to *Here Come the Brides, Planet of the Apes*, and the 1973 cult film, *Please Don't Eat My Mother*, Kartalian's role as Bruce W. Wolf in 1976's *Monster Squad* has also brought him considerable recognition. "That was kinda fun," remembers the actor. "It shoulda run longer than it did; the director just let it die. People liked it. I still get mail from people about that. The beauty of *Monster Squad* was Dracula, Frankenstein, the Wolfman — we were stumble bums. We went to fight crime, but we always screwed up. We weren't really heroes, we had our frailties. We made mistakes, got stuck, got in worse positions."

In addition to still performing, Kartalian somehow finds the time to attend conventions and shows honoring motion pictures like *Planet of the Apes.* "Last April, I got a call from England," says the actor. "Birmingham. They were doing this huge science-fiction show, and I've done about fifteen to twenty of them in the States — Florida, here, there. You go there. You bring your pictures from *Planet of the Apes,* you sign autographs, talk to the people — enthusiastic fans. Well, they called me. They said Linda Harrison, who did *Planet of the Apes,* would be coming. She's in her sixties now. They asked her, 'Who else would be good for this?' She said, 'Well, how about calling Buck? He had a flashy part that stands out — he was the jailer.' So they called me. I said, 'I want to take my wife. I can't leave her.' They said, 'That's all right.' So, they paid all our expenses to Birmingham, and put us up in a beautiful hotel. And they had a big poster of me as Julius in *Planet of the Apes.*"

Buck Kartalian considers himself very fortunate to have enjoyed the sort of career he's had. "A lot of this is hitting the right things at the right time," notes the actor. "The field is overcrowded — *way* overcrowded. There're just not that many parts for the thousands. I was lucky. But now I do commercials because my agent dropped their theatrical department.

"I gotta look for another agent."[5]

1. Biheller – 2008
2. Ben Bard – IMDB Mini Biography – by Bartley Bard – accessed June 20, 2008, 2:29 p.m. EST
3. Biheller – 2007
4. Balduzzi – 2007
5. Kartalian – 2008

"The crew people should never be forgotten. They're wonderfully helpful and good to actors. Without them, we wouldn't be able to do anything. The crew is very, very important."[1]

*Here Come the Brides* guest star Susan Silo

Part Four
# *Behind The Scenes*

"Renee is my mentor and my big sister."

*Here Come The Brides* semi-regular Karen Carlson

# Chapter 15
# *Renee Valente:*
# *"I Love Actors!"*

"She was able to be a woman while competing in a man's world. She could absolutely walk the walk and talk the talk with the men and often would be the only woman seated at a table at Fox or wherever. She could absolutely keep 'em beat for beat and yet the soft side of Renee was still intact. She was really a champion for actors. You know she was the only person that Frank Sinatra would work with. When they approached him about doing this movie for television — *Cherry Hill Street*, I think it's called, Renee was the only producer…he would only do it if she would be the producer. I think that says something, I think that says a lot. And she has never… I don't think Renee has ever been acknowledged properly as she should have been. I think people… I would love to do something that would acknowledge what she brought to the industry."[1]

That was strong testimony from *Here Come the Brides* semi-regular Karen Carlson concerning the series' executive in charge of casting, Renee Valente. The same Renee Valente who put former *Gunsmoke* regular Burt Reynolds in his first series as star (*Hawk*), the same Renee Valente who was a major player in the superb 1973-77 Screen Gems anthology, *Police Story,* the same Renee Valente who produced the aforementioned Frank Sinatra TV-movie, *Contract on Cherry Street*, and so many other TV-movies.

During the course of her career, a career which still continues, Renee Valente served as production manager, production supervisor, and executive producer. So it should have come as no surprise that, in time, she would form her own production company, Renee Valente Productions. Nor should it have come as a surprise that when Valente began her career in entertainment, she began it with one of the best: producer/talk show host David Susskind.

"I started in New York with David Susskind Talent Associates," says Valente. "I was part-time secretary to a story editor [assigned] to Joyce Robinson. One of my duties was to walk her poodle (whose name was Chermudley) on Park Avenue every afternoon when I came in. I just wanted a part-time job, because I was still going to school. But a couple of years later, they asked me to go on full time. I said, 'No. I really want to get my degree.' They said, 'Well, don't you want to hear what we have to offer you?' I said, 'Well…Okay.' And they said, 'Well, you have the chance to be the exchequer.' I said, 'No, I'm very good at math, but I hate it.' They said, 'Don't you want to hear the money we would pay you?' I said, 'Well…okay.' When they told me, I said, 'Well, I could always get my degree…'"

At that point in her career, "I never, in New York, went into casting," points out Valente. "I was in production. I was with David thirteen years, and I became head of production and development, and associate producer, and producer. I was a line producer — I was involved with how you shoot it, getting the script, breaking it down for budget, what you were gonna do with it, how much it was gonna cost, how many days you needed, just everything but casting. Then, at a certain point in time, I left David and went to work for Columbia/Screen Gems. Did a pilot for them called *Hawk* with Burt Reynolds. When that sold, they asked me to continue and produce it. That's when I found I really started to be involved with acting."

Fighting for Burt Reynolds to be the star of *Hawk*, "and that's a whole big story in itself," states the producer, when *Hawk* was canceled, Valente was asked by Screen Gems executive in charge of production Jackie Cooper to come out to California and take charge of the company's talent program. "I said, 'I've never done anything with talent, Jackie. I can't do that,'" remembers Valente. "He said, 'I met you when I was an actor. You were absolutely wonderful. You could do it.' So, I went out."

At that point Valente really got going. "I was the first woman vice-president of any major motion picture television studio," states Valente. "I was 'Head of Talent,' meaning writers, actors, directors — just took to all talent. Jackie Cooper was wonderful…I talked to him about forming a talent program, which we did, for actors, and we paid them. Which was rare then. Instead of giving them dance lessons, I gave them karate. It was a great program. David Soul was in it. He came out of that program."

As head of Screen Gems talent, Vice-President Valente instituted an "open-door policy," and had "casting directors, who worked with me. We created a very loving, nurturing department which was rare and, I guess, still is. We loved actors. It wasn't difficult for them to come and see us, and let us get to know them. It was wonderful. I spent seven or eight years doing that."

Valente's approach was atypical. "When I first came out to California, it was 1968, there were I think, one hundred and three agents at the time," says the producer. "I called each and every agent. I said, 'I want to see your clients.' Most of them didn't know what to think. They had no idea who this woman from New York was who called to see all their clients. But I thought since I was going to get involved in the casting business, I better know who the actors were. So for four days a week, I saw mostly actors, because with writers, I could read their scripts, and with directors, see their films, and go to the theater. With actors, I had to meet them and have them do scenes. By the end of the year, I pretty well knew all the actors in town. When I interviewed actors, I wanted to get to know them. I wouldn't discuss acting, cuz they came in wanting to prove to me that they were terrific; they hid who they really were. Well, what I wanted to find out was who they really were."

Valente didn't learn this by asking actors for their views on such things as politics, religion, or sex. "Instead, I would say to them, 'Do you ride motorcycles?' That would throw them. Or, 'Do you ride horses?' I talked about anything other than acting, because that showed me immediately when they came alive. I could see in their eyes, in their body language, where they really were, and it gave me hints as to what they really could do or wanted to do. From that interview, I would decide on what part to read them for."[2]

According to Karen Carlson, reading for Valente was much easier than reading for other casting executives. Explains the actress, "One of the really wonderful things about Renee was that if you went in to read for her, and maybe you didn't do such a great job for whatever reason, well, there were a lot of casting people…that's what they would remember. So, when your name came up again, they would say, 'No. Pass.' But Renee would, after a period of time, she would always give credit to the fact that an actor had worked and studied and kept going. She would always give them another chance and realize that maybe that [bad reading day] wasn't just a good day for them. Or whatever. There weren't a lot of people in casting who did that. I think because of that ability to really be on the side of the actor — that's what made her such a phenomenal producer. She's the one who discovered Burt Reynolds and gave him his first break when she was casting out of New York. So many actors — she gave them their first shot."[3]

Valente's talent for picking the right actors was very much evident in the pilot of *Here Come the Brides*. "My main casting was in the pilot," she states, "getting all the running stars, and the series players. The peripheral actors [semi-regulars like Dick Balduzzi and Cynthia Hull] — a lot of would them come and go. They were cast by my casting director, Burt Metcalfe or Ernie Losso, who did all my day-to-day casting."

Major guest stars like Don Pedro Colley and Meg Foster were a different matter.

"The guest-casting was normally something that I got involved with," says Valente. "On the weekly episodes, my main interest was the guest stars. I'd help the company and the producers get the guests. The producer would say, 'I'd like to get XYZ and I can't,' because we had to get approval from the network for the stars. So producers like Bob Claver would get to know the people at the network and he would say, 'Hey, I'd like to use XYZ and they would say, 'Okay.' Then the guest star had to come, and we'd have to try to make a deal. That's when I came in, or, if I read the script, which I did all the time, I would call the director or the producer and say, 'You know who would be great for that? XYZ.' So, I read every script and I came up with ideas for guest stars. I'd have them come in and read if they weren't *star* stars, but mainly I wanted to read everybody. It's only these days that people cast by looking at DVDs. But, if you look at something they've already done, and it doesn't fit in with the image you have of the role, that's unfair. You need to really meet someone personally, and get the feeling of who they are. When they're with you and read, you can say, 'Well, that was okay, but now try to do it this way.' That's the way I've always felt about casting. I like to have someone come in, meet them, see them. If I don't really know their work, well, I'll have them read. If I've seen them in something I love, or see them on stage, and really know they don't have to read, that's something else."

Given the versatility she displayed in her television, stage, and motion picture work, "A Jew Named Sullivan's" Linda Marsh would seem to fall in that category. "I still wanted her to read," remembers Valente. "That's interesting casting. I don't remember if she was somebody I wanted or not. It's always a collaborative decision. I like to work in a collaborative way in everything I do. And you had to get approval from the network. Even for the guest casts. You better believe it."

Valente's discernment when it came to knowing good actors from bad actors proved invaluable when last-minute casting changes were made in the second season's "Land Grant." In that case, Lou Antonio was the last-minute replacement. "He was a wonderful actor," praises Valente. "A very good actor. Then he became a very well-known, respected television director."

Making casting executive Valente's job easier was Screen Gems programming executive Jackie Cooper. "Jackie Cooper was the one responsible for me going out to California, and for my entire career in California," notes Valente. "I owe him a great debt of gratitude. Jackie Cooper would back me up on a lot of things. He was absolutely wonderful to work with, and for. Having been an actor, he understood acting and the business, and how actors should be treated. It was just wonderful to work with him. And I loved Swack. He was terrific. We had no problem. I've had very few problems — there're maybe two or three people in my entire career who have been problems; I've been very fortunate."

Being the executive producer of *Here Come the Brides*, it was only natural that Bob Claver have reservations about Valente using performers from her New Talent program. "I was using a lot of people from my [New] Talent Program," admits Valente, "But I wouldn't think of using them if they didn't deserve it. But when you have Joan Blondell and Robert Brown, you know, *serious* players, you couldn't get name actors, who, in those days, were used to making more money [to play smaller parts]. The license fees in those days [were] not very much, so you had to fill the other roles with unknowns. The running cast was pretty much young and new in the business. So they'd do anything without complaining. And there was such camaraderie on the set. It was very easy for Robert Brown and Mark Lenard and Joan Blondell to tell the kids different things and teach them, and whatever. It was kind of — at least from my point of view, a lovely atmosphere to work in. I think that the cast on that series became a family. They really all worked to help each other. A lot of shows have a lot of 'Oh, they're getting more lines than we are. They're getting this. They're getting that.' There really wasn't much of that. All of them were so happy to be working."

Renee Valente was aware of such things because "I visited the set all the time. It was a very hard show to do. There was a lot of physical labor on that. Between the horses and the chopping of the wood, it was not an easy show to do. We had to do them in seven days, and you didn't rehearse ahead of time; if you went over a day, it was hell to pay."

Fortunately, since cast and crew truly liked one another, things generally went very smoothly. "We were all very friendly," says Valente. "David's one of my best friends to this day. One of his sons was practically at my home at least two or three times a week. And Karen is still a good friend of mine. She was a very lovely actress. She did *The Candidate* with Robert Redford. That's the first time I had seen her. Then I read her and used her as much as I could. She was a very lovely girl and now she's a very lovely woman. She and David are still very good friends, but now she lives in Tennessee. She has a landscaping business, Mother Earth. She's just super."[4]

In addition to maintaining close contact with Carlson, Valente saw *Brides* regular Susan Tolsky following the series cancellation. "Susan Tolsky was going with a friend of mine, so we'd see each other socially," explains the producer. "She was doing a lot of commercials. She was the new girl on TV commercials. Susan wanted to do more, like any actor. You know, give them six lines — they want twenty-six lines. If they're happy with six lines, it's not gonna work for them. That's not how they're gonna get ahead."

"I don't know that Bridget ever complained," reflects Valente. "To me she was always Maureen O'Hara. Just bubbly and wonderful and line-perfect. She was oh so happy with any role she could bite into and do something with, just so long as it had something that you could shout about."

"Bridget had enthusiasm. That was the whole tenor of that show. It had Bridget's kind of enthusiasm. It was a happy show."[5]

1. Carlson – 2007
2. Valente – 2007
3. Carlson – 2007
4. Valente – 2007
5. Valente – 2007

"We were real close to the crew — they were our family. We saw them more. I had a boyfriend at the time, and I saw these people more than him. The crew was wonderful. We had a twenty-five- or twenty-year reunion when the cast and crew got together, and for me, working on a show, or anything that I did from that point on, I hung with the crew. Those people to me were the heart of any series."[1]

Here Come the Brides regular Susan Tolsky

# Chapter 16

# On The Set

## Wardrobe man Steve Lodge

"The head of wardrobe on *Here Come the Brides* was a gentleman who was about my age, Pat McGrath," says Steve Lodge. "His father had been a very good friend of Tommy Dawson's, and Tommy put him on that show. Tommy Dawson ran the Columbia costume department, and it was like the old studio system — the department head hired the individual costumers. That's where I got my start. Working for him. [Prior to that] I did the pilot of *Farmer's Daughter*. If you ever see the pilot, you'll see Bill Windom get into an elevator. I'm the elevator operator. I have one line: I say, 'Good morning, Senator.' Anyway Tommy had never been able to use me, because I worked three days. Then they called me to go to work on *The Fugitive*. Then I did *Family Affair*, and at the end of the summer of 1968, I was called to go to work at Columbia on *Here Come the Brides*. I got on in the middle of the first season. Did that till the end of the first season, and then I did the whole second season. I was the set man, basically. Which means I got to stay on the set all day; Pat had to go prepare the shows."

Being on the set all day, Steve Lodge often had a different take on *Brides* episodes than did the show's story editor, William Blinn or the executive producer, Bob Claver, etc. Steve Lodge knew who kept the streets of Seattle muddy; he knew of the conditions under which "A Christmas Place" was shot; he was aware of the studio spies. Lodge also had his own opinions as to who was a good director, and who was not. One who fit into the former category was Bob Claver. "Bob Claver was a very good guy," praises Lodge. "Whenever he directed a show, it was probably even more fun than when Swack did. Swack was the big one that was there all the time, and he was married to you know who. Claver would come in and direct here and there, and Dick Kinon, I remember him. Jerry Bernstein was kind of a schmuck, but Kinon was a sweetheart. He was great. Great to work with. We had some pretty nice directors on the show."

Including line producer Paul Junger Witt. "Paul Junger Witt was all right," says Lodge. "A bit snooty. But he was nice. Paul's father was an attorney for Columbia Pictures in New York, and right after I left the mail room at Columbia Pictures, Paul went to work in the mail room. Then I got a job. I went into publicity. I got a job with David Swift on [Screen Gems'] *Camp Runamuck* as an assistant to his producer. At the same time, Paul got a job with Bob Claver, as assistant to Bob Claver. So we kind of compared notes. Well, I didn't get along with my producer — he was kind of an asshole, so I quit that show, but Paul stayed with Bob, and you know where Paul's career went. Then, I got a job in [costuming] and stayed there for a while."

Because he was involved with *Camp Runamuck*, Steve Lodge knew the *Brides* set was already somewhat built before the show even began filming. "The whole set was built for *Camp Runamuck*," he explains. "They built all these two basic sets. One side was Camp Runamuck [the boy's camp], the berm went around that, the next berm was [the girl's camp] Camp Divine. On *Here Come the Brides,* the Camp Runamuck set turned into the cabins, where they all lived, and then between, where the berm came down, was the totem pole. On the left of that, which had been Camp Divine, they built Seattle — and the dock there; Clancey's ship was on rollers, and they would roll that up."

At one time the brother-in-law of *Fugitive* star David Janssen (the two worked together on that show, and again on the 1976 TV-movie, *Mayday at 40,000 Feet*), Steve Lodge fit very easily into the *Brides* set-up, having worked on another comedy-drama: the excellent Brian Keith/Sebastian Cabot CBS series, *Family Affair,* co-starring young actors Kathy Garver, Anissa Jones, and Johnnie Whittaker. "Kid actors are easy to work with," notes Lodge. "Kids are fine. The only one that ever gave me some shit was Johnnie Whittaker. He asked me to tie his shoe. I said, 'How old are you?' He said, 'I'm seven years old.' I said, 'You tie your own shoe.'"

As for Brian Keith, "he was a sweetheart," says Lodge. "And Anissa Jones was fine. I became very good friends with her family. In fact, I used to go over and cook tacos for Anissa and Paul and their mother. I remember I was invited to her eighteenth birthday party, so I went down there to the beach. She seemed fine. I don't believe her death was a suicide. If anything I think it was an o.d. [drug overdose]; Anissa was just sweet. What she wanted the most was to be a normal little girl. So, once that show was over she didn't want anything to do with the business. I remember, I'd written a script for a friend of mine. I wrote it for Anissa and Jack Elam. Jack Elam was ready to do it, then we went to talk to Anissa. We gave her the script. She read it. She says, 'I just don't want to be in the movies anymore. Thank you.' I mean, she turned down the Linda Blair part in *The Exorcist* before Blair got it. She said, 'I wouldn't do that. Masturbating with a cross.'"

*Family Affair* was already into its third season when Steve Lodge was called to work on *Here Come the Brides* in late 1968. Among the first-season episodes he did: "A Christmas Place," "A Man and His Magic," "Wives for Wakando," "The Firemaker," "My ex-wife [Jill Janssen — half-sister of David Janssen) was in *Brides,*" says Lodge, "Jill worked every show. I didn't work with Karen Carlson, but she would come back and see David all the time. And by the time I got there, Bo Svenson was gone. I worked with Bo later on. I guess he enjoyed the show."

Of the three series stars, "David Soul was the nicest one," notes Lodge. "Bobby was a close second. Bobby and David were the nicest guys in the world. They'd sit around and play guitar between shots and sing, and have a ball. David was kinda shy, but he still was a singer. He'd play his guitar. Always had his guitar with him. Then there was always Henry Beckman [Clancey]. On every show, we'd go into the saloon one day to do all of the scenes from that particular episode. So, toward the end, toward the afternoon, Bobby and Robert and David, and Clancey, were always half in the bag. They'd all be half in the bag, and it would start…you know that kind of laughter you get when you're in school? They'd get that way, and they would break up shots, and it was rather funny. But not to Seymour Friedman, of course, who was back at the studio. And there was obviously a spy on the set who would call him every time [that happened], because we'd hear from Seymour."

Spies on studio sets were not uncommon. "The production manager of the studio has to know what's going on," explains Lodge. "So they have a spy. There are people who are very happy to be spies, people very happy to tattle on the stars. I did a show called *Dundee and the Culhane* one time, and one of the stars had a little problem with drinking, so one of the extras went right up to the production manager and told him. He says, 'You gotta really be happy that I did this last night. I drove your actor home last night, cuz he was so drunk.'" "You know," Lodge remarks sarcastically, "That's really nice to do."

As for *Here Come the Brides'* two female stars, Joan Blondell and Bridget Hanley, "I never got to know Joan that well. I knew Bridget somewhat. Bridget was fine. She was great. She was a trouper. If they walked through the mud, she'd walk through the mud. And every night the girls' dresses would have to be sent out — they'd be all muddy at the bottom. And keeping that street muddy…we had a special effects man on duty all the time, with a fire hose. Between shots, he'd just water that street down, because they wanted to make mud-holes, and water holes, all that kind of stuff. So we supplied galoshes, big rubber boots, everything for the crew."

The fire hose and so much mud caused the crew members to resort to some rather juvenile, tension-breaking antics. Remembers Lodge: "In the middle of summer, somebody would grab the fuckin' hose from the special effects guy and squirt [DP] Fred Jackman. Then Jackman would pick up a bucket and throw it. We had huge water fights sometimes on the set with that hose and the mud. One or two times, they'd dig a big hole and fill it with water, then they'd come over and ask one of the stand-ins or somebody to stand right over there. So he'd step in it, and go right up to his waist in water. You know, it was just stuff to kill the time."

Setting the juvenile mood of the crew was the show's regular director of photography Fred Jackman. "Fred Jackman was the biggest prankster," chuckles Lodge. "He had a great personality. Everybody liked him. The mood of the crew is kinda what Fred was. Fred was kind of the leader; the cameraman is kind of the leader of that thing, but Fred was not young. He'd been around for a long time; he had a lot of experience, he'd been a director, too." (On Screen Gems series, like *Route 66*.)

When it came to the show's assistant directors, with the exception of Jim Hogan, who went on to serve as the unit production manager for *Brides* in its second season, the two most frequent were the sons of famous directors: Michael Dmytryk (son of director Edward) and David Hawks (son of director Howard.) "Jimmy Hogan was a sweetheart," praises Lodge, "a real nice guy, much nicer than most production managers. Most of them are so worried about their budget and their this or that. Mike Dmytryk was fine. He was a muscle guy, and had a temper. I think he got into it with Brown a few times. David Hawks was a very gentle man. A very pleasant man. And David wore a Red River D buckle. He had worked on *Red River* with his old man when he was a kid. Then we had Sonny Jones. He was one of the extras. Sonny had been with some country singer. And Danny Borzage worked as an extra. Danny Borzage was John Ford's guy — he was the guy that always played the accordion. When John Ford would step out of the car, he would play the 'Yellow Ribbon' theme or something. I don't know what it was. Danny Borzage was [director] Frank Borzage's brother. Then our script girl, Julie Pitcannon, was married to Buzz Bechins, who was a producer at AIP."

One of the interesting things brought up by series co-star Bobby Sherman in his autobiography, *Still Remembering You*, was how he, Bridget Hanley, and Susan Tolsky helped the *Brides* extras make a little more money by giving them a 'bump.' Explains Lodge: "If you [the actor] made an extra more than an extra, if you gave them a bit, by saying something to them, and they reacted, they would get a 'bump.' David Janssen did that one time, and he scared the crap out of this one extra. He asked him a question, and the extra answered. Then the extra went, 'Oh, shit.' Because he knows the director will get pissed off at him."

During the run of *Brides*, Sherman wanted to change Jeremy's wardrobe. "The jacket that Bobby Sherman wore in the first year — kind of a gray jacket with a corduroy collar — you can see that on Mickey Callan in *Cat Ballou*," reveals Lodge. "The second year, Bobby was a much bigger star and he wanted to wear his own…he wanted to have a flare in his pants, and he wanted to wear a suede jacket. So we let him get by with that. It wasn't really period, neither were the flares, but they just said, 'Okay, let him wear it. Fuck it.' That was his dress outfit."

"They spent most of their money in the beginning," continues Lodge. "The pilot they shot at MGM on lot three where they had this big ocean front. We'd start out the season, going up to the mountains behind La Crescenta. We'd shoot the real trees and all that kind of stuff. Then, in the middle of the season, we ended up going to Franklin Canyon, and by the last of the season, we were doing it on the lake — the lagoon set — on the stage, and we never left the lot. See, they'd spend a lot of money in the beginning, then they'd realize that they had to cut down. So, by the end, they were just scrimping by, to get the last shows made."

Lodge tried to help by coming up with his own script for *Brides*. "I had it all figured out," he remembers. "You put the ship on the stage and put a black backing [background] up. You do it at night so nobody knows where you are; the whole scene takes place at sea at night. They hadn't done that [story] yet. Well, it wasn't more than two weeks after they turned me down that we were putting that boat on the sound stage, and we were at sea…fuck 'em. That happened to Tommy Dawson's son Gordon Dawson, who made all the *Maverick* remakes. Gordon Dawson wrote an *Empire* once [*Empire* was a drama set on a ranch in New Mexico — it too was produced by Screen Gems]. He turned it in. He said, 'They didn't even have the courtesy to change the fuckin' [guest character] names. They just put somebody else's name on it." [That "somebody else" received credit for writing the story.]

Besides forming a friendship with Robert Brown stunt double Dave Cass, Steve Lodge became quite close to *Brides* semi-regular Hoke Howell. "Hoke Howell and I got along great," enthuses Lodge. "He and I wrote a movie [the 1975 half-hour short, *One Block Away*]. I directed it, and he starred in it." While Lodge found *Brides* "a very happy set," unlike his friend, Dave Cass, he got along none too well with series star Robert Brown. "Dave Cass was Robert's stuntman and stand-in," says Lodge. "He saw him from a different angle. He didn't have to worry about 'This thing doesn't fit!' I'd say, 'Well, Robert, you put on some fuckin' weight.' You know, it was that kind of stuff. But, everybody sees Robert from a different angle. To me, he was arrogant."

Still, "*Brides* was fun," continues Lodge. "I mean we had a lot of fun on *The Fugitive* but *Brides* was a different kind of fun than *The Fugitive* because *The Fugitive* was a drama. *Brides* was fun because it was outdoors, and we were on the same set every day, in the mud."

And of course there were those *HCTB* football games. "I took my camera out to the park, at the Columbia ranch because we had a big football game there," says Lodge. "I took mostly people on the sidelines. I still have pictures of that — the *Brides* people playing football."[2]

# Stunt double, stunt coordinator, actor, director Dave Cass

"[The cast and crew of *Brides*] was just a wonderful, big family," asserts Dave Cass. "It truly was. I always say that these crews and these casts get to be one big dysfunctional family after a while. That show was not dysfunctional at all. Everyone got along."[3]

*Brides* started Cass on his way towards becoming a television director; career-wise, Dave Cass started BIG! Right out of high school, he went to work for Robert Shelton of Old Tucson Studios. Created in July 1939 by Columbia Pictures, who reserved $250,000 to create a realistic-looking set for the filming of *Arizona* (starring William Holden and Jean Arthur), Old Tucson was frequently used as a filming location for such pictures as *The Bells of St. Mary's*, *Winchester '73*, and *Gunfight at the O.K. Corral*. By the late 1950s, the location had fallen out of favor and was in danger of becoming a ghost town. Then Midwest carpenter Robert Shelton leased the land in 1959 and turned Old Tucson into both a studio and theme park. A year later, Shelton presented this new attraction to the public. Thanks to his Old Tucson studio hosting four separate John Wayne pictures — *Rio Bravo* (1959), *McClintock* (1963), *El Dorado* (1967), and *Rio Lobo* (1970) — the location soon became very popular with motion picture and television productions. Among the television shows to use the locale: *Bonanza*, *High Chaparral*, and *Petrocelli*. Dave Cass couldn't have asked for a better start to his entertainment career.

"I was working as a gunfighter on the streets of Old Tucson," he remembers. "I worked as an extra in some pictures that came to town, did some old-fashioned melodrama, and acted a little bit in a little theater there in Tucson, and performed in the stunt shows. Then *McClintock* came to town with John Wayne. Robert Shelton introduced me to John Wayne. I think that was [in]'62. John Wayne gave me a part in the movie. So I kind of got hooked by the golden bug of the motion picture industry, and shortly thereafter, moved out to Hollywood. I thought I was gonna do it on my own for a while. But after about sixty days, I decided, 'You can't do that.' Well, Wayne had given me his office number, and his secretary's name, Howard St. John. I called there. They said, 'The Duke's been wondering where you're at.' So I went down to see him in Hollywood. We talked for about forty-five minutes, then he told me, 'Go back to Burbank.' I did. By the time I got back to Burbank, I had a telephone call from a wardrobe man on *Gunsmoke* — he said, 'We expect you here for a wardrobe fitting tomorrow morning.' I mean those wonderful, velvet tentacles of John Wayne and some of those other guys just stretched into this community. So I went to work, and through Wayne, I met other directors, and it just kind of perpetuated my career. I went to actors, stuntmen…years later I became a stunt coordinator, second-unit director, and now I'm a director."

Like many who worked with him, Dave Cass was a big fan of the Duke: "John Wayne was badly maligned because of his conservatism," states Cass, "but we didn't have conservatives and liberals in those days really. Wayne just believed in this country. It's that simple." Nor was Wayne prejudiced. "There wasn't an anti-Semitic bone in his body," says the former stuntman. "He had an assistant director named Al Murphy — his name was actually Al Horowitz, and on *McClintock* one day, I think I remember somebody saying something like, 'He's really a little Jew.' Wayne turned on them like a bulldog. He said, 'He may be a Jew, but he's MY Jew! Leave him alone!' So he was very protective of the people who worked for him. If he didn't like you, but you did your job and just stayed away from him, you wouldn't have a problem in the world. It was the people who would try to get too close to him that he didn't want to get too particularly close to him — those were the people who had problems with him, and who thought he was standoffish. He wasn't standoffish at all. It was just…he could discern a phony when he saw one."

Another down-to-earth star was Robert Mitchum. "I doubled him on a couple of shows," remembers Cass. "We were kinda friends. He was a journeyman actor. He never went to school really to be an actor. One time they asked him how it felt to be a movie star. He said, 'Lassie's a movie star.' You know, most of those guys came up the hard way. They appreciated what they had and where they were in the world."

While Dave Cass never worked with John Wayne again — "I got so busy," explains Cass. "I met Vince and Bernie McEveety through Duke Wayne. Andy McLaglen did *McClintock*, and he was doing *Gunsmoke*, so I met Vince and Bernie there. Then Vince brought me in to Universal to guest on *Buck Rogers* [*in the 25th Century*]. I played a satyr."

Another Wayne connection was producer/director/writer/actor/composer Andrew J. Fenady. "A.J. Fenady!" exclaims Cass. "What a great guy he is! I met Andy because of Duke because Andy was producing *Hondo* [the TV series starring Ralph Taeger and Kathie Browne] with Bob Morrison, who is John Wayne's brother [Wayne's real name was Marion Michael Morrison]. So that started *that* connection. Then A.J. used me to do parts." Most of which were in TV series like *Hondo*, *Branded*, and TV movies like *Black Noon*. "I did more television than I did features," admits Cass, "ended up in the TV world — [I] don't dislike it. That was fine because they had all those action shows and the adventure shows. All three networks had hours of drama — it kept me busy working. I did *Gunsmoke, Six Million Dollar Man, Streets of San Francisco*... and I met my two mentors. They mentored me in directing. One was Virgil Vogel. The other was Burt Kennedy. Burt Kennedy was a wonderful writer-turned-director. He did *Train Robbers* with John Wayne and Ann-Margret. I ended up directing second units and coordinating for Burt in later years. And Virgil Vogel was probably the hottest director in town. He was an editor for Orson Welles on *Touch of Evil*. I met Virgil on *Here Come the Brides* in 1969, continued to work for him until, basically, the day he died. I got on the Quinn Martin shows because of Virgil. Quinn was a nice guy to work for. I only met him twice. He was very prolific. He and Aaron Spelling — they were the kings of television. I did [Martin's] *The FBI, Bert D'Angelo, Superstar*, I think I did *Most Wanted*. And I worked on *Mission: Impossible* three or four times for Virgil Vogel."

Another director for whom Cass worked was Robert Butler. "Bob Butler was a sweetheart of a guy," praises Cass. "He was a very prolific television director, a very nice guy that knew what he wanted, and very confident. He ran a very nice set-up. There was a different breed of director then — [of] course, the business was different, too, but the director was captain of a ship." Especially if he was someone like actor Vic Morrow. "Met Morrow on *Treasure of Matecumbe*," recalls Cass. "Went to work for him on two shows he directed. I also worked with Harry Harris [frequent *Gunsmoke* director, and an Irwin Allen favorite] and William Claxton."

Being a stuntman, Dave Cass naturally ran into a lot of actors who enjoyed doing their own stunts. Such as Chuck Connors. "Chuck Connors was great," enthuses Cass. "I had only worked with him that one time on *Branded*, then on *Gambler Four* [*The Gambler Returns: The Luck of the Draw*], Kenny Rogers ran into all these famous TV characters [Bat Masterson, Bart Maverick, Kwai Chang Caine, The Westerner, et al], they had Chuck as *The Rifleman*. Well, they sent Chuck to me on second-unit, and Dick Lowry was directing scenes with Chuck...Chuck came up to me; he said, 'I know you. You worked on *Branded*.' And you're talking about something that was thirty years before that movie! Chuck was just kind of a regular guy. He would just say what he thought. He saw me limping at one point. He said, 'You need a new hip.' I said, 'Yeah.' He said, 'I just got one. I'll give you the name of my doctor, Dave. Don't suffer anymore.' But Chuck was very physically fit. He liked to do his own stunts. He could do them, too. He was tough as a nail."

Another actor who loved to do his own stunts, in particular his own fist-fighting, was *Bonanza* star Michael Landon. States Cass, "When you're young, you're ten feet tall. So, when you see Michael Landon fighting on *Bonanza*, ninety percent of the time, it's Michael Landon. Unless he's getting thrown through a door, or out a window. They wouldn't let him do that. The insurance company wouldn't let him do that. Michael liked to do all his stunts — yeah. He didn't want to rob the audience of anything. Those three guys [Landon, Lorne Greene, Dan Blocker], they put their heart and soul into that show."

Cass did *Bonanza* as an actor. "I played the same deputy two or three times," he says. "They had Bing Russell in the town, and then Ray Teal. For some reason, they would bounce 'em back and forth. Whenever it was Ray Teal, who basically only walked onto the set to do dialogue at that point in his career, if somebody had to get hit on the head, or do some riding or something, they cast me as his deputy." Following the cancellation of *Bonanza*, Dave Cass moved on with Michael Landon to other series. "I went on because of Michael and Jack Lilly, who was an old friend of his," says Cass. "Michael did that spin-off [from *Little House on the Prairie*], *Father Murphy* with Merlin Olsen. I did that a couple of times as an actor. Then I did *Highway to Heaven* probably four times. It was all because of Michael and Jack Lilly. Michael always wanted to have the same old faces around."

Prior to *Bonanza,* Cass served as the stunt double for Robert Brown on *Here Come the Brides.* "I came in the second season," says Cass. "A fella named Reg Parton had doubled Robert the first season, and I was actually a really good double for Robert. I was in my twenties then; Steve Lodge got me that job. I had met Steve on [the short-lived 1967 CBS western] *Dundee and the Culhane* in Arizona. He brought me in to interview. I was literally…in those days, you could work, you had the Screen Actors Guild and the Screen Extras Guild, they were two separate entities so I would go to work every day as a stand-in photo double for Robert Brown. If there were stunts to do, they'd bump me up to stuntman. And, once in a while, they'd give me a part to do. I mean, in 1969, I made almost thirty thousand dollars. We did twenty-five shows that year." (It was actually twenty-six.)

Dave Cass was very impressed by the "look" of *Here Come the Brides.* "The photography on *Brides* was really amazing, given the era, and what they had to work with — old film and all that stuff. It was gorgeous. You believed it was in Seattle. We only went to the mountains once or twice. And at that time, in that era in Hollywood, what was Warner Bros. and is Warner Bros. again, there's…I believe it was the Burbank Studios — I'm not sure — and off a pass in Riverside, was a backlot for that studio and that whole little town. The *Brides* set was built on that backlot, then there was a berm they put up, big mound of dirt, with evergreen trees, you could never see [any] of that. Captain Clancey's boat would pull into the front, it actually was on wheels; they'd roll it in, and they always shot across it to the town, to the dock. They had stock shots of the boats, of Captain Clancey's schooner — we never went out on the water."

While "a lot of the exterior in that show was shot right there in the mountains, they did some of it [the exterior] on the backlot," continues Cass. "They built these big berms of dirt, and you'd have a T intersection — you could ride to the right, or to the left, and they had pine trees on the set, in the town. By using a Chapman crane, you could go from the top of the pine tree right down."

The series' directors and directors of photography (Fred Jackman, Brick Marquard, and Irving Lippman) further created the illusion of the Seattle forests and countryside by mixing shots of the town with shots in the mountains and forests. "We'd ride out of town," explains Cass, "through one of the berms and disappear. Then they'd pick us up in Franklin Canyon or somewhere. In Franklin Canyon — there's a big reservoir that overlooks Beverly Hills. It's up at the top, right off Mulholland Drive. It's city property — you can't go in the water, because it's drinking water for Beverly Hills, but it looks like a big foresty kind of area, with pine trees and hills and everything."

Like his fellow stuntman and second unit-director Bill Catching, Cass is very informative when it comes to how certain visuals were done on *Brides* and other series of the 1960s and '70s. "In those days they used the big arc lights," explains Cass. "They actually had a negative positive carbon that you had to strike — it threw out all this light. I believe the nine lights came in — that gave you a lot of light, and the ten-to-one zoom lens had just come in so they weren't all hard and set lenses. When they put a ten to one on, which goes from a 25 millimeter to a 250 millimeter lens, they can change the lens size just with the twist of the lens. [For example] you'd be in a shot with three people talking, the camera would just zoom in on somebody's face. Because they had the zoom lens, they thought it was cool to do it like that. They don't do it anymore. But what it saves is, instead of having to take a lens off, and put another lens on, you can just adjust that lens, and it gives you a wider or tighter shot." Since *Brides'* E.W. Swackhamer and other directors enjoyed doing dolly shots, that meant laying down a dolly track. "We'd go out and do it in the forest," remembers Cass, "it looked like a railroad track. They'd put down this metal track and they leveled it; they put wedges under it and apple boxes. They can build one on the side of a hill if they want to."

As the executive producer of *Here Come the Brides*, Bob Claver did much to establish the tone and spirit of the show. "Bob Claver, for the kind of producer he was — he had a hit TV show, [yet] he never bossed anybody around," states Cass. "He was part of the team. He'd come to the set maybe once a day, twice a day. [Line producer] Paul Witt was young, he was ambitious, and Chris Morgan [the son of Harry Morgan], he was a second assistant director on that show."

Cass has very good things to say about the series' assistant director/unit production manager, Jim Hogan. "Jimmy Hogan was a solid-gold guy," says Cass. "He did his budget, would tell you how much he had to spend. If, after meeting with the director, you went back and said, 'Look, Jimmy here's what he wants to do,' he would say, 'Let me go talk to him.' And he'd talk to him; he would never put pressure on any of us as an individual. He'd always take it to the top. He took all the pressure for us. Which was, even in those days, a great thing to do."

Cass got along with the camera crew as well. "Fred Jackman was the cameraman. He had his crew and everybody...you were there to do your job. If you did your job, you stayed. And you were welcome. You just felt like you were at home with a bunch of people who enjoyed their work and who were happy to be there."

Among them, David Soul. "He was the unknown singer, bag on his head, and all that stuff," remembers Cass. "I worked with David on *Starsky and Hutch* and *In the Line of Duty*. He was a very good actor. He was there to do his job." Though both Soul and Bobby Sherman were eager to do their stunts, they did have their stunt doubles. At least Sherman did. "Gary Epper doubled Bobby Sherman," remembers Cass, "and then there were two fellas — Eddie Heiss was one of the doubles, and Buddy Joe Hooker also doubled Bobby Sherman. They were great guys. Great young guys."

While Cass got along very well with series star Robert Brown there were some problems doubling Brown when it came to wardrobe. "Robert had these shoulder pads put in the leather shirt that he wore," says Cass, "so they put 'em in my double shirt, but, it didn't fit me right because my shoulders were bigger. So Steve Lodge went in and cut 'em out one day because I was having a hard time getting on a horse. Well, when we cut the shoulder pads out, the whole shoulder dropped down, so the scene was way down on my bicep. [The pads] had to go back in."

Like many of the guest stars who did *Here Come the Brides*, Cass found the entire *Brides* cast a pleasant group. "I don't remember anybody on that show being temperamental," he says. "Which helped a lot. Cuz when a guest star came on, you had this real laid-back cast, regular cast. Nobody else wanted to be temperamental, because the regular cast wasn't temperamental. And Bridget Hanley was just great. She was wonderful. Bridget was just salt of the earth. She and Swack — that was a good marriage. [Of all the "brides"], Bridget and Susan Tolsky are the two who stick in my head. There was another blonde-headed gal who was on the show from time to time, but those were the two basic young leads. Susan was a character. She had a great sense of humor. She was a very fine actress. To pull that part off, she had to be a fine actress…played that little airhead.

"I miss those guys." [4]

1. Tolsky – 2007
2. Lodge – 2007
3. Cass – 2007
4. Ibid

"We went off the air far too soon. You had a hundred girls, a hundred stories. I think we could have had a good five-year run."[1]

*Here Come the Brides* series regular Susan Tolsky

Part Five

# *The Original Run of*
# Here Come the Brides

In the appendix of this book, the reader will find a complete listing of every ABC-TV affiliate that carried *Brides* during its original network run. Secondary affiliates (TV stations that carried more than one network during the time) are included in this list, as are stations that became ABC affiliates during *Here Come the Brides'* original run.

As readers will also note, the episode guide for the first season covers the period from December 30, 1967 (the first known publicity for *Brides*) to September 3, 1969; the guide for the second season begins with September 13th, 1969, and ends with November 1970. (This was about the time the teen magazines so began lessening their coverage of the series.) Through this chronicling of the *Here Come the Brides* series on a week-by-week basis, plus the inclusion of the guest appearances of the *Brides* stars on game shows, music shows, etc., I hoped to create a feeling that you, the reader, have been taken back to the time of *Brides'* original network run. Whether or not I succeeded in this task, only you can say.

*Author's note: For those unfamiliar with the terms, "teaser" and "tag," the former refers to the opening of the show preceding the writer/director/producer credits. The latter refers to the brief sequence before the end credits.*

# Season One
# December 30, 1967 (pre-publicity)
# to September 3, 1969

Dec. 30, 1967 – *TV Teletype: Hollywood*
Joseph Finnigan Reports that *Farmer's Daughter* producer Bob Claver is doing another pilot, *Here Come the Brides,* starring "100 eager women who go West in search of a husband.[1]

March 2, 1968 – *The Doan Report: Networks Set Fall Programs*
Richard K. Doan reports that definitely in ABC-TV's fall schedule is the "logging-camp comedy"[2] *Here Come the Brides.*

March 16, 1968 – *TV Teletype: Hollywood*
Joseph Finnigan Reports that "David Soul and Bridget Hanley (two members of Screen Gems' new-talent program) will be appearing in the new ABC series, *Here Come the Brides.* The show stars ROBERT BROWN, whom you probably never heard of either..."[3]

May 11, 1968 – *TV Teletype: Hollywood*
Joseph Finnigan reports that Joan Blondell will be playing a saloonkeeper in the new ABC series, *Here Come the Brides.*

June 2, 1968 – WBLG-TV, Channel 62 in Lexington, Kentucky, signs on as an ABC-TV affiliate.

July 1968 – The magazine *Photo Screen* informs its readers of a new television western on ABC-TV entitled *Here Come the Brides*.

August 24, 1968 – *TV Teletype: New York*
Neil Hickey Reports that Henry Beckman (Barbara Parkins' father on *Peyton Place*) will "show up regularly as a roguish ship's captain"[4] on the new ABC series, *Here Come the Brides*.

Sometime in 1968 – Signet Books publishes *The Only Complete Guide to TV 69* (a guide to the 1968-69 television season). The text regarding *Here Come the Brides*: "For those who may remember that movie musical of years ago, *Seven Brides for Seven Brothers*, there will be an air of familiarity about this new series, although it isn't based on the movie. Like the movie, however, it deals with the shortage of women among the loggers of the old northwest, and the efforts to bring some distaffers from the east, New Bedford, to be exact.[5]

WBKB, Channel 7 in executive producer Bob Claver's hometown of Chicago, Illinois, becomes WLS-TV.

KTVM-TV, Channel 5 in Medford, Oregon (a secondary affiliate carrying both ABC and NBC programming) becomes KOBI-TV.

WDXI-TV, Channel 7 in Jackson, Tennessee, becomes an ABC affiliate. It will become WBBJ-TV in 1969.

Fall 1968: "Mass Marriage"
*Movieland & TV Time* – Fall Annual.

September 14, 1968 – *TV Guide's* Fall Preview Issue
A description of new ABC-TV series, *Here Come the Brides*, on page 50. Pictured in background, all smiling, are, left to right, David Soul, Robert Brown, Bobby Sherman; in foreground, with backs to camera, wearing wedding gown and veil are a number of "brides." Magazine informs reader that series will debut on September 25. On page 51 is program grid which informs reader that *Brides* will air at 7:30 p.m. on ABC-TV, preceding the half-hour drama, *Peyton Place*, at 8:30, and the two-hour *ABC Wednesday Night Movie* at 9:00.

September 18, 1968 – *TV Guide*
7:30 p.m. Wednesday – underneath the listing for *The Avengers*, reader is told that *Avengers* will be moving to 7:30 p.m. on Monday. A new television series, *Here Come the Brides*, will be airing in this time slot.

September 25, 1968 –
7:30 p.m. Wednesday, ABC-TV – Premiere: *Here Come The Brides*

## Episode #1: "Here Come the Brides" *September 25, 1968*

*Lottie:* A hundred girls! I don't know how you did it. But it's done.
*Jason:* Just the beginning, Lottie. Just the beginning.

Writer . . . . . . . . . . . . . . . . . . . . . . . . . . . . . . . . . . . . . . . . . . . . . . . . . . N. Richard Nash
Director. . . . . . . . . . . . . . . . . . . . . . . . . . . . . . . . . . . . . . . . . . . . .E.W. Swackhamer
Film Editor . . . . . . . . . . . . . . . . . . . . . . . . . . . . . . . . . . . . . . . . . . . . . . Asa Clark
Assistant Director . . . . . . . . . . . . . . . . . . . . . . . . . . . . . . . . . . . . . . Marvin Miller

### The Brides

Franny. . . . . . . . . . . . . . . . . . . . . . . . . . . . . . . . . . . . . . . . . . . . . . . Carol Shelyne
Ann . . . . . . . . . . . . . . . . . . . . . . . . . . . . . . . . . . . . . . . . . . . . . . . . .Cynthia Hull
Sally. . . . . . . . . . . . . . . . . . . . . . . . . . . . . . . . . . . . . . . . . . . . . . . . . .Diane Sayer
Debra. . . . . . . . . . . . . . . . . . . . . . . . . . . . . . . . . . . . . . . . . . . . . . Elaine Joyce
Mary Ellen . . . . . . . . . . . . . . . . . . . . . . . . . . . . . . . . . . . . . . . . . .Karen Carlson
Emmaline . . . . . . . . . . . . . . . . . . . . . . . . . . . . . . . . . . . . . . . . . Jeanne Sheffield

### Jason's Men

Canada . . . . . . . . . . . . . . . . . . . . . . . . . . . . . . . . . . . . . . . . . . . . James Almanzar
Billy Sawdust. . . . . . . . . . . . . . . . . . . . . . . . . . . . . . . . . . . . . . . . Dick Balduzzi
Corky. . . . . . . . . . . . . . . . . . . . . . . . . . . . . . . . . . . . . . . . . . . . . Robert Biheller
McGee . . . . . . . . . . . . . . . . . . . . . . . . . . . . . . . . . . . . . . . . . . . . . Barry Cahill
Sam. . . . . . . . . . . . . . . . . . . . . . . . . . . . . . . . . . . . . . . . . . . . . . . Buck Kartalian
Pebbles. . . . . . . . . . . . . . . . . . . . . . . . . . . . . . . . . . . . . . . . . . . . . .Andy Romano
Logger. . . . . . . . . . . . . . . . . . . . . . . . . . . . . . . . . . . . . . . . . . . . . . Vic Tayback

### Unbilled

Reverend . . . . . . . . . . . . . . . . . . . . . . . . . . . . . . . . . . . . . . . . . . . . Lou Frizzell
Townswoman. . . . . . . . . . . . . . . . . . . . . . . . . . . . . . . . . . . . . . . . . . Nora Marlowe
Frank (the storekeeper) . . . . . . . . . . . . . . . . . . . . . . . . . . . . . . . . . Hollis Morrison
Mocking sailor. . . . . . . . . . . . . . . . . . . . . . . . . . . . . . . . . . . . . . . . . Gordon Jump

**Teaser:** Jason, his men *(dubbed "The Magnificent Seven" by E.W. Swackhamer)*, Josh, Jeremy, Big Swede, Aaron, Reverend, Miss Essie.

**Tag:** Jason, Josh, Jeremy, Candy, Biddie, Frannie, Ann, Sally, Mary Ellen, the Brides, Aaron, Lottie, Clancey, Jason's men, Frank, the people of Seattle.

**Competition:** *Daktari* ("A Family for Jenny"), CBS; the first hour of the ninety-minute *The Virginian* ("Silver Image," guest-starring James Daly and Geraldine Brooks), NBC.

**Photography:** the opening shot of the mountain; Jason (in long shot) cutting off part of the tree; Jason (in close-up) at top of tree; Jason's walk into Seattle picking up more people as he proceeds (the camera pulling back and going to long — and then crane-shots as more and more people join him); the brides of New Bedford encountering the Bolts (the sequence is similar to the 'walk into Seattle' sequence); the slow pan over the brides at the town meeting listening to Jason; the tracking shot of the brides sleeping in the stalls on Clancey's ship; long shots of the ship with the Bolts and the Brides — the camera coming in closer as the ship nears the dock; the little vignettes as the town prepares to meet the brides; the slow pan over the loggers, the

*The Bolt brothers make their pitch to the single ladies of New Bedford — left to right: Bobby Sherman, Robert Brown, David Soul, Carole Shelyne in constable's uniform.*

slow pan over the brides; the gangplank being lowered; the concluding sequence, as it moves from one couple to another.

**Notes:** The teaser preceding the writing, directing, and producing credits makes clear two things: first, this new television series, *Here Come the Brides*, is an ensemble piece; second, the stories will concern the town of Seattle, its development, and its citizens. Among the locales in the Teaser: the Bolt Brothers camp on Bridal Veil Mountain, the town jail, and the church. In short order, the audience meets all three Bolt Brothers; their nemesis, Aaron Stempel; Bolt employees including Corky, Billy Sawdust, Sam, McGee, and Big Swede; the town schoolmarm, Miss Essie; the town's reverend; and so on.

The brides from New Bedford add further diversity to the series — Candy Pruitt is a fire-engine mechanic, Franny works as a police constable, Ann is a storekeeper. Despite the very detailed plot and multitude of characters, all of the characters seem well defined — Jason is something of a con artist who treats women in a casual and cavalier manner, his brother Josh exhibits similar feelings. Jeremy is more attuned to the women's feelings. Like Lottie Hatfield (frequently the voice of reason in the show), Jeremy knows and appreciates the great sacrifice the women are making in journeying to New Bedford. Being a great deal like his brother, Jason, Jeremy knows just how to handle Candy Pruitt. Candy is no less adept in dealing with Jeremy.

In addition to the romance that quickly develops between Candy and Jeremy, Big Swede has begun to court Miss Essie. Among the running gags introduced: two

*Jason Bolt, his brothers Jeremy and Josh, and their men march into Seattle — left to right: Barry Cahill(?), Buck Kartalian (behind Bobby Sherman), Sherman, Robert Brown, James Almanzar (behind Brown and David Soul), Soul, Robert Biheller (second from right), Dick Balduzzi, Vic Tayback (behind Balduzzi).* PHOTO COURTESY DICK BALDUZZI]

people talking over one another in heated tones – in this case it's Jason and Clancey: Clancey's heavy drinking and belching, Jason and Stempel in competition.

*HCTB* "Man of the Family" guest Angel Tompkins' point that *Here Come the Brides* could have done a story about each bride is somewhat demonstrated through the pilot's tag sequence. During the tag, a number of vignettes are presented, each depicting the personality of the supporting brides. For example, Karen Carlson's Mary Ellen is a Presbyterian, as are all of the "brides." She is romantically linked with Hollis Morrison's Frank, has an aggressive streak, and may be in the process of converting Frank to Presbyterianism. Diane Sayer's Sally seems to be attracted to Barry Cahill's McGee. She doesn't explain to him when she turns the light off — before she gets in bed, or when she gets in bed. Based on her earlier behavior towards both Josh and Jeremy, Sally is one of the more flirtatious brides. Cynthia

Hull's Ann is a feisty, loud, wisecracking girl. Andy Romano's Pebbles has taken a shine to her.

As for Carole Shelyne's strong-willed Franny, who, back in New Bedford, had been a police constable: she wants logger Vic Tayback to take a bath — that's the only way she'd consent to marry him.

*Series Star Robert Brown:* "They didn't film in continuity — they couldn't afford to; these things were done for not much money. We did some great pilot exteriors on the old MGM lot — it's no longer there — the dock in New England, that was right — that's where *Gone With the Wind* was filmed. In that section. The old structures and the street scenes, those backlots were really beautiful when they were alive and shooting that way."

*Brown On Being Compared To Burt Lancaster* (In the sequence where Jason Bolt makes his pitch to the New England brides, Brown's manner of speaking and his demeanor calls to mind Burt Lancaster's role as *Elmer Gantry* in the 1960 film of the same name): "Lancaster said exactly the same sort of thing to somebody when I lived in Malibu. He said, 'If I were free, I'd be doing it, because this guy's (Brown) doing it the way I'd be doing it.' So, to be thought of as Lancaster, that ain't bad."[6]

*These three shots of Bridget Hanley from the Brides pilot prove that the Candy Pruitt character was anything but one-note, all photos but Candy holding the gun.* COURTESY BRIDGET HANLEY

*Leading Lady Bridget Hanley:* "We were out at the MGM backlot for part of it; they gave it a nice, lengthy shoot; we came to work in the dark and we left in the dark. We only saw daylight when we were shooting outside, but we did have some night shoots. If we were gonna shoot really late, we'd shoot on a Friday. Usually we finished about five-thirty or six, and we'd have a little toast to each other, and then head home.

"We did reshoot some stuff, so if it was longer, that's why. I felt that the shoot was kind of normal. I was thrilled to be at MGM, on the backlot, in these wonderful costumes — it just was so fun, then we shot a lot of it at the ranch.

"The shot that wasn't in the pilot, it was all of us brides standing — we were out at the MGM lot, which is no longer there — it's all condominiums now. We had to shoot at night, and we were out on the backlot, and MGM just had, I think ghosts, wonderful ghosts everywhere — it was just magical to be there, and just to be in the wardrobe department, and being on these little, round, raised, velvet-covered tufts that moved around...I was just so excited that I got to have a taste of that whole time. It wasn't like when Joan was there, but they still had their own costume department.

"Anyway, it was nighttime, and all the brides, and all the extras who were to play brides were getting on the boat, Swack did a very slow pan down the whole line — first of all; I think he showed the line from behind, and then he slowly did a pan shot of all of our faces, with our anticipation, with our fears, with our joys, with everybody waiting to get on that ship to start our new life — it was absolutely phenomenal... They had to cut it out of the pilot. It was too long.

"I have the *Here Come the Brides* pilot in a can in the garage. I've never been brave enough to take it in someplace to see if it that scene's there. I should."[7]

*Series Regular Susan Tolsky:* "We shot the pilot in December [1967] — it was the coldest December in the history of California in the last thirty-two, thirty-four, thirty-five years. It was so cold. Oh, dear God, it was freezing. Yeah, that was an experience.

"When we were at MGM, shooting exteriors, when we were on the boat getting ready to leave New Bedford (you know, to go to Seattle), we were shooting out at MGM on the cobblestone pier — in the old city — and it was the middle of the night. Well, they watered down the cobblestones, and we had our little 'Mary Jane's' and those shoes froze to the cobblestones. We were sticking to the cobblestones.

"There was a hole in the side of the boat and we had to shoot on one side — the side with the hole in the boat. We had a hundred petticoats — we had that on, then the dress, then the jacket, and then the hat, and then the purse; I had three hairpieces which weighed more than I did. Bridgie had like five. We would have sunk to the bottom of the sea — we would have gone directly down, there would have been no way to retrieve us. And the crew on the boat was sick.

"The boat later sank in San Pedro Harbor, not at sea; it sank in San Pedro Harbor, while sitting there!"[8]

*Semi-Regular Karen Carlson:* "I remember us being out on the ship — on location on this old Swedish vessel — I want to say it was off of Newport. We spent a day shooting on it because we actually had to get footage of being out on the water. So we were on this thing, and it felt like 105° with these petticoats and the bustles and the dresses and the gloves and the hats and all this stuff. We're out in this choppy water — most of us just heaving over the sides, and then, in order to make our entrance onto deck, we had to go down into the hull and come up out of there and that was where...

"So I just remember being…Absolutely one of the most miserable days physically that I've ever endured was one of those days. So we got the day done. Then we get back. I think it was maybe two or three days later that boat sank. Sank in the harbor."[9]

*Semi-Regular Mitzi Hoag:* "There was a very beautiful woman playing one of the brides — she ended up marrying David Soul — Karen Carlson. What they did was they had all the men who were waiting for the ship to dock. Swack put Karen up on a crane, and then panned slowly — the crane moved Karen slowly across this group of men — high in the air, [the finished shot] was as if they were looking at the ship-load of brides, but they wanted something up high so the men were looking up. So they're all yelling and screaming, 'Yay, they're here,' all that kind of thing and every-thing. Swack cut — made a signal for them to stop, and then slowly panned [their faces] with Karen sitting on the crane, moving parallel, but higher across the group of men, and they all…I was watching the scene — I could see them — they were all just looking kind of awestruck. So they had one specific thing to look at. Acting has to be specific — if you're looking off in the distance, you have to look at something specific or it just looks weird. So that was what Swack chose to do."[10]

> September 28, 1968 – *HCTB* Publicity – *TV Guide* – Wednesday program listing for October 2: "New show – *Here Come the Brides* – ABC-TV – In Color 7:30 p.m., pictured: David Soul, Robert Brown, Bridget Hanley.

> Below the guest cast for *A Crying Need:* "Will Robert Brown become a TV matinee idol? See next week's TV GUIDE."[11]

> October 1968 – *Tiger Beat* article, "TV's Brightest New Stars and Shows"; *TV Radio Show* article, "The Story of their Romance"; *TV/Radio Mirror*: Show Biz" a discussion of new shows; *TV & Movie Screen* article: Down Mexico Way – South of the Border, Part 2"; *Movie Stars* article, "What's New on TV"; *Modern Movies* article, "Preview of New TV Shows – Fall '68."

## Episode #2: "A Crying Need"          *October 2, 1968*

> *Jason:* "A woman trying to do a man's job must expect
> a certain amount of difficulty."
> *Dr. Allyn Wright:* "Expect it, Mr. Bolt? I've lived it!"

Writer . . . . . . . . . . . . . . . . . . . . . . . . . . . . . . . . . . . . . . . . . . . . . . . . . . . . . . .Skip Webster
Director. . . . . . . . . . . . . . . . . . . . . . . . . . . . . . . . . . . . . . . . . . . . . . . . . . . . Bob Claver
Film Editor . . . . . . . . . . . . . . . . . . . . . . . . . . . . . . . . . . . . . . . . . . . . . . . . Asa Clark
Assistant Director . . . . . . . . . . . . . . . . . . . . . . . . . . . . . . . . . . . . Michael Dmytryk

*Guest Cast*

| | |
|---|---|
| Dr. Allyn E. Wright | Kathleen Widdoes |
| Dr. Booth | Arthur Space |
| Emily | Dolores Mann |
| Millicent | Karin Wolfe |
| Emmaline | Jeanne Sheffield |
| Holly | Pat Delaney |

**Teaser:** Brides, Biddie, Sally, Brides, Candy, Jason, Josh, Jeremy, Aaron.

**Tag:** Jason, Josh, Jeremy, Candy, Dr. Allyn Wright, Big Swede.

**Competition:** *Daktari* ("Clarence the Lionhearted"), CBS; the first hour of the ninety-minute *Virginian* ("The Orchard," guest-starring Burgess Meredith, Brandon DeWilde, and William Windom), NBC.

**Photography:** The opening shot with the slow pan over the brides; the pan over the logs in the log jam and up the river bank to Jeremy and Corky; the jiggling up-and-down camera pan over the Bolts and their men as they wait while Dr. Wright tends to the ailing Jeremy; Candy telling the brides that their new doctor is a woman, then blowing out her candle as the others (IN THE DARK) reveal their bigotry towards the idea of a woman doctor.

**Notes:** Semi-regular Hoke Howell begins his role as general store owner Ben Perkins, Dolores Mann makes the first of two appearances as his wife, Emily.

Jason Bolt's respect and admiration of Dr. Wright adds yet another layer to Robert Brown's already-multidimensional character; Candy's guilt over the ultimatum she delivers to Jason and his brothers at the beginning of the story (they have just six weeks to find a doctor or the brides will leave Seattle), plus her acting as spokeswoman when the brides apologize to Dr. Wright, adds considerable dimension to Bridget Hanley's characterization. Because Candy has talked the other brides into signing the "No Marriages until Jason Gets us a Doctor" proclamation, because she has partially brought about the tongue-lashing of the brides from Jason, she seems to feel the need to be reprimanded. Candy's willingness to put herself in such a position (despite being the first bride to embrace and welcome Dr. Wright) makes her a very interesting character.

There are new dimensions to Josh and Jeremy as both try to prove their manhood. Ditto Clancey; thanks to the strong-willed Dr. Wright, Clancey's attitude towards women is now beginning to change. As proven by the tag in the pilot, Clancey was already starting to change his attitude towards women. For writer Skip Webster to catch this brief moment in the pilot, and build onto that with this script speaks highly for Webster's skill as a writer.

*HCTB* guest star Lynda Day George's belief that "people need to think when they are watching television"[12] is key to understanding Dr. Allyn Wright's closing speech to the brides. Though some *HCTB* fans feel this speech is out of character for the doctor, were one to put oneself in Dr. Wright's place, were one to consider the incredible daily stresses and the numerous obstacles this woman is guaranteed to face given the era in which she is working, this speech (and Dr. Wright's behavior) make perfect sense.

For starters, Dr. Allyn E. Wright has chosen to enter a profession where she is likely to make a number of life and death decisions. She will be making other tough decisions as well –whether or not to perform amputations, for example. Moreover, as Dr. Wright points out to Jason, being a female doctor has exacted an emotional toll: twenty-two colleges rejected her before she was accepted by the one in San Francisco. To make matters worse, her father (who was himself a doctor) has fought her at every step. As did the men running the college from which she graduated; despite being #1 in her class, she was unable to accept her diploma in public.

No less importantly, Dr. Wright has chosen to establish her practice on the frontier, and in a town that is just beginning to grow. The likelihood of finding cultured and educated women (and men) is pretty remote. Clearly, as evidenced from Kathleen Widdoes' performance, a key factor in the doctor's decision to set up practice in Seattle is the fact that a number of women from New England (women like herself) have chosen to make a life there. But, as the doctor's soliloquy makes quite clear to the audience, these women aren't nearly as advanced and as open-minded as Dr. Wright.

"You know," explains the doctor to Candy, Biddie, and the other few brides, "when I came here, I didn't expect to find the end of the rainbow. But I was counting on you women to help me. You say you want me to stay. How many of you? Eight? Ten? Well, that still leaves ninety unaccounted for, doesn't it? Can you tell me how long it's going to take before they…accept me? Because I'll tell you something. I'm not strong enough to prove myself day after day to everyone in this town. Whether it's because I'm a doctor, or, because I'm a woman, I need to be believed in."

Widdoes' delivery of this soliloquy underscores Dr. Wright's great disappointment with the women of New Bedford. Encountering opposition from men…Allyn Wright is accustomed to that. But to encounter opposition and hostility from women close to one's own age — women, who like the doctor, have shown great courage and determination in willingly taking on a new kind of life — that's nothing short of emotionally devastating. Indeed, of all the people in Seattle, those who should be most receptive to the idea of a female doctor are the forward-looking women of New Bedford, Massachusetts.

To ask Dr. Wright to take on the extraordinarily burdensome task of winning over every one of these bigoted women, when she already has so much stress in her life, is not only unreasonable of Candy and the others, it's ridiculous. The fact that the strong-willed, courageous Dr. Allyn E. Wright has no intention of putting up with such bigotry, the fact that she finally reaches her breaking point, adds great dimension, and an enormous amount of realism to Kathleen Widdoes' character. At the time when it really counts, Dr. Allyn E. Wright's greatest degree of support comes from the initially chauvinistic Jason, Clancey, Josh, and all the men of Seattle. Robert Brown is superb in the scene where Jason lets the brides from New England know what he truly thinks of them.

As made clear by this second-aired episode, the *Here Come the Brides* television series would not be placing its title characters on a pedestal.

*Executive Producer Bob Claver:* "I have a copy [of the show] here. It was Bobby Sherman in an explosion and all kinds of stuff. I was about to make that shot, and it was a really complicated shot with four cameras, five cameras or something, and my daughter called, and she wanted me to bring home a Marks-A-Lot pen, and of course, what else would be more important than her Marks-A-Lot pen? I said to my wife, 'I've got a hundred and fifty people waiting here for me to make this shot, and she actually called me…' We both thought it was very funny."[13]

*Story Editor William Blinn:* "I think Robert's idea that Jason's having a romance with one of the brides would take away from the show is absolutely correct. A lot of the girls were eighteen, nineteen, twenty, and Robert was a man of a few more years. There's a little awkwardness…If you were to accept that situation as real, Jason Bolt would have been pretty stupid if he'd romanced one of those girls. He was better off with Kathleen Widdoes — that kind of age range and sophistication was more… was easier for the Robert character to get to. Of the romances [Jason has] that was probably the best for him.

"I liked that [show]. That was okay. Again, it wasn't anything that was break-through stuff, but we needed to answer…'Wait a minute, we've got a hundred new people just come to town, a hundred new females just come to town, certainly we're gonna have marriages, we're gonna have babies, is there a doctor in this town?' It wasn't a question of let's bring in a female doctor — it was 'Where's the doctor? Who's the doctor?' And so from that, came this episode. I thought within the realm of the overall series, it was okay. Screen Gems was fine with that."

*Blinn On The Log-Jam Sequence:* "Screen Gems was a notoriously cheap studio, and when you start to do action-adventure…Well, we did one [episode] with a log jam, and the log jam had to be blown up. We shot it fairly well – it was shot out in the lagoon of the Columbia Ranch, which is maybe fifty yards across, and so when you had scenes throughout the entire river, then, 'My God, what terrible problems this is going to bring to our community.' But [because of what could be done on the budget], you kinda looked down and thought, 'It's not going to be that big a deal. It just looks to me like maybe two hundred logs stacked up there, and we ought to be able to work that out.' So we suffered for that."[14]

## Writer Skip Webster

Starting his writing career with situation comedies like the late-1960s Eve Arden/Kaye Ballard series, *The Mothers-In-Law*, and the early '70s hit, *The Partridge Family*, Skip Webster's first script for *Brides*: A Crying Need" proved that the writer was capable of more than silly comedy. In his April 3, 1974 episode of *Doc Elliot*, "Things that Might Have Been," a facially scarred Lane Bradbury has been saving money for years so as to afford cosmetic surgery. Then Bradbury's hopes are dashed by her father Tim O'Connor's critical illness.

Webster guaranteed himself a place in *Harry O* series history by writing the story for the first-season's "For the Love of Money" (January 16, 1975). That was the episode that introduced Anthony Zerbe as private detective Harry Orwell's (David Janssen) friend, and nemesis, Lt. KC. Trench, along with Trench's sidekick, Sgt. Roberts (Paul Tulley). Webster's March 25, 1975 *Barnaby Jones* episode, "Poisoned Pigeon," more than likely pleased series producer Philip Saltzman, as it had a storyline concerning a female criminal (played by guest star Penny Fuller). Saltzman felt that female criminals were more interesting than their male counterparts.

Before becoming executive story consultant/producer of *Fantasy Island,* Webster wrote one of the first season *Wonder Woman* classics: The Bushwhackers" (January 29, 1977, ABC), guest-starring Roy Rogers.

*Story Editor William Blinn:* "Skip Webster was one of the family. He had worked for Bob Claver before as a PR guy. He'd worked in public relations and publicity, I think for Screen Gems, and I think for Bob Claver, but he didn't like PR – it's certainly very limiting for a writer. He wanted to get into writing. He loved writing, and he was doggedly persistent. He would write six, seven, eight, nine, ten drafts of a script to get it to the point where someone would say, 'Yeah, we really like this now,' and then he was also a big boy when you said, 'Now, Skip. This isn't getting it. What do we do?' He managed to put his ego aside, and just be as hard-nosed about his work as one could possibly be. And he loved going down to the set without being intrusive ever. He was a very, very sweet human being. It surprises me not at all that Bridget liked him so much because she's outgoing and intelligent and bright and full of fun. Skip responded to that; I'm sure she responded to his ongoing humanity.

"I used him on *The Rookies* when I did *The Rookies,* and when I left *The Rookies* at the start of the third season, Skip took over as producer. He was a good guy, a hard worker, doggedly determined to get it right. He'd rewrite it fifty times if he had to. He was right for *Brides* in particular, because he had a droll sense of humor. He didn't take it seriously in terms of professionalism, but his attitude as a human being was much more optimistic and sunny, so he was good casting for *Brides.*

"Later on, I did a show at Warner Bros. called *The New Land* with Kurt Russell and Bonnie Bedelia. Skip did a couple episodes for me there. He passed away fifteen, sixteen years ago."[15]

*Leading Lady Bridget Hanley:* "Skip Webster I remember because I knew him, and I loved his scripts. He was a charming man and funny and had great humor."[16]

*Series Regular Susan Tolsky:* "I remember him being just a real jovial guy – he wrote well for me. When I saw his name on a script, I always felt I'd be treated well. For me to remember Skip Webster's name, you have to know that it made some sort of impression on me.

"So when I hear his name, I remember that they were funny scripts, not that others weren't, but it must have meant I had some good stuff or some good lines, because I do remember when I saw his name on a script I knew I was okay — I knew I had funny stuff to do."[17]

## *Editor Asa Clark*

*Executive Producer Bob Claver:* "Asa Boyd Clark goes back to *Farmer's Daughter.* He was good, he was a whiny old guy, but he was good at what he did. He was always complaining — especially about my directing. 'I don't like the coverage, and you didn't do this, and you…' He was funny; I didn't get angry at him. He was trying to be helpful, he was a good editor. His brother, Jim, is a good director — James B. Clark."[18]

*Leading Lady Bridget Hanley:* "Oh, I loved Asa. Asa loved Swackhamer, too. He did mostly what Swack did. What a wonderful guy."[19]

*Story Editor William Blinn On Semi-Regular Hoke Howell:* "The guy who played Ben — Hoke Howell, I knew back in New York, we'd gone to school together. I had him in to read, he got the part. He was terrific."[20]

## *Guest Star Kathleen Widdoes*

According to *Brides* fans, more fan fiction has been written about Dr. Allyn E. Wright than any other one-time *HCTB* character. Executive producer Claver said that he "loved" Kathleen Widdoes in the part.

Born March 21, 1939 in Wilmington, Delaware, the eighteen-year-old Widdoes made her stage debut as Alma in *Bus Stop* at the Robin Hood Playhouse in Wilmington. Following this, she toured Canada, working in both stage and TV, before moving to Paris, where she studied at the Sorbonne under a Fulbright scholarship; she also studied mime at the Universite au Theatre des Nations in Paris.

Returning to the U.S. in 1959, Widdoes began doing many on-and-off Broadway plays. In addition, she garnered excellent reviews for her work in such

*"A Crying Need" star Kathleen Widdoes with Sam Waterston in a 1974 PBS broadcast of Joseph Papp's New York Shakespeare Festival Production,* Much Ado About Nothing.

Joseph Papp/New York Shakespeare Festival plays as *Henry V, Measure for Measure, A Midsummer Night's Dream,* and *The Tempest.* Television work included a regular role on the soap, *Young Dr. Malone* and a guest shot on the Roald Dahl anthology, *Way Out.*

By the time Widdoes made her film debut in 1966's *The Group* (based on the novel by Seattle born author Mary McCarthy — sister of actor Kevin), she'd appeared in multiple episodes of the critically acclaimed Herbert Brodkin series, *The Defenders* and *The Nurses.* After moving to Hollywood, Widdoes displayed her versatility in the role of Irina Zavanoff in the QM Productions/*12 O'Clock High* third-season episode, "Massacre," and as small-town Kansas schoolteacher Ellen Woods in the QM Productions/*Invaders* first season episode, "Nightmare." In that one, which also featured future *Brides* guest stars Jeanette Nolan and Irene Tedrow, Ellen has a hard time getting anyone to believe her incredible story of being attacked by carnivorous insects!

Post *Brides*, Widdoes' lady golfer Margaret Kane found herself being romanced by murderous, bogus Vietnam War vet Chad Everett in the QM/*FBI* fourth-season episode, "The Hero"; then the actress reunited with *Invaders*/ "Nightmare" director Paul Wendkos for his 1971 QM horror classic, *The Mephisto Waltz*, and played Anna Kosovo — the wife of a deranged Michael Pataki in the 1972 *Bonanza* episode, "Frenzy."

By the late 1970s, Widdoes moved into television daytime drama, playing running parts on such series as *Another World, Ryan's Hope*, and *As The World Turns.* She continues to work on stage.

*Leading Lady Bridget Hanley:* "Swack was so excited when she came out to do the part. Talk about…She is like such a lady, but with such spirit and such spine, but gentle humor and an absolute huge, huge body of work. Absolute skill to match"[21]

*Series Regular Susan Tolsky:* "Kathleen I remember being…A NEW YORK ACTRESS! At the time it was so different — you either were L.A. or New York. Most people headed for stage. But it was always my ambition to come out West — I did not want to do stage. My feeling about Kathleen was it was a very New York feeling. She was not intimidating. One was one coast, one was the other; New York was stage, Hollywood was film. I didn't find her offensive or anything, but it was like 'Oh, she's stage trained.' And I'm camera trained.

I certainly had stage background, but I didn't go and do Broadway."[22]

*Casting Director Burt Metcalfe:* I certainly knew who Kathleen Widdoes was — that sounds like somebody who'd I'd be pushing for. She was from New York — a very good actress."[23]

## Guest Star Arthur Space

In motion pictures since the early 1940s (credits included Abbott and Costello's *Rio Rita*, the drama, *Random Harvest*, the biopic, *Wilson*, the war dramas *Wing and a Prayer* and *Thirty Seconds Over Tokyo*), Arthur Space also had such television shows as *The Adventures of Superman, Zorro, Perry Mason, Wagon Train, Voyage to the*

*Bottom of the Sea,* and *The Wild Wild West* to his credit by the time he guest-starred on *Here Come the Brides.*

Post *Brides,* Space appeared in the well-done *Cade's County* episode, "Company Town," (guest-starring *Brides* guest alum Will Geer as a brutal mob boss), the Disney movies *Bedknobs and Broomsticks, Herbie Rides Again,* and *The Strongest Man in the World,* and guest starred in such '70s and '80s series as *Little House on the Prairie, Baretta, The Waltons, Charlie's Angels,* and *Lou Grant.* He died of cancer on January 13, 1983.

> October 5, 1968 – *HCTB* Publicity: The First Real Hunk of Man Since Errol Flynn" by Fritz Goodwin – pgs 16, 17, 18 – *TV Guide* –Vol. 16, No. 40, October 5, 1968, Issue #810.

## Episode #3: "And Jason Makes Five"        *October 9, 1968*

> "You got it all wrong. You don't want to get married. But you're gonna get married. Yeah, you can count on that, Mr. Bolt."
> *Holly Houston to Jason Bolt*

Writers. . . . . . . . . . . . . . . . . . . . . . . . . . . . . . . John O'Dea and Jay Simms
Director. . . . . . . . . . . . . . . . . . . . . . . . . . . . . . . . . .E.W. Swackhamer
Film Editor . . . . . . . . . . . . . . . . . . . . . . . . . . . . . . . . . Jim Faris
Assistant Director . . . . . . . . . . . . . . . . . . . . . . . . . . . . Jim Hogan

*Guest Cast*

Holly Houston . . . . . . . . . . . . . . . . . . . . . . . . . . . . . Jennifer West
Judge Young. . . . . . . . . . . . . . . . . . . . . . . . . . . . . . .Bill Zuckert
Thorne . . . . . . . . . . . . . . . . . . . . . . . . . . . . . . . . . . Eric Shea
Melody . . . . . . . . . . . . . . . . . . . . . . . . . . . . . . . . Linda Sue Risk
Laurel . . . . . . . . . . . . . . . . . . . . . . . . . . . . . . . . Maralee Foster

*Teaser:* Holly Houston, Thorne, Laurel, Melody, Frank.

*Tag:* Aaron, Jason, Josh, Jeremy.

*Competition: Daktari,* "African Heritage," guest-starring Allison Price as a writer who, seeking adventure, disrupts the compound, CBS; *The Virginian,* "A Vision of Blindness," headlining series regular Sara Lane in a strong performance, and guest-starring John Saxon, Ben Johnson, and the popular singing group, The Irish Rovers, NBC.

*Photography:* "THEY'RE DOIN' *[HCTB]* CHOREOGRAPHY": This episode features four striking examples of director E.W. Swackhamer's skill at choreography. In the first, Candy and four other brides (including Biddie and Franny) run from the kitchen in the brides' dormitory up to the second floor where they find Holly Houston's three children. Swackhamer begins the sequence at the bottom of the steps, where we see five stocking-clad pairs of legs running up the stairs, moves to the top of the stairs where all five women turn the corner, then ends the sequence with the five brides coming to a stop in front of the children's beds, all five women have their backs to the camera with Candy ending up in the middle.

In the second sequence (where Candy and the brides insist that Jason take care of Holly's abandoned children), the director has all three of the Bolt brothers holding a child. Jason is in the middle, holding Holly's "son" Thorne. As he and his brothers argue with Candy (who is again in the middle of the women), the camera keeps

*Unknown actress, Bridget Hanley, Joan Blondell, and Carole Shelyne (behind Blondell) in "And Jason Makes Five."* PHOTO COURTESY BRIDGET HANLEY

cutting back and forth, the women always shushing Jason in unison every time he raises his voice.

In the third sequence, (Jason dragging Holly into Lottie's saloon for a bath), Swackhamer begins the scene at the exterior top floor of the dormitory with four brides washing one window apiece, each woman is shown cleaning a window in the exact same spot at the exact same time. Even better is the fourth and last sequence: after rebuking Candy and the others for their harsh judgment of Jason, Lottie then tells them to "come along." Two by two, the brides turn, in perfect step, to follow Lottie and Candy.

**Music:** Another clever touch in this episode is composer Hugo Montenegro's background scoring. When Holly's three children nod their heads, they do so to the accompaniment of a harpsichord. When Candy whispers in Jeremy's ear, the rapid pace of the harpsichord shows she is talking to him very fast.

**Notes:** *Brides'* first comic outing, "And Jason Makes Five" introduces a frequently recurring theme – one or more of the men becomes involved with a dishonest woman.

In the skillfully directed opening sequence, E.W. Swackhamer takes the viewers on a full tour of the growing town of Seattle as the camera follows the wagon of Holly Houston. Viewers go inside the Bolt's cabin for the very first time; they also hear the brides' first choir practice. To *TV Guide*'s Cleveland Amory, the scene in which Lottie prepares to give Holly a bath, was quite possibly the episode's best scene.

Robert Brown proves himself more than up to the challenge of playing both straight man to Jennifer West and matching (and at times topping) her comic performance — for example, the "Sit" and "Stay" scene in the buckboard wagon. Like West, Brown has some dramatic moments — despite Holly's accusation that he is the father of her children, Jason comes to admire Holly's determination to do right by the kids. Candy's suspicion of Holly's story (and her giving Jason the benefit of the doubt) brings a new layer to the Jason Bolt/Candy Pruitt relationship. Bobby Sherman's skill for comedy is very evident in the scene where a frustrated Jeremy attempts to teach Holly's three "children" the letter "C."

While this episode continues the previous show's negative presentation of the brides, it also proves the men of Seattle are pretty judgmental as well. In fact, with the exception of Lottie and his brothers, everyone in Seattle (including an uncertain Candy), believes Holly's accusation that Jason is the father of her children.

*Story Editor William Blinn:* "Jennifer West really got into the part. She was very over the top. That's probably why Henry [Beckman] didn't do that show. When you've got someone that big and that energetic, then putting Henry in the same scene, and in the same frame with her, is just gonna take the believability and totally pitch it out the window.

"I thought it was cute. Putting a guy like Robert with kids is a good television idea. It's standard operating fare, but it's also kind of fun."[24]

### Editor Jim Faris

*Executive Producer Bob Claver:* "Jim Faris was a good editor, too. With an hour show, you need two guys. Blinn might have suggested him — if Bill suggested an editor, I would go with that." (Faris was editor on Blinn's previous TV series, *Shane*.)

### Assistant Director/Unit Production Manager Jim Hogan

*Executive Producer Bob Claver:* "Jim Hogan was [a member of Alcoholics Anonymous] and he'd been dry for six or seven or eight years. I needed a guy, when I had *Interns* and *Partridge*, I needed a guy to work both shows. I hired Jim, and he went off the wagon. When you go off the wagon, when you're an alcoholic, it is a progressive disease, it progresses even when you don't drink. So, by that time, I remember my wife and I driving through the valley and looking for him in back yards, and finding him — it was awful. He was a wonderful, wonderful unit manager and Gil [Mandelik] was solid, but Jim would be the guy you would pick to do two shows."[25]

(The people at Universal Studios probably agreed. Although *The Partridge Family* was still in production when the studio's 90-minute *Mystery Movie* series, *Banacek* began, they hired Hogan as the show's Unit Production Manager.)

## Guest Star Jennifer West

Playing the female lead in Broadway's *Diamond Orchid* (a fictionalized drama based on the life and death of Eva and Juan Peron), appearing in a television version of actor Charles Aidman's 1963 theatrical adaptation of Edgar Lee Masters' *Spoon River Anthology*, and the April 5, 1964 *Du Pont Show* ("Jeremy Rabbitt, the Secret Avenger"), Jennifer West had guest-starred on such TV series as *Sugarfoot, 77 Sunset Strip, The Many Loves of Dobie Gillis, Dr. Kildare, The Defenders,* and *Hawk* by the time she played Holly Houston on *Here Come the Brides.* Prior to her reprising the role of Holly in the second-season *Brides* episode, "Debt of Honor," West guest starred in *The FBI.*

Following her second *Brides,* and a 1970s *Gunsmoke* guest shot ("Hackett"), West disappeared from television. Attempts to determine her whereabouts by this author have proved unsuccessful.

*Star Robert Brown:* "She was a character, she had the set going. You expected to see much of her again. She was that person."[26]

*Leading Lady Bridget Hanley:* "Oh, what a hoot. We had more fun…she was 'Yee Haw,' and we all felt like that with her. She was more fun — 'Get on over here!' [Jennifer would say] — That was just really fun and I knew she did other things — she was just a great…did a terrific job with that part.

"Yeah. Very over the top. But not without reality — there was a human side — it was not, 'Let's see how big I can go and have nothing to fall back on.'"[27]

*Casting Director Burt Metcalfe:* "I remember her. I had also known her in a whole other framework — before I became a casting director, I was an actor, and it seems to me I knew her then. I think we did something in summer stock. She played bad girls a lot. She was a very good actress, but very offbeat…kind of different, an interesting personality."[28]

## Writers John O'Dea and Jay Simms

Announcer on the mid-1950s game show, *High Finance*, writer of late-1950s B-horror flicks (*The Killer Shrews, The Giant Gila Monster*), Jay Simms had done quite a few westerns (*Laramie, Gunsmoke, Rawhide, Laredo*) by the time he teamed up with John O'Dea for the *Here Come the Brides* comedic episodes, "And Jason Makes Five" and "One Good Lie Deserves Another."

O'Dea's pre-*Brides* credits included the comedies *Killer Dill* (1947), *The Admiral Was a Lady* (1950), the 1955 Reverend Billy Graham drama, *Wiretapper*, and the series,

*Sky King, Surfside 6, T.H.E. Cat, The Girl from U.N.C.L.E., Mission: Impossible,* and *The Iron Horse.* Together, he and Simms wrote *The Second Hundred Years* episode, "Right of Way," and two episodes of *The Big Valley*: Bounty on a Barkley" and "Lightfoot."

Big Valley *Producer Arthur Gardner on* Valley *series writer Jay Simms:* "Jay Simms had a marvelous sense of humor. He was a very, very likable guy. Jay wrote a lot of scripts for us. Humor stories were his specialty."[29]

*Trivia:* Holly Houston is one of the *Brides'* fans' favorite guest characters.

This episode reunites child stars Eric Shea and Maralee Foster; the two had previously worked together in the 1968 Lucille Ball/Henry Fonda comedy, *Yours, Mine, and Ours.*

Pre-*Brides*, Eric Shea (the brother of child actor Christopher Shea), had played the memorable role of the cowboy-worshipping Andy in the *Batman* spoof of the Alan Ladd classic, *Shane* ("Come Back, Shame"/ "It's How You Play the Game"). Ironically, Christopher Shea played Joey in the TV series version of *Shane* — on which *Brides'* William Blinn served as story consultant.

Post *Brides,* Eric Shea appeared in the Irwin Allen blockbuster, *The Poseidon Adventure,* in addition to playing whiz kid Alvin Fernald in the *Wonderful World of Disney* two-parters, *The Whiz Kid and the Mystery at Riverton,* and *The Whiz Kid and the Carnival Caper.* In the latter, Shea falls for not-so-bad girl Jaclyn Smith. The kid certainly had good taste!

October 16, 1968 – episode #4 airs

October 17, 1968 – David Soul is guest on *The Merv Griffin Show*

October 18, 1968 – Bobby Sherman is tentatively scheduled for *The Joey Bishop Show*

## Episode #4: "Man of the Family"                     *October 16, 1968*

"I think I know what you're going to say next.
And I'm not ready to hear that. Not yet."
*Polly Blake to Reverend Randolph Gaddings*

Writer . . . . . . . . . . . . . . . . . . . . . . . . . . . . . . . . . . . . . . . . . . . . . . . . . . . . . Jo Heims
Director. . . . . . . . . . . . . . . . . . . . . . . . . . . . . . . . . . . . . . . . . . . . . .E.W. Swackhamer
Film Editor . . . . . . . . . . . . . . . . . . . . . . . . . . . . . . . . . . . . . . . . . . . . . . . . Jim Faris
Assistant Director . . . . . . . . . . . . . . . . . . . . . . . . . . . . . . . . . . . . . . . . . . . Jim Hogan
*Guest Cast*
Rev. Randolph Gaddings. . . . . . . . . . . . . . . . . . . . . . . . . . . . . . William Schallert
Polly Blake. . . . . . . . . . . . . . . . . . . . . . . . . . . . . . . . . . . . . . . . . .Loretta Leversee

Tommy Blake . . . . . . . . . . . . . . . . . . . . . . . . . . . . . . . . . . . . . Stefan Arngrim
Debra Whitfield . . . . . . . . . . . . . . . . . . . . . . . . . . . . . . . . . . . Elaine Joyce
Jenny . . . . . . . . . . . . . . . . . . . . . . . . . . . . . . . . . . . . . . . . . . . Angel Tompkins
1st Mate. . . . . . . . . . . . . . . . . . . . . . . . . . . . . . . . . . . . . . . . . Karl Lukas
Woman . . . . . . . . . . . . . . . . . . . . . . . . . . . . . . . . . . . . . . . . . Elaine Fielding
Man. . . . . . . . . . . . . . . . . . . . . . . . . . . . . . . . . . . . . . . . . . . . . Don Kennedy

**Teaser:** Clancey, mate, Candy, Biddie, Miss Essie, Lottie, Jenny, Debra, Aaron, Reverend Gaddings, Polly, Jason, Josh, Jeremy, Big Swede.

**Tag:** Miss Essie, Big Swede, Debra, Jason, Clancey, Tommy, Reverend Gaddings, Polly, Candy, Biddie, Lottie, Josh, Jeremy, Aaron, Jenny, Sally.

**Competition:** *Daktari*, "The Outsider," guest-starring Diane Shalet and William Jordan, CBS; *The Virginian*, "The Wind of Outrage," a drama based on Canadian history, guest-starring Ricardo Montalban and Lois Nettleton, NBC.

**Photography:** Long shot of the church tightening in for a close-up, the little boy opening the church door with the intention of playing hooky, his mother grabbing him and taking him [and the audience] inside the church, the camera then taking the audience down each row of the church pews to stop at the podium/altar for a two-shot of Reverend Gaddings and organist Polly Blake. The shot through the pine trees of Tommy Blake making his way towards the Bolt Brothers' logging camp.

**Notes:** Superb performances from William Schallert, Loretta Leversee, and, (especially Stefan Arngrim), plus excellent work from series semi-regulars Mitzi Hoag, Elaine Joyce, and supporting guest Angel Tompkins make this one of the most durable *HCTB* episodes. The scripting, as one situation piles on top of another, is also very effective.

Though both William Schallert and Loretta Leversee bring dimension to their parts, the lion's share of the story goes to child actor Arngrim. Robert Brown's scenes with Arngrim much more vividly illustrate story editor William Blinn's point that "putting Brown with kids is a good television idea." For example, after Tommy Blake smears his nice new suit with mud, Jason asks, "Is that the fashion in New Bedford?" "It's my suit," sneers Tommy. "Guess I can do whatever I want to it." "Guess you can," Jason agrees, whereupon he invites Tommy to jump in a nearby mud-puddle, and "make a thorough job of it." This 'tough love' approach to Tommy, and Jason's talking to Tom like one adult to another is the ideal approach for the boy. Thanks to Jason's child psychology, Tommy comes to accept Reverend Gaddings; thanks to Tommy's change of mind, the Reverend and Tom's mother, the widowed Polly Blake, can now marry.

This episode provides a fine example of how to arouse and maintain an audience's curiosity — by the close of the teaser, there are already two questions in the audience's mind: One – What is the "precious little cargo" to which Captain Clancey refers? Two – Why, when it is obvious she is attracted to him, is Polly Blake opposed to accepting the Reverend's proposal of marriage? As the story continues, more questions and more problems surface.

Besides the romance between Reverend Gaddings and Polly, (which results in the series' first onscreen wedding), making the episode further unusual is the fact that a character (who has nothing to do with Aaron Stempel) creates the possibility of the Bolts losing their mountain.

Complimenting the Gaddings/Blake romance are the Jason/Jenny romance, and the Essie/Swede/Debra triangle. Though both Jenny and Debra are very attractive, Debra is less than kind to the plain-looking Essie and it is clear that Jenny, who has romantic designs on Jason, would very much like Polly to leave them alone.

*Left to right: Robert Brown, Bridget Hanley, and Stefan Arngrim as the title character in the series' fourth-aired episode, "Man of the Family."*

There is also good comedic chemistry between Bobby Sherman and Bridget Hanley in this story. Candy's exclamation of "Oh, my" when Jeremy fails to understand why Jason and Jenny don't wish to join the group picnic makes for a very funny moment.

For reasons never explained, the curtain behind the podium in the church changes from red to blue, then back to red during the course of this show.

*Story Editor William Blinn:* "By and large, it was a little slow. [But writer] Jo Heims worked a lot. I don't recall any problems. It was very pabulum-esque, very white-bread, kind of predictable. There wasn't anything very memorable about it.

Bob Claver wasn't thrilled with Arngrim. He didn't like working, as a director or producer, with kids." [30]

*Henry Beckman (on the Marriage Scene):* "It was a total off-the-wall. The script said: 'pronounce you man and wife.' The director was so enamoured [*sic*] of the scene, he delayed calling 'cut,' so I saw the camera was still running and added: 'and may God have mercy' etc. then the director hollered 'cut.' I said: 'Sorry, just couldn't resist it.' Wherupon [*sic*] he yelled 'leave it in — print it!' and a classic scene was born. I guess I was well into the Clancey mode at the time and he was thinking of the past marriage(s) he'd been subjected to. Who knows how these things work? If YOU know, please tell me." [31]

## Guest Star William Schallert

Off-screen announcer of the *Here Come the Brides* second-season promotion (accompanying the Meg Foster episode, "Two Worlds"), William Schallert began his movie career back in the late 1940s with such films as *The Foxes of Harrow* (1947) and *Mighty Joe Young* (1949). Among Schallert's many TV guest credits: *The George Burns and Gracie Allen Show, You Are There, Zorro, Maverick, Richard Diamond: Private Detective, Twilight Zone, Sea Hunt, Thriller, Perry Mason, Combat, The Virginian, Marcus Welby, M.D., The Partridge Family, The FBI, Kung Fu, Police Story, Ellery Queen, Archie Bunker's Place, Matt Houston,* etc. In addition to his series as regular or semi-regular: *The Many Loves of Dobie Gillis, The Patty Duke Show, The Hardy Boys/Nancy Drew Mysteries,* Schallert served as president of the Screen Actor's Guild from 1979-81.

*Leading Lady Bridget Hanley:* "He is just the love of the world — he is just a gentle soul, [who] has the talent of the angels." [32]

*Story Editor William Blinn:* "I liked it because I liked William Schallert. Schallert was very good — he always was.

"I liked the fact that we were playing a minister as someone who wasn't just about Scripture, and just about God, and being good, and so forth. He had moments of confusion and short-temperedness, a few more facets than most ministers showed in television in that day and age. He was kind of like Richard Todd's Peter Marshall in *A Man Called Peter* — he [Gaddings] had an astonishing amount of charm. He wasn't a minister and therefore perfect. He was an imperfect man attempting to be a minister." [33]

## Guest Star Loretta Leversee

Unforgettable as a deaf mute desperate to maintain custody of her adopted child in the superb 1967 *Judd, for the Defense* episode, "To Love and Stand Mute" (written by *Here Come the Brides* "A Dream that Glitters" co-writer Gerry Day), native

Chicagoan Loretta Leversee had attended the New School for Social Research Dramatic Workshop in New York, studied with Lee Strasberg at the Actors' Studio, and worked in such 1950s dramatic anthologies as *Robert Montgomery Presents, Philco Television Playhouse,* and *Studio One* by the time she played Polly Blake on *Here Come the Brides.* Post Brides, Leversee appeared in *Bonanza, Medical Center,* and *The Silent Force.* She later became executive director of the Fifth Street Studio Theatre in Los Angeles, and served on the boards of the Windsor Square-Hancock Park Historical Society, the Goethe Institute, and the White House Millennium Committee. She passed away from cancer on December 27, 2005 in Los Angeles, California.

*Bridget Hanley on Loretta Leversee:* "I remember really liking her a lot."

*Bridget Hanley on Stefan Arngrim:* "Oh, what fun! I was supposed to see him not long ago, after all these years. I just loved him. It was hard not to — I just wanted to be his mother. He was just terrific."[34]

## Guest Star *Angel Tompkins*

Beginning her performing career as a Chicago-area model in the early 1960s, gorgeous Angel Tompkins had only one credit to her name (criminally inclined actress Marcia Dennison in the 1968 *Wild Wild West* episode, "The Night of the Death-Maker") before playing Jenny in the *HCTB* episode, "Man of the Family." Jenny's sophistication and seductive manner make her a very good romantic partner for Jason Bolt.

Post Brides, Tompkins guaranteed herself a permanent place in *Bonanza* history when she portrayed Janie Lund — a troubled pyromaniac who is soon to marry Virginia City Deputy Sheriff Clem (series semi-regular Bing Russell) in the September 13,

*"Man of the Family" guest Angel Tompkins in a Universal publicity portrait.*

1970 twelfth-season opener, "The Night Virginia City Died." Written by the series' story editor and frequent episode writer John Hawkins, "Died" gave Tompkins the unique opportunity to burn the entire town of Virginia City down to the ground. (The episode was devised by Hawkins for the express purpose of destroying the old

Virginia City sets at Paramount Studios; the *Bonanza* company then moved into their new home at Warner Bros.) Tompkins was excellent as Janie, and garnered plenty of audience sympathy, thanks to flashbacks which showed how the young Janie has been tortured by her pyromaniac father. Unfortunately, as was so often the case with the serious love-interests of the Cartwrights and their friends, Janie did not survive to the end of the story.

Two years later, Angel Tompkins began the regular series role of telemetry specialist Gloria Harding in the 1972-73 Gene Roddenberry-created, Hugh O'Brian/ Doug McClure/Tony Franciosa spy adventure *Search*. Her frequently jealous wisecracks concerning O'Brian's flirtation with Elke Sommer gave the series' 1972 pilot some of its funniest and best scenes.

Other memorable television work included the 1971 *O'Hara, U.S. Treasury* premiere episode, "Operation: Big Store" and "The Concrete Jungle Caper," a 1974 guest shot on Dennis Weaver's tongue-in-cheek *NBC Mystery Movie* series, *McCloud*. One of the actress's very best performances came in the 1973 cult classic, *Little Cigars*. This one-of-a-kind crime drama had gangster's girlfriend Tompkins joining forces with five midget criminals to rob a string of banks. During the crime spree, Tompkins falls in love with the midget's leader, Billy Curtis.

*Leading Lady Bridget Hanley:* "She was another great beauty. I look at her now, and I think of all the gifts she's given to the Screen Actor's Guild. She gets in there. She's a mover and a shaker. She gets things accomplished. I think that's really terrific. I can't tell you how honored I am as a member of Screen Actor's Guild that she is doing all that she has done, and is doing to help all of us. She's really remarkable — really terrific. And she's very strong-willed. She plays aggressive women."[35]

*Guest Star Don Pedro Colley:* "I did a western heritage show in Asheville, North Carolina, and met Angel Tompkins there. She had a husband — I wish she hadn't — she was so much fun. She really seemed to like me — she came over and threw her arms, her whole body around my neck and crushed me, 'Oh God, Angel,' and she's really a lively person — very lively person. She was just a fun gal — she liked to dance and skip along merrily with her little braids in the air — she was just a total fun person — everybody loved the hell out of her. She was couch bait in some of those assholes' minds, and she doesn't go for that. Women have such a hard way to go with that."[36]

*Angel Tompkins on the series' premise:* "I'm the proverbial optimist — in spite of my knowledge. When I was cast for the show, when I read for the show, I just thought it was a wonderful opportunity that I considered an equal cast. Women have yet to be seen on television...according to a 2000 survey, we're half the population, so we should be doing half the roles. I found this just a great opportunity for interaction of men and women, girls and boys, in that kind of show. I loved the premise — a wedding a week — that's how it was pitched, and that's how it was played. But they never lived up to their initial pitch.

"I think the only thing that limited that show, when I look back at it, was the narrowness of the scripts themselves. The storyline lost its focus, it needed that — it really needed that story — a wedding a week. Dealing with forests and lumber... it really needed some second-unit work — the camera angles just got shorter and shorter, and there was more talking, and I think that...well, *Gunsmoke* and *Bonanza* always kept the story out and wide, and *Here Come the Brides*, which had a lot of promise of doing that, of becoming a cultural city within a city – it didn't happen. I don't know why it didn't happen.

"If you did those stories today, the story now, in retrospect, certainly would have been about maybe the women themselves — their pasts, their stories, and I don't recall, but I think maybe men were writing those stories. Mail-order brides, at that particular time, if they had brought more reality [and explored] the reason why women would even answer such an ad, and go through the condition and the situation of getting there, hopefully alive, and not diseased, and not injured by the elements, their stories would have been... if they were told more truthfully, a bigger story, a more interesting story; it wouldn't be, 'Here is one tall lady,' it would be, 'Here is a woman on her last leg, the woman abused by her stepdad; running away, half-breed women who didn't fit anywhere. It could have been storylines of women looking to fit, looking to make a contribution, looking to have a life, looking to build their own home, looking not to get married, but just living in a community differently than where they had come from; [securing] more work opportunities; hopes of maybe getting a husband or not, [or] taking someone's money on false pretenses to go set up their own business, their own store, the bride — at the last minute — telling the truth. Those kinds of stories would have been authentic soap opera of that time and era."[37]

To help illustrate her point, Tompkins brings up the example of the real-life Harvey Girls (popularized in the 1946 Judy Garland MGM musical, *The Harvey Girls*). The Harvey Girls (who hailed from North, South, and Midwest America) were brought to the Southwest portion of the country to work in the chain of restaurants/hotels businessman Fred Harvey established along the Santa Fe railroad line in the late 19th Century. Harvey's purpose was to offer passengers on the Santa Fe a good meal at a reasonable price in comfortable surroundings. Recruiting women from 18 to 30 through newspaper ads, Harvey demanded that they be of good morals, somewhat educated — at least possessing an eighth grade education, exhibit good manners, and be clean and articulate. Those hired had to agree to a six-month contract, to not marry during this time, and follow all company rules and regulations. Upon employment, each woman was given a rail pass so as to reach the restaurant the Company had chosen for her.

"*The Harvey Girls* showed how women were brought on a train, conditioned to standards of conduct and dress [and learned] how customers [in a restaurant] need to be treated," explains Tompkins. "They set the tone, later on in years, for retail in the service industry, to get [for] the person who could afford a ticket or a hotel or a meal outside of their own home a way of being serviced that was consistent. They [Harvey Girls] could be relied upon. They created a reputation for the owners of a store or restaurant or the service company, created the basis for our retail. When you think about that, that's what the Harvey Girl was kind of doing — letting the world know there are ways of producing standards and practices that allow customers to come back and seek satisfaction. As opposed to, 'Take it or leave it. We have one lovely bride. Either you want them or you don't.' Those stories in *Here Come the Brides*...and I don't think television was ready for it, maybe William Blinn, who is a terrific writer, maybe those are things he pitched.

"Where was the storyline about the woman who came under false pretenses just because she wanted to be on her own? Or, somebody who just turned around and changed her mind, and said, 'You know what? I just don't think I'm interested. In fact, I like one of the girls here.' Where were lesbians during that time? I don't know. It wouldn't have been new to me, but it certainly would have been bold. It would have caused a ruckus. Lesbians at the time would have been the old maid — too attached to her sister. That's how lesbianism [was depicted then]...

"I still look at that storyline — that series, watched it after I guest-starred. I grew up on stories — on many women's stories — that's how I decided I was gonna be an actress. That's why I didn't get to do *Wonder Woman*. Had I known if I'd just combed out my hair naturally and not highlighted it so it looked blonde, I might have had a chance. But you went with what sold at the time, and being pretty at the time — is a blonde image. Sure I watched it. I got [the first-season DVDs]...the reason why I mainly watch it is because in that episode, in that moment, for me, they on the set epitomized everything that I thought women were supposed to be like."

*On "Man of the Family" Director E. W. Swackhamer:* "Unlike some others, who are really technicians, he was always open to rehearsing, he was always open to trying something different and new. He had a great...I considered his mind kind of like a Cinemascope mind. He always had limited...on the backlot in the Columbia ranch, he had a limited amount of camera-moving space. He always made the shots look larger and bigger and gave it an open feeling of the countryside."

*On the three male stars:* "David Soul was always in his trailer practicing on his guitar, and Bobby was always singing and strumming in another corner, and Robert Brown, who was a remarkable man, was always busy on the phone with his brother, who eventually went out and bought oil tankers. What a world."

*On Robert Brown:* "He was a very sweet man. He was the male lead, but, unlike most Hollywood style handsome male leads, he had a warmth about him, rather than just a sexual edge. When he looked at you, he actually spoke at you, and spoke to you. As opposed to Hugh O'Brian; Hugh O'Brian never passed a mirror that he didn't admire and examine his teeth. Robert wasn't like that. He was just really comfortable in his skin. Robert Brown was just there and he appreciated terrific actors, and he appreciated the other actors who did well, and he loved to interact; Robert was in the moment. Good acting, good actors, are always together, in the moment. He didn't worry about his hairdo, he didn't worry about his clothes; he didn't have a lint brush around him. Nobody did. Everybody was there.

"A lot of the lines had to go to Robert, and, so he was constantly working on his lines. He was also constantly working with his brother on the phone, and a few years later on, when I saw him, I asked, 'How come you're not doing a series?' because I think if anybody had a lifelong career, to go into one show to the next, it would have been him. He said, 'Oh, my oil tanker's with my brother in Hong Kong.' So, they were in the oil-trucking business.

Told of the alternative title Brown thought might have applied to *Here Come the Brides: The* Way it Ought to Have Been," Tompkins replies, "He's right. He's right. But, that's also the way he was. He was very unpretentious. He was a genuinely personable and good man. His character had the same persona without the tinge of evil that the character on *Nip and Tuck*, on *Charmed...* [had] — he plays the devil. He [Brown] surprisingly just had other choices that he chose to make in life — not just be an actor. But I thought he would have been one of the finest."

*On co-star Bobby Sherman:* "Bobby was very, very intense and professional. He was concerned about hitting his mark and doing the best job that he could — he had to be, because he played one of the younger brothers; he had to be energetic and enthusiastic. Any time he got a chance to sit down and be quiet, [he did so]."

*On co-star David Soul:* "David Soul was the one who talked to himself most of the time. I'd say he was learning to play the guitar. He was kind of introverted, kind of introspective. That he later went on to do *Starsky and Hutch* was a surprise because he had to be so outgoing."

*On Leading Lady Bridget Hanley:* "Bridget was just a charming lady. She expressed to me that she was just glad to be there, and was surprised that she was there. She wasn't dating Swack at the time. There was some kind of affection, at least in eye contact. I don't think that anything had transpired."

*On Veteran Actress Joan Blondell:* "The woman who was remarkable was Joan Blondell. She was just a live wire and a pistol and a grand lady. She was gracious with her time — she loved talking about acting. She was fully there at every take. Nothing shy about her at all. I really admired her."

*On her portrayal of Jenny:* "I was told at the time that I was being hired to be the love interest of Robert Brown. When you're the love interest of a star, you think you're gonna be brought back, if nothing else, someone to remember. There's a storyline that they could have picked up, a thread somewhere, but evidently, I was not gonna get lucky after that. I wasn't gonna have anymore than a glimpse and a taste at the picnic. There was sort of a hope and a promise that I had, that I'd given myself — if I really do, if I really do a good job, you get that from your agent, you move forward every week on hope, and a promise to yourself. I hoped that I had done a good job, that, since my character wasn't being married off, I was just being introduced, that if the show continues, I could be brought back as a regular. But the show moved on and got canceled. Until I actually saw the DVD, I didn't appreciate how good I was."

*On the lasting appeal of* Here Come The Brides: "I didn't see a lot of marketing for the show, and I don't know why. If the [first-season] DVD is selling well, then guess what? Today's audience is looking for that. For that time. Looking for that presence. Looking for that era. For something that touches them."[38]

## *Writer: Jo Heims*

Born January 15, 1930 in Philadelphia, Pennsylvania, Jo Heims had written the movies, *The Girl in Lovers Lane, The Threat, The Devil's Hand,* and *Navajo Run* before moving into TV to write for such series as *The Fugitive* and *Bonanza.* Heims' *Fugitive* episode, "Corner of Hell" (guest-starring future *HCTB* guest R.G. Armstrong) was one of the series' classics. The story had Dr. Richard Kimble's (David Janssen) perpetual nemesis Lt. Philip Gerard (Barry Morse) following him into the backwoods moonshine country. There Gerard is suddenly thrust into a situation which closely mirrors the circumstances which turned Dr. Kimble into a fugitive. Post *Brides,* Heims penned such movies and TV-movies as *Play Misty for Me, Breezy,* and *Nightmare in Badham County.* She died April 22, 1978 in Los Angeles, California.

***Trivia:*** KSTW (Channel 11 in Seattle) used the scene of Miss Essie falling in the mud puddle in their on-air promotions for the series; Gaddings was the last name of the reverend in the 1961 movie musical script for *Brides.*

***End Note:*** Given the number of women in "Man of the Family," and the little portraits that are presented of Angel Tompkins' Jenny and Elaine Joyce's Debra Whitfield, in addition to the fuller one of Loretta Leversee's Polly Blake, it's understandable why Tompkins felt the show could have done a "bride a week" story. The number of bride characters she has sketched above while discussing the series' premise, is fascinating. Had *Brides* followed this route, an even more unusual television series would have resulted.

October 19, 1968 – Joan Blondell on *The Dating Game*

October 20, 1968 – Bobby Sherman on *The Joey Bishop Show*

October 21, 1968 – Joan Blondell on *The Joey Bishop Show*

## Episode #5: "A Hard Card to Play"                 *October 23, 1968*

"And Jason…when those cards come and I charge, brother, step aside!"
*Joshua Bolt to his brother, Jason*

| | |
|---|---|
| Writer | William Blinn |
| Director | Bob Claver |
| Film Editor | Asa Clark |
| Assistant Director | Michael Dmytryk |

*Guest Cast*

| | |
|---|---|
| Lorenzo Mack | Phil Bruns |
| Felicia Mack | Sheree North |
| Lucy Dale | Helen Page Camp |

Corky . . . . . . . . . . . . . . . . . . . . . . . . . . . . . . . . . . . . . . . . . . . . . . . . . . Christopher Stone
Bear . . . . . . . . . . . . . . . . . . . . . . . . . . . . . . . . . . . . . . . . . . . . . . . . . . . . . Allen Jaffe

*Teaser:* Corky, Big Swede, Jason, Josh, Jeremy, Jason's men, Candy, Biddie, Lorenzo Mack, Felicia Mack, Clancey, Bear, Lottie.

*Tag:* Jason, Josh, Jeremy, Aaron.

*Competition:* National Geographic special, "America's Wonderland: The National Parks," CBS; *The Virginian*, "Image of an Outlaw," guest-starring Don Stroud and Amy Thomson, NBC.

*Notes:* The first of many episodes written by story editor William Blinn, "A Hard Card to Play" does much to establish the Joshua Bolt character. During the course of this episode, it is revealed that Josh is the practical and patient member of the family. He is the one who sets up the Bolt Brothers' logging camp books, the one to set up the timetables and schedules for the completion of projects. Being quieter and lower-key than Jason, and more cautious than Jeremy, Josh is the ideal Bolt brother to take on a professional gambler. In fact, the scene in which an irritated Josh finally releases his pent-up frustration with the reckless and enthusiastic gambling of his brothers, is perhaps the best scene in the entire show. David Soul plays it for all its' worth.

"All right, Jason, I'll say it," Josh begins after Jason asks him to explain why he's been so annoyed with their gambling. "You're both rotten poker players. Look, I watched you last night. Jason, you don't care what happens. You just want to be SPECTACULAR! You bluff too much and you, you stay with cards that don't have a prayer. And *you*," Josh says to Jeremy, "you never listen to the other bets and you don't know the odds on helping in a draw. Fact is, you're both the worst kind of card players. You don't care if you win or lose. You just want to look good." Soul's gestures and expression as he delivers the last line is priceless. The performances of Robert Brown and Bobby Sherman add further to the scene.

Henry Beckman and Susan Tolsky also have some fine moments (the scene in which 'Biddie Cloom' teaches the brides how to play poker adds yet another wrinkle to an already-interesting character) as does new supporting semi-regular Lindsay Workman (beginning his role as Reverend Adams), and Bridget Hanley. Candy's unselfish donation of her mother's valuable silver to help the Bolts cover their bet suggests that, in the future, Candy Pruitt is going to be a very valuable ally for the brothers. Character actress Helen Page Camp (in the role of town busybody Lucy Dale) does very well, too.

Like the previous episode, the beginning of "A Hard Card to Play" has the audience asking themselves two questions by the close of the Teaser: first, why, given his previous behavior in the pilot episode, does Joshua Bolt so disapprove of his brothers and their men gambling? Second: why does professional gambler Lorenzo Mack keep smoothing his hair?

Two elements introduced in this show are to be used in future episodes: the "It's a ship, not a boat"/Clancey gag, and the fact that there currently exists the "Seattle Code of Civil Behavior." According to Rule 84 (on page 28), no gambling is permitted within the city limits of Seattle.

The tag of this episode sets up perfectly the episode to follow. In the tag, Jason and his brothers make it clear to Aaron Stempel that they hold no grudges against him for bringing professional gambler Lorenzo Mack to town. After all, thanks to this particular Stempel scheme, the three brothers have grown closer, the brides and the townsmen are on a new footing, and two of the Bolt brothers have "learned the value of patience."

*Story Editor/Episode Writer William Blinn:* "I enjoyed that show. Sheree North was terrific — she was very underrated. Though what she had to do wasn't all that demanding. Phil Bruns was fine. He was good.

"One of the goals [of the episode] was to give David something to do. It was pretty obvious what Robert Brown was going to do, and it was pretty obvious what Bobby Sherman's appeal was, and David was good-looking and blond. We had to find something that he brought to the table that no one else did. So this was the way we went.

"That [show] was well shot, and well done and well cast, and a whole bunch of things, and then we got to the very end. I don't know if it was the actors, or the director, or a combination of both, but the people on the set just chickened out, because originally the gambler…in my original script, was to bet his toupee, his teeth, his girdle and his lifts, so that, at the end, he was bald, without teeth, and about six inches shorter and thirty pounds heavier than he had been throughout the entire show.

"It really was…you know they tell this story about Brian Donlevy — you'd see this bald, kind of fat, short man walking in and going into the dressing room. Twenty minutes later, Brian Donlevy walked out. Well, in this show, they stopped at the toupee."[39]

## Guest Star Sheree North

20th Century Fox's "next Marilyn Monroe," after a couple of uncredited bits in Red Skelton's *Excuse My Dust* (1951) and Bob Hope's *Here Come the Girls*, Sheree North found much better employment opportunities in television. In addition to such Quinn Martin series guest shots as *The Fugitive, Barnaby Jones, Cannon* and *The Streets of San Francisco*, North played Lou Grant's girlfriend Charlene on *The Mary Tyler Moore Show* and Archie Bunker's prostitute friend, Dotty Wertz, on *All in the Family* and its sequel, *Archie Bunker's Place*. Among her 1960s motion picture credits: *Madigan*, Elvis Presley's *The Trouble with Girls*; among her 1970s films: *Telefon* and John Wayne's swan song, *The Shootist*. She died on November 4, 2005.

*Bridget Hanley on Sheree North:* "She was just lovely, just a wonderful, wonderful, wonderful woman. Such a skilled performer and so unique, and so quiet. There was no show-off there, she was just the real thing, what a personality. Whatever she did and created, who knows whether it was God or her, both of them did a good job."[40]

### Guest Star Philip Bruns

Beginning his television career on Jackie Gleason's variety show, *Jackie Gleason and His American Scene Magazine*, Philip Bruns had such quality TV series as *The Defenders, East Side, West Side*, and *Hawk* to his credit by the time he guest-starred on *Here Come the Brides*. Post *Brides*, Bruns did well-regarded films like *Midnight Cowboy* and *The Out-of-Towners*. His *1975 Streets of San Francisco* episode ("Trail of Terror," guest-starring future *HCTB* guest Meg Foster) was an excellent episode of that series; Bruns' other post *Brides* TV credits include *The Rookies, M\*A\*S\*H*, and *Hill Street Blues*.

*Bridget Hanley on Philip Bruns:* "Oh, what a good actor. Just a wonderful actor, and that face, that face. An Oooohh face. A nice 'Oooohh,' not an Uhhhh 'Ooooohh.' Just a pleasure, a delighted 'ooooo.' I didn't know that he'd played football. If I'd known that, I would have told him about my dad and my uncle."[41]

## Episode #6: "Letter of the Law"                     *October 30, 1968*

"We've never had a sheriff here before.
The whole thing is sort of...an experiment."
*Aaron Stempel to Sheriff Emmet Wade*

Writer . . . . . . . . . . . . . . . . . . . . . . . . . . . . . . . . . . . . . . . . . . . . . . . . . . .Skip Webster
Director. . . . . . . . . . . . . . . . . . . . . . . . . . . . . . . . . . . . . . . . . . . . .Paul Junger Witt
Film Editor . . . . . . . . . . . . . . . . . . . . . . . . . . . . . . . . . . . . . . . . . . . . Asa Clark
Assistant Director . . . . . . . . . . . . . . . . . . . . . . . . . . . . . . . . . . Michael Dmytryk
*Guest Cast*
Emmett Wade. . . . . . . . . . . . . . . . . . . . . . . . . . . . . . . . . . . . . . . . John Marley
Ethan Weems . . . . . . . . . . . . . . . . . . . . . . . . . . . . . . . . . . . . .Michael Murphy
Judge Cody . . . . . . . . . . . . . . . . . . . . . . . . . . . . . . . . . . . . . . . . Larry D. Mann
Becky Hobbs. . . . . . . . . . . . . . . . . . . . . . . . . . . . . . . . . . . . . . . .Heidi Hunt
Claude Dupre . . . . . . . . . . . . . . . . . . . . . . . . . . . . . . . . . . . . . . . James Almanzar

**Teaser:** Candy, Biddie, Becky Hobbs, Brides, Dupre, trappers, Jason, Josh, Jeremy, Aaron, Big Swede, Emmett Wade.

**Tag:** Judge Cody, Jason, Josh, Jeremy, Candy, Aaron, Big Swede, Ben, Miss Essie, Lottie, Clancey, Ethan Weems, Becky Hobbs.

**Competition:** *Daktari*, "Adam and Jenny," guest-starring Louis Gossett and Maidie Norman, CBS; *The Virginian*, "The Heritage," guest-starring folk singer Buffy Sainte Marie (in her acting debut) as a Shoshone Indian, and also guest-starring Ned Romero, Jim Davis, Karl Swenson, and Jay Silverheels, NBC.

**Photography:** in classic TV and movie western style, Big Swede makes the rounds of the town square, checkin' to make sure there're no varmints about. As he walks around the corner, headin' for the brides dormitory, the camera takes the viewer along the side of the dormitory then past the trees behind the dormitory, coming into the clearing to stop at the town jail.

*Notes:* Line producer Paul Junger Witt's first *Brides* episode as a director, "Letter of the Law" provides good character development for both Mark Lenard and Bo Svenson, and some fine comic moments for Henry Beckman, Susan Tolsky, and Lindsay Workman. With this episode, the relationship between Lenard's Aaron Stempel and Robert Brown's Jason Bolt changes for the better. Locked in a battle of wills with their new town sheriff, Emmet Wade, Aaron and Jason find themselves working together to keep Wade in check. Interestingly, Aaron has more reservations than Jason (or the other town council member, Ben Perkins) about hiring Wade. Events soon prove Aaron's reservations justified.

Also getting a lot to do in this episode is Bo Svenson. Depressed that his fiancée, Miss Essie, is considered a professional while he is seen as nothing more than a working man, he jumps at the opportunity to serve as Sheriff Wade's deputy. Swede really enjoys his new job — he calls Jason "Pardner," and is more than happy to go over the 'Wanted' posters, as per Wade's request. In fact, Swede's need to be a professional is so great that he willingly arrests such friends as Clancey. The question, and dramatic hook in this episode, is, 'Just how far will Swede go?' As this story reveals, pretty far.

Even when it came to its minor supporting characters, *Here Come the Brides* was exceptionally good in the matter of continuity. In the previous episode, Reverend Adams was shown to have played the shell game years ago in the missionary. In this episode, he winds up in the pokey on a charge of gambling — he conducted a church raffle. "Collections down again, Walt?" his old friend Judge Cody asks.

Like his predecessor, Reverend Gaddings, the Reverend Adams is a human being, only he's funnier. Not only does the Reverend whisk off Captain Clancey's hat when all of Sheriff Wade's "criminals" stand up as Judge Cody approaches the bench, he's pretty good with a comeback. "I'll drink to that," Clancey declares when the Reverend compliments Judge Cody on so quickly dispensing with Wade's absurd charges. Hearing Clancey, Wade shoots him a dirty look. "Oh, no you won't," the Reverend tells Clancey.

In addition to introducing a musical "lumbering" theme for Big Swede, and featuring black townspeople, this episode has Bridget Hanley in some great costumes. In her dress and white gloves, Candy is beautiful in the scene in which the townspeople throw a welcoming party for their new sheriff.

Moreover, in what is to become an *HCTB* tradition, a semi-regular plays a role other than his semi-regular character — in this case it's James Almanzar (the logger, Canada) as the leader of the trappers, Claude Dupre.

Ernest Losso makes his debut as *Brides'* casting director with this episode.

*Star Robert Brown:* "John Marley was a great friend — I saw him a lot. He played with me when I played in [Thornton Wilder's] *Our Town.* I was George, the young boy. Marley was the stage manager — he was the narrator, the old guy talking to the audience, telling them about this and that. *Skipper Next to God* was where we met. That's where we got to be friends. Marley was in the same group that I was in — the improvisational group. I helped him get that part in *Brides*." [42]

*Story Editor William Blinn:* "That was not my favorite episode. Johnny was good, and we did some good things in it. But it was kind of one-note in its development — there were no major surprises and no major plot twists and turns. He [Wade] came in, he was overbearing, he remained overbearing, he got more overbearing. It was well shot and well acted, though. I think the fault lies with Skip [Webster]. It was not as good as it ought to have been."

With the exception Blinn notes, of the change in Mark Lenard's character Aaron Stempel: "There's a problem with having ongoing villains," states Blinn, "and Mark Lenard...well, if you think of *The Fugitive*, it's one thing to have Lt. Gerard chasing him [Dr. Kimble] for six or eight years, or however long it ran, because he's got a job to do, and he remains convinced of the doctor's guilt, etcetera, etcetera, but they rarely had scenes together. Well, with Mark and Robert, they always had scenes together. Because they're both in the town." (As a result, Stempel became a nicer character.)

"So I think Mark's character was in some respects, a richer character [than Robert Brown's]. When Aaron was drawn to be kind to Candy, that was a little bit of a headline. When Robert was, it was just Jason being Jason." [43]

### Guest Star John Marley

Probably best known as the movie mogul who wakes up to find the severed and bloody head of his beloved horse lying next to him in his bed in the hit 1972 film, *The Godfather,* John Marley began his film career with two other crime classics: 1947's *Kiss of Death* (starring Victor Mature and one of William Blinn's favorite actors, Richard Widmark) and 1948's *The Naked City.* No surprise then that when Marley began working in television, he guest-starred on many crime dramas: *Tightrope, Peter Gunn, Bourbon Street Beat, The Untouchables, Surfside 6, 77 Sunset Strip, Hawk, T.H.E. Cat,* and *Mannix.* Marley's craggy features and tough voice and manner also made him a natural for westerns. Among his credits in that genre: *Law of the Plainsman, Rawhide, Sugarfoot, The Rebel, Laredo, Gunsmoke, Branded,* and *The Virginian.* Marley also was one of the first actors to do TV-movies — in 1968, he made the Louis Jourdan World War II drama, *To Die in Paris* and the Gene Barry/Senta Berger/Mary Ann Mobley secret-agent thriller, *Istanbul Express.*

Post *Brides,* Marley began working even more in crime dramas, along with some medical and lawyer shows (*Medical Center, Petrocelli*). He also did quality TV films like 1971's *The Sheriff,* starring Ossie Davis and Ruby Dee, played 'Moses' in 1978's *Greatest Heroes of the Bible,* Marilyn Monroe's lover, Joe Schenck, in 1980's *Moviola: This Year's Blonde,* and Leonard Bernstein in a 1981 spoof of *The Godfather* on NBC's late-night series, *SCTV Network 90.* John Marley died on May 22, 1984.

*Bridget Hanley on John Marley:* "Oh, Robert and John and Swack. John Marley — he scared the pee out of me when I first met him. He said [imitating a deep, gruff, clipped voice] 'Yeah! Hi!' What a cottonball — this [man] was like a pussycat. The first time I met him, I just thought, 'Oh my gosh,' and Robert [first time she met him], I almost fainted. He was so gorgeous!

"But John Marley. What a guy! What a guy! What a performer and what a man!"[44]

## Guest Star Michael Murphy

Appearing in more Robert Altman films and television productions than any other actor, Michael Murphy began his television career with two 1963 episodes of the critically acclaimed WWII series, *Combat;* he followed that with the 1964 TV-movie, *Nightmare in Chicago.* Shot on location in Chicago by director Altman, the movie aired as an episode of the Universal anthology series, *Kraft Suspense Theatre.* Murphy then appeared in three episodes of the critically acclaimed medical drama, *Ben Casey,* as well as Elvis Presley's 1967 feature, *Double Trouble,* played the role of a white man married to an Indian woman (*Gilligan's Island's* Dawn Wells) in the excellent ninth-season *Bonanza,* "The Burning Sky."

Post *Brides,* Michael Murphy began appearing almost exclusively in films. Among his TV-features was the critically acclaimed *The Autobiography of Miss Jane Pittman* in 1974. Among his big-screen efforts: *M\*A\*S\*H, What's Up, Doc?,* and *Manhattan.*

## Guest Star Larry D. Mann

Hilarious as the gold (and SILVER!) digging prospector, Yukon Cornelius, in the Rankin-Bass Christmas classic, *Rudolph the Red-Nosed Reindeer,* Canadian-born actor Larry D. Mann began his career playing Captain Scuttlebutt and Flub-a-Dub in the *Howdy Doody* TV series. Moving on to more dramatic fare by the 1960s, including *Big Valley, Ben Casey,* the five-part *77 Sunset Strip* episode, "5," and six episodes of the TV western, *Shane,* Mann had such films as *Robin and the 7 Hoods, Dead Heat on a Merry-Go-Round,* and *In the Heat of the Night* to his credit by the time he played Judge Cody on "Letter of the Law." Post *Brides,* Mann guest-starred on *Bonanza, Green Acres* (three times), and *Columbo,* in addition to doing much cartoon voice work.

November 1968 – KPLM, Channel 3 in Palm Springs, California, signs on as an ABC affiliate. *Tiger Beat* articles: South of the Border," "Bobby Sherman and David Soul – South of the Border"; *TV & Screenworld* article, "Pocket Guide to the New TV Shows"; *TV and Movie Play* article, "New Series Sneak Preview"

November 2, 1968 – *HCTB* PUBLICITY: *TV Guide* crossword – #3 Down: _____ Come the Brides (Vol. 16, No. 44, Issue #814). In November 2, 1968 issue, *TV Guide's* Richard K. Doan reports that *Daktari* (*Brides'* competition on CBS) will be leaving the air at year's end.

## Episode #7: "Lovers and Wanderers"        *November 6, 1968*

> "There're lots of mountains. Only one Miss Essie."
> *Jason Bolt to his brother, Josh*

Writer . . . . . . . . . . . . . . . . . . . . . . . . . . . . . . . . . . . . . . . . . . . . . . . . . . . . William Wood
Director . . . . . . . . . . . . . . . . . . . . . . . . . . . . . . . . . . . . . . . . . . . . .E.W. Swackhamer
Music. . . . . . . . . . . . . . . . . . . . . . . . . . . . . . . . . . . . . . . . . . . . . . . . . Paul Sawtell
Casting . . . . . . . . . . . . . . . . . . . . . . . . . . . . . . . . . . . . . . . . . . . . . . Burt Metcalfe
Film Editor . . . . . . . . . . . . . . . . . . . . . . . . . . . . . . . . . . . . . . . . . . . . . .Jim Faris
Assistant Director . . . . . . . . . . . . . . . . . . . . . . . . . . . . . . . . . . . . . . . . . Jim Hogan

*Guest Cast*

Tessa . . . . . . . . . . . . . . . . . . . . . . . . . . . . . . . . . . . . . . . . . . . . . . . . . . .Majel Barrett
Steve Weller . . . . . . . . . . . . . . . . . . . . . . . . . . . . . . . . . . . . . . . . . . . Mills Watson

*Teaser:* Jason, Josh, Jeremy.

*Tag:* Big Swede, Miss Essie, Jason, Josh, Jeremy, Lottie, Candy, Aaron, townspeople.

*Competition: Daktari,* "A Man's Man," guest-starring Stephen McNally and Eddie Applegate, CBS; *The Virginian,* "Ride to Misadventure," guest-starring Joseph Campanella and Katherine Justice, NBC.

*Photography:* The fade-out on Miss Essie sitting in the dark as the song, "Wish I Knew" performed off-camera by Mitzi Hoag, comes to an end. In the fight scene between Big Swede and Jason in Essie's house, hand-held camerawork enhances the action of the scene. And, of course, there is the unforgettable shot of Miss Essie and Jason looking down on the people of Seattle — despite Miss Essie's living in a one-story house!

*Notes:* The situation in "Lovers and Wanderers" is one of chain reaction. Thanks to the recklessness of Joshua Bolt, the loud mouth and short temper of his brother Jason, the pushiness of Miss Essie's friend Candy Pruitt, and the smooth, ego-boosting talk of Aaron Stempel, lovers Miss Essie Halliday and "Big Swede" Olaf Gustafson are driven apart. The continuous misunderstandings result in a lot of nice people getting hurt. Having created the mess, it's up to Jason and his brothers to patch up the quarrel between Essie and Swede. That's a none-too-easy task given Essie's misreading of Jason's kindnesses towards her, and Jason's troublemaking Scottish logger, Steve Weller (memorably portrayed by *Misadventures of Sheriff Lobo* comedian Mills Watson).

This episode is rich in detail concerning both Big Swede, and especially Miss Essie. It also wraps up the storyline, begun in the pilot episode, of Essie's strong feelings for Jason. Not to mention the same episode's storyline of the romance between Swede and Essie — in fact, the two marry at the close of Act Four.

Since Aaron Stempel tells Swede that he's the most important member of Jason's crew, one can't help but wonder if Jason mentioned this to Aaron during their battle of wills with Sheriff Wade in the previous episode. Swede being the most important member of his crew, was exactly what Jason had told Miss Essie in that story.

Robert Brown delivers a very funny performance in this show; ditto Bobby Sherman during the sequence in which Jeremy travels to Clearwater. In the ultra-clichéd, minor role of the prostitute with the heart of gold, *Star Trek* semi-regular Majel Barrett is only adequate.

*Story Editor William Blinn:* "I liked William Wood a lot — he was a good writer. Very good writer. Very good guy. And I always had — and deservedly so, a reputation for doing a lot of rewriting. With William Wood, you didn't need to do much at all. He understood the show — he was a very...poetic is the wrong word. He definitely understood the soft edges of our show. And he wrote them very, very well. Mitzi Hoag and Bo were terrific in their roles. That was very close to the kind of show that we definitely should have kept trying to do."[45]

*Semi-Regular Mitzi Hoag:* "I made a bad mistake once. There's a scene where Swede and Jason are fighting in Miss Essie's house. I was meant to hit Robert, and I had what looked like a bedpan — it was made of heavy cardboard, but it was meant to be lightweight. Robert said, 'Whatever you do, Mitzi, don't hit me in this ear,' because I had to slap his face. Well, I was very nervous about this whole scene — we had stuntmen to play the fight itself when they were breaking everything up, but I was nervous and untrained in stunt work. You're not often called upon to do things like that. I said to the stuntman, 'I'm a little nervous about this.' He says, 'You're nervous! I'm nervous working with actors!' Well, of course, I hit Robert's ear. He said, 'Ohhh. You did it.' But he didn't get angry. I never saw him do that [get angry]."

*On her song, "Wish I Knew":* "I'm not a singer. I ended up singing 'Oh, What a Lovely War,' and that was better than the Miss Essie thing. I apologized to the man; he said, 'Well, I wish you had six months of lessons.' He was just a technician who was enhancing the song. They do a lot of tinkering to make it sound better than it really sounds."[46]

## Guest Star Mills Watson

Probably best known as Deputy Perkins on the Glen Larson hour-long comedies, *BJ and the Bear* and *The Misadventures of Sheriff Lobo*, Mills Watson started appearing on television in 1968, mostly in westerns like *Gunsmoke*, *High Chaparral*, and, of course, *Here Come the Brides*. Besides guest-starring in *Gunsmoke's* only three-parter: "Gold Train — The Bullet," and ten other episodes of that series, Watson had the honor of guest-starring in the *Alias Smith and Jones* premiere episode, "The McCreedy Bust" (this episode resulted in two sequels). Watson also did the two-hour Lou Antonio *McCloud*, "Man with the Golden Hat" (Dennis Weaver's Sam McCloud being the aforesaid man) and had an interesting role as a Vietnam vet/psychiatric patient who enjoys feeding pigeons in the park in the second-season *Harry O* ("Group Terror"). His work in the 1975 Quinn Martin TV-movie, *Attack on Terror: The FBI vs. the Ku Klux Klan*, afforded him another honor. Including commercials, the movie was four hours long!

*Semi-Regular Dick Balduzzi:* "Mills I worked with again — we did another show together. He was very good in that show ["Lovers"]. He played this shit-kicker kind of character. We had a lotta laughs."[47]

*Casting Director Burt Metcalfe:* "Mills Watson I had used several times and I was very happy when he got this. You always…when you're in casting, you point with pride to certain people that you've kind of nurtured and that you really went to bat for and advocated very strongly — he was one that I would characterize that way. He went on to do *Lobo* [formerly *The Misadventures of Sheriff Lobo*] — he was good at playing dumb hicks — backwoods kind of yokels. He had a very interesting face, and he was a good actor, a very bright guy, but he really was good at playing those kinds of things, so eventually he did."[48]

## Guest Star Majel Barrett

Guaranteed a place in TV series history thanks to her association on-and-off camera with the *Star Trek* franchise, Majel Barrett co-starred with *Here Come the Brides* semi-regular Mitzi Hoag and Danielle Aubry as one of the "Three Brides for Hoss" in the 1966 *Bonanza* comedy of the same name. Barrett's second appearance on *Bonanza*, "Three Brides" featured her as tough cowgirl Annie Slocum. In Barrett's first *Bonanza* — the third season's "Gift of Water," she, farmer husband Royal Dano and their daughter, Pam Smith, receive invaluable help from all three of the Cartwright boys, not to mention their father, Ben, as the group looks for the water Dano believes to exist beneath his arid land.

## Writer William Wood

Credited writer and uncredited actor in the 1963 Debbie Reynolds/Cliff Robertson/David Janssen comedy, *My Six Loves,* William Wood had five *Kraft Suspense Theatre* episodes, plus a *Fugitive,* a *Cimarron Strip* and two *Greatest Show on Earth*s to his name prior to writing "Lovers and Wanderers." Post *Brides,* Wood wrote the December 3, 1970 *Immortal* episode, "Dead Man, Dead Man," (guest-starring *Here Come the Brides* regular Henry Beckman), in addition to contributing stories to such series as *Mission: Impossible* and *The Mary Tyler Moore Show*. Among his TV-movies: *Harpy, Outrage,* and the 1979 actioner, *Death Car on the Freeway.*

*Mitzi Hoag on William Wood:* "William Wood wrote "Lovers and Wanderers." We knew one another in New York. He was writing a novel at the time, nearby where I was living. We just kept in contact [through the years]. He came out here first [when Hoag came out]; we re-connected: I was doing a play he came to see. Since we were friends, he wrote that ("Lovers and Wanderers"). They showed the pilot to writers, then the writers [would] submit scripts. He chose to write about Miss Essie. I thought it was beautiful."[49]

## Composer Paul Sawtell

Paul Sawtell was the composer of some 312 film and television scores. Among the former: *A Date with the Falcon, Tarzan's Desert Mystery, Sherlock Holmes and the Scarlet Claw, San Quentin, The Devil Thumbs a Ride, Dick Tracy Meets Gruesome, Four Faces West, Davy Crockett, Indian Scout, Denver and Rio Grande, Kansas City Confidential, Inferno, Kronos, The Story of Mankind, The Fly, The Big Circus, Return of the Fly, A Dog of Flanders, The Lost World, Five Weeks in a Balloon, The Last Man on Earth, Faster, Pussycat! Kill! Kill!,* and *The Christine Jorgenson Story*; among the latter: *Cheyenne, Broken Arrow, African Patrol, Colt. 45, Lawman, Bourbon Street Beat, Surfside 6, Hawaiian Eye, Voyage to the Bottom of the Sea* (also the 1961 film), *The Time Tunnel, Land of the Giants.*

The Polish-born conductor/musical director/orchestrator/stock music composer began his amazingly prolific career as a composer with the 1939 Republic Pictures feature, *Woman Doctor,* starring Frieda Inescort as the title character. A year earlier, Sawtell had conducted the music for the MGM Travelogue, *Glimpses of Argentina.*

No matter the genre — be it a western, an adventure, a mystery, a horror picture, a drama, science-fiction, etc., Paul Sawtell never failed to come up with a good score. His theme and background music for Irwin Allen's *Voyage to the Bottom of the Sea* added enormously to the show (and was recently featured by one of the guest hosts on *The Rush Limbaugh Show*). Ditto his scores for *Here Come the Brides.* Given how prolific he was throughout his life, it is not surprising that after his death on August 1, 1971, there were Paul Sawtell film scores yet to be released.

***Trivia:*** Fans of the New Christy Minstrels will recognize the "Acres of Land" tune in the tag sequence of this episode. In the New Christy Minstrels' version of this tune, the song is entitled "Denver." The lyrics of "Denver" (telling of a man who's been rambling about the country, with no intentions of settling down, and then meeting a woman who causes him to do just that) would have made an ideal storyline for an episode of *Here Come the Brides.*

November 9, 1968 – *HCTB* Publicity: *TV Guide* – Television Crossword – answer to puzzle of November 2 – 3 Down: 'Here'; in the November 9, 1968, *TV Guide,* (Vol. 16, No. 45, Issue #815), Richard K. Doan reports that *The Glen Campbell Show* will replace *Daktari on* January 29, 1969.

*Author's note: As no sources are available which reveal when the following station started broadcasting* Here Come the Brides, *I have chosen to present this information with the date of the station's founding:*

*November 12, 1968 – A new station begins broadcasting, and will soon be airing HCTB:* On November 12, 1968, KSEL-TV, Channel 28 in Lubbock, Texas, begins broadcasting as an independent station; it will then begin broadcasting some ABC programs, which had previously aired on

CBS affiliate KLBK (Channel 13) or NBC affiliate KCBD (Channel 11). KSEL-TV became a primary ABC affiliate sometime in 1969.

November 13, 1968 – *Brides* pre-empted by special, *Sense of Nature* (based on the works of Rachel Carson and narrated by Helen Hayes)

November 16, 1968 – *HCTB* Publicity – in Wednesday, November 20, 1968 program listings of *TV Guide* (Vol. 16, No. 46, November 16, 1968, Issue #816), a half-page ad by Mattel Toys: "Tonight, see Major Matt Mason on 'Here Come the Brides.'"

*Author's Note: Mattel advertised on a number of series the week of November 16-22. Although the company also advertised on* Daktari *the night of the 20th, only* Brides *was mentioned in larger type for that particular night. Other series which received the large-type treatment for the week of Nov 16-22, 1968:* Get Smart, Gentle Ben, I Dream of Jeannie, The Mod Squad, The Ugliest Girl in Town, Operation: Entertainment.

## Episode #8: "A Jew Named Sullivan"                    *November 20, 1968*

"When I came out here, I thought, no — I *knew* —that I wouldn't meet any Jewish men. But I said, 'Well, I won't be Jewish anymore. And I…I thought I could do it, too. I…I was never the most religious girl in my family. But it meant more to me than I knew. It's the history. It's where I come from. And my mother, and her mother before her, and on back, thousands and thousands of years. I'm proud of that. I can't turn my back on it."
*Rachel Miller to Candy Pruitt and Lottie Hatfield*

Writer . . . . . . . . . . . . . . . . . . . . . . . . . . . . . . . . . . . . . . . . . . . . . . . Oliver Crawford
Director . . . . . . . . . . . . . . . . . . . . . . . . . . . . . . . . . . . . . . . . . . . . . Jerry Bernstein
Casting . . . . . . . . . . . . . . . . . . . . . . . . . . . . . . . . . . . . . . . . . . . . Ernest Losso
Film Editor . . . . . . . . . . . . . . . . . . . . . . . . . . . . . . . . . . . . . . . . . . . Jim Faris
Assistant Director . . . . . . . . . . . . . . . . . . . . . . . . . . . . . . . . . . . . . . . Jim Hogan
### *Guest Cast*
Rachel Miller . . . . . . . . . . . . . . . . . . . . . . . . . . . . . . . . . . . . . . . . . . . Linda Marsh
Will Sullivan (Sully) . . . . . . . . . . . . . . . . . . . . . . . . . . . . . . . . . . . Dan Travanty
Amanda . . . . . . . . . . . . . . . . . . . . . . . . . . . . . . . . . . . . . . . . . . . . . Kristina Holland
Grace . . . . . . . . . . . . . . . . . . . . . . . . . . . . . . . . . . . . . . . . . . . . . . . . Mary Wilcox
Logger (Hutch) . . . . . . . . . . . . . . . . . . . . . . . . . . . . . . . . . . . . . George Renschler
Ann . . . . . . . . . . . . . . . . . . . . . . . . . . . . . . . . . . . . . . . . . . . . . . . . . . Cynthia Hull

*Teaser:* Candy, Jeremy, Rachel, Josh, Biddie, Amanda, Grace, Jason, Clancey, Hutch, Sully, Lottie.

*Tag:* Josh, Jason.

*Competition: Daktari,* "African Showdown," guest-starring Alan Hale and Tony Monaco, CBS; *Hallmark Hall of Fame,* "A Punt, a Pass, and a Prayer," starring Hugh O'Brian and Shelly Novack, NBC.

*Notes:* Take an extraordinary and superb actress the caliber of Linda Marsh, a terrific television series writer like Oliver Crawford, mix with one accommodating male guest star such as Daniel J. Travanti, and the result is a great piece of television. "A Jew Named Sullivan" is a vivid example of director Ralph Senensky's belief that all 1960s and '70s dramatic television series were anthologies, and an equally perfect illustration of *Here Come the Brides'* executive producer Bob Claver's feeling that "each story particularly has to be about one person's problem so the audience can focus on it, and have something to pull for."[50] "A Jew Named Sullivan," despite its title, is very definitely the story of Rachel Miller (Marsh). Every character in the episode, every dramatic element in the show, is somehow or other connected to Rachel.

Rachel Miller is a very well-written, very well-played, multi-dimensional character — a woman with more than one flaw, quite a few doubts, and a sensitivity and compassion towards other people. Rachel Miller is also a character who grows. During the course of the story, she changes from a woman who isn't very religious to one who is very proud of both her religion and her heritage.

This isn't the only change. As the story continues, Rachel's feelings towards Sully switch from outright hostility to deep, affectionate love. A key factor in this change: Lottie's sudden and very serious illness. As Dr. Allyn E. Wright is out of town, it's up to Rachel (who's had some training as a nurse) to bring Lottie back to health. While Rachel doesn't believe she has the ability to save Lottie, Candy, Jason, and the rest of the town, with the exception of a few bigoted brides, are behind her all the way. "You're in charge," Jason tells Rachel. "Tell us what to do, and we'll do it." The pep talk from Captain Clancey, who makes it very clear to Rachel he admires the Jewish people, is equally surprising. The men of Seattle certainly seem to be changing their opinions when it comes to the brides of New Bedford.

But what really gives Rachel the ego boost she needs is the behavior of her would-be suitor, Will Sullivan. Given the prejudice of her former friend Amanda and some of the other brides, for all Rachel knows, Jason, Clancey, and the others may just be trying to compensate with acts of kindness. Such is not the case with Will Sullivan — after all, like Rachel, Sully is a Jew. Even more importantly, Sully is blunt and honest with Rachel. "Are you prepared to take orders from me, Mr. Sullivan?" Rachel asks Sully when he offers to stay in the sickroom and help her treat Lottie. "Long as they're the right ones, Miss Miller," he replies.

To writer Oliver Crawford and actress Marsh's credit, at no point in the story does Rachel Miller ever seem anything but human — in fact, while certainly an extraordinary woman, Rachel cannot resolve the story's most serious problem: the prejudice from Amanda and the other brides. That task falls to Jason, who, in one of the best moments of this episode (and one of Robert Brown's best scenes in the entire series), gives the extremely bigoted Amanda the talking-to that she needs.

In addition to featuring the show's first multi-dimensional one-time female character, "A Jew Named Sullivan" opens up a new dramatic area for the show — romantically involving Joshua Bolt with an interesting female character — usually somewhat troubled, and wounded in some way. (In this particular instance though, the Josh romance is merely a dramatic device to set up the love story of Rachel Miller and Will Sullivan. David Soul's failure to remember Linda Marsh underscores this point.)

Like Joshua Bolt, the Captain Clancey character is also starting to grow; indeed, when it comes to all of the people in Seattle, Clancey seems to know more about the Jewish people and their religion than anyone else.

In the first of her two guest appearances as bride Amanda, Kristina Holland delivers an excellent performance.

This episode has two great tear-jerking sequences; the first is Biddie's admission to Candy of her prejudice towards Jews, and the reasons for this prejudice; the second is the conclusion of Act IV in which the forgiving and compassionate Rachel tosses the bridal bouquet to Amanda. Through her willingness to attend the Jewish wedding of Rachel and Sully, the very bigoted Amanda has made a giant step; Rachel has the sensitivity to recognize this.

Special attention needs to be given to the aforementioned Biddie/Candy scene — this scene, perhaps more than any other Biddie/Candy scene in the entire run of *Here Come the Brides*, reveals just how close the two young ladies are. Even more importantly, it shows just what a fine actress Susan Tolsky is — no matter how many times one watches this scene, it is impossible not to be moved by her performance. Bridget Hanley's reactions throughout the scene are just right — Biddie's admission of her prejudice is, without question, Susan Tolsky's moment. Hanley does nothing to take it away.

*Executive Producer Bob Claver:* "I loved the whole idea. It was such a hip idea for a western — to start doing a story about a Jew. I thought the whole thing was very brave, and I was very surprised that we didn't get a lot of crap from the network. But there were no problems — they liked the show. I loved that episode — I just loved everything about it, because I'm a Jew. But I don't know that part of the Jewish religion, because she was really Orthodox. And once you get into — start bathing and all that...I just thought it was a terrific show; I'd never seen anything like that in a western. We all liked that show. It was kind of unique."[51]

*Story Editor William Blinn:* "Linda Marsh was excellent, and obviously, Dan Travanti was terrific. I liked that episode. That did have, for example, a curve in it. That isn't what you expect to see in a 'western comedic setting.' That was a change of pace that still kept the integrity in the series, and showed some diversity within the dormitory. Kristina Holland's being prejudiced — that put a little salt into the pabulum, and I think that's a good thing — because we were doing a very sweet show. If it's unremittingly sweet; it just tends to wear you down after a while.

"That was one of my favorite episodes, one of the titles I liked. We never got any flack about that show from either the network or the studio. I thought they might say it was too tightly focused on the religion for a broad audience. We never heard a word.

"One of the things that was consistent within the series was a demand for honesty and a demand for respect almost…I can't say totally, but almost regardless of what belief system we were dealing with. 'A Jew Named Sullivan' was treated with respect."[52]

*Series Star Robert Brown:* "It was an important thing to see, because we weren't talking, in our country, about prejudice, and maybe we still aren't — in a poetic way. Poetic meaning the way we did it; we told the story of what we hoped we would be like."[53]

*Leading Lady Bridget Hanley:* "'A Jew Named Sullivan'! There are times when the stars together in the universe, and I think that happens in film — certain actors have that magic, certain shows [episodes] have that, too — all the elements combine and create this magic. I think when all the stars are in alignment, and I mean the stars in the constellation — there's magic that can happen, and one doesn't even know exactly why. It's a combination of elements, and when it all works — and, of course, a lot of it happens in the cutting room, too, I'm not discounting that — but it's everybody from craft service to the final cut; if everything is in alignment, there is magic. And it ['A Jew Named Sullivan'] was very well done. That does make a difference. There's no question that it was a wonderful, wonderful story."[54]

*Series Regular Susan Tolsky:* "I remember the title. I remember the episode, because it was quite daring. You couldn't get away with a title like that nowadays, because nowadays, you'd be hauled into court, because it's 'politically incorrect.'

"I remember Linda Marsh being on the show. The story was not an ordinary story. The fact that they would allow a character like Biddie…to write in her that kind of depth that was a credit to them because they had to do the work [of selling the episode to the network and the audience]. The fact that they would even have considered that is something to give them credit because you're talking about an hour comedy-adventure. The fact that they went to that level is something you don't often find in not only half-hour shows, but hour shows."[55]

## Director Jerry Bernstein

Starting out as an assistant director on a number of Three Stooges comedy shorts like *Bedlam in Paradise* (1955) and *Pies and Guys* (1958), once Jerrold (a.k.a. Jerry) Bernstein started working on such Screen Gems situation comedies as *The Donna Reed Show*, *Gidget* and *I Dream of Jeannie*, he moved up to series director. As can best be determined, *Here Come the Brides* was the only dramatic series which Bernstein directed. His last known credit was the October 16, 1971 *Getting Together* episode, "Singing the Blues." Bernstein died on April 24, 1979.

*Susan Tolsky on Jerry Bernstein:* "Jerry came on. He was so reliable, extremely reliable. He knew what he was doing. He was prepared. It was like *bim-bam-boom*. We did it. I don't remember conflict with him at all. It was like he knew what he was there to do, and we knew what we were there to do. That's why he did a lot of them. He was affable and you could talk to him and laugh with him."[56]

*A Jerry Bernstein anecdote from* The Farmer's Daughter's *William Windom:* "Remember the Carl Betz show — *The Donna Reed Show?* They had a very tough, first assistant director named Bernstein, and they said to me, 'Be very careful. He's like a top sergeant. He brooks no nonsense. ACTORS! — *UGGGH!'* — You know, he was one of those guys.

"Now, in those days, I used to roll my own cigarettes out of pipe tobacco. It was before pot was well known — that was what it [the cigarettes] looked like, but it was pipe tobacco. And people reacted two ways when they saw those. Either they said, 'Oh, that's nice. Could I try it?' Or they said, 'You want a REAL cigarette?'

"So that was what Bernstein did to me — 'You want a REAL cigarette?' So I thought, 'I'll get even with him.' Well, I found one of these dried cow 'pies' on location one day. I think it was a buffalo 'pie' — very dry and crumbly, and I put a little chip of it into my pocket. It was a costume pocket and [I] brought it back to the set. I crumbled it up and I rolled a cigarette out of it. I knew what was gonna happen. He said…Finally one day he said to me, 'Roll me one of those goddamn things.' I said, 'Okay.' I went back in my dressing room and I rolled him one out of buffalo dung and myself one out of pipe tobacco, and by this time, everybody in the company knew, except him, and I lit them both and everybody silently waited to see what would happen. He took a long drag. He said, 'Ugggh! Kinda strong, ain't they?'

"Well, the company blew up, and he couldn't figure out why.

"About two days later, I'm sitting in a car with Donna Reed, with a process going on behind us, and he comes charging over just before the take. He grabs me by the shirt and lifts me up out of the car. 'You son of a bitch!' he said. 'I just found out what was in that cigarette!'

"I didn't want to start any trouble. I'm sitting next to Donna Reed, and I was [in the] wrong anyway. I said, 'Listen. Relax. I just did a *Ben Casey*, and I talked to a doctor on the set there, and he said it was perfectly harmless.' 'Yeah?' he said. 'Well, I couldn't find any buffaloes.' BAM! So he got the best of me after all.

"He told me later. He said, 'You know. I never smoked again from that day on.' So, that was a cure."[57]

### Guest Star Linda Marsh

Born February 8, 1939 in New York City, New York, Linda Marsh began her television career on *The Howdy Doody Show* playing the role of Native American Princess Summerfall Winterspring (a role originated by *Jailhouse Rock*/Elvis Presley leading lady, Judy Tyler). Princess Summerfall Winterspring was the only *Doody* puppet character to be turned into a live-action person during the 1947-60 run of the *Howdy Doody* series.

Following this, Marsh began appearing on numerous television series, playing all sorts of nationalities (Greek, French, Italian, Mexican) and everything from a mute (*Wild Wild West*, "The Night of the Howling Light") to a Native American, guitar-strumming folk-singer (*Mannix*, "Who Will Dig the Graves?"). She also appeared in the movies *America, America* (1963, for which she received a Golden Globe nomination for Supporting Actress) and *Che!* (1969), and portrayed the role of Ophelia in the 1964 John Gielgud-directed Broadway version of the Shakespeare play *Hamlet*, starring Richard Burton.

*Linda Marsh ("A Jew Named Sullivan") in the Elia Kazan Warner Brothers feature,* America, America.

Post *Brides*, Marsh continued to guest star on television, portraying the old flames of lead characters Steve Austin and Harry Orwell in, respectively, the *Six Million Dollar Man* episode, "Lost Love," and the first season *Harry O*, "The Last Contract." She also did a considerable amount of work for producer Quinn Martin, guest-starring, more than once, on the QM series *Cannon* and *The Streets of San Francisco*. Following the Bette Davis TV-movie/miniseries, *The Dark Secret of Harvest Home*, Marsh pretty much retired from acting, turning to her long-held dream of becoming a writer. Beginning as a scriptwriter for such popular situation comedies as *One Day at a Time*, Marsh then became one of the staff writers on the even more successful *The Facts of Life*. *Life* focused on a number of teenage girls attending a private girl's school. During the course of this series, Marsh (who co-wrote many a script with her writing partner, Margie Peters) moved up from writer to series producer to executive producer.

One reason Linda Marsh was so convincing and so good in the role of "A Jew Named Sullivan's" 'Rachel Miller' was that she was actually Jewish. Director Elia Kazan cited this as one of the reasons he cast Linda, Paul Mann, and Harry Davis in his 1963 motion picture, *America America*. "All of them know oppression, they all have uncles from the 'Old World' and have an affectionate relationship towards their forbears," [58] stated the director.

*Executive Producer Bob Claver:* "I'm sure that somebody like Linda Marsh, we read. I wasn't as much a fan of Linda Marsh until that episode ended. I didn't know who she was. I loved her looks — she has an intelligence, and that is a very big turn-on to me. I mean other people are into other parts of the body. I think the head is where all the appeal is. And, she's a pretty lady."[59]

*Star Robert Brown:* "It's people like Linda Marsh who make the shows."[60]

*Leading Lady Bridget Hanley:* "Linda Marsh! What a great lady. She was just terrific! We had fun. We would see each other [in] other places, too – just run into each other. She's a terrific actress. There are certain people that you hitch onto, and others that you don't...she was fabulous!"[61]

*Series Regular Susan Tolsky:* "I remember Linda being very, very nice. She was just kind of a...there was a really nice kind of soft ingénue feel about her. They hired a lot of that — a lot of those girls were like that – very soft young ingénue. She had a Susan Howard kind of look. I remember her being very nice, very pleasant."[62]

*Semi-Regular Mitzi Hoag:* "Linda Marsh did a good dialect. It was convincing because she didn't overdo it — it was a suggestion of a dialect, and that usually works better. She was good at that, but then she was doing a dialect she was familiar with already.

"Her mom [Liska March] was a secretary at the Actor's Studio in New York and so she [Marsh] was around, and she became part of the Actor's Studio; she was around actors all the time and so she...that (becoming an actress) certainly evolved out of it. But she wanted to write and be a producer. For one thing you make a lot more money; you have more control over the product, you're more in charge and she was a really strong woman. To make that jump in what was essentially a male-dominated world, was admirable.

"I remember the last conversation I had with her was after the Northridge Earthquake. She had quite a bit of damage to her house, and it was terrifying. She said, that was it, she was leaving 'L.A. and going back to New York.'"[63]

## Guest Star Daniel J. Travanti (a.k.a. Dan Travanty)

Later known as Daniel J. Travanti, the actor firmly established himself as a New York performer thanks to guest shots on such critically acclaimed series as George C. Scott's *East Side, West Side*, and Herbert Brodkin's *The Defenders* and *The Nurses*. That he was capable of comedy was more than proven by his performance as a "space hippie" on the ridiculous-but-fun third-season *Lost in Space* episode, "Collision of the Planets." The story had the long-haired Travanti and the other space hippies driving "space" motorcycles and endangering the Robinsons' survival.

Post *Brides*, Travanti guest-starred on such series as *Lancer* (his guest shot, "The Escape," co-guest-starring *HCTB*'s Robert Biheller, is held in very high regard by series producer, Alan A. Armer), *Barnaby Jones, Mission: Impossible*, and *The FBI*. In the late '70s, he hit it big with the role of Captain Frank Furillo on NBC's long-running *Hill Street Blues*.

*Bridget Hanley on Daniel J. Travanti:* "When he got on *Hill Street Blues*, I was just so happy for him because he's a wonderful guy, and an incredible actor. He was just, oh boy, he was magical and fun and dear. You meet so many wonderful people on your journey as a performer, and each time, you meet, it's like a family, especially if you're doing a series. A big, huge, special family, but every time you do anything, depending on the configuration of the cast and all of that, it's like a family, too. He just — oh, boy — I wanted to always have him in my family. Just a wonderful actor and a wonderful man and everything. I was so thrilled when *Hill Street Blues* happened for him, because he just really deserved a huge break — a big break like that on his own. He's done a lot of wonderful work."[64]

## Writer Oliver Crawford:

Story consultant for Screen Gems' *The Iron Horse*, MGM's excellent *Medical Center* and Richard Widmark's too short-lived Universal *NBC Mystery Movie* series, *Madigan*, Oliver Crawford also wrote the first-season *Star Trek* series departure, "The Galileo Seven," the first season *Fugitive* ("Ticket to Alaska" the only episode in the series where all four 'Acts' and the 'Epilog' were introduced by series narrator William Conrad), and the same series' fourth-season entry, "There Goes the Ball Game." Crawford's feature film credits included the 1953 Glenn Ford feature, *The Man from the Alamo*.

Blacklisted during the McCarthy era, Crawford had made quite an impressive comeback by the time he wrote "A Jew Named Sullivan." Post *Brides*, he then wrote for such series as *Love, American Style*, *Land of the Giants*, *Kojak*, and *Petrocelli*. In 1985 he produced the small screen version of his own novel, *The Execution*. In 2003 he published the sci-fi novel, *The Last Generation*.

A longtime baseball fan and baseball player, Oliver Crawford died on September 24, 2008, aged ninety-one. Fortunately, this author had the chance to inform him of the high regard in which the makers of *Here Come the Brides* hold his one and only episode of the series before his passing.

*Executive Producer Bob Claver:* "Oliver Crawford? That's not a Jewish-sounding name. I would have to guess he isn't. But that's an interesting place to go for a writer. Imagine doing a western on a subject like that! It was dynamite!"[65]

*Story Editor William Blinn:* "Oliver Crawford was interested in the Jewish culture. That is true, that's absolutely true. As I recall, that's a big part of Oliver's nature and character, and where the story came from, I don't recall. I'm sure Ollie came in and pitched it. I don't remember doing a huge rewrite on that, but it's been awhile. Ollie was always a good guy to work with. He can be a curmudgeon (as *Fugitive* co-producer George Eckstein has stated). But that's fine. If you know that going in, it's not a problem."[66]

*Series Regular Susan Tolsky:* "You couldn't do what Oliver Crawford did in that show now — you can only do it now in a [documentary]. You really couldn't write stuff like that. To have something said like that, you'd have to do a documentary. You can't put that stuff in a show now, because of politically correct [attitudes], because somebody's gonna get up and start picketing the studio. It's just stupid — it's gonna be offensive to somebody. You know I wish these people would go get a life, and stop worrying about where they can picket."[67]

Big Valley *Producer Arthur Gardner:* "Oliver Crawford is terrific. He's still a dear friend of mine — I still talk to him occasionally. He was a neighbor of mine. Oliver and his wife and my wife were very, very friendly. He was, *is,* a very, very solid writer, a nice man. I can't praise him enough."[68]

*Bridget Hanley on The Series' Guest Writers:* "For a lot of the guest writers, it's easier to create your own character than it is to keep fresh characters that were created by someone else. I'm not trying to take anything away from anyone — what I'm saying is it's kind of a gift to create their own person in the midst of all the givens. I would think that for any guest writer, it's nice to be able to create your own. For all of the other characters, you have to try to go with some of the givens, you can't just recreate them — you have to give them the same essence and the same persona in certain respects. You can go outside the boundaries, but you can't reinvent. But with your own guest characters, you're free. It's like being given your own dream."[69]

November 23-29, 1968: Henry Beckman plays Brown in "The Governor's Mansion" – this week's episode of the religious drama, *Insight.*

## Episode #9: "The Stand-Off"      *November 27, 1968*

> *Candy Pruitt:* Ooohh. If there were only some way of
> keeping men from doing stupid things.
> *Essie:* There is. But it's mean.

| | |
|---|---|
| Teleplay | Don Tait & Skip Webster |
| Story | Don Tait |
| Director | James B. Clark |
| Casting | Burt Metcalfe |
| Film Editor | Asa Clark |
| Assistant Director | Michael Dmytryk |
| Music | Paul Sawtell |

### Guest Cast

| | |
|---|---|
| Charlie Bates | Gary Dubin |
| Chips | Gordon de Vol. |
| Lu Ann | Stefanianna Christopherson |
| Ox | Don Pedro Colley *(Special Guest Star)* |

*Teaser:* Josh, Jeremy, Aaron, Ox, two toughs.

*Tag:* Candy, Jeremy, Ox, Lottie, Jason, musicians.

*Competition: Daktari,* "Once Upon a Fang," guest-starring Glynn Turman and Adolph Caesar, CBS; *The Virginian,* "Dark Corridor," guest-starring Judy Lang and ventriloquist Paul Winchell, NBC.

*Notes:* If "A Jew Named Sullivan" called attention to the *Here Come the Brides* series by taking the television western in an uncommon direction, the following episode, "The Stand-Off" underscored the unique qualities and dramatic possibilities that came with a large, regular female cast. Only in *Here Come the Brides* could such a storyline have worked.

*Robert Brown and Gary Dubin in "The Stand-Off."*

"The Stand-Off" is *HCTB's* version of the anti-war Greek comedy, *Lysistrata* — loosely meaning "she who disbands armies." In the original play, written in 411 B.C. by the Greek playwright Aristophanes (the "Father of Comedy"), the title character leads the story's other female characters into barricading the public funds building and withholding sex from their husbands so as to end the Peloponnesian War and ensure peace. To achieve her objective, Lysistra takes her plan to the women of Sparta, Boeotia, and Corinth. Initially, they are opposed to the idea, but in time, all agree to the plan and swear an oath of allegiance to the cause.

Not too surprisingly, the *Lysistrata* storyline was used in more than one Hollywood film. The earliest known version was the 1955 Twentieth Century-Fox musical comedy, *The Second Greatest Sex,* starring Jeanne Crain, George Nader, singer Kitty Kallen, singer/comedian Bert Lahr, and '50s sexpot Mamie Van Doren. In this version, Crain played Liza McClure (Liza being short for Lysistrata) — the fiancée of Matt Davis (Nader).

In 1961 a German TV version of the story was produced under the title, *Die Sendung der Lysistrata,* starring Barbara Rutting and Romy Schneider. The same year, E.Y. (Yip) Harburg of *Wizard of Oz* and *Finian's Rainbow* fame, brought to Broadway his version of *Lysistrata* — *The Happiest Girl in the World.* Running for a total of 96 performances at the Martin Beck Theatre, *Happiest* starred Cyril Ritchard, Janice Rule (the one-time wife of *Here Come the Brides* creator N. Richard Nash), and Bruce Yarnell.

The following year (1962) came what was probably the best version of *Lysistrata* to date — MGM's *Jessica*, starring Angie Dickinson, Maurice Chevalier, Agnes Moorehead, and the very sexy (and often very funny) Yugoslavian actress Sylva Koscina. Directed by *Three Coins in the Fountain/How to Marry a Millionaire's* Jean Negulesco, *Jessica* made for a pretty amusing comedy.

Six years later, *Here Come the Brides* did its version of *Lysistrata* with the ninth-aired episode, "The Stand-Off." "The Stand-Off" was just as good, if not better, than its predecessors. Indeed, if taken as an individual hour of television, rather than an episode in a certain series, "The Stand-Off" holds up well, thanks to the performances of Bridget Hanley, Mitzi Hoag, and Susan Tolsky, plus the comic vignettes in which the brides rebuff the sex-starved men of Seattle.

If viewed in the context of the series, the episode is even better. By this time, all of the characters and their relationships were pretty well defined — as a result, "The Stand-Off" added yet another chapter in the Candy Pruitt vs. Jason Bolt storyline, the Candy-Jeremy romance, the marriage of Miss Essie and Big Swede, the Biddie's affection for Corky storyline, and so on.

But, good as the sex-strike angle of this episode is, the character who makes the strongest impression is Don Pedro Colley's Ox. Thanks to the performance of Colley, the friendship between former slave-turned-professional tough Ox, and young Charlie Bates (Gary Dubin) becomes just as important a plot in the show as the sex strike. The Ox character's relationship with Aaron Stempel is even more fascinating. Stempel may be a villain at this point in the series, he may be out to get the Bolt Brothers' mountain, but one still has to admire Aaron for his lack of prejudice concerning Ox. Not only does Aaron put Ox in charge of all his professional toughs; in all his conversations with him, Aaron never once talks down to the man — if anything, he respects his opinions. For his part, Ox has great respect for his opponents, the Bolt brothers. Just as is the case with Aaron Stempel, Ox considers the Bolts his equals, not his superiors. "You're a brave man," Ox tells Jason when they first meet; "Kinda dumb, but brave. I'll give you that."

A particularly nice touch in this episode is the fact that it is Candy — not Jason, not Josh, and not Jeremy — who keeps the Bolt brothers from losing their mountain. When it comes to the physical stuff, Candy Pruitt is certainly no slouch. Even when she's carrying a heavy axe, Candy can run pretty well. She's also adept at dodging folks who get in her way.

In addition to providing Ox with his own musical theme (a theme used in later episodes), this episode is the first to make extensive use of the lake. The tag of this show, where an accordion plays the series theme, as Candy and Jeremy slowly stroll across the square to the dormitory, makes for a great episode finale.

### Guest Star Don Pedro Colley

"I'm just plain Ox Nobody," Don Pedro Colley will say when introducing himself to *Here Come the Brides* fans at conventions and so forth. But 'Nobody' hardly describes the forceful elements Don Pedro Colley has brought to his television and motion picture characters, much less his supremely confident attitude towards just about anything, or anyone.

The son of a professional musician, "who played piano like Art Tatum, Teddy Wilson," in "gambling joints and houses of ill repute," and a politically minded woman who "worked her way up to Northwest Regional Chairman for NAACP for the state of Oregon, Washington and Idaho," the Klamath Falls, Oregon-born Colley planned on a career as an architect before a stay with friends in San Francisco, and then Sausalito, ignited his interest in acting.

*Don Pedro Colley ("The Stand-Off") as voodoo god Baron Samedi in American International Pictures' Sugar Hill.*

At a friend's suggestion, Colley auditioned for a part in a Shakespearean play. "I ended up getting one line in *Merchant of Venice*," he recalls. "It was the one line that got the biggest laugh through the entire show, so I was hooked. It hooked me right there…So the next five years I spent in San Francisco learning my craft [by studying] avant-garde writers and artists of the nineteenth century — Jean Anouilh, Chekov, Ibsen, Shaw and Shakespeare and others — I compiled quite a list in about a year and a half there. And it was a time… what they called theater of the avant-garde [what the term meant was] if you could do a part that didn't necessarily mean [or require that] you had to be Caucasian or Asian or black or whatever, you got hired. That afforded me a lot of these complete roles — it gave me a chance to paint my picture — paint the picture as it should be painted. I then began to form a plan of attack, that each time I did a play it would be a little bigger part in a better theatre in San Francisco. So, in that period, I was able to work through all of the good theaters in San Francisco. My last years or so were in the Actor's Studio where we were doing Bertolt Brecht, people like that. Pretty good stuff."

From this point on, Colley did television guest shots (*Cimarron Strip, Daktari, The Bill Cosby Show*), TV-movies (*Cross-current*), and motion pictures (*Beneath the Planet of the Apes, THX 1138*). TV series roles as a regular included the Canadian trapper Gideon on *Daniel Boone*, and the no-nonsense Sheriff Little on *The Dukes of Hazzard*. A man who always held his own and who was never intimidated by big stars like Charlton Heston or Clint Eastwood, Colley won the *Dukes* part of Sheriff Little in his usual forceful way. "I had to go and meet Paul Picard — the producer on the show at that time," says Colley. "I said, 'Well, I'm gonna give 'em a little extra effort.' Now, when you gotta meet the people that you're going to be hired by, you usually try and bring in not only the essence of the character that you're essaying, but sometimes almost a full-blown performance. So, I went home and got my cowboy boots — tallest ones I had. I put on my slacks and a dark shirt and a cowboy tie, big leather jacket and a cowboy hat, and went over to the office for the interview. He's in the inner office, so I'm sitting with my hat in my lap and flirting with the secretary. Then she says, 'Okay, Mr. Colley, you can go in now.' So, I put my hat on, took a couple of deep breaths and when I walked in the door, I walked in the door and slammed it behind me, and just stood there, ice-cold! He was fiddling with papers on the desk and so forth, and it so shocked him he had to stop and look at me, and when he looked up, his eyes got as big as saucers. I didn't move. I didn't let it go at all. Then he starts fumbling. He says, 'Oh. Your name is Don Pedro Colley, isn't it?' I didn't answer him. 'Oh, let's see. Oh, yes. You're reading [for] Sheriff Little, aren't you?' I didn't answer him. I'm just standing there — ICE-COLD! Like, 'Any minute, you will be arrested, buddy! Cuz that's what I'm here for. I'm just waiting for you to mess up, cuz I'm gonna take you off to jail!' And he's fumbling and fumbling, and it was funny. So, we started to read the script, and he had to read with me — one section, it called for me to cock my shotgun. At the same time, I'm saying to Roscoe and Boss Hogg, 'COWCHIPS! You guys are lying to me! COWCHIPS!' I'm thinking, 'Well, I don't have a shotgun, but, if I focus the concept of [the word] 'cowchips,' you can almost make it sound like a shotgun cocking. So, we got to that part, and that's what I did, I said, 'COWCHIPS!' He jumped in his chair. When he said, 'Okay, that's it. That's the end of the scene. Thank you,' that's when I broke. I took my hat off. I said, 'Thank you,' walked over and shook his hand, 'Thank you, Mr. Picard.' He was completely dumbfounded. I left the office. I went back over to Leonard Kaufman's office. I said, 'Thank you for giving me the opportunity.' By the time I got home, I had a phone call. They said, 'Get back over to the studio and start getting fitted for costumes.' 'Oh, all right.'"

"So," notes the actor, "I got twelve episodes out of 147 that were devoted to, or focused around, Sheriff Little. [And in those twelve episodes], something may be going on. You may only see me twice, or three times, in that particular episode, but whatever's going on, everybody's running and hiding and trying to get around Sheriff Little. That was a good show."[70]

As was *Here Come the Brides*' "The Stand-Off."

*Guest Star Don Pedro Colley: "Here Come the Brides* was great fun. They had originally wanted Woody Strode to play this character [Ox]. But Woody said, 'I only do movies.' 'Well, yeah,' they said, 'but it's a guest star…Special Guest Star…' He said, 'NO!' He didn't want to. There was that stigma that, 'You're only a television actor.' He felt that, and in those days it was true, that, if you're a movie star, you don't go backwards and do television. It was kind of an unwritten whatever — if you came up through television, and you could make it into the movies and be a movie star, you wouldn't go back to television. Well, that's not really the essence of acting, but that's how it went down. So they wanted Woody Strode, and he said, 'No,' and I was second in running for this part. I came in and gave 'em a pretty strong audition. They said, 'Okay, let's go to work.'

"My God!" Colley exclaims. "It was really fantastic! The character was incredible in that it was like a theater production — a theater piece. It had a beginning, a middle, and a climax at the end, so it was a complete character in the script. Each level...you could perform each level, and the audience had a chance to see him changing from being just a hired-for-money dummy to somebody with a real feeling, a real soul for his friend Charlie Bates — the orphan in the town."[71]

Colley's performance as Ox illustrates just how much an intelligent, thinking, guest star can improve an episode.

"I was a 'good' bad guy," states the actor, "So, I figured, okay, you can be two levels, but why not make it six or eight levels? Okay, I'm the bad guy hired by Aaron Stempel, but, he [Ox] meets this orphan boy, and they have this nice, long talk, and they find that they're both orphans, really, sitting there fishing and talking about life and things — there's levels three and four right there. Ordinarily most bad guys in the movies...you never see that. So each time I went to a new level, I tried to give it another shading of the main character. So, in the end, the transition, when he stops everybody and says, that 'I cheated and I used my father's axe,' it doesn't come as such a shock, but it answers your questions right there. [*TV Guide*'s] Cleveland Amory got the idea, and gave me a good write-up. When Cleveland Amory reviewed the show [*Brides*], he said there was this one episode, and he gave me the whole paragraph. I was floored — pretty proud, but I was floored cuz, even today, when things come back my way, I do not expect them so I'm totally honest about it. Wow, that's too neat."[72]

Colley's work also impressed executive producer Bob Claver, as Colley recalls: "He was an average-sized guy with thick horn-rimmed glasses — black horn-rimmed glasses, as I kind of remember. I didn't speak to him too much, but some, and he was very supportive of me. I had tremendous respect because I was with my first agents, and my agency had tremendous respect for character people throughout the industry — that always gave me a kind of first class wherever I went. I never tried to abuse it ever. Anyway, the few times that I spoke to Claver...well, it's a pretty unique thing when a producer, or writer, comes up and says, 'I really like your work, and I really like what you're doing.'"[73]

When Colley showed the episode to other people, and they saw "the really wonderful scene, when Charlie comes to stop me when I'm walking out of town — it was a good, touching..., they said, 'It brings tears to my eyes.' Oh, well, I think I did my job then."

Colley definitely enjoyed working with child actor Gary Dubin. "He was trying very hard to be a performer, and we talked about it a little bit and I came up with, 'Just relax and be natural. Just be natural. Don't act it out. We'll work off of each other,' and it was fun. Because Gary comes into my tent the first time, then we go fishing, and we talk about our backgrounds — it was very touching and very nice. Very nice. Although he was a little hard to run with like he was a football under my arm there. There were so many innovative things that we did on that. That's what made it so much fun."

During the shoot, Colley spotted singer/actor Dean Martin. "Warner Bros. had a little ranch just about five blocks from the main studio — it was called the Columbia Ranch originally. Columbia Pictures used it a lot. While we were doing that, Dean was on the set doing something or other. I was very shocked at how short a guy he was — a little guy. Couldn't have been five-foot-seven, five-foot-eight."

Although Colley had scenes with her, "I didn't know who Joan Blondell was until years later. I had no idea. It wasn't until later after seeing her in other things that I realized she was in *Here Come the Brides*. Cuz I just basically came to work and did my job. I said 'Hello' to Bridget and told her I remembered her from San Francisco, had a few quick laughs with Sue Tolsky."[74]

*On Series Star Robert Brown:* "They hired Robert Brown because he sounded a bit like Richard Burton, and he looked a bit like Richard Burton. He wasn't what you call a real strong actor, but he had the English accent – he had the same kind of voice timbre that Burton did. That's how he got in the job, I think. He was kind of locked into that strait-jacket. It was kinda tough. He got the best out of it for what it was. Whether it could have taken a little more strengthening in the writing or the filming of it can be debated on many different levels. He got the best out of it that he could. Maybe a stronger performer could have found other things to do.

"He was a nice guy. The sequence where we're supposed to chop down the tree as part of the big thing, I met him years later, and he was laughing. He said, 'Goddamn, the day we had to chop down that tree…I thought we were gonna do the tree-chopping thing — I thought we'd go out and hit the tree with an axe and take a couple of whacks, knock off a little piece of bark or whatever, and it'd be okay.' He says [to the people around them], 'He's got this huge monster — pieces of wood flying off the edge of this tree — bang, bang.' He says, 'You were actually trying to bring that tree down, weren't you?' I said, 'Well, yeah. I'm a lumberjack and I've done this thing before.' He said, 'You were about to embarrass me. I'm kind of throwing the axe at the tree like an actor.'

"I was actually chopping the tree down! I really did want to do that. We had a big laugh over that."

*On co-star Bobby Sherman:* "Bobby Sherman. He was just a young kid that was there. The few fans that came around — they would go crazy over Bobby Sherman and I didn't know…he was this young rocker or whatever. He was just a… when we all rehearsed the scenes that we had to do, he was trying to learn — he was learning everything he could possibly learn; he really wasn't an actor. He was just this musician kind of thing that fell into [acting]."

*On co-star David Soul:* "That was the first time I met David Soul. I got along with David. David was blond and pretty and thought the world should stop around David Soul. Even his partner, [Paul Michael] Glaser, was a little bit like that — Glaser was a bit erratic at times. David Soul might have been a little out of the circuit because Bobby Sherman was so well known; David was trying to be a star. David was off being a star."

*On co-star Mark Lenard:* "That was really fantastic. That [*Brides* episode] was the second time I worked with Mark. When we did *Midsummer Night's Dream* at the Inter-City Cultural Center, he played Oberon, the king of the fairies, and I said, 'Gee, this guy's got a wonderful voice — deep, wonderful resonance to it, and he's an actor, a really good actor.' When he got the part of Aaron Stempel on the show and I got on the show, God, it was old home week. It was all hugs and kisses and jumping up and down. 'Wow! Great to be working with you again!'

*On leading lady Bridget Hanley:* "Most of the gals on the show were friends. I had known Bridget Hanley. I had seen her work in San Francisco before I got to L.A. and I said, 'Gosh, this girl has…Boy, she's got it!'"

*On series regular Susan Tolsky:* "Sue Tolsky! The cute, funny one. Cute as she could be."

*On semi-regular Mitzi Hoag:* "And one of the other gals…Mitzi Hoag, I thought, 'She's gonna be really good, too. She's got a real craft.' They never really allowed her to apply it a lot. Those three gals I can remember the most: Sue, Bridget and Mitzi."

*On semi-regular Buck Kartalian:* "Bucky Kartalian! He was in the *Planet of the Apes*. I didn't know him then. I met him when we were doing *Here Come the Brides*. We started conversations, started talking. I met him several different times at these conventions. He was always full of energy and jumping up and down. Buck is a nice guy. I really did like him. He had a chance to act — to be an actor, as it were."[75]

*Leading Lady Bridget Hanley:* "He was so lovely and fun and big, just big — a wonderfully sensitive guy. He was really — he was just a lovely human being and a wonderful actor. And fun. I remember there were a lot of jokes and quips and things which made it really, really fun. I've run into him through the years just a couple of times. As we age, we change. He doesn't really. Or didn't. We'd give each other a big hug."[76]

*Semi-Regular Mitzi Hoag:* "Don Pedro Colley is a really nice man. I remember we had some nice conversations."[77]

## Director James B. Clark

The brother of *HCTB* film editor Asa Clark, James B. Clark had edited nearly sixty films from the late 1930s to the mid 1950s (among them *How Green Was My Valley, Leave Her to Heaven,* and *The Desert Fox*) before beginning a career as a film and television director. Among the motion pictures he directed: *My Side of the Mountain* and *Flipper;* among his many television series: *My Friend Flicka, Lassie, Bonanza, Wild Wild West, High Chaparral,* and *Batman.* For the latter, Clark directed episodes featuring Riddler, Joker, Catwoman, King Tut, and Marsha, Queen of Diamonds.

Clark's first *Wild Wild West* ("The Night of the Hangman") was quite a departure for that series. In "Hangman," secret agents James West (Robert Conrad) and Artemus Gordon (Ross Martin) race against time to save convicted killer (Harry) Dean Stanton from the gallows. Although West has testified against Stanton, the case against the man seems too perfect — and this arouses West's suspicions. Unlike almost every other episode of the popular 1965-69 series, West and Gordon are not working for the U.S. government on this occasion — they simply walk into the situation when they decide to visit town.

James B. Clark's work on the excellent, much too short-lived 1966-67 ABC western, *The Monroes*, was unusual as well. Thanks to the on-location filming in Wyoming's Grand Tetons, the show's photography was always memorable. Clark's "The Forest Devil" (September 28, 1966), was particularly striking — at times the episode was presented from the title character — a wolverine's — point of view!

James B. Clark worked with Don Pedro Colley again in the December 13, 1968 *Wild Wild West* episode, "The Night of Miguelito's Revenge," which marked the very last appearance of the series' all-time favorite villain, Dr. Miguelito Loveless, (the little person/actor Michael Dunn). Dr. Loveless shrinks Jim West to little-people size, poses as Robin Hood and a knight in armor, and, develops a way for people to enter paintings in previous episodes. Don Pedro Colley couldn't have asked for a better *WWW* guest shot.

*Trivia:* "The Stand-Off" is the first of two shows where David Soul's arm is in a cast. According to William Blinn, Soul broke his arm during one of the *HCTB* cast and crew football games.

In 1971, Gary Dubin (Charlie Bates) played the role of Milton — the first date of Bobby's little sister, Jenny (Susan Neher) in the "All Shook Up" episode of the Bobby Sherman situation comedy, *Getting Together*.

Stefanianna Christopherson (Lu Ann) was the original voice of Daphne Blake (one of those "meddling kids") in the *Scooby-Doo* cartoons.

*Critical acclaim for HCTB Guest Don Pedro Colley:*

*TV Guide* – December 28, 1968-January 3, 1969 – From Cleveland Amory's review: "Here again, what might have been another bust-'em-down and shoot-'em-up became something very different, when one of the ruffians named Ox (Don Pedro Colley) turned out in the end to be not only the hero, but also to give one of the most memorable performances we've seen this year."[78]

December 1968: Down Mexico Way – Again"
*Tiger Beat*, Bobby Sherman article in *FaVE!*

## Episode #10: "A Man and His Magic"        *December 4, 1968*

"When you live my kind of life, one place is the same as another.
I've never stopped anywhere long enough to leave a mark."
*Merlin to Lottie*

Writer . . . . . . . . . . . . . . . . . . . . . . . . . . . . . . . . . . . . . . . . . . . . Gerry Day
Director . . . . . . . . . . . . . . . . . . . . . . . . . . . . . . . . . . . . . . . . . Harvey Hart
Casting . . . . . . . . . . . . . . . . . . . . . . . . . . . . . . . . . . . . . . . Burt Metcalfe
Film Editor . . . . . . . . . . . . . . . . . . . . . . . . . . . . . . . . . . . . . . . Jim Faris
Assistant Director . . . . . . . . . . . . . . . . . . . . . . . . . . . . . . . . . Jim Hogan
Music . . . . . . . . . . . . . . . . . . . . . . . . . . . . . . . . . . . . . . . . . Paul Sawtell

### Guest Cast

Jack Albertson . . . . . . . . . . . . . . . . . . . . . . . . . . . . . . . . . . . . . . . Merlin
Harve . . . . . . . . . . . . . . . . . . . . . . . . . . . . . . . . . . . . . . . . . George Sims
Paulie . . . . . . . . . . . . . . . . . . . . . . . . . . . . . . . . . . . . . . . . Darryl Seman

*Teaser:* Brides, Loggers, Lottie, Aaron, Jason, Josh, Jeremy, Harve, Merlin, Clancey.

*Tag:* Jeremy, Candy, Paulie.

*Competition: Daktari,* "Strike Like a Lion," CBS; *The Virginian,* "The Mustangers," guest-starring James Edwards and John Agar, NBC.

*Photography:* Act 1: Slow pan over the brides' windows in the dormitory, then down the roof to the porch where Biddie and Candy are watching Merlin; the shot of Merlin through the rails of his brass bed frame; three-shot of Merlin, Jason and Jeremy through the bed frame; tent show sequence featuring Merlin and Jeremy, Candy in background in soft focus in every shot featuring Jeremy; shot of Harve and Jeremy with bottles of elixir in foreground; shot of Jeremy being put in jail by Stempel; Paulie running around jail and through huge puddle.

Act 2 opening: Jason and Paulie come into town, walking through puddle; Jason and Jeremy walking back to camp, puddle in foreground;

*Jeremy's first apology to Candy:* totem pole at right, Jeremy at left, his back to camera, Candy in middle of shot at clothesline.

*Jeremy asks Merlin to cure him:* shot through trees of Jeremy (in profile) then shot of Jeremy walking towards camera, two-shot (through trees) of Jeremy and Merlin walking, then stopping with Merlin (back to camera) facing Jeremy, then vice versa; shot of trees as Jeremy and Merlin walk away.

*Jeremy's second apology to Candy:* shot through the steps of the brides' dormitory as Jeremy enters. Jeremy and Candy's dispute, after he quits stuttering: Candy outside dormitory, at the top of the steps at door of dormitory; the shot begins from Candy's point of view, she and the camera looking down at Jeremy; the shot switches down to Jeremy when he begins climbing up the steps to Candy, the camera moving up with him through the trees, then going down with him after he and Candy have their argument.

Act 3 concludes with a freeze-frame on Jeremy — he's just learned that Merlin has skipped town, and feeling the man is a "fake," Jeremy has now lapsed back into his old habit of stuttering. This scene in the Bolt brothers cabin, begins with Josh and Jeremy in their bunk beds, Jeremy in the lower bunk, Jason is seen through the frame of the beds.

*Notes:* Of all the *HCTB* episodes, "A Man and His Magic" is the one most similar to creator N. Richard Nash's *The Rainmaker*. Like *The Rainmaker's* Starbuck, Merlin promises he can work miracles with the weather, only, in this case, it's to *stop* the rain. This is the only episode in the series where the audience actually sees it raining in Seattle.

This is also one of the few episodes where the photography is truly outstanding. Like E.W. Swackhamer, "A Man and His Magic" director Harvey Hart is one of the few *HCTB* directors able to stage visually striking scenes which, at the same time, personalize the dramatic situation for the audience. Hart also makes good use of the sets and props – the clothesline scene featuring Jeremy and Candy calls to mind the clothesline scene between the two in the series pilot. The tent show sequence in which Jeremy is talking to Merlin underscores how much Candy is on Jeremy's mind. No matter what angle Hart chooses to shoot the sequence from, Candy Pruitt is in the background of every Jeremy shot!

*Bobby Sherman in "A Man and His Magic."*

In addition to advancing the Jeremy/Candy romance, this episode reveals that Biddie likes to drink, and further develops the Joshua Bolt character – after Merlin skips town, Josh, with no suggestion from Jason, goes after Merlin and brings him back to help Jeremy understand just who it was that cured his stuttering.

Jeremy began stuttering with the word "Amen." This same word figures very prominently in the moving second-season entry, "Absalom."

A nice aspect of this episode is the fact that Jeremy Bolt exhibits some negative qualities. Not only does he talk incessantly, he fails to keep his dinner appointment with Candy. He also has a short temper. And Candy may have a jealous streak – now that he's cured of his stuttering, Jeremy has the confidence to talk to the other brides.

*Story Editor William Blinn:* "Gerry Day [the writer of "A Man and His Magic"] was a lady. Gerry was one of the few ladies who was writing westerns. She was writing a lot of *Gunsmoke*s and stuff. Gerry was someone I had known from the old *Gunsmoke* office. She [and actress] Bethel Leslie worked [wrote] a lot together."[79]

### Guest Star Jack Albertson

Veteran of vaudeville, burlesque and Broadway, winner of an Oscar, a Tony and an Emmy, former musical star Jack Albertson had two motion pictures to his credit (1938's *Next Time I Marry* and 1940's *Strike Up the Band*) before playing the memorable bit part of the post office mail sorter in the 1947 Christmas classic, *Miracle on 34th Street*. A few years later, after doing a number of variety shows like *The Ed Sullivan Show* and *The Colgate Comedy Hour*, Albertson began guest-starring on TV comedies like *I Love Lucy* and *Our Miss Brooks*, plus more dramatic fare such as *Riverboat, Dr. Kildare,* and *The Twilight Zone*. Movies included *Man of a Thousand Faces, Days of Wine and Roses*, Elvis Presley's *Kissin' Cousins* and *Roustabout*, the Jack Lemmon-Virna Lisi-George Axelrod comedy, *How to Murder Your Wife*, and George C. Scott's *The Flim-Flam Man*.

Post *Brides*, Albertson played the title (magician) character in the amusing *Land of the Giants*, "Return of Inidu," then the role of Dr. Walter Koster – a doctor hoping to replicate the unusual, life-saving blood possessed by Ben Richards in the excellent *Immortal* episode, "Reflections on a Lost Tomorrow." There was also his memorable performance as Judge Hadley in the great *Alias Smith and Jones* entry, "Jailbreak at Junction City," Grandpa Joe in the 1971 children's fantasy, *Willy Wonka & the Chocolate Factory*, Manny Rosen in the Irwin Allen disaster classic, 1972's *The Poseidon Adventure*, and of course, "The Man" Ed Brown — in the 1974-78 NBC situation comedy, *Chico and the Man*. Jack Albertson continued to work until his death in 1981.

*Leading Lady Bridget Hanley:* "I just wanted to bow down and kiss his toes. Man, what a guy! With great style and talent and to be working with these people was just amazing. The fact that everybody...when you're working, you all have the same intent — to bring the script to life — in addition to the life that it already has on the page, but to enhance it and everything, that's really an actor's purpose. He just was like an actor beyond actors, and we had a number of them on the show. Some of them became the actor upon actors, as their career progressed — it's just wonderful to watch people grow and change, and blossom and bloom and go from one format to the other — it's really been wonderful. Every once in a while, you run into somebody and you kind of remind each other, and it's like... there're these screams — 'Oh!' which is just lovely, and sometimes there's just a nod, and sometimes there's big hugs. It's an incredible world — it ain't all perfect, and it's full of hurts and disappointments and joys and boundaries and capacities — it's just everything."[80]

*Series Regular Susan Tolsky:* "The guys I remember cuz I hung out with the guys. I remember Jack Albertson, I remember Ed Asner — these were guys who had such track records, especially Jack Albertson. Jack Albertson at that time was enormous — he had done films, he had done so many films that he was now relaxing in television."[81]

## Director Harvey Hart

Starting his career in 1952 as part of the Canadian Broadcasting Corporation's talent pool, Harvey Hart had episodes of both *Peyton Place* and *The Alfred Hitchcock Hour* to his credit by the time he directed Ann-Margret and Michael Parks in the musical comedy, *Bus Riley's Back in Town*. Though he continued to direct big-screen features, most of Hart's best work as a director came in television — among the series for which he directed: *Wild Wild West, Ben Casey, T.H.E. Cat, Judd, for the Defense* (the pilot episode, "Tempest in a Texas Town"), *The Felony Squad, The FBI* (Hart's episode, "Nightmare Road" was a favorite of the real-life bureau), *The Bill Cosby Show, Mannix, The Young Lawyers, Dan August, Columbo*. Hart directed a number of TV-movies as well, five of them (1974's *Murder or Mercy* and *Panic on the 5:22*, 1977's *The City*, 1978's *Standing Tall*, and 1980's *The Aliens are Coming*) were for Quinn Martin Productions.

*Leading Lady Bridget Hanley:* "I loved Harvey [Hart]. He was wonderful. And I did something else for Harvey too — he was just…we all wanted him to come back. I just was enamored. We all were. You know — it was, 'What do you want us to do? We're there.' Because he just had that kind of personality and that skill. That's an enormous, enormous talent. To have all of those components in one person is really unique. I mean, the photography in that is fabulous!

"Swack was like that, but he was noisier than Harvey. Lustier. He was louder. Harvey had great humor, like Swack, but he was more constrained and that's just the demeanor I was talking about. But they both were striving for the same thing."[82]

*Semi-Regular Dick Balduzzi:* "Harvey Hart did a lot of heavy episodes of things. I think I first met him when he worked with Cassavettes. Then I think he started doing a lot of episodic things, like *Police Story*; he did family things, too. He was nice — I enjoyed working with him. Some of these guys are so creative, and they know how to work with actors. That's when you enjoyed working on the shows. When you had people like that directing.

"He was very astute, really on the ball, knew his work, did his homework, and [was] very good with actors. I enjoyed him; he always had a respect for actors. He was one of those kind of directors who really worked with them well because he was an actor. He'd worked in Canada. Good directors, they pretty much know…a good director has his storyboard pretty well set in advance and knows exactly from day to day what he's gonna shoot."[83]

*Actor Peter Mark Richman:* "Harvey was a close friend of mine. We had worked together in Canada. He was very simpatico to actors — he was an actor's director, loved actors, loved what they bring to a picture. He was patient, very kind.

"Harvey was a wonderful director, well-trained from live television in Canada. He could do real long takes. He had a tendency to move the camera from one thing to the next and try to get long takes without cuts. He liked that. That's from live television — moving cameras back and forth from A to B to C to D to E to F. He died about ten, twelve years ago. Used to smoke like crazy, chain-smoker."[84]

*Director Robert Butler:* "Harvey Hart had a theatrical background, plus live television experience. His orientation was — and I remember this to be pretty true in the shows I saw of his — it was character oriented. He wasn't interested or experienced in action and production — by that I mean complex shows physically. His strength was character."[85]

## Writer Gerry Day

Co-head writer of the long-running soap opera, *The Secret Storm*, Gerry Day was writing scripts for episodic television by the early 1960s. Among the series to which she contributed: *Peyton Place, Big Valley, Judd, for the Defense, Court Martial, Laredo,* and *Wagon Train.* Post *Brides*, Day wrote for *High Chaparral, Barnaby Jones, McCloud, Hawaii Five-O, Spenser: For Hire.* Her last-known credit: *Columbo: Undercover.*

*Trivia:* Jason is heard whistling "Acres of Land" (the tune from episode #7: "Lovers and Wanderers") in the scene in the Bolt tent.

December 11, 1968 – *HCTB* episode "The Firemaker" will not be seen tonight.

## Episode #11: "A Christmas Place"       *December 18, 1968*

> *Lizbeth:* Jeremy said the Perkins baby would be just like Jesus.
> *Marcia:* If it got born on Christmas.
> *Lizbeth:* Don't you remember what the grown-ups did to Jesus?
> *Marcia:* They wrapped him in swaddling clothes.
> *Lizbeth:* First they did. But then, when it was Easter, they killed him!

Writer . . . . . . . . . . . . . . . . . . . . . . . . . . . . . . . . . . . . . . . . . . . . . . .William Blinn
Director. . . . . . . . . . . . . . . . . . . . . . . . . . . . . . . . . . . . . . . . . . Richard Kinon
Film Ed . . . . . . . . . . . . . . . . . . . . . . . . . . . . . . . . . . . . . . . Norman Wallerstein
Assistant Director . . . . . . . . . . . . . . . . . . . . . . . . . . . . . . . . . . . . Jim Hogan
Director of Photography . . . . . . . . . . . . . . . . . . . . . . . . . . . . . .Irving Lippman
                                         *Guest Cast*
Michael Bell . . . . . . . . . . . . . . . . . . . . . . . . . . . . . . . . . . . . . . . . . . . Roger
Emily. . . . . . . . . . . . . . . . . . . . . . . . . . . . . . . . . . . . . . . . . . . . . .Dolores Mann
Lizbeth . . . . . . . . . . . . . . . . . . . . . . . . . . . . . . . . . . . . . . . . .Christie Matchett
Marcia . . . . . . . . . . . . . . . . . . . . . . . . . . . . . . . . . . . . . . . . . . . . . .Erica Petal

*Teaser:* Jason, Lizbeth, Marcia, Ben, Jeremy, Josh, Candy, Biddie, Brides.

*Tag:* Ben, Jr. (the baby), Biddie, Clancey, Jason, Lizbeth, Marcia, Roger, Ben, Emily, Candy, Lottie, Jeremy, Josh.

**Competition:** *Daktari*, "The Discovery," guest-starring Mike Road and June Vincent, CBS; *The Virginian*, "Big Tiny," a comedy headlining David Hartman, and guest-starring Julie Sommars and Roger Torrey, NBC.

**Notes:** When it comes to thought-provoking, and intelligently written religious

*A Christmas Place" left to right: Robert Brown, Joan Blondell, Dolores Mann, Hoke Howell, Bridget Hanley, Susan Tolsky.*

dramas, William Blinn's "A Christmas Place" is right up there with such big-screen features as *A Man Called Peter* and 1961's *King of Kings* and TV-series episodes like *Harry O* ("Mortal Sin"), and Blinn's own seventh-season *Bonanza*, "All Ye His Saints." The subject matter of "A Christmas Place" is rather shocking — using two little girls as his villains, Blinn underscores the problems one might create in telling the story of the Crucifixion to one's child. Based on the conversation between widower Roger Hale's two young daughters (which closes this episode's teaser,) Roger and his late wife haven't done a very good job of telling this story to their children. Roger does not sense what's troubling his daughters — nor do Jason, Jeremy, Biddie, Ben, or Candy. That's because everybody is excited about the impending birth of the Perkins baby. The viewers are the only ones who know what's troubling the girls.

Wanting to protect the Perkins baby from the adults following his birth, the two little girls abduct the baby. Since the child was born on Christmas Day, the girls fear he will meet the same fate as Jesus. Interestingly, nobody in Seattle ever learns why the two kidnapped the infant (at least not on screen). Nor is there any explanation as to why Lizbeth and Marcia later exchange the child for the small statue of Jesus in the manger (in the church).

Featuring a strong performance from Dolores Mann whose Emily Perkins character unfortunately disappeared after this episode, and enhanced by some fine moments for Susan Tolsky, and the too under-used Carole Shelyne and Cynthia Hull, "A Christmas Place" is another human and winning episode for *Brides*. Other nice moments in this episode: Jeremy telling Candy she'll have to make her own Christmas in Seattle; Candy looking upward and thanking God when she learns the Perkins baby is safe; Josh tenderly putting the tiny statue of Christ back in the manger bed; Josh and Jeremy singing "The Holly and the Ivy" in the episode's tag.

This was the first of many episodes directed by Richard Kinon.

This episode also has four great tearjerker moments. In the first, Candy, Biddie, Ann, Franny, and the other brides receive Christmas presents and cards from their families in New Bedford, Massachusetts. As they read their letters and cards, the brides' mood changes from excited to sad and somber. The enormity of what they have done: left their families and homes for a new way of life, makes a sudden and powerful impact on every one of them.

In the second tearjerker, Biddie gives Candy a Christmas present.

In the third: despite the loss of her baby, Emily Perkins is determined to go to church, because "it's Christmas." Moved by her spirit and determination, the people of Seattle, and, in particular, the brides, follow suit.

Fourth, and maybe best of all, Biddie carefully puts an ornament on the tree.

*Story Editor/Episode Writer William Blinn:* "I think my favorite episode is probably the Christmas episode. I enjoyed that. I thought it was fun. It has one of my favorite jokes when Biddie rushes in and says, 'The baby's born!' They say, 'What is it?' She looks at them for a second, and then runs out again. I thought that was a really cute show. It was properly corny and sentimental at the end, but it all played.

"'How does a parent tell their child about the Crucifixion without scaring them?' was definitely one of its purposes. It's not up there in neon letters, but it's part of the fabric of the show. I liked that episode on paper, and I liked it on film.

"If there was concern about this show, I don't recall it. I think if it had been expressed to me, I would have recalled it. Cuz I would have to fight to get my way. I don't remember any big arguments — I know Bob liked the script a lot. I don't recall any major overt blowups about [the script] that had taken place. I guess I must be interested in those kinds of religious subjects, but it's a very unconscious [thing], cuz you're talking to someone who's an agnostic, if I have to define myself. Maybe [because] that's a question I haven't answered for myself, I keep trying to answer it on paper, I don't know…I think raising the question [concerning how to tell the story of the Crucifixion] made for some pretty good television — I recall liking that episode a lot."[86]

*Bridget Hanley on William Blinn's "A Christmas Place":* "'A Christmas Place' — that was fun. Bill was wonderful. He just keeps writing all these theater pieces and they're wonderful, and Lee Meriwether and I are gonna read in one of them soon. I love to read his stuff — he's just very, very talented."[87]

## Director Richard Kinon

Starting with *Four Star Playhouse*, Richard Kinon had such TV-series credits as *The Rogues*, *Burke's Law*, *The Farmer's Daughter*, *Bewitched*, *The Second Hundred Years*, and *I Dream of Jeannie* to his credit by the time he became one of the regular *Here Come the Brides* directors. Post *Brides*, Kinon did such series as *Love, American Style*, *Barney Miller*, *Wonder Woman*, and *Love Boat*.

*Executive Producer Bob Claver:* "Richard Kinon was frequently in anything I did. He is a perfect director. He's prepared, he's good, he's tasteful, he had a great sense of humor, he's a terrific director. He never stopped working, he's just one of those guys, that when you're a producer, you say, 'Well, Kinon's working next week.' So, you don't have to show up on the set. You don't have to do anything cuz it'll be fine. I thought he was a wonderful director."[88]

*Leading Lady Bridget Hanley:* "Dick Kinon I worked with tons prior to *Brides*. I mean, so much stuff! So many episodes of so many different things, and then after, too. He was always so funny. But he didn't mean it. It was part of him — it was part of his energy. We'd all say, 'Okay,' and jump on board and go. We'd all have a good time. But it was led by him. The director kind of sets the pace, sets the tone, and he always set this kind of crazy, nutty tone — I loved him. Great personality. Great persona. Great energy. And he was funny. Kind of sacrilegious in his own way. We all just enjoyed him so much cuz he created such a light. And Dick Kinon was very respectful of the writing. He'd always try to make it fun and energy-filled so that everybody was kind of at their peak in terms of their mental acuity. You really kind of totally concentrated on having a good time. He had a really good skill. He just was funny."[89]

*Series Regular Susan Tolsky:* "Dick Kinon was wonderful. I always enjoyed seeing his name come up — I was always, 'Oh, Dick Kinon's working!' I enjoyed working when Dick was working because I knew that I'd feel safe and good and it would be an easy shoot. He was a fun director. He was one of the directors that liked actors. If we did something funny, he laughed. To have a director react like that is like, 'Gosh, Wow.' He was the sweetest man. Always nice and quiet; I don't remember him [ever] raising his voice. He was just gentle and sweet and nice. And totally prepared."[90]

*Wardrobe Man Steve Lodge:* "Kinon was a sweetheart. He was great — great to work with. We had some pretty nice directors on the show."[91]

## Guest Star Michael Bell

Long active as a voice artist in animated cartoons, Michael Bell guest-starred on quite a few series before moving into that field. In addition to his two appearances as Bill Duncan — the former husband of Kate Jackson's Sabrina Duncan in the first season *Charlie's Angels* episodes "Target: Angels" (directed by Richard Lang) and "The Blue Angels" (directed by future *HCTB* guest Georg Stanford Brown), Bell guest-starred on the *Cannon/Barnaby Jones* two-parter, "The Deadly Conspiracy." He also worked in the excellent, and much too short-lived James Franciscus series, *Longstreet*, the third-season *Mission: Impossible* series departure, "The Exchange" (in which IMF agent Cinnamon Carter is captured while on assignment), the 1969 *Big Valley* "Joshua Watson" (Lou Rawls as the title character — a super cowboy/rodeo rider), four episodes of *Petrocelli*, five *Ironsides*, etc. Among his movie credits: *Airport, Brother John;* among his TV-movies: *A Clear and Present Danger* (concerning the subject of air pollution.)

*Bridget Hanley on Michael Bell:* "I know Michael very, very well, and so does Susan; he became a great voice-over person. He got married, and then had a child; she went to school very close to here, so we used to run into each other quite often. One day, there was this honking, honking, I was walking down the street, and — he'd pulled over to the curb, and there he was with his glorious daughter. And his wife is a very talented person. She's an actress and a painter. She did a lot of theater and a lot of television. He's a terrific guy. He works really, really diligently and hard for the Screen Actor's Guild."[92]

## Director of Photography Irving Lippman

Starting his career as an assistant cameraman on a 1922 Roscoe 'Fatty' Arbuckle comedy, Irving 'Lippy' Lippman enjoyed an over twenty-year career as a still photographer on such famous motion pictures as 1937's *Lost Horizon* (starring future *HCTB* guest Jane Wyatt), 1939's *Mr. Smith Goes to Washington*, the 1942 Fred Astaire/Rita Hayworth musical, *You Were Never Lovelier*, the early Marilyn Monroe feature, *Ladies of the Chorus* (1948), the 1949 Robert Rossen/Broderick Crawford classic, *All the King's Men*, and the 1953 blockbuster, *From Here to Eternity*, before moving to the more important position of series director of photography with the 1955 Screen Gems western, *Tales of the Texas Rangers*. Doing quite a few motion pictures (like the 1957 *Hellcats of the Navy* starring future U.S. president and first lady Ronald and Nancy Reagan) prior to his longtime association with the ground-breaking Screen Gems series, *Route 66*. Lippman did a couple of Three Stooges features before working with English director Robert Day on *Tarzan and the Valley of Gold*, and *Tarzan and the Great River*. *Gold* was filmed in Mexico City, Mexico; *River* in Brazil. Somehow during this time, Irving Lippman managed to squeeze in fifty-six of the fifty-eight episodes of TV's first "music video" series, *The Monkees*.

After a two-episode stint on *Here Come the Brides*, Lippman moved on to another music-based series, Screen Gems' *The Partridge Family*. After that came the Barry Newman *Rashomon*-style lawyer series, *Petrocelli*, then the sci-fi series, *Fantastic Journey* and *Logan's Run*. (On both, future *Brides* writer D.C. Fontana served as story editor/consultant).

Challenging himself to the end of his career, Irving Lippman's last two series were the huge, all-star guest cast anthologies, *The Love Boat* and *Fantasy Island*. Unique for switching back and forth between two or three stories during their running time, *The Love Boat* and *Fantasy Island* (with their multi-character stories, intricate camera set-ups, and, in the case of *Island*, increasingly bizarre plots) were the perfect coda to an amazing career. Seven days after his one-hundredth birthday (on November 8, 2006), Irving Lippman passed away.

***Trivia:*** Christie Matchett went on to play Melissa Marshall – the daughter of defense lawyer Owen Marshall (Arthur Hill) in the David Victor/Universal series, *Owen Marshall: Counselor at Law*.

December 21, 1968 – *TV Guide* Crossword – 19 across – Here Come the _____ (Vol. 16., No. 51, December 21, 1968, Issue #821)

December 24, 1968 – WJBF-TV, Channel 6 in Augusta, Georgia, becomes a primary ABC affiliate, and secondary NBC affiliate when WATU-TV, Channel 26, signs on and begins broadcasting NBC programming. Prior to this time, WJBF had been a primary NBC affiliate, with some ABC programming.

December 25, 1968 – Episode #3: "And Jason Makes Five" goes down in *HCTB* rerun history as the very first *Brides* episode to be repeated. It competes against a repeat of *The Virginian* seventh-season premiere, "Silver Image" on NBC, and a repeat of Vladimir Horowitz – First TV Recital At Carnegie Hall on CBS.

On this same day, *HCTB* regular Joan Blondell guest stars in the Darren McGavin series, *The Outsider*, in the episode, "There Was a Little Girl" on NBC, one half-hour after the conclusion of "And Jason Makes Five."

December 28, 1968 – Cleveland Amory gives very positive review of *Here Come the Brides* in *TV Guide*, Vol. 16, No 52, Issue #822.

Underneath the Wednesday program listing for *Brides* is the following: "Read the article about this series in next week's TV GUIDE."

On last page of Friday program listings is half-page ad for next week's issue with *Brides* cast of Bobby Sherman, David Soul, Bridget Hanley, and Robert Brown pictured counter-clockwise. The ad tells of how *Brides* is a "surprise hit," and how the show "isn't hip, it just has down-to-earth 'soul.'"

January 1969 – Three Bobby Sherman articles in *Tiger Beat*: His Secret Shyness," "A Happy Rainy Day with Bobby Sherman" (featuring scenes from "A Man and His Magic"); articles on Sherman and David Soul in *Flip Teen*. Robert Brown in *Photoplay Annual*: TV's New Faces," article on Brown in *Movie Stars*; Henry Beckman in *TV Star Parade*; Bridget Hanley in *TV Radio Show*, Mark Lenard tidbit in *Screenland*.

## Episode #12: "After a Dream Comes Mourning"    *January 1, 1969*

"There's only one difference between Seattle and New Bedford. New Bedford is a dream that's finished, completed. Seattle is a dream that's yet to come. And if you think building a dream is easy…"
*Jason Bolt to Candy Pruitt*

Writer . . . . . . . . . . . . . . . . . . . . . . . . . . . . . . . . . . . . . . . . . . . . . . . . . . . . William Blinn
Director . . . . . . . . . . . . . . . . . . . . . . . . . . . . . . . . . . . . . . . . . . . . . . . . E.W. Swackhamer
Film Editor . . . . . . . . . . . . . . . . . . . . . . . . . . . . . . . . . . . . . . . . . . . . . . Asa Clark
Assistant Director . . . . . . . . . . . . . . . . . . . . . . . . . . . . . . . . . . . . . Michael Dmytryk
*Guest Cast*
Dmitri . . . . . . . . . . . . . . . . . . . . . . . . . . . . . . . . . . . . . . . . . . . . . . Marvin Silbersher

*Teaser:* Biddie, Clancey, Lottie, Big Swede, Corky, Jason, Josh, Jeremy, Candy, loggers.

*Tag:* Clancey, Lottie, Jason, Josh, Jeremy, Candy, Candy's rabbit, brides, Biddie.

*Competition:* Daktari, "Jungle Heartbeat," guest-starring jazz percussionist Ed Thigpen on CBS; Orange Bowl-Kansas Jayhawks vs. Penn State's Nittany Lions at Miami on NBC.

*Photography:* Jason, Jeremy, and Corky take the brides on a trip "around and around the mountain," the sequence cuts from Jason to Jeremy to Corky, and back again, the next character in the new cut finishing the previous character's line; the long shot of all the brides sitting on the log, talking amongst themselves, their backs to camera; Jason's hunt for Candy, her yelling 'Help!' the camera then swinging around from Candy to the trees. In Clancey's ship — the slow pan over and up the brides to stop at Franny (left), Lottie (center), and Candy (right) as Lottie talks about men and Seattle; the long aerial shot of the town square as the brides, loggers, and Stempel's men all circle the "cornered" Dmitri; the long shot of Jason and Dmitri saying "Farewell," which closes out Act 4.

*Notes:* During the first season of a television series, a good bit of time is spent defining the characters, and their relationships. Through trial and error the writers find what kinds of stories work, and those that don't. As the series proceeds, its makers then begin tackling questions that need to be answered — for example, when *The Fugitive* began, its title character, Dr. Richard Kimble, was already living the life of a fugitive. But at some point, it was vital that the series' producers explain how the doctor became a fugitive; they didn't make this explanation until the Christmas Day aired episode, "The Girl from Little Egypt."

A similar situation arose when it came to the living quarters for the single, marriageable women from New Bedford in *Here Come the Brides*. By not answering the question of where the brides' dormitory came from right away, the show had a good "hook" to keep the audience watching. To answer the question with an episode which flashed back to the brides' arrival in Seattle was a brilliant move on episode writer William Blinn's part.

This episode also provides some information concerning the early life of the Bolt brothers. Not only do we visit their old cabin on the east side of Bridal Veil Mountain, we learn that Jeremy was two, Josh was six, and Jason was thirteen when they were living in the cabin.

*Bridget Hanley, and her "wee friend" in "After a Dream Comes Mourning."*

PHOTO COURTESY BRIDGET HANLEY

This is the first show in which Biddie drinks (she has quite a bit), and it is the second and last episode in which Clancey burps and belches. The pilot episode was the only other show where Clancey did this. As the story continues, Clancey and Biddie (in the present-day flashback-framing scenes), grow more and more drunk. "You couldn't do that [kind of comedy] now," says Blinn.

Lottie's description of Seattle reflects the lyrics to the series' theme "Seattle"; in the song there is the line, "Like a beautiful child, growing up free and wild." Lottie describes Seattle as a still-growing "child."

*Story Editor/Episode Writer William Blinn:* "The pilot that I saw was an hour, without question. It was not a two-hour show; this was not the second half of the pilot. That ["After a Dream Comes Mourning"] was one of my favorite titles. This [episode] was just done, essentially…we'd answered the question, 'Where's the doctor?' Well, the next question: 'Was there a dormitory when the brides arrived?' – no one had the answer to it. Well, if the answer was, 'No, there was no dormitory,' well, hell, then they would turn around and leave, [and] not sleep out in the woods all night. So that became an interesting premise for an episode, and a question to try to solve."[93]

*Guest Star Marvin Silbersher:* "Swack brought me into the show. We were buddies at drama school. I think it was very early in the shooting. It was one of the funniest episodes. I don't think it was midway through the series — I believe it was right at the top. They edited the show because it ran too long. It was like a double-story, so they held it back.

"David and Bobby Sherman and I had so much fun singing together. We were kind of like three brothers, David, Bobby and me, off-camera. We never stopped singing — all of us had guitars. We knew the same folk songs — 'Careless Love.' We loved to sing. We did crazy things and songs. We became like an off-camera comedy team. We used to do improv together back and forth.

"We did the finale in the town square, as I remember, in one take. Maybe it was two takes, but it was very concise. We were all so…Swack was very good about treating us right. He made sure the cast was comfortable and fed and rested. So, when he said, 'Action,' it happened.

"The wrap party was wild and grand. Happy."

## *Guest Star Marvin Silbersher*

"I had the 'call' when I was thirteen years old," says Marvin Silbersher. "There was a radio program long ago — you may recall this, called *Let's Pretend* (March 24, 1934-October 23, 1954; *Let's Pretend and the Golden Age of Radio,* a history of the series written by series guest Arthur Anderson, was published by Bear Manor in 2004.) It was a program of fairy tales, a national CBS show [featuring] very gifted teenage kids. You could write in for an audition, and I got an audition. Did a six-minute sketch I wrote myself — about a newsboy delivering his papers to eight different people of different accents — like Greek and Irish and Russian. At the end of my audition, the producer — her name was Nila Mack, came running into the office. 'My God,' she says, 'You're a little genius! Who are you? Where've you been?' It was like God had smiled on me. I just walked in, did the audition. She said, 'You're good enough. You're part of the company.' So I began with *Let's Pretend.* I had a whole career in radio."

Marvin Silbersher had a satisfying career in early television, too. Working mainly as a director and sometimes an actor, Silbersher was "both in front of and in back of the camera." In the '60s he did religious series like *Lamp Unto My Feet* and *Look Up and Live,* as well as the long-running variety series, *The Ed Sullivan Show.* On the latter, he served as assistant director.

An actor-director who, during the course of his ongoing career, has "discovered" such talents as Tony Curtis, Stiller and Meara, and Mary Travers (of Peter, Paul, and Mary fame), Marvin Silbersher's description of the United States of America made him an ideal guest star for *Here Come the Brides.* "America is a romance," says

Silbersher. "That's why this country came into being. There's no other explanation. I mean, if Washington hadn't been a romantic, there would be no America. To put up with what he put up with…most of the Revolution… they had to believe in romance about life, about God, about people, this country."[94]

*Marvin Silbersher on the series:* "The whole series was just a happy occasion. Everybody was in such a good mood. It was such a triumphal series. Everybody was pleased by their work and the way the series was received, and the whole atmosphere, which was created really by Swack and Bridget and Bob Brown."

*On reuniting with old friends E. W. Swackhamer, Robert Brown, and Mark Lenard:* "Oh, my God, it was like a reunion of all of us: Bob Brown and Mark Lenard — Mark was one of my actors at CBS — he was playing the villain — so we were all together. These people are so dear to me because we all shared the same struggle and the same world of creativity."

*On Director E. W. Swackhamer:* "I was well aware of how good he was and prepared — to the point of how [quickly] he got to the essence of what he had to do once we started rolling. I guess we did everything in one take, well, he did live television. He was so good and everybody was so prepared, Mark and David and Bobby Sherman, and of course Bridget. 'Let's do it again.' 'No, no, we got it. We got it. Print it!'"

*On series star Robert Brown:* "Bob Brown was larger than life, the old-fashioned hero type. He had the same kind of verve and panache as Errol Flynn, but he was bigger [physically] than Errol."

*On co-star Bobby Sherman:* "Bobby Sherman is a darling, wonderful guy, another talent like David Soul. He was a very talented kid. He could do imitations."

*On co-star David Soul:* "David Soul is one of my favorite people — a big talent, a wonderful guy. He was funny and gifted, a terrific boy. He never objected to [not getting as much attention as Sherman or Brown]. He was a very objective, fair-minded person. Very outgoing and charming. Most outgoing and charming and funny. This thing about [his being] shy — first time I hear this — maybe that was his way of surviving. I don't remember him showing an interest in directing at the time."

*On leading lady Bridget Hanley:* "I can't say enough about Bridget. Bridget is so beautiful. She was wonderful, the most talented. That girl is so gifted. She should be on top. She's a good actress, great actress. She doesn't have a venue which really shows her off. She's a great character actress now. I don't know why she's not the most celebrated actress in America, really — she is so gifted. I've asked her to do a one-woman show — she'd be so marvelous — to show the range of what she can do, how good she is. She's doing all these things that don't really show her to her true gifts that she has — she's an amazing person. She's outstanding. We've been talking about doing a show where she's an Irish madwoman; there're so many aspects of character she can play, she does the funniest imitation of Katharine Hepburn, she reads from Hepburn's book about me, (doing Hanley doing Hepburn): 'I'm reading this book about me, it's about me. Spencer and I were having a love affair on the floor of my kitchen, yes.' Funny — she's so funny. I don't know why she…she should be at the top of the entire business. The venue doesn't allow for the many talented people to arrive where they should be. It's luck, or whatever it is. This business loses so many people who should be elevated up to stardom.

*On Co-Star Mark Lenard:* "Mark must have worked for me thirty times before I went to do *Brides* with Swack. He was a wonderful actor — marvelous actor who never got the occasion to show all the sides that he could do. I mean, he could play anything. We just had a grand time. Mark and I used to talk over all the things that we did at CBS; he did some great stuff. He was a paratrooper in Europe."

*On Bridget Hanley and E. W. Swackhamer:* "Swack and Bridget were madly in love. When Bridget touched a page of Swack's shooting script, it would burn, or vice versa, Swack would touch her script — it would just fill with smoke. God, they were crazy about each other!"

*On veteran actress Joan Blondell:* "I grew up admiring her. Suddenly there she is — Joan Blondell — another of my movie favorites. She was always extraordinary — there's none better than Joan Blondell. Glenda Farrell and Joan Blondell. I was just delighted to be working with her."

*On series regular Henry Beckman:* "Another talent. A very gifted man. He could play all kinds of characters. I think this was the first time we were together." [95]

January 4, 1969 – First issue of *TV Guide* for 1969 (Vol. 17, No. 1, Issue #823) features on its cover *Brides* cast of Bobby Sherman, David Soul, Bridget Hanley and Robert Brown, all smiling. Hanley is in character as Candy Pruitt – she's biting her nails. Sherman is in foreground, the others are behind him. In same issue is article on *Hawaii Five-O* star Jack Lord, who won the part of *Five-O* chief Steve McGarrett – the part for which Robert Brown had been seriously considered. Pages 20-23 – same issue – *Brides* article, "Making Sin Palatable" by Dwight Whitney.

## Episode #13: "The Log Jam"                     *January 8, 1969*

> *Billy:* Well, we knew we couldn't keep them waiting forever.
> *Lew:* Jeremy Bolt don't get married we could. Lots of men
> been known to stumble walkin' up the aisle.

Writer . . . . . . . . . . . . . . . . . . . . . . . . . . . . . . . . . . . . . . . . . . . . . . . . Albert Beich
Director . . . . . . . . . . . . . . . . . . . . . . . . . . . . . . . . . . . . . . . . . . . . . . Jerry Bernstein
Film Editor . . . . . . . . . . . . . . . . . . . . . . . . . . . . . . . . . . . . . . . . Norman Wallerstein

Assistant Director . . . . . . . . . . . . . . . . . . . . . . . . . . . . . . . . . . . . . . . . Jim Hogan
*Guest Cast*
Sam Melville . . . . . . . . . . . . . . . . . . . . . . . . . . . . . . . . . . . . . . . . . . . . . . . . . .Lew
Pamela Dunlap . . . . . . . . . . . . . . . . . . . . . . . . . . . . . . . . . . . . . . . . . . Abigail
Tommy . . . . . . . . . . . . . . . . . . . . . . . . . . . . . . . . . . . . . . . . . . . . . .Todd Garrett

*Teaser:* Jason, Lew, Josh, Jeremy, Corky, Billy, loggers.

*Tag:* Candy, Jeremy, Biddie, Ann, Franny, Jason, Josh, Lottie, Lew, Abigail.

*Competition: Daktari,* "A Tiger's Tale," episode about a Bengal tiger named Sarina, CBS; *The Virginian,* "Stopover," guest-starring Herb Jeffries, John Kellogg, and Jan Shepard, NBC.

*Notes:* The title of this episode refers to the fact that there haven't been any weddings in Seattle for a while. Clancey no longer seems to have an objection marrying people aboard his ship — in fact, he and general store owner Ben Perkins have gone into the marriage-deal business. And the brides of New Bedford are certainly changing things in Seattle — women have never played horseshoes in the town before, so, when Abigail teams with Jason she establishes a new tradition.

As Abigail, Pamela Dunlap is both cute and touching. Not to mention strong — the minute Jason makes a crack about Lew, Pamela rushes to the defense of her man. But Abigail is no weak-willed female — when she hears that Jason and Lew are having a kicking contest — and *she's* the prize — she verbally blasts the two of them, and books passage with Captain Clancey out of Seattle. The scheme which Jason and company concoct to reunite Abigail and Lew allows Bridget Hanley a rare chance to display her comedic abilities. Excellent performances from the regulars in this one, and Dunlap and Melville are terrific. Dick Balduzzi has some fine moments, too.

According to this story, Biddie is now up to five when it comes to catching bridal bouquets!

*Trivia:* Sam Melville later starred in the William Blinn series, *The Rookies.*

January 11, 1969 – *TV Guide* – Vol. 17, No. 2, Issue #824 – *TV Guide* Crossword – 8 Down – Lottie on *Here Come the Brides.*

## Episode #14: "The Firemaker"                    *January 15, 1969*

*Aaron:* Lulu has to agree to marry one or the other within a week.

*Jason:* Fair enough.

Writer . . . . . . . . . . . . . . . . . . . . . . . . . . . . . . . . . . . . . . . . . . .James Amesbury
Director . . . . . . . . . . . . . . . . . . . . . . . . . . . . . . . . . . . . . . . . . Richard Kinon
Film Editor . . . . . . . . . . . . . . . . . . . . . . . . . . . . . . . . . . . . . . . . . . .Jim Faris
Assistant Director . . . . . . . . . . . . . . . . . . . . . . . . . . . . . . . . . . . . . . Jim Hogan
Music. . . . . . . . . . . . . . . . . . . . . . . . . . . . . . . . . . . . . . . . . . . . Paul Sawtell

*Guest Cast*

Raymond Bass.................................... Monte Markham
Balter............................................Edward Asner
Lulu Bright ....................................... Stefani Warren
Davey Hingle .....................................Hagan Beggs
Omar Freeman ................................... James McCallion
Marshall ..............................................John Dolan

*Teaser:* Jason, Aaron, Omar Freeman, Matthew Balter, Lulu, Davey Hingle, Raymond Bass, Josh, Jeremy.

*Tag:* Biddie, Josh, Bride, Jeremy, Candy, Jason, Lottie, Aaron, Brides.

*Competition: Daktari,* "Judy Comes Home," the last episode of the series, CBS; *The Virginian,* "Death Wait," guest-starring Harold J. Stone, Murray MacLeod, Sheila Larkin, and Conlan Carter, NBC.

*Notes:* Good performances from guest stars Monte Markham and Edward Asner add a lot to "The Firemaker." But it is Stefani Warren as bride Lulu Bright who adds so much to the show. Like Rachel Miller in "A Jew Named Sullivan," Lulu is a very interesting character. Indeed, finding a bride who works in Lottie's saloon is a pleasant surprise. Finding a bride who can dish out wisecracks to the likes of the highly educated and self-satisfied Aaron Stempel is even more enjoyable. For example, when Stempel tells Lulu that she should marry his man, Davey Hingle, because "Stempel men make the best husbands," Lulu asks him, "How many Stempel men have you been married to, Mr. Stempel?" The fact that, in the end, Lulu picks Hagan Begg's very sympathetic (and pathetic) amateur arsonist, Davey Hingle, over Monte Markham's unjustly accused (but very conceited) Raymond Bass, adds further to the richness of the actress' character. It's unfortunate Stefani Warren wasn't given more screen time.

Robert Brown is great in the closing sequence where the angry people of Seattle almost hang a clearly repentant Davey Hingle; amidst all the commotion and yelling, one hears Bridget Hanley's horrified screams. Hanley's screams really register on the viewer.

*Photography:* the sweeping shot of the trees as Act 1, featuring Lulu and Davey, begins.

*Writers:* Prior to writing three scripts for *Here Come the Brides,* James Amesbury penned two episodes of the *Bonanza* series: "The Conquistadors" and "The Greedy Ones," both of which aired in 1967.

### Guest Star Monte Markham

Deciding to become an actor during his high-school years, Monte Markham had done summer stock, received a master's degree in drama from the University of Georgia, played the Globe Shakespeare Theatre in San Diego, the Shakespeare Festival in Ashland, Oregon, worked in the Actor's Workshop and spent a year in the repertory company at the Pasadena Playhouse before playing the dual role of late-nineteenth century prospector Luke Carpenter and his grandson Ken in the 1967-68 Screen

Gems/Bob Claver-produced situation comedy, *The Second Hundred Years*. An actor not lacking in confidence, a quality he brought to the role of Raymond Bass in *Here Come the Brides* episode, "The Firemaker," Markham worked in theater so that he could do character roles or play strong character leads. "That's why I went to the Actors Workshop in San Francisco," the actor told *TV Guide*'s Robert de Roos, "because they would cast you out of type to stretch your mind and capabilities."[96]

Post *Brides*, Markham did some very interesting guest shots. His October 11, 1970 *FBI*, "The Architect," had him playing a super-brilliant criminal so terrified of human contact, he'd rather die; in the March 11, 1975 *Barnaby Jones* episode, "Doomed Alibi," the actor played two characters; in *The Six Million Dollar Man* November 1, 1974 episode, "The Seven Million Dollar Man," Markham played a bionic villain. In the '90s, Monte Markham moved into writing, directing, and producing.

*Leading Lady Bridget Hanley:* "Monte Markham was a very dear friend. I worked with him on *The Second Hundred Years*. He's just…what a guy! We used to have dinner all the time. His wife, Claire…whenever he'd do a series, she'd cook lunches and bring them in to the whole crew, and she just is a physically beauti-

Brides *guest stars Monte Markham ("The Firemaker"), Stefanianna Christopherson ("The Stand-Off") and R. G. Armstrong ("The Deadly Trade") in the November 14, 1969* Mr. Deeds Goes to Town *episode, "Wedding Bells for Mr. Deeds".*

ful and spiritually beautiful woman, and they're a great family — the son and daughter and Monte and Claire. They're just wonderful, and they're so happy.

"He's a terrific actor, and really fun to work with. He and I were in San Francisco at the same time, but at different theaters. We didn't meet each other until *Second Hundred Years* until I got down here. He just was a big theater actor and a wonderful film and television actor, and now he's producing all these incredible things. He was a good friend of Ray Bradbury's."[97]

*Series Regular Susan Tolsky:* "I loved talking to those guys, there were so many girls on the set, when a guy came on, you thought, 'Oooh!' I think I'll go talk to Monte.' Monte was just a sweetheart. To this day, he will come up and grab me like…He's just a dear."[98]

### Guest Star Edward Asner

Before he played Matthew Balther on *Here Come the Brides*, Ed Asner's credits included stage work in the plays of Shakespeare and Bertolt Brecht, and television appearances in such series as *Studio One* (his television debut), *Route 66*, *The Outer Limits*, *The Fugitive*, *The Felony Squad*, and *Judd, for the Defense*. Post *Brides*, Asner was Lou Grant on the long-running sitcom, *The Mary Tyler Moore Show*, and then its dramatic spin-off, *Lou Grant*. Then he became a part of TV history by appearing in both *Rich Man, Poor Man* and *Roots* (the two miniseries which firmly established the miniseries format), Quinn Martin's first TV-movie, the two hour/fifteen minute flashback-laden shocker, *The House on Greenapple Road*, and *The Police Story*, the 1973 pilot film for the excellent dramatic anthology, *Police Story*.

Among the many Asner guest shots worth checking out: *The FBI* ("The Tormentors"), *Rat Patrol* ("The Life Against Death Raid"), *The Fugitive* ("Run the Man Down"), *Route 66* ("The Opponent, Shoulder the Sky, My Lad"), *Police Story* ("A Dangerous Age").

In the 1990s, Ed Asner moved into voice work, doing such cartoons as *The Real Adventures of Jonny Quest*, and animated films like 1997's *A Christmas Carol*. Now in his late seventies, he remains an active and outspoken member of the motion picture and television industry.

*Story Editor William Blinn:* "One of the guys who got punished, and I've said this to him, for being a good actor, was Ed Asner. Cuz there were times when I would have a speech or a scene where there just had to be a ton of exposition laid out, which is the worst — so hard for an actor, when I could throw it to Ed, I'd throw it to Ed, because he would go in there like a terrier — he'd bite into that speech, and he'd just plow right on through it, and get all the points made. I went down and said to him, 'This is why you're getting it.' It's a backward compliment to say you're getting the bad speech because you're a good actor, that's the fact of the matter, that's the reality. I wasn't telling him anything he didn't know."[99]

*Leading Lady Bridget Hanley:* "Ed Asner did one of our shows. He's kind of a crusty old guy. I wasn't sure he liked me. God knows, he had huge success after *Brides*. He seemed to have a great time on our show. We loved his character, and what he did with it. I think he's a terrific actor."[100]

*Series Regular Susan Tolsky:* "There were tons of brides, but Ed...These guys I loved talking to, and I loved being around them. They were pros. They'd been around. It was really neat talking to the guys."[101]

*Semi-Regular Mitzi Hoag:* "Edward Asner. He was wonderful; he was an actor's actor. He liked actors, and I liked him a lot. On *The Mary Tyler Moore Show*, he was brilliant."[102]

*Wardrobe Man Steve Lodge:* "Ed is the sweetest thing. Like a big old bear. We have totally different political opinions. He was a good friend of Steve Ihnat's."[103]

January 18, 1969 – *TV Guide* – Vol. 17, No. 3, Issue #825 – *TV Guide* Crossword – 8 Down – Answer: Blondell

*Left to right: Susan Tolsky, guest star Susan Howard, and Bridget Hanley on the run from the Indians in "Wives for Wakando".* PHOTO COURTESY BRIDGET HANLEY

## Episode #15: "Wives for Wakando"                    *January 22, 1969*

"Jason Bolt pay — we pay. It is fair."
*Chief Wakando to the brides*

Writer . . . . . . . . . . . . . . . . . . . . . . . . . . . . . . . . . . . . . . . . . . . . . . . . . . . Don Balluck
Director . . . . . . . . . . . . . . . . . . . . . . . . . . . . . . . . . . . . . . . . . . . . . . Richard Kinon
Film Editor . . . . . . . . . . . . . . . . . . . . . . . . . . . . . . . . . . . . . . . . . . . . . . . Asa Clark
Assistant Director . . . . . . . . . . . . . . . . . . . . . . . . . . . . . . . . . . Michael Dmytryk
Music . . . . . . . . . . . . . . . . . . . . . . . . . . . . . . . . . . . . . . . . . . . . . . . . Paul Sawtell
*Guest Cast*
Wakando . . . . . . . . . . . . . . . . . . . . . . . . . . . . . . . . . . . . . . . . . . .Michael Ansara
Kitana . . . . . . . . . . . . . . . . . . . . . . . . . . . . . . . . . . . . . . . . . . . . . William Smith

Willard . . . . . . . . . . . . . . . . . . . . . . . . . . . . . . . . . . . . . William H. Bassett
Jane . . . . . . . . . . . . . . . . . . . . . . . . . . . . . . . . . . . . . . . . . . Susan Howard
Sylvia. . . . . . . . . . . . . . . . . . . . . . . . . . . . . . . . . . . . . . . . . .Mary Angela
Indian Sentry. . . . . . . . . . . . . . . . . . . . . . . . . . . . . . . . . . . . . Bert Santos

*Teaser:* Candy, Biddie, Jane, Wakando, two braves.
*Tag:* Jason, Josh, Lottie, Aaron, Jeremy, Candy, Jane, Willard.
*Competition: Voyage to the Enchanted Isles* ("The Galapagos") – narrated by Britain's Prince Phillip, CBS; *The Virginian*, "Last Grave at Socorro Creek," guest-starring Steve Ihnat, Lonny Chapman, Ellen McRae, and Kevin Coughlin, NBC.

*From a December 1968 letter from Mark Lenard to his fans:* "One last show that I'd like to mention is one that many people have mixed feelings about. Some of the 'brides' are kidnapped to replenish a depleted Indian tribe with women. Well…it's called 'Wives for Wakando,' and I would be interested in your reactions."

*Notes:* There is no question that "Wives for Wakando" is a very funny episode. Robert Brown and Bobby Sherman have some great comic moments, Bridget Hanley gets in a risqué one-liner at the end of Act Four, semi-regular Hollis Morrison has a good bit, and Diane Sayer (as bride Sally) has one of the best lines in the entire run of the show. Guest stars Michael Ansara and William Smith are funny, too; so are Susan Tolsky and Henry Beckman.

The opening of Act One is pretty remarkable. After brides Candy, Biddie and Jane close the teaser by running away from the pursuing Indians, when the act opens to show them still running (following the opening credits), they are in the place where they probably would have been had the episode continued to show them running.

Of all the *Brides* episodes to air, "Wives for Wakando" is the one that plays best if the viewer watches it as just a single television production, rather than as an episode of the series. For, when viewed as part of the series, one starts to wonder just exactly why Candy Pruitt, who up to this point in the program has been a strong-willed, fearless, and resilient woman, suddenly turns into a cowering, helpless female the minute she encounters an Indian. In fact, the only time Candy behaves like Candy is in the kidnap scene (but at the time Candy doesn't know who's abducting her). Given that Chief Wakando has already told Candy and the other brides that he and his people are friendly, it's strange that Candy doesn't even try to escape or argue with Wakando, much less discuss a means of escape with her fellow kidnapped brides, Jane and Biddie. Candy depending on Jeremy and his brothers to rescue her is pretty un-Candyish behavior, to say the least. As for Susan Howard's Jane, it's doubtful any Howard fan would put "Wakando's" Jane in their favorite Susan Howard characters' list.

In fact, Susan Tolsky's Biddie is the only kidnapped bride who makes any sense; she's the only one of the three to show no fear. Being kidnapped by a bunch of Indians is more than okay with Biddie. They're men, aren't they? Tolsky's performance definitely adds a lot to this story.

Back in town, though, the other brides are behaving like Candy and Jane — totally out of character. Suddenly, all of these courageous, intelligent young women from New Bedford have become a bunch of scared rabbits. Not to mention the biggest gang of empty-headed morons who, without question, swallow the biggest whopper Jason Bolt has ever told. Joan Blondell's reaction to that whopper is priceless.

Stretching credibility even further is the incredible stupidity of Michael Ansara's Chief Wakando, and his fellow Indians. Given that Seattle took its name from the real-life Indian chief, Seattle, one might have expected *Brides'* first American Indian-themed tale to be an intelligent drama presenting the subject with respect. Particularly since Chief Seattle was a remarkable man. Known for his bravery, daring and leadership in battle, Seattle (who was also something of a gifted orator) had become the leader of six separate Indian tribes, thanks to his ability to handle times of crisis. Like his father, Schwaebe, Seattle was on very good terms with the Europeans who'd chosen to settle in the area. After becoming good friends with forward-thinking businessman Doc Maynard, the chief later saved Maynard from an assassination attempt by another Indian. He also helped protect the white settlers in the area from attacks by other Indians. Thus, when it came time to name their new town, Doc Maynard insisted to his fellow settlers that it be called Seattle. All agreed.

Considering the positive presentation of the American Indian Michael Ansara had rendered in the 1950s series, *Broken Arrow* and *Law of the Plainsman*, one might have expected his Chief Wakando to be a Chief Seattle sort of Indian. Unfortunately, as noted below by *Here Come the Brides* story editor William Blinn, leading lady Bridget Hanley, and series regular Susan Tolsky, a dignified portrait of the American Indian did not result in this particular episode.

*Story Editor William Blinn:* [Groaning when asked about this episode], "I hated "Wives for Wakando." [Writer] Don Balluck was a good guy. It was just one of those ideas that sounded much better on paper than it ever turned out to be on film. I mean, you end up casting Michael Ansara as the Indian and then William Smith! Michael Ansara was a very good actor, and had an ethnicity that…he could play Indians and play them very well, but that's an issue of political incorrectness where we have advanced. We had some good comedy, but what would you learn from this episode that was about drama? I'm not saying it's without drama. There's all sorts of action-adventure stuff in it. But I keep talking about, keep mentioning the unexpected and the curve-ball and so forth and so on; again, this is like "Marriage: Chinese Style" — it's an old-fashioned western episode. Absolutely old-fashioned. It doesn't take the old-fashioned premise and turn it on its ear, or take the old-fashioned premise and suddenly lead you up to a third act ending that you hadn't anticipated. That was not our finest hour."[104]

*Leading Lady Bridget Hanley:* "I loved all the episodes of *Here Come the Brides* — with the exception of "Wives from Wakando." If you want to say anything about that, all I could do is…just a deep low laugh. I mean, I don't want to offend anyone.

I don't want to offend any of the actors, but, it was like the Hollywood tribe. It was just the teepees and the Indians, and just the fact we did an Indian dance. The actors were all great. We all had a great time, but it was hard to keep a straight face.

I thought it was a bad story. William Smith — he and I...he was a hunk! I saw him at an autograph signing, and I kind of reintroduced myself, and he was just like blank. Just blank!

*To quote Bridget Hanley: "Ha-ha-ha-ha-hee-hee."* PHOTO COURTESY BRIDGET HANLEY

"I think we were all a wreck when we were doing that show. Because we weren't making fun of people on *Here Come the Brides*. We weren't poking fun at anything, and we weren't trying to be a rip-off. We approached the series with fun, but we approached it with a certain integrity to the truth. But this show...it just felt hokey to me, and demeaning, and there weren't that many...the series was romantic comedy, obviously, but it didn't feel hokey. I mean, those other stories came from a real place.

You know, you think of all the shows that might have had a real place to come from that could have been [about] the Indians in Seattle. On this one, I think they must have accepted the first script that came down the pike."

Hanley is stunned to hear that the writer of this episode was *High Chaparral* story editor Don Balluck. (One of executive producer David Dortort's objectives in making *High Chaparral* was to present a non-Hollywood portrait of the American Indian. Besides serving as story editor, Balluck wrote episodes of *Chaparral.*) "My God, *High Chaparral*, which I loved!" states the actress. "I remember, Dick Kinon [the director of "Wakando"], he would always say, 'Well, let's see what we can do with this piece of shit' and we had a lot of laughs on this one. I don't know whether they were good. But he would…he rolled his eyes a lot on this one." As for the aforementioned risqué moment from Hanley, "you had to do something!"[105] she laughs.

*Series regular Susan Tolsky:* "Oh, that was fun. That was fun. That damn costume! We were in Angeles Crest, and that damn costume! Oh dear Lord! I mean, of all the stuff we had to wear…! They hook us up with, Oh God, the beads, and they had me looking like a total…! Didn't I look stupid? Didn't I have that Indian costume on? Yeah, she's [Biddie] real pretty. I just remember being in Angeles Crest, because we went there a lot. I remember it being a fun shoot — because we had a big cast, we had a lot of people, and it truly was because we got out of those hideous dresses, and Bridget, to this day, our waist, they had us cinched in, please, dear God, but it was fun having a different outfit and playing something different. That was a fun one because we also were on location. I knew Susan Howard so well – it was just…I know we hung. We all laughed and carried on and hung. Just hanging around the set, and chewing the fat."[106]

## Guest Star Michael Ansara

Starting his career with an uncredited bit in the 1944 feature, *Action in Arabia*, Michael Ansara was working in television by the early 1950s. Guest-starring on *Terry and the Pirates* and *Dangerous Assignment*, the Lebanese-born Ansara then scored with two series where he presented a very positive portrayal of the American Indian: *Broken Arrow* — where he played the Apache Chief, Cochise, and, a season later, *Law of the Plainsman*. In that series, Ansara was Harvard-educated, Apache-turned-U.S. Marshal, Sam Buckhart. Ansara was very proud of both series. "I think *Broken Arrow* should be revived," he told *TV Scout Feature* writer Joan Crosby. "Or even *Law of the Plainsman*. I think they were both ahead of their time."[107]

Following the cancellation of *Plainsman*, Ansara began doing numerous guest appearances on such series as *The Outer Limits, Branded, Perry Mason,* and *The Farmer's Daughter.* Motion pictures included George Stevens' 1965 epic, *The Greatest Story Ever Told*, and Elvis Presley's *Harum Scarum.* The actor also guest-starred in all four of Irwin Allen's sci-fi/adventure series: *Voyage to the Bottom of the Sea, Lost in Space, The Time Tunnel,* and *Land of the Giants,* in addition to working with "Wives for Wakando's" Susan Howard in one of the better third-season *Star Trek* episodes, "Day of the

Dove." The same year he did "Wakando," Ansara appeared with "Firemaker" guest star Monte Markham in the *Magnificent Seven* sequel, *Guns of the Magnificent Seven*. 1970s guest shots included *Mission: Impossible* ("The Western") *Police Story* ("Requiem for an Informer," the first of the Don Meredith as Bert/Tony Lo Bianco as Tony *Police Story* episodes), 1974's *The First Woman President*, the 1975 Bill Bixby-directed pilot *The Barbary Coast*, E.W. Swackhamer's great 1976 *McCloud*, "Our Man in the Harem"

(with Ansara as Sheik Ramal), the 1978 David Janssen-narrated miniseries, *Centennial* (Ansara as 'Lame Beaver'), and the *Buck Rogers in the 25th Century* episode, "Escape from Wedded Bliss," in which Ansara played Kane; the actor reprised the role in three *Buck Rogers* episodes in 1980.

Michael Ansara's 1970s motion pictures included 1973's *The Doll Squad*, 1976's well-regarded *Mohammed: The Messenger of God* (also featuring *Brides* guest Michael Forest), and one of the better eco-terror B-pictures, 1977's *Day of the Animals*. Working throughout the 1980s and '90s, with credits that included *Mike Hammer, Murder, She Wrote*, and *Star Trek: Voyager*, Ansara is now retired from the business.

*John Lupton and Michael Ansara ("Wives for Wakando'") in the '50s TV series,* Broken Arrow.

*Bridget Hanley on Michael Ansara:* "Michael Ansara was terrific, and he was married to Barbara [Eden]. He was a great guy. What an actor! What a guy. A terrific actor and a gentleman and skilled."[108]

### Guest Star William Smith

Beginning his career as a child actor in motion pictures of the early 1940s, fluent in Russian, German, French and Serbo-Croatian, direct descendant of Kit Carson and Daniel Boone, boxer, weightlifter, semi-pro football player, motorcycle rider... one-time "Marlboro Man" William Smith had served in the Army during the Korean War and received the Purple Heart by the time he entered television in the early 1950s. ABC-TV's first choice for the role of Kwai Chang Caine in *Kung Fu*, Smith had such diverse motion pictures as *The Ghost of Frankenstein, The Song of Bernadette, Going My Way, Meet Me in St. Louis*, and *A Tree Grows in Brooklyn* on his list of credits by the time he guest-starred on that series.

When Smith began his regular role of Texas Ranger Joe Riley on Universal TV's 1965-67 comic western, *Laredo*, he'd already guest-starred on shows like *Combat*, *Broadside*, *The Farmer's Daughter*, and *The Alfred Hitchcock Hour*. Following the cancellation of *Laredo*, Smith went back to guest shots, appearing on shows such as *The Second Hundred Years*, *Batman*, and *I Dream of Jeannie*. After the *Brides* comedy, "Wives for Wakando," William Smith appeared in early '70s drive-in fare: *C.C. and Company* (with Ann-Margret and Joe Namath), *Invasion of the Bee Girls*, and quality TV like *Columbo*, and *Rich Man, Poor Man-Book I* and *Book II.*

Beginning the 1980s with the regular role of James "Kimo" Carew on the hit crime drama, *Hawaii Five-O*, Smith later appeared on David Soul's *The Yellow Rose*. Other '80s guest appearances included *Benson*, *Masquerade*, *Knight Rider*, *The Fall Guy*, *Matt Houston*, and *Scarecrow and Mrs. King*; in 1988, Smith was seen in *HCTB* semi-regular Hoke Howell's movie, *B.O.R.N.* (The movie also featured *HCTB* guest alum Ross Hagen, who directed, and his wife, *HCTB* guest alum Claire Polan).

Moving into the role of writer and producer (in the 1970s), then director (in the 1980s), William Smith is still working today.

## Guest Star Susan Howard

Making her TV debut in the April 10, 1967 *The Monkees* episode, "Monkees, Manhattan Style," Susan Howard guaranteed herself a place in *Star Trek* history, and for that matter, television history, when she played the role of Mara, the wife of Michael Ansara's Klingon Commander Kang in the third-season *Trek* episode, "The Day of the Dove." Howard was the only woman in the original *Trek* to play a Klingon. Howard's role of Mara foreshadowed the gutsy, strong-willed 'Maggie Petrocelli' — the character the actress portrayed on the 1974-76 NBC lawyer drama, *Petrocelli.*

Nora Dawson, the mental patient Howard played on the sixth season *Mission: Impossible* episode, "Committed," was another fine part for the actress. Nora's' knock-down, drag-out fight with brutal prison matron Ma Brophy was a definite highlight of the episode. As was the conclusion which had the men: IMF agents Jim, Barney, and Willy leaving the women (IMF agent Casey and the fully recovered Nora) completely in charge of putting away the assorted villains.

Following her two-year stint as the wise-cracking secretary/wife Maggie Petrocelli on the aforementioned *Petrocelli*, Howard then began an eight-year run as Donna Culver Krebs on the hit prime-time soap opera, *Dallas*. During the course of the series, Howard began writing for the show. When the series producers later wanted the married Donna to begin an affair with another character in 1988, Howard balked and left the show. Shortly after moving back to her home state of Texas, Howard was then appointed as a commissioner for the Texas Parks and Wildlife Department by then-governor, George W. Bush.

In 2000 Susan Howard, an active member of the Writer's Guild of America and a member of the board of directors of the National Rifle Association, appeared as a spokesperson for the NRA in a thirty-minute advertising spot for the organization; it aired throughout the year. She remains a staunch supporter of conservative causes.

*Leading Lady Bridget Hanley:* "Susan Howard was a dear friend. We were really close and we had a lot of fun — the two Susans and me — crazy times together. She went on to other things — to *Dallas*; religious efforts, I think, are her thing now." [109]

*Series Regular Susan Tolsky:* "Susan was from Texas — there were a huge amount of University of Texas people that migrated out here. When I came out, we have to go back to the Eddie Foy story — it sounds like an Annette Funnicello story — but I truly was discovered. When he [Foy] let me join the New Talent Program, even though I was not under contract, Susan Howard was [also] in the New Talent Program. She was very beautiful. That's when they had the pretty people. They did not have character people in the New Talent Program. They were not nurturing character people — they were nurturing young starlets, and the David Soul kind of look.

"Susan and I got to be friends — she's from Marshall, Texas, and I'm from Houston, and we got to be friends, and we were roommates. Then one summer, Calvin Chrane, who was a friend of mine, who I went to the University of Texas with, came out, and we had a network where anybody who came out from the university — you know, we looked each other up. So Calvin came over one day to see me and visit; he met Susan and they got married. She was doing *Brides* at that time." [110]

### Writer Don Balluck

Executive story consultant/editor on *The High Chaparral*, Don Balluck had previously written for the John Mills series, *Dundee and the Culhane* and the primetime soap, *Peyton Place* before writing his one and only episode of *Here Come the Brides*: "Wives for Wakando." Following *The High Chaparral*, Balluck wrote multiple episodes of Michael Landon's *Little House on the Prairie* prior to becoming the executive story consultant on that series. In addition to writing for another Landon series, *Father Murphy*, Balluck did such TV series as *Hawaii Five-O*, *Police Woman*, and William Blinn's *The Rookies*.

January 25 1969 – Jackie Cooper's corrections appear in *TV Guide* – Vol. 17, No. 4, Issue #826 – Cooper rebukes the magazine for not including Joan Blondell and Henry Beckman in their cover picture, and points out that it was Steve Blauner who believed in the idea for the series.

## Episode #16: "A Kiss Just for So"              *January 29, 1969*

"Ah, darling. If courage were a belt, you'd need suspenders."
*Gallagher to Jason Bolt*

Teleplay . . . . . . . . . . . . . . . . . . . . . . . . . . . . . . . . . . . . . . . . . . . . . . . . James Amesbury
Story . . . . . . . . . . . . . . . . . . . . . . . . . . . . . . Albert Beich and James Amesbury
Director . . . . . . . . . . . . . . . . . . . . . . . . . . . . . . . . . . . . . . . . . . . Jerry Bernstein
Film Editor . . . . . . . . . . . . . . . . . . . . . . . . . . . . . . . . . . . . . . . . . . . Asa Clark

Assistant Director . . . . . . . . . . . . . . . . . . . . . . . . . . . . . . . . . . Michael Dmytryk
Director of Photography . . . . . . . . . . . . . . . . . . . . . . . . . . . . . .Irving Lippman
Music. . . . . . . . . . . . . . . . . . . . . . . . . . . . . . . . . . . . . . . . . . . . .Warren Barker

*Guest Cast*

Dana . . . . . . . . . . . . . . . . . . . . . . . . . . . . . . . . . . . . . . . . . . . . . Kathryn Hays
Gallagher. . . . . . . . . . . . . . . . . . . . . . . . . . . . . . . . . . . . . . . . . Michael Forest
Bishop Newkirk. . . . . . . . . . . . . . . . . . . . . . . . . . . . . . . . . . . . . Rhys Williams
Peter . . . . . . . . . . . . . . . . . . . . . . . . . . . . . . . . . . . . . . . . . . . . . Barry Williams
Lenny . . . . . . . . . . . . . . . . . . . . . . . . . . . . . . . . . . . . . . . . . . . . .Ralph Mara
David. . . . . . . . . . . . . . . . . . . . . . . . . . . . . . . . . . . . . . . . . . . . . . Gary Pillar

*Teaser:* Jason, Josh, Jeremy, Lottie, Gallagher, Aaron, Clancey, David, Dana, Peter, Bishop Newkirk, Ben, Candy, Lenny, townspeople, Amish people.

*Tag:* Jason, Dana, David, Peter, Bishop, Candy, Jeremy, Josh, Ben, Clancey, Lottie.

*Competition: The Glen Campbell Goodtime Hour* (premiere), with guests the Smothers Brothers, Bobbie Gentry, Pat Paulsen on CBS; *The Virginian*, "Crime Wave at Buffalo Springs," guest-starring Tom Bosley, Yvonne DeCarlo, James Brolin, Carrie Snodgress, Ann Prentiss, and The Irish Rovers, NBC.

*Notes:* While a traditional western story (*Bonanza* had done such a tale on October 8, 1960 with episode #37, "The Hopefuls"), this is nonetheless a good *Brides* outing thanks to the performance of lead guest Kathryn Hays, the interesting casting of *The Brady Bunch*'s Barry Williams as an Amish boy, and most especially, second-billed Michael Forest. Forest is so good as Gallagher, in fact, that he even steals scenes from Henry Beckman. While Forest is the chief villain in the piece, he is at least a charming villain.

Robert Brown makes the most of his character's rare opportunity to resort to violence. Bridget Hanley receives short shrift, however. With the exception of standing in the crowd to welcome and bid farewell to the Amish visitors, her character has nothing to do.

*Story Editor William Blinn:* "I probably liked it more then than I would now, only because I know a little bit more about the Amish and how insular they are; not in a harsh, people sense, but they are not racing toward outsiders with an embrace. I remember the Jason Bolt angst, and the decision to be made, and her telling him he couldn't make the decision because he was kidding himself [and] all that stuff. I remember liking the episode then, looking back on it now, I think I might think it a little bit heavy-handed. What we did was a television cutesy-version."[111]

## Guest Star Michael Forest

"When people say, 'Gee, I'd love to work in this business,' I say, 'Well — maybe — and maybe not!' It just depends on how everything kind of works out for you, because, there are some very good actors who never go anywhere, and then there are some actors that should never have gone anywhere, and they seem to be getting all the breaks."

Michael Forest was in the former category. During the course of his career, Forest worked with such luminaries as Richard Burton and director Joseph Losey (*The Assassination of Trotsky*), studied with character actor Jeff Corey, dubbed over five hundred films while living overseas, taught acting, and guest-starred in numerous television series of the 1950s and '60s.

Born Gerald Michael Charlebois, the young actor decided that a name change was a necessity. "A lot of people said, 'Gerald Michael Charlebois? Boy, that's a mouthful!'" laughs Forest, "and a lot of casting people would say to me when I would come in, 'Ah, Gerry, or Gerald, you speak with a French accent?' And I'd been talking with them for five or six minutes or so.' I said, 'Do I sound like I speak with a French accent when I'm speaking English?' They said, 'Well…' I said, 'I do speak French, but I don't speak English with a French accent.' That's when I began to get the idea that maybe I'd better change my name. Well, Michael was my middle name. Bois is 'Forest' or 'Wood' in French. And I decided I'm 'Forest' as opposed to 'Michael Wood.'"

Living in Seattle, Forest began performing on stage at "the Seattle Repertory Playhouse. The people there were originally from New York. They had a theater in New York. During the Federal Theatre days [the Federal Theatre Project (FTP) was a New Deal project to fund live artistic performances in the United States during the Great Depression] they came to Seattle, and opened the repertory playhouse. I was there with them in the '40s. That's where I began the kind of basic instruction in theater. I did Shakespeare in Seattle. That's when I was first introduced to it. It was very good the way they presented it. I was a neophyte type of actor at the time, and I was willing to absorb anything anybody said to me. Later on I came to California. I went to San Jose State, and I worked there in Shakespeare because the department was particularly good in that area. Twice I performed at the Old Globe in San Diego, so I've had fairly extensive work in Shakespeare. When I was teaching at USC, I taught acting in Shakespeare, at USC."

Forest's first film, Roger Corman's *The Viking Women and the Sea Serpent* gave the actor very little to do. "It was a real turkey," he laughs, "but it was fun to do." Forest did quite a few features with Corman, including *Beast from the Haunted Cave, Ski Troop Attack,* and *Atlas.*

By the time *Atlas* was released, Forest had done a great number of television westerns, among them, *Death Valley Days, Tombstone Territory, Adventures of Wild Bill Hickok, Zorro, Have Gun, Will Travel, 26 Men, The Rifleman, Bronco, Bat Masterson, The Westerner, Maverick, Cheyenne, Tales of Wells Fargo,* and *Bonanza.* At one point considered for the lead in Levy/Gardner/Laven's *The Rifleman,* Forest has a very good attitude about the people working in television.

"Everybody in television was perfect," he laughs. "In the early days, nobody took a slam at anybody. You couldn't offend anybody. A lot of shows were always under the gun. You had to get it done. You were always fighting the light, or fighting for time."

When it came to on-screen fist-fights, Forest "always did a lot of my own. A lot of times when the director would ask them, 'Can Mike handle this?' the stunt coordinators would say, 'Oh, yeah. Mike can handle it. He knows what he's doin'. And I was pretty good. I could handle myself in fight scenes. I knew how to throw a punch, and I could do the rough and tumble stuff, for the most part, as well as the stunt guys. But when it came to the real crashing around, that was the stunt doubles because they were hired to do that, so they'd better earn their money. A lot of times the stunt doubles would come in and handle the really rough stuff because they didn't want the actors to get hurt. If you bang up your face or something like that — you're out, for whatever length of time, you're out. They didn't want that to happen. So when it came to the hard falls downstairs and stuff like that, the stunt guys were being paid to do that, and that's fine with me. I didn't really know how to do that without getting hurt."

Perhaps best known for his role as Apollo in the second-season *Star Trek* episode, "Who Mourns for Adonais?" Forest exhibits no regrets over his onscreen work. "Whatever I've done, I did, you know, and good, bad, or indifferent, that's what I... whatever legacy I have, that's it. And I have to say that a lot of the people in this country would give their left arm to have done some of the stuff that I did. I was lucky enough to be part of it, and most of the time, it was really pleasant, really pleasant. It was hard sometimes, and difficult, but always you enjoyed...[I thought to myself] I'm getting up. I'm going to work this morning — *Wow*! This is *great*! It was something you could look forward to."[115]

*Michael Forest on Series Star Robert Brown:* "Robert Brown was a little stand-offish, a little bit uneasy, a little uncomfortable with me. For whatever reason, I don't know why particularly. I got along with him all right, but we didn't really get along like buddy-buddy type. Maybe that was fine as far as the characters were concerned. He was okay, he was fine. He was a good actor, but I always had the feeling he was kind of like standing away from me a little bit for whatever reason, I really don't know why. I hadn't set up anything in an effort to try to usurp his position, nor could I — he was the star of the show and I was just coming — jobbing in — as I always did."

*On co-stars David Soul and Bobby Sherman:* "I never got to know David Soul very well. He was certainly easy to work with. He was affable and pleasant, and he knew what he was doing. Bobby Sherman was the same way. I never had a problem with any of these guys. I always got along with most of the people. Very rarely did I get into a beef."

*On leading lady Bridget Hanley:* "I see Bridget every once in a while at theater. She's a very talented lady; she's always fun to be around."

*On fellow guest star Kathryn Hays:* "I didn't know Kathryn Hays was in it. I saw her years later in New York. When I met her again, when I did *As the World Turns*, I thought I was meeting her for the first time. Then one day I saw that segment — I said, 'My God, Kathryn Hays! I didn't even know that I had worked with her before; I had a whole big scene with her."

*On the inspiration for* Brides: "The original idea for that — they say it came from the Greek — the Sabine Women, basically. Well, I was in a musical in Seattle called

*Calico Cargo*, and that to my knowledge, was the original modern version of *Brides*. *Seven Brides for Seven Brothers* also came from that musical. The musical was done in '45 or '46 — they tried to sell it down here [Hollywood], and somebody had optioned it. Then nothing happened with it. I think the idea came from that script originally called *Calico Cargo*, because the basic idea is based on what actually happened in the Northwest in Seattle, with the Mercer Girls. And some of the characters in *Brides* were out of that book [*Roger Conant's Journal of a Voyage Aboard the Continental*, 1866.) I do know that that whole idea came from that original musical.

"*Brides* started out as a musical? That ties in with the original *Calico Cargo*, which was a musical. It [*Calico*] was quite good, and very well received in Seattle because of the locale and its historical significance. No, there weren't any famous performers in *Calico Cargo* [other than Forest]. Those were just local people."

*On the weather in Seattle:* "I can tell you that I spent a lot of time in Seattle and its environs, and I don't think I ever saw anything that resembled what was in *Brides*. Because they didn't shoot up there. They shot here in town. Maybe they would go out and get some kind of establishing shot someplace, but it was always in the mountains here, not in the Seattle environs. Not that it's that much different. I mean trees are trees, and rocks are rocks, but when they said, 'This is Seattle,' I said, 'Mmmm. Okay. If that's what you believe, that's fine.' If you say it loud enough and long enough, people will believe it, I guess. It didn't matter to me. It was believable. One would believe it. It wasn't that far off the mark as far as the way the terrain looks around Seattle and in the mountain areas and so forth, but for those of us who had grown up there, and been outdoors a lot, you knew that it was not quite the same. Not quite. But that's okay. That's what film is all about anyway.

"It never rained on *Brides*, [except in "A Man and His Magic"] and believe me, when you have forty inches of rain a year, every year, and sometimes more, then you know that something is a little amiss when it doesn't ever rain. It *always* rains. There're probably about two, maybe two and a half months out of the year when it doesn't rain and then the rest of the time…it's not always raining day and night, but I know we used to go to the movie; you'd go in, the sun would be shining, you'd come out two or three hours later, and it was pouring rain. And vice versa –you'd go in, it's pouring rain – you'd come out, the sun is out. So, you never knew in the Seattle area – it wasn't called the 'Rainy Marine Area' for nothing.

"And you know when I grew up there, I didn't know any different. When it was raining in Seattle, I thought it was raining everywhere. You do that as a kid. You know it's raining here, then it's gotta be raining in the rest of the world. I found out later on that was not true. Anyway, I learned to play golf in the rain. If you didn't play golf in the rain, you didn't play golf. It was as simple as that – it was a given – it's gonna rain. Not all day long. Or every day. But you knew there'd be rain sometime during the week. In the wintertime particularly."[112]

*Leading Lady Bridget Hanley:* "I remember thinking, 'Wow! What a tall, handsome man!' And he was in the first and second season, so I probably didn't look at him as lovingly the second season. I got married between the first and second season.

He's a wonderful actor, and very handsome, and he's just charming. I've seen him off and on, at the theater, or somewhere. Kind of a warm, wonderful feeling when I think of him."[116]

*Wardrobe Man Steve Lodge:* "Michael Forest was fine. He worked a couple of shows. Just a big, muscular guy. No big ego problems there."[117]

### Guest Star Kathryn Hays

Probably best known as the title character Gem in the interesting third-season *Star Trek* episode, "The Empath," former model Kathryn Hays established herself as an actress who enjoyed doing the offbeat from the very beginning of her career. In her earliest-known TV credit: the February 21, 1962 *Hawaiian Eye*, "Total Eclipse," after she's been found not guilty of murdering her husband, Hays is still suspected by private detective Tom Lopaka (Robert Conrad). The "Gaslight" treatment to which Hays is then subjected has something to do with the upcoming "total eclipse."

*Robert Brown and Kathryn Hays in "A Kiss Just for So".*

Hays' May 17, 1963 *Route 66* episode, "Shadows of an Afternoon," proved to be years ahead of its time (unfortunately) in depicting the appalling treatment to which former Vietnam soldiers were subjected upon their return to the States. In "Shadows," Vietnam vet Linc Case (series star Glenn Corbett) is accused by an elderly woman of attacking a dachshund with a pair of garden shears. It is Hays, not her boyfriend Todd Stiles (series star Martin Milner) who gets Linc a defense lawyer. The lawyer clears Linc with the help of two little girls (played by the daughters of executive producer Herbert B. Leonard).

That same year, Kathryn Hays was seen in Frank Perry's independent film, *Ladybug, Ladybug*, in which the staff and students at a rural school are warned of an imminent nuclear attack. They have no idea whether the threat is imagined or genuine. 1966's *Ride Beyond Vengeance* continued the offbeat nature of Hays' work. The movie, co-starring *Brides'* Joan Blondell, and *Brides* guest-star Paul Fix (playing a farmer with the last name of Hanley) was told in double-flashback. The following year, Hays played cellist Annabelle Rice in the Universal WWII drama, *Counterpoint. Counterpoint* starred Charlton Heston as a famous orchestra conductor, who, when captured by the Germans, is forced to put on private concerts for the Nazi generals.

Also appearing on such 1960s and '70s series as *Mannix, The High Chaparral, Marcus Welby, M.D., Night Gallery,* and *Cade's County* (starring one-time husband Glenn Ford), Kathryn Hays can now be seen in the recurring role of Kim Sullivan Hughes on the long-running daytime serial, *As the World Turns.*

Note: A Kathryn Hays guest shot well worth checking out is her June 17, 1965 *Kraft Suspense Theatre,* "Kill Me on July 20th." Co-starring Jack Kelly and *Brides* guest Stefan Arngrim, "Kill Me" is a typically atypical Hays story.

*Leading Lady Bridget Hanley:* "She was in it a lot. She was from New York."[113]

*Series regular Susan Tolsky:* "She was lovely, a lovely lady. Just a very nice lady, and very quiet. She wasn't, 'Let's all jump on a horse and go play around the ranch.' I also associated her with an Eastern feeling. A very nice, very pleasant, very pretty lady. And she still has a beauty about her. I saw her on something not too long ago. I'm just thrilled when I see people [I knew] working, especially forty years later."[114]

## Guest Star Rhys Williams

Making his film debut in the 1941 John Ford film, *How Green Was My Valley,* on which he also served as technical advisor and Welsh language consultant, Shakespearean actor Rhys Williams followed that classic with other excellent motion pictures, including *Random Harvest, The Corn is Green, The Spiral Staircase, The Farmer's Daughter,* and *Plymouth Adventure.* Television included *The Adventures of Superman, Four Star Playhouse, The Millionaire, Alfred Hitchcock Presents, Wagon Train, Maverick, Bonanza, Adventures in Paradise, Peter Gunn, 12 O'Clock High, The FBI, Mission: Impossible, The Invaders,* and *Mannix.*

In 1961 Williams co-starred with Jane Wyman in the pilot, *Dr. Kate,* based on the long-running radio series about a woman doctor. He died on May 28, 1969 in Santa Monica, California.

## Guest Star Barry Williams

Guaranteed television immortality thanks to his role as Greg Brady on the 1969-74 hit situation comedy, *The Brady Bunch,* Barry Williams might well have become another Dean Stockwell had he not been so identified with *Brady.* Like Stockwell, Williams had some very unusual roles as a child actor. In the March 12, 1968 *Invaders,* "The Pursued," (co-starring future *Brides* guest Will Geer), he was an alien invader posing as a newsboy; in the October 1, 1968 *Lancer,* "Blood Rock," Williams played a young man who hero-worships his outlaw father (J.D. Cannon). The 1968 cult film, *Wild in the Streets,* had Williams' character exhibiting a talent for coming up with homemade explosives. In the February 4 and 11, 1969 *It Takes a Thief* two-parter, "A Matter of Gray Matter" (also guest-starring *Brides* guest Michael Forest), Williams was the one with the gray matter. As for the February 1, 1970 *Mission: Impossible*, "Gitano," King Williams masqueraded as a little girl.

## Composer Warren Barker

Perhaps best known for his *77 Sunset Strip* score, Oakland, California-born Warren Barker played piano and trumpet in school before moving on to saxophone. Majoring in music at UCLA, Barker started working in radio after serving in the Army Air Corps; in the Corps, he played in a band. Beginning his radio, television, and motion picture career with NBC as the chief arranger for their musical show-case, *The Railroad Hour*, Barker later moved to Warner Bros., where he composed the theme songs and background scores for such series as *Hawaiian Eye* and the afore-mentioned *77 Sunset Strip*. He also served as the musical director and conductor on the *77* soundtrack album.

In the 1960s, Barker composed music for such Screen Gems series as *Bewitched, That Girl,* and *The Flying Nun.* In 1970, he won an Emmy for his work on the James Thurber-inspired situation comedy, *My World and Welcome to It.* In the mid-seventies Barker wrote 'A Little Bit Country, A Little Bit Rock-n-Roll,' the theme song for the *Donny and Marie* (Osmond) variety series.

*Trivia:* The "Ox" musical theme returns.

Sometime in 1969 – Bobby Sherman article in *Teen Stars Yearbook* "HCTB Synopsis": Who's Who in Movies," Robert Brown in *TV Yearbook.*

February 1969 – Bobby Sherman article in *16 Magazine;* Bobby Sher-man article in *FaVE!;* Bobby Sherman article in *Tiger Beat,* "I Visit the Stars – Part 1"; *Tiger Beat,* "Meet Robert Brown and David Soul" *16 Magazine;* Brown and Soul tidbits in *TV Radio Talk;* Henry Beck-man in *TV Picture Life;* "Why TV's Top Stars are Over 40,"

*TV and Movie Play;* Robert Brown and Joan Blondell – *16 Magazine;* Robert Brown and Bridget Hanley – *TV Picture Life;* Robert Brown – *TV Radio Show;* Robert Brown – *TV Star Parade;* Robert Brown article in *Movieland and TV Time;* Robert Brown – *Screen Stars.*

February 1, 1969 – *TV Guide* – Vol. 17, No. 5 – Issue #827 – *TV Guide* Crossword – 13 Down – star of *Here Come the Brides* (2 words)

February 5, 1969 – episode #17 airs; Robert Brown guests on *The Merv Griffin Show;* comedian Al Hamel is the guest host.

## Episode #17: "Democracy Inaction"          *February 5, 1969*

*Jeremy:* Jason, we're doing the right thing for the wrong reason.
*Jason:* Winning is an excellent reason.

"And it starts...with the sacred right — TO VOTE!"
*Candy Pruitt to the women of Seattle*

Writer . . . . . . . . . . . . . . . . . . . . . . . . . . . . . . . . . . . . . . . . . . . . . . .William Blinn
Director. . . . . . . . . . . . . . . . . . . . . . . . . . . . . . . . . . . . . . . .R. Robert Rosenbaum
Film Editor . . . . . . . . . . . . . . . . . . . . . . . . . . . . . . . . . . . . . . . . . . Asa Clark
Assistant Director . . . . . . . . . . . . . . . . . . . . . . . . . . . . . . . . . Michael Dmytryk
Music. . . . . . . . . . . . . . . . . . . . . . . . . . . . . . . . . . . . . . . . . . . . . Paul Sawtell

### Guest Cast

Bundy . . . . . . . . . . . . . . . . . . . . . . . . . . . . . . . . . . . . . . . . . . Raymond Kark
Leonard Spencer. . . . . . . . . . . . . . . . . . . . . . . . . . . . . . . . . . . . Logan Ramsey

*Teaser:* Lottie, Spencer, Jason, Jeremy, Josh, Candy, Biddie, Bundy.

*Tag:* Biddie, Bundy, Candy, Jeremy, Big Swede, Josh, Miss Essie, Ann, Clancey, Lottie, Jason.

*Competition: Glen Campbell's Goodtime Hour* guest-starring John Wayne (in a cameo), Jeannie C. Riley, and The Monkees who sing "Last Train to Clarksville" and "Tear Drop City" CBS; *Hallmark Hall of Fame*, "Teacher, Teacher," starring David McCallum, Ossie Davis, and George Grizzard, NBC.

*Notes:* Though a fine comedy/drama, like quite a few other *Brides* episodes of the first season ("And Jason Makes Five," "A Man and His Magic," "Wives For Wakando," "A Kiss Just for So," "A Dream that Glitters," "The Crimpers," "A Man's Errand," and "Marriage: Chinese Style"), this episode has some similarities to an earlier-aired *Bonanza* episode. This might have been one reason *Brides* moved to a more serious format in the second season.

In the case of this episode, the mayoralty race gimmick had been done before in the October 28, 1968 tenth-season *Bonanza*, "The Last Vote." "Democracy Inaction" is nonetheless an original episode, thanks to the women's suffrage angle, and the many vignettes involving the people of Seattle. In "Democracy," the brides of New Bedford aren't just decoration or empty-headed; they have something concrete to do, and display the independence and intelligence one would expect from a group of women who've survived the six-month voyage from New Bedford, Massachusetts, to Seattle, Washington.

In her last portrayal as Miss Essie, Mitzi Hoag leaves the series in grand style. Bo Svenson has some good scenes as well, and Henry Beckman is wonderfully funny in the "campaign rules" sequence, the "Seattle casts its vote" montage, and just about every other scene in which he's featured. The entire cast, in fact, does good work, particularly Bridget Hanley.

This was the only episode of *Brides* to be directed by R. Robert Rosenbaum. An associate of E.W. Swackhamer, Rosenbaum shows a very Swackhamer-like style through the sequence in which Candy, Essie, and Lottie walk out of the saloon and slam the door, not to mention the scene of the women marching through town as the brides close the dormitory shutters.

*Photography:* The pan over the dormitory windows as the brides close the shut-

*Left to right: Mitzi Hoag, Susan Tolsky, and Bridget Hanley in "Democracy Inaction".*
PHOTO COURTESY BRIDGET HANLEY

ters, spelling out the slogan, "Miss Essie for Mayor"; the pan back and forth over the townspeople (Candy Pruitt rocking back and forth on her heels) as they wait for the election results.

*Story Editor/Episode Writer William Blinn:* "Democracy is a terrible system — it just happens to be the only one that works. The only reason that came up at all was, we hadn't had anything political, not in any serious sense, we hadn't done anything about elections, and so forth and so on. Well, maybe two or three years earlier, Mike Gleason and I had written an episode for *Laramie* and the premise of the episode, was that Wyoming was the first state in the Union where women could vote. [Women received the right to vote in Wyoming on December 10, 1869.] We weren't in Wyoming, so the women couldn't vote. I thought, well, if the women can't vote, that's obviously going to be a major problem. That became the premise for what happened in the episode.

"That was probably not my favorite episode, but I think it's probably the best episode in terms of serving all the characters and serving the premise. And also, because Bo Svenson — 'Big Swede' — was a guy who needed serving, too. Not because he was demanding of it. I knew Bo a little bit because my wife was also Swedish. He was such a presence — six-foot-four, strapping guy, handsome in a rugged manner. If you had him in the scene, the audience was looking at him and saying, 'Who's that? He looks interesting.' So, he was a character that needed to be served."

Blinn is not surprised that some of the *Brides* fans were not happy with the fact Essie chooses her marriage over her political career. "I recall having a conversation with a friend or two [about the episode]," says the writer. "I said, 'Well, are we not set in 1873?' Is not that the reality of 1873?' What's the old Freud thing, 'There are times when a cigar is just a cigar.' I think that's where we finally came up. You know, life is gonna have some times when it's just contradictory and ambiguous. There's not gonna be one answer for everybody. If there's a lady in Iowa who's married and got four children, and is living the fulfilled life in the world, more power to you. If there's a lady who's a stockbroker, and my daughter is, and has got two kids, and is somehow making it all work, more power to you. We seem to want one size fits all — only one answer for every question."

Blinn enjoyed the hypocrisy the male characters displayed in "Democracy Inaction." "The men saying they can't give women the right to vote, and the women know more about it," laughs Blinn. "God! That's been true forever. The number of times...and it came up in *Roots* a couple of times, and we talked about it in other shows."[118]

*Semi-Regular Mitzi Hoag:* "I really liked 'Democracy Inaction.' I remember us all marching in. It was fun marching in with the banner and Susan and Bridget and all the brides. She [Essie] didn't really put her marriage above her political career. I thought that sort of stole from the...Judy Garland [and, before that, Janet Gaynor] movie [*A Star is Born*, in which the actress is playing] Mrs. Norman Wayne. I remember that scene. It seemed a little bit like that. It also seemed appropriate for the time.

"I didn't like the conclusion. I think I rushed the scene a bit because I didn't like it. I didn't take my time with it. Sometimes that happens when you're acting — you resist the material a bit, and I think, in fact, when I saw that scene with Jamie, my grandson...well, television is fast, and they don't...This is what happens, too, when actors are regulars, at least it happened a bit when I was working on *We'll Get By.* When you don't do something well, you want to do it over, and there's not really time.

"I liked what they did in that final scene. That made it okay, because they had us all working as a committee. I thought that was a really good solution, the sort of thing that really could be done effectively in small communities. I did like that they were all arguing away. That was satisfying. You know, it was okay — she was still part of the process there. It wasn't hard to do the scenes where everyone was talking at once, because it's something people do, and no, it was not hard — we were improvising. That was all ad-lib — they'd made this compromise where all these people were on the town council, and this was the result.

"Bob Rosenbaum pretty much left me to do what I chose to do. He was supportive and quick, kind of like Virgil Vogel."[119]

*Bridget Hanley on Politics:* "My mother-in-law — when she was living out here near us — I would take her to vote, because she couldn't walk too well. I'd walk her in, and she'd vote, and she'd come out crying, and it was the most extraordinary sight, because she was born when there was no voting. It made me realize that no matter how one votes, it's so important to take that challenge and make it your own, and do it. My girls [Megan and Bronwyn] are so good about voting. I don't care how they vote or whatever — just the fact that they take that seriously. Anyway I just remember her [my mother-in-law] crying — she was just so overcome with the joy of being allowed a voice. She was just an amazing woman — started off in horse and buggy days, her father had a lumber camp...

"I love the battle, so I do love politics. I remember in college, when Nixon and Kennedy were running against each other, my roommate — on the inside of her closet door, she had a big poster of John Kennedy, and I had a big picture of Richard Nixon. And what we'd do every night when we would go to bed, we would just open our closet doors. We wouldn't say a word, just let the two guys look at each other, then close our doors and go to bed. We never fought about it.

"My parents were very Republican; I'm more pro-Democratic [now]. I think that was something that I acquired parentally — we all are different; we're all entitled. I did really kind of change my feelings [from Republican to Democrat] through the years, because of my husband, and all of that."[120]

## Guest Star Logan Ramsey

Memorable as Proconsul Claudius Marcus in the second-season *Star Trek* episode, "Bread and Circuses," Logan Ramsey and his actress wife, Anne, established and operated Philadelphia's Theatre of the Living Arts, before embarking on motion picture careers. While often cast as a bigot or coward in the movies, Logan Ramsey fared much better in television.

Among the Ramsey guest shots worth checking out: *Route 66* ("To Walk with the Serpent"), *Mission: Impossible* ("The Falcon," Parts 1, 2, and 3), *Alias Smith and Jones* ("Six Strangers at Apache Springs"), *Petrocelli* ("The Sleep of Reason"), and *Charlie's Angels* ("Dancing in the Dark").

February 8, 1969 – *TV Guide* – Vol. 17, No. 6 – Issue #828 – answer to *TV Guide* Crossword – 13 Down: Robert Brown.

## Episode #18: "One Good Lie Deserves Another"    *February 12, 1969*

"It's got nothing to do with how much Clancey has had to drink,
Joshua. It's got to do with being alone and the kind of fear that that
brings. And it's got to do with not being Matthew Muncey."
*Jason Bolt to his younger brothers, Joshua and Jeremy*

Writers. . . . . . . . . . . . . . . . . . . . . . . . . . . . . . . . . . . John O'Dea and Jay Simms
Director. . . . . . . . . . . . . . . . . . . . . . . . . . . . . . . . . . . . . . . . . .Paul Junger Witt
Film Editor . . . . . . . . . . . . . . . . . . . . . . . . . . . . . . . . . . . . . . . . . Asa Clark
Assistant Director . . . . . . . . . . . . . . . . . . . . . . . . . . . . . . Michael Dmytryk
Music. . . . . . . . . . . . . . . . . . . . . . . . . . . . . . . . . . . . . . . . . . . . .Shorty Rogers
### *Guest Cast*
Matthew Muncy . . . . . . . . . . . . . . . . . . . . . . . . . . . . . . . . . . . . . . . .Lew Ayres
Dewey . . . . . . . . . . . . . . . . . . . . . . . . . . . . . . . . . . . . . . . . . . . . .Gene Tyburn

*Teaser:* Lottie, Clancey, Candy, Jeremy, Josh, Franny, Jason, Aaron, Biddie, Barney, Matthew Muncey.

*Tag:* Clancey, Lottie, Jason, Aaron, Candy, Jeremy, Biddie.

*Competition: The Glen Campbell Goodtime Hour* with guests Jose Feliciano and comedy team Jack Burns and Avery Schreiber, CBS; *The Virginian,* "The Price of Love," guest-starring Peter Deuel and Skip Homeier, NBC.

*Photography:* The close of Act I with Clancey sitting in his galley having dinner all alone — the camera slowly pulls back from Clancey at the table, the scene slowly fades out.

*Notes:* In a foreshadowing of what's to come in the second season, this episode focuses on the series' supporting players — in this case, Joan Blondell and Henry Beckman. Guest Lew Ayres is the old flame from Lottie's past who caused problems for her back then; he's likely to do so again. Even more importantly, being an old flame, Ayres arouses Clancey's jealousy. Just how much Clancey has come to care for Lottie, and vice versa, becomes very evident in this episode. Since the story focuses on Lottie, Clancey, and Ayres, it comes across as a very adult, very well-written show. The only scene to strain credibility is when the more-experienced and older Lottie goes to the much-younger Jason and states how she's always running to him for advice. This was hardly the relationship between Jason and Lottie when the show began.

Highlights in this episode are the voiceovers between Jason and Aaron, then the free-for-all talk-over between Jason, Aaron, Lottie, Candy, and Biddie as Dewey ("Dewey from Clearwater") tries to introduce himself to Jason. Susan Tolsky's expression upon first meeting Dewey is priceless!

Henry Beckman's "Riff Raff" remark in response to the loggers' teasing when they see him all "duded-up" is fun; his mud-fight with Lew Ayres' dapper Matthew Muncy is absolutely hysterical.

### Guest Star Lew Ayres

A member of the Henry Halstead Orchestra, Lew Ayres, who played tenor-banjo, long-neck banjo, and guitar in that orchestra, began his motion picture career in 1927.

Three years later, Ayres became a star thanks to his role as Paul Baumer in the

*Left to right: Joan Blondell, Lew Ayres, and Robert Brown in "One Good Lie Deserves Another".*

Lewis Milestone anti-war classic, *All Quiet on the Western Front*. Eight years after this, Ayres began what was to be a four-year run as Dr. James Kildare in MGM's *Dr. Kildare* movie series. A total of nine *Kildare* pictures were produced. In between, Ayres worked in such features as *These Glamour Girls* with Lana Turner and *Broadway Serenade* with Jeanette MacDonald. Later features included *Johnny Belinda* (1948) and the Harold Robbins trash classic, *The Carpetbaggers* (1964).

Unlike so many other big-name stars from the '30s and '40s, when the new medium of television began, Ayres exhibited no objections towards doing it. In addition to his unforgettable role as the Nazi hunter Bartlett in *Route 66* ("Man on the Monkey Board"), the actor guest-starred in the first season *FBI*, "The Tormentors," twice on *The Big Valley*, played Barbara Harper Douglas' father, Professor Harper in the "Mister X" episode of *My Three Sons*, guest-starred in two *Hawaii Five-O*s, and played the governor of Hawaii in the pilot, "Cocoon." Other TV guest shots included *Columbo, Kung Fu, McMillan and Wife, The Fantastic Journey, The Bionic Woman, Wonder Woman, Battlestar Galatica, Flying High, Fantasy Island, Love Boat, Quincy, Highway to Heaven, The A-Team,* and *Fame.*

TV-movies included *Marcus Welby, M.D.* ("A Matter of Humanities," the two-hour pilot for the *Welby* series), *She Waits, The Questor Tapes, The Stranger.* Ayres passed away on December 30, 1996.

*Story Editor William Blinn:* "That was fun, and I worked with Ayres, he did an episode of *Fame* for me, and he was…somehow I had the preconception of Lew Ayres that he would be a little bit cold, stuffy, proper. He was a great deal of fun. He loved doing that kind of thing, cuz he knew it played against what his presentation seemed to be to a lot of people. He was great fun to work with."[121]

*Leading Lady Bridget Hanley:* "I just…I thought…who ever would have thought they'd meet Lew Ayres in their entire lifetime? And I was shy about certain people. But, because of Joanie, and she would include us in stuff – we really had some lovely conversations. He was so dear. But mostly, I was there with my mouth hanging open. I was a kid, and meeting people I thought I would never even meet in my life."[122]

## Composer Shorty Rogers

Born Milton Rajonsky in Great Barrington, Massachusetts, in 1924, Milton "Shorty" Rogers began his musical career when he was only five years old. One day, a young man who worked for his father came into Mr. Rajonsky's small tailor's shop in Lee, Massachusetts, and handed little Milton a trumpet to see if he could play it. As it turned out, Milton could. A few weeks later, the little boy was playing in the newly organized local drum and bugle corps. From age five to age thirteen, the young man played in different bugle and drum bands.

Just before Milton Rajonsky turned thirteen, his father asked him what he'd like for a bar mitzvah present. Milton said a trumpet. From that point on, caught up in the big band music of the era, Milton "Shorty" Rogers had no question as to what he wished to do. Inspired by such jazz musicians as Louis Armstrong, Roy Eldridge, and Dizzy Gillespie, Rogers entered the High School of Music and Art in New York City. Thanks to his performance on trumpet during a high school dance, he received an offer of employment from the high school dance's guest star, jazz band leader Will Bradley.

After leaving the Bradley band, Rogers worked with legendary vibraphonist Red Norvo. Then it was on to Woody Herman, who invited the musician to join his band as soon as he completed his WWII service. In the Herman band, Rogers met a number of famous jazz musicians, including future television and movie composer Neal Hefti.

In the early '50s, thanks to recommendations from his fellow musicians, Pete Rugolo and Shelly Manne, Rogers joined the Stan Kenton band. By this time, Rogers had developed a considerable talent for arranging and composing.

Upon leaving Kenton's band to form his own group, The Giants, Rogers recorded a series of albums for RCA, among them *The Cool and the Crazy* and *Shorty Courts the Count*. Then, when the West Coast jazz scene began to lose popularity in the early '60s, the musician turned to composing scores and background music for movies and TV. Among his motion picture soundtracks and scores: 1965's *Young Dillinger*, the 1966 remake of *Stagecoach*. Among the TV series for which he composed: *Occasional Wife*, *The Partridge Family*, *The Interns*, *The Rookies*, and *Starsky and Hutch*.

February 15, 1969 – TROUBLING RATINGS FOR *Here Come the Brides* – in *TV Guide*, Vol. 17, No. 7, Issue #829, the magazine reveals that in the ratings for Wednesday, January 29, 1969, the debut of *The Glen Campbell Goodtime Hour* scored a powerful 26 in the ratings. Coming in second: *The Virginian*, with a score of 16; coming in last: *Brides*, which received 13.

## Episode #19: "One to a Customer"                    *February 19, 1969*

> "Eventually I hope to shelter and cherish twenty-six wives.
> The same number as espoused by our leader, Brigham Young."
> *Mormon Adam Wilson to Jason Bolt*

| | |
|---|---|
| Writer | John McGreevey |
| Director | Jerry Bernstein |
| Film Editor | Norman Wallerstein |
| Assistant Director | Jim Hogan |
| Music | Shorty Rogers |

*Guest Cast*

| | |
|---|---|
| Adam | Peter Jason |
| Amanda | Tina Holland |

*Teaser:* Loggers, Jason, Corky, Adam.

*Tag:* Jason, Josh, Jeremy, Candy, Franny, Ann, Biddie, Adam, Amanda.

*Competition: The Glen Campbell Goodtime Hour* guest-starring Roger Miller and Stevie Wonder, CBS; *The Virginian*, "The Ordeal," guest-starring Robert Pine and Michael Masters, NBC.

*Notes:* Given *Here Come the Brides'* dramatic situation, the story of the pioneer Mormon women (whose accomplishments were astonishing, to say the least) was tailor-made for the show. Unfortunately, there are no Mormon female characters in *Brides'* sole Mormon tale, "One to a Customer." Though the episode somewhat plays Adam Wilson's practice of polygamy for laughs, it still treats the character with dignity and respect, thanks primarily to the attitude of Kristina Holland's Amanda Forrester. Unlike the other three brides courted by Adam (Candy, Biddie, and Ann), Amanda doesn't like the idea of the brides using Adam as a pawn to get back at the self-assured, conceited men of Seattle — even though Adam was less than honest with the brides when he first approached them.

"He was really just doing what his religion calls for," she explains to the other women. "You can't blame somebody for that." This from the same Amanda who'd been so prejudiced towards Jewish bride Rachel Miller in the earlier "A Jew Named Sullivan." Clearly, the serious talking-to Jason Bolt gave Amanda in "Sullivan" registered with the young woman. Thanks to Jason's lesson, Amanda Forrester is now looking at another person's religion with an open mind. Kristina Holland is just magnificent in the part.

Despite its silly title, "One to a Customer" is a quality *Brides* outing.

*Story Editor William Blinn:* "John McGreevey I had never worked with before. But his reputation preceded him. He was a constantly working writer, and he had so many credits. If John McGreevey was available and interested, he was someone you went after.

"[Having worked on *Family Affair* and *My Three Sons*, McGreevey] would fit into the show well. I was okay with that. A lot of the stuff just had its own limitations because of the Screen Gems budget, and I think we could have...I think we did okay with it. The LDS (Latter Day Saints), the Mormons, were just coming into popular awareness at that time."[123]

## Guest Star Peter Jason

Making his film debut in the John Wayne/Howard Hawks picture, *Rio Lobo*, Peter Jason originally planned to be a football player. He decided upon an acting career after playing the lead in a high school production of the George S. Kaufman play, *The Man Who Came to Dinner*. Following a season of summer stock at the Peterborough Playhouse in New Hampshire, Jason enrolled as a drama major at the Carnegie Institute of Technology in Pittsburgh, Pennsylvania.

Among Peter Jason's early TV work: the homosexual-themed *Judd, for the Defense* episode, "Weep the Hunter Home," *Daniel Boone* ("Bickford's Bridge") *Land of the Giants* ("The Secret City of Limbo") and *Gunsmoke* ("Gentry's Law," an excellent sixteenth-season episode written by soon-to-be *HCTB* writer Jack Miller. Jason also appeared in William Blinn's two-part 1979 *Starsky and Hutch*, "Targets without a Badge," as well as *The Incredible Hulk*, *Hart to Hart*, *Cagney and Lacey*, and *Remington Steele*. He was recently seen as gambler Con Stapleton in the cable TV western, *Deadwood*.

*Leading Lady Bridget Hanley:* "Peter Jason is one of the funniest men that I have ever met in my life. Instant funny. He doesn't even have to think. He's such a good actor. He came to see *Lion in Winter*, and when he was doing *Deadwood* — we did a musical together called *You Haven't Changed a Bit and Other Lies* at the White Fire Theater, then at the theater on the West Side. There were two companies and we alternated; I ended up playing the last month or so with both companies so I got to play with Peter a lot. We just had the best time — he is just unscrupulous with his humor, it is so ever ready and fresh and funny — he's just a lovely man, just a lovely man. And I also did *Kung Fu Revisited* with him up in Canada, with David Carradine. Peter is really a character. He was always in the moment; it was fun to watch him at work."[124]

*Semi-Regular Dick Balduzzi:* "On *Hallmark Hall of Fame*– "A Bell for Adano" I played a soldier. Worked with this young actor named Peter Jason. We did these little scenes — vignettes — there were these little parts showing different soldiers. Peter Jason was a funny guy; we became good friends. You know you see these people for years and then all of a sudden, you don't see them anymore. Peter used to come to the house for dinner because he was a bachelor. My wife didn't ever know who I was bringing home cuz I'd see someone on the set who didn't have anywhere to go. I'd bring them home for dinner or something."[125]

## *Writer John McGreevey*

Writer/Director/Producer John McGreevey started out writing at age seven in Logansport, Indiana, and continued to write through high school and college. Studying English at Indiana University, McGreevey soon began writing plays and radio scripts. Not long after his marriage in 1944, he moved to Arizona, where he worked as both writer and announcer for radio station KTAR in Phoenix. There he created, wrote, and directed the southwestern regional network radio series, *Arizona Adventure*, from 1948-'52. During this same time, McGreevey published a number of stories in magazines, and produced scripts for such radio series as *Cavalcade of America* and *Dr. Christian*.

By the 1950s, McGreevey was contributing scripts to such live television anthologies as *Armstrong Circle Theatre*, *General Electric Theatre*, and *Westinghouse Studio One*. By the late 1950s, he was turning out stories for filmed television series such as *Trackdown, Broken Arrow, Tombstone Territory,* and *Laredo*. Then it was on to '60s sitcoms: *Hazel, My Three Sons, The Farmer's Daughter, Gidget,* and *The Flying Nun,* and '60s dramas: *Route 66, Adventures in Paradise, 12 O'Clock High, Court Martial,* and *Arrest and Trial.*

Greatly influenced by his Midwestern upbringing, McGreevey was the perfect writer for the comedy-drama, *Family Affair*. In *Family Affair*, four of the five regular characters hailed from Terre Haute, Indiana. Shortly after the cancellation of *Family Affair*, John McGreevey began writing for another popular CBS series, *The Waltons*. Like *Affair*, *The Waltons* was a gentle series extolling old-fashioned values.

McGreevey also wrote TV-movie scripts. Among his credits: *Crowhaven Farm, Ruby and Oswald, Sergeant Matlovich vs. the U.S. Air Force,* the four-hour miniseries, *Murder in Texas,* and the 1979 *Roots* sequel, *Roots: The Next Generations.*

## Episode #20: "A Dream that Glitters"          *February 26, 1969*

*Jeremy:* He would have never found any gold in there. We both know that.
*Candy:* No, we don't know that. And neither does he.

Writers. . . . . . . . . . . . . . . . . . . . . . . . . . . . . . . . . . . . Gerry Day and Ila Limerick.
Director. . . . . . . . . . . . . . . . . . . . . . . . . . . . . . . . . . . . . . . .Herb Wallerstein
Film Editor . . . . . . . . . . . . . . . . . . . . . . . . . . . . . . . . . . . . . . . Asa Clark
Assistant Director . . . . . . . . . . . . . . . . . . . . . . . . . . . . . . Michael Dmytryk
Music. . . . . . . . . . . . . . . . . . . . . . . . . . . . . . . . . . . . . . . . . . .Warren Barker

*Guest Cast*

Benjamin Pruitt. . . . . . . . . . . . . . . . . . . . . . . . . . . . . . . . . . . . . Will Geer
Man. . . . . . . . . . . . . . . . . . . . . . . . . . . . . . . . . . . . . . . . . . . .Ed McReady
Bride #1. . . . . . . . . . . . . . . . . . . . . . . . . . . . . . . . . . . . . . .Mary Angela

*Teaser:* Ben, Clancey, Jason, Josh, Jeremy, Biddie, Aaron, Benjamin Pruitt, Lottie, Candy.

*Tag:* Jason, Josh, Aaron, Lottie, Benjamin Pruitt, Jeremy, Candy, Biddie, Ben, Clancey.

*Competition: The Glen Campbell Goodtime Hour* guest-starring Cree Indian folk-singer/composer Buffy Sainte-Marie, Gary Puckett and the Union Gap, and John Byner, CBS; *The Virginian,* "The Land Dreamer," guest-starring James Olson, Don Francks, and Cloris Leachman, NBC.

*Notes:* The performances of Bobby Sherman and Bridget Hanley, plus a clever twist, breathe new life into the oft-told western tale of the old prospector who thinks he's struck it rich. The twist this time: the old prospector is Candy Pruitt's grandfather, Benjamin Pruitt. Throughout his life, Benjamin Pruitt has always dreamed of discovering the mother lode. So, when the old man is seriously injured in a "gold" mine cave-in, Candy, with the help of Jeremy, convinces Benjamin he's struck it rich.

Unfortunately, after Benjamin Pruitt recovers and word gets out that he and his business partner, Lottie Hatfield, have found gold, "gold fever" hits Seattle. Because Candy is the originator of the lie, it's up to her to confess. But she can't. So Benjamin confesses, telling Seattle that he, rather than Jeremy and Candy, salted the mine. His reason: he's always wanted to realize his dream of striking it rich. Later, Jeremy steps forward to tell Seattle the real truth.

The beautiful irony of the story is that Benjamin Pruitt really *believes* he's discovered gold. His reason for claiming otherwise is very simple: he wants Candy and her husband-to-be Jeremy to have the gold in the mine as a safety valve should they ever run into financial difficulties. Knowing this, neither Candy nor Jeremy attempts to correct him. The closing scene of the young woman fighting back tears as she waves goodbye to her grandfather is unforgettable.

Besides giving the audience a vulnerable and flawed Candy Pruitt, the fun of this story is the fact that Candy's reasons for not coming forward with the truth are never made clear to the viewer. The viewer has to furnish his own explanation.

## Guest Star Will Geer

Once described as the "world's oldest hippie"by Helen Hayes, Indiana-born William Aughe Geer began his acting career in tent shows and on river boats. Appearing in a total of thirty-one Broadway plays from 1928-1971, Geer's Broadway works included *110 in the Shade*, the musical version of *The Rainmaker*, John Steinbeck's *Of Mice and Men* (in which Geer played Slim), and Shakespeare's *The Merry Wives of Windsor*. In various stage and screen productions, Geer also portrayed the legendary writers Robert Frost, Walt Whitman, and Mark Twain.

Both folksinger and, in his own words, 'folklorist,' during the Depression, the six-foot-two, 230-pound Geer traveled around the country with his friends Woody Guthrie and Burl Ives singing at government work camps. Proud of being a lifelong agitator and radical, Geer was later blacklisted during the McCarthy era when he refused to name names before the House Committee on Un-American Activities. During this time, Geer built the Will Geer Theatricum Botanicum in Topanga, California; this allowed him to combine his two passions: acting and botany.

It was also around this time that audiences saw Geer in the 1951 Universal Pictures feature, *Bright Victory*. A year earlier the actor appeared in two classic movie westerns in 1950: *Winchester '73* (in which he portrayed Wyatt Earp) and *Broken Arrow*.

In the 1960s and early'70s, before really hitting it big with his role as Grandpa on *The Waltons*, Will Geer became a very active television guest star. Not too surprisingly, his guest shots were as colorful as the man himself. In the second-season *Mission: Impossible*, "The Town," Geer was the villainous doctor who headed an international assassination ring. The actor was equally good as brutal town boss Hurley Gaines in the bizarre September 26, 1971 *Cade's County* episode, "Company Town." Less than two weeks later, audiences saw him as the old prospector Seth in the October 7, 1971 *Alias Smith and Jones*, "Smiler with a Gun." Then there was Geer's role as chemist Len McNeil in the March 11, 1973 *Harry O* pilot film, *Such Dust as Dreams Are Made On*. In this, 'Len' gives private detective Harry Orwell (David Janssen) — and the audience — a detailed crash course on how to make heroin!

*Bridget Hanley on Will Geer:* "Will Geer [played] my grandfather! That was the thrill of a lifetime! And he and David Soul struck up a friendship. Will was just a phenomenon. We had a lovely time. He was very socialistic, but I never experienced that. I often go to his daughter's…the arena theatre outdoors. They used to call it 'Hippie Heaven.' It's kind of a hideaway."[126]

## Director Herb Wallerstein

Getting his start at Columbia Pictures in the mailroom, Herb Wallerstein served as assistant director on such Screen Gems sitcoms as *Hazel, I Dream of Jeannie,* and *The Farmer's Daughter* before moving up to the position of director on the two latter series. Wallerstein then started doing Screen Gems hour-long shows like *Brides* and *Iron Horse,* and Paramount series such as *Star Trek* and *Mission: Impossible.* He had the honor of directing an episode of *Wild Wild West* ("The Night of the Diva," which guest-starred real-life opera star Patrice Munsel). Then, on September 11 and 18, 1972, audiences saw Wallerstein's superb two-part *Gunsmoke,* "The River." Shot on location on Oregon's Rogue River, the episode was written by *Brides* alum Jack Miller, and featured *Brides* semi-regular Patti Cohoon. Other series Wallerstein helmed in the '70s: *Petrocelli, Six Million Dollar Man, Happy Days, Wonder Woman,* and *Tabitha.*

Spring 1969 – *HCTB* article in *16 SPEC.*

March 1969 – Bobby Sherman article in *16 Magazine,* "Bobby Sherman Story, Chapter 1"; two Bobby Sherman articles in *FaVE!;* "Set Secrets" *FaVE!;* "Best New Shows on TV" *TV Radio Mirror;* general article in *Teen World;* Bobby Sherman article in *TV and Movie Screen;* Bobby Sherman article in *Movie Mirror;* "I Visit the Stars, Part 2" *Tiger Beat;* Robert Brown article in *Screen Stories;* Brown tidbit, *Screen Stories; Inside TV,* "Hollywood Women's Press Club Picks 'Stars of the Year!'" (featuring Robert Brown) – *TV Radio Mirror.*

## Episode #21: "The Crimpers"    *March 5, 1969*

> "Don't tell me that you're actually concerned
> about the welfare of the Bolt brothers."
> *Captain Clancey to Aaron Stempel*

| | |
|---|---|
| Writer | Don Tait |
| Director | Paul Junger Witt |
| Film Editor | Asa Clark |
| Assistant Director | Michael Dmytryk |
| Music | Paul Sawtell |

### Guest Cast

| | |
|---|---|
| Amy Fletcher | Rosemary DeCamp |
| Thorpe | Jack Perkins |
| Bartender | Warren Munson |
| Eddie | Dennis Fimple |
| Murphy | Ben Alisa |

*Teaser:* Jeremy, Josh, Corky, Thorpe, Bartender, customers, dancing girls.
*Tag:* Aaron, Jason.
*Competition: The Glen Campbell Goodtime Hour* featuring Joey Bishop, Judy Carne, and Bobby Goldsboro, CBS; *The Virginian,* "Eileen," guest-starring Debbie Watson and Richard van Vleet, NBC.

*Notes:* While "The Crimpers" is similar to the first season *Bonanza* comedy, "San Francisco," unlike "San Francisco," "The Crimpers" contains elements of drama. For example, when Candy learns that Jeremy has disappeared in the town of Port Angeles, she is determined to go there with Jason and Aaron and assist in the search. Lottie tells her not to — she'll only be in the way. Candy is so upset at not being able to help that she comes close to bursting into tears. But, Candy being Candy, she doesn't want to do anything so personal in front of anybody. So she runs off, looking for some private place to cry. But, no matter where she goes, there are people — and, all the while, Biddie is practically on her heels. Why she keeps following Candy becomes clear once Candy finds the one place she can cry in private — the lavatory. Biddie is there to lend emotional support.

Adding further drama to the episode is the fact that the Bolts' sometime-nemesis, Aaron Stempel, is helping Jason free his shanghaied brothers. Aaron claims he's doing this since he needs all of the Bolts to help him fill his latest order; his actions and conversations with Jason prove otherwise.

Like "One to a Customer," this is another *Brides* episode in which semi-regular Robert Biheller is used to good effect. Director Paul Witt's shooting of the teaser, part of it from the drugged Jeremy's point of view, makes for very involving television. The fight in the dark when Josh and Jeremy overpower attempted rescuers Jason and Aaron is another memorable bit. Rosemary DeCamp's unusual casting as the head of the crimpers adds to the fun.

## Guest Star Rosemary De Camp

Rosemary De Camp's role as Amy Fletcher in *Here Come the Brides*, "The Crimpers," is the sort of role the actress always played well. De Camp had been playing this sort of character ever since she'd made her film debut in 1941's *Cheers for Miss Bishop*. In that movie, the thirty-year-old De Camp played a sixty-five-year-old woman! That was just four years after she'd began her seventeen-year run as Judy – the nice nurse on the *Dr. Christian* radio serial.

Thanks to her work on radio, De Camp developed a vocal quality which allowed her to sound much older than she was. She was so good at this that in 1942 she was cast as the mother of James Cagney's George M. Cohan in the Warner Bros. screen biography, *Yankee Doodle Dandy*; Cagney was fourteen years older than DeCamp! Three years later, the actress played composer George Gershwin's (Robert Alda) mother in Warner's *Rhapsody in Blue*. De Camp was just one year older than Alda!

Despite these less than glamorous roles, De Camp was the favorite of the 475th Squadron, USAAF in World War II. To these men, De Camp was the girl next door, or the wife that waits. There was also a Rosemary De Camp Fan Club with chapters all over the U.S. which published a magazine with the motto, "Rosemary De Camp— our candidate for stardom." A regular feature in the magazine was a letter from the actress, "Rosemarily yours," in which De Camp brought her fans up to date on her career. An industry insider, DeCamp was a director of the Screen Actors' Guild for twelve years, and later served as the Guild's vice president.

On television, DeCamp appeared in two popular early sitcoms, *The Life of Riley*, in which she portrayed Peg Riley, the wife of Chester A. Riley (Jackie Gleason). In the more successful *Love that Bob*, De Camp was Margaret MacDonald, sister of the lecherous, girl-chasing photographer Bob Collins (Bob Cummings) The 1960s found DeCamp playing Helen Marie, Ann's mother on *That Girl*; the Bradley girls' Aunt Helen on *Petticoat Junction*; and Priscilla Rolfe Alden-Smith-Standish on *The Beverly Hillbillies*. She also served as substitute host on the western anthology, *Death Valley Days*, for her longtime friend, Ronald Reagan.

In addition to a seventeen-year position as commercial spokesman for *Death Valley Day's* sponsor, 20 Mule Team Borax, Rosemary De Camp wrote newspaper columns and children's books. Later she played Grandma on the '70s hit, *The Partridge Family*. De Camp's other TV series guest shots included *Dr. Kildare, Rawhide, Burke's Law, Longstreet, Mannix, Marcus Welby, M.D., Police Story, Family, Simon & Simon*, and *Hotel*. She passed away on February 20, 2001 in Torrance, California, at the age of ninety.

*Bridget Hanley on Rosemary Decamp:* "She was already a star [when she appeared on *HCTB*]. All I remember is like…I was kind of like…the mouth dropped open. It was like Joan Blondell time. When you meet somebody who had a career, or is having a career, your mouth drops open and you kind of breathe, and hope that they think you're okay." [127]

## Writer Don Tait

Starting out editing the segments of the *Woody Woodpecker* cartoon series in 1957, Don Tait moved on to *Maverick* and then more serious fare like *The Virginian, Felony Squad*, and *The Green Hornet* by the mid-1960s. After writing a few action screenplays (*Hell's Angels '69, One More Train to Rob*) in the early'70s, Tait then went to work for Walt Disney Studios, turning out scripts for such popular Disney comedies as *The Apple Dumpling Gang* and *The Shaggy D.A.*

*TV Guide* – March 8, 1969 – Vol. 17, No 10, Issue #832 – Jerry Buck: TV Jibe – Dialogue I'd Love to Hear" From *Here Come the Brides* – dialogue between Lumberjack and Miss Essie: Lumberjack asks Miss Essie to marry him. Essie tells him she didn't come to Seattle to work over a "hot stove." She's going to get a job at Boeing.

# Episode #22: "Mr. and Mrs. J. Bolt"        *March 12, 1969*

"Welcome to the family, Mrs. Bolt."
*Joshua Bolt to Peggy*

Writer . . . . . . . . . . . . . . . . . . . . . . . . . . . . . . . . . . . . . . . . . . Richard Bluel
Director . . . . . . . . . . . . . . . . . . . . . . . . . . . . . . . . . . . . . . . Richard Kinon

Film Editor . . . . . . . . . . . . . . . . . . . . . . . . . . . . . . . . . . . . . . . Norman Wallerstein
Assistant Director . . . . . . . . . . . . . . . . . . . . . . . . . . . . . . . . . . . . . . . . Jim Hogan
Music. . . . . . . . . . . . . . . . . . . . . . . . . . . . . . . . . . . . . . . . . . . . . . . Shorty Rogers

*Guest Cast*

Jebediah. . . . . . . . . . . . . . . . . . . . . . . . . . . . . . . . . . . . . . . . . . . . . . . Henry Jones
Peggy. . . . . . . . . . . . . . . . . . . . . . . . . . . . . . . . . . . . . . . . . . . . . Mary Jo Kennedy

*Henry Jones and Robert Brown in "Mr. and Mrs. J. Bolt".*

**Teaser:** Josh, Jeremy, Jason, Candy, Peggy.

**Tag:** Jason, Jeremy, Josh.

**Competition:** *The Glen Campbell Goodtime Hour* guest-starring Leslie Uggams, Ken Berry, Merle Haggard, and Tom and Dick Smothers, CBS; *The Virginian,* "Incident at Diablo Crossing," guest-starring Gary Collins and Kiel Martin, NBC.

**Notes:** *Mission: Impossible — Here Come the Brides*-style — with Jason as the mastermind, Josh and Peggy masquerading as a newly married couple, Jeremy and Candy keeping Clancey from the bottle, and Lottie getting Aaron out of town.

Target of the group's deception: Peggy's ne'er-do-well uncle and guardian, Jebediah Thornley. This is a funny, funny show, with terrific performances all around. Best sequence: Jeremy downs glass after glass of whiskey in an attempt to keep Clancey from getting drunk.

An interesting touch concerning the teaser and tag of this episode is that both take place at the same location (the exterior of the Bolt cabin), where Jason waxes philosophical about the importance of all three brothers sharing the work. Only it is Josh and Jeremy who are doing the work!

*Story Editor William Blinn:* "Dick Bluel I had met. I had never worked with him before. That was kind of a crap shoot. By that I mean, 'Let's see how it works out.' He was good — he's a good writer. He was an excellent writer and dependable and all this and that, but he was a carpenter, he wasn't an architect, at least for me. There was a lot of restructuring that went on after Dick walked out of the office. It was a worthwhile effort — kind of bizarre and strange. If you do corny stuff with enough belief, sometimes it can really work, and that's what we were trying to do with this one. I think my attitude towards this show is based on the fact that I knew how bad it was before we got there. But there was some good stuff in there, absolutely. And it was a chance for David to get out from under the shadow of Bobby, and he made the most of it. When we gave him those episodes, a lot of it was we wanted to try to bring him forward. Forget about his career problems, we needed to have another leading man on the show because Bobby was just getting overworked, and to some degree, Bobby was weary, doing eighteen-hour days, on the weekend doing concerts and records, and so forth and so on. We needed to give him some time off.

"That was a good episode."[128]

## Guest Star Henry Jones

Making his stage (and Broadway) debut as Smoky Flynn in the farce, *She Lived Next to the Firehouse*, Philadelphia-born Henry Jones followed that with the role of Doctor Glenn in Theodore Dreiser's *An American Tragedy* at the Hedgerow Theatre in Moylan, Pennsylvania. He then returned to Broadway to play the dual roles of Reynaldo and the second gravedigger in Shakespeare's *Hamlet*. Jones' many other Broadway credits included William Saroyan's *The Time of Your Life*, the comedy, *My Sister Eileen*, the musical fantasy, *Alice in Wonderland*, the comedy, *The Solid Gold Cadillac*, and the dramas, *The Bad Seed*, *Sunrise at Campobello*, and *Advise and Consent*.

Following his film debut as the soldier, Mr. Brown in the 1943 Warner Bros. musical, *This is the Army*, more than a decade later, Jones appeared in the Glenn Ford/ Van Heflin 1957 western, *3:10 to Yuma*. In Alfred Hitchcock's *Vertigo*, he was a coroner; in the 1968 William Castle science-fiction/spy thriller, *Project X*, he was Dr. Crowther, the head of a scientific team who sends secret agent Christopher George into the year 2118 to help defeat a threat posed by a foreign power. The 1969 James Garner comedy-western, *Support Your Local Sheriff* offered Jones as a preacher. The same year's Paul Newman/Robert Redford mega-hit, *Butch Cassidy and the Sundance Kid*, featured him as a bicycle salesman.

Thanks to the fast pace of television, Jones had an opportunity to play an even wider variety of roles. In the 1961 *Thriller*, "The Weird Tailor," the actor played the title role. The April 20, 1962 *Route 66*, "Two on the House" took him to Cleveland, Ohio, to portray the role of Asa "Ace" Turnbull, captain of the boat which takes passengers on a tour around the city. Jones then played the title character in the 1965 *Honey West*, "The Abominable Snowman." The same year, audiences saw him as Secretary of State Hamilton Fish on *Profiles in Courage*. Then there was Nick Barkley's former Union commander, General Alderson, in the March 6, 1967 *Big Valley*, "Court Martial," Mr. Pem in two fourth-season *Voyage to the Bottom of the Seas*, and Dr. Zachary Smith's Southern-accented cousin, Jeremiah Smith, in *Lost in Space*, "Curse of Cousin Smith." Jeremiah made the underhanded, unscrupulous Dr. Smith look like a saint.

"Unforgettable" described Jones' role as King Arthur (he rides around on horseback in full armor) in the December 20, 1964 *Bonanza*, "A Knight to Remember." Then there was robot maker Dr. Chester Dolenz in three memorable episodes of the mid-'70s hit, *The Six Million Dollar Man*, and Judge Jonathan Dexter during the two seasons of *The Mary Tyler Moore Show* spinoff, *Phyllis*. Other 1970s guest shots included *The Partridge Family*, *Vegas*, *Project U.F.O. Love Boat*, and *Fantasy Island*. Eighties appearances included *BJ and the Bear*, *Cagney and Lacey*, *Mr. Belvedere*, and *Murder, She Wrote*.

*Bridget Hanley on Henry Jones:* "Henry Jones! I later...I got to meet him again, in a social situation, and he is, just was, just the most divine man. He was funny — I was shy of him, and Swack knew him, and Bill Windom knew him, but I didn't know that he and Bill were so close. What a team together — Windom and Jones."[129]

(William Windom and Henry Jones worked together in the August 18, 1981 situation comedy pilot, *Quick & Quiet* — the last television production from TV giant Quinn Martin.)

### *Writer Richard Bluel*

Probably best known for producing the 1966-67 Bruce Lee cult series, *The Green Hornet*, Richard Bluel began his more than twenty-five year television career as a story supervisor on the mid 1950s anthology, *DuPont Theater* — a.k.a. *Cavalcade of America*. By the late 1950s, Bluel was writing for the action-filled Charles Bronson series, *Man with a Camera*. Following that, he wrote for the early '60s detective drama, *Bourbon Street Beat*, then the WWII drama, *The Gallant Men*. After helping to get the post Civil War sitcom, *F Troop* off the ground, Bluel became producer of *The Green Hornet*. Following this, he did the Monte Markham Screen Gems comedy, *The Second Hundred Years*.

Alternating between producing *Goliath Awaits*, *The Impostor*, and writing *Raid on Rommel*, *The Castaway Cowboy*, *Owen Marshall: Counselor at Law*, and *Banacek*, Richard Bluel died in 1992.

March 15, 1969 – *TV Guide* Crossword – 12 down – Here Come the
_____ (Vol. 17, No 11, Issue #833)

## Episode #23: "A Man's Errand"          *March 19, 1969*

"Don't let this thing between you and Candy tip the scales too much."
*Jason to Jeremy*

Writer . . . . . . . . . . . . . . . . . . . . . . . . . . . . . . . . . . . . . . . Lee Oscar Bloomgarden
Director. . . . . . . . . . . . . . . . . . . . . . . . . . . . . . . . . . . . . . . . . . Jerry Bernstein
Film Editor . . . . . . . . . . . . . . . . . . . . . . . . . . . . . . . . . . . . . . . . . . Asa Clark
Assistant Director . . . . . . . . . . . . . . . . . . . . . . . . . . . . . . . . . . . . Jim Hogan
*Guest Cast*
Silas. . . . . . . . . . . . . . . . . . . . . . . . . . . . . . . . . . . . . . . . . . . . . John Anderson
Ward . . . . . . . . . . . . . . . . . . . . . . . . . . . . . . . . . . . . . . . . . . . Jeff Pomerantz
Ashley . . . . . . . . . . . . . . . . . . . . . . . . . . . . . . . . . . . . . . . . . Larry D. Mann

*Teaser:* Clancey, Jeremy, Jason, Josh.

*Tag:* Candy, Silas, Jason, Josh, Jeremy.

*Competition: The Glen Campbell Goodtime Hour* guest-starring Jim Nabors and Bobbie Gentry, CBS; *The Virginian,* "Storm over Shiloh," featuring the regular cast, NBC.

*Notes:* Reminiscent of the fourth-season, September 30, 1962 *Bonanza* episode, "The Quest" (in which the youngest Cartwright, Little Joe, seeks to prove himself by winning and fulfilling an important timber contract for the Ponderosa), Lee Oscar Bloomgarden's *Here Come the Brides'* "A Man's Errand" begins with the youngest Bolt, Jeremy, seeking to prove *himself* by winning an important contract for the Bolt brothers logging operation. "Begins" is the key word. Although Bobby Sherman cited this manhood test as an important development for the Jeremy character in his autobiography, *Still Remembering You,* "A Man's Errand" actually places more emphasis on the Jeremy/Candy romance.

Up to this point, the Jeremy/Candy romance, while frequently used, had never really dominated a story. The situation in "A Man's Errand" creates a perfect opportunity to have the couple dominate a show — a good way to do this is to put them at odds. Thanks to this scenario, some negative qualities are brought to sweet, good-guy Jeremy. Though the audience's sympathy is with him in the beginning, it soon transfers to Candy.

Bobby Sherman is just terrific in this change-of-pace role. John Anderson does his usual fine work as Silas Harmon, and Larry D. Mann (Judge Cody from "Letter of the Law") is fun as a cigar-smoking, self-satisfied, Northern California lumberman.

In this episode we learn what varieties of trees grow on Bridal Veil Mountain. They are: Oak, Spruce, Douglas Fir, and Maple. We also see Candy behaving in a more outwardly vulnerable manner. She cries openly in the presence of her new friend, Ward Kimberley.

Fans of *Bonanza, Lancer, The Wild Wild West,* etc. will recognize the stock shot of San Francisco in this episode.

## Guest Star John Anderson

Graduating with a master's degree in drama from the University of Iowa, John Anderson began his performing career on the Mississippi River showboat, *Goldenrod*. His first onscreen acting job was for Curad band-aids; only his finger was used. After serving in the Coast Guard during World War II, Anderson spent a year at

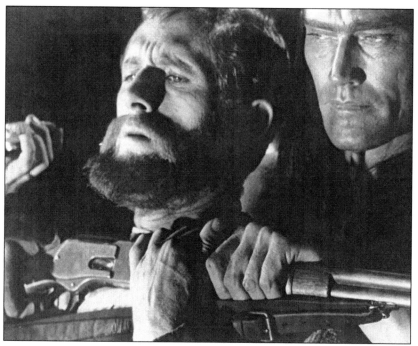

*"A Man's Errand" star John Anderson with Chuck Connors in the Levy/Gardner/Laven western,* Geronimo.

the Cleveland Play House, then he moved to New York, where he appeared in such Broadway shows as *Cat on a Hot Tin Roof*.

An assistant director on the 1946 B-movie, *Dick Tracy vs. Cueball*, Anderson made his film debut in the 1952 Burt Lancaster feature, *The Crimson Pirate*. He then became a very active TV guest star, appearing on '50s series such as *Sea Hunt, Richard Diamond, Private Detective, Mike Hammer, Peter Gunn, Trackdown*, and *Have Gun, Will Travel*. In the '60s, the prolific Anderson guest-starred on *Adventures in Paradise, Dr. Kildare, Route 66, The Outer Limits, The Great Adventure, Mannix, Rat Patrol, Perry Mason, Occasional Wife, Tarzan*, etc. Seventies credits included *Hawaii Five-O, Cannon, Kung Fu, The Bob Newhart Show, Little House on the Prairie*, and *The Family Holvak*.

In addition to his work in such motion pictures as *Psycho, Geronimo, 5 Card Stud*, and *The Lincoln Conspiracy*, Anderson's TV-movies included 1974's *Smile, Jenny,*

*You're Dead* (the second pilot for David Janssen's *Harry O* series), 1975's *Death Among Friends*, (in which Anderson's Captain Lewis hands out the assignments to homicide detective Kate Reid and her partner, A Martinez), the 1930s-era gangster drama, *The Manhunter*, 1978's *Donner Pass: The Road to Survival*, and an adaptation of the James Fenimore Cooper classic, *The Deerslayer*. Among Anderson's miniseries: *Backstairs at the White House*, *Rich Man, Poor Man, Book II*, the E.W. Swackhamer-co-directed *Once an Eagle*.

One of Anderson's most unusual TV productions was the 1969 Roy Huggins/Universal feature, *The Profane Comedy* (a.k.a. *Set This Town on Fire*.) Offbeat in its story, characters and presentation, *Profane* was co-produced by its editor, Carl Pingitore. The movie reunited Anderson with frequent co-star Chuck Connors. Anderson played town drunk Henry Kealey. Henry's actions in *Profane* are quite bizarre, to say the least.

*Bridget Hanley on John Anderson:* "John Anderson was one of our closest, closest, closest friends. He and Swack...Swack directed him, and an actor named Alex Nicol, in the touring company of *Cat on a Hot Tin Roof.* So they knew each other before I even knew of Swack. He (Anderson) was a New York guy — they all were. He and his wife Pat, and their daughter, Kelsey, and their son, Jeff — they lived here in the Valley. We saw them all the time. So I knew him before the show. He's just an extraordinary actor.

"His wife passed away before him. I miss them. I still make her recipe for caviar pie. And a number of other things. Swack loved John — I just adored him, too. I was in awe when I first met him; I had seen him on so many things. So I would just kind of hang back. We dined together — at the Brown Derby, after going to the theater together. It was a whole different Hollywood, you know. The Andersons — I cannot say enough about — they knew Henry [Beckman], too. There was a smaller gang then. A lot of them knew each other and knew each other well. They had done tons of movies together — a lot of television [also].

"I feel honored to have been part of it. It was really unique. How I ever was brave enough to put my toe in the water here...I am so glad I did. I just kept thinking, I think I can, I think I can I think I can — like the little red engine, and I kept getting enough successes that it kind of spurred me on to the next round."[130]

*TV Guide* – March 22, 1969 -Vol. 17, No 12 Issue #834 – *TV Guide* Crossword – Answer – 12 down – *Brides*

March 23, 1969 – Mark Lenard guest stars on *Mission: Impossible* in the episode, "Nitro."

## Episode #24: "Loggerheads"                          *March 26, 1969*

> "I thought being a lawyer would mean helping people. That's not
> what's happening. That's why I told you. I had to tell somebody,
> Biddie. If I had to tell, I'm glad you were here to listen to me."
> *Barnabus Webster to Biddie Cloom*

Writer . . . . . . . . . . . . . . . . . . . . . . . . . . . . . . . . . . . . . . . . . . . . . . . . . . .Skip Webster
Director. . . . . . . . . . . . . . . . . . . . . . . . . . . . . . . . . . . . . . . . . . . . . . Richard Kinon
Film Editor . . . . . . . . . . . . . . . . . . . . . . . . . . . . . . . . . . . . . . Norman Wallterstein
Assistant Director . . . . . . . . . . . . . . . . . . . . . . . . . . . . . . . . . . Sheldon Schrager

*Guest Cast*

Barnabus . . . . . . . . . . . . . . . . . . . . . . . . . . . . . . . . . . . . . . . . . . . . . . Hal England
Victor. . . . . . . . . . . . . . . . . . . . . . . . . . . . . . . . . . . . . . . . . . . Alan Oppenheimer
Judge Weems. . . . . . . . . . . . . . . . . . . . . . . . . . . . . . . . . . . . . . William Zuckert
Dutch . . . . . . . . . . . . . . . . . . . . . . . . . . . . . . . . . . . . . . . . Christopher Stone

*Teaser:* Biddie, Candy, Jeremy, Barnabus, Clancey, Lottie, Josh, Jason, Victor.

*Tag:* Biddie, Barnabus, Victor, Jason, Josh, Jeremy, Candy, Clancey, Aaron, Lottie.

*Competition: Africa Special — Adventures at the Jade Sea*, hosted and narrated by William Holden, CBS; *The Virginian*, "The Girl in the Shadows," guest-starring *Brides* guests Jack Albertson and Brenda Scott, NBC.

*Notes:* "The first thing we do, let's kill all the lawyers," says Dick the butcher to villain Jack Cade in Shakespeare's *Henry the Sixth*–Part II, Act IV. This might well be the thinking of the people of Seattle considering the way Victor Webster and his attorney brother, Barnabus, spread dissension in Seattle.

A somewhat comedic (but actually more dramatic) late first-season entry with comedienne Susan Tolsky playing a very moving Biddie in love, "Loggerheads" presents viewers with a very hostile Joshua Bolt. During the course of the story, the disagreement between Joshua and his two brothers becomes worse and worse as the episode progresses. Because of their falling out, the Bolts are in danger of losing their mountain. Saving it and reuniting the three Bolts, both directly and indirectly, is — of all people — Biddie Cloom!

In this episode, we learn that the name of the Bolts' father is Jonathan, and that under the terms of his will, all three brothers own a third of the mountain. The only way anyone else can claim the mountain is if all three brothers agree to release their share.

William Zuckert, who played the judge in episode #3 ("And Jason Makes Five") plays the same character again; Robert Brown is at his best in the trial scene where he resorts to hour after hour of reciting American poetry as part of his "defense."

While every member of the cast does good work, the touching moments, of which there are many, all go to Susan Tolsky. She is excellent in this episode. As Barnabus Webster (the man who loves her), Hal England is just right.

*Story Editor William Blinn:* "It was okay. I wish we could have been more clever. You know, the actors, I think, occasionally the writers get tired, too. I think it was a little forced. I've said a number of times, 'If you give me a pound of ground round, and a hamburger bun, and some Swiss cheese, and a little bit of seasoning, the best thing I can do is make a cheeseburger. I can't make it into Dover sole. And I think sometimes we suffered with the *Brides* — the material that we were given just didn't give us the opportunity to go any further. I don't think the show ever got to where I thought it ought to be. I think we kind of got intrigued with the whole legal lawyer aspect thing, and obviously got tied up in a message because it was the message of the show. Somehow the topic overshadowed the fact that we were dealing with character. Not that it was bad; it just wasn't what it ought to have been."[131]

*Series Regular Susan Tolsky:* "My great love scene and I've got the cramps. I had terrible cramps. The only kiss I ever had, and there's a heating pad on my belly, and [they] had to shoot me tight two-shots. Truly. There were extension cords, and the thing that's funny is if the camera pulled back, you would see extension cords. It was just a funny sight to do the shot so you wouldn't see it. It's funny now, but it was painful then."[132]

## Guest Star Alan Oppenheimer

Beginning his lengthy career while still a teenager (he was the voice of Mighty Mouse in the *Mighty Mouse* shorts of the mid-'40s), Alan Oppenheimer then played the villainous cat, Oil Can Harry, in the CBS 1955-66 Saturday morning cartoon, *The Mighty Mouse Playhouse.* Soon after that, Oppenheimer was guest-starring in numerous sitcoms: *Hogan's Heroes, I Dream of Jeannie, The Partridge Family,* and dramatic shows such as *Judd, for the Defense, The Name of the Game, The FBI,* and *Lancer.* He also played recurring roles on *I Spy* (Colonel Benkovsky), *He and She* (Murray Mouse), and *The Six Million Dollar Man* (Dr. Rudy Wells). Motion pictures included the Japanese monster flick, *Gammera the Invincible, In the Heat of the Night, Star, The Maltese Bippy, Little Big Man,* and *Westworld.*

On March 22, 1971, audiences saw Oppenheimer as disguise expert Edgar Winston in the *Mission: Impossible* spy spoof, *Inside O.U.T.* Directed by *Mission's* Reza S. Badiyi, this half-hour Screen Gems pilot co-starred *I Dream of Jeannie/ The Bob Newhart Show's* Bill Daily, and an up-and-coming young Screen Gems discovery named Farrah Fawcett. Oppenheimer's other '70s TV work included the *Bonanza* comedies, "A Deck of Aces," "The Customs of the Country," and "A Visit to Upright," *Medical Center,* "The Fourth Sex" (Parts 1 &2), *Harry O,* "The Acolyte," and the sitcoms *Happy Days, Here's Lucy, SOAP,* and *What's Happening.* Miniseries included *Helter Skelter* and *Washington: Behind Closed Doors.*

Continuing to do voices in cartoons while guest-starring on series such as *Knight Rider* and *Matlock* in the 1980s, Alan Oppenheimer is still acting and doing voice work, as of this writing.

*Bridget Hanley on Alan Oppenheimer:* "I know Alan very well. From Theater West. Crazy Alan. He's just a great, great guy. What an actor! A fabulous actor. And funny. And wry. And witty. Wonderful to be around as a fellow actor and as a friend."[133]

## Guest Star Hal England

Making his Broadway debut in the 1958 Betty Comden/Adolph Green musical comedy, *Say Darling*, at the ANTA Playhouse, North Carolina-born Hal England was a member of the company during Joseph Papp's first season of Shakespeare in the Park in New York in 1957. During that season, England appeared in such classic works as *Romeo and Juliet*, *Two Gentlemen of Verona*, and *Macbeth*. England's television debut came in *The Clear Horizon* — a short-lived CBS soap-opera focusing on astronaut Roy Selby (Ed Kemmer) his family, and co-workers at Cape Canaveral. England played Lt. Douglas Merrill. Among the other well-known performers appearing in regular roles: Lee Meriwether (Enid Ross), Beau Bridges (Eddie Tinker), Ted Knight (Colonel Tate), and Jan Shepard (Betty Howard).

Following this series, England began doing many situation comedy guest shots — among them: *The Many Loves of Dobie Gillis*, *F Troop*, *Occasional Wife*, and *The Flying Nun*. It wasn't really until the '70s that England began doing dramatic series. His credits included *Cannon*, *Barnaby Jones*, *The Streets of San Francisco*, *Tales of the Unexpected*, *Marcus Welby, M.D.*, *The Mod Squad*, and *Police Woman*. In the '80s, England guest-starred on fantasy/sci-fi series including *Manimal*, *Fantasy Island*, *Quantum Leap*, *Otherworld*, and *Beauty and the Beast*.

A longtime member of the Actor's Studio, one of England's greatest successes came when he played the lead role of J. Pierpont Finch in the national tour of the Broadway hit, *How to Succeed in Business Without Really Trying*. He died of a heart attack at age seventy-one in Burbank, California.

*Bridget Hanley on Hal England:* "Hal England was one of my dearest, dearest, dearest friends. He was just the best. There's a cookbook…we all — it was to save my grandparents' house which was going to be demolished. [England contributed a recipe to the cookbook.] Hal and I worked together many times — a lot of Theatre West, a lot at the Actor's Studio, and I think we did a couple other shows. He was a fantastic man and actor, and friend. I mean, I just miss him every day. Fabulous, fabulous guy. We did a play together called *The Innocents of Summer*. Another dear friend, who is no longer with us, directed. We played brother and sister. I played this drunken, boozy, wonderful Southern lady, and Hal was my brother. We just had… theatrically, and on film, I had some of the best experiences of my life with that man. He just had a great…everybody loved Hal.

"I was a pallbearer at his funeral. I was the only woman. I was so honored. I just felt so honored to be one of his closest friends, and to help carry him to Heaven. That was so sad, and I get…oh boy, I still can't believe it — being a pallbearer. It was a memorial, a celebration for an incredible life as an actor, a human being, and a darling friend. It was amazing. It was just amazing. We could laugh. We could swear with each other, tell each other the truth. I don't know whether people have that many friendships. I have a lot of female friends, and they've become deeper and richer as the years have gone by. But this [friendship] was a guy and a lady — actors first, and then a friendship from that. We were just clear with each other, and had so many laughs, and so much fun. And then the deep sadness — I was so honored to be asked to share his final performance. His final bow.

"Having him on the show, he was just…He was 'Hail Fellow Well Met.' He just came on the set, and you just went…'Oooo. I want to work with you.' He was just like that. He was cheery and confident, but vulnerable. To be a performer, there's a certain vulnerability that you need, but you don't want to let it cut the other part out. He just knew how to do it."[134]

> March 29, 1969 – *TV Guide* – Vol. 17., No. 13 – Issue #835 – TV Tele-type: Hollywood – Joseph Finnigan Reports: And Here Come the Brides concentrates less on the new "brides" next fall and more on anthology-type stories of the Pacific Northwest."

> April 1969 – Bobby Sherman article in *Inside TV;* "Bobby Sherman Story, Chapter 2"
> *Tiger Beat;* Bobby Sherman article in *Tiger Beat;* two Bobby Sherman articles in *FaVE!;* Bobby Sherman article in *16 Magazine;* "I Visit the Stars, Part 3"
> *Tiger Beat;* "Frenchy's Freakies Presents HERE COME THE BRIDES"
> *16 Magazine;* Henry Beckman in *TV and Movie Screen;* Robert Brown article – *TV and Movie Screen, TV Star Parade, Movie Life;* Bridget Hanley – *Tiger Beat.*

> April 2, 1969 – *Brides* pre-empted by rerun of *Jacques Cousteau Special – The Unexpected Voyage of Pepito and Cristobal.*

## Episode #25: "Marriage: "Chinese Style"              *April 9, 1969*

"I am Jeremy Bolt's Toy."
*Toy Quan (Linda Dangcil) to the ladies of Seattle*

Writer . . . . . . . . . . . . . . . . . . . . . . . . . . . . . . . . . . . . . . . . . . . . . . . .Skip Webster
Director. . . . . . . . . . . . . . . . . . . . . . . . . . . . . . . . . . . . . . . . . . . . Richard Kinon
Film Editor . . . . . . . . . . . . . . . . . . . . . . . . . . . . . . . . . . . . . . . Norman Wallerstein
Assistant Director . . . . . . . . . . . . . . . . . . . . . . . . . . . . . . . . . . . . . . Jim Hogan
Music. . . . . . . . . . . . . . . . . . . . . . . . . . . . . . . . . . . . . . . . . . . . . . . .Warren Barker
*Guest Cast*
Toy Quan . . . . . . . . . . . . . . . . . . . . . . . . . . . . . . . . . . . . . . . . . . .Linda Dangcil

Lin. . . . . . . . . . . . . . . . . . . . . . . . . . . . . . . . . . . . . . . . . . . . . . . . . . . . . . Bruce Lee
Chi Pe . . . . . . . . . . . . . . . . . . . . . . . . . . . . . . . . . . . . . . . . . . . . . . . . Richard Loo
Kang . . . . . . . . . . . . . . . . . . . . . . . . . . . . . . . . . . . . . . . . . . . . . . . Weaver Levy
Lucy . . . . . . . . . . . . . . . . . . . . . . . . . . . . . . . . . . . . . . . . . . . . . . . Helen Kleeb
Chu . . . . . . . . . . . . . . . . . . . . . . . . . . . . . . . . . . . . . . . . . . . . . Hideo Imamura
Capt. Hale. . . . . . . . . . . . . . . . . . . . . . . . . . . . . . . . . . . . . . . . . Jeff DeBenning
Maude . . . . . . . . . . . . . . . . . . . . . . . . . . . . . . . . . . . . . . . . . . . . . .Myra deGroot
Mrs. Bronson. . . . . . . . . . . . . . . . . . . . . . . . . . . . . . . . . . . . . . . Nora Marlowe
Donovan . . . . . . . . . . . . . . . . . . . . . . . . . . . . . . . . . . . . . . . . . . .Jack Perkins

*Teaser:* Jeremy, Tacoma townspeople, Toy Quan, Donovan, Captain Hale, Mrs. Bronson.

*Tag:* Clancey, Lottie, Biddie, Josh, Candy, Jeremy, Jason.

*Competition: The Glen Campbell Goodtime Hour* guest-starring Ray Charles, singer Lynn Kellogg, Jack Burns and Avery Schreiber, CBS; *The Virginian,* "The Stranger," guest-starring Shelly Novack, John Doucette, Michael Conrad, NBC.

*Notes:* The situation of Jeremy Bolt coming back from Tacoma with a Chinese girl whom he's rescued, and who claims he now owns her, is definitely clichéd, but it allows for some of the naughtiest and raciest dialogue ever heard on the series — such as: "He picked her up in an alley by the waterfront."

Susan Tolsky gets some of the best lines in the entire show. For example, when Josh is telling the ladies of Seattle that Jeremy paid the sea captain $300 for Toy Quan (Jeremy was trying to protect the girl and enable her to meet her intended, Lin), Jeremy corrects him, pointing out it was only $275. Cracks Biddie to Candy, "Some people will haggle over anything." Later, when the ladies of Seattle find Toy Quan in the Bolts' cabin, with a bare-chested Jeremy, the blue-nosed Lucy exclaims, "Well, I never!" "Ooooh," replies an overwhelmed Biddie, "None of us has."

Top-billed guest Linda Dangcil, whom *Brides* leading lady Bridget Hanley describes as "charming" and "delightful" adds even more to the fun of this show. Fans of *The Waltons* will recognize *Waltons* semi-regular Helen Kleeb in the part of Lucy. Guest composer Warren Barker's score exudes an Oriental flavor.

*Story Editor William Blinn:* "We did one where there was a logging contract that took place in San Francisco — they had to go to San Francisco, and we did another where we had a Chinese heavy, and it got to be cartoony. It got to be really cartoony, which would have been okay, if that's how it was played, but it was played for a reality basis. I disliked that show. I was the story editor. I approved it, so I have no one to blame but it was very much like an old-fashioned *Bonanza* — you know the Oriental person saying, 'Oh, you saved my life. Therefore, blah, blah, blah, blah, blah. And A. That's not true — it was a television myth, and B: It doesn't take you anywhere — it was kind of like an hour sitcom as opposed to a half-hour sitcom. I was not a fan of 'Marriage: Chinese Style.' I just thought it was such a traditional, corny western plot. I recall going in there, trying to put some little curve on it, some little shine on it. Whether I was successful or not, I don't know, but I know there was a lot of work done on that. If it's not right at the foundation, it's never gonna be right at the roof."[135]

## *Guest Star Bruce Lee:*

Martial arts trailblazer, actor, philosopher, and instructor, Bruce Lee was sent to the United States at the age of eighteen after getting into a fight (which he won) and clashing with the police. Completing his high school education in Seattle and receiving his diploma from Edison Technical School, Lee enrolled at the University of Washington, where he studied philosophy, drama, and psychology. Though featured in motion pictures when he was a baby, Lee had no plans of becoming an actor. But when he presented a high-profile, martial arts demonstration at the 1964 Long Beach Karate Tournament, in attendance was the hairdresser of *Batman* executive producer William Dozier.

Dozier was planning another super-hero series, *The Green Hornet*; because of his lightning-fast moves, Lee won the role of the Hornet's chauffeur and fellow crime-stopper, Kato. While the series lasted just one season, it has amassed quite a following, thanks to the cult-hero status of Lee.

Following the cancellation of *The Green Hornet*, Bruce Lee appeared in guest-star roles on such series as *Here Come the Brides* and *Ironside*. Then he played the role of Li Tsung, the martial arts instructor to blind insurance investigator Mike Longstreet (James Franciscus) in both the *Longstreet* pilot movie, and the 1971-72 series. Executive produced by — and at times written by — Stirling Silliphant (who had been one of Lee's martial arts students), *Longstreet* even featured an episode ("The Way of the Intercepting Fist") in which Lee's character described his approach to the martial arts. By this time, Bruce Lee had appeared in his first American picture, the James Garner detective drama, *Marlowe*.

After being turned down for the role of Shaolin priest-turned-fugitive Kwai Chang Caine in the excellent 1972-75 ABC series, *Kung Fu*, Lee went to Hong Kong where he soon became a martial arts star. Unfortunately, Lee did not live to see the release of *Enter the Dragon*, the movie that made him a mega-star in both America and Europe. Three weeks before the picture's release, the thirty-two year old Lee died under mysterious circumstances. To this day, the exact cause of death is unknown. His wife Linda, whom he met at the University of Washington, had him buried in her hometown of Seattle, at Lakeview Cemetery.

*Leading Lady Bridget Hanley:* "I wasn't even aware who Bruce Lee was. He was fabulous. I was stunned when I realized that that was the Bruce Lee I later got to watch."[136]

*Wardrobe Man Steve Lodge:* "Bruce and I had a deal…I don't know how it ever started. I would be sitting in a chair reading a newspaper, Bruce walked by. I said, 'Hi.' He says, 'Hi,' and then he went 'Hi-yah!' and he kicked at me — a karate kick — two inches from my face! I could feel the gravel on the bottom of his boots, come up and hit me in the face like a shotgun. So, whenever he would see me, he would come up and 'Hi-yah!' He had a great sense of humor. He had a neat sense of humor."[137]

April 12, 1969 – *TV Guide* – Vol. 17., No. 15 – Issue #837 – Series regular Joan Blondell to be profiled in the following issue.

## Episode #26: "The Deadly Trade"        *April 16, 1969*

"Twenty-four hours, Mr. Bolt. Give me that boy, or Seattle comes down."
*Lijah Harmon to Jason Bolt*

Writer . . . . . . . . . . . . . . . . . . . . . . . . . . . . . . . . . . . . . . . . . . . . . . . . . . . . . William Blinn
Director . . . . . . . . . . . . . . . . . . . . . . . . . . . . . . . . . . . . . . . . . . . . . . . . Paul Junger Witt
Film Editor . . . . . . . . . . . . . . . . . . . . . . . . . . . . . . . . . . . . . . . . . . . . . . . . . Asa Clark
Assistant Director . . . . . . . . . . . . . . . . . . . . . . . . . . . . . . . . . . . . . . . . . . Jim Hogan
Music. . . . . . . . . . . . . . . . . . . . . . . . . . . . . . . . . . . . . . . . . . . . . . . . . . . Warren Barker

### *Guest Cast*

Lijah . . . . . . . . . . . . . . . . . . . . . . . . . . . . . . . . . . . . . . . . . . . . . . . R.G. Armstrong
Jobe . . . . . . . . . . . . . . . . . . . . . . . . . . . . . . . . . . . . . . . . . . . . . . . . . Ross Hagen
Stoker . . . . . . . . . . . . . . . . . . . . . . . . . . . . . . . . . . . . . . . . . . . . . . Ronald Feinberg
Dorne . . . . . . . . . . . . . . . . . . . . . . . . . . . . . . . . . . . . . . . . . . . . . Murray MacLeod
Will . . . . . . . . . . . . . . . . . . . . . . . . . . . . . . . . . . . . . . . . . . . . . . . William Bassett
Joseph . . . . . . . . . . . . . . . . . . . . . . . . . . . . . . . . . . . . . . . . . . Christopher Shea
Johnny Wolf . . . . . . . . . . . . . . . . . . . . . . . . . . . . . . . . . . . . . . . . . . . X Brands
Linda. . . . . . . . . . . . . . . . . . . . . . . . . . . . . . . . . . . . . . . . Jacqueline Scott *(Special Guest)*

*Teaser:* Loggers, Jason, Josh, Jeremy, Will Harmon, Johnny Wolf.
*Tag:* Lijah, Stoker, Jobe, Dorne, Clancey, Jason, Josh, Jeremy, Linda, Joseph.
*Competition: The Glen Campbell Goodtime Hour* guest-starring Nancy Sinatra, Al Martino, Tim Conway, Robert Goulet, CBS; *The Virginian,* "The Heritage," (rerun) guest-starring Buffy Sainte-Marie, Ned Romero, and Jim Davis, NBC.
*Notes:* Brilliantly done, the teaser of "The Deadly Trade" begins like many first-season episodes — it's lighthearted and comic. Then the comic situation turns tragic. Logger Will Harmon is dead — thanks to the antics of Joshua and Jeremy Bolt.

Will's death is quite jarring — when the log slides down the flume and hits the logger, his back is to the camera — physically, Will and the viewer are in the same position: facing the approaching log.

With such visual elements as Biddie attired in black, Clancey standing watch over Will's body and (later) holding a gun on Lijah Harmon, "The Deadly Trade" prepares the viewing audience for the grimmer *Brides* of the second season. The tag is the longest one ever presented on the series — it clocks in at nearly six minutes.

Best known for her role as Donna Kimble Taft (the sister of unjustly accused Dr. Richard Kimble on *The Fugitive*), Jacqueline Scott is the first performer on *Brides* to receive an onscreen billing as 'Special Guest.' Supporting guest stars Ross Hagen and Ronald Feinberg will return in the second season.

**Photography:** The hand-held camera work in the lunch-box toss sequence; Clancey reminiscing to the Bolts about Will Harmon; the Harmon family riding into Seattle; Jason and Clancey, behind Will's closed casket, greeting Lijah and Jobe Harmon as they enter the church; long shots of the Bolts, Linda and Joey Harmon, walking through the forest out of town; rippling shots of Candy, and Biddie looking at the fire the townsmen have set as a signal to the Bolts; Jason's fight with the mute Stoker.

*Story Editor William Blinn:* "It was grim. That was the result of ABC trying to slowly transition us into a different kind of show. It was certainly a change of pace. It was, I think, in order to demonstrate to ABC that 'If you want us to go this way, we can go this way. We can be more serious. We can be more gritty and real.' I didn't dislike the episode. I thought the episode was okay. It was just…I wish someone at Screen Gems would have said to ABC, 'Look. We did not cast for this. You're asking our players to change in mid-stream, and they might be able to do it, but I don't know how the audience is going to respond to it.' But the fact of the matter is, it's the network's bat at ball, and they make the rules."[138]

*Leading Lady Bridget Hanley:* "It [the teaser and the episode] really…it made the transition. It was really quite wonderful. You can't make a joke out of those things. The fact that we could be…not just a comedy, but also, have a humanity, and that there was a certain philosophy about certain things…It just depended on how it was handled. I think it was important — obviously — that they handled it that way."[139]

*Guest Star R. G. Armstrong on series star Robert Brown:* "Robert Brown. Yeah. He was a handsome lookin' guy and I had a scene with him at a bar where he came in and did something. I was s'posed to backhand him, and they had the camera set. I came around and backhanded, and there's s'posed to be…'Keep it pretty close,' the director said. He kept telling me, 'about four or five inches, come at him like that.' I came up and backhanded him [Brown], and my finger just clipped his nose, and man, he turned…I barely touched him, but I clipped his nose, and he whirled around and caught his face. God! He made such a fuss I couldn't believe it. It was an hour before they could get him back to work. Really!

"He had that handsome look and the profile. He was protecting it. I said, 'I'll be damned.' I couldn't help it. I mean I've been socked in fights that went on (laughs), you know, ROUGH STUFF! I had to sort of…I remember on a show we were doin' — well, it was a *Gunsmoke,* on that show, I did a fight with Pernell Roberts. It took us two days to shoot a fight scene, all the way across the porch of a western set, down across the road, then up against somethin' else, and we wuz fightin'. The doubles would lay it all out, and the stunt guys, but we had to get in there and do it almost as rough as they did, and so that really hit me that he (Brown) raised such a ruckus over it; me just barely clippin' the end of his nose. He grabbed it — Man! It was like, 'I've gotten…' I barely even touched him."

*Veteran Star Joan Blondell:* "Joan Blondell! She really had great, big blue eyes — huge, and talked just like she did in the film…I used to like Joan Blondell when I was a kid. I'm workin' with people out here who come in and do things like Joan Blondell when I was a kid and went to movies. That's what I remember about that."

*Co-Star Henry Beckman:* "Henry Beckman was an actor from Canada, and I talked to him a little bit. He was a good character actor. I think I had lunch with Henry Beckman. He was very cordial and friendly and was goin' back to Canada, but I don't know whatever happened to him. He had a great career out here."

## Guest Star R.G. Armstrong

R.G. Armstrong (the 'R.G.' stands for Robert Golden) was one of those actors who hadn't planned on entering the profession. "I'd made one gesture toward that as a matter of a prayer," Armstrong admits. "When I came home from a movie — I think Paul Muni was in it. I forget which one it was, but it was in the late '20s. Maybe it was a Greta Garbo-John Gilbert movie, *Flesh and the Devil.* Anyway, it so touched me that it just overwhelmed me, and I fell on my knees on that dirt road home — about six or seven miles out in the country, and made a secret prayer — 'Just let me be an actor.' I promptly forgot it. I thought it was absurd. You know what I mean? Me prayin' to the heavens! And by and large, it was more or less somethin' of a puzzlement why I did become an actor after wishing for somethin' so desperately, and not being able to practice it by way of school. People would put me in a play — I'd write something in college, and they'd put it on, like three one-act plays, in Harvard College, now Sanford, and I played the lead — Simon Ayres in *Shoemaker's Holiday* — it was like a Shakespeare bawdy comedy. [And] all the time not dreamin' that any of this had any connection to that prayer I made on the road."

Hoping to become a writer, military veteran Armstrong used the G.I. Bill to continue his college education. "Went to the University of North Carolina at Chapel Hill," he says. "That gave me four more years of college. I got my master's, and then taught a year up near Asheville. I taught American Literature, English Literature, and American History, and a freshman English course, which I hated. I had to study it every night, memorize and get familiar with all those eight parts of speech, and all that stuff again — you know, dependent clauses and independent clauses, and all the mechanics of writing. I'd forgotten it, but you use it, some of it, pretty correctly and naturally, but dependent clauses and two independent clauses together, all that, and eight parts of speech, and I had to study it every night, the lesson next day, like I was a student or somethin'. So that really helped along the way."

Like so many actors, Armstrong performed on Broadway. "I went to New York in 1952," he remembers. "I was there five years. Got into the Actor's Studio through friends of mine who'd been at the University of North Carolina. Eva Marie Saint auditioned with me and helped me get into the Actor's Studio, and from there, Jack Garfield had taken me to play the general in *End as a Man* — a Calder Willingham novel. Willingham was a Southern writer. I played it on Broadway till it closed. It didn't run too long. Then they cast me in *Cat on a Hot Tin Roof*, playin' the doctor and understudyin' Burl Ives, and before I knew it, I was playing the lead in a hit play on Broadway, playin' Big Daddy — you know, sometimes two weeks in a row. Cuz Burl'd go off and do concerts and stuff, and it was a tough part. So he'd miss out four performances or something like that. I got to play that part so much an agent happened to see me doing it one day or one night. Called me in and wanted to represent me for movies. I said, 'Movies?' She says, 'Yeah. Movies.' And then she mentioned a name — I didn't know that she already had something in mind, cuz within a week, she called me up, and I'm on my way to Hollywood to do a screen test for a movie called *From Hell to Texas* (this was 1957) with Don Murray, Chill Wills, Diane Varsi. It was based on a novel called *The Hell Bent Kid*. And [director] Henry Hathaway, when we went in to the meeting, I was shaking still from the flight — eight-hour flight; they didn't have jets back then. He sits there, lookin' at me and talkin' to me. He had Don Murray come in. I just read a passage with him — something with him. And the writer was there. He was from Virginia — Robert something, but anyway, he [Hathaway] says, 'You got the part. Go over and get wardrobe.' And that was it! In four days, I was up in Bishop, North Carolina, on a horse, shooting a major western movie at Fox. And I know people who are trying hard, still trying hard in New York. I'm not saying that they didn't do it right to develop and grow as they needed to grow. But I seemed to be thrown in there and I had to learn how to act, how to get free to be an actor while I'm working. I didn't feel that I was up to the part. I wasn't an actor yet, and I kept trying."

Movies soon led to television. The more TV he did, the more practical Armstrong became regarding this often too casually dismissed medium. "When you're in New York, you don't make much money on Broadway unless you're starring, or, unless they really want you," he explains. "I mean, I worked in *Cat on a Hot Tin Roof*, playing the doctor for $125 a week, and that's eight performances a week. Then, when I did Big Daddy, which I did when Burl was out — it'd be four performances, and then he was on vacation for two weeks one time. I got $300 a week. Well, that's just very small out here — small salary, and I remember making the money out here. A lot of actors were gettin' the chance to make a living out here. That's one of the main things I was thinking when I was in Hollywood raisin' a family. It took me a good while to look at acting on a TV show as anything but just an exercise to get better as an actor. I didn't take 'em seriously. That is in terms of being like when you went on a movie project. But I got over that. I realized that wherever I am, and whatever I'm in, it's still: 'You gotta do the best you can anywhere.' I knew that they were limited, limited by money, limited by who they could get, and all that."

One thing that was very important to Armstrong when he was doing a television series was whether or not the people with whom he was working liked him. "That was comin' out of the South all screwed up myself," he states. "I wanted to be liked. [Then, Armstrong would ask himself] 'What do you care about whether anybody likes you or not?' That was all part of me acting — helping me. Actually, acting was like a huge, big psychodrama ward somewhere. I got a chance every once in a while to come out of my cave, and go on, and do a scene that helped me out of my fixation, (laughing), my 'purgatin' my…repressed hostility. So a lot of acting for me was releasing that in those parts, in the villains. I never looked at myself much as an actor anyway. But I liked to get out and do that cuz I felt so refreshed after I finished one. Especially when I have to do a scene over and over and over, and finish the thing. Am I glad when that's over. So, that's one of the things I grabbed [television shows]. Television shows ran six days or seven. [As opposed to] two months on a movie."

Because television was geared more towards the small, personal drama, Armstrong had to develop a much subtler, and quieter, acting style. "That was a lesson to me," he admits. "I didn't really have to put that much voice into my work, just take it easy, just talk; all those were part of me learnin' how to just not overact, and not do too much. Actually, less is better, I learned. They learned me: 'Less is better.' They kept saying, 'Less is better, R.G. You got too much — *Macbeth* wouldn't contain all that stuff you're bringin' in. It's just a television show.' (Laughs.) 'Less is better.' I never will forget that phrase they used. The directors — not all the time — but every once in a while, they'd come up, 'Less is better, R.G. Remember, less is better.'"

Though R.G. Armstrong did work in one television series as a semi-regular (the 1966-67 NBC crime-drama, *T.H.E. Cat*) and another as a recurring character (the late 1980s horror anthology, *Friday the 13th, the Series*), "I was tryin' really to get out of TV," he laughs. "I wasn't that interested, but I had four children, and I had to work, and I've got four novels, twelve or thirteen plays, and some screenplays I wrote with people.

"A writer was what I wanted to be. Movies, and acting was supposed to give me time to be a writer, and it did in a way. But when you get so involved with a series, you don't have much time, and I just dropped out. [In the case of *Friday the 13th, the Series*], I said, 'I don't want to keep doin' this.' The way I did it — they were only paying me $500 a week. I said, 'I want $750,' and they dropped me. That was my way of getting' out. I knew they were cheap ass."[140]

Suffering from macular degeneration at the time he was interviewed by this author (in 2001), R.G. Armstrong has now retired due to blindness. His vivid performance in *Here Come the Brides'* "The Deadly Trade" is one not easily forgotten.

*Bridget Hanley on R.G. Armstrong:* "He was a known commodity, and a wonderful known commodity, and how lucky for us to have him.[141]

*Bridget Hanley on Jacqueline Scott And William H. Bassett:* "Jacqueline Scott and I still see each other. I didn't even know her then, but I have since then got to know her better. We had fun on the show, then we would see each other at auditions and things. We have a nice, wonderful, lovely friendship.

"Bill Bassett was a member of Theater West and we were very close friends. He was one of the first to do organic gardening. He helped with tree people. He was always with an acting group, with my friend, Robert Ellenstein."[142]

April 19, 1969 – *TV Guide* – Vol. 17., No. 16, Issue #838: "Joan Blondell: Miss Elevator of 1969" by Robert de Roos, pgs. 35, 36, 38 & 40. TV Crossword – 7 Down – Character on *Here Come the Brides.*

April 23, 1969 – *Brides* repeats begin with "A Crying Need" vs. *The Glen Campbell Goodtime Hour* with guests Johnny Cash, June Carter Cash, singer Vikki Carr, and comedian Bob Newhart, CBS; *The Virginian*, "The Saddle Warmer," guest-starring Ralph Bellamy, Tom Skerritt, Chris Robinson, and the musical group, The Irish Rovers (performing "Come In" and "Don't' Mind If I Do"), NBC.

April 26, 1969 – *TV Guide* – Vol. 17., No. 17, Issue #839 – TV Crossword – 7 Down – Answer: Jason.

April 30, 1969 – *Brides'* "The Stand-Off" vs. *The Glen Campbell Goodtime Hour* guest-starring The Beatles, The Righteous Brothers, Liza Minnelli, and Waylon Jennings, CBS; *The Virginian*, "The Orchard," guest-starring Burgess Meredith, Brandon De Wilde, William Windom, NBC.

May 1969 – Bobby Sherman in *16 Magazine;* "Bobby Sherman Story, Chapter 3"
*Tiger Beat;* Bobby Sherman article in *Tiger Beat;* Bobby Sherman article in *Flip Teen;* Bobby Sherman article in *16 Magazine;* "I Visit the Stars, Part 4"
*Tiger Beat;* "Life-Lines –Stars of *HCTB*"
*Tiger Beat;* Joan Blondell in *Movie Stars;* Robert Brown – tidbits – *Screenplay, TV Star Parade, Modern Movies, TV Picture Life;* Robert Brown article in *Movie Stars;* Robert Brown in *Inside TV; TV Radio Mirror, Motion Picture,* 'Screenland, *Screen Stars;* David Soul tidbit in *TV Star Parade;* Bridget Hanley in *Tiger Beat.*

May 3, 1969 – *TV Guide* – Vol. 17., No. 18 – Issue #840 – TV Crossword – 23 Across – *Here Come the Brides* man

May 7, 1969 – Brides' "A Man and His Magic" vs. *CBS Playhouse*, "Shadow Game," starring Daniel Massey, William Shatner, and William Windom; *The Virginian*, "The Winds of Outrage" guest-starring Ricardo Montalban, NBC.

May 10, 1969 – *TV Guide* – Vol. 17., No. 19 – Issue #841: "Bridget Hanley: She plays 'Candy' – with a difference" by Melvin Durslag, pgs. 21, 22, 24; TV Crossword – 23 Across – Answer: Jason

May 14, 1969 – *Brides* pre-empted by rerun of *Jacques Cousteau – Sunken Treasure* special.

May 17, 1969 – *TV Guide* – Vol. 17., No. 20 – Issue #842 – TV Crossword – 37 Down –Robert Brown's TV role.

May 21, 1969 – *Brides*' "Letter of the Law" vs. rerun of *The Glen Campbell Goodtime Hour* guest-starring the Smothers Brothers, Bobbie Gentry, CBS; *The Virginian*, "Storm Gate," guest-starring Burr DeBenning, Susan Oliver, and Scott Brady, NBC.

Week of May 24-30, 1969 – Bobby Sherman guests on *The Dating Game*.

May 24, 1969 – *TV Guide* – Vol. 17., No. 21 – Issue #843 – TV Crossword – 37 Down – Answer: Jason.

May 28, 1969 – *Brides*' "Man of the Family" vs. *The Glen Campbell Goodtime Hour* rerun guest-starring Jim Nabors and Bobbie Gentry, CBS; *The Virginian*, "Big Tiny," comedy guest-starring Roger Torrey, and Julie Sommars, NBC.

Summer 1969 – Bobby Sherman in *16 SPEC*.

June 1969 – Bobby Sherman articles in *TV Radio Talk*, *16 Magazine*, two articles in *Tiger Beat*; "Bobby Sherman Story, Chapter 4" *Tiger Beat*; Three Bobby Sherman articles in *FaVE!*; Bobby Sherman article in *TV Radio Mirror*; Bobby Sherman article in *Flip Teen*; "I Visit the Stars, Part 5," *Tiger Beat*; Bobby Sherman article in *Movie Stars*; Bobby Sherman and David Soul – Second Banana Roundup" *Teen*; Robert Brown – tidbit – *Screen Parade*; Bridget Hanley in *FaVE!*, *Tiger Beat*.

May 31, 1969 – *TV Guide* – Vol. 17., No. 22, Issue #844 – TV Crossword – 12 Across – Gal on *Here Come the Brides*.

6-4-69 – *Brides*' "A Hard Card to Play" vs. *Tarzan*, "A Life for a Life," on CBS (*Tarzan*, starring Ron Ely as Tarzan had aired on NBC from 1966-68); *The Virginian*, "Ride to Misadventure," guest-starring Joseph Campanella, Katherine Justice, and Joe Maross, NBC.

June 7, 1969 – *TV Guide* – Vol. 17., No. 23, Issue #845 – TV Crossword – 55 Across ____ *Come the Brides*; TV Crossword from May 31, 1969 – 12 Across – Answer: Lottie.

June 8, 1969 – Emmy Awards – Robert Brown presents Emmy to Barbara Bain for her role as Cinnamon Carter on *Mission: Impossible* during *Mission: Impossible* timeslot on CBS.

June 9-13, 1969 – David Soul and Karen Carlson guest on game show, *It Takes Two,* with Michael Landon and his wife, Lynn, and Shari Lewis and her husband, Jeremy Tarcher.

June 11, 1969 – *Brides'* "Lovers and Wanderers" vs. *Tarzan*, "The Day the Earth Trembled" guest-starring Susan Oliver and *Brides* guest John Anderson – CBS; *The Virginian*, "A Vision of Blindness," guest-starring John Saxon, Ben Johnson, and the Irish Rovers, NBC.

June 14, 1969 – *TV Guide* – Vol. 17., No. 24 – Issue #846 – TV Crossword – 36 Down – Lady on *Here Come the Brides*; TV Crossword from June 7, 1969 – 55 Across – Answer – 'Here'; underneath the listing for "The Firemaker" announcement that series regular Susan Tolsky is to be featured in the following week's issue.

June 18, 1969 – *Brides'* "The Firemaker" vs. *Tarzan*, "Leopard on the Loose," guest-starring Russ Tamblyn and Ken Scott, CBS; *The Virginian*, "Last Grave at Socorro Creek" guest-starring *Brides* guest Steve Ihnat, Lonny Chapman, and Ellen McRae, NBC.

June 21, 1969 – *TV Guide* – Vol. 17., No. 25 – Issue #847: She took off her glasses and…nothing happened" (Susan Tolsky of *Here Come the Brides*), pgs. 10-13 – by John Wasserman; TV Crossword – 53 Across – He's Joshua on *Here Come the Brides;* TV Crossword from June 14, 1969 – 36 Down – Answer: Lottie.

June 25, 1969 – *Brides*, "A Jew Named Sullivan," vs. *Tarzan*, "The Three Faces of Death," guest-starring Woody Strode and Ena Hartman, CBS; *The Virginian*, "Nora," guest-starring Anne Baxter and Hugh Beaumont, NBC.

June 28, 1969 – *TV Guide* – Vol. 17., No. 26 – Issue #848 – TV Crossword from June 21, 1969 – 53 Across – Answer: Soul.

July 1969: Bobby Sherman Story, Chapter 5"
*Tiger Beat;* "Bobby's Dream Girl"
*Tiger Beat;* Two Bobby Sherman articles in *Flip Teen;* general article in *Movie TV Pinups;* Joan Blondell article in *Movie Stars;* Robert Brown tidbit – *Photoplay;* Robert Brown in *FaVE!, Movieworld, Photoplay, Modern Screen, Motion Picture, TV Radio Mirror, TV Star Parade, Tiger Beat, TV and Movie Play, Screen Life, Movie TV Pinup;* Bridget Hanley – *FaVE!, Tiger Beat.*

July-2, 1969 – *Brides'* "The Log Jam" vs. *Tarzan*, "The Ultimate Weapon," guest-starring Andrew Prine, Jock Mahoney, and Sheilah Wells, CBS; *The Virginian*, "The Mustangers," guest-starring John Agar, James Edwards, and Don Knight, NBC.

July 5, 1969 – *TV Guide* – Vol. 17., No. 27, Issue #849 – *Brides* mentioned on pg. 33 of "She worked with Orson Welles when he was thin (Rosemary De Camp of *That Girl)*" by Dick Hobson; "The Amorys" *TV Guide* reviewer Cleveland bestows his own awards – Joan Blondell wins "Amory" for Best Supporting Actress, Dramatic Series, for *Brides*.

July 9, 1969 – *Brides'* "One Good Lie Deserves Another" vs. *Tarzan*, "The End of the River," guest-starring Michael Whitney, Robert J. Wilke, and Jill Donohue, CBS; *The Virginian*, "Crime Wave at Buffalo Springs," guest-starring Tom Bosley, Yvonne De Carlo, James Brolin, and Ann Prentiss, NBC.

July 12, 1969 – *TV Guide* – Vol. 17., No. 28, Issue #850 – TV Crossword – 54 Across – *Here Come ___ Brides*

July 16, 1969 – *Brides*, "And Jason Makes Five," vs. *Tarzan*, "Village of Fire," guest-starring Nobu McCarthy and Joel Fluellen, CBS; *The Virginian*, "The Girl in the Shadows," guest-starring *Brides* guests Jack Albertson, Brenda Scott, and Ken Swofford, NBC.

July 19, 1969 – TV Guide – Vol. 17., No. 29, Issue #851 – TV Crossword – 32 Across – ___ *Come the Brides;* TV Crossword of July 12 – 54 Across – Answer: The.

July 23, 1969 – *Brides'* "The Deadly Trade" vs. *Tarzan*, "The Last of the Supermen," guest-starring Alf Kjellin, Antoinette Bower, and Michael Burns, CBS; *The Virginian*, "The Land Dreamer" guest-starring James Olson, Don Francks, and Cloris Leachman, NBC.

July 26, 1969 – *TV Guide* – Vol. 17, No. 30, Issue #852 – TV Crossword of July 19-32 Across – Answer: Here.

July 30, 1969 – *Brides*, "A Dream that Glitters," vs. *Tarzan*, "Mask of Rona," guest-starring Martin Gabel, Leslie Parrish, Nancy Malone, and Jock Mahoney, CBS; *The Virginian*, "Fox, Hound, and the Widow McCloud," guest-starring Troy Donahue and Victor Jory, NBC.

August 1969 – Bobby Sherman and Bridget Hanley on cover of *Tiger Beat;* "Bobby Sherman Story, Chapter 6"
*Tiger Beat,* "Bobby Takes You on Tour"
*Tiger Beat,* "Bridget Tells All on Bobby, Part 1"
*Tiger Beat;* "I Visit the Stars, Part 6"
*Tiger Beat;* Bobby Sherman article in *Teen World;* "The Bobby Sherman I Know and Love" by Bridget Hanley in *Flip Teen;* Bobby Sherman article in *Modern Screen;* Three Bobby Sherman articles in *FaVE!;* Joan Blondell article in *TV Movies Today;* "Win Robert Brown's Gloves" *Movie Stars.*

August 2, 1969 – *TV Guide,* Vol. 17, No. 31, Issue #853 – TV Crossword – 20 Across – Robert Brown's TV role; TV Teletype: Hollywood – Joseph Finnigan Reports – *Brides* mentioned in blurb about the show's executive producer Bob Claver making a big-city hospital pilot called *The Interns.*

August 6, 1969 – *Brides'* "After a Dream Comes Mourning" vs. *Tarzan,* "The Fire People," CBS; *The Virginian,* "Stopover," guest-starring Herb Jeffries, John Kellogg, Jan Shepard, and Jay C. Flippen, NBC.

August 9, 1969 – *TV Guide* – Vol. 17, No. 32, Issue #854 – TV Crossword of August 2 – 20 Across – Answer: Jason.

August 13, 1969 – *Brides'* "Loggerheads" vs. *Tarzan,* "Jai's Amnesia," guest-starring John Dehner, CBS; *The Virginian,* "Ordeal," guest-starring Robert Pine and Michael Masters, NBC.

August 16, 1969 – *TV Guide* – Vol. 17, No. 33, Issue #855 – TV Crossword – 27 Across – Man on *Here Come the Brides.*

August 20, 1969 – *Brides'* "One to a Customer" vs. *Tarzan,* "The Fanatics," guest-starring Diana Hyland and William Smithers, CBS; *The Virginian,* "Death Wait," guest-starring Harold J. Stone, *Brides* guest Murray MacLeod, and Sheila Larkin-NBC; also on August 20, 1969, WKPT-TV – Channel 19 (Kingsport/Johnson City, Tennessee; Bristol, Tennessee/Virginia) signs on as an affiliate of ABC-TV.

August 23, 1969 – TV Guide – Vol. 17, No. 34, Issue #856 – TV Crossword of August 16, 1969 – Answer: Jeremy.

August 27, 1969 – *Brides'* "Democracy Inaction" vs. *Tarzan,* "The Maguma Curse," guest-starring Barbara Luna and Simon Oakland, CBS; *The Virginian,* "Storm Over Shiloh," NBC.

Fall 1969 – Two Bobby Sherman articles in *16 SPEC;* Bridget Hanley in *16 SPEC.*

September 1969: Bobby Sherman Story, Final Chapter"
*Tiger Beat;* "Bridget Tells All on Bobby, Part 2"
*Tiger Beat;* Bobby Sherman article in *Teen Life;* Two Bobby Sherman articles in *Flip Teen;* "Shows that Made It"
*TV Star Annual;* Robert Brown presents Emmy to *Mission: Impossible*'s Barbara Bain"
*Movie Stars;* Brown presents Emmy to Bain– *TV Star Parade;* Henry Beckman in *TV Picture Life;* Joan Blondell article in *Modern Screen;* David Soul article – *Tiger Beat;* "An In-Depth Talk with David Soul, Part One"
*Tiger Beat;* Robert Brown articles in *Movieland and TV Time, Screenplay, TV and Movie Screen;* Bridget Hanley – *FaVE!;* Bobby Sherman and Bridget Hanley on *Tiger Beat* cover.

September 1, 1969 – Bobby Sherman guests on *The Merv Griffin Show.*

September 3, 1969 – *Brides'* "A Man's Errand" vs. *Billy Graham* special on CBS; *The Virginian,* "Dark Corridor," guest-starring Judy Lang and Paul Winchell, NBC; it's revealed that *Brides* will move to new time slot of Friday at 9 p.m. for second season. *Brides'* time slot will be filled by *The Flying Nun,* and a new show, *The Courtship of Eddie's Father.*

1969: Who's Who in TV"
1969-70 – Another Synopsis – Season 2.

Fall 1969 –KXIX-TV – Channel 19 goes on the air as a satellite of Corpus Christi station KIII-TV – Channel 3.

September 1969: An In-Depth Talk with David Soul," Part 1 – *Tiger Beat.*

# Season Two
## Prologue: A Change in Direction

Said Mark Lenard to his fans about *Brides'* upcoming season in early 1969: "The first year of a television serials (*sic*) is a time of confusion, indecision, and is generally a mess. It usually takes a year to get the direction of the series and the characters and where they are going straightened out. *Here Come the Brides* is now in the midst of severe creative birth pains. We expect considerable format changes for the coming year."[143]

"They were chasing an audience," explains *Brides* star Robert Brown. "They must have gotten the feeling, from whatever research is done when a series is on, they must have gotten that feedback that they wanted to broaden it. I think they wanted to make it more popular, not just for the kids; they wanted to bring the older group in, maybe change it so it would not just be *giggle, giggle* for the young women who liked Jeremy. I don't know if it changed or if it helped."

To many *Brides* fans, the change from what Brown has also described as "Bobby Sherman and giggly, googly girls,"[144] to more serious and grim situations — such as Captain Clancey being attacked by a bear the night of his birthday (episode 29, "The Soldier") was not a good idea. Story editor William Blinn agreed with the fans. "I think the difficulty in the show wasn't the number of characters," reflects Blinn. "They were all very specific and quite different, so we weren't worried about duplicating anything. The difficulty in writing the show, if there was a difficulty, was in keeping the odd tone of the sentimental comedy. Which is why, I guess, eventually the network pushed us into the action-adventure thing. Which was much harder. I mean, the notion of Robert pulling a gun would just make you laugh; the same thing with Bobby and David — maybe less so David because David was more comfortable in the action-adventure area. On *Bonanza*, that was less of a problem because *Bonanza* was a western, and they're walking around with guns on their hips everywhere they go — it's just part of the potential of every scene. So the only time we ever got into trouble was the second year because the show was cast and meant to be a comedy-drama. Or a sentimental comedy, if you will. That's probably closer."

"[The early success of] the first season was not a surprise to us," continues Blinn. "It was the kind of show we set out to do — a funny story, and oddly touching. God knows you have someone like Henry Beckman, he was so out of the tent, but that was okay. In the first season, that was funny old Clancey. Joan Blondell — same kind of thing. Joan was never hard-edged — certainly at that age. Maybe she was able to do it in the Warner days. But Joan was the chubby lady with all the dogs in the trailer — having a sweet time. When it got to be serious and grim, we did not have the tools with which to work. Both in terms of production and terms of cast. And maybe in terms of the writers, too. We did bring in some writers that had largely done westerns, but we weren't doing a western. That isn't how we started out. So it wasn't challenging in the first year because we were always dealing with actors who were in a generally comedic mode. They were easy there, they were comfortable there. They could do that, and sometimes we were doing stories that were very, very little; by that I mean, 'Democracy Inaction.' Technically, it wasn't about anything that was life and death, and all this and that, but it was about something that these characters were passionate about."[145]

Still *Here Come the Brides* was set in the primitive Northwestern Washington territory in the late nineteenth century. The harshness of the West at that time was a reality. More importantly, Blinn's feeling that the first season wasn't challenging because the actors were comfortable wasn't exactly a good thing. When a television series' cast wasn't challenged, when they kept doing the same thing over and over, that didn't promise a long run for a show. While the cast members and writers (and viewers) of *Brides* had yet to get bored, the potential was there. The fact that the series was starting to slip in the ratings, that *Brides'* competition (*The Virginian* and *The Glen Campbell Goodtime Hour*) had been getting better ratings, made it clear that some kind of change was necessary.

"In the second year, we started to get pressure from ABC to concentrate more on action," explains William Blinn. "Neither Robert nor Bobby...that was not their strong point. As actors, they had enough facility to carry it off, but you don't cast Charles Bronson in a British teacup drama, and neither would you cast Robert Brown in a hard-boiled, bloody action-adventure. Robert was a leading man, in the classical sense, a leading man. Drop-dead handsome. He had a touch of the poet to him in his presentation — he was comfortable with that. So, when it came into the second season, and we started doing more of those episodes, it was uneasy because the writers didn't have any choice. I mean, that was the dictum that went out, and we were trying to fulfill that. But when it got to be that real nitty-gritty...we got misdirected. I think, had we been allowed to try to stay doing an hour sentimental comedy, we would have had a lot more success and might have had a couple more seasons. We didn't want the actors to feel that they were being misused, or abused, and unfortunately, to some degree, they were."[146]

Adds *Brides* leading lady Bridget Hanley, "What bothered me about the second season was not the going into the character study stuff [of both the regular and guest characters] because that was kind of wonderful, but that they changed it from the mud and rain to horses and guns. That, to me, explains the differences in the two seasons. But I was thrilled with whatever I got to do. I had a great time within those versions. They had a right to do whatever they wanted."[147]

"As the second season came along it was done a little differently," agrees Robert Brown; "[there was] a different attitude. We tried to give it a more...they had a gun, and there was some danger. It wasn't just the sweetness of the women, it was about issues. I thought it was maybe necessary, and added more to the show. If things were different, it seemed to be a little more for the older crowd, and not just for the youngsters."[148]

Nothing made that plainer than the switch from Wednesdays at 7:30 p.m. to Fridays at 9 p.m. To *Brides* fans, this seemed a terrible idea. Leading lady Hanley did not agree. "They moved to a later time slot because they wanted to include the whole family," explains the actress. "Or the adults that didn't have kids."[149]

Still, moving a popular series to a Friday 9 p.m. slot seemed somewhat destructive. After all, Friday evening was one of those evenings people went out on dates — that was, then and now, a night people partied. Friday night was also movie night on CBS. For the ABC network to put the one-hour *Here Come the Brides* up against splashy big-budget CBS-aired features such as *The Guns of Navarone, The Music Man,* and *Viva Las Vegas* seemed to practically guarantee the death of the series. The experience of *Judd, for the Defense,* the ABC series that had occupied the same Friday night time slot the season before, proved otherwise. In fact, *Judd, for the Defense* had premiered in one of the worst time slots for any television series – Friday nights at 10 p.m.

Created and executive produced by *Peyton Place*'s Paul Monash, *Judd, for the Defense* starred *The Donna Reed Show*'s Carl Betz as Texas-bred, defense lawyer Clinton Judd, a mixture of such famous attorneys as F. Lee Bailey, Clarence Darrow, Melvin Belli, and Earl Rogers. Going into its first season (1967-68), *Judd* had four strikes against it. First, it had been created by a man who'd executive produced a soap opera! Second: It was to be executive produced by that man. Third: The star of the show had been a co-star on a popular series for eight seasons — being a co-star, there was no guarantee he could carry a show. Four: This co-star had performed on a light, situation comedy. To expect an audience to accept this former co-star (Carl

*Carl Betz in the well-regarded 20th Century Fox/ABC-TV series,* Judd, for the Defense — *the series whose time slot* Brides *filled in its second season.*

Betz) as a defense attorney taking on unpopular cases which bring him into conflict with the law, his fellow attorneys, and even his junior partner, Ben Caldwell, this was asking an audience to accept a lot.

No wonder ABC gave *Judd, for the Defense* the Friday night 10 P.M. death slot. No wonder the series soon became one of the seventh lowest-rated shows on the ABC network. But, what the know-it-alls failed to take into account was the intense dedication and belief star Carl Betz would bring to his part. Or executive producer Paul Monash doing controversial and offbeat stories — stories dealing with abortion, mercy killings, a deaf couple wishing to adopt a child who could hear. Stories about modern-day witchcraft, rape, draft evasion, immaculate conception, the Hollywood blacklist, homosexuality. Stories where Clinton Judd defended a syndicate boss on the charge of murder. The show's ambiguous endings were another surprise. On *Judd, for the Defense*, things never turned out well. Even when Clinton Judd won a case, he really didn't win, because there was always that downbeat, realistic twist where Judd's client was left facing an unpleasant situation. Laughs *Judd* fan Lynda Day George: "It was kind of discouraging. You'd be like (plaintively), 'Come onnn! Win one!'"[150]

As a result of this unusual approach and the believability and intensity with which Betz played his role, *Judd, for the Defense* won for itself a big audience. Before its first season had ended, the often critically acclaimed series was placing in the Top 40! This, despite playing against hit movie musicals, such as *Seven Brides for Seven Brothers,* action features like *The Great Escape* and Hitchcock's *North by Northwest,* comedies starring Bob Hope, westerns with John Wayne — all on *The CBS Friday Night Movie.*

For ABC-TV to put *Here Come the Brides* into *Judd's* new 9 p.m. Friday time slot was a great compliment to *Brides* – it underscored how much faith ABC had in the *HCTB* series. Moreover, to give *Brides* the green light for a full second season, when so many other ABC series (old and new) were being dropped, that *really* was a compliment!

Had William Blinn known this, he might have been less uneasy about ABC's "growing up" the *Brides* characters. "When you're doing light comedy," explains Blinn, "most of the characters are about twelve years old. If you're doing farce, they're about four, and in a broad stroke kind of way, I think there's some truth to that. Well, our characters were about seven or eight in many instances. But, as long as you bring the integrity of a seven-year-old belief system to it, it works. I think that's what we had the first season. Well, the second season, the network decided they were all really eighteen. And we… the boat sailed at that point."[151]

Robert Brown saw things differently. "The second year, the scripts got more developed, I guess," muses Brown. "They had more to do with the society that we were in, dealt with current events. I changed the costume; we took the frills off the green leather. [Brown's friend, director Robert Altman, didn't like the frills and the green leather], but I didn't judge any of it. I was always accepting of what they were doing. I didn't try to redo it. Whatever it was, was what was needed. The other [the first season's approach] was lighter and more virginal. This [version] was less contrived. We could have gone on for many years."[152]

"We coped with the problem [the more serious and grim tone] by focusing a little bit more on the guest star characters," remembers Blinn. "If you're not gonna be doing the sentimental comedy within the community, well, then, you're gonna be bringing in some bad guys from the outside."[153] Having bad guys and villains on *Brides* was a very good idea – they gave the show an edge. As did stories out of town. When a character was away from the safety and comfort of Seattle [Jeremy Bolt in the aforementioned "The Soldier"], the potential for danger existed. Of course, this sort of thing wasn't necessary the first season thanks to the villainous Aaron Stempel character. But, by the end of that first season, Stempel had become a pretty nice person.

As the folks who made *Bonanza* could have told the makers of *Here Come the Brides*, to go into their new season with no villain or villains, no kind of edge or contrast to the very nice people of Seattle — THAT was a recipe for disaster! The eighth and ninth seasons of *Bonanza* proved that. In the eighth season, Lorne Greene, Dan Blocker, and Michael Landon had carried the show; in the ninth season, David

Canary joined the trio in the recurring role of the Cartwright's new ranch-hand Candy. Soon after Canary's addition to the series, *Bonanza*'s ratings (which had gone down during the eighth season) picked up considerably. Having watched *Bonanza* throughout the years, *Bonanza/Brides* guest star Lynda Day George knew why. Notes the actress: "I guess probably half of the *Bonanza*s that I saw had Pernell Roberts in them. When Pernell was on *Bonanza*, it had an edge. When Pernell was not on *Bonanza*, it didn't. Well, when David Canary got on the show, he added the edge again. But, when [Canary's] Candy went away, the show got soft. That show needed a hard edge because there was an awful lot of softness in that show. If you've got just softness and no edge, you don't know the softness from the softness. You can't separate softness from softness. You've got to be able to do that. Otherwise, the show is one level. And when you're watching a television show, you have to have contrast. Without the contrast, without an edge, a show gets very one level; it doesn't have what is needed to capture viewers' attention. So, when there was a contrast, or, an edge, on *Bonanza*, the ratings went up."[154]

Somebody at ABC-TV might have been thinking similarly when it came to *Here Come the Brides*. When *Brides* began its second season on September 26, 1969, it had an edge. In the person of the series' new characters: Candy's little brother and sister, Christopher and Molly Pruitt.

# Season Two
# September 13, 1969 (new time slot)
# to September 18, 1970 (the final telecast)

September 13, 1969 – *TV Guide* – Vol. 17, No. 37, Issue #859 – underneath Friday listing for *Judd, for the Defense*, "An Elephant in a Cigar Box," it is noted that *Brides* will be taking over the canceled *Judd*'s time slot. In the same *TV Guide*'s "What's New in Old Shows" section, it is revealed that Bridget Hanley's Candy Pruitt will be getting a brother and sister. Playing the children are nine-year-old Eric Chase and ten-year-old Patti Cohoon.

## Episode #27: "A Far Cry from Yesterday"          *September 26, 1969*

"Those two children...aren't going home again."
*Jason Bolt to Captain Clancey*

Writer . . . . . . . . . . . . . . . . . . . . . . . . . . . . . . . . . . . . . . . . . . . . . . . . . William Blinn
Director . . . . . . . . . . . . . . . . . . . . . . . . . . . . . . . . . . . . . . . . . . . . . . . . Bob Claver
Film Editor . . . . . . . . . . . . . . . . . . . . . . . . . . . . . . . . . . . . . . . . . Norman Wallerstein
Assistant Director . . . . . . . . . . . . . . . . . . . . . . . . . . . . . . . . . . . . . . . . David Hawks

*Guest Cast*

Homer Shagrue..................................... William Schallert
Sheriff Bond ........................................ Scoey Mitchell

**Teaser:** Lottie, Ben, Aaron, Biddie, Candy, Jason, Josh, Jeremy, Clancey, Christopher, Molly.

**Tag:** Molly, Christopher, Candy, Jeremy, Jason, Lottie, Josh, Biddie.

**Competition:** *The CBS Friday Night Movies* – *The Guns of Navarone* (first hour of two hour conclusion; Part 1 aired Thursday at same time); *Name of the Game*, "A Hard Case of the Blues," starring Robert Stack as Dan Farrell, and guest-starring Sharon Farrell, Keenan Wynn, Sal Mineo, and Russ Tamblyn, NBC.

**Photography:** the "boat is in" teaser; hand-held camera work on Candy after she learns of the death of her mother; Candy telling her brother and sister about their mother's death; Candy debating about marrying Jeremy following his proposal – the camera moving in for close-ups on Candy.

**Notes:** Like "The Deadly Trade," (the last episode of the first season) "A Far Cry from Yesterday" opens on a happy note – Jeremy and Candy are finally getting married — Jeremy's even bought her an engagement ring. But the death of Candy's mother, who's sent Candy's little brother and sister for a "visit," results in Candy postponing the wedding; Candy must now become a mother to her brother and sister. Though Jeremy is still willing to marry her, Candy doesn't wish to place him under the burden of raising a family. The scenes of Candy reacting to the unexpected death of her mother are powerful, the sound and sight of the exploding firecrackers vividly illustrate the realm of emotions she is experiencing. Also exceptional is the sequence in which Candy reflects on the past year she has spent with Jeremy. Bridget Hanley is superb throughout these scenes.

Both Patti Cohoon and Eric Chase do well in their debut as *Brides'* new semi-regular characters, Molly and Christopher Pruitt. Chase's Christopher is the more comical of the two; Cohoon's Molly very much takes after her big sister. The two children running off so Candy can marry Jeremy immediately wins the viewer over to the two new characters. Just like the people of Seattle, Molly and Christopher show a compassion and sensitivity towards others — in this case, it's their big sister, Candy, and her intended, Jeremy. In the next episode, the beneficiary of the two children's compassion will be the kidnapped Captain Clancey.

William Schallert's Homer Shagrue makes for an amusing villain; comedian Scoey Mitchell has some fun scenes as a town sheriff. And Bridget Hanley looks great in the costume Candy is wearing when she, Aaron, and the Bolts ride off on horseback in search of her little runaway brother and sister.

Things have certainly changed in Seattle after a year. Thirty-seven of the ladies from New Bedford have become brides, sixteen are engaged, and the population has increased to three hundred: seven babies have been born.

Composer Hugo Montenegro's tender score for Candy and Jeremy (as the two discuss their new relationship) will be used quite a few times during this season. The name of Candy's little sister comes from Bridget Hanley. Hanley's little sister was named Molly. First-season assistant director Jim Hogan becomes the show's new unit production manager.

*Story Editor/Episode Writer William Blinn:* "It was...I think the powers that be could sense, we were a little adrift. I think "Deadly Trade" showed it as well. And one of the ways you can pump up some new energy into a show is usually bring some kids in.

*Bridget Hanley's Candy Pruitt with her little sister Molly (Patti Cohoon) and brother, Christopher (Eric Chase), in the second-season premiere, "A Far Cry from Yesterday".*
COURTESY BRIDGET HANLEY

It does give you a different storytelling element. The kids were well cast — Patti Cohoon and Eric Chase. It was kind of like putting the same meal on the table with a different presentation.

"Claver was not a big fan of it. I'm pretty sure it was a network request, and I kind of went along, but, if I had to vote, I would have voted with Claver. It did give us more opportunity to go to Candy, and it gave Candy a little bit more to do, but it also tended to make the storytelling more childlike. I'm not sure that's a good thing."[155]

*Series Semi-Regular Eric Chase:* "William Schallert was just a very professional, great actor. We had to do a scene where we were eating stew and we did it about six-thirty in the morning. They kept re-doing the shot and re-doing the shot, and I kept wolfing down more stew — it was actually pretty good, and I remember — he just looked at me once and he goes, (in a Homer Shagrue voice), 'How can yew eat ALL THAT STEW? At this time of the morning?' I don't know if they got it on camera — but he was doing his line, the director had said, 'Cut' or something, and he [Schallert] looked down at me, he's got this perplexed look on his face. Everybody was just laughing — this little kid down there wolfing all this stew.

"We had a little campfire going, but it was kind of an indoor shot. We were around a campfire — it was supposed to be out of doors, and it was supposed to be nighttime, but it was really the crack of dawn. Sometimes I had to get up really early, you had to be on the road by 5:30 in the morning — you got there when they wanted you there. It just depended on what was the schedule for the day.

"Schallert was a little playful. I think like most people he enjoyed working. I think most people who are actors seem to love their work."[156]

*Executive Producer Bob Claver on New Assistant Director David Hawks:* "David Hawks was very quiet. There was something very classy about David Hawks. He was kind of nice-looking, slender. I liked Michael Dmytryk, too. That was a tough act to follow — that father. Eddie Dmytryk was a big-deal director."[157]

## Candy and the Kid (Brother): Second Season Semi-Regular Eric Chase

"Every time I go down and put on a case in front of a jury, I scratch my head and I think to myself, 'If I were in a jury box, would I fall asleep listening to me? How can I capture their interest?' So I have to…when I'm cross-examining a witness, when I'm on direct examination with a witness, my witness, the questions that I ask are couched to keep the attention and the interest of the jury. I build exhibits to do that, too. Exhibits are there and they're highlighted, and they've got the bullet points, the diagrams, pictures, models, whatever it is, it's really there to put on a show for the jury so that they're interested. Because if they stay focused and interested, and they like your presentation, then they're gonna like your case. If they like your case, then you're gonna win. Isn't that what any TV show is trying to do? It's trying to keep the interest of the audience so they'll watch the commercial and buy the product. So it's all the same stuff."

That is how former actor-turned-lawyer Eric Chase describes his work as an attorney. Chase's noting the similarities between a TV series and a jury case is not surprising — very early in his life, Chase exhibited the same sort of practicality and intelligence. It was very much evident during his one season on *Here Come the Brides*. Case in point: the "key light" incident during the shooting of one episode. Laughs Chase: "The only time I remember somebody coming just unglued was when we were gonna shoot the scene and some clown had knocked the plug out of one of the key lights. The director said, 'We've gotta shoot the scene. Somebody plug in that plug.' Somebody said, 'No, we can't. The electrician has to do it under the union rules.' The director said, 'Okay, Well, where's the electrician? Have him plug it in.' The guy says, 'He's on his mandatory fifteen-minute break. Just started his break; he just went out the set door.' The director said, 'Well, go get him and have him plug it in.' The guy goes, 'Nope. That's against the union rules.' He [the director] just started screaming and yelling, and cussing, 'Nobody can plug in that GODDAMN PLUG? I've got two hundred people standing around here! You know what the cost is per hour? And there's one plug!' He was just so upset. I mean the guy just came unglued! It was the only time I ever saw anyone come unglued in the time that I was there. Well, I walked up to the director. I said, 'I'll plug in the plug.' But I don't think I did because there were always union guys standing around watching — they didn't want… it had some union rule implication. I think we had to stand around and wait until the guy got through with his cigarette outside. And I remember thinking, as a little kid, 'Well, this is about as stupid as it gets.' I was only like ten years old, and I could figure that out. But that poor director — red face, cussing and yelling about that."

Another puzzle to Chase was the need for so much makeup. "They put such heavy makeup on," the former actor remembers. "I never liked it. It felt like it was a quarter inch of makeup all over you — it just felt gummy. It was like wearing frosting all day. They said they needed it because they had these high-intensity lights that would wash you out unless they put on the dark makeup. I could never figure it out, but I thought to myself, If you need to put on makeup to keep me from being washed out by the high-intensity light, why not just use a lower intensity light? They had it all figured out, but you'd think those things."

Then there was the "Christopher Pruitt hat mystery." Chuckles Chase: "I remember I had...I don't know where I left it, but I had to wear a hat, then I lost the hat and the wardrobe guy was going crazy because we couldn't find the hat. When the hat was lost, I was thinking to myself, Well, that's not a big deal. Who cares about the hat being lost? But this guy just went crazy. He was beside himself. It was almost like...it was like he had lost the deed to his house or something. Anyway he found another hat, and he spray painted it brown, and they stuck it on my head. It wasn't exactly the same hat, but it was close enough. The wardrobe guy had a very difficult job, because they've gotta be very conscious of the flux that you're trying to portray. The odd part is that you wear kind of the same clothes from show to show almost. Which seems odd. It doesn't seem like that's what people would normally do. But back then they had the feeling that it provided continuity for people who were watching the show — that they'd go, 'Oh, *that's* the person!'"

This practicality and common sense of Eric Chase's may have explained why he was so convincing in that scene from "A Bride for Obie Brown" in which Christopher Pruitt and his sister Molly pose a thought-provoking question to guest Cicely Tyson — a question which results in Tyson deciding to make a new home in Seattle. But good as he was in this and other *Brides* episodes, Chase hadn't planned on being an actor.

"I was part of I guess what would be a seemingly typical Hollywood story fantasy," he laughs. "There was a pair of agents named Lynne and Jerry Rosen. They were very Hollywood like; she had a big bee[hive]-style hairdo, and they smoked those long tips — long cigarette holders, and they wore those weird cat-eye sunglasses and dressed in those outfits that you see back then. They were a very colorful couple. Well, one Saturday my mother was shopping at a health-food store, and Lynne Rosen was in there. She saw us, [Chase and his brother] and ran up and started raving about how cute we were and how we would be great in show business and pictures. She gave us her card, wanted us to come and see her. My mother had no concept of what was going on. She said, 'Sure, let's go down and check it out, and see what she has to say.' As it turned out, the Rosens were quite flamboyant and pushy so a lot of people banned them from the set. We didn't know that. But they were the kind of people who would call you 'darling,' and grab your face, they were very, very flamboyant. They would say, 'Baby.' They were quite a couple. He was the agent for the gal who played the lead on *Gilligan's Island* [Tina Louise]. She was one of his main clients. They were generally adult agents. But my brother and I Lynne Rosen was really interested in. My brother did a couple of little things, then [he] kind of fizzled out."

According to Chase, his obtaining acting work in the beginning "wasn't really talent. It was just the look. I did commercials, little parts. I had done a few jobs before

I'd gone in and got the *Here Come the Brides* show. I interviewed for *The Brady Bunch*. They had a cattle call for billions of kids. They probably interviewed a couple thousand kids for a particular part. It all boiled down to Michael Lookinland and I [when it came to casting] the kid who played Bobby Brady. They brought us down there to an interview with Robert Reed one night. We sat there for four or five hours going back and forth, they would call one kid in, then send him out, then they'd call in the other kid. I remember sitting there for about an hour and a half with nothing going on, with the door shut, all these guys inside talking. Then finally, it was probably ten at night. They said, 'We just can't…hardly make a decision. We just like you both. But in the end, we think Michael Lookinland looks just a little more like Robert Reed, so we're going with him.' So for perhaps a flip of the coin the other way, I would have been in a totally different direction."

Chase has good memories of his *Brady Bunch* tryout, which involved reading with Reed in front of the producers, casting people, etc. "They were nice guys," he recalls. "gracious people. Reed was a very nice guy and smiled. He said, 'Good job.' The other guys seemed enthusiastic. I was the last part of the children to be cast. [Casting Bobby Brady] seemed to be an agonizing decision for them. To have it boiled down to two kids, to be there for hours and hours while they debated over that, that never happened to me before that or after that."

Not long after his *Brady Bunch* audition, Chase was cast in the role of Candy Pruitt's little brother, Christopher Pruitt, on the second season of *Here Come the Brides*. "That was another cattle call," states Chase. "They decided they needed to have a better mix after that first year. Bob Claver was the one that ultimately selected me. He just loved me to pieces. He was another guy that was warm and fuzzy about my looks as a little kid. I guess it was a 'look' thing."

Playing Chase's sister, Molly Pruitt, was established child actress Patti Cohoon. "Patti was blonde and I was a brown-haired kid," laughs Chase. "I'm not sure we looked all that much alike. I guess we did a little bit because we had freckles. I really think that was the thing because he [Claver] just loved freckles. He thought that was…I remember him commenting about that. For some reason that was a look that he really liked."

Eric Chase very much enjoyed working for Bob Claver. "He was such a nice guy," praises the actor-turned-lawyer. "A very Hollywoodish, very people guy. He was the type that would roll in and hug people, and smile, and 'How you doing?' and a lot of enthusiasm. He's a very enthusiastic kind of guy. When we did something right, he'd do the Hollywood thing — just full of praise — 'That's Beautiful, Baby!' Made me feel like…you know you always want to feel like you're pleasing whoever it was. So he probably did a good job of drawing a little more out of people, just because he was slow to criticize, and quick to praise. I'm sure he had a lot of pressure, but he did not let it [get] to him. I'm sure they had a huge production cost and pressure as time flies, but he was upbeat, and kind of got everybody into a happy mood. Which is nice."

Particularly given the demands of the show. "The actors on *Here Come the Brides* worked long days," says Chase. "They would have early morning set calls. Until late at night. There were no rules, of course, once you hit eighteen as to how long you could work. Children could only work nine hours, three of that had to be for schooling. They had to plan around us a little more. We had to have three hours of schooling every day. And we had to have a private teacher — they'd assign special teachers for me from Los Angeles School District. These are basically set teachers, and they float around. Oftentimes, you'll get different teachers, but sometimes, if you like a teacher, they can get a job, and you get continuity. I had one teacher for quite a while. Generally the teachers were very focused and attentive, and part of their job was as a welfare worker. They would hang out on set and make sure all the rules were met. If it was time for you to have a meal, they would go up and say, 'Hey! We need a break. These guys have to go out and eat.' I didn't pay much attention to it because I was a little kid. They were running around, taking care of you, watching out for your interests, and they still do. Probably more so today than before.

"A lot of that comes from the Jackie Coogan days [in the silent film era]," continues Chase. "On *Our Gang* — the pictures that they made where they really didn't have much oversight, questionable things happened. They were pretty brutal to the kids. By the time the '60s and '70s rolled around, which was when I was kind of out there, we were much more socially conscious to our children."

Being Candy Pruitt's little brother and sister, Eric Chase and co-star Patti Cohoon had a lot of scenes together. "We were pretty close," the actor remembers. "During the breaks, we would play together, and we were in school together, and we would do…we had a great time together. We were buddy-buddies."

Watching over both children were their respective mothers. "Both my mom and Patti's mom were on the set," explains Chase. "They were buddy-buddies. We all did stuff together. We'd go to lunch. We'd take some of the stand-ins, two ladies who were stand-ins. Sometimes we'd go with them. Sometimes we'd go with other people."

Chase's mother was very well liked by cast and crew. "My mother was such an easy-going person," states the former child actor. "Stage mothers are very interesting because you get some stage mothers that are…they're like something out of a movie. They're butting in, arguing constantly about whether their kids should get in that shot, whether the lighting was right for that kid. But my mom was a low-key person. She would just turn me over to the gang and sit over in the corner and crochet, or something. If someone came up to her, she was just gracious. She would just say, 'Oh, thank you. Sure.' I remember Chris Morgan — he was second assistant [director]. He just loved my mother. He would…a lot of times — he had that same voice that his dad [actor Harry Morgan] did. He'd say (in a Harry Morgan voice), 'Well, there she is. The Hollywood mother of the year.' He liked to joke with my mom."

Things didn't go as well for Chase's father. "There was one time where my dad had to take my mother's place," remembers the actor. "He had to come down and watch me for the day because she had some important event. He probably was not… my mother was quietly conscious of what was going on around her; she made sure that we were where we were supposed to be and doing what we should. My dad, on the other hand, was pretty oblivious to the process. Now, I was supposed to be on a set filming, but we had a break. [After the break] I was supposed to be back at a particular time to film something, but [during the break] I went over and visited with Joan Blondell. Joan Blondell had a really decked-out trailer that they'd made for her, with a garden around it, and she had these two old dogs that were in there — pug dogs. And Joan, of course, she was an old-time vaudevillian actress, and she always kind of dressed a little flamboyantly and Hollywoodish. Anyway, she liked me, and I had this downtime, and I wasn't really aware of when I was supposed to be back. So I went over to Joan's to visit her — I don't remember why she had downtime, but I wanted to play with the dogs. So, I was in there, and she made me something to drink and got me cookies — she was a very friendly person. I didn't know when I was supposed to be back. I figured somebody would come and get me. Well, the scene that I was in was supposed to be filmed, and I wasn't there! So they were looking around, and my dad was on the set, and he didn't know where I was. So they spent about an hour looking for me; I think that they thought I'd been abducted — they had a full studio search going on. Whoever the director was, he was going crazy because I was holding up production. But when they found me, he wasn't upset at me. He brought me back in, treated me — 'Oh! I'm so happy we…' but I know he took my dad, chewed him up one side and down the other — 'Your kid! You're responsible! You're supposed to know where he's at! What are you doing to me?' Cuz you don't want to yell at the kid because he's gonna be upset and blow his lines; that's only gonna take more time."

Like Joan Blondell, Bridget Hanley was very good to both Eric Chase and Patti Cohoon. "Bridget was very kind to us kids," remembers Chase. "She treated us very sister-like. Always made sure that we were happy. Got us little things, little trinkets. Bridget was married to Swack, the director. As I understand it, they had a wonderful relationship — I think she was married to him till he died. He was a distant acquaintance in the sense that I saw him and that I observed. My recollection was that they had a very nice marriage."

Originally meeting a few of the *Brides* regular actresses and female extras when they were dressed in full costume, Eric Chase was at times shocked when he saw them in street dress. "I was always amazed cuz these ladies would come in in the morning dressed in a certain way," he explains, "then the makeup people would work on 'em, and by the time they got through and were finished with them, they were completely different people. They would add on hair pieces, do all this makeup, change their wardrobes out of whatever Sixties style dresses they were wearing to Eighteen Hundred style. By the time they got done, they were just…almost, like on a lot of them, you'd see a picture of them on the street, then take a picture of them with their makeup on — you would never think that they were the same person. It was amazing. That was the case with Bridget to some extent because they added a big hairpiece on her, the way they highlighted her cheeks, and then they put all that mascara stuff on — by the time they got done, she was pretty lit up. She looked pretty good. She was a nice-looking gal anyway, but they knew how to get the most out of her."

Chase never had any trouble recognizing Hanley when she was out of costume, but "a couple of times, I would see the women, some of the extras, and they would come up, and 'Hi, Eric. How you doin'?' and I was just, I didn't know who they were, then they'd get their makeup on and I'd go, 'Ooohh. I should have known that.' So it was interesting to see the transformation."

Series regular Susan Tolsky was in a class all her own. "She was almost the same personality off the camera that she was on the camera," Chase remembers. "She was always giggling, had that laugh — kind of high energy — she's running a million miles an hour. That was her personality, and I think that she was able to market it in a lot of different situations. On the show, and in other jobs."

Like the *Here Come the Brides* guest stars, Eric Chase found the regular cast of the series a very nice bunch of people. "I was looking at things through kind of different eyes," he explains. "It didn't appear to me, you know, I've worked many different jobs, done many things in my life, and seen many work environments, but I never saw any animosity, or any acrimony, never saw any jealousy. Robert did like to be sort of patriarchal in a weird way. He did like to walk around and kind of oversee — nobody minded. He wanted to be paternalistic, he was always looking after people. He was always kind of looking after people to make sure that they were comfortable, but he also wanted to be the center of attention — he wanted all the cameras on him. He was a bit of a chicken, too. I remember once we had a wagon scene. They had pulled a cable off through the...across the little road there — you know, one of those cables, and I think the horses mistook it for a snake or something. They just went crazy and started jumping around, and we were on the back of the wagon; Robert was on the front, and he bolted. He was at the top of the wagon — he was afraid the horses were going to run off, and without even thinking, he just jumped off the wagon. There was no one holding the reins then — it was a real wagon, real horses, real reins. I remember I grabbed the reins to steady the horses, just reached up and grabbed them, and held on till one of the wranglers came up and grabbed them. Robert was pretty embarrassed — he took a lot of egging from the crew for the next hour, everybody started making fun of him. That wasn't quite the image he was trying to portray. But he was sure likable. They [Brown, Bobby Sherman, David Soul] were all likable.

"Bobby Sherman was a very pragmatic individual," continues Chase. "He was sort of one of those teen idols, and he knew those things are fleeting so he was trying to capitalize on it, took the money that he saved, and invested in like a recording studio that he was planning on using as a future business once the teenyboppers moved on to the next idol. He wasn't the type of kid that was running around, blowing everything that he took in. I felt like Bobby was always a humble person. Even though really Bobby was the hottest item on the show, he seemed to remain very low-key. He was the type of guy that anybody could walk up to and have a nice conversation with. He was...he never seemed to lose the 'I'm the average guy on the street' attitude. That was a little unusual — when you get that kind of attention — Hollywood drives you into this scene. Once you're there, people fawn over you, and they always want something from you, and then you develop an attitude, and once you do that, you feel like you can do whatever you want, unless you have great discipline. A lot of people were not able to handle that real well, and made some poor choices."

"David Soul made some hard choices," Chase believes. "I think life beat him up quite a bit, probably some of those guys had experiences like that, but back then,

David Soul was just a boy. Almost angelic in the sense that he was very enthusiastic, excited to be working, excited to be there. He was just a nice, nice boy. He liked to ride his own horses, and do his own work. He was a kid. And he was enthusiastic, and he was just…he was very athletic and energetic. I used to see him out during the down times playing basketball, and he just…he wanted to move. He was just…I've met him once or twice since then, and I almost wish you could go back and bottle and capture that boy that he was."

As for the show's villain, Mark Lenard, and its comedian, Henry Beckman, "Mark Lenard was one of the gang," says Chase. "Nice to everybody. Upbeat kind of a guy, good actor. I remember he would joke a lot on the set. He seemed to have a lot of fun doing what he did. Didn't seem to have a particularly big ego, and he played a guy with a big ego. He really didn't exhibit that ego. But the one that was always intriguing to me was Henry Beckman because he acted almost the same as a character as he did as a non-character. He did enjoy the bottle. I remember when I saw him at the twenty-year reunion he didn't look one bit different than he did twenty years before. Very little change — he was just a funny guy. They definitely had some people with character on that show. I remember Hoke Howell. He was involved in some kind of political…seems to me he was involved in some kind of…not Habitat for Humanity, but some charitable kind of thing. He was a very nice guy."

During the filming of one second-season episode, a fire broke out on the set. According to Chase, he was perhaps the first *Brides* cast member to realize there was a fire. "We were coming back from lunch," he remembers. "I looked across, walking down the lot at Columbia — it's a big, huge studio, and I could see over on the western town — there was an outdoor western set. I could see smoke coming out, and I said to [one of] the gals, 'Look! I think there's a fire over there. We should call…' She said, 'No, it's not. There's no fire over there. They're probably just burning trash on the backlot.' I kept watching, and they kept yakking about…nothing. I kept watching smoke getting bigger and bigger. I said, 'No. I think it's a fire.' They said, 'No, no. It's not a fire.' Finally, I saw a flame come over the top of the set. I said, 'There's a flame coming over the top of the set. They're not burning trash!' The lady said, 'Ohhhh! There is!' The next thing I knew the whole damn lot was on fire. There were wranglers trying to get horses out and people running all over the place, and they were trying to get people out and the fire department in. It was a massive fire. I think we ended up over at the *Bewitched* set. I think they were able to get it out before it got to our set, but they lost a lot of stuff. What had happened was they had a lot of dry old sets out there. A guy had put one of the light lamps down in one of the sidewalk areas of the western set. In the sidewalk areas, there's a lot of wood, and they had [put down a] magnifying glass, and it caught the wood on fire. It was a huge fire. A huge fire! And there were loose horses running around and wranglers chasing things. It was wild. I don't think anyone got injured, but after that lady [alerted by Chase] called, somebody else comes running out from somewhere, 'There's a fire!' And I remember Susan [Tolsky] screaming and yelling. She got real excited. You can imagine what that was like — that energy — it was totally uncorked during the fire."

Being a kid, Chase wanted to go watch the firefighters battle the flames. "There were some people that came over and kind of scolded me, herded me the other way," the former actor relates. "We were taken…I don't know how we got out — maybe on little carts. We stood on the *Bewitched* lot for several hours while the fire trucks went by in both directions, and, of course, everybody was out there talking. The flames were high — it was a big fire. I think they burned down *The Flying Nun* set in that fire — quite a bit of damage. I'm sure it was many millions of dollars worth of damage. I think it got pretty close to our stage, but not our outdoor sets — it was quite an event. I think Bridget came up and hunted us down — she was very concerned, wanted to make sure that the kids were all right. Whoever the director was, he was kind of running around and making sure that all the *Here Come the Brides* people were out of the way. If you had people on the soundstage, that could have been a problem. For as bad a fire as it was, I think it was lucky that they didn't have any real injuries."

During his one season on *Brides,* Chase appeared on other Screen Gems series, such as *Bewitched.* "I did a couple of *Bewitched*s mainly because I was already on the set," he explains. "They said that they would need somebody for something, and they pulled me off. They had all these things going on; in general, it was just an interesting place. It was fun to walk around the studio, when you had lunch, or you had a break, and see all the different things that were going on — they had a lot of things that they were shooting. You could walk over to the *Bewitched* set and watch them film there a little bit, or you'd walk over and watch…they were filming a *Monkees* commercial, all the Monkees were riding horses.

It was either while working on, or visiting the *Bewitched* set that Chase had conversations with veteran actress Agnes Moorehead. "Joan Blondell was fun because she would tell me all her stories, and she had a lot of stories about old acting days, and Agnes Moorehead was another who would tell you stories," says Chase. "She claimed that she got cancer, the Duke [John Wayne] and all the others — they were doing all these Hollywood westerns. They would shoot them in southern Utah, where they were testing all these nuclear warheads. She always talked about how a lot of the people that she worked with got cancer and died. She blamed it on that. But she smoked like a chimney!"

Chase very much enjoyed his one season on *Here Come the Brides.* "It really was a congenial group of people,' he states, "they were an interesting bunch. They were anti-war and very Democrat-like, and anti-Nixon. But my family was a Republican family. My dad was very much into business and low taxes."

Yet Chase's political leanings had nothing to do with his leaving the entertainment business. "I got out of acting voluntarily because I got tired of going to malls," he explains, "just got tired of going to the beach, got tired of going everywhere, seeing people come up and ask you questions, following me around. I didn't like all that attention, and I quit at a time when I was doing really well. A lot of people were calling me [because] you get to the point where they don't have to interview you anymore; you get called, they want you to do a job, a commercial."

Shortly after he stopped acting, Chase became an attorney. "Acting prepared me to be a lawyer," he notes, "and I've been a lawyer for a long time. I'm a trial lawyer so I spend a lot of time in court and I spend a lot of time arguing cases. There's no difference between what I do now and what I did then. It's all…you get a case, and a case is a set of facts, and the set of facts is put together in a particular way that best suits your client. Then it really forms into a play. You are putting on a play, playing out a script, in front of a jury — with a judge, whoever you're presenting the case to — it's a stage, the courtroom is a stage, the jurors are the audience. It's a show."[158]

October 1969: Bobby Sherman: His Mother's Story' – *TV Radio Talk;* ("Meet Bobby's Dream Girl"; "You Interview Your Fave – Bobby Sherman" "Your Returning TV Fave"; 'My Son, Bobby" by Mrs. Robert Sherman; "An In-Depth Talk with David Soul, Part 2"; David Soul tidbit) – all of these articles in *Tiger Beat;* "Where You Can Find Bobby Sherman"

*Flip Teen;* Bobby Sherman article in *TV Picture Life;* Three Bobby Sherman articles in *FaVE!;* Bobby Sherman article in *Teen World;* Bobby Sherman article in *16 Magazine;* Robert Brown article in *16 Magazine;* David Soul article in *Screen Stars;* Bridget Hanley in *FaVE!* and *Teen World;* "Coming Back" blurb about the series in *TV Preview.*

October 1, 1969 – Mark Lenard guest stars on *Hawaii Five-O,* "To Hell with Babe Ruth" 10 p.m., CBS.

## Episode #28: "The Wealthiest Man in Seattle"        *October 3, 1969*

"I committed the three unpardonable sins. I lied to me brother,
to a priest, and worst of all, to a fellow Irishman."
*Captain Clancey to Jason Bolt*

| | |
|---|---|
| Teleplay | Charles Watts, Paul Stein, and Allen Clare |
| Story | Watts and Stein |
| Director | Richard Kinon |
| Film Editor | Asa Clark |
| Assistant Director | Michael Dmytryk |

### Guest Cast

| | |
|---|---|
| Father Ned | Bernard Fox |
| Gil | Ken Swofford |
| George | Mills Watson |
| Claude | Hagan Beggs |
| Mark | Felton Perry |
| Dutch | Dick Balduzzi |

*Teaser:* Lottie, barman, Jason, Clancey.
*Tag:* Clancey, Jason, Aaron, Lottie, Jeremy, Candy, Josh.

**Competition:** *CBS Friday Night Movie: Double Trouble* starring Elvis Presley; *The Name of the Game*, "Blind Man's Bluff," with Tony Franciosa as Jeff Dillon, guest-starring Jack Klugman, Broderick Crawford, Coleen Gray, Denny Miller, and Michele Carey, NBC.

**Notes:** A more dramatic Captain Clancey having been presented in the first season's "A Jew Named Sullivan" and "One Good Lie Deserves Another," this episode continues with that theme. Only here, it has to do with the Captain's pride. Clancey's need for self-worth, his desire to be something more than the hard-drinking captain of a boat is a subject he'll discuss only with Lottie. "Darlin'," he tells her. "I'm a man who likes good times and I like to hear the sound of people's laughter. I want them laughin' *with* me, not *at* me! I'll be any man's friend. But no man's clown."

While there are a lot of tender and emotional moments in this episode, there's also a great deal of humor. Much of it comes from villains Ken Swofford (in his first *Brides*) and Mills Watson (in his second.) Seeing all the businesses Clancey "owns," Swofford, Watson, and their gang kidnap the captain while he's walking across the town square. "We seen them there Clancey signs on every business in Seattle," Swofford's Gil tells Clancey. "You done real good for yourself and now you're gonna do real good for us, too." Swofford is just great in the part.

Though he is no longer on the show, Bo Svenson's Big Swede is referenced in the teaser.

*Story Editor/Episode Writer William Blinn:* "*I'm* Allen Clare. That's one of my *nom de plumes*. If my name was on it — for the story editor to get a credit — that means it was a major rewrite. I sort of liked that one. It was overtly sentimental and obviously "The Wealthiest Man in Seattle" all deals with the people who care for Clancey, and are there for Clancey, and support Clancey, and love Clancey and so forth and so on, and that's pretty corny. And if it works, it's not corny, and if it doesn't work, it is corny. I thought for what it was, it was okay."[159]

*Series Semi-Regular Dick Balduzzi on Guest Star Bernard Fox:* "Bernard Fox was a very close friend of Gavin MacLeod's. He used to come and see [A Funny Thing Happened on the Way to the] *Forum* all the time because he loved the show, and he was a friend of Gavin's. [Balduzzi and MacLeod were playing in *Forum* at the time.] We played it for nine or ten performances — I think he [Fox] was there about seven or eight times."

*Dick Balduzzi on Guest Ken Swofford:* "Ken Swofford is a great guy. I like Ken. I did a show on *Mary Tyler Moore* that he never forgot — I played Philly, the drunk — friend of Lou's. He used to comment on that to me all the time. Swofford is a wonderful actor. He's a really nice man, and a really good actor. He's great at those lieutenant and chief of police [characters]. He can do anything, really. He's good on heavies."[160]

*A Ken Swofford memory from William Blinn:* "I loved to do this…I love to find that offbeat thing for a character that the audience thinks they know. I recall in *Fame,*

Ken Swofford played the principal of the school and there was…one of the teachers was just enraged at something he had done, and she went charging in to his office to have a confrontation with him. She found him in tears at his desk because his dog had died that morning, and he started talking about his dog. Those are the kind of curveballs I think are just terrific to throw at the audience, but, in order to do that, like a pitcher, you have to set the batter up with fastball, fastball, fastball, fastball, then, curveball. When you can do that, it is great fun."[161]

October 6-10, 1969 – Robert Brown is a guest celebrity on the daytime version of *Hollywood Squares*.

## Episode #29: "The Soldier"                                    *October 10, 1969*

"You're fit for nothing. And that's precisely what you're going to do. I'm relieving you of all responsibilities. You will eat, sleep, and collect your pay. But twenty-four hours a day, you will do absolutely nothing."
*Captain Hale to Sergeant Noah Todd*

"We're not talking about an 'it,' Josh. We're talking about a man.
And I'm not sure he can wait."
*Jeremy Bolt to Joshua Bolt*

"When that animal died, what was left of my army career died right with it."
*Sergeant Noah Todd to Jeremy Bolt*

Writer . . . . . . . . . . . . . . . . . . . . . . . . . . . . . . . . . . . . . . . . . . . . . . . . . . . . . . . Skip Webster
Director . . . . . . . . . . . . . . . . . . . . . . . . . . . . . . . . . . . . . . . . . . . . . . . Paul Junger Witt
Assistant Director . . . . . . . . . . . . . . . . . . . . . . . . . . . . . . . . . . . . . . . . Floyd Joyer
Film Editor . . . . . . . . . . . . . . . . . . . . . . . . . . . . . . . . . . . . . . . . . . . . . . Asa Clark
Music . . . . . . . . . . . . . . . . . . . . . . . . . . . . . . . . . . . . . . . . . . . . . . . . . . Shorty Rogers
### Guest Cast
Noah Todd . . . . . . . . . . . . . . . . . . . . . . . . . . . . . . . . . . . . . . . . . . . . . . Steve Ihnat
Captain Hale . . . . . . . . . . . . . . . . . . . . . . . . . . . . . . . . . . . . . . . . . . . . James Sikking
Hart . . . . . . . . . . . . . . . . . . . . . . . . . . . . . . . . . . . . . . . . . . . . . . . . . Christopher Stone
Braddock . . . . . . . . . . . . . . . . . . . . . . . . . . . . . . . . . . . . . . . . . . . . . . George Clifton
Sentry . . . . . . . . . . . . . . . . . . . . . . . . . . . . . . . . . . . . . . . . . . . . . . . . . William Engle

**Teaser:** Clancey, Lottie, Jason, Josh, Jeremy, Ben, Candy, Corky, Biddie.
**Tag:** Lottie, Jason, Josh, Aaron, Sgt. Noah Todd, Candy, Jeremy, Corky, Biddie, Clancey.
**Competition:** *The CBS Friday Night Movie: Doctor, You've Got to be Kidding* starring Sandra Dee and George Hamilton; *The Name of the Game*, "The Emissary," starring Gene Barry as Glenn Howard, guest-starring Charles Boyer and Craig Stevens, NBC.

***Photography:*** Biddie running up steps of dormitory; shots of townspeople walking out of Lottie's to dead bear; Candy and Jeremy amongst the flowers; the daylight, left profile of Candy; the nighttime, right profile of Candy.

***Notes:*** The first character study of the season, and the show's first hard-edged villain, defines for viewers how the Bolts and the rest of Seattle will behave towards the people who wish them harm. Introducing this theme is the show's sweetest character, Jeremy Bolt. Setting the standard for the sympathetic villains to follow is the magnificent character actor, Steve Ihnat.

In his first action piece, Bobby Sherman is just excellent. The sequence in which Candy has a nightmare about Jeremy is equally excellent.

Christopher Pruitt's interruption, then resumption of his bedtime prayer provides a nice, lighthearted touch. The inebriated Clancey being attacked by a bear the night of his birthday party makes for a jarring teaser. First-season semi-regular Cynthia Hull (playing bride Ann) has a good, albeit brief, scene.

*Series Semi-Regular Eric Chase on Director Paul Junger Witt:* "He was very Hollywoodish. He had those long sideburns, and dressed in those very wide collars and bellbottoms that they wore back in the '60s. He would be a laughingstock today from a fashion perspective. But nice — an upbeat guy."[162]

## Guest Star Steve Ihnat

Fleeing his native Czechoslovakia with his family at the age of five, Steve Ihnat became interested in acting around the age of fourteen. Often cast as villains, most notably as the demented Garth of Izar in the third-season *Star Trek*, "Whom Gods Destroy," Ihnat was unforgettable as the Indian-hating Mr. Ganns in the twelfth-season *Bonanza*, "Terror at 2:00." Other good Ihnat performances: *The Outer Limits*, "The Inheritors," the 1967 spy spoof, *In Like Flint*, and the much lauded third-season *Mission: Impossible* "The Mind of Stefan Miklos."

A screenwriter and director (in the late '60s he directed and starred in the underground film, *Don't Throw Cushions in the Ring*) Ihnat fared much better with the 1972 picture, *The Honkers*. Sadly, on May 12, 1972, while attending the Cannes Film Festival, Steve Ihnat died of a heart attack. He was only thirty-seven years old.

*Leading Lady Bridget Hanley:* "I loved Steve Ihnat and I knew his wife. I loved him. I just loved him. He was so talented and sexy, such a wonderful male presence."[163]

*Story Editor William Blinn:* "Steve, of course — who died much, much too young — was a fabulous actor. He was…one of the things that I observed in westerns is that a lot of young actors tend to overanalyze this kind of thing. You have to buy the fable, and you have to know what the legend is, and you just have to play the legend. Steve did that. That's why he was one of *Gunsmoke*'s most popular guest stars. He did a lot of those, directed a couple of westerns that were very good, and he was just immensely bright, immensely talented, died much too young."[164]

*Series Semi-Regular Robert Biheller:* "I was very good friends with Michael Pataki, and they [Pataki and Ihnat] were friends. That's how I met Ihnat. Ihnat would always ask me, 'What did you think? How did I do?'"[165]

*Wardrobe Man Steve Lodge:* "My writing partner, Steve Ihnat, was considered for the part of Jason Bolt. It would have been a totally different look because Steve was a much ballsier, rougher guy than Robert. Robert was a musical kind of looking guy. That's something that Ihnat told me himself. I wrote *The Honkers* with Steve. And there's a very famous episode of *Star Trek* that he did: Whom Gods Destroy" where he plays Garth. That's one that people talk about a lot. Believe it or not, that was the absolutely only *Star Trek* I ever worked on.

"Every time we worked with each other, Steve and I always used to say, 'What are you doing? What are you doing?' Because I would be writing, and he would be making his little movie on the weekends, and all that kind of stuff. Somehow we finally got together to write.

"The 'Bear' show with him — the one where Bobby Sherman shoots this bear, where Steve was the old sergeant, he was only thirty-four, thirty-five years old when he did that. And he was playing this seventy-year old man!"[166]

## Episode #30: "Nest Week, East Lynne"          *October 17, 1969*

"Oh, Jason, this isn't being done for the loggers. It's being done
for the brides. And they want Shakespeare."
*Candy Pruitt to Jason Bolt*

"The way of the artist is hard."
*Marlowe, in an aside to the audience*

Writer . . . . . . . . . . . . . . . . . . . . . . . . . . . . . . . . . . . . . . . . . . . . . . . . . . . Henry Slesar
Director. . . . . . . . . . . . . . . . . . . . . . . . . . . . . . . . . . . . . . . . . . . . . . . Irving Moore
Film Editor . . . . . . . . . . . . . . . . . . . . . . . . . . . . . . . . . . . . . Norman Wallerstein
Assistant Director . . . . . . . . . . . . . . . . . . . . . . . . . . . . . . . . . . . . David Hawks
### Guest Cast
Marlowe . . . . . . . . . . . . . . . . . . . . . . . . . . . . . . . . . . . . . . . . . . . . . . Donald Moffat
Eleanor . . . . . . . . . . . . . . . . . . . . . . . . . . . . . . . . . . . . . . . . . . . . . .Jayne Meadows
Pierre LeBeau . . . . . . . . . . . . . . . . . . . . . . . . . . . . . . . . . . . . . . . . . . Ian Ireland
Ada Moon. . . . . . . . . . . . . . . . . . . . . . . . . . . . . . . . . . . . . . . . . . . . . .Susan Silo
Boniface. . . . . . . . . . . . . . . . . . . . . . . . . . . . . . . . . . . . . . . . . . . . . . Paul Marin
Knight. . . . . . . . . . . . . . . . . . . . . . . . . . . . . . . . . . . . . . . . . . . . . Gordon DeVol
Laertes. . . . . . . . . . . . . . . . . . . . . . . . . . . . . . . . . . . . . . . . . . . .Peter Lawrence
Marshall . . . . . . . . . . . . . . . . . . . . . . . . . . . . . . . . . . . . . . . . . William Phillips

**Teaser** *(in Tacoma):* Jason, Josh, Candy, Mr. Boniface; Teaser *(in Seattle):* Jeremy, Ben, Lottie, Aaron.

**Tag:** Jeremy, Jason, Josh, Candy, Lottie, Biddie.

**Competition:** *The CBS Friday Night* Movie, *Where Angels Go, Trouble Follows,* starring Rosalind Russell and Camilla Sparv; *Name of the Game,* "Chains of Command," Robert Stack as Dan Ferrell, guest-starring Dorothy Lamour, Pernell Roberts, Sidney Blackmer, and *Brides* guests Steve Ihnat, Jay C. Flippen and Paul Fix, NBC.

**Photography:** Slow pan over the brides, loggers, Aaron, Ben, Lottie, Jeremy, Biddie.

**Notes:** While it has its funny moments, "Next Week, East Lynne," *Brides'* first comedy of the season, suggests that perhaps ABC-TV was justified in pushing the series in a more dramatic direction. Over the top acting is definitely the right approach to this tale, but when actors go over the top, they often go too far. That seems to be the case with Jayne Meadows at times, and to a lesser degree, Donald Moffat. While Ian Ireland seems to be pushing it as the dashing Frenchman, Pierre LeBeau, Susan Silo is much better as the obviously-not-thirteen-year-old Ada Moon. Perhaps one reason Silo comes off so well is that she often has a mug of beer in her hand.

The weakest part of the story is the sequence where Marlowe introduces the members of his troupe. That Lottie is the only one in Seattle not to believe that Ada Moon is thirteen stretches credibility to the limit. Are general store owner Ben Perkins, "bride" Biddie Cloom, and the other people of Seattle truly that naive?

Maybe so. In one of the funniest moments in the episode, Meadows' Eleanor Tangiers tells Marlowe that robbing the safe in the general store will be no problem. "It hasn't got a back," she remarks with a loud laugh. "They just shove it up against the wall."

Former Shakespearean actor Robert Brown has fun in the scenes where his Jason Pruitt (brother of Candy) joins Marlowe's Great Western Shakespeare Company as new leading man, Jason Winthrop. David Soul has some good comic moments, too.

*Story Editor William Blinn:* "I thought it was cute. I didn't think we cast it particularly well. It was so bizarre, not unlike the Jenny Lind show, made up out of whole cloth, but those traveling troupes were a big deal, and it was fun to get into the theatrical mode. Robert did that sort of thing very well."[167]

*Series Star Robert Brown:* "It was like all the other episodes, one I recall more vividly, because I was in costume. It was something I felt comfortable in."[168]

*Wardrobe Man Steve Lodge:* "The guy who wrote that [Henry Slesar] — he wrote that way all the time. It was a very special way of writing — the way he described things — that was fun. We went on Western Street. That was supposed to be another town in Washington [Tacoma]. When we went to another town, it was always Western Street."[169]

## Guest Star Susan Silo

A graduate of New York's High School of Performing Arts, Susan Silo has been an actress since the age of four; she has performed in radio, television and theatre, (both on and off Broadway). At one point a teenage pop star, Silo's talent for different voices and accents kept, and keeps, her, very busy in the entertainment industry.

Because her mother was an actress, and her father, Jonathan Silo, was "an amazing character actor," Silo grew up in New York among theatrical people. "Accents for me... it was a given," she explains, "a 'you either have it or you don't' type of thing. I spoke and sang in different languages, too. I really didn't have to study that much. I would be coached, not by [dialect coach] Bob Easton (the 'Henry Higgins of Hollywood'), but by other people. When I did [the pilot] *The Five Hundred Pound Jerk* with Alex Karras...we were two athletes, I was a gymnast, and he was a weightlifter, or whatever it was, and I was supposed to be a Russian gymnast. So, I had to study Russian. And I studied with someone who was Russian. When I did French or anything like that, I was hired over the French girls

*"Next Week, East Lynne" guest star Susan Silo as the Riddler's aide, Mousey, in an episode of* Batman.

because nobody could understand them. I remember this one actress said to me 'Why are you doing the French thing, rather than the French girl? You're not French.' I didn't want to tell her that I was told because they could understand me. So I was an American doing the French [dialect]; the French girl they couldn't understand.

Once Susan Silo started working in television, she guest-starred on such series as *Gunsmoke, My Three Sons, Dr. Kildare, The Wild Wild West, Bonanza, Combat, Route 66, Hawaiian Eye, Sea Hunt, The Many Loves of Dobie Gillis*, and most memorably, *Batman*. She was also a series regular on the comedies *Occasional Wife* and *Harry's Girls* (The latter was the TV version of the Gene Kelly feature, *Les Girls*). Larry Blyden was Harry, while Silo, Dawn Nickerson, and future *HCTB* guest Diahn Williams were his "girls."

"I was a trained actor," states Silo, "I came from Broadway, and all of that, and when we got into television, we hoped that some of the craft would be used, and that they'd allow us to play. You'd work hand in glove with the director, but you hope you can bring something to the party. And, when I did Mousey on *Batman*, I was having a good time playing with that kooky role. I mean, I really — that came from my theatrical training from the High School of Performing Arts. And, in that show, because it was 'high camp,' remember those words, 'high camp?' they allowed us to go nuts — to go over the top. And bless his heart, my Riddler, Frankie [Gorshin], you'd look at those shows, and...Tell me he's not over the top. Are you kidding? He was amazing. He was so funny, but Frank, unfortunately, never achieved what he wanted to achieve. Which was being a great actor. Which he could have been. But people just wouldn't forget the Riddler. And they wouldn't forget that he was an impressionist. I mean Kirk Douglas and Burt Lancaster, he didn't look like them but suddenly he did. It was something that really...it was an amazing thing to see.

"Frank and I were friends for years," continues Silo. "We did [Screen Gems'] *Empire* with Ryan O'Neal and Terry Moore, and Richard Egan. He was Red Adair — the oil firefighter, I was his dumb country-bumpkin wife. I remember Frank would always tell me...in later years, when I would see Frank, he would always tell me he wanted the career of an actor. And when Frank died, they had a picture all over the world of Frank and me, and I'm in the foreground. So people thought I died. My mother called up. She said, 'Are you okay?' I went, 'Yeah, Ma. I saw the obit. It's ridiculous.' Someone said, 'You know, it's such a good picture of you, you oughta have it for your own obit.'"

Because of her talent for accents and different voices, Silo's guest shots were always colorful. "I did this *Gunsmoke*, 'The Long Night,'" remembers the actress, "all men, and me, as a half-breed. I shot someone, and we all were in Miss Kitty's saloon, all night long." In the mid-'70s, Silo starred in a comedy pilot with William Windom — *Heck's Angels.* "I was the German-French spy who was his girlfriend," she recalls, "and I think it was World War I. It was a riot. It was wonderful working with Bill. He's a darling man, a very bright man. He did his one-man show, *Thurber*, for years."

By the mid-1970s, Susan Silo found herself becoming more and more involved in voice work, often for cartoons. "They came to me," she recalls. "It kind of just morphed into something. I have kind of an unusual voice in itself. So people would request me because I was with agents that represented different aspects of voice-over. I kind of got thrown into it at Hanna-Barbera just because I was an actor. They liked to use actors if they could, not just people with funny voices, but people who could act and do voices. And it just, as I said, grew like topsy. I started out with the Hanna Barbera shows, doing the *Smurfs* and all that kind of stuff, and before you knew it, my career just grew and grew and grew. I'm very blessed, because I've done features as well as [video] games. I do a lot of game stuff, a lot of television animation, a lot of cartoon shows. I'm doing a wonderful show over at Nickelodeon called *El Tigre* and that's really marvelous — it's a very funny show with very talented people in it. And Joanie [Van Ark] and I were cows for a long time for Land O'Lakes margarine, I believe it was. It went on for years. It was Joanie Gerber, Joan Van Ark, and Susan Silo as three cows. For Land O'Lakes. I'll tell you something: That sucker ran for at least ten to twelve years.

One thing Susan Silo does not miss as she continues to do work as a voice artist is the actor/actress' makeup call. "We'd come in early for makeup," she laughs. "Way early, ridiculously early, and we'd be there all day. Into the night sometimes." Other than that, Silo very much enjoyed her years onscreen. "The studios were really studios," she states. "Now, it's really gotten corporate. There's not a sense of history with some of the young people of today. I remember growing up and of course knowing about the older stars that my parents knew. We had a sense of history."

As do some of the fans Silo encounters. "It's amazing how many people remember all of the things that I've done," she says. "I had really the best of times and the best of experiences in my work. I can't even really recall anything personally. I was always happy to be there. I loved my work. And the people around me were always so wonderful. I hate to be Pollyanna, but it really was a great time. Sometimes you don't realize it when you're living it. What a wonderful time we had, what wonderful people. I'm just so glad that's what I can remember."

Very happy with her voice-artist career, Susan Silo doesn't even entertain the thought of leaving the business. "None of us, I think, if we have our druthers, would retire," says the actress. "To retire from what? Retire from love – the love of our lives? The passion? It's like my right. I don't know how not to act. That's what I do, that's how I live, that's how I breathe. It's just in our blood."[175]

### *Susan Silo's memories of her* Brides *shoot*

"It was a delightful experience. It was such a happy set. People were having a lot of fun. In this particular show — because it was a theatrical show within a show. We were acting in an acting show, and it had a kind of double meaning for all of us actors. We were laughing at ourselves, saying, 'God, can you imagine being an actor in those days?' And a robber at the same time? And, of course, I was playing a young girl — younger than myself, who was a beer-swigging lunatic — this was Juliet on acid! It was hysterical. We had such a wonderful time dressing up in those costumes; I remember wearing a page costume, like a young boy, with a page-boy wig. It was adorable. I had so much fun doing all of this play-acting. It was like doing dress-up when you're a kid. I do remember in one scene she was drinking beer, and beer cannot be emulated. You can emulate wine with something else, or liquor, but beer is beer. So I got to drink real beer in the morning — it was a riot, and everyone was laughing and joining in; everyone was feeling pretty wonderful by the end of the day because we all had beer. That was a different era. Everyone threw parties; everyone was treated in a certain way.

"Donald Moffat! What a wonderful man he is. What a wonderful actor. I was in awe of him. I was amazed at Donald Moffat, because he was so well known as a theatrical actor, that he was even gonna do television…It was just amazing that this man would do this show — he was so well thought of. The 'theatah' is the queen of everything. Doing good theater to an actor was always so important, especially in those days. Today, too. You see a lot of people who do movies wanting to go to the stage. And, for a while, TV was held in contempt, absolutely. It was like doing commercials. None of us at that time would have done commercials Can you believe that? Now it's like, oh my God, all these stars doing everything. But in those days, it was like the kiss of death. Can you believe that?

"I loved Jayne Meadows Allen. Jayne was a hoot! Jayne had to put me under her wing at that time. I had recently gotten married, was a young little bride, and

Jayne was just lecturing me on how to be a good wife. Oh, it was a riot. She really was Mother Hen to me. She was a hoot. She's just larger than life. A very, very, very theatrical, wonderful woman. They threw away the mold with somebody like that. I remember Steve [Allen, her husband] coming to visit us on the set, and he was a very quiet, gentle man. She was the bombastic, out-there lady, but he was very, very, very quiet. Very self-effacing, very nice man. And, of course, a genius.

"And Irving Moore. What a nice man. He was a terrific director."[170]

*On series star Robert Brown:* "Bob Brown and I have been friends since I was seventeen. Oh, what a sweetheart he is, wonderful man. Smart man. Married to a wonderful artist. They're terrific people. They were very close friends of Carroll O Connor who was my English teacher at the High School of Performing Arts. Robert Brown was great friends with Carroll O Connor. They were closer as pals than I was because I was a kid. They were thrilled with what I did, and I was thrilled to be doing it."

*On series star Bobby Sherman:* "Bobby Sherman I remember was having a career as a singer, too. Bobby was kind of a youngster on the way up. We could relate because we were kids. That was kind of neat."

*On co-star David Soul:* "David Soul was a very interesting actor. He worked with my ex-husband [Burr DeBenning] on *Starsky and Hutch.*"

*On leading lady Bridget Hanley:* "Oh, Bridget's a sweetheart. I've known Bridget for years. She's still at Theater West and doing work there. She was a delight. She's a talented lady. She's more theater than me. I went into voice-over. She kind of went back to the theater."

*On veteran actress Joan Blondell:* "Joan Blondell! Oh, my God! She was wonderful, too. A very mothering, nurturing woman. A very, very sweet, very available woman, I enjoyed her very much. Good lady. And a very good actress — and, I think, underrated. I really do. I think she was a very, very good actress, and I think she was kind of overlooked in that character vein she was in. I think she could have gone on to do some very wonderful things."

*On series regular Henry Beckman:* "Henry Beckman! What an amazing actor, and what a lovely man, too. He did so much work on television. He worked steadily. I think he could have broken through the ranks to have been bigger. Maybe it wasn't the time."

*On series regular Susan Tolsky:* "Susan and I have known each other through the years. She's had quite a career. I knew her later on basically through the voice-over world."

*On Director E.W. Swackhamer:* "What a terrific director and a great guy he was. He died way too young. That was a shame. We were all there for that [Swackhamer's memorial]. That was very, very sad for Bridget and her children. But she's a strong lady. She keeps going."

*On Director of Photography Fred H. Jackman and the Crew Members:* "The director of photography is very important. Makeup is very important, and I loved our makeup people, all of them, and the hairdressers and everything, 'specially when they did period stuff — they were amazing because what they had to do wasn't contemporary stuff, but your DP, if you get somebody who lights you well, you look gorgeous. So the actresses used to take their photographers, their cameramen with them on the film [for a photo shoot], it wasn't necessarily the makeup or hair, it was the cameramen because they knew how to light them and shoot them. Fred Jackman. He was amazing. He was terrific.

"But the people that we associated with were the makeup people, the hair people, our own actors, and the director, basically. At the end, when there'd be a party or something, then you'd mix it up with everybody, and the crew people should never be forgotten. They're wonderfully helpful and good to actors; without them, we wouldn't be able to do anything. The crew is very, very important, but basically we did not talk so much to the cinematographer. It's the director who says, 'Let's shoot it this way. Let's do it.' We had nothing to do with it."[171]

*Susan Tolsky on Susan Silo:* "Oh, God, Susan! Susan is just… years and years of knowing Susan. She's a hoot and a half. I don't think she has changed one iota. Always reliable. Always good. Right there. We've had more contact because she does voice stuff. Tons of voice stuff as a voice actor."[176]

*Leading Lady Bridget Hanley on Guest Star Jayne Meadows:* "What a hoot. I found out that she and Swack had gone to New School together. We just had a ball talking. Sometimes, I was in shock that I was standing next to this person and doing a scene with them, you know, it was so turned around."[172]

*Series Regular Susan Tolsky on Guest Star Jayne Meadows:* "Jayne Meadows Allen! Jayne and Steve. You can't separate them. They were both…having been around him, I just see them together. Lovely, lovely lady. I remember Jayne was at a convention, and Bridget and I went to see her. Beautiful lady. She looked the same forever. She just remained, just beautiful. Gracious, lovely lady. The two of them were just always together. Just seemed to adore each other and be happy with one another. Happy Hollywood couple. Very pleasant, very delightful. I just loved them together. It was like Laurel and Hardy."[173]

*Bridget Hanley on Guest Star Donald Moffat:* "How lucky we were to get him. He was a wonderful actor."[174]

## Writer Henry Slesar

Author of the novels and short-story mystery collections, *Murder at Heartbreak Hospital, A Classic Case of Murder, The Thing at the Door, The Gray Flannel Shroud, Murders Most Macabre, Clean Crime and Neat Murders, Enter Murderers, The Veil, A Crime for Mothers and Others, Foul Play & Cabernet, Murder Makes a Call,* and *Inspector Cross,* Henry Slesar is a familiar name to fans of *Alfred Hitchcock Presents,* and *The Alfred Hitchcock Hour.* (For the former, he wrote around sixty episodes; for the latter, about fifteen).

The man who coined the term "coffee break," advertiser-turned-author Slesar wrote many short stories (often under the pseudonym, O.H. Leslie) during the course of his lengthy career. Starting in television as the head writer on the daytime soap, *Search for Tomorrow* (he performed similar duties on the soaps *One Life to Live, The Edge of Night,* and *Somerset*), Slesar wrote for *Batman, Ghost Story, Roald Dahl's Tales of The Unexpected,* and the original and new *Twilight Zone.* Movies included *Two on a Guillotine,* and an adaptation of Edgar Allan Poe's *Murders in the Rue Morgue.* He died on April 2, 2002.

## Director Irving Moore

Director of some of the best episodes of *Wild Wild West,* Irving J. Moore began his Hollywood career assistant directing such well known 1950s films as *The Solid Gold Cadillac, Run Silent, Run Deep* and *Bell, Book and Candle.* Moore's work in television began with his helming such Warner Bros series as *Maverick, Cheyenne, Surfside 6, 77 Sunset Strip,* and *Hawaiian Eye.*

In the 1960s, when not doing *Wild Wild Wests,* Moore directed *Lost in Space, Laredo,* and *Gunsmoke.* In the '70s, he directed many episodes of *Dallas* and *Eight is Enough.* On the latter, he received an unusual tribute. One of Nicholas Bradford's (series regular Adam Rich) best friends was named Irving J. Moore!

## Episode #31: "A Wild Colonial Boy"        *October 24, 1969*

> *Flynn:* No matter what the cost, our cause is a noble one. A cause
> more important than any individual. Do you understand me, darling?
> *Bridget:* I hear ye. But I'm not sure about the understandin' part.

Writer . . . . . . . . . . . . . . . . . . . . . . . . . . . . . . . . . . . . . . . . . . . . . . . Michael Fisher
Director . . . . . . . . . . . . . . . . . . . . . . . . . . . . . . . . . . . . . . . . . . . . Paul Junger Witt
Film Editor . . . . . . . . . . . . . . . . . . . . . . . . . . . . . . . . . . . . . . . . . . . Asa Clark
Assistant Director . . . . . . . . . . . . . . . . . . . . . . . . . . . . . . . . . . . Michael Dmytryk
### Guest Cast
Flynn . . . . . . . . . . . . . . . . . . . . . . . . . . . . . . . . . . . . . . . . . . . . . . . . . . . Art Lund
Bridget . . . . . . . . . . . . . . . . . . . . . . . . . . . . . . . . . . . . . . . . . . . . . . . Brenda Scott
Pat . . . . . . . . . . . . . . . . . . . . . . . . . . . . . . . . . . . . . . . . . . . . . . . Donnelly Rhodes
Dennis . . . . . . . . . . . . . . . . . . . . . . . . . . . . . . . . . . . . . . . . . . . . . Allan Arbus

*Teaser:* Clancey, Pat, Flynn, Dennis, Lottie, Ben, Loggers, Jason, Josh, Bridget.
*Tag:* Clancey, Josh, Bridget, Jason, Jeremy.
*Competition: The CBS Friday Night Movie: The Last Challenge* starring Glenn Ford and Chad Everett; *Name of the Game,* "Goodbye, Harry," starring Gene Barry as Glenn Howard, and guest-starring Darren McGavin, James Whitmore, and Strother Martin, NBC.

*Photography:* Josh carrying Bridget over the mud puddle; close-up on Clancey yelling at his crew; Josh walking along dock, looking at Bridget on the *Seamus O'Flynn* as the boat moves further and further away; long shot of the town with the three Bolt brothers walking back to their cabin.

*Notes:* Future story editor Michael Fisher's first episode skillfully blends two historical realities of the time into a very fascinating show. The first is the ugly practice of child labor. The second involves the Fenian Brotherhood's dedication to establishing, by armed revolution, a free and independent Ireland. Founded by Irish nationalist John O'Mahoney in the late 1840s, the Fenian Brotherhood was the American branch of the Irish Republican Brotherhood, the forerunner of the Irish Republican Army (IRA). Shortly after the Civil War, the Fenians (many of whom had fought in the war) made a series of raids into Southern Canada, at the time under British rule, in the hopes of holding this part of Canada hostage. Their aim was to pressure Britain into granting Ireland its independence. The plan failed.

Bridget, the Brenda Scott character, was a child laborer; she is the stepdaughter of Kieran Flynn, leader of the Fenians.

The traditional Irish tune, 'The Wild Colonial Boy' provides the title for this episode. The episode gives the audience a look at the Bolt's supply shack (where they keep their dynamite) and shows more of the interior of Clancey's ship.

Leading lady of *The Road West* TV series, and guest star on such series as *The Fugitive*, *Bonanza*, *The Virginian*, and *Route 66*, Brenda Scott is the grand-niece of silent screen star Mae Busch. Alan Arbus is best known as Major Sidney Freedman from *M*A*S*H*. Donnelly Rhodes played Dutch on *SOAP*.

*Story Editor William Blinn:* "Michael [Fisher] was the oldest young man. Probably eight, ten, twelve years younger than I was, and he was stolid and straightforward, and I think most of his shows were like that. 'Wild, Colonial Boy' had nice moments to it, and Lund was pretty good. Brenda was fine. Again, probably done under the pressure of trying to be more dramatic, trying to be more serious, made a good episode. I don't know if it should have been an episode of *Here Come the Brides*. Art Lund dying — that's not happy and foot-tapping."[177]

*Wardrobe Man Steve Lodge:* "Art Lund was another nice guy. Brenda I knew from high school. She could make you cry in an instant — with her acting. I think they hired her in parts that had crying."[178]

## Guest Star Art Lund

Graduating from Westminster College in his native Salt Lake City, then from Eastern Kentucky State Teachers' College (he would teach mathematics at a Kentucky high school), six-foot-four-inch Art Lund went on to receive a master's degree in aerological engineering from the United States Naval Academy. Despite this extensive education, Lund later became a lead baritone with the Benny Goodman Orchestra.

Earning five gold records for such songs as "Mam'selle," "Blue Skies," and "My Blue Heaven," Lund's tour with the Goodman band was interrupted by military service in WWII (he was in the Navy in the South Pacific). After returning to the Goodman band following this service, Lund then became a solo performer, playing the role of Joey, the foreman, in the musical, 'The Most Happy Fella' in 1956. Two years later, he was Lennie in an off-Broadway musical adaptation of Steinbeck's *Of Mice and Men*. Other stage plays included *Fiorello*, *No Strings*, and *Destry Rides Again*.

On television, Art Lund guest-starred in such series as *Wagon Train*, *The Name of the Game*, *Little House on the Prairie*, and *Baretta*. Movies included *The Molly Maguires*, and *The Last American Hero*. Sadly, in 1969, the year he guest-starred on *Here Come the Brides*, Lund lost his first wife, Kathleen Virginia Bolanz, in an automobile accident. Not long after remarrying in 1989, Lund passed away of cancer. He was seventy-five.

*Series Star Robert Brown on Allan Arbus:* "Allan Arbus had been a very famous photographer in New York, and he had done some plays in New York. I got him interested in acting. He had a lot of talent. He came out, and he was in one of the episodes. Played an Irish guy dancing on the tabletop with his violin. That got him into the union — Screen Actors' Guild. Then he became a very famous guy, lots and lots of films, and he was in the series, *M\*A\*S\*H* — played a psychiatrist. Alan stayed with me at my house until he got his own place. We're still very close friends."[179]

*Leading Lady Bridget Hanley on Allan Arbus:* "Allan Arbus. Wonderful, wonderful actor, extraordinary human being. I just briefly met Allan when he worked on the show."[180]

## Episode #32: "Hosanna's Way"          *October 31, 1969*

"Bolt, I think you're in for some trouble."
*Aaron Stempel to Jason Bolt*

"Jeremy. It doesn't make any difference how old he is.
They're taught from birth to be killers."
*Aaron Stempel to Jeremy Bolt*

Writer . . . . . . . . . . . . . . . . . . . . . . . . . . . . . . . . . . . . . . . . . . . . Rick Tobin
Director. . . . . . . . . . . . . . . . . . . . . . . . . . . . . . . . . . . . . . . . Virgil W. Vogel
Film Editor . . . . . . . . . . . . . . . . . . . . . . . . . . . . . . . . . Norman Wallerstein
Assistant Director . . . . . . . . . . . . . . . . . . . . . . . . . . . . . . . . . David Hawks
*Guest Cast*
Hosanna . . . . . . . . . . . . . . . . . . . . . . . . . . . . . . . . . . . . . . . . . . Ric Natoli
Trapper . . . . . . . . . . . . . . . . . . . . . . . . . . . . . . . . . . . . . . . .Eddie Firestone
Billy Gumm . . . . . . . . . . . . . . . . . . . . . . . . . . . . . . . . . . . . . . . .Joe Perry
Sheriff . . . . . . . . . . . . . . . . . . . . . . . . . . . . . . . . . . . . . . . . Kelly Thordsen

```
Dr. Harris . . . . . . . . . . . . . . . . . . . . . . . . . . . . . . . . . . . . . . . . . . . . . . . Roy Engel
Hank Garrone. . . . . . . . . . . . . . . . . . . . . . . . . . . . . . . . . . . . . . . . . . . . Jon Shank
Jean Claudeaux . . . . . . . . . . . . . . . . . . . . . . . . . . . . . . . . . . . . . . . Paul Sorensen
```

*Teaser:* Jason, Josh, Jeremy, Hosanna.

*Tag:* Jason, Josh, Jeremy, Molly, Christopher, Candy.

*Competition: The CBS Friday Night Movie: Come Fly With Me,* starring Pamela Tiffin; *The Name of the Game,* "Give Till it Hurts," starring Robert Stack as Dan Farrel, guest-starring Dennis Weaver, Diane Baker, Larry Storch, and Sue Ane Langdon, NBC.

*Photography:* Shot of Ben through candy jar in general store; zoom in — slow, on Hosanna — the light on his face going dark; zoom in on Billy; pull back from Billy in cell; zoom in on Hosanna, then shot of him through general store window, walking up to store to attack trapper Eddie Firestone; shot of knife; Hosanna running through forest, shot through trees, hand-held camera at tops of trees; shot from Hosanna's point of view; zoom in on grave.

*Notes: Brides'* second Indian-themed tale is nothing like the first season's "Wives for Wakando." Comic situations are few and far between in this grim story of an orphaned Apache boy, who, after trappers murder his family, tries to fit into the world of the white man — with the help of the Bolts, and in particular, Jason. A bit heavy-handed at times, but not bad.

First-season guest Joe Perry has a memorable role as former mental hospital inmate-turned-prison attendant Billy Gumm. Jeremy's compassion for Billy, who's terrified of being in a locked room in the dark, makes for some good moments.

In the friendship they quickly develop with Ric Natoli's Hosanna, Patti Cohoon and Eric Chase do some fine work as well.

Given the meaning of the word "Hosanna" (the people's recognition of Jesus as the Messiah when he entered Jerusalem), and the savage (but understandable) actions of Ric Natoli's character in this story, writer Rick Tobin might have come up with a better name for the character. Character actors Eddie Firestone, as the high-pitched, laughing trapper, Kelly Thordsen, as the sheriff in Tacoma, and Roy Engel, as the doctor at the hospital, all add to this episode.

*Story Editor William Blinn:* "Rick Tobin was a friend I'd gone to school with, and he'd come in with the idea. He did not end up being a writer, and I think that says that he was not, in fact, a writer. It got done, and it was okay, and it was probably not my finest hour. It would probably be a little politically correct; in that process, we lost the story-telling."[181]

## Director Virgil Vogel

Starting out as an assistant editor at Universal Studios in the 1950s, Virgil Vogel (a.k.a. Virgil W. Vogel) launched his lengthy career as a director in 1956 with the science fiction-thriller, *The Mole People.* While he made a few other B-pictures at Universal, it was in television, particularly the television western and crime drama, that Vogel truly made his mark. His output on Levy/Gardner/Laven's *The Big Valley* was outstanding. In addition to directing the two-part shows "Legend of a General" and "Explosion," Vogel did quite a few episodes showcasing either series star Barbara Stanwyck ("Alias Nellie Handley," "A Day of Terror," "Top of the Stairs"), co-star Linda Evans ("Brother Love," "Day of the Comet") or both actresses (the very funny, "The Great Safe Robbery"). In fact, Vogel seemed to do quite well directing women on *The Big Valley*. Besides "Alias Nellie Handley," which had Victoria going undercover to investigate deplorable conditions at a women's prison, there was "Hell Hath No Fury" Carol Lynley as the leader of an outlaw gang, "They Called Her Delilah" Julie London as the title character.

Other series where Virgil Vogel directed many episodes: Quinn Martin's *The FBI*, *The Streets of San Francisco*. Vogel and Martin met at Universal during their film-editing days.

The director also did a few episodes of *Mission: Impossible*, *Police Story*, and *Magnum P.I.* He died on New Year's Day, 1996 in Tarzana, California.

*Executive Producer Bob Claver:* "Virgil Vogel was like Bill Russell — a get-it-done guy. He knew how to direct, he knew how to plan it, and get the job done, and that was fine. He worked a lot in westerns. He was okay. I had no problems with him. Claxton was upscale from there."[182]

*Story Editor William Blinn:* "Virgil Vogel! To this day…I worked with Virgil, and he did a couple *Brides*. He always showed up on the set absolutely so pumped up with enthusiasm and energy, almost more so than Swack, that it was infectious. Even when he was wrong, you went along with him because he was so…he just brought so much energy to his point of view, and God knows he could shoot film like Claxton — it always went together. Virgil would always like to fine-tune stuff. He was very creative and had a lot of input, not necessarily in terms of story construction, but maybe in terms of how the scene was gonna play. He'd say, 'Instead of playing it all in the bar, can we start it in the bar and move it upstairs, and out on to the balcony, and cut it up into five small scenes?' That kind of thing."[183]

*Leading Lady Bridget Hanley:* "Virgil was a sweet man. He was so dear. He directed quite a few [shows]. You almost thought he was gonna let you do what you wanted. He had all those irons in the fire. He had a vision, and he went for it."[184]

*Series Semi-Regular Eric Chase:* "There were a few directors who were all over the place, very into it. He was that way — he was a nice guy."[185]

*Wardrobe Man Steve Lodge:* "Virgil was another sweetheart. He's even been to my house. He loved Dave Cass — said he could be more than just a stunt man."[186]

*Robert Brown Stunt Double Dave Cass:* "Virgil loved hand-helds. If you're doing a fight or something, and you're inside with the actors fighting, let's just say you've done the stunt doubles fighting in the wide shots. You want to go in closer on the real actors — they go in there hand-held. And the DP in television, even to this day, runs the set, but in those days, they had a little more respect for the director, and they would listen to them, because some of these guys like Vogel who came to those shows had so much experience under their belt that they'd listen to 'em and they'd learn from 'em. But Freddie [Jackman] was not a spring chicken at the time.

"Little Virgil who was a very small man, was the same way. [Vogel was just six years younger than Jackman.] He'd say, 'Come on, kid,' and he put me behind my first camera. He had Jackman give me a camera and their loader at lunchtime, and made me learn lenses — the size of the lens and all that stuff. He told me, 'You're too creative to be falling on your head the rest of your life. Let's get you going doing something.' So he and Burt Kennedy were my two big mentors. And every day I take them to work with me. Everything I do, I do nothing original. People will say, 'That's a great shot,' I say, 'Learned it from Burt Kennedy in 1973.' Or, 'That's a great camera move.' 'Yeah, Learned it from Virgil Vogel in 1970.' Because they would do things then that nobody else would do."

Cass was not the only young director to think so highly of Virgil Vogel. "Bogdanovich had a script," remembers Cass, "[I] believe it was the original story for *Lonesome Dove*. He wanted to make a western in the Big Bend country in Texas, that's how long ago that script was around. He wanted to make a feature with John Wayne and Jimmy Stewart, and I had worked in the Big Bend Country. Peter got ahold of me. He said 'You need to tell me about the Big Bend country. I'm thinking about doing a show there about these two old Texas Rangers.' So I said, 'Fine.' I had lunch with him. [I] was working at Warner Brothers at the time. [I] was walking back to the set, and we were talking. Here came Virgil. 'Dave,' he says, 'you're on your way back?' I said, 'Yeah.' 'I'll walk back with you,' Virgil says. I introduced the two guys…Bogdanovich was like a little kid in a candy store. He said, 'My God! Virgil Vogel! Have you read my book? There's a whole chapter about you in my book!'

"You know, Virgil Vogel was sold short. I don't think all his credits…they can't be put on IMDb."[187]

The Big Valley *producer Arthur Gardner:* "Virgil was terrific. I can't praise him high enough. Thoroughly professional. Brought everything in on budget, pleasant. He knew everything — fine director. Knew every phase of the motion picture business. Virgil was a very, very nice man, very sweet guy; he would encourage talent."[188]

*Director Bruce Kessler:* "Virgil Vogel could get it done fast. His shows looked great. Virgil was an amazing guy. Very uncommunicative director, but a very talented guy. Put on a good-looking show."[189]

November 1969 – Bobby Sherman article in *TV Star Parade;* "Bobby's Dream Girl Comes to Hollywood"
*Tiger Beat;* "Bobby's High School Days"

*Flip Teen;* "Bobby Sherman, Going Places – Fast"
*Screen and TV Album;* David Soul: Facts About Your FaVEs"
*FaVE!;* "My Son Bobby by Mrs. Robert Sherman," Part 2 – *Tiger Beat;*
two Bobby Sherman articles in *Teen Life;* David Soul article in *Teen Life;* "An In-Depth Talk with David Soul," Part 3 – *Tiger Beat;* Robert Brown: Facts About Your FaVE's"
*FaVE!;* Robert Brown – article in *Photo Screen; TV Radio Mirror, Flip Teen;* Bridget Hanley articles in *Teen Pin-Ups, FaVE!, Teen Life, Tiger Beat.*

November 1, 1969 – *TV Guide* – Vol. 17, No. 44 – Issue #866 – TV Teletype: Hollywood – Joseph Finnigan Reports that *Brides* has been renewed by ABC. The show will run through the end of the season.

November 3 – Bobby Sherman guest hosts *Music Scene,* with guests Johnny Cash, Lulu, and Buffy Sainte-Marie.

## Episode #33: "The Road to the Cradle" *November 7, 1969*

> *Lottie:* You sound like a man who has never had —
> or known — the love of a child.
> *Harry Smith:* You're wrong — on both counts.

| | |
|---|---|
| Writer | Ken Trevey |
| Director | William Claxton |
| Film Editor | Norman Wallerstein |
| Assistant Director | David Hawks |

### Guest Cast

| | |
|---|---|
| Harry | John Anderson |
| Blackburn | Ross Hagen |
| Pinkie | Dal Jenkins |
| Albright | Michael Stanwood |
| Bethany | Susannah Darrow |
| Stebbins | Charles Seel |
| Chinook | Henry Wills |

*Teaser:* Loggers, Lottie, Jason, Josh, Jeremy, Chinook, Pinkie, Blackburn.
*Tag:* Josh, Chinook, Pinkie, Jason, Blackburn, Jeremy, Gentlemen Harry, Lottie.
*Competition: The CBS Friday Night Movie: How to Stuff a Wild Bikini* starring Frankie Avalon, Annette Funnicello, and Buster Keaton; *The Name of the Game,* "The Perfect Image," starring Gene Barry as Glenn Howard, and guest-starring Hal Holbrook, Ida Lupino, Clu Gulager, Diana Hyland, Joanna Barnes, and Edward Asner, NBC.

**Notes:** *The Fugitive* — *HCTB* style with John Anderson. Like Kimble, "Gentleman" Harry is on the run; like unjustly convicted murderer Kimble, genuine criminal Harry is basically a good guy. On *The Fugitive*, the villains were often law-and-order types. The bad guys in this story are bounty hunters turned U.S. Marshals Blackburn, Pinkie, and Chinook.

Further similarities to *The Fugitive* — like Dr. Richard Kimble, "Gentleman" Harry Smith is a widower who's lost his one and only child. But he's had enough medical training, as had Kimble, to safely deliver a baby. Unfortunately, in performing this good work, just like Kimble always did on *The Fugitive*, Harry endangers his life.

John Anderson is very good in the part, especially when he tells Lottie that his deceased daughter is aged "seven. Seven for all eternity," and when he talks about spending the rest of his life in the "stony lonesome." Ross Hagen and Dal Jenkins are wonderfully slimy as marshals Blackburn and Pinkie; *High Chaparral* stunt coordinator Henry Wills is properly menacing as their silent Chinook Indian associate.

A definite plus in this episode is the considerable use of Joan Blondell. The sympathy she shows a half-conscious Jeremy when he temporarily slips back into his childhood and calls her 'Mom' makes for one of the episode's best moments. As does the final shot with Jeremy patting Lottie's hand as the two watch Harry leave for prison, in the custody of Jason and Josh.

*Robert Brown Stunt Double Dave Cass:* "Bill Claxton came over to direct one, and he brought some of his crew — some of his stunt guys from the *High Chaparral* [including] Henry Wills, who was his second-unit director/stunt coordinator. Henry was my mentor in the stunt world. Henry is playing this Eskimo guy on a horse; he's riding his horse, Kilroy, and Robert's supposed to run out, tackle this horse, and pull the horse and the rider down. Well, of course, I [not Robert Brown] did it. Well, Kilroy was one of those horses that liked to fall so Henry couldn't show him the hand before he was supposed to fall. And, somewhere there's this picture of me, going through the air — I've got my hand out — I don't quite have it on the horse's head, and the horse I've already gone over. It was kind of a thrill for me to do that show because here was my mentor from *The High Chaparral* comin' to work on the show with us. And Billy Claxton. I loved Billy. He cast me I don't know how many times in *The High Chaparral* and *Bonanza*."[190]

## *Director William Claxton*

A favorite of Michael Landon's — he directed multiple episodes of *Bonanza* and *Little House on the Prairie*, plus Landon's later series, *Father Murphy* and *Highway to Heaven*, William F. Claxton worked as an editor and agent before moving into a very successful career as a television director. Besides working for William Blinn on the writer/producer's series, *The Rookies*, *Fame*, and the Blinn-developed *Eight is Enough*, Claxton helmed episodes of *Rawhide*, *Perry Mason*, *Route 66*, *Gunsmoke*, *Love, American Style*, and *The Blue Knight*. Claxton's motion picture credits include the one-of-a-kind 1972 sci-fi thriller *Night of the Lepus*. In *Lepus,* mutant killer rabbits menace stars Stuart Whitman, Janet Leigh, Rory Calhoun, and *Star Trek's* DeForest Kelley.

*Story Editor William Blinn:* "I believe I brought him in to *Brides*. I loved the guy's work, and loved the guy himself. He was such a quiet, consummate professional, and I knew Screen Gems loved him because Bill did not just go over budget. He just did not. He found a way to make it work and he did it without drawing attention to himself or getting into any overblown production problems. He knew what he could accomplish in the time he had.

He was always one of those directors…if you give him the material he will get all the essence and all the juices out of the material. If he doesn't have the material to work with, okay, then it's not gonna be there. He's not a writer, he's not a story-teller in a technical sense, but as a human being he had so much humanity…he was one of my favorite people of all time.

"When I used Claxton in a series called *Our House*, we were gonna do a Christmas show. It was bloody complicated, moving here, moving there, moving…it was really tough, and the production guy came in and said, 'This is a nine-day show. We'll never shoot this in seven days.' And Bill Claxton was one of the great people in my life, he rarely talked — he was very, very quiet. So the production guy is explaining to me why 'this is too difficult, and that's too difficult,' and 'we'll have to trim here and trim there, and do this and that,' Claxton just cleared his throat, and said, 'I'll shoot it in seven days.' The guy looked at him…Claxton said, 'I'll shoot it in seven days. I'll shoot it in seven days…it'll be fine.' And that's exactly what happened. He shot it in seven days. And it was fine. Because he knew so much about film. He wasn't gonna shoot every piece that I had written full. He'd get the establishing shot — 'Fine. We're done. Let's move on.' I mean, some of the actors just hated him because he would not pamper actors. They'd say, 'Why am I saying this?' 'Because you're playing…Miss Jones?' 'Yes.' 'Okay, that's what they say Miss Jones says. That's why you're saying it.' He was never rude to people and actors ended up loving him, because they would then see the film and see how good it was and think, 'Maybe this old curmudgeon knows what he's doing.'"[191]

*Leading Lady Bridget Hanley:* "William Claxton! I liked him a lot. He was smart. He was good. He was very insightful in terms of… I really liked him a lot. And he was very cheery. He was like alive, and interested, and it helped us, too. Very smart. I felt very honored to work with him. We were all very…I felt…generous to anybody who was brand new, just coming on for the first time. We all kind of bent over backwards, if they wanted to have conversation or whatever, sometimes people just wanted to study their stuff. We had to be smart about that — not trying to make it happy hour."[192]

### Writer Ken Trevey:

Ken Trevey had written for seven westerns (*Bonanza, Tales of Wells Fargo, Wagon Train, The Iron Horse, Dundee and the Culhane, Gunsmoke, The Big Valley*) prior to

*Here Come the Brides.* For *Valley,* he wrote four scripts: "Down Shadow Street," "Into the Widow's Web," "Under a Dark Star," and "By Fires Unseen." Like his *Wagon Train,* "The Geneva Balfour Story," Trevey's *Big Valley*s tended to focus on female characters.

Post *HCTB,* Trevey wrote for producers David Victor (*Marcus Welby, M.D.*), Quinn Martin (*Cannon*), Irwin Allen (*Swiss Family Robinson*) and Andrew J. Fenady (the offbeat 1974 TV-movie, *The Hanged Man*') Among his other TV-movies: *The Weekend Nun* (Joanna Pettet as the title character) and *Banjo Hackett: Roamin' Free.*

*Story Editor William Blinn:* "Ken Trevey was very much a western writer. I think I'd met him over at *Gunsmoke.* This for him was a little bit of a change of pace, because it was a little lighter, a little more sentimental. Most of his stuff on *Gunsmoke* was hard-edged and the kind of thing that *Gunsmoke* did very well, which was a very tough western, usually with some kind of bittersweet frame around it. Ken, whom I liked a lot — big guy — six-foot-eight, I think, enjoyed doing the show, and did it well. He was fun to work with."[193]

*Big Valley* *producer Arthur Gardner:* "Ken Trevey was a terrific guy. Not only a good guy, but personally. He was one of our most respected writers, and we employed him whenever Ken was available. He could write anything — love stories, action tales. Fast writer. I think he may have written some *Rifleman* scripts. I enjoyed working with Trevey."[194]

## Episode #34: "The Legend of Big Foot"          *November 14, 1969*

"BIGFOOT'S AFTER MEEEE!"
*Biddie Cloom to all of Seattle*

Writer . . . . . . . . . . . . . . . . . . . . . . . . . . . . . . . . . . . . . . . . . . . . Richard Bluel
Director . . . . . . . . . . . . . . . . . . . . . . . . . . . . . . . . . . . . . . . . Herb Wallerstein
Film Editor . . . . . . . . . . . . . . . . . . . . . . . . . . . . . . . . . . . . . . . . . Asa Clark
Assistant Director . . . . . . . . . . . . . . . . . . . . . . . . . . . . . . . Michael Dmytryk
*Guest Cast*
Caleb . . . . . . . . . . . . . . . . . . . . . . . . . . . . . . . . . . . . . . . . . . . . . . . Paul Fix
Matt . . . . . . . . . . . . . . . . . . . . . . . . . . . . . . . . . . . . . . . . . . Edward Asner
Carver . . . . . . . . . . . . . . . . . . . . . . . . . . . . . . . . . . . . . . . . Richard Bull
Forbes . . . . . . . . . . . . . . . . . . . . . . . . . . . . . . . . . . . . . . . . . Noam Pitlik
Marshall . . . . . . . . . . . . . . . . . . . . . . . . . . . . . . . . . . . . . . . Larry Haddon
Big Foot . . . . . . . . . . . . . . . . . . . . . . . . . . . . . . . . . . . . . . Mickey Morton
Townsman . . . . . . . . . . . . . . . . . . . . . . . . . . . . . . . . . . . . . . . Sonny Jones

*Teaser:* Clancey, Jason, Josh, Jeremy, Candy, Aaron, Biddie, Ben, Forbes, Lottie, Molly, Christopher, Carver.

*Tag:* Matthew, Caleb, Clancey, Molly, Christopher, Aaron, Jason, Josh, Candy, Jeremy, Lottie, Biddie.

*Photography:* the towering Bigfoot looking down at Candy, Christopher, and Molly — the scene is presented from Bigfoot's point of view.

*Competition: The CBS Friday Night Movie: Penelope* starring Natalie Wood, Peter Falk, and Jonathan Winters; *The Name of the Game,* "The Prisoner Within," starring Tony Franciosa as Jeff Dillon, and guest-starring Steve Forrest and Ron Hayes, NBC.

*Notes:* Bigfoot having made its way into popular culture by the late 1960s, and the unexplained being a good way to hook an audience, writer Richard Bluel may have thought a story about Bigfoot would be right for the series. It wasn't!

At the time this episode aired, Bigfoot — said to stand seven to nine feet tall, and to weigh from six hundred to nine hundred pounds — was definitely in the public's mind. The country had just recently heard of the creature thanks to the Patterson-Gimlin film (a.k.a. the Patterson film). The Patterson/Gimlin film was a movie lasting just a few seconds which showed an ape-like creature moving across a clearing near Bluff Creek in Northern California.

Often referred to as "Sasquatch" (the Indian term for "hairy giant") the Bigfoot creature had been mentioned in quite a few American Indian legends. The first sighting of the creature by white men came in 1811 near Jasper, Alberta Canada. Sightings of 'Bigfoot' seemed to be most prevalent in Canada and the Pacific Northwest.

The American public grew very interested in Bigfoot in 1958 after bulldozer operator Jerry Crew found enormous footprints near where he was working in Humboldt County, California. After Crew made a cast of the footprint and a local newspaper ran the story of his discovery with a photo of Crew holding the cast, the story was picked up by other papers. The name "Bigfoot" came from the photo of the enormous footprint.

A cast of a big foot figures into this episode — one in which Eric Chase's Christopher Pruitt has a good bit to do. Susan Tolsky and Henry Beckman have some very funny comic bits.

Richard Bull (later to portray Mr. Olson on *Little House on the Prairie*) played the semi-regular role of the Seaview doctor in Irwin Allen's first hit series, *Voyage to the Bottom of the Sea.* Paul Fix is best known for his role as Micah Torrence on Levy/Gardner/Laven's *The Rifleman.*

*Story Editor William Blinn:* "I don't think one of our more successful episodes frankly. I think we were…sometimes you look at a show, and you say, 'Boy, they were really laboring there, weren't they?' I think that was one of the episodes where in fact we were there laboring. It was a little bit of a reach — one that I guess a twelve-year-old would get to, but an adult might say, 'I think I'll go in the other room.' In golfing terms, that was a 'shank' as far as we were concerned."[195]

*Series Semi-Regular Eric Chase:* "That was a fun one to shoot. That was a lot of fun. They would shoot all those outdoor scenes with water over at the reservoir — Franklin

Canyon — a lot of pretty trees around there; it was interesting how they could duplicate Seattle in Southern California. It was fun to hang out by the reservoir, we were out there running around in the trees; the scenes were a lot of fun. A couple of the workers would go fishing on the break. The actor [Mickey Morton] was playful. He'd pick me up and run around in circles. It was very hot in that old suit he was wearing."[196]

*Trivia:* Dominic Frontiere's *Outer Limits/Invaders* score returns to *Brides* in the sequence in which Molly and Christopher go out looking for Bigfoot. The score was first heard in episode #12 "After a Dream Comes Mourning," in the scene where Candy, Jason and Dimitri enter the Bolt cabin where the brothers had first lived with their parents.

November 15, 1969 – *TV Guide*, Vol. 17, No. 46, Issue #868 – TV Crossword – 1 Down – Family name on *Here Come the Brides*.

November 17-21 – Robert Brown guests on game show, *Name Droppers;* other guests include Polly Bergen and Jim Backus.

November 19, 1969 – WENY-TV – Channel 36 (Elmira, New York) signs on as ABC affiliate.

## Episode #35: "Land Grant"                    *November 21, 1969*

*Josh:* My name is Joshua Bolt, by the way.
*Telly:* Your name is 'land thief,' by the way, and you get off our land
before we bust your head.
*Candy:* He certainly has a way with words, doesn't he?

Writer . . . . . . . . . . . . . . . . . . . . . . . . . . . . . . . . . . . . . . . . . . . . . Larry Brody
Director . . . . . . . . . . . . . . . . . . . . . . . . . . . . . . . . . . . . . . . . . Virgil W. Vogel
Film Editor . . . . . . . . . . . . . . . . . . . . . . . . . . . . . . . . . . . . . . . . Asa Clark
Assistant Director . . . . . . . . . . . . . . . . . . . . . . . . . . . . . . . Michael Dmytryk
Music . . . . . . . . . . . . . . . . . . . . . . . . . . . . . . . . . . . . . . . . . . . .Warren Barker
*Guest Cast*
Telly . . . . . . . . . . . . . . . . . . . . . . . . . . . . . . . . . . . . . . . . . . . . .Lou Antonio
Iona . . . . . . . . . . . . . . . . . . . . . . . . . . . . . . . . . . . . . . . . . . . . .Mitzi Hoag
Stephanos . . . . . . . . . . . . . . . . . . . . . . . . . . . . . . . . . . . Michael Baseleon
Janitor . . . . . . . . . . . . . . . . . . . . . . . . . . . . . . . . . . . . . . . . Ken Swofford
Avery . . . . . . . . . . . . . . . . . . . . . . . . . . . . . . . . . . . . . William Wintersole
Judge . . . . . . . . . . . . . . . . . . . . . . . . . . . . . . . . . . . . . . . . .Bill Zuckert
Land Agent . . . . . . . . . . . . . . . . . . . . . . . . . . . . . . . . . . . . Jim Goodwin
Ed . . . . . . . . . . . . . . . . . . . . . . . . . . . . . . . . . . . . . . . . . . . .Dave Cass

***Teaser:*** Josh, Telly, Iona, Stephanos, Greek settlers.

***Tag:*** Telly, Stephanos, Candy, Jeremy, Iona, Biddie, Jason, Josh, Lottie, Aaron, the whole town, the Greek settlers.

***Competition:*** *The CBS Friday Night Movie: Fanny* starring Leslie Caron, Horst Bucholz, and Maurice Chevalier; *Hallmark Hall of Fame*, "The File on Devlin," starring Dame Judith Anderson, Elizabeth Ashley, and David McCallum, NBC.

***Photography:*** Tracking shot on Jeremy and other Seattle men as the Greek men invite the brides to their celebration; hand-held close-ups on Candy, Biddie, brides, Stephanos, Greek men during dance; hand-held shots on Jeremy fighting janitor Ken Swofford as the straw burns in barn; moving in for close-up on Candy and Jeremy as the two watch the Greeks dance.

***Notes:*** Writer Larry Brody's very first TV script, "Land Grant," takes *Brides* in a very different direction by creating the possibility of some new semi-regular characters — the nearby Greek settlers. A mixture of both drama and comedy, Brody's original presentation of the Telemachus Theodakis character was considerably altered for television. Brody's original idea was to do a character study, rather than a comedy.

*Story Editor William Blinn:* "If there was a ton of rewriting, I would usually say, 'Well, let's go find somebody else so we don't have to write.' We heard about Larry Brody and had him come in, and kicked around some story ideas, and he delivered an outline, and we then put him in the script. We had conversations about it a number of times before he sat down at the typewriter.

"I think it was his agent that told me about him. I thought the notion of getting a young guy in who was part of the science-fiction world might give us a whole new take on what we were trying to do, might come in with a point of view that none of us had. It was a pretty young group around there. Larry came up with the Greek characters."[197]

*Guest Star Lou Antonio:* "They had hired an actor, Neville Brand, because he promised he was a good boy and wasn't drinking, I think. Two days before shooting, he got drunk, I'm told, and tore up a bar in Malibu, and they needed somebody quick. Somebody said, 'Lou Antonio's Greek.' They said, 'Well, you'd never know from his name.'

"The Greek accent should have come easy to me. My father had one. I was too young so I curled my hair with bobby pins at night. They sprayed a little gray on it and I rushed into it.

"It was all a rush job, and I was doing my best to put pin curls in my hair at night, and I think, all I did was do my job. I didn't look up and get to know anybody, really. I don't schmooze a lot when I go on a set as an actor. I keep pretty much to myself, and it's just that I was working with such good actors. They were just good actors — particularly Joan Blondell, whom I'd admired so much as a younger man. She was very friendly. And Henry Beckman — boy, what a character! He was terrific. The young guys were just young guys — the pretty boys — David and Bobby.

"Virgil Vogel was terrific. He was funny, one of the funniest guys — inadvertently funny — that I ever saw. He called me 'Tony.' Hey, Tony. Over here." I said, 'Mr. Vogel, it's Lou, if you don't mind.' 'Oh right, right, Tony, I don't mind. Yeah, right.'"[198]

*Guest Star Mitzi Hoag:* "Lou tried to use a dialect, but it didn't work too well, and I didn't even try. I didn't feel we were very convincing Greeks. It's hard to play a character with a dialect, and you may have some dialects you can use easily but you often don't, and the time between when you're cast and when you go to work is quite short. Stars can go to a dialect coach, or in the theater you can, but in television, you don't have time. When I did Irish and English plays, the accent evolved out of the rehearsal process, but when you have to do that Greek or Italian and you don't have that accent, it's very hard to get. But Lou was up there trying — he took the risk. I didn't even take the risk. We were fighting time."[199]

*Episode Writer Larry Brody:* "*Zorba the Greek* was one of my favorite books at the time, and I wanted to bring someone like Zorba to TV. *Brides* was my first chance to do that. If I'd been working on, say, *Hawaii Five-O* at the time, I would've pitched an episode about a life-loving Greek getting in trouble on Maui. (Written by Nikos Kazanfzakis, the title character in *Zorba the Greek* is a zesty, lusty, sixty-five-year-old man who urges the book's college-educated, thirty-five-year-old narrator to get the most out of life each and every day.)

"I worked very hard to get Telly's speech pattern right. Lots of listening to Greek-speaking actors in foreign film. Lots of reading of Greek grammar books! I was very proud of the fact that I'd created a character who spoke English the way a Greek immigrant would. So I've got to say that what I disliked about the episode most was the fact that Bill [Blinn] changed all of Telly's dialog into what I thought of as 'stage Greek.' No one who watched that episode heard one line of my Telly dialog. I also wasn't too thrilled about the fact that Telly was cast so young. Remember, I was trying to recreate Zorba." [200]

*Wardrobe Man Steve Lodge:* "We did this episode with Dave Cass as a logger, Brown throws him in jail…Vogel was directing. Well, I got this great idea, and raced over to the wardrobe department, and I wrote a scene, with Robert and this character [Ed] and gave this character a bunch of lines. I put it on yellow paper. I said, 'This came from the studio, and we need to…just give it to him.' So the director went over and gave it to him. He said, 'Here, y'gotta learn these lines, Dave.' Dave went, 'Oh, shit' because it was a whole page. Robert Brown was in on the joke; he thought it was a great joke. Well, Dave learned the lines. And we rehearsed it. It was very quiet because everybody knew the joke, and it got out of hand. But we rehearsed it. Then Virgil said, 'Let's shoot the son of a bitch.' Then the phone rang. It was [Screen Gems executive] Seymour Friedman. The spy [on the set] had called him, and told him what we were doing."[201]

*Guest Star Dave Cass:* "They wanted Neville Brand to play that role, and they called Neville, and I knew Neville. I drank with him in those days, cuz I'd done *Laredo* with

Neville, and Bill Smith and Philip Carey at Universal. Well, Neville drank pretty heavy, so they called Neville to get his sizes, and they said, 'Hat?' Neville said, 'Size 2.' Shirt — '36, 42' then he goes through this whole thing. They write all this down. They call the producer, Bob Claver. They said, 'Look, we know his agent says he's sober, but these are the sizes that he gave us. You better go meet this guy.' So Claver came to the set, and he (Brand) was white as a sheet and drunk. Well, they replaced him in that show with Lou Antonio."[202]

## Writer Larry Brody

*On Executive Producer Bob Claver:* "Bob Claver had what, to me, was a huge office, with a big meeting room in it, and talked about his European vacations. That scared the hell out of me, since I'd never been anywhere. He also was the Big Boss, which also scared the hell out of me at the time. Fortunately, I only met with him a couple of times. Although years later, in the early '80s, when I was the Big Boss of a series called *Automan*, I found out that Bob was available as a director and hired him for that show. It wasn't until then that I got to know him and discovered that he was a good guy, and very eager to please me."

*On Line Producer Stan Schwimmer:* "Stan Schwimmer's the guy who actually hired me. I was a thrilled newbie, but to me he seemed like an unhappy, disappointed old man (although I don't think he was much more than forty at the time), always talking about how much he hated his office and the studio and the neighborhood it was in, that kind of thing. Always telling me he was going to quit. I was relieved when he stopped meeting with me and turned me over to Bill (Blinn). In retrospect, after a thirty-year career of my own, I understand Stan much better. I hope he's still alive and happy now."

*On Line Producer Paul Junger Witt:* "Paul Junger Witt and I didn't interact much on *Brides*. He was a producer-director, and he didn't direct or actively produce any of my episodes. So, in a situation where everyone was busy as hell, we had no reason to talk. In later years, Paul and I worked together on a couple of things and became friends. In the '90s, when I was teaching screenwriting at The College of Santa Fe, Paul flew down there to talk to my students. When I came back to L.A. after that, Paul and I would get together for lunch a lot and talk about projects we wanted to do with each other. They never happened, but the talking always was fun."[203]

## Guest Star Lou Antonio

"I planned on becoming an actor," said Lou Antonio, who is still working as a director as of this writing. "When I graduated from college, I went right into summer stock," he explains. "I did about a dozen shows in New York, seven on Broadway, six off Broadway: *Garden of Sweets* — opposite Katina Paxinou, *The Lady of the Camellias*, directed by Franco Zefferelli, with Susan Strasberg, *Andorra* with Horst Bucholz and Hugh Griffith, *Ready When You Are, C.B.*, directed by Josh Logan, *Ballad of the Sad Café* — Edward Albee's adaptation, opposite Colleen Dewhurst. My debut was off-Broadway in *The Buffalo Skinner* — got a Theatre World Award for that for Most Promising Actor, did *Brecht on Brecht* off-Broadway, *Choir of the Raindrop* off-Broadway, played Faustus in *The Tragical History of Dr. Faustus.*"

Making his Broadway debut at the Plymouth Theatre on March 2, 1960 in *The Good Soup,* where he played the roles of The Shady One, The Third Patron, and Lecasse, Antonio had previously worked on Broadway as an assistant stage manager in *HCTB* creator N. Richard Nash's *The Girls of Summer.* That was from November 1956 to January 1957.

"I studied with Lonny Chapman and Lee Strasberg and Curt Conway in their private classes," says the actor/director. "Then I was accepted into the Actor's Studio. I did television in New York — *Naked City*s — I did two in one season. I did four *Naked City*s, three *Defenders,* Army training films, a soap opera called *Love of Life* — they had a half-hour Saturday series with Phyllis Newman — I did about three of those — that's kind of where you learned film acting. And, actors could be extras in New York, but you had to be a member of the Screen Actor's Guild. So I did *The Power and the Glory* with Olivier and George C. Scott. (This 1961 TV production was co-produced by David Susskind and future *HCTB* executive casting director Renee Valente.)

Although Lou Antonio appeared in quality television like Reginald Rose's *The Defenders,* "nobody took it very seriously," he says. "In those days we didn't appreciate it like, 'Oh. Gee. It's Reginald Rose.' Young actor, it was just a job, and a good part. We were used to good writing. We didn't have anything to compare it with that was inferior. It was just a good gig — particularly for a young actor. Good people, good work, and low pay. I was [also] in the very last closing episode of *For the People* — *A Competent Witness* (May 9, 1965) — William Shatner, Jessica Walter, and Lonny Chapman. Stuart Rosenberg directed. He was terrific. Directed *Cool Hand Luke.*" [204]

*Cool Hand Luke* was released in 1967. The same year Antonio embarked on his continuing career as a television series/TV-movie director. He made his directorial debut with the Ivan Tors series, *Gentle Ben,* thanks to the series star, Dennis Weaver.

*Executive Producer Bob Claver:* "He turned into a good director, and a good actor, too. He was very easy to get along with." [205]

*Leading Lady Bridget Hanley:* "Lou's so great. Swack loved him as an actor. He said, 'Antonio, you're a wonderful director, too — but the *acting*! Just gonna miss ya.' They [Antonio and actress-wife Lane Bradbury] were really close friends — our kids kind of grew up together." [206]

*Executive Casting Director Renee Valente:* "Lou Antonio! He became a very well-known, respected television director. A very good actor. Before he directed, he was a wonderful actor." [207]

*Guest Star Mitzi Hoag:* "Lou Antonio was a friend. I knew him very well, knew him from the Actor's Studio, and Swack and Bridget would have these grand 4th of July parties. We were always together there." [208]

*Wardrobe Man Steve Lodge:* "We liked Lou a whole lot. He was a good guy. I knew him afterwards — worked on shows with him afterwards. Did some *Young Rebels,* and then I did a movie of the week with him, with Mean Joe Greene."[209]

*Guest Star Dave Cass:* "Lou Antonio! He was great. He was wonderful. Lou was one of the finest actors you ever worked with."[210]

*Director Bruce Kessler:* "Lou Antonio's quite a gifted director."[211]

## Introducing a New Talent in Television: Larry Brody

As noted earlier, *Here Come the Brides* was the very first TV series for which Larry Brody wrote. Below, Brody further discusses his association with the series.

"I wasn't around until after the series was on the air, so when I realized I was going to have to know about the show I managed to watch an episode before the meeting with Stan [Schwimmer]. At that meeting he gave me half a dozen scripts and sent me home to come up with a solid idea for an episode."

While he wasn't happy with the way William Blinn rewrote the dialogue for Telly Theodakis, Brody found his association with the *Brides* story editor invaluable.

"Bill was the first TV writer I ever worked with," explains Brody. "He was an honest, blunt-spoken man who knew his stuff. My first *Brides* assignment was cut off at story, but Bill wanted to see it go so much that, after I'd screwed up two tries at an outline, he wrote a new one from scratch. Seeing the way he put the moves together, and where he took the idea, was instrumental in putting me in a more filmic (and less novelistic) frame of writing mind.

"On the other two episodes [only one made it to the screen], I learned simply by hearing his notes, which were suggestions and not orders, as most notes are in TV and film today, and by seeing what he did to the scripts with his final rewrite. I saw what he took out and what he left in and a pattern emerged so that I could see the 'why' behind his actions. I learned to keep things short and simple. Not to have my characters try to explain things to the audience that they wouldn't have to explain to each other. That sort of thing. It was a great learning experience, and it continued long after *Brides* as I went with Bill to other shows he story edited and produced."

Like many others to work on *Here Come the Brides,* Larry Brody found the experience very enjoyable.

"I liked everything about writing for *Brides* because it was my first out, so what's not to like?" he asks. "It wasn't my favorite series, by any means. Too soft. I felt like I was writing a musical (à la *Seven Brides for Seven Brothers*) and kept thinking I should be putting in music cues. But here I was, twenty-three years old and writing words that were going to be heard by millions. And some of them were going to be said by Joan Blondell, who, in my mind, had been a big movie star.

"Although I didn't know it at the time, writing for *Brides* was very pleasant compared to some other shows, primarily because Bill Blinn always presented everything in the most positive light. He protected me – and, I assume – the other freelance writers — from all the network negativity that would get in your face at other places."[212]

*Story Editor William Blinn:* "The fact that Larry did more than one…Larry's a good writer and a very bright human being."[213]

*Executive Casting Director Renee Valente:* "Larry Brody — he's wonderful to work with. Very exciting to work with because he came up with exciting ideas. And was just extremely talented. That's why he went over to *Police Story*. [Brody was story editor/writer on *Police Story*.] Terrific guy, very talented."[214]

*Trivia:* underneath *TV Guide* listing for this episode it's noted that guest star Mitzi Hoag played the schoolteacher in the series' first season.

November 22, 1969 – *TV Guide*, Vol. 17, No. 47, Issue #869 – TV Crossword – 1 Down – Answer: Bolt.

## Episode #36: "The Eyes of London Bob"          *November 28, 1969*

"He was a thief, a liar, a pirate…He was all those things.
In most people's eyes."
*Jason Bolt to his brothers, Jeremy and Joshua*

Writer . . . . . . . . . . . . . . . . . . . . . . . . . . . . . . . . . . . . . . . . . . . . . . Ken Trevey
Director. . . . . . . . . . . . . . . . . . . . . . . . . . . . . . . . . . . . .E.W. Swackhamer
Film Editor . . . . . . . . . . . . . . . . . . . . . . . . . . . . . . . . . . Norman Wallerstein
Assistant Director . . . . . . . . . . . . . . . . . . . . . . . . . . . . . . . . . . David Hawks
### Guest Cast
London Bob . . . . . . . . . . . . . . . . . . . . . . . . . . . . . . . . . . . . . .Peter Whitney
Michael Forest. . . . . . . . . . . . . . . . . . . . . . . . . . . . . . . . . . . Mike Donegan
Richard Peabody . . . . . . . . . . . . . . . . . . . . . . . . . . . . . . . . . . . Zach Perch
Joseph Bernard . . . . . . . . . . . . . . . . . . . . . . . . . . . . . . . . . . Gideon Perch

*Teaser:* Jason, Jeremy, London Bob.

*Tag:* Clancey, Gideon, Zach, Donegan, Jason, Josh, Jeremy.

*Competition:* (This may have been pre-empted by special on 'M Company' Third Battalion, Seventh Marine Regiment in South Vietnam.) If not, the *Competition: The CBS Friday Night Movie: Please Don't Eat the Daisies* starring Doris Day, David Niven, and Janis Paige; *The Name of the Game*, "The Civilized Men," starring Robert Stack as Dan Ferrell, and guest-starring Jack Kelly, Rod Cameron, and Jill St. John, NBC.

*Photography:* Shot on Bob from waist down, walking through the forest; Bob looking down at unconscious Jason – scene going in out and of focus, scene is shot from Bob's point of view; crane shot on Donegan walking out of Seattle towards accomplices in forest; shot moving down from trees and on to Candy and Biddie; slow crane shot, going down, down, down to Jason and Bob; another scene of Bob looking down at unconscious Jason — the shot going in and out of focus, this shot is different from the first, underscoring that Bob's eyesight is growing worse as the story continues; profile of bride walking out of brides dormitory — camera shooting her from side then moving behind her to follow her progress across square, which puts Lottie's saloon in foreground of scene; shot of London Bob and Jason scaling down the mountain; long shot of Jason and Bob at lagoon; crane shot on Jason and Bob — on their backs, then shot of them coming towards viewer as they come up the mountain; long shot of Jeremy, Josh, and Clancey coming into clearing; long shot of Jeremy, Clancey, Josh, and their men coming down coast; dimly lit scenes of Jason, then villains entering the cave in search of Bob; long shot of Jason pounding in the cross at Bob's grave.

*Notes:* A story of two men who begin as enemies, but do not remain that way, "The Eyes of London Bob" is an interesting tale of a man rapidly losing his eyesight. Because of the way director E.W. Swackhamer presents this story and the approach both Robert Brown and Peter Whitney take to their characters, in the end, one feels sympathy for, rather than anger toward, London Bob — a man, who, at the start of the tale, is very brutal and cruel.

First-season guest Michael Forest returns in the colorful part of lead bad-guy Donegan. Susan Tolsky has an amusing bit when she sees how the frightened Candy is being comforted by Jeremy. Henry Beckman has some fun in the tag when he learns Donegan is not a true Irishman. The many outdoor scenes in this episode (quite a few of them on the coast) add enormously to the very strong visuals of this story.

Guest star Peter Whitney played Mexican bandit El Diablo in the 1967 *Monkees* episode, "A Nice Place to Visit." Whitney's talent for accents allowed him to play Swedish characters: Lars Holstrom in *The Virginian* comedy, "A Bride for Lars," Arabian — Sheikh Achmed in *The Rogues,* "Death of a Fleming," German — Alex Schumann in the 1941 Warner Bros. feature, *Underground.* Identifiable by his very bushy eyebrows, one of Whitney's best known parts is the no-account backwoods bum Lafe Crick in the first season of the long-running CBS sitcom, *The Beverly Hillbillies.*

*Story Editor William Blinn:* "That was one where they pushed us into grittier, more life-and-death situations. Swack did the very best one could do. There were just profound limitations — we had a pound of hamburger, and they were telling us they wanted trout. We did the best we could, but it never really came to fruition."[215]

*Wardrobe Man Steve Lodge:* "We went down to the beach to finish that up — down at some cove near Malibu. Peter Whitney, Michael Forest, Richard Peabody — he was great."[216]

*Guest Star Michael Forest on Director E.W. Swackhamer:* "They had a program there at Columbia in which they had people who wanted to direct, come in and learn some of the craft, so I had applied for that. I used to come in on shows I wasn't working on as an actor. I was there on the set the whole day watching Swack and following him and asking him questions and asking the cameraman questions about lenses and one thing and another just to acquaint myself with the rudiments of directing in film. And Swack was very helpful — he really was. He would say, 'Now here's what I do, and some people do it this way, and others don't, but this is the way I start a scene.' And he'd show me how he would do it and how he would set it up — all of the little things that you don't think about when you're first trying to learn the craft. He was a good teacher.

"I was working primarily on *Brides* because Swack was there most of the time — he was one of their stock directors — that's why I kept following him around and it was great. It was really good — I enjoyed it. He would point out that there were certain lenses they were using — you know, certain sizes depending on whether it was a close-up or an establishing shot, whatever. We didn't really get into any of the new innovations, but what he did say was that there are constantly new innovations being introduced into the business. And he says, 'But it's not anything that dramatic that you're going to have to take a course in it or anything like that.' He says, 'You'll pick it up. You'll learn it. As I'm learning it.'"

*Guest Star Michael Forest on Peter Whitney:* "I did a show with Peter Whitney [*Tombstone Territory*]…it's over so many years, you work with so many people, it all becomes kind of a blur. But he was somebody I didn't forget because I'd seen him before I came to Hollywood. I'd seen him in films. When I suddenly realized I was gonna be working with him…we had a good rapport, as actors do in any given…in most of the things that you do, you always have a good rapport with actors. I can't even remember once having any real problem — well, maybe one or two, but you get along with everybody, or you try to anyway. I always did. I figured it was better to do that than not to."[217]

December 1969: My Dream Date with Bobby Sherman"
*Tiger Beat;* "Dream Date Gossip"
*Tiger Beat;* Bobby Sherman article in *Inside TV;* "Bobby Sherman – Going Places – Fast"
*Screen and TV Album;* "1969 Emmy Awards"
*TV Movie Parade;* "My Son Bobby by Mrs. Robert Sherman"
Part 3 – *Tiger Beat;* Two more Bobby Sherman articles in *Tiger Beat;* "Your FaVE' Answers You – David Soul"
*FaVE!;* Robert Brown Birthday Gift Guide – *16 Magazine;* Robert Brown – *TV Movies Today, Flip Teen;* Bridget Hanley – *Teen World.*

## Episode #37: "The Fetching of Jenny"          *December 5, 1969*

*Candy:* Look. If having Jenny Lind here was a good idea two days ago, what makes it such a bad idea now? Well, wouldn't a concert with Jenny Lind help get back some of that money that was stolen? And make a favorable impression on the governor?"

*Aaron:* That makes sense. Listen to what she's saying, Jason.
It really makes sense.
*Lottie:* That's right.

Writer . . . . . . . . . . . . . . . . . . . . . . . . . . . . . . . . . . . . . . . . . . . . . Henry Sharp
Director . . . . . . . . . . . . . . . . . . . . . . . . . . . . . . . . . . . . . . . . . .E.W. Swackhamer
Film Editor . . . . . . . . . . . . . . . . . . . . . . . . . . . . . . . . . . . . Norman Wallerstein
Assistant Director . . . . . . . . . . . . . . . . . . . . . . . . . . . . . . . . . . . . David Hawks
### Guest Cast
Big Luther. . . . . . . . . . . . . . . . . . . . . . . . . . . . . . . . . . . . . . . . . . . Alan Hale
Peale . . . . . . . . . . . . . . . . . . . . . . . . . . . . . . . . . . . . . . . . . . . . Paul Lambert
Barnum . . . . . . . . . . . . . . . . . . . . . . . . . . . . . . . . . . . . . . . . . . . .Ivor Francis
Governor Stuart . . . . . . . . . . . . . . . . . . . . . . . . . . . . . . . . . . Byron Morrow
Guard . . . . . . . . . . . . . . . . . . . . . . . . . . . . . . . . . . . . . . . . . . . Jack Bannon
Receptionist. . . . . . . . . . . . . . . . . . . . . . . . . . . . . . . . . . . . . . Allison McKay
Jenny Lind. . . . . . . . . . . . . . . . . . . . . . . . . . . Mala Powers *(Special Guest)*

*Teaser:* Biddie, Aaron, Candy, Jason, Lottie, Josh, Jeremy, Ben.

*Tag:* Jenny Lind, Aaron, Governor, Jason, Lottie, Ben, Candy, Josh, Jeremy, Molly, Christopher, Biddie, Ben, the whole town.

*Competition: The CBS Friday Night Movie: Having a Wild Weekend* starring the Dave Clark Five; *The Name of the Game,* "High Card," starring Gene Barry as Glenn Howard, and guest-starring Barry Sullivan, Gene Raymond, and Martine Beswick, NBC.

*Photography:* Zooming in to Lottie's — shot at night; close-up on Biddie, pulling away from her to show Aaron, Candy, Jason, Lottie, Jeremy, Josh; long shot of Molly and Christopher running over to dormitory from the side of the church; Candy and Jeremy waving goodbye, then longer shot of ship leaving dock, past totem pole, etc.; long, sweeping shot of San Francisco; zoom-in on Big Luther, then shot of cab rolling up for him; long shot of Jason and Aaron being thrown out of Barnum's rolling down steps; long, tracking shot on Biddie — starting at tops of trees, then moving down on Biddie; tracking scene on Clancey's ship — beginning with feet of Jason, Aaron, Clancey, pulling back to identify the three, moving up to mast to become long shot of Jason, Aaron, Clancey, running, leading Big Luther and his men away from Clancey's ship, then moving down to show Lottie and Candy, in capes, leaving Clancey's ship; angular shot of Jason leading Big Luther astray in streets of San Francisco; tracking shot on Candy and Lottie in women's wardrobe room at Barnum's; long shot on fountain in park as Jason and Jenny walk towards fountain; long shot on Jason returning to Clancey's ship; nighttime scene, in long shot, as Clancey's ship returns to Seattle; Jason speaks to town — long shot — in dark; long shot — town takes down banner welcoming Jenny Lind, then on to stagecoach arriving; pull back on Jenny as Jason introduces her to Seattle; long shot on Jenny — beginning on her, pulling away and down to whole town, moving in for close-up on Aaron, Governor, Jason, then back, and up to Jenny, then down to Candy, kids, and other in town, then back up to Jenny, then down to town.

***Notes:*** Pure fiction in regards to when "Swedish Nightingale" Jenny Lind really toured the U.S. (1850-1852), and where she actually went (the Eastern part of the country), "The Fetching of Jenny" is very accurate in terms of the famous singer's professional association with P.T. Barnum. Thanks to Jason's being in San Francisco, Jeremy's staying in Seattle, and Candy and Lottie also traveling to San Francisco, director E.W. Swackhamer has all manner of locations in which to shoot, as noted above in the *HCTB* Photography section.

The "Homer Shagrue" theme (from the second season premiere, "A Far Cry from Yesterday") plays as Ben enters Lottie's, then plays with the introduction of Big Luther, and at other times when Luther is shown. Clancey's comic bit about the "grapnel hook" is writer Henry Sharp poking fun at his former series, *The Wild Wild West.* Grapnel hooks were often featured on *West.*

Bridget Hanley sings the famous Scottish song, "Annie Laurie." (Hanley's singing "Annie Laurie" on board Big Luther's boat is of particular interest — this very popular song was closely associated with Jenny Lind. Luther mistakes Candy for Jenny Lind.)

The music from "Next Week, East Lynne" (the scene in which the Shakespearean actors arrive in Seattle) plays as the stagecoach carrying the real Jenny Lind and Governor Stuart arrives.

Susan Tolsky's importance on the series continues to grow. When Candy leaves, she puts Biddie in charge of her brother and sister; Biddie also takes over for Lottie as temporary manger/bartender of the saloon.

Best known for the role of Roxanne in *Cyrano de Bergerac,* Mala Powers' casting as Jenny Lind makes for a further parallel to Henry Sharp's former series, *Wild Wild West.* Powers played the role of would-be actress Lily Fortune in the second season *West* episode, "The Night of the Big Blast." In "Blast," mad scientist Ida Lupino turns U.S. Secret Service agents Jim West and Artemus Gordon into walking time-bombs.

*Story Editor William Blinn:* "I remember the episode very well. I liked the episode a lot. I thought it was funny, the kind of thing — the kind of little bit larger than life romance that this show did very well, in particular, the kind of thing Robert did very well, cuz it was very much what the pilot was in terms of the guy going off to perform this Superman kind of feat. Robert liked doing that kind of stuff."[218]

*Leading Lady Bridget Hanley:* "I did 'Annie Laurie,' and Joan gave me a gold record. Joan Blondell got a black record and had them paint it gold. In the black label, she wrote, 'Bridget Hanley Sings Annie Laurie.' I still have it. I'm gonna frame it and put it up."[219]

*Bridget Hanley on Mala Powers:* "She had dated my husband, and actually, they were very nice friends. I knew Mala and her husband, and I used to see her quite often. We'd run into each other and liked each other a lot. She was a terrific actress — I admired her talent enormously. I think that was her singing."

*Bridget Hanley on Alan Hale:* "He was so great. Now there's a 'Hale' fellow well met. He was just so fun. He worked always — but it was so great to watch him just go on and on and on. He was just fun and dear."

*Bridget Hanley on Ivor Francis:* "Ivor Francis was a good friend of my husband's. He was just a lovely, wonderful, charming man — brilliant actor, and I believe he was also a very good friend of Bill Windom's. He was just like the essence of class. I was just again…felt like the new kid on the block, but the one who had gotten the prize — to be able to work with Ivor and people like that."[220]

### *Writer Henry Sharp*

Story consultant/story editor on the aforementioned 1965-69 CBS secret agent/ western, *The Wild Wild West,* Henry Sharp had *The Man from U.N.C.L.E.* and the sitcoms, *Bewitched* and *The Addams Family* to his credit prior to "The Fetching of Jenny." Post Brides, Sharp went back to work for *West* producer Bruce Lansbury in the early 1970s, during the producer's years on *Mission: Impossible.* Sharp's sixth-season *Mission,* "Nerves," co-written with Carrie Bateson, gave the series one of its best sixth-season outings.

The Wild Wild West/Mission: Impossible *producer Bruce Lansbury on Henry Sharp:* "He was an artist before he was a writer. His scripts were always very visual. Very, very visual and imaginative."[221]

December 8-12 – Robert Brown guests on game show, *It Takes Two.* Marty Allen, Darren McGavin, and Kathie Browne also guest.

## Episode #38: "His Sister's Keeper"          *December 12, 1969*

"Candy, I've heard an awful lot about Jeremy's older brother.
I think that it's about time we met."
*Julie Stempel to Candy and Biddie*

Writer . . . . . . . . . . . . . . . . . . . . . . . . . . . . . . . . . . . . . . . . . . . . .Skip Webster
Director. . . . . . . . . . . . . . . . . . . . . . . . . . . . . . . . . . . . . . . . . . . Jerry Bernstein
Film Editor . . . . . . . . . . . . . . . . . . . . . . . . . . . . . . . . . . . . . . . . . Asa Clark
Assistant Director . . . . . . . . . . . . . . . . . . . . . . . . . . . . . . . . . . .Michael Dmytryk
*Guest Cast*
Julie. . . . . . . . . . . . . . . . . . . . . . . . . . . . . . . . . . . . . . . . . . Katherine Crawford
Stacey . . . . . . . . . . . . . . . . . . . . . . . . . . . . . . . . . . . . . . . . . . William Lucking
Reverend Adams. . . . . . . . . . . . . . . . . . . . . . . . . . . . . . . . . . . Lindsay Workman

*Teaser:* Aaron, Julie, Candy, Biddie.
*Tag:* Biddie, Ben, Clancey, Josh, Jeremy, Lottie, Jason, Candy.

*Competition: The CBS Friday Night Movie: Paris — When It Sizzles* starring William Holden and Audrey Hepburn; *The Name of the Game*, "The Power," starring Robert Stack as Dan Farrell, and guest-starring William Conrad, John Ireland, and Broderick Crawford, NBC.

*Notes:* The second episode to focus on Aaron Stempel, "His Sister's Keeper" reveals that Aaron has a younger sister. Like Aaron, she lives in Seattle. Aaron has a great deal of control over his sister's future — her choice of a husband must be approved by him. This episode introduces some new sets — the interior and exterior of the Stempel home; as well as the never-before-seen "Lover's Lagoon."

A highlight of this show is the fight, initiated by both Ben and Clancey, between Aaron and Jason. The sprawling fight sequence, which covers many exteriors, allows the series to illustrate the diversity of Seattle; during the fight, the audience sees elderly people, quite a few Indians, Aaron's Chinese servant, etc.

Candy and Biddie now seem to be working at Ben Perkins' general store; they're also working at Lottie's. First-season semi-regular Lindsay Workman returns in the role of Reverend Adams.

Guest star Katherine Crawford is the daughter of the late Universal vice-president and executive producer Roy Huggins, and the wife of one-time Universal executive producer Frank Price. Despite her familial connections to Universal, Crawford had to prove herself in order to obtain work at the studio. A look at her excellent performances in such Universal productions as *Suspense Theatre* ("The Easter Breech") and *The Virginian* ("A Bride for Lars") reveals Crawford to be quite versatile. She certainly had strong credentials. Determined to be an actress, Katherine Crawford enrolled at the Royal Academy of Dramatic Art in London.

*Story Editor William Blinn:* "I think that was one of Skip's [Webster] best. Because he wrote so many, he was really part of the family of the people doing the show. So he was aware of the currents, you know, 'Let's try this, let's do that.' He had an overview that a lot of guys just doing episodes probably didn't have. That episode could have been better, had we had more time and more dollars. Again, I think because of the physical constraints of the Screen Gems television budget, it didn't really fly. We may have bit off physically more than we could chew."[222]

*Wardrobe Man Steve Lodge:* "Version of *The Quiet Man* in the fight between Jason and Stempel. We did [the fight] over and under, up and down, in and out, through the town, at Franklin Canyon, everywhere. It required a lot of set-ups. Kathy and I went to high school together. We did a senior play; she and I and Brenda Scott — we were all at the same school. It was always fun to see them."[223]

*Robert Brown Stunt Double Dave Cass:* "I remember doing a fight between Robert Brown and Mark Lenard. And Bernstein wanted it to be a fight like *The Quiet Man*. Well, there's a dam up in the Hollywood Hills, off Mulholland, called Franklin Canyon Dam — we used to shoot up around that lake. I hired a fella named Bobby Herron to double Mark Lenard, and he and I…I felt like we fought for four days.

We started on the set (at Screen Gems' backlot), did the end there, we did the middle of the fight all through Franklin Canyon Reservoir. It was a lot of work. I'd never been so tired in all my life.

"I remember I was sitting one day, and had this Popsicle, and I was in Robert's clothes — I think it was Bernstein who came up and said, 'Would you be eating that in front of John Ford?' I said, 'Yeah. Yeah, of course I would.' I could never understand why...it wasn't like I wasn't ready to do my job. He was funny. I could never figure out why he asked me that question."[224]

## Episode #39: "Lorenzo Bush"          *December 19, 1969*

"God made the land. Belongs to Him. You ain't got no right to ruin it."
*Lorenzo Bush to the Bolts and their men*

Writer . . . . . . . . . . . . . . . . . . . . . . . . . . . . . . . . . . . . . . . . . . . . . . . . . Jack Miller
Director . . . . . . . . . . . . . . . . . . . . . . . . . . . . . . . . . . . . . . . . . . . . Jerry Bernstein
Film Editor . . . . . . . . . . . . . . . . . . . . . . . . . . . . . . . . . . . . . . Norman Wallerstein
Assistant Director . . . . . . . . . . . . . . . . . . . . . . . . . . . . . . . . . . . . . David Hawks

*Guest Cast*

Lorenzo . . . . . . . . . . . . . . . . . . . . . . . . . . . . . . . . . . . . . . . . . . . Ronald Feinberg
Wesley . . . . . . . . . . . . . . . . . . . . . . . . . . . . . . . . . . . . . . . . . . . . . Dennis Cooney
Keenan . . . . . . . . . . . . . . . . . . . . . . . . . . . . . . . . . . . . . . . Lawrence Montaigne
1st Man . . . . . . . . . . . . . . . . . . . . . . . . . . . . . . . . . . . . . . . . . . . . David Draper

*Teaser:* Jason, Josh, loggers, Lorenzo Bush.

*Tag:* Clancey, Biddie, Lottie, Josh, Candy, Jeremy, Jason, Wesley.

*Competition: The CBS Friday Night Movie: Seven Brides for Seven Brothers* starring Howard Keel and Jane Powell; *The Name of the Game*, "Laurie Marie," starring Tony Franciosa as Jeff Dillon, and guest-starring (Peter) Mark Richman, Antoinette Bower, John Kerr, Barry Atwater, and Carla Borelli, NBC.

*Notes:* Future *Gunsmoke* executive story consultant Jack Miller's first show for *Brides*, "Lorenzo Bush" features a favorite Miller theme: the primitive, old man (or woman) who's sickened by what civilization is doing to the land of the West. While Miller certainly did not originate this theme, his coming to the defense of the "baddies" in this case, the tree-chopping Bolts, is definitely a departure from the environmental messages that were beginning to permeate both television and motion pictures.

Jeremy Bolt being the sweetest character in *Brides*, he is the perfect spokesman to defend the lumbermen's profession to Molly and Christopher, who have taken Lorenzo's "save the trees" message to heart. Without trees, Jeremy explains to the two, their big sister Candy wouldn't have the cedar chest she so treasures. Without trees, there would be no books. Or no Bibles.

Writer Miller's presenting both the need to protect the environment and the dangers of environmental extremism makes it very clear that when it comes to storytelling, *Here Come the Brides* is becoming a very mature, and rich, adult drama. Like the next episode, "A Bride for Obie Brown," in terms of its subject matter, "Lorenzo Bush" was years ahead of its time.

Besides introducing the "Biddie Theme," this episode shows the Susan Tolsky

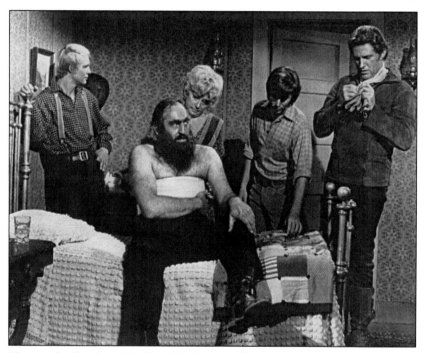

"Lorenzo Bush": *left to right: David Soul, Ronald Feinberg, Joan Blondell, Bobby Sherman, Robert Brown.*

character to very good effect. Aaron's stepping up on behalf of the young woman when she is upbraided by Wesley is one of the nicest moments in this show; it also plays further into the possibility that as time goes along Aaron and Biddie might get together romantically. Biddie's thanking Aaron for defending her, and her remark to the group at Lottie's that "Sometimes it's just no fun being a Biddie" is another nice moment.

"*Story Editor William Blinn:* "I kind of liked that — maybe it's liking the ugly child better than the other ones. I recall sort of liking maybe that Jack tilted my perception a little bit. In terms of the environmental [issue]. It's a pre-runner of the Al Gore movie, maybe. I would hope that it does present both sides. I don't want to get into presenting only one viewpoint."[225]

*Series Regular Susan Tolsky:* "I remember sitting there filming this scene, and I remember the impact it had because it was quiet. It was between me and Ron Feinberg. There's a scene where I'm talking to him, and he's in jail, and we're talking through the bars, that scene is maybe two minutes — I'm proud of that scene."[226]

## Guest Star Ronald Feinberg

Guest star in the two-part 1968 *Cowboy in Africa,* "African Rodeo," the two-part 1969 *It Takes a Thief,* "A Matter of Gray Matter," the 1969 *Judd, for the Defense* two-part, "The Holy Ground –The Killing"/"The Holy Ground –The Killers," Ronald Feinberg is the only guest star in *Here Come the Brides* to appear in three separate episodes. Interestingly, his third and last *Brides,* "Two Worlds," was co-written by "Lorenzo Bush" writer Jack Miller.

Post *Brides,* Feinberg achieved another unusual television record: guest-starring (for four seasons in a row) on an episode of *Mission: Impossible.* A few years later, the actor began working as a voice artist on *Hong Kong Phooey* and *The Scooby-Doo/Dynomutt Hour.* Among the other series on which he guest-starred: the much too short-lived lighthearted adventure, *The American Girls,* the daytime soap-opera comedy, *Mary Hartman, Mary Hartman,* the tongue-in-cheek adventure *Bring 'Em Back Alive,* and the sitcom, *Night Court.* TV-movies included *Hijack, The Missiles of October,* and the wonderful *The Man in the Santa Claus Suit.* In the '90s, the majority of Ronald Feinberg's credits were in voice work. He died on January 29, 2005.

*Leading Lady Bridget Hanley:* "Oh, I loved him. He was terrific. Crazy Big Ron. That's the one I remember most: Lorenzo Bush." Crazy Big Ron, but with a heart like a big soft marshmallow. He was so dear, and he probably had to be. He was a wonderful actor. And what an imposing presence — physically — 'Here he comes!' Kind of like Robert [Brown] but Robert had more poetry about him. Ronald had a kind of earthy quality — and that was what made it more imperial in its majesty and its bigness."[227]

*Series Semi-Regular Eric Chase:* "That was another fun one; that had a little bit of drama to it. He was, of course, very different from his [character]. He was a nice guy — cultured. My recollection was he was a low-key guy. My recollection was that he was respectful, did his lines, listened. He did a good job. He came across exactly as they wanted him to. I remember him mentioning that this was his second round on the show. When you get somebody who is a known quantity, somebody who's easy to work with and will do the job, you find a slot for him and bring him back."[228]

*Story Editor William Blinn:* "I liked that episode because I kind of liked Ron as an actor. He was offbeat, and strange, and certainly non-traditional. He was in *Brian's Song* years later, playing one of the football players."[229]

## *Writer Jack Miller*

Creator of *Dirty Sally*, the character portrayed by *HCTB* guest Jeanette Nolan in the January-April 1974 CBS series of the same name, executive story consultant on *Gunsmoke* from 1971-75, Jack Miller had written for both *Dundee and the Culhane* and *The Invaders* ("The Pit") before *Here Come the Brides*. Miller's three stories for *Brides:* "Lorenzo Bush," "Two Worlds," and "Two Women" foreshadowed the sorts of tales he would write (and later approve, once he moved into the position of story consultant), on *Gunsmoke*. Other series for which the late Miller wrote: *Three for the Road;* the John Mantley-produced, James Arness mini-series, *How the West Was Won;* creator/producer David Dortort's long-running *Bonanza;* the Bob Claver/William Blinn drama, *The Interns.*

*Story Editor William Blinn on Jack Miller:* "I liked Jack's writing. It was a kind of offbeat, quirky episode, and I tend to respond in a positive way to anything like that. Whereas something like "Marriage: Chinese Style" or "Wives for Wakando," I'm definitely not on the same page.

"Jack liked *Brides*, because it was such a change of pace from what he had been doing for the other westerns that were on the air, particularly *Gunsmoke*, and also he liked the group who was doing *Brides*. Jack and I got along well. He liked to come to the set. He and I would go down to the set, and he just liked the feel of the storytelling."[230]

December 26, 1969: A Bride for Obie Brown" originally scheduled to air.

1970 – Bobby Sherman article in *Photoplay;* Bobby Sherman article in *TV Radio Album*, "Bobby Sherman Hits Pay Dirt in the Pacific Northwest."
WNBE-TV, Channel 12 (New Bern/Greenville/Washington, North Carolina) becomes (ABC affiliate) WCTI-TV sometime in 1970.

January 2, 1970 – *Brides* pre-empted by NBA Basketball – New York Knicks vs. Milwaukee Bucks.

January 1970: Bobby Dream Girl Tours Hollywood"
*Tiger Beat;* "Bobby's Groovy Presents"
*FaVE!;* "Bobby Sherman, Going Places – Fast"
*Screen and TV Album;* Bobby Sherman article in *Rona Barrett's Hollywood;* Bobby Sherman article in *Movie World;* Joan Blondell article in *Modern Movies;* two Bobby Sherman articles in *Flip Teen;* Bobby Sherman article in *Tiger Beat;* Bobby Sherman article in *Teen World;* David Soul article in *TV Star Life;* Robert Brown – *Chicago Tribune* TV Week Preview; Bridget Hanley – *Tiger Beat, FaVE!, Movie Time, Teen Life, Silver Screen.*

## Episode #40: "A Bride for Obie Brown"          *January 9, 1970*

*Lucenda:* Are there any black families in Seattle?
*Obie:* Not...so you'd notice.
*Lucenda:* Then you would be the first?
*Obie:* Pretty much.
*Lucenda:* Doesn't the thought scare you?
*Obie:* Not...nearly as much as the thought of being alone.

Writer . . . . . . . . . . . . . . . . . . . . . . . . . . . . . . . . . . . . . . . . . . . . . . . Bob Goodwin
Director. . . . . . . . . . . . . . . . . . . . . . . . . . . . . . . . . . . . . . . . . . . Richard Kinon
Film Editor . . . . . . . . . . . . . . . . . . . . . . . . . . . . . . . . . . . . . . . . . . Asa Clark
Assistant Director . . . . . . . . . . . . . . . . . . . . . . . . . . . . . . . . . . . David Hawks
Music. . . . . . . . . . . . . . . . . . . . . . . . . . . . . . . . . . . . . . . . . . . . . . .Warren Barker

### Guest Cast

Lucenda. . . . . . . . . . . . . . . . . . . . . . . . . . . . . . . . . . . . . . . . . . . . . . Cicely Tyson
Obie . . . . . . . . . . . . . . . . . . . . . . . . . . . . . . . . . . . . . . . . . Georg Stanford Brown
Johnnie Mae . . . . . . . . . . . . . . . . . . . . . . . . . . . . . . . . . . . . . . . . Ketty Lester

*Teaser:* Josh, Jeremy, Obie.

*Tag:* Obie, Jason, Josh, Jeremy, Lucenda, Candy.

*Competition:* *The CBS Friday Night Movie: Sole Survivor* starring Vince Edwards, Richard Basehart, William Shatner and *Brides* guests Lou Antonio and Dennis Cooney; *The Name of the Game*, "The Brass Ring," starring Robert Stack as Dan Farrell, and guest-starring Van Johnson and Celeste Holm, NBC.

*Notes:* Something of a foreshadowing of ABC's 1977 blockbuster miniseries, *Roots* (it was *Brides'* William Blinn who adapted the Alex Haley novel of the same name for television) "A Bride for Obie Brown" is undeniably authentic in regards to the historical references in the story. During the course of the show, Lucenda tells Molly and Christopher about the African-American tradition of oral history; she mentions such notable blacks as Hiram Rhodes Revels: the first black to serve as a U.S. senator (from the state of Mississippi — 1870-71), and Jonathan Clarkson (J.C.) Gibbs — Florida's first black Secretary of State (1868-72.) The reason the episode is so accurate is that it was written by African-American Robert Goodwin.

Lottie's remark to Josh that his brother Jason is "always talking about the future," hearkens back to such first-season episodes as "A Crying Need" and "A Jew Named Sullivan." Lucenda and Obie's discussion of how Obie and whatever woman he marries would be the first black family in Seattle further emphasizes "the growing town of Seattle and its future" theme. This also applies to Molly and Christopher's pointing out to Lucenda that, if she goes back to her native Africa, the history of the black people's accomplishments in America will not be passed on to future generations — of blacks — and whites.

This time, it's the children who teach the guest character the important lesson.

*Story Editor William Blinn:* "Bob Goodwin couldn't have been a sweeter guy. [He] was, at that time, one of the few working African-American writers in town, at least that I knew of, and also one of the few who, when he worked, wasn't always bringing you stories that dealt with a black lead. I think we called him about "Obie Brown," cuz it just made sense, 'If we're gonna do it,' to try to have a black guy at the helm. And he did a good job, and it turned out to be a good episode. Georg was a

*"A Bride for Obie Brown"* — *left to right: David Soul, Bobby Sherman, Robert Brown, guest Georg Stanford Brown.*

good actor, and a good director. I used Georg as one of the leads on *The Rookies*, and it worked out very well. We never got any flack about it from either the network or the studio."[231]

*Robert Brown Stunt Double Dave Cass:* "I can remember Georg Stanford Brown. He guest-starred on a show where he was a black logger looking for a bride, and this African princess comes to town, and that was Cicely Tyson. We all said, 'Gosh! This little gal can really act!' That must have been one of her first jobs in town."[232]

### Guest Star Cicely Tyson

A very successful model who appeared on the covers of both *Vogue* and *Harper's Bazaar* in the late 1950s, Cicely Tyson started on the path to what proved to be a very successful and well-regarded acting career thanks to a black character actress by the name of Evelyn Davis. While the movie Davis convinced Tyson to do (*The Spectrum*) would never make it to theatres (due to lack of production funds), it wasn't long before Tyson was appearing in features like *Odds Against Tomorrow* and *Twelve Angry Men*, not to mention off-Broadway plays like Jean Genet's controversial, *The Blacks*.

*The Blacks* attracted the attention of George C. Scott, who wanted Tyson to play the regular role of Jane Foster – office secretary to his social worker character Neil Brock in the critically acclaimed, though short-lived series, *East Side, West Side*. Because of the quality of the series, Tyson accepted.

Following the cancellation of *East Side*, Cicely Tyson began guest-starring on different series, but only if a series presented either its regular or guest black characters in a positive and intelligent light. Tyson refused to do stereotypes. As a result, she guest-starred on such series as *I Spy* and *Mission: Impossible*, as well as the Ivan Tors/Chuck Connors African-western, *Cowboy in Africa*. Frequently examining African culture and customs, and co-starring black child actor Gerald Edwards, almost every episode of *Cowboy in Africa* featured at least one black actor (Paul Winfield, Louis Gossett, Jr., Yaphet Kotto, James McEachin, etc.) in the cast. Tyson's guest shot, "Tomorrow on the Wind," featured her as a teacher of African children.

In the 1970s, Cicely Tyson's television work consisted mainly of TV-movies and miniseries. With a few notable exceptions, like the 1972 classic, *Sounder*, most of the actress's work has been in TV. To this day, she will not appear in any television or movie production which does not offer a positive image of blacks.

*Leading Lady Bridget Hanley:* "I just think she's divine, and what a skillful, wonderful talent. I have watched almost everything that she's done. I remember working with her, thinking that she was a woman of great grace and great talent."[233]

*Series Regular Susan Tolsky:* "I remember hearing when Cicely did [the critically acclaimed 1974 TV-movie, *The Autobiography of*] *Miss Jane Pittman*, she stayed in character all day long, I remember Cicely. I thought she was wonderful. I know she had marvelous training. A good background."[234]

*Series Semi-Regular Eric Chase:* "The one I remember the best was Cicely Tyson. She was such a gracious person. I remember my mother was distressed because somebody called and they had the flu or were sick, or some illness. I don't remember what it was. So my mother was upset because she wasn't at home, and she was in tears. Cicely Tyson came over and comforted her. Then she got on the phone and she had some remedy or recommendation to solve whatever the problem was. She spent quite a bit of time with whoever was at home taking care of the kid, and she helped solve the problem. My mother was always very grateful and touched by the fact that this person would come over and take the time to help her. That was the kind of person that she was. I don't remember if she was a big star at the time or not. She really seemed to take notice of things going on around her and was kind and helpful. Whatever it was that she recommended, it worked."[235]

## Guest Star Georg Stanford Brown:

Beginning his acting career by enrolling in the theater program at Los Angeles City College in 1962, (he wanted to take something easy), Georg Stanford Brown discovered that he liked acting so much that he pursued it further at the American Musical and Dramatic Academy in 1964. There he met fellow student, and future wife, Tyne Daly.

Brown's first professional acting came in a Joseph Papp Shakespeare production in Central Park – he played the role of a spear carrier in a mob scene. After that, the actor moved to more substantial parts in such Shakespeare works as *Measure for Measure*, *Richard III*, and *Macbeth*.

Soon appearing in motion pictures like *The Comedians* and *Bullitt*, Brown had guest-starred in such series as *It Takes a Thief*, *Judd, for the Defense* and *Julia* before playing the role of Obie Brown on *Here Come the Brides*. Not long after this he co-starred as Officer Terry Webster on Spelling/Goldberg's *The Rookies*. During the run of *The Rookies*, Georg Stanford Brown made his directorial debut.

After playing the role of Tom Harvey in the 1977 blockbuster miniseries, *Roots*, and its 1979 sequel *Roots: The Next Generations* (he directed part of that sequel), Brown found himself very much in demand as both an actor and director.

*Leading Lady Bridget Hanley:* "Wonderful actor and wonderful gentleman. We used to see each other a lot – Georg and Tyne and Swack and me. Georg worked with Swack a lot (on *The Rookies*). I did a *Rookies*, too, and Tyne was part of our theater group that we tried to start; Barbara Bosson was part of that group, and David [Soul] was part of the group, too, and it finally came to be that they got a theater. We were all too busy to be a part of it; we kind of got disenchanted along the way."[236]

## Writer Robert L. Goodwin:

Actor/Producer/Director/Writer Robert L. Goodwin had guest-starred on *Laredo* and written for *Bonanza*, *Insight*, *Big Valley*, *Tarzan*, and *Julia* prior to writing for *Brides*. Post *Brides*, Goodwin wrote for the Quinn Martin/Burt Reynolds series, *Dan August*. He also wrote, produced and directed the 1971 film, *Black Chariot*. He died on February 13, 1983 in San Diego, California.

*Story Editor William Blinn:* "He was just... a sweet, dear, gentle, bright guy with a wonderful sense of humor. When he was in the room, it was a good place to be. If you didn't like what he'd written, he could handle that. He wrote well. He had an understanding of race. Just a dear, good guy. I brought him in from *Bonanza*."[237]

January 10, 1970 – *TV Guide* – Vol. 18, No. 2, Issue #876 – *Brides* mentioned on pg. 16 of profile of *Brides* guest Stefan Arngrim.

# Episode #41: "To Break the Bank of Tacoma"          *January 16, 1970*

"Well, that's how it goes. First your money, and then your clothes."
*A rhyme used when someone is swindled — which happens many times in this story.*

Writer . . . . . . . . . . . . . . . . . . . . . . . . . . . . . . . . . . . . . . . . . . . . . . . . Michael Fisher
Director. . . . . . . . . . . . . . . . . . . . . . . . . . . . . . . . . . . . . . . . . . . . . . . Jerry Bernstein
Film Editor . . . . . . . . . . . . . . . . . . . . . . . . . . . . . . . . . . . . . . . Norman Wallerstein
Assistant Director . . . . . . . . . . . . . . . . . . . . . . . . . . . . . . . . .Christopher Morgan

### Guest Cast

Simon Bill. . . . . . . . . . . . . . . . . . . . . . . . . . . . . . . . . . . . . . . . . . . . . . . .Bill Mumy
Harry Miles. . . . . . . . . . . . . . . . . . . . . . . . . . . . . . . . . . . . . . . . . . . . Larry Linville
Peter Savage. . . . . . . . . . . . . . . . . . . . . . . . . . . . . . . . . . . . . . . . . . . . . . Sid Haig
Bean . . . . . . . . . . . . . . . . . . . . . . . . . . . . . . . . . . . . . . . . . . . . . . . . . .Ed Gilbert
Big George . . . . . . . . . . . . . . . . . . . . . . . . . . . . . . . . . . . . . . . . . . .Julian Burton
Felix. . . . . . . . . . . . . . . . . . . . . . . . . . . . . . . . . . . . . . . . . . . . . . . . Felton Perry
Mrs. Hobbs . . . . . . . . . . . . . . . . . . . . . . . . . . . . . . . . . . . . . . . . . Geraldine Wall
Cyrus Malone . . . . . . . . . . . . . . . . . . . . . . . . . .Harold Gould *(Special Guest Star)*

*Teaser:* Harry Miles, Josh, Jeremy, Felix, saloon patrons.
*Tag:* Simon Bill, Cyrus, Mrs. Hobbs, Jeremy, Josh, Jason.
*Competition: The CBS Friday Night Movie: Robin and the 7 Hoods* starring Frank Sinatra, Dean Martin, Sammy Davis, Jr., and Bing Crosby; *Name of the Game,* "Island of Gold and Precious Stones," starring Tony Franciosa as Jeff Dillon, and guest-starring Lee Meriwether, Hazel Court, Yvonne DeCarlo, and *Brides* guest Henry Jones, with cameos by Rudy Vallee, Edward Everett Horton, and Estelle Winwood, NBC.
*Notes:* Bill Mumy's role as Simon Bill, who knows how to open the safe, work the roulette wheel, etc. brings to mind Mumy's famous role as whiz-kid Will Robinson on the 1965-68 CBS series, *Lost in Space.* Harold Gould as lawyer Cyrus Malone is a familiar characterization for the actor. Gould often played a lawyer when guest-starring on such series as *The Fugitive* and *The Invaders.* Later, in the 1974-76 NBC lawyer drama, *Petrocelli,* he played the recurring role of attorney Haskell "Foxy" Fox.
A definite high-point in this episode is the Horace Morris one-man band.

*Story Editor William Blinn on Bill Mumy:* "Billy Mumy could handle it [child stardom] better than most kids. My recollection is that Billy came from a show business family. He had a little bit of armor-plate around the edges; he was not easily bruised."[238]

*Leading Lady Bridget Hanley on Harold Gould:* "Harold I know very well. He's a member of Theater West. I remember when I first joined Theater West, it was the first time I had seen him, since that time [Gould's *Brides* guest shot], and we ended up doing *A Christmas Carol* – Steve Allen's version of *A Christmas Carol*, and he [Gould] played Scrooge, and I played many characters – one of them was the 'Ghost of Christmas Past.' We got caught on this…there was this platform that we were both standing on. It was wheeled over, and one night, it shook so badly that we didn't know whether to leap for safety. We finally…we just were hysterical by the time we finally got off. Nobody could see what we were doing. I said, 'If that ever happens again,' it was just…

"He is a wonderful, wonderful actor, and I did a couple of things with him after that. It was such a pleasure to get to know him, because I didn't really get to know him on *Brides* – he's such a wonderful, brilliant actor."[239]

## Episode #42: "Debt of Honor"                              *January 23, 1970*

> *Biddie:* Well, Holly, you're no match for that kind of man.
> *Holly Houston:* Cloom, I'm a match for any man.

| | |
|---|---|
| Writer | Skip Webster |
| Director | Herschel Daugherty |
| Director of Photography | Brick Marquard |
| Film Editor | Norman Wallerstein |
| Assistant Director | Christopher Morgan |

*Guest Cast*

| | |
|---|---|
| Jennifer West | Holly Houston |
| Pat Harrington, Jr. | J. Montague Morgan |
| Guy Raymond | Amos Higgins |
| Larsen | Vic Tayback |
| Bartender | Leon Lontoc |

*Teaser:* Reverend Adams, Ben, Aaron, Jason, Biddie, Candy, Josh, Lottie, Holly.
*Tag:* Aaron, Ben, Holly, Jason, Biddie, Josh, Jeremy, Candy, Lottie.
*Competition: The CBS Friday Night Movie: Wake Me When It's Over* starring Ernie Kovacs, Dick Shawn, Jack Warden and Don Knotts; *The Name of the Game,* "The Take-over," starring Gene Barry as Glenn Howard, and guest-starring Anne Baxter, David Sheiner, Gloria Grahame and *Brides* guest Michael Ansara, NBC.
*Notes:* Jennifer West returns as the still-single Holly Houston; there are some great comic moments from West — both physical and verbal. Leon Lontoc played the chauffeur, Henry, on *Burke's Law.* Pat Harrington, Jr. is best known as Schneider, the girl-chasing superintendent on the 1970s CBS situation comedy, *One Day at a Time.*

*Story Editor William Blinn:* "Skip was the epitome of being dependable. There were probably writers that had more flash and more flair, might be more difficult to work with. Skip was the guy who would always get you three yards, and there's something to be said for that, and, hopefully, if I can get in there after Skip and turn in the five yards…Being a member of the family, there was very little about the show he didn't know. He knew other people's episodes, and knew what had been said in which episode, and 'Well, Jason might not say that because don't you remember earlier he said so and so.' So, to that degree, he was sort of like — as close as anything to a staff

writer as we had. He loved writing for Henry and he loved writing for Joan. He was a happy camper. If he wrote sequels well, it's because he was very fond of, and close to, the show."[240]

*Leading Lady Bridget Hanley:* "She [Jennifer West] was the same wacky, wonderful woman that I loved in the first one. She's just wonderful. She was fun to be around and sacrilegious. She was kind of carefree."[241]

*Leading Lady Bridget Hanley on Pat Harrington, Jr.:* "One of my dear friends. Pat and his wonderful wife. He is just wonderful — we did a Ray Bradbury piece called 'Falling Upward.' He is so darn funny. I was just so thrilled. He worked with my husband a lot — and Monte Markham — they did a *Mr. Deeds*

Brides *guests Jennifer West ("And Jason Makes Five," "Debt of Honor") and Dennis Cooney ("Lorenzo Bush") in the late'60s stage play,* Tiger at the Gates. *Cooney is next to West. Also pictured: Tony Van Bridge, Philip Bosco (at left).*

*Goes to Town* pilot together. They used to come to the St. Patrick's Day party; cook all the crazy Irish food. Pat's also a Member of Yarmy's Army — formed for my dear friend Dick Yarmy, who was dying of lung cancer — Dick was also a very close friend. Dick started this group of a few people whom he loved and thought were funny, to gather around him to make him laugh. They'd meet once a week at a restaurant; my husband was included and Pat and Ronnie Schell, and Peter Marshall, and now, it's gotten even bigger. They still meet and they do good work. They do benefits and they give money to charities, or to somebody who's ill."[242]

### *Director Herschel Daugherty*

Starting out as a dialogue director on such 1940s Warner Bros. films as *Edge of Darkness,* and *Night and Day,* Herschel Daugherty began directing television series in the early 1950s – among them *Biff Baker, U.S.A.* A very active TV director for

Universal Studios, his Universal series included *Alfred Hitchcock Presents, The Alfred Hitchcock Hour, Thriller,* and *The Virginian,* Daugherty directed one of the earliest TV-movies, *Winchester '73.* Other non-Universal series Daugherty directed: *Dr. Kildare, Star Trek, Hawaii Five-O, Bonanza.*

### Director of Photography Brick Marquard

Beginning his career at ZIV-TV in the 1950s, Brick Marquard did a few episodes of *Bat Masterson* in the early '60s, then such 1960s B-pictures as *Castle of Evil* and *Destination Inner Space* before becoming the regular director of photography on the 1966-68 WWII series, *The Rat Patrol.* "Debt of Honor' was his first of two *Brides* episodes.

*Leading Lady Bridget Hanley:* "I knew him. He had a red face. I remember him as being very lively, but he was working all day — it wasn't like there was a lot of interaction. He had a great humor, but that's all I remember."[243]

## Episode #43: "The She-Bear"                    *January 30, 1970*

"Sometimes a marriage dies even before you know it's sick."
*Lottie to Molly and Christopher*

Teleplay . . . . . . . . . . . . . . . . . . . . . . . . . . . . . . . . . . . . . . Don Tait and Allen Clare
Story . . . . . . . . . . . . . . . . . . . . . . . . . . . . . . . . . . . . . . . . . . . . . . . . . . Don Tait
Director . . . . . . . . . . . . . . . . . . . . . . . . . . . . . . . . . . . . . . . William F. Claxton
Director of Photography . . . . . . . . . . . . . . . . . . . . . . . . . . . Brick Marquard
Film Editor . . . . . . . . . . . . . . . . . . . . . . . . . . . . . . . . . . . . . . . . . . Asa Clark
Assistant Director . . . . . . . . . . . . . . . . . . . . . . . . . . . . . . . . . . David Hawks
#### Guest Cast
Jack Crosse . . . . . . . . . . . . . . . . . . . . . . . . . . . . . . . . . . . . . .Bob Cummings
Pryor . . . . . . . . . . . . . . . . . . . . . . . . . . . . . . . . . . . . . . . . . . .J.C. Flippen
Evans. . . . . . . . . . . . . . . . . . . . . . . . . . . . . . . . . . . . . . . . . Logan Ramsey
Stanhope . . . . . . . . . . . . . . . . . . . . . . . . . . . . . . . . . . . . . . . Ned Glass
Deckhand . . . . . . . . . . . . . . . . . . . . . . . . . . . . . . . . . . . . Gene Rutherford

*Teaser:* Jeremy, Josh, Stanhope, Jack Crosse.
*Tag:* Clancey, Candy, Biddie, Evans, Jason, Judge, Josh, Lottie.
*Competition: The CBS Friday Night Movie: The Venetian Affair* starring Robert Vaughn, Elke Sommer, and Lucianna Paluzzi; *The Name of the Game,* "The Garden," starring Robert Stack as Dan Farrell, and guest-starring Richard Kiley, Anne Francis, and *Brides* guest Brenda Scott, NBC.
*Notes: HCTB's* first murder mystery and murder trial, with Lottie as the defendant. The victim is her former husband, Jack Crosse. The episode also reveals that Lottie has a daughter named Katherine, and that when Lottie and her husband separated,

she started working in saloons to support herself and her daughter. Her first job was at Schroeder's Beer Parlor and Dance Emporium on the Barbary Coast.

Nighttime scenes of Clancey's ship, and scenes in the darkened Lottie's saloon bring a touch of *film noir* to the episode (as does the story point concerning the smuggling of opium). Given the negative and at times, ugly tone of many a *Rat Patrol*, *Rat*'s regular director of photography, Brick Marquard is the ideal DP for this downbeat episode.

Jay C. Flippen played judges a number of times towards the end of his career; character actor Ned Glass is probably best known for his role as Doc in the 1961 musical, *West Side Story*.

*Story Editor William Blinn:* "Bob Cummings…playing kind of a ne'er-do-well rogue — that came out okay. I suspect that if I had been in charge at the network, I would have said, 'I don't know. If we're gonna do a love story with Lottie and Bob Cummings, I don't know if that addresses the audience that tunes in to see Bobby Sherman and David Soul every week. It was okay — I don't think Bob Cummings at that time was the finest actor Hollywood had to offer. He was excellent in *Kings Row*, but I think if there's a Bob Cummings memorial, this will not be in the time capsule."[244]

## Guest Star Bob Cummings

Studying for an engineer's degree at several colleges, including Carnegie Tech, before deciding to become an actor, Robert Cummings learned his craft at the American Academy of Dramatic Arts. After some early rejections, the Joplin-born Cummings thought his chances of obtaining work in Hollywood might be better were he to pass himself off as British actor Blade Stanhope Conway. The ruse worked. Cummings resorted to the same scheme when he looked for work on Broadway. On that occasion, he was rich Texan Bruce Hutchens. Again, the masquerade was successful.

But it was under his own rather common name of Bob Cummings which really established the actor's reputation. This was due in part to two excellent 1942 features: *King's Row* and *Saboteur*. It was also under the name of Bob Cummings that he played his best-known role: womanizing fashion photographer Bob Collins in *The Bob Cummings Show* (a.k.a. *Love that Bob*).

Bob Cummings played quite a few characters like Bob Collins after this 1950s TV hit. Among them, sleazy Hollywood agent Dan Pierce in 1964's *The Carpetbaggers*, womanizing scientist Dr. Bob McDonald in the 1964-65 sitcom, *My Living Doll*, girl-watching photographer Bob Mitchell in 1967's *Five Golden Dragons*, and beauty pageant host Dan Carson in the 1973 Spelling-Goldberg TV movie, *The Great American Beauty Contest*. Cummings also visited the town of Hooterville, playing the role of award-winning journalist Mort Warner in the January 10, 1970 *Green Acres* episode, "Rest and Relaxation."

*Leading Lady Bridget Hanley:* "I just thought Bob Cummings was wonderful. I knew him from *The Bob Cummings Show*."[245]

*Wardrobe Man Steve Lodge:* "It was a treat to work with Bob Cummings. I had grown up watching his TV shows — he was such a gentleman. I remember telling him the shows I liked on *The Bob Cummings Show* — him playing 'Grandpa,' the two parts."[246]

January 31, 1970 – Joseph Finnigan – TV Teletype Hollywood in *TV Guide* (Vol. 18., No. 5, Issue #879) reveals that Bobby Sherman will be guest-starring on Perry Como's February 22 NBC special. Underneath the listing for the February 6 episode, "Another Game in Town," it is noted that Sherman will be featured in the next week's issue.

February 1970 – Bobby Sherman article in *Tiger Beat;* "Bobby's First Gold Record"
*Tiger Beat* (also pictured is Robert Brown, in costume); Bobby Sherman article in *Screen Stars;* Bobby Sherman article in *Screen Scene;* Bobby Sherman article in *Teen World;* Susan Tolsky tidbit in *Screenland;* Bridget Hanley: You Can Be an Actress," Part 1 – *Tiger Beat* (Hanley on cover, with Bobby Sherman and others); Hanley also in *TV and Movie Screen.*

## Episode #44: "Another Game in Town"          *February 6, 1970*

"I run a dance hall and those are my girls. And the next time anyone in Seattle buys them a drink, it's going to come out of my stock. Oh, but don't worry. If your business gets too bad, I'll be happy to buy you out."
*Patricia Vanderhof to Lottie Hatfield*

"It seems that everything anyone does ends up hurting someone."
*Candy Pruitt to Jeremy Bolt*

Teleplay . . . . . . . . . . . . . . . . . . . . . . . . . . . . . . . . . . . . . . . . . . . . Larry Brody
Story . . . . . . . . . . . . . . . . . . . . . . . . . . . Seymour Friedman and Larry Brody
Director . . . . . . . . . . . . . . . . . . . . . . . . . . . . . . . . . . . . . . . . Louis Antonio
Film Editor . . . . . . . . . . . . . . . . . . . . . . . . . . . . . . . . . . . . . . . . Asa Clark
Assistant Director . . . . . . . . . . . . . . . . . . . . . . . . . . . . . . . . . . David Hawks
*Guest Cast*
Patricia. . . . . . . . . . . . . . . . . . . . . . . . . . . . . . . . . . . . . . . Diahn Williams
Barney . . . . . . . . . . . . . . . . . . . . . . . . . . . . . . . . . . . . . . . Steve Gravers
Billie . . . . . . . . . . . . . . . . . . . . . . . . . . . . . . . . . . . . . . . .Cynthia Hull
Pat's Girls . . . . . . . . . . . . . . . . . . . . . . . . . . . . . . . . . . . Barbara Noonan,
                    Nadia Sanders, Claire Hagen, Roberta Collins

*Teaser:* Clancey, Josh, Barney Alton, Patricia Vanderhof, Pat's girls.
*Tag:* Jason, Patricia, Aaron.

**Competition:** *The CBS Friday Night Movie: Cutter's Trail* starring John Gavin and Nehemiah Persoff; *Hallmark Hall of Fame,* "A Storm in Summer," starring Peter Ustinov, Peter Bonerz, and Marlyn Mason, NBC.

**Photography:** Slow pan over the brides; slow pan over the men in saloon; pan back in other direction, pan over the emporium.

**Notes:** This episode allows Aaron Stempel a romance. That alone makes the episode worthwhile. Aaron has good taste — Patricia Vanderhof is a knockout! First-season semi-regular Cynthia Hull returns as Billie, one of Pat's girls. Co-writer Seymour Friedman was a production supervisor at Screen Gems.

Guest Star Diahn Williams played 'Terry' on the 1963-64 sitcom *Harry's Girls* — co-starring on that series was *HCTB* guest Susan Silo. Henry Beckman, David Soul, and Bobby Sherman all have some great comic moments in this episode. As do Robert Biheller and Susan Tolsky.

*"Another Game in Town"* — *Diahn Williams in a bit of comic cheesecake.*

*Story Editor William Blinn:* "My guess is Seymour came into Bob Claver's office, and said, 'You know. Have you guys thought about doing such and such story where such and such happens? You could shoot it all on the ship or shoot it all here, and Claver would say, 'You know, that's not such a bad idea,' and passed it on to me, and I passed it on to Larry Brody, and he and Seymour shared story credit. Good ideas come from a whole bunch of places, and wherever you find one, you go with it, absolutely."[247]

*Episode Co-Writer Larry Brody:* "I've written and produced thousands of TV episodes since that time. Frankly, I have absolutely no memory of what that episode was about. The story, however, would have been Seymour's because what I do remember is that Bill called me in one day and handed me a *Brides* script that Seymour had written on spec. He was the head of production for Screen Gems. Now that I think about it, I also remember the name of Seymour's version: 'Why Buy a Cow?' Funny that would come back to me.

"I was hired to rewrite him, which I did. And then Bill rewrote me. This is common in TV and films. And although it might seem strange to have a new writer rewriting someone who's been around, that's also common. I think it's because newbies work cheaper. At least, I did back in the day."[248]

February 7, 1970 – *TV Guide* (Vol. 18, No. 6, Issue #880): Bobby Sherman, Master of the Big Bounce – The Wheel Takes Another Turn" by A.S. "Doc" Young.

## Episode #45: "Candy and the Kid"                    *February 13, 1970*

"I'm a man who goes after what he wants, Candy."
*Richard "Rafe" Holliday to Candy Pruitt*

Writer . . . . . . . . . . . . . . . . . . . . . . . . . . . . . . . . . . . . . . . . . . . . Daniel Ullman
Director . . . . . . . . . . . . . . . . . . . . . . . . . . . . . . . . . . . . . . . . . . . . Jerry Bernstein
Film Editor . . . . . . . . . . . . . . . . . . . . . . . . . . . . . . . . . . . . . . Norman Wallerstein
Assistant Director . . . . . . . . . . . . . . . . . . . . . . . . . . . . . . . . . .Christopher Morgan
                                    *Guest Cast*
Richard "Rafe" Holliday . . . . . . . . . . . . . . . . . . . . . . . . . . . . . . . . .James Davidson
Drifters . . . . . . . . . . . . . . . . . . . . . . . . . . . . . . . . . . . . . . . . . Ken Tilles, Porter Fowler

*Teaser:* Jeremy, Richard "Rafe" Holliday (the Kid).
*Tag:* Jason, Josh, Aaron, Jeremy, Candy.
*Competition:* The CBS Friday Night Movie: *Hatari, Part II,* starring John Wayne, Elsa Martinelli, and Red Buttons; *The Name of the Game,* "Tarot," starring Gene Barry as Glenn Howard, and guest-starring Jose Ferrer, William Shatner, David Carradine, and Bethel Leslie, NBC.
*Photography:* Rafe out riding horse, encounters Christopher and Molly; Sheriff Rafe out making the rounds in Seattle; long shot of Candy and Jeremy; final shot — Rafe riding horse at sunset.
*Notes:* A very "western" episode, making great use of exteriors, "Candy and the Kid" is a somewhat sympathetic character study of a notorious outlaw who has the potential to become a productive, law-abiding citizen. Besides playing one of the two title characters in this episode, actor James Davidson earns himself a special place in *HCTB* history: he gets his own musical theme — one which would not be used again.

*Story Editor William Blinn:* "I hated it. Bridget was good, and Bobby was good. It was up there with "Marriage: Chinese Style." It was such a traditional western deal. I don't know, did we do it better than *Gunsmoke?* No. Better than *Bonanza?* No. If we couldn't do it better than the other shows that were doing those kinds of shows, then I don't think we should have been doing them. But I also suspect that it was towards the end of the year, and everyone had their tongue hanging down around their knees, and 'Let's see if we can try to pull this thing together.'"[249]

*Leading Lady Bridget Hanley:* "I remember being a little nervous because other than Jeremy, Candy hadn't had any great romances. We got on great — he [Davidson] was a very generous actor. We felt very comfortable with each other and able to act together well, I thought. I had so much to do in that episode. I was kind of thrilled with him. 'Candy and the Kid' was fun because it was about Candy and the Kid. Each one had its own charm for me, and was a delight to be in."[250]

*"Candy and the Kid" — left to right: Hoke Howell, Bridget Hanley, and guest James Davidson.*

## Writer Dan Ullman

Daniel Ullman had written a number of western film screenplays (*Cherokee Uprising, Outlaws of Texas, Kansas Territory*) and television western episodes (*Adventures of Jim Bowie, Trackdown*) before moving into the science-fiction and adventure genres in the 1960s. Writer of *The Fugitive* episode, "Wife Killer," in which Dr. Richard Kimble obtains positive proof that the one-armed man murdered his wife, Ullman also wrote the amusingly titled *Wild Wild West* "The Night of the Flying Pie Plate," *The Felony Squad*, "Hit and Run Run Run" (a favorite of *Felony* series producer Philip Saltzman), and *The Rat Patrol*, "The Bring 'Em Back Alive Raid" (featuring *HCTB* guest William Schallert as a Josef Mengele-type doctor). Ullman's sixth-season *Mission: Impossible*, "The Miracle," was another offbeat story. In "The Miracle," the Impossible Missions Force convinces "mark" Joe Don Baker (a hit man with a lifelong hatred of religion) that he's had a heart transplant — from a priest!

## Episode #46: "Two Worlds"                    *February 20, 1970*

"Sometimes, Callie, things are worth the pain."
*Joshua Bolt to Callie Marsh*

Writers. . . . . . . . . . . . . . . . . . . . . . . . . . . . . . . Jack Miller and Shelley Mitchell
Director. . . . . . . . . . . . . . . . . . . . . . . . . . . . . . . . . . . . . . . . . . Louis Antonio
Film Editor . . . . . . . . . . . . . . . . . . . . . . . . . . . . . . . . . . . . . . . . . Asa Clark
Assistant Director . . . . . . . . . . . . . . . . . . . . . . . . . . . . . . . . . . David Hawks

*Guest Cast*

Jacob . . . . . . . . . . . . . . . . . . . . . . . . . . . . . . . . . . . . . . . . . . . . .Gene Evans
Haynie. . . . . . . . . . . . . . . . . . . . . . . . . . . . . . . . . . . . . . . . Ronald Feinberg
Callie. . . . . . . . . . . . . . . . . . . . . . . . . . . . . . . . . . . . . . . . . . . . Meg Foster
Dr. Bryce . . . . . . . . . . . . . . . . . . . . . . . . . . . . . . . . . . . . . . . . Don Hanmer
Goff. . . . . . . . . . . . . . . . . . . . . . . . . . . . . . . . . . . . . . . . . . Rance Howard
Hawkins . . . . . . . . . . . . . . . . . . . . . . . . . . . . . . . . . . . . . . .John Czingland

*Teaser:* Jacob, Callie, Jason, Josh, Jeremy.
*Tag:* Josh, Candy, Callie, Mr. Hawkins, Lottie, Jeremy, Jason.
*Competition: The CBS Friday Night Movie: The Challengers,* starring Darren McGavin, Anne Baxter, Richard Conte, and Sal Mineo; *The Name of the Game,* "The King of Denmark," starring Tony Franciosa as Jeff Dillon, and guest-starring Joseph Cotten, Margaret Leighton, and Noel Harrison, NBC.
*Photography:* Tracking shot with Josh and Callie walking in woods; tracking shot on board Clancey's ship and down from mast; pull-away from Josh and Callie; tracking shot as Josh and Callie leave Clancey's ship and walk through streets; Callie regaining sight; shot on building moving down to Callie; shot on flowers; shot on board Clancey's ship from cabin to deck where table awaits Callie; tracking shot as ship returns to Seattle; pan across dormitory — brides looking down; Callie's first glimpse of Seattle — littered with broken crates, boxes, etc.; tracking on lake-trees reflected in water, and up to Josh and Callie; close-up on Callie tearing off her glasses after she's unintentionally shot her father; long crane shot of Marsh cabin-Josh arriving, trappers leaving; moving in for close-up on Josh and Callie; tracking and pan on Clancey and ship; long shot of Callie and Bolts.
*Notes:* The most moving episode of the series, "Two Worlds" vividly illustrates to the viewer the peculiar joys of being blind, and the disadvantage of being able to see. As her sighted father, Jacob Marsh, knows, having always been blind, Callie Marsh has never been witness to the destruction her fellow men can create, and the pain people can inflict. So Jacob is greatly opposed to Joshua Bolt taking his daughter to San Francisco for an operation which will remove her cataracts. Josh and his brothers (and the viewer, for that matter) are puzzled by Jacob's attitude.
    While Callie's introduction to her new "sighted" world in San Francisco is wonderful and happy and somewhat fits the storybook picture she has painted in her mind, ironically it is when she, Clancey, and Josh return to Seattle that the ugliness of the

sighted world sets in. Surveying a town square littered with broken crates, boxes, and so forth (the result of the booze-hungry trappers' looting of Clancey's just-returned ship), a dejected Callie remarks to Josh, "I didn't think that it would look like this." Hugo Montenegro's score for this scene is highly appropriate.

Callie is similarly disappointed when she sees the cabin where she and her father Jacob live. "When I couldn't see," Callie explains to Josh, "my poppa and me, we lived in a castle, and it was big and full of secret places. But it ain't like that at all. It's dark, poor, dirty. My poppa — he don't look anything like I thought he would."

Later accidentally killing her father when the two are attacked by trappers, Callie is so horrified by the sight of him dying, she no longer wants to look at her new world. "You're ugly and the whole world's ugly," she tells Josh. "I don't want to see any more. I should have stayed blind." Having done so much to bring to Callie Marsh the gift of sight, it's up to Joshua Bolt to make Callie fully understand the joys sight can bring.

As Callie, Meg Foster hits just the right note each and every time. David Soul is equally excellent in his very sensitive and measured portrayal; Gene Evans is good as Jacob, and Rance Howard's Goff makes for a very funny trapper. The scene in which he and Jeremy discuss why he stuck his hand in the spittoon is priceless. As for director Lou Antonio, his work is absolutely amazing.

Though he is billed as co-writer with Shelley Mitchell, given his previous episode, "Lorenzo Bush," and his third and last *Brides*, "Two Women," it's likely that the majority of this story, and, in particular, the character of Callie Marsh, comes from Jack Miller.

*Story Editor William Blinn:* "I liked it because I liked Meg so much, she was just a compelling presence; she was fun to work with. I enjoyed it. My guess is it was kind of a community idea, 'What can we do? What can we do? What can we do?' three or four people in the office coming up with this thing. I was and am so taken with Meg Foster, I recall liking it a lot; I'm probably not very objective about it. I liked Jack, always. I guess one of the reasons why I liked it, and again, this is personal prejudice — or personal something…I have been dodging visual problems all my life; I've managed to do it okay — but I can't tell you how many operations, and that's been like since I was ten. So I suspect anytime a show comes along and it deals with visual failings, I'm automatically, 'Oh, that sounds interesting,' because I've gone through a little bit of it, not a lot, nothing in a tragic way, but in a mental way, surely explored what that's gotta be like. So I suppose that's a prejudice that leads me to maybe like an episode that normally I might not — but again, Meg Foster's such a good actress."[251]

*Director Lou Antonio:* "Meg Foster had these [light blue] eyes, and they were so cheap at Screen Gems that they wouldn't show the dailies in color except maybe for a twenty-second swatch of color from the master so the cameraman could check the color. The rest [of the dailies] were in black and white. They saved the print cost. Well, Meg Foster's…those blue eyes — in black-and-white, [they] made her look like a beautiful space person. They were like slate-bright gray eyes — most unusual thing I've ever seen. She was just beautiful — the black and white really showed her off.

"Now Robert Brown…in those days there were no cell phones, and they had a phone — always had a phone on the set, up against the wall, and Robert Brown would always be on the dadgum telephone when we were ready because, 'Okay. We're ready!' And he'd be across the sound stage. 'Okay, just a minute. I'm on the phone.' So, we would wait, and he would leisurely walk across the stage and get into the scene. I said to the script supervisor one day, 'Look, do me a favor. I'm gonna see how much time he costs us, getting off the phone, and onto the set, in a day's time.' As I recall, it was forty-eight minutes. I said, 'That's close-ups. That's coverage that I'm losing,' and so I dropped…when I couldn't…I would just not shoot his close-ups — to teach him a lesson. The producers of course came roaring down on me — that guy, not just Claver, [but] Paul Witt. They used to call him 'The Shiv.' He always had a knife out for somebody. I said, 'Look,' and I told them the story. They said, 'Well, Lou…' Well, let's just put it this way — I was never invited back to do another one. The star is the star. I thought I was doing them a favor in teaching him a lesson. Well…they taught me a lesson."[252]

*Series Semi-Regular Karen Carlson:* "I do remember her [Foster] having the most amazing eyes — those eyes were just unbelievable. That was a special show." [253]

## Guest Star Meg Foster

Making her onscreen debut in *Here Come the Brides,* "Two Worlds," Meg Foster soon became a favorite at Quinn Martin Productions, guest-starring three times on *Barnaby Jones* and *The FBI,* twice on *Dan August,* and once on *Cannon* and *The Streets of San Francisco.* Very active in other crime-dramas of the 1970s, Foster was then seen as Hester Prynne in a 1979 television adaptation of Nathaniel Hawthorne's *The Scarlet Letter.* She followed that by playing Katrina Van Tessel in a 1980 TV version of the Washington Irving short story, *The Legend of Sleepy Hollow.* Although she was the actress who originated the role of Detective Christine Cagney in the hit police series, *Cagney & Lacey,* Foster was soon replaced by Sharon Gless; the powers that be thought Gless was more "feminine"! Following this setback, Meg Foster continued to work as a television series guest star; she also appeared in movies.

*Leading Lady Bridget Hanley:* "All I can remember are her eyes. We all adored her. I remember her so strongly, and we would re-meet on other occasions — just socially, or just run into each other. But I remember not being able to take my eyes away from her eyes, ever. They were deep — I've never seen a human being with those eyes. So I guess that's what I remember about that episode with her. She was gracious and fun and funny — and we had a great time. She was like one of the girls, but the eyes! I just couldn't help — you almost had to put on dark glasses.

"I think they — David and Meg — had a great chemistry together. I think it was very platonic between them, but I think it was very fabulous between them as actors."[254]

*Series Regular Susan Tolsky:* "Meg Foster! The gal with the scary blue eyes! Meg was getting to be very pronounced at that time — she was working a lot. She was just an amazing-looking person with those eyes — you couldn't look away. I don't remember her being really warm or approachable. I don't remember that. She could have been, but I could have been just intimidated. She had such a mysterious demeanor about her. Her eyes were astonishing! I've never seen anybody with eyes like that. So I don't remember going, 'Oh! Let's go get some coffee together.' I don't remember that. I don't remember a real approachability with her."[255]

*Trivia:* Callie wears the same dress that Dr. Wright wore in "A Crying Need." When she is wearing the dress, Callie is going from Seattle to San Francisco; when Dr. Wright wears the dress, she is coming from San Francisco to Seattle.

## Episode #47: "To the Victor"          *February 27, 1970*

"Telly and Bolts now on opposite sides of the middle of the roads."
Telly Theodakis to Jason Bolt

Writer . . . . . . . . . . . . . . . . . . . . . . . . . . . . . . . . . . . . . . . . . . . . . .Skip Webster
Director. . . . . . . . . . . . . . . . . . . . . . . . . . . . . . . . . . . . . . . . . . . .Virgil Vogel
Film Editor . . . . . . . . . . . . . . . . . . . . . . . . . . . . . . . . . . . . . . . . . Asa Clark
Assistant Director . . . . . . . . . . . . . . . . . . . . . . . . . . . . . . . . . . . . Mel Swope

### Guest Cast
Telly. . . . . . . . . . . . . . . . . . . . . . . . . . . . . . . . . . . . . . . . . . . . . . . . .Lou Antonio
Stephanos . . . . . . . . . . . . . . . . . . . . . . . . . . . . . . . . . . . . . . . Michael Baseleon
Astasia. . . . . . . . . . . . . . . . . . . . . . . . . . . . . . . . . . . . . . . . . . . .Arlene Martel
Jenkins. . . . . . . . . . . . . . . . . . . . . . . . . . . . . . . . . . . . . . . . . . . .James Sikking
Fowler . . . . . . . . . . . . . . . . . . . . . . . . . . . . . . . . . . . . . . . . . . . Eddie Ryder
Petros. . . . . . . . . . . . . . . . . . . . . . . . . . . . . . . . . . . . . . . . .Shephard Sanders

*Teaser:* Astasia, Lottie, Biddie, Josh, Ben, Stephanos, Telly, Jason, Clancey.
*Tag:* Jason, Josh, Stephanos, Clancey, Telly, Jeremy, Candy, Biddie.
*Competition: The CBS Friday Night Movie-Peyton Place-Part II* starring Lana Turner, Diane Varsi, and Hope Lange; *The Name of the Game*-"The Skin Game," starring Robert Stack as Dan Farrell, and guest-starring Suzanne Pleshette, Charles Drake, Hari Rhodes, and Rossano Brazzi, NBC.
*Notes:* Coming right after the exceptional "Two Worlds," the premise of "To the Victor" seems rather pointless. Reprising the role of Telly Theodakis, Lou Antonio is once again good in the part; as for Arlene Martel, she does what she can with the

rather silly role of Josh's and Stephanos' love, Astasia. An interesting moment in this episode comes when general store owner Ben Perkins shows up in a Confederate Army uniform. Ben is leading a detachment of men some in Union Blue, some in Confederate Gray. They are preparing to do battle with the Greeks.

*Story Editor William Blinn:* "I remember Michael Baseleon very, very well. I thought that was okay. I was initially, I think, wary of continuing the Larry Brody sequel, if you will, but I think Skip did a good job on it, and we tightened it up — Skip tended to be a little loose in terms of construction. I was okay with that."[256]

*Telly Theodakis' Creator Larry Brody:* "[Not being asked to write the sequel] really bummed me out. Made me feel rejected. And I don't think there were any mandatory character creation payments in those days, so I didn't even get a mention or a check for that. I thought I'd failed — and my definition of failure then was disappointing Bill Blinn. When he brought me on to his next show, *The Interns*, I was very relieved."[257]

*Guest Star Lou Antonio:* "They called the character back. Again, six-day shoot, everybody was in a hurry. My character had to ride up on a horse. The horse reared up, and I dismounted. The stuntman said, 'Look, we gotta put a stuntman for when the horse rears up.' I said, 'Naw, I can do it. I'm a horseman.' So, now get this — they used the stuntman in the close-up of rearing it up, and for some reason, put me on for the wide shot. It was just very peculiar."[258]

*Writer Larry Brody on the Episode that never made it to the screen:*

"My favorite [*Brides*] episode was the one that didn't get finished because it had the most *oomph* to it. It was about Jason Bolt befriending a gunfighter who's been hired by Stempel to kill him. Jason and the gunfighter become friends before the gunfighter finds out Jason's the target. Now that I'm telling the story, I know why we could never figure out a satisfactory plot. The primary problem was the guest's and not the star's. When you're paying a star a whole lot of money (and have a ton of stars every week), you want to make sure the episode is about HIM."[259]

February 28, 1970 – WUTR-TV-Channel 20 (Utica, New York) signs on as an ABC affiliate.

Spring 1970 – *Tiger Beat* Spectacular – Bobby Sherman Issue.

March 1970 – Bobby Sherman article in *Tiger Beat;* "*Brides* Canceled!" *Teen Screen;* Bobby Sherman article in *Flip Teen* – Sherman on cover of magazine; "Spend a Day with Bobby on the 'Brides' Set" *Flip Teen;* Bobby Sherman: My New Year's Resolutions" *Flip Teen;* Bobby Sherman article in *Movie Life;* "David Soul – My New

Year's Resolutions"
*Flip Teen;* Robert Brown in *Flip Teen;* Bridget Hanley – *FaVE!* (cover, with Sherman), *Teen Life* (cover, with Sherman), Bridget Hanley: You Can Be an Actress," Pt. 2 – *Tiger Beat;* Hanley in *Screen Stars.*

## Episode #48: "How Dry We Are"     *March 6, 1970*

"It's booze we're after. Come on, let's cast off."
*Captain Clancey to Jeremy Bolt*

Writer . . . . . . . . . . . . . . . . . . . . . . . . . . . . . . . . . . . . . . . Roberta Goldstone
Director . . . . . . . . . . . . . . . . . . . . . . . . . . . . . . . . . . . . . . Nicholas Colasanto
Film Editor . . . . . . . . . . . . . . . . . . . . . . . . . . . . . . . . . . . . . David Berlatsky
Assistant Director . . . . . . . . . . . . . . . . . . . . . . . . . . . . . . Christopher Morgan

*Guest Cast*

Benet . . . . . . . . . . . . . . . . . . . . . . . . . . . . . . . . . . . . . . . . . Alan Oppenheimer
La Fond . . . . . . . . . . . . . . . . . . . . . . . . . . . . . . . . . . . . . . . . Marcel Hillaire
Renee . . . . . . . . . . . . . . . . . . . . . . . . . . . . . . . . . . . . . . . . . Monica Evans
McKay . . . . . . . . . . . . . . . . . . . . . . . . . . . . . . . . . . . . . . . . . Johnny Seven
Tom . . . . . . . . . . . . . . . . . . . . . . . . . . . . . . . . . . . . . . . . . . . Quinn Redeker
Jim . . . . . . . . . . . . . . . . . . . . . . . . . . . . . . . . . . . . . . . . . . . . Lou Robb
Turner . . . . . . . . . . . . . . . . . . . . . . . . . . . . . . . . . . . . . . . . . Timothy Scott

*Teaser:* Lottie, Jeremy, Jason, Josh, Clancey, Benet, loggers, brides.

*Tag:* Lottie, Jeremy, Candy, Clancey, Aaron, Jason, Josh, Biddie, people of Seattle.

*Competition: The CBS Friday Night Movie: The Sandpiper* starring Elizabeth Taylor, Richard Burton, Eva Marie Saint, and Charles Bronson; *The Name of the Game,* "Man of the People," starring Gene Barry as Glenn Howard, and guest-starring Vera Miles, Fernando Lamas, Robert Alda, Jackie Coogan, James Gregory, *Brides* guest Gene Evans, and Patricia Medina, NBC.

*Notes:* A funny tale of the folks in Seattle being taken to the cleaners by a group of liquor-supplying con artists. First they supply it, then they steal it. Great comic moments from both Henry Beckman and Susan Tolsky. And a good bit of the action takes place in Canada. Returning guest Alan Oppenheimer plays the head of the con artists.

*Story Editor William Blinn:* "Roberta Goldstone was Bob Claver's secretary — I could be wrong about that. But a lot of times you'll have people work on a show, and they're in the office, or in the editing room, or wherever the heck it may be. After a while they become so immersed, they go, 'You know. What would be fun to do…' And, the best *Fame* episode I did was based on an idea one of our editors came up with — it was a sensational episode.

"My recollection [concerning "How Dry We Are"] is that Roberta came in very... she almost backed into the office. She said, 'Can I pitch you a story idea?' She was a sweet lady, and very bright. I said, 'Well, let's take a shot, and see what happens,' and that's what happened."[260]

*Series Regular Susan Tolsky:* "Oh, Gosh — Swack and I giggled and laughed on that one — they hit me with Fuller's Earth. The still exploded. They put all this Fuller's Earth on me, and then they said, 'Okay, we're gonna hit your face.' You had to squeeze your eyes and purse your mouth when they hit your face so it looked like you closed your eyes. I said, 'Let me know before...' and they didn't hear that I was saying something — they hit me in the face. My mouth was open, and my eyes were open. So, I had a mouth full of Fuller's Earth. I went, 'Let's try this again now, with my mouth shut!'"[261]

March 7, 1970 – *TV Guide*, Vol. 18, No. 10 – Issue #884 – underneath Friday program listing for *Brides,* it's noted that series regular Mark Lenard will be profiled in the next week's issue. Sad news – In "The Doan Report," Richard K. Doan notes that *Brides* is one of nine ABC-TV series to be canceled. Also, WXOW-TV-Channel 19, in La Crosse, Wisconsin (a satellite sister of Madison, Wisconsin station WKOW-TV, Channel 27) signs on with ABC.

## Episode #49: "Bolt of Kilmaron"                    *March 13, 1970*

"What does a man do when he's head of the clan and
his land is no more? Where does he go?"
*Uncle Duncan Bolt to Jason Bolt*

Writer . . . . . . . . . . . . . . . . . . . . . . . . . . . . . . . . . . . . . . . . . . . . D.C. Fontana
Director . . . . . . . . . . . . . . . . . . . . . . . . . . . . . . . . . . . . . . . . Nicholas Colasanto
Film Editors . . . . . . . . . . . . . . . . . . . . . . . . . . . David Berlatsky, John B. Woelz
Assistant Director . . . . . . . . . . . . . . . . . . . . . . . . . . . . . . Christopher Morgan
*Guest Cast*
Duncan . . . . . . . . . . . . . . . . . . . . . . . . . . . . . . . . . . . . . . . . . . . Denver Pyle
Jenkins. . . . . . . . . . . . . . . . . . . . . . . . . . . . . . . . . . . . . . . . . . . . . Bobby Hall

*Teaser:* Candy, Biddie, Uncle Duncan, Jason, Josh, Jeremy.
*Tag:* Uncle Duncan, Lottie, Clancey, Biddie, Candy, Jeremy, Aaron, Josh, Jason.
*Competition:* The *CBS Friday Night Movie: Two on a Guillotine* starring Connie Stevens, Dean Jones, and Cesar Romero; *Hallmark Hall of Fame,* "Neither Are We Enemies," starring Van Heflin, Kristoffer Tabori, J.D. Cannon, Ed Begley, Kate Reid, and Leonard Frey, NBC.
*Notes: Star Trek* story editor Dorothy C. Fontana's one and only *Brides* opens a new direction for the series: stories about the Bolts' relatives. By this time, viewers had

met and gotten to know Candy's grandfather and, of course, her younger brother and sister were semi-regular characters on the show. The audience had met Lottie's former husband, and learned of her daughter; they'd met Aaron's younger sister, Julie, and Clancey's brother, Father Ned. They'd even heard of Biddie's Aunt Irene. Ironically, the only regular characters on the series not to encounter a relative, much less talk about one, (with the exception of their parents), were the lead characters Jason, Joshua, and Jeremy Bolt. Thanks to D.C. Fontana, this episode remedied that oversight.

During the course of this story, viewers learn that Kilmaron has been the home of the Bolt clan for six hundred years. Had Uncle Duncan not lost the land, Kilmaron would have gone to Jason. There's also a reference to Candy's grandfather visiting last year. (i.e., last season.)

With this episode, *HCTB* writer Michael Fisher comes on board as the series' new story consultant. This, plus the three remaining shows Fisher did, suggests that had *Here Come the Brides* been renewed for a third season, there would have been an even greater emphasis on drama. Given her view of *Brides*, Dorothy C. Fontana might well have written more episodes for the series.

According to one of the *Brides* fans, a person doesn't play the Highland Bag Pipes seated. Nor does one play them on a stagecoach, or indoors.

*Former Story Editor William Blinn:* "I think Mike Fisher worked in *Bonanza*. Mike's dad was also a writer — Steve Fisher. Steve Fisher was the guy who wrote *I Wake Up Screaming*, and Steve, I think, was working at Paramount doing a lot of the B-westerns for A.C. Lyles, and that may have been how I got to know Mike. Mike was younger than I was.

"My offhand memory is that I was writing the pilot for *The Interns* — Screen Gems at that time was making a big push to try to get into the hour field, and they had a feature that had come out; I think it was called *The New Interns*. Anyway they wanted to try to spin that off into a TV series, which lasted a year — too many leads, just got confused, which was really my fault. When I went off, they brought Mike to fill in."[262]

*Episode Writer Dorothy C. Fontana:* "Bill Blinn [and the others] invited me in to pitch stories when the show first went into production. I pitched a number of them, and they finally chose the one about the Bolts' uncle coming from Scotland to mess up their lives. There was a screening so we could see who the characters were, how the actors portrayed them, etc. As I recall, it was not an individual screening for me alone, but rather for a number of writers who were possibles for assignment."

Fontana's decision to do a story about the Bolt brothers' uncle "was a last second pitch," she explains. "I had exhausted the other stories I came to pitch, which weren't thrilling the producers, so I pulled a rabbit out of a hat and suggested the uncle who came from Scotland, having lost everything there, and trying to throw his influence around in the new world with his nephews who were building a new business and a new life. I am part-Scottish on my mother's side of the family. Norman (her mother's maiden name) is a sect of the clan MacLeod." (Fontana did not know, nor did anyone tell her, that star Robert Brown was of Scottish descent.)

Writer Fontana was very happy with the production, and casting of the episode, and very pleased with the show that aired. "I usually write about love — between family, between friends, between people and pets, etc," she says. "I don't think humans function very well without that element in their lives. I felt it was well produced, and well acted; it was a story about family relationships that came across. Denver Pyle was a legend as a character actor, and he played the role to the hilt — and to perfection. All the characters had their moments, and I thought it had dramatic impact with some good comedy moments. [Moreover] at the time there were not many shows with an abundance of female characters. Certainly it was nice to be able to write for them and not just the strong leading men! [Writing for the show] was a terrific experience. I enjoyed it immensely. I did not meet any of the *Brides* cast. Most freelance writers didn't get to go to the set — on any show. Not just this one."

(One of the curious things about *Here Come the Brides* is that many of its fans are also fans of *Star Trek*. The two shows had quite a lot in common.) "There was always a sense of family on *Star Trek* because the crew was so well-knit," states Fontana. (That same sense of family existed on *Brides*.) The actors conveyed that well, and we writers wrote about it often. The U.S. Northwest was a frontier, as was space. Any time you venture out onto a new frontier, there is danger, there is opportunity, and there are stories to tell."[263]

*Leading Lady Bridget Hanley:* "We were singing a song — we were all around the table. We were singing this song, and it was way up high. I said, [to director Nicholas Colasanto], 'Nick, could I sing this lower?' And he just blew. And I found out later that he blew because I asked him three or four times and he didn't pay any attention to me. I didn't want to ruin the shot.

"Anyway he thought I meant quieter. And he finally said, 'No, goddammit!' — something like that. He just laid into me. Laid into me, and Robert, Bobby, and David confronted him later. They said, 'How dare you! How dare you treat our friend like that!' That was just a misunderstanding, but it was very hard. He was just mercurial as hell. Talk about 'gusto.' He had more than his share. He was the only director that ever blew up at me."[264]

*Series Semi-Regular Robert Biheller:* "I didn't want to be around Colasanto. My friend, Dal Jenkins, he did one of the *Brides* [the-earlier aired, "The Road to the Cradle"] — he was out on the set. Nicholas saw him and was intrigued. He got Dal's name and hired him; did a show with Dal. Dal reminded me that he [Colasanto] carried a riding crop. I don't remember that, but I wouldn't put it past him. He was kind of like Otto Preminger."[265]

## *Guest Star Denver Pyle*

Abandoning a planned career in law to work in the oil fields of Oklahoma (and then moving from that to work on a shrimp boat in Galveston, Texas), former NBC radio studio page Denver Pyle was inspired to become an actor by a mute oilfield co-worker who communicated with others through body language. Studying with such performers as Maria Ouspenskaya, Pyle was soon finding work on the television westerns of Roy Rogers and Gene Autry. Other TV series were to include: *Route 66, Checkmate, Ben Casey, The Virginian, Perry Mason, Bonanza, The Waltons, Cannon, The Family Holvak, Barnaby Jones, Petrocelli.* Among Pyle's motion pictures: *To Hell and Back, The Horse Soldiers, The Alamo, Cheyenne Autumn, Shenandoah, Bonnie and Clyde, Bandolero.* During the run of *Brides*, Pyle was playing Buck Webb on *The Doris Day Show.* Soon after he played the role of Mad Jack on the mid-seventies series, *The Life and Times of Grizzly Adams,* a few years later, Pyle hit the big time — he was cast as Uncle Jesse on the soon-to-be hit series, *The Dukes of Hazzard.*

## *Writer Dorothy C. Fontana:*

"I wanted to become a writer from the time I was eleven years old," states Dorothy (D.C.) Fontana. "I started off writing short stories and wanted ultimately to write novels. I majored in business in high school and took an Associate Arts degree in business at Fairleigh Dickinson University. My first job after college was at Screen Gems [then the TV arm of Columbia Pictures] in New York. When I read my first script there, I decided I could do that. Several months later, I moved to California, found my first job at Revue Studios [now Universal] and approximately eight months after that, sold my first story to television — *The Tall Man.*

"The first four sales I had were to *The Tall Man,*" continues the writer. "My boss, Samuel A. Peeples, was very open to reading any submissions I made and encouraged me greatly, as well as mentoring me in this kind of writing. During that period I also did a script rewrite on *Shotgun Slade* and sold a story to *Frontier Circus* (again Sam Peeples). After that, there was a period of about two years when I could not manage to sell a script. There had been a shift in the types of shows on the air — from half hours to hours and from westerns to more contemporary shows. I also decided that I possibly was being held back by the fact I was a woman, so I changed my credit to 'D.C. Fontana.' (All other scripts/stories had been under Dorothy C. Fontana.) I wrote a spec script for *Ben Casey,* a show I liked, and my agent put it in. The producer, Irving Elman, liked it and bought it. During the period of two years when Gene Roddenberry was making two pilots for *Star Trek,* I got a script assignment on *Slattery's People* (which was canceled before my script could be done) and on *The Road West,* a new hour-long western starring Barry Sullivan (who had also co-starred on *The Tall Man*). These new credits were helpful in establishing me outside of the original arena in which I had worked. I enjoyed working on them all, but especially the contemporary shows, which gave me new experience and a more rounded credits list."

Fontana's involvement with *Star Trek* is "an old story that everyone knows," she says. "I was working at MGM on *The Lieutenant* for the Associate Producer, Del Reisman. Gene Roddenberry was the producer of that show. For a while, while his own secretary was ill, I worked with Gene directly and he came to know that I had written scripts that were produced and that I wanted to become a writer. When he created and sold *Star Trek*, he asked me to come and work as his executive secretary on the show.

"Gene asked me what story I wanted to write when *Star Trek* went into production in 1966," continues the writer. "I chose 'Charlie X.' Then I wrote an original script called 'Tomorrow is Yesterday.' After 'Tomorrow,' I decided I wanted to become a full-time writer, not a secretary, so I left the show. However, Gene called me and gave me an opportunity to rewrite a script that was in trouble. He said if I rewrote it to his satisfaction and NBC's, he would back my hiring as story editor. The script turned out to be 'This Side of Paradise.' Gene liked it, NBC liked it, and I became the show's story editor for the rest of the first season and all through the second season."

Though D.C. Fontana was strongly identified with the science-fiction genre, thanks to the incredible popularity of *Star Trek,* she wrote in many other genres: westerns, crime-drama, medical, etc. "In my mind, there was no difference beyond the genres, plus (again) the tone and style of the shows," says the writer. "*Ghost Story* (which later dropped its host and became *Circle of Fear*) was an anthology show from William Castle. I worked with Jimmy Sangster on both the scripts I did for them, both of which were adapted from short stories. The first one starred the marvelous Helen Hayes, the second was adapted from a short story by my old friend, Harlan Ellison ('Shattered Like a Glass Goblin'). An anthology, of course, has no running characters, so I was free to develop the stories and write the scripts as I chose. 'Earth, Air, Wind and Fire' (adapted from 'Glass Goblin') was shot on my first draft only. I was thrilled that I had accomplished that. Normally, it's a required second draft and a polish as well.

"*Six Million Dollar Man,* for which I did two scripts, was a joy to work for, as Harve Bennett was an excellent producer and knew his show well," continues Fontana. "I worked as story editor on both *Fantastic Journey* and *Logan's Run* for producer Leonard Katzman. That was an excellent experience — again working for a fine producer. Leonard didn't know much about science fiction when he took on *Journey,* but he learned quickly and soon became an expert on the genre. I didn't write any scripts for *Journey* — as story editor my job was to work with writers, develop the scripts and rewrite where needed. We were thrown into production on it very quickly and had to really scramble to keep up the production schedule. My biggest contribution on it was the development of the character of Jonathan Willaway, played by Roddy McDowall. On *Logan,* Leonard again asked me to be story editor, and I felt we had a good series going, except for the fact that both Leonard and I were often over-ruled and rewritten by the executive producers — who claimed they knew nothing about science fiction and since we did, we would be left alone to do the show. Not so — and it hurt us. It also hurt us that CBS kept putting the show on after football and then moved it around without letting the audience know where it would be (i.e. on-air ads, *TV Guide* ads, etc.) It was too bad that it was canceled, as I thought it should have had a much longer run.

Like so many others who worked for Quinn Martin, Dorothy C. Fontana never met the producer. "I worked primarily for Bill Yates on *Streets* and *The Runaways,*" she says. "John Wilder was the producer on the first *Streets* I did, while Bill was Associate

Producer (as I recall). On the other two scripts I did for *Streets,* Bill was the producer. Both men were wonderful to work with — smart, good notes for changes and fixes, good guides to understanding the show. *Runaways* was a single script assignment and the series did not last long. I did like writing the script for it — but *Streets* was more fun. How can you beat writing for actors like that?? As I recall, I only did a story for *Superstar."*[266]

As of this writing, Dorothy C. Fontana is still working in the business.

March 14 – *TV Guide* – Vol. 18, No. 11, Issue #885: When is a Villain Not a Villain? – Consider the problem of Mark Lenard" by Leslie Raddatz, pgs. 35-36; TV Crossword – 35 across – Girl on *Here Come the Brides.*

March 16 – 1970 – ABC affiliate WLBW-TV – Channel 10 (Miami/ Fort Lauderdale, Florida) becomes WPLG-TV.

## Episode #50: "Absalom"                           *March 20, 1970*

"You freed that boy yesterday from that cage. He trusts you.
You've earned that trust. There's no one in the whole world
that can help him any more than you can."
*Jason Bolt to his brother, Jeremy*

Writer . . . . . . . . . . . . . . . . . . . . . . . . . . . . . . . . . . . . . . . . . Michael Fisher
Director . . . . . . . . . . . . . . . . . . . . . . . . . . . . . . . . . . . . . . .Paul Junger Witt
Film Editor . . . . . . . . . . . . . . . . . . . . . . . . . . . . . . . . . . . . . . . Asa Clark
Assistant Director . . . . . . . . . . . . . . . . . . . . . . . . . . . . . . . . . . . Mel Swope
Music. . . . . . . . . . . . . . . . . . . . . . . . . . . . . . . . . . . . . . . . . . . .Shorty Rogers
*Guest Cast*
Oliver Tray . . . . . . . . . . . . . . . . . . . . . . . . . . . . . . . . . . . . . . Steve Ihnat
Absalom. . . . . . . . . . . . . . . . . . . . . . . . . . . . . . . . . . . . . . . . Mitch Vogel
Sister Agnes . . . . . . . . . . . . . . . . . . . . . . . . . . . . . . . . . . . . .Mitzi Hoag
Beef. . . . . . . . . . . . . . . . . . . . . . . . . . . . . . . . . . . . . . . . . . . . Mills Watson
1st Logger . . . . . . . . . . . . . . . . . . . . . . . . . . . . . . . . . . . . . . . Don Steele
Howard Tray . . . . . . . . . . . . . . . . . . . . . . . . . . . . Steve Ihnat *(Uncredited)*

*Teaser:* Townspeople, Absalom, Beef, Jeremy, Lottie, Clancey.
*Tag:* Oliver Tray, Absalom, Jason, Josh, Jeremy.
*Competition: The CBS Friday Night Movie: Rio Conchos* starring Richard Boone; *The Name of the Game,* "Echo of a Nightmare" starring Robert Stack as Dan Farrell, and guest-starring Arthur Hill and Ricardo Montalban, NBC.
*Photography:* Flashback to Absalom with his late father; eating at table in flashback; eating at Lottie's table in flash-forward to present; moving in for close-up on

Jason and Clancey on board Clancey's ship; Jason voice-over as Jeremy and Absalom are shown; pan from Sister Agnes to Absalom; moving in for close-up on Absalom; night scene of Jeremy and Tray walking; nighttime scene of Bolt cabin (this particular angle on the cabin was never presented before in the series); shot of Absalom and Jeremy from bunk bed; shot on memento being looked at by Absalom; crane shot on Absalom and Jeremy in cabin; the musical montage featuring Absalom, Jeremy, Candy, Molly, and Christopher; shot with Jason and Josh, back to camera, the two looking at Jeremy, Christopher, and Candy; nighttime sequence of Jeremy leaving Bolt cabin, riding out of Seattle, then through forest to Absalom's cabin; Jeremy finding Absalom in cabin — Jeremy in light, Absalom in dark; hand-held camera on Jeremy and Absalom fighting; slow motion when Absalom clouts Jeremy with log upon mistaking Jeremy for his father; Jeremy riding away, then Absalom crying out, "Amen"; Jeremy and Absalom returning in dark; Absalom waving goodbye to Bolts.

**Notes:** One of Bobby Sherman's favorite episodes, "Absalom" features strong performances from both Sherman and Mitch Vogel as the mute Absalom. The sequence in which Absalom confuses Jeremy with his late father is well edited by *Brides* most frequent film editor, Asa Clark. Vogel joins the small band of *Brides* guests who gets his own musical theme.

The song performed by Bobby Sherman, "Take a Giant Step" was on the very first Monkees album; Sherman's version of the song is quite different. According to Mitch Vogel's conversation with *Brides* fan Kim, when he was smashing up the furniture, etc. in the Bolt cabin, there was one chair which wouldn't break — it took a number of takes before it did. Vogel found playing a mute very difficult.

Like the previous episode, this story provides further details about the Bolt family — in this case, the pain Jeremy went through during the many years he stuttered.

Jeremy's way of teaching Absalom how to talk is quite fascinating — when he says a word to Absalom, such as "chair," he points at the chair, at the same time he puts Absalom's hand on his throat. That way the boy can feel the vibration of Jeremy's throat when Jeremy says the word, "chair." Once he's done this, Jeremy then puts Absalom's hand on Absalom's own throat and repeats the word, "chair." By watching Jeremy's lips when he says the word, "chair," the deaf and mute Absalom begins learning how to form the word; through the vibration in his throat, he will know when he says the word correctly.

The panicked Absalom's later crying out the word, "Amen," in the scene in which Jeremy rides away from the Tray's cabin, is yet another example of *Here Come the Brides'* very good continuity. As revealed in the first-season's "A Man and His Magic," "Amen" is the word Jeremy could not say when standing at his mother's grave; it was at that moment when Jeremy began stuttering.

*Leading Lady Bridget Hanley on Mitch Vogel:* "He was just adorable. We've seen each other off and on. Wow, to be that talented! A lot of people went right over my head. I didn't watch much television."[267]

*Series Semi-Regular Eric Chase:* "We went to lunch with him a few times; he was a soft-spoken kid, and very bright, and knew his job, and did his job. Kind of a fun guy to hang out with. It seemed like people who came on were professional and courteous."[268]

Brides *guest Mitch Vogel with Rupert Crosse in the Steve McQueen Cinema Center Films feature,* The Reivers.

March 21, 1970 – *TV Guide* – Vol. 18, No. 12, Issue #886 – 37 across – TV Crossword – Robert Brown's TV Role; answer to TV Crossword of March 14 – 35 Across – Answer: Candy.

## Episode #51: "The Last Winter"     *March 27, 1970*

*Jason:* Is your death more important than the life of a young man?
*Old Indian:* Your brother's life means nothing to me.

"You don't care about Jeremy. I don't care about your customs."
*Candy Pruitt to Old Indian*

"How can we get a dead man to talk?"
*Jason Bolt to his brother, Josh*

Writer . . . . . . . . . . . . . . . . . . . . . . . . . . . . . . . . . . . . . . . . . . . . . . . . Tim Kelly
Director. . . . . . . . . . . . . . . . . . . . . . . . . . . . . . . . . . . . . . . . . . . . . . . . Jim Hogan

Film Editor . . . . . . . . . . . . . . . . . . . . . . . . . . . . . . . . . . Norman Wallerstein
Assistant Director . . . . . . . . . . . . . . . . . . . . . . . . . . . . . .Christopher Morgan
*Guest Cast*
Ma Oates. . . . . . . . . . . . . . . . . . . . . . . . . . . . . . . . . . . . . . . . . Jeanette Nolan
Junior. . . . . . . . . . . . . . . . . . . . . . . . . . . . . . . . . . . . . . . . . . . Zooey Hall
Old Indian. . . . . . . . . . . . . . . . . . . . . . . . . . . . . . . . . . . . . . .Richard Hale
Eben . . . . . . . . . . . . . . . . . . . . . . . . . . . . . . . . . . . . . . . . . . . Joshua Bryant
Magistrate . . . . . . . . . . . . . . . . . . . . . . . . . . . . . . . . . . . . . . . .Bill Zuckert
Phelps . . . . . . . . . . . . . . . . . . . . . . . . . . . . . . . . . . . . . . . . .Robert Foulk
Drummer. . . . . . . . . . . . . . . . . . . . . . . . . . . . . . . . . . . . . . . . . Bart La Rue

*Teaser:* Biddie, Phelps, Drummer, Jeremy, Junior, Ken, patrons in Lottie's saloon.

*Tag:* Old Indian, Jeremy, Josh, Jason.

*Competition: The CBS Friday Night Movie: Where the Boys Are* starring Connie Francis, George Hamilton, Yvette Mimieux, Paula Prentiss, and Jim Hutton; *The Name of the Game,* "Jenny Wilde is Drowning," starring Tony Franciosa as Jeff Dillon and guest-starring Pamela Franklin, Frank Gorshin, Gavin MacLeod, and Ann Prentiss, NBC.

*Photography:* hand-held camera work during some of the fight between Jeremy and Junior, shot of Jason and Josh walking; shot on table in the Oates cabin; shot from totem pole; final scene — long shot of the three Bolt brothers watching Old Indian walk away.

*Notes:* Unit production manager Jim Hogan's one and only *Brides* as a director, "The Last Winter" is, according to the story, that time in an old Indian's life when his tribe no longer finds him useful. As a result, (again, according to the story), this Indian leaves the tribe and begins to live out his "last winter." When an Indian enters this phase, he already considers himself dead.

At the time of this story, the old Indian is on his journey to live out his "last winter" when he sees Jeremy standing over the dead body of Phelps — as a result, he can clear Jeremy of the murder charge. But, in asking the Old Indian to come to Seattle and clear Jeremy, Jason, Josh, Candy, and the others run the risk of intruding upon and showing disrespect to the man's customs and religious beliefs. By putting the life of one of the *Brides* characters at risk, "The Last Winter" puts to the test the credo by which the characters on the series have come to live: to respect and honor another's religious beliefs, customs, etc. When Jeremy's life is at stake, just how far will his brothers' and his fiancée's commitment to such respect and honor go?

This episode also allows the series to make amends for its cartoonish portrayal of the American Indian in the previous season's "Wives for Wakando." At one point, Biddie dresses up as an Indian maiden, telling Jason she learned a lot about the American Indian when she was held captive by Wakando and his tribe last year. Because of her "knowledge," Biddie believes she can talk the Old Indian into testifying on Jeremy's behalf. When the Indian learns that the "feast of welcome" Biddie has prepared for him was made with this intention, he is greatly offended. "You have made feast of welcome another white man lie," he tells the young woman.

Guest star Zooey Hall was one of the regulars on television's one and only forty-five minute series — the Aaron Spelling-produced, Rod Serling-created, *The New People* (September 1969-January 1970).

Because of his appearance, guest star Richard Hale was often cast as Native American and Middle Eastern characters. Among two of Hale's more unusual roles: the alien Fred Wilk, Sr. in *The Invaders*, "The Trial," the rapidly aging Philip Sedgewick from *The Wild Wild West*, "The Night of the Sedgewick Curse."

Character actor Robert Foulk is best known for his roles as Hooterville phone company owner, Mr. Roy Trendell, and Mr. Wheeler (father of Eb's intended, Darlene) on *Green Acres*. Other series on which Foulk worked as a semi-regular: *Lassie* (Sheriff Miller) and *Bonanza* (various sheriffs).

*Story Editor William Blinn:* "Tim Kelly [the writer], I think, was from *Gunsmoke*. Jeannette [Nolan] could play a hard type better than anybody. Bobby accused of murder, and the only one who can clear him is an old Indian...sounds like something we shouldn't go to too often."[269]

### Guest Star Jeanette Nolan

Wife of actor John McIntire, mother of actors Tim and Holly McIntire, radio/stage actress Jeanette Nolan made her motion picture debut in the 1948 Orson Welles feature, *Macbeth*. For a time, she performed with Welles' Mercury Theatre troupe. Nolan followed *Macbeth* with the role of Mrs. Hart in the fictionalized Richard Rodgers and Lorenz Hart musical bio, *Words and Music*.

By the early 1950s, the actress was working in television. Her first series role — Annette Deveraux — came in the 1959-60 Earl Holliman western, *Hotel de Paree*. She followed that with the 1963-64 anthology, *The Richard Boone* Show, on which she, Boone and nine other actors (Robert Blake, Lloyd Bochner, Laura Devon, June Harding, Bethel Leslie, Harry Morgan, Ford Rainey, Warren Stevens, and Guy Stockwell) played different characters from week to week. Three years later, Nolan began the semi-regular role of Holly Grainger, wife of Shiloh Ranch owner Clay Grainger (John McIntire) on the long-running series, *The Virginian*.

A year after leaving *The Virginian*, Nolan originated the role of Dirty Sally — a character created by *Brides* writer Jack Miller in the 1971 two-part *Gunsmoke*, "Pike." Three years later, Nolan reprised that role in the short-lived 1974 series, *Dirty Sally*. Among the many series on which the actress guest-starred: *Thriller, The Real McCoys, Combat, Dr. Kildare, Perry Mason, F Troop, The Invaders, Marcus Welby, M.D., My Three Sons, Cade's County, Hec Ramsey, Harry O, The Waltons, Love Boat, Charlie's Angels, Incredible Hulk, Misadventures of Sheriff Lobo, Fantasy Island, Matt Houston, The Golden Girls,* and *Dear John*.

## Writer Tim Kelly

Starting out as a writer, then story consultant, then story editor on the David Dortort western, *High Chaparral,* Tim Kelly began writing film scripts in the 1970s. Among his few features – *Cry of the Banshee, The Brothers O'Toole, Sugar Hill,* and *Black Fist.* Kelly is best known, however, as America's most prolific playwright. His works (which include comedies, dramas, one-acts, mysteries, melodramas, children shows, and musicals) have been performed by New York's Student Ensemble Theatre, Aspen Playwrights' Festival, the Seattle Repertory Company, and countless other theaters around the world. Tim Kelly died in 1998.

April 1970 – Bobby Sherman article in *16 Magazine;* Joan Blondell article in *TV Radio Show;* "HCTB Set Gossip – Headed for Junk Heap?" *Inside TV;* "What's In a Name?"
*16 SPEC;* "My Brother, Bobby," Part 1 – *Tiger Beat;* Bobby Sherman article in *Teen World;* Bobby Sherman/Robert Brown – Gossip concerning fan mail: TV Picture Life"; Bridget Hanley – *FaVE!;* Bridget Hanley: Teen Pin-Up," *FaVE!, 16 SPEC, Teen World, Tiger Beat;* Bridget Hanley: You Can Be an Actress," Part 3 – *Tiger Beat.*

March 28, 1970 – *TV Guide* – Vol. 18, No. 13, Issue #887 – TV Crossword – 37 across – answer: Jason.

April 3, 1970 – episode #52 (the last episode to be produced) airs.

## Episode #52: "Two Women"                                   *April 3, 1970*

"Wait till Seattle sees Miss Emma Peak and Miss Valerie Watkins.
We're two women they won't forget for a while.
Not for a good long while, I sincerely hope."
*Emma Peake to her niece Valerie Watkins*

*Valerie:* Josh. I don't want to hurt you.
*Joshua:* Then don't. I'm asking you to marry me.
*Valerie:* If you'd only said that two days ago.
*Joshua:* What could have happened in two days?
*Valerie:* I don't know how to say it without sounding cruel.

*Jeremy:* There's gotta be an answer, Josh. We just can't tear our family apart.
*Joshua:* It's already been done.

Writer . . . . . . . . . . . . . . . . . . . . . . . . . . . . . . . . . . . . . . . . . . . . . .Jack Miller
Director. . . . . . . . . . . . . . . . . . . . . . . . . . . . . . . . . . . . . . . . .E.W. Swackhamer
Film Editor . . . . . . . . . . . . . . . . . . . . . . . . . . . . . . . . . . . . . . . . . . Asa Clark
Assistant Director . . . . . . . . . . . . . . . . . . . . . . . . . . . . . . . . . . . . . Mel Swope

*Guest Cast*

Emma Peak. . . . . . . . . . . . . . . . . . . . . . . . . . . . . . . . . . . . . . . . . . . . Jane Wyatt
Valerie Watkins . . . . . . . . . . . . . . . . . . . . . . . . . . . Lynda Day (Special Guest Star)

*Teaser:* Clancey, Emma, Valerie.

*Tag:* Josh, Valerie, Jason, Jeremy.

*Competition: Don Knotts' Nice, Clean, Decent, Wholesome Hour* starring Knotts, guests Juliet Prowse and the Establishment, and Special Guest Andy Williams, CBS; *The Name of the Game,* "One of the Girls in Research," starring Gene Barry as Glenn Howard and guest-starring Brenda Vaccaro and *Brides* guests Will Geer and Sheree North, NBC.

*Photography:* Teaser: opening shot — Clancey's boat shrouded in mist (just half of the screen is in mist); pan down from mast to Valerie and Emma

Act One, beginning: Emma, Valerie, and Clancey stepping off ship — mist over Emma, then, montage with Emma voice-over, during which the camera swings from Candy to Valerie. During the Josh and Valerie fall in love sequence, David Soul and Lynda Day do voice-overs as the couple's romance is depicted; Valerie's report to Emma ends Act I.

Act Two: Tracking back and forth at beginning to the scene where Valerie invites Jason to lunch; close-up on Emma as Jason and Valerie leave; swing down from Lottie's sign to Jason and Valerie leaving Lottie's saloon; swing from Josh and Jeremy to Jason as they see Valerie kissing Jason; pull back from Josh as Jason walks up to him and Jeremy, then up and across church to the Peak/Watkins hotel room and move towards and in through window, Emma walking across room as Valerie enters; the "sundowning/wandering" sequence begins with Emma at window, Valerie totally out of focus throughout her scenes with Emma; Emma hearing voices as she wanders off to burned-down Peak House. *(Special Note: The terms "sundowning" and "wandering" will be explained in the author's profile of the Emma Peak character.)*

Act Three, beginning: swing from Josh's finger on candy box and up to him; Josh running from general store over to the Bolt cabin — long shot of this action in distorted angle; Josh leaving Bolt cabin, making way towards Lottie's; long shot: swing up through trees as Jeremy leaves Bolt cabin and begins running up path to logging camp, then down from trees at camp for tracking shot on Aaron as he walks over towards Jason; pan down from staircase in Lottie's, Emma halfway down the stairs, and on to Josh, Jason, and men; pan from Jason, Aaron, and others and up, moving in for close-up on Emma, then down to profile of Jason looking up in Emma's direction as she goes back up stairs.

Act Four: Josh in dark standing up, moving into light, camera moving with him; moving in for close-up on Jason in general store; moving in for close-up on Jason and Jeremy in dark at totem pole; moving in for close-up on Clancey in ship; pulling back from close-up on Jason to two-shot of Jason and Emma; Emma's point of view — Jason blurring out of, then into, focus, and close-up on painting of Jonathan Bolt.

Tag: Pull back on Josh and Valerie, camera on Josh's feet as he bends down, camera moving up with Josh and on him and Valerie; low angle shot on Josh and Valerie as they walk away from Peak's Bluff; pulling back on Jason as Josh and Valerie join him, Josh and Valerie saying their silent goodbyes; swinging up and around Clancey's ship and into wide angle, including shot of town as the Bolt brothers make their way to cabin.

*Notes:* At the time of filming, nobody knew that "Two Women" was to be the last *Brides* episode made. Fortunately, under the direction of E.W. Swackhamer, the episode took the series out in style. Featuring some of the show's most unusual photography, "Two Women" is the only *Brides* episode where the guest cast is all female — Jane Wyatt and Lynda Day George. By this time in their careers, both George (then billing herself as Lynda Day) and Wyatt had made names for themselves as trail-blazing actresses in television. Wyatt's forceful portrayal of Margaret Anderson on the 1954-60 series, *Father Knows Best* began a long run of Screen Gems series where the top billing was virtually always given to women (*The Donna Reed Show, Bewitched, I Dream of Jeannie, Gidget, The Farmer's Daughter*, etc.); she also had the honor of appearing in the very first-aired TV-movie: Universal's *See How They Run* (October 7, 1964).

As for George, 'first' certainly described the bulk of her television work. The actress was among the earliest performers to appear in network television's first attempt at quality children's programming: the 1963-73 *The NBC Children's Theatre*. She had a prominent part in the first fact-based TV-movie — Universal's December 10, 1968 NBC feature, *The Sound of Anger* and was the leading lady in television's first horror picture (NBC/Universal's March 3, 1969 offering, *Fear No Evil*). The following year, George appeared in the flashback-laden *The House on Greenapple Road*. The first of many TV-movies from television great Quinn Martin, *House* had the most unusual running time of any TV-movie ever shown: in its initial broadcast, *House* ran a total of two hours and fifteen minutes (including commercials).

In between her first (and only) two television series as a regular (the September 1970-'71 ABC series, *The Silent Force*, in which she played television's first female expert of disguise, Amelia Cole, and the sixth and seventh seasons of CBS' 1966-73 *Mission: Impossible*, in which she portrayed Casey, TV's *second* female expert of disguise), in March of 1971 Lynda Day George appeared in the back-to-back TV movies, *Cannon* and *The Sheriff*. Back to back because during this time in TV-movie history, there were no other new TV-movies to air between these two features.

The actress's work as a guest star was just as impressive, if not more so. Through series such as *Flipper, Route 66, The Fugitive, The FBI*, and *Bonanza*, George quickly built a reputation as "the series departure actress." She also established herself as a performer specializing in "quirky, complex characters."[270] Such as the harpist who possesses an extraordinary knowledge of WWII British aircraft. Or the previously paralyzed former champion water skier who continues to remain in the wheelchair she no longer needs and harbors strong suicidal tendencies. On another occasion, George had her audience wondering if she was an alien married to another alien, or a human married to another human, or a human married to an alien. (If the latter was true, was George's infant son then part alien?) Then there was the woman who doesn't wish to commit murder, but does. A short time before that, audiences saw the actress as a newly graduated registered nurse who believes she is incapable of handling life-threatening situations. Other memorable roles included: the conceited amateur photographer who flies her own airplane.

Whatever the role, a Lynda Day George television performance was always worth catching. Her portrayal of Valerie Watkins in *Here Come the Brides*, "Two Women," is no exception. The episode gives the actress a rare credit — a "last show of the series" guest shot. George further earns herself a place in *Brides* history by becoming the only guest actress to kiss both Robert Brown and David Soul. George's Valerie is also the only woman in the series to whom Soul's Joshua Bolt proposes marriage.

The scene in which Henry Beckman asks Josh not to break up the Bolt family is a favorite moment for quite a few fans. The Miss Essie theme ("Wish I Knew") plays briefly (and cleverly) in the scene where Aunt Em (as Valerie calls her) confuses Valerie with a woman they both know (or knew) named Frannie.

*Wardrobe Man Steve Lodge:* "[Director of photography] Fred [Jackman] had been around so long — he knew all the tricks. He could make anything look real. Even the shot of Jane Wyatt. Even when she was standing up on the hill, and the wind was blowing, that was on the lagoon set; on the other side of the hill was the Hollywood freeway. I'm sure the cars going by could see her standing up there.

"David loved that show. That made him very happy. Of course. Didn't he get to kiss Lynda? Actors love that — it makes them look like they're masculine, I guess. That was a big deal for David, that episode. It was kind of a dreamy thing. I think that's what it required. I wouldn't have been surprised at all that Robert wasn't happy with that episode. He wanted the show to be about him, that's the way he was then."[271]

*Series Regular Henry Beckman:* "To my knowledge, it was the first time Captain Clancey ever ASKED anything of anyone, rather than demanding it. Where are those wonderful writers who MADE that series — where are they now that we truly need them?"[272]

*Bridget Hanley on David Soul's work with* Brides *guest actresses Meg Foster and Lynda Day George:* "Well, listen. Who wouldn't go for either one of them [Foster and George]? But I have to be wise and say that they went for each other in an artful, artistic sense. Swack, when he was directing David and Lynda, was probably egging them on. I wish I could be Swack or maybe I would be very grateful if I didn't know what was going on in his head."[273]

*Author's note: In order to give the most balanced and objective view of* Here Come the Brides *as possible, I will preface my analysis of "Two Women" (definitely the oddest episode in the entire series) with the comments of story editor William Blinn and the* Brides *fans.*

*Below, ten separate fans comment on the show; following their remarks are the comments of Mr Blinn.*

*Fan #1:* "I've always had such trouble taking in the facts as presented in the Emma Peak episode. It seems like a script written for a different show that had the *Brides* cast penciled in when it didn't sell. No one was in character – and Emma's version of early Seattle was mind-boggling to say the least. But since it was aired, then it has to be true."

*Fan #2:* "I don't accept Emma's version of early Seattle, and I don't think that's illogical, or a denial of the show's canon. I just think the woman is nuts! There 'was' no Seattle forty years before the time period of the episode. It wasn't even called Seattle until 1852, or so. And there was no 'there' there until, what, 1851? I think that the Bolts were the only ones there before the Denny party arrived, and I think Emma's memories are of a town a bit further up or down the coast, where Jonathan visited a few times and caught her eye. Somebody oughtta've said to her, carefully, so as not to set off an insane rage, 'No, honey, you're thinking of Tacoma…'"

*Fan #3:* "Even if you consider this episode a stretch it really showed growth in the characters it involves; Joshua became more than a two-dimensional character used to promote the story line, as happened in many other stories. It also gave all three [Bolts] a chance to grow. There so many subplots in this episode that could provide grist for stories. The writers did a marvelous job in giving us glimpses into the past lives of the Bolt family and their interconnections with the community. I still get chills at the end when the bullet is lodged in Jonathan's picture…and that picture, too, has become important in stories because of this episode. It must have touched more lives than just mine."

*Fan #4:* "I enjoyed 'Two Women' because of its departure. It showed us different traits and that certainly gave us lots to consider in our own stories. It's a very emotional episode, too. I love that. The scene between Josh and Jeremy, as Josh is packing to leave, and Jeremy is in tears. It showed us just how connected these brothers are, and how tender-hearted. I think the whole thing with Valerie and Jason could have been done better, though."

*Fan #5:* "This episode really did throw a monkey wrench into things, didn't it? I do think that woman was a touch n-u-t-s, but it's fun trying to work with the information she tells us.

"For me, the big problem is the forty-year thing. I think if you go back forty years in Seattle's history, you would not find big houses or lavish, posh parties."

*Fan #6: (As the story Fan #6 wrote was based on "Two Women," the fan's take on this episode is given in her description of her story.)*

"As some of you know, Emma is in my story, and I have to deal with this very issue. [Emma Peak's distorted history of Seattle.] If you recall, the Peak house was quite large and at some point burnt down. In my story, Seattle was just getting built up – it had long been a popular spot for trappers and fishermen, but no real settlement until Captain Ambrose Peak moved there with his wife and two daughters. He was drawn to the area because it was a natural harbor and sought to put money into the town to help it grow. Thus, it was Captain Peak's money that caused the livery, trading post and blockhouse to be built.

"Emma was infatuated with Jonathan and her family encouraged it, because compared to the trappers, he was quite the catch. There was a great party one night – Emma referred to it in 'Two Women.' Alas, Jonathan was eager to go home to Scotland to see if his fiancée awaited him and skipped the party in order to gather his things to travel home. He did not bother to explain, until out at sea, he wrote Emma a note of apology.

The Peak house burned that very night. I suspect Emma did it. She had assumed that Jonathan would be announcing their engagement that night. After the fire, the Peaks moved south. (Now, you might be asking just why did Captain Peak choose to put his family in such an odd location, but then again, knowing Emma was a bit touched, one might assume that it either ran in the family or Captain Peak sought a place where she could live her life in peace.)"

*Fan #7:* "'Two Women' had to be the strangest episode of them all. I don't believe any of the characters were acting true to type in that one. How could Jason not have wondered why Valerie planted a big old smacker on him in front of God and everyone? He dismissed it as a kiss for the brother of the man she loves. Sure, as if any of us believed that! Valerie was a wacko, Emma was the chief wacko, and the Bolts were incredibly naïve."

*Fan #8:* I have another chronology question: Emma Peak said that she had left Seattle '41 years ago.' Since *Brides* is sometime in the mid-to-late 1860s, that would put her living there with her family in the 1820s, before there was a Seattle. But even if we ignore that, when the ship comes into port she exclaims to Valerie how much the town has grown, and talks about how 'this used to be there, etc.' As Seattle is pretty small in the show (compared to Tacoma, Auburn, Olympia), imagine how small it would have been when she lived there. Yet her family owned this 'huge' house up on the bluff, they gave fancy parties, and she had dresses shipped in from Paris! This sounds more like the high society life of the East Coast. Is there a logical explanation for all this?"

*Fan #9:* Amen to that! Too bad that was the last episode ever shown. It was too strange...why would Josh believe that Jason was going behind his back after his girl? Why would a seemingly intelligent girl like Valerie go along with her aunt's deluded plans for revenge? Why would Josh break down like that, and try to punch out Jason, in front of the whole gang at Lottie's?"

*Fan #10:* "I've always thought that the 'Great Seattle Fire' was caused by Miss Emma. And that's why she left town…her father shipped her off so she wouldn't be tried and convicted…or institutionalized.

Just one thing, when they spoke of Emma Peak's clothes being from Paris, wasn't the voice-over referring to her wedding dress only that she sent away for to Paris, in her lame presumption that Jonathan was going to marry her? Let's face it, this woman had lived in a dream world since her early years, and had craved revenge for many more ('Valerie, I raised you for this,' or something to that effect.) As a teenager, this episode did not affect me too much, other than I knew she wanted to hurt the Bolt Brothers. When I saw it again in 1987, I was deeply moved by the episode. Clancey's scene near the end when Josh is going to leave and Clancey begs him 'not to do this thing.'"

*Story Editor William Blinn:* "It doesn't work. Not for me. I think you hate to put together an episode where the audience has to have watched about three quarters of the prior episodes to understand what's going on. It's like *Lost,* I'm told it's a terrific series, but by the time I tuned in to watch an episode, so much had gone on, and so many character relationships had been established, I just couldn't keep up. It's not a knock on the show. I think dealing with so much back-story, requires an awful lot of the audience."

*On the guest casting of Lynda Day George:* "I think someone like that takes the audience out of the story. They maybe didn't know Lynda Day George at that time, but they knew that incredibly pretty face from a thousand commercials that were playing all the time. I think Bob and Screen Gems were under pressure to pump up the heat. It was an opportunity for David to do a love story, and they'd never really done one, certainly not to that degree."

*On episode writer Jack Miller:* "One of the reasons Jack liked writing for *Brides* was that he liked to try to find the softer side of his writing which, in *Gunsmoke,* was just never invited. He enjoyed the process of trying to write a different tone and timbre. Jack became story editor on *Gunsmoke.* I worked with him as a freelance writer when he was story editor there.

"It ["Two Women"] was bittersweet. Jack did those kinds of things very well. He would do the episodes on *Gunsmoke* where you learned a little bit more about Matt than you might have known before, or Kitty, or somebody. He liked to do that kind of thing. What he didn't try to do, wasn't part of the guy, was anything humorous and parental/sentimental, which is why he was so good for *Gunsmoke.* The episode he did was good, but it wasn't what we did. If you're Jack Miller, the story was good; if it's for *Here Come the Brides,* maybe it wasn't beneficial. But if you evaluate it as just a story, it's good. Jack was a good writer. I always liked working with him. Matter of fact, Jack Miller, a few years later did a series [*Dirty Sally*]. I think Jack wrote good parts. I don't know if he did romantic ingénues (Lynda Day George as Valerie?), but the offbeat and the bizarre, and the 'Dirty Sallys' of this world. But it was well-written, and I think one of the reasons David did like it was that David was not used that much. He certainly wasn't used to the degree that he should have been used, but he was always there, and a great-looking guy, and terrific."[274]

## "Two Women": The Author's Interpretation
### The Source

Based on its characters and Gothic settings, "Two Women" seems to be *Brides'* version of Charles Dickens' *Great Expectations*. In this version, David Soul's Joshua Bolt is Pip, Jane Wyatt's Emma Peak is Miss Havisham, and Lynda Day George's Valerie Watkins becomes Estella Havisham, the adopted daughter of Miss Havisham.

There are two things Joshua Bolt has in common with *Great Expectations'* Pip — First: He's the target of an embittered older woman; second: he's madly in love with a beautiful young woman who is at the core of the older woman's plan to destroy him.

As for the similarities between Miss Havisham and Emma Peak, both are wealthy, eccentric women who live in the past. But, unlike Miss Havisham, who was definitely jilted by her fiancée, there is no proof in "Two Women" (other than her own statement) that Emma Peak and the Bolts' late father, Jonathan, were planning to marry. In fact, given Emma's mental condition, this may be pure fantasy.

Perhaps also pure fantasy is Emma's claim that she brought up her niece Valerie to wreak vengeance on the brothers Bolt. Though Valerie is similar to Estella Havisham in that she carries out her aunt's wishes, and — like Estella — feels some degree of obligation to the older woman who has raised her, Valerie does not seem to like hurting the male sex — in this case, Joshua Bolt. The fact that *Brides* fan#9 sees Lynda Day George's Valerie as an intelligent woman and wonders why she would participate in her aunt's insane plan would please the actress — Lynda Day George always wanted her audience asking questions about her characters. Chances are, "Two Women" writer Jack Miller would also have been pleased at the way this episode puzzled *Brides* fans. Like Special Guest Star George, Miller was very much interested in the subject of mental illness.

### Writer Jack Miller

In reviewing the television series episodes penned by Jack Miller, there is one character type that emerges again and again — the person who is cut off from, or does not fit into, the regular world. Sometimes, this cutting off and not fitting in is a voluntary choice on the character's part — for example, 'Lorenzo Bush.' Sometimes, forces out of the character's control cut him off and prevent him from fitting into the regular world. Three of Miller's *Gunsmoke*s illustrate this latter point. In the first, "The Lost," Kitty Russell (series regular Amanda Blake) finds a cabin housing two bizarre people who keep a mute girl locked up in a cage; from time to time, they exhibit the girl as a wild animal. In the second *Gunsmoke,* "New Doctor in Town," gunsmith Newly O'Brien (series regular Buck Taylor) has a bone fragment pressing on his brain – this causes him to have hallucinations. In the third *Gunsmoke*, "Mirage," the hallucinations story point returns, along with the favorite series television disease of amnesia. Suffering from both hallucinations and amnesia is *Gunsmoke's* most comical character: Festus Hagen (Ken Curtis).

Jack Miller also dealt with hallucinations in *The Invaders* episode, "The Pit." Like *Gunsmoke*, "The Lost," *The Invaders*, "The Pit" has more reality than the *Gunsmoke's* "New Doctor in Town" and "Mirage" since the afflicted person is the guest character, rather than the regular character. In "The Pit," the afflicted individual is scientist Charles Aidman. Suffering from hallucinations as the story opens, Aidman sees alien saucers and alien beings everywhere he looks. Naturally, his claim that his assistant is an alien is viewed with skepticism by the *Invaders* viewer. Writer Miller and actor Aidman further increase viewer doubt by having Aidman accuse the show's hero: the alien-hunting and alien-exposing David Vincent (series star Roy Thinnes) of being an alien. Since Vincent has spent the entire *Invaders* series trying to defeat the villainous aliens, the viewer can't help but conclude that Aidman is insane. But maybe he's not!

Although well written and well acted, "The Pit" is not in the same league as Miller's later *Here Come the Brides'* "Two Women." With "Two Women," Jack Miller, Jane Wyatt, and Lynda Day George took the insanity theme to extraordinary lengths.

## An ahead-of-its-time study of Alzheimer's?

At the time of "Two Women's" original broadcast, very little was known about the disease of Alzheimer's. No information was available to the general public about what caused it; a name hadn't even been put to the illness. Whether Jack Miller knew someone who suffered from this illness, or whether his fascination with (and probable research into) different forms of insanity, resulted in his creating a character as ahead-of-her time as Emma Peak, are questions only the late Miller could answer.

At any rate, when one considers the symptoms displayed by Emma Peak in *Here Come the Brides*, "Two Women," it's astonishing to note their similarity to the symptoms displayed by the Alzheimer's patient who is undergoing Stages Five and Six of the disease: Middle-Stage/Moderate to Late-Stage/Severe Alzheimer's.

In Stage 5, problems with memory and thinking become very apparent. Symptoms include an inability to remember such basic things as one's home address, phone number, and important details about one's own background; there is also confusion as to time and place. In Stage 6, the patient begins exhibiting changes in personality and behavior, and memory continues to worsen; the sufferer not only fails to recall recent events, but has difficulty recognizing close friends and family members. The patient also begins to experience "sundowning" and "wandering," exhibits hostility and suspicion, and often repeats the same behaviors or words.

As noted earlier by *Brides* fans #1, #2, #5, #8, and #10, Emma Peak's recollection of Seattle is rather confused and distorted. When the story begins, she is already having problems with both memory and thinking; as fans #2 and #8 so astutely point out, she is also disoriented to both time and place. Being in the fifth stage of Alzheimer's,

Emma is therefore mixing up one time and place with another. Given fan #2's speculation that Emma may be thinking of another town further up or down the Pacific coast, and given how his previous *Brides* episodes, "Lorenzo Bush" and the co-written "Two Worlds" presented viewers with a duality ("Lorenzo" tackled both sides of the environmental question; "Two Worlds" had Meg Foster living in both the world of the blind and the sighted), one can't help but wonder if writer Miller had familiarized himself with the history of Seattle prior to the writing of "Two Women." Having Emma deliver a history of Seattle which the people who lived there knew, was highly inaccurate, was a very clever way to call attention to the character and her illness.

Later in the story, Emma fails to recognize her niece, Valerie, the one person who has been living with her for so many years. She also accuses Valerie of abandoning her, (thanks to the "voices" she hears). These are two signs Emma is now in the sixth stage of Alzheimer's. Other indications include her "sundowning" and "wandering." The former is shown when Emma becomes angry with Valerie, and strikes her. It is further illustrated by the scene where Emma hears voices in the wind-blown trees. Prior to this, Emma is shown dancing in the mud-spattered streets of Seattle. This dancing, and the subsequent journey-to-Peak's Bluff sequence, might be described as "wandering." When wandering is combined with sundowning, the result may be the dangerous situation of "elopement at night." Those experiencing this might be lost out of doors (which Emma Peak most definitely is), dressed inappropriately (Emma's clothing does not provide adequate protection from the inclement weather), and unable to take responsibility for their own safety and security. The conclusion of this particular Act leaves Emma Peak in such a condition.

Given the bizarre and colorful requirements of her role, it's no wonder the late Jane Wyatt had fond memories of guest-starring on *Here Come the Brides*. As did her fellow guest star, Lynda Day George.

## Lynda Day George

"Always keep 'em guessing." *Lynda Day George as Valerie Watkins*

"You remember Myrna Loy? *The Thin Man?*" Lynda Day George queries as she begins to describe her approach to acting. "Well, very early in my career, I worked with Myrna Loy onstage, and one of the things she told me was 'one of the most exciting things about a performance, or a movie, is the part you can't see.' She said that, 'If you leave something to the imagination, and allow people to get into their own minds, what they come up with, or what they see in their minds, will be much more exciting to them than anything that you can do on camera.' And that very same thing was said to me by, of all people, Gypsy Rose Lee, when I worked with her in *Auntie Mame*. I remember, she was always saying, 'Leave them guessing. Leave them guessing. Leave 'em…[wanting] to see more.'"[275]

As the comments of *Brides* fans #4, #7, #9, and #10 reveal, Lynda Day George's performance as Valerie Watkins in "Two Women" clearly has the viewers of this episode "getting into their own minds" and looking for some kind of answer when it comes to her character's strange behavior. In the case of *Brides* Fans #4 and #7, each is confounded by the very passionate and very obvious kiss Valerie gives Jason in front of the entire town of Seattle. This action comes out of nowhere; like many other things in the story, it is never explained. As a result, fan#4 says the scene should have been handled differently, while Fan#7 comes to the perfectly logical conclusion that Valerie is insane. By contrast, finding Valerie a sane and intelligent person, Fan #9 wonders why Valerie is going along with her clearly deluded aunt's insane plans. Like *Brides* Fan#10, who is thinking about Emma Peak's (and by extension, Valerie Watkins') background, Fan#9 is get-

ting very close to what Lynda Day George always hoped her audience would do — imagine themselves as her character.

An actress whom director Robert Butler says, "works behaviorally and psychologically on her characters,"[276] Lynda Day George's original plan was to become a doctor, specifically a psychiatrist. It was her late mother, Betty, who wished her to become an actress. Entering the acting profession reluctantly, by the time she reached her late teens, Lynda made a decision that would ultimately lead to the realization of her mother's (and her own) dreams. Recalls the actress, "when I was sixteen or seventeen, and started noticing how my acting was affecting the people around me, I redefined for myself the process of what healing is all about. The idea of being a doctor, a healer, a communicator, they all run together. Acting gave me an ability to be with people in a way that gives them expression

*"Two Women" guest Lynda Day George and Lancer star James Stacy in a bit of comic publicity that had absolutely nothing to do with the situation facing George's character in her Lancer guest shot, "The Escape." Also guest-starring in "The Escape" were* Brides *semi-regular Robert Biheller and guest star Daniel J. Travanti.*

of who they are. I looked at acting as a kind of healing. I thought of it as a healing, not just for myself, but for other folks. I mean, people can see themselves in characters, and sometimes, if you do it right, people can experience themselves as a result of a piece of work you've done. Not that I was in the category of people who did these magnificent things and changed people's lives necessarily, but I think that sometimes people got a glimpse of who they were through one of the things I'd done. So, one of the things I wanted to do in my career was to give people a piece of the puzzle that they hadn't had before. I wanted people to imagine themselves in my shoes — that's how I wanted them to respond. That they could actually be this person or this character, that they could foresee themselves as this person, and because of that, maybe extract some little bit of information about themselves. You know, we go through life, we go through our lives without an inkling of who we are, or who we could be, so, part of what I wanted to do as an actress was to give people an idea of who they could be."[277]

As far as director Butler was concerned, George accomplished such goals. "Because of Lynda's great interest in psychiatry, and the way she played her characters, you always felt that you were getting inside those characters," states the director. "You knew what they were thinking. Her analysis of acting — the fact that she was able to notice the effect that her acting was having on others — that's fascinating to me. That's just a total amalgamation of the sender (actor) and the receiver (audience). Of course, that's what psychiatry is trying to do. Lynda's analysis of acting is exceptional. That sounds like her. That analysis — it's quite broad, it kind of runs human experience and healing and susceptibility, and strength and weakness, it runs them all together into a sort of collaborative collision. It's a very broad view of who we are and what we do. It's a very compassionate view. It's pretty clear she's a humanitarian."

Continues Butler: "The most natural thing that happens in acting is that the actor submerges himself in the process and can't see out all that well. Lynda's process is to see out! I've never thought about that before. I don't think many actors do that, but that's what she's doing. It's funny…she isn't the fly on the wall. It's a bigger view than that. Her kind of acting, the way she thinks, as she amalgamates the actor and the audience, the sender and the receiver, she's thinking of the world around her, her environment, the people in her world. She kind of includes the voyeur, the sender and the receiver she kind of melds together. It's not one-sided, it's multi-sided, it's both sides, it's the pitcher and the catcher both."[278]

As a result, Lynda Day George was the ideal actress to play a character as complex and as contradictory as Valerie Watkins. For only by imagining oneself as Valerie Watkins, only by looking at things from Valerie's point of view, can one satisfactorily resolve the strange goings-on and characters of "Two Women."

*Lynda Day George on* Here Come The Brides: "On the rare occasions when I did get to watch *Here Come the Brides*, I would watch it cuz I thought it was fun. I liked the music, too. I loved the background music. I really enjoyed it.

"Oh, God — I loved doing *Here Come the Brides*! I really enjoyed doing that show! As far as I know, they called me, and asked me to do the job, and sent me a script. I said, 'Sure! I'd love to!' I did enjoy the show. I thought it had good values. It seemed to me that it was one of those shows that was really fun. I didn't know that this was the last episode. I do not remember anyone saying that this would be the last show. I don't think anybody expected that."

*On the comparison between* Brides *and* Bonanza (both series cast guest actresses in unusual parts): "There was really no comparison between *Brides* and *Bonanza*. They're like apples and oranges. They didn't have anything to do with one another as far as the show was concerned. As far as classification is concerned, or any of that.

*Bonanza* was a drama — it was a family drama, and *Here Come the Brides* was really much more light-hearted, much more fun. Just much more fun. It had a totally different perspective. It certainly had a different perspective than *Bonanza* — *Bonanza* was more of a drama. So, as far as I'm concerned, trying to compare those two shows is like comparing apples and oranges. There is no comparison between the two."

*On being made an honorary member of the* HCTB *fan club:* "How sweet of them to do that. I love that!"

*On the show's setting of Seattle, Washington:* "I love Washington! I love it there. I can't think of anywhere on this continent or on another continent that I would rather be. We are moving up there. I am not [comfortable in] California! We were just not meant for this place!"

*On Episode #17 ("Democracy Inaction"):* "I loved *Democracy Inaction*! I did like that one. That was good."

*On the cast and crew:* "I never had any trouble fitting in as the guest star. They were very, very good folks — very friendly, very open. I never felt a moment of discomfiture on the show at all. Not to say that any of the shows that I worked on were really miserable, but there were a couple that were really miserable. Oh, my goodness!

"You know, on any series where people are thrown together, perhaps not knowing one another, prior to beginning the show, there's a great deal of…you spend an awful lot of your life with these people, and you must develop a real fondness for them. Otherwise, you will make your life miserable. Well, they all seemed very fond of each other. They had a lot of wonderful…you know, you develop little jokes that get carried on and on and on and on and down through the whole series, that you play on off-times, when you're off-camera. So filming was a great deal of fun. We had a lot of fun, and it was very comfortable. I just enjoyed very much working on that show because the people were great fun, and there were a lot of laughs. I would say it was one of the happier sets I worked on. They were very, very good folks — very friendly, very open. I just think they were a great bunch of folks. They were a delightful group of people."

*On Robert Brown:* "Robert Brown. I think at the time he was…there was something going on, and I'm not real sure what it was. I think it had something to do with production. He didn't seem too, too happy at that time. Not that…I don't know that that was the way he was all the time, and if…I recall some of the cast members mentioning that he was very upset, and 'He's just not like this.' I would have to say that I think he was probably upset about one thing or another, and unfortunately, he wasn't able to keep that out of his performing day. Even though I don't think his performance necessarily reflected that. I think that the time that we spent on the set somehow reflected that. I think he was just unhappy at the time for some reason or another. I don't know what it was."

*On Bobby Sherman:* "Bobby Sherman! Holy mackerel! Bobby Sherman's career was taking off…his singing career. Bobby Sherman was, is, a dynamo, and my recollection of him is that he was so dynamic and so out there all the time that it was really quite exciting. He was very, very…he seemed very dear. Hard-working person. All of this was very important to him, so, doing well, and doing it appropriately, all of that was important. He did work hard, and you have to respect that, and I did."

*On David Soul:* "I enjoyed very much working with David Soul. This was like one of the first things that he had ever done, and he was very shy and tentative at times. I'm sure that he's not that — or hasn't been that for quite some time. But he certainly was at that time — a very endearing, a very dear person."

*On Bridget Hanley:* "Bridget was delightful. Bridget was terrific. So energetic, and excited. Bridget was like Lee Meriwether. I wouldn't say she was a non-stop talker, but she could talk."

*On Bridget And Bobby:* "I believe that Bridget and Bobby really had a great relationship. They seemed like they had a great time working together. So, it was my experience that they really enjoyed having this show, and having this fun relationship with each other. Bobby and Bridget got along well."

*On Mark Lenard:* "I have to tell you that I didn't know that he was Spock's dad. (George was/is a great fan of *Star Trek*. Spock is her favorite character.) I did not recognize him in that way. I mean he didn't have his ears on! He was very distinctive looking — a very, very elegant man. Very composed, very in control of himself and what was going on around him — he was completely conscious all the time. That's something that's very difficult to do. I really, really liked him. He was an awfully nice man, and he seemed to really have a handle on what was going on. I liked him a lot. It wasn't until after I finished the show that I realized who he was [Sarek ]. I was really annoyed with myself…I'm…'What have I done?' I threw away that opportunity." (George would have liked to tell Lenard how much she loved *Star Trek*.)

*On Henry Beckman:* "Oh, Henry Beckman! Amazing!"

*On Susan Tolsky:* "Susan Tolsky was wonderful! She was just so sweet and funny."

*On Joan Blondell:* "I absolutely loved her! Absolutely loved her. She was so…in fact she may have been the spirit of the show. She was just fabulous! She kind of set the tone of the show. She absolutely was the spirit of the show! I just loved her on it — I thought she was great. I asked her about the *Topper* movies that she did. She was great in those, and I just loved those. She said, 'My God! I've had a lot of people come up to me and ask me about different things that I've done, but hardly anybody has ever asked me about those.' So, took her by surprise? Yes, I did. Yes, I did. She really enjoyed them. And, she told me some things that were unprintable. She was a risqué sort. She said, 'I've been around long enough. I don't have to worry about it.'"

*On E.W. Swackhamer:* "The director, Swack, was also the husband of Bridget Hanley. He was fun. He was really a nice man, and he enjoyed so much working on that show. I think he really enjoyed working with his wife a lot. Swack was great!"

*On Director of Photography Fred H. Jackman:* "Fred Jackman was great. He was amazing!"

*On Jane Wyatt:* "I recognized her as Spock's mom. She always intimidated me a little bit. She was so…she was just so vivacious and alive. I thought she was wonderful. Sometimes when you're doing stuff like that, and you come across somebody that you have always admired…for me, one of the things that I was able to do was just watch, and it was really a pleasure, really a pleasure to watch her, and to watch her from the perspective of really having enjoyed her for all of my life. Not just in *Lost Horizon*, in things like…just about everything that she's done. You bet I watched *Father Knows Best.*"[281]

*Executive Producer Bob Claver:* "Lynda's pretty. She's pretty, and she's bright. Lynda was one of the trailblazers in the business. She absolutely was. She was really not a star in a real sense of the word, ever. She was kind of a television person that worked a lot – a leading lady who was a character actress. There were probably a fair number of people like that."[282]

*Leading Lady Bridget Hanley:* "Lynda was just lovely. Lovely. We met in the wardrobe trailer, and I went, 'Oh, she is the most gorgeous woman I have ever seen!' Made me want to be in the other room, I think I was in kind of a raggy costume. I can't remember, and I said…we had a little conversation, and she just was charming and warm and very dear. It was just a really lovely time. She was just heaven. Everybody adored her. She was just so dear, and just so lovely, and so approachable. And everybody felt the same way.

"Swack loved working with her and Chris. I was familiar with some of the things she'd done. Oh, yeah. But particularly that she worked all the time, and did movies and television. And mostly movies. I was also a bit in awe. She's just…wouldn't every young woman dream to be her? Just the whole package. She was like to me the epitome of everything that is beautiful and good, and how many can achieve that? Beautiful. Talented. And gracious – no, that's not the right word. Not everybody is that. I wish we had gotten a chance to work together again. I adore her. I think she's phenomenal."[283]

*Series Regular Susan Tolsky:* "I remember Lynda doing the show. Talk about a regal lady! She was a lady of television. I remember her being very present and very accessible. I can remember her just smiling and being very cordial. A lot of times when people as guest stars come onto a show, they're coming into a family that they don't know, and I didn't feel any hesitation on her part. I didn't feel any overbearance on her part, cuz some people come on and try to go, 'Ha ha ha. I'm the guest star.' Please. Give me a break. I just remember her coming in and merging. She was just there, and it wasn't like, 'Oh, that's Lynda Day George!' She was one of us, and we were one of her. That's what I remember about Lynda. I would not put her…if you dropped her down in Oshkosh, I'm sure she'd be fine. Just drop her anywhere. But there was just something very elegant about her. But I did not associate the New York stage with her."[284] (George did plays on and off Broadway.)

*Executive Casting Director Renee Valente:* "Lynda…she was wonderful. She was married to Chris George at the time. She's such a lovely, lovely, lovely woman. She was terrific. It was a joy to work with her. She was very professional. Just, just wonderful. One of the top ten actresses in television. You bet. You bet. Very, very underrated. She always was.

"What was most important to her was her husband. They had a wonderful marriage. She was terribly distraught when he passed away. Her life was not just acting. "I am a big fan of hers. She's very special."[285]

*Wardrobe Man Steve Lodge:* "Lynda's never had a bad performance, I don't think. She's very pretty. I like her."[286]

*Leading Lady Bridget Hanley on Jane Wyatt:* "Jane Wyatt! She was just like Mother Earth, but funny, and fun, and dear. And that's my remembered feeling of her. Because I had seen her on television — there's something more approachable about television than movies. Film at that point for me, I went, 'Oh my God!' And television…I felt like she was one of that family [the Andersons from *Father Knows Best*] in a way. I think television does that, because it's on every week, and they were on forever. But she was fun. I felt honored [to be working with her]."[279]

*Series Regular Susan Tolsky on Jane Wyatt:* "Jane Wyatt. Jane was very quiet and reserved. I don't remember her as being accessible. We, as the regulars always wanted to make everybody feel comfortable, and we did…all of us approached every new cast member and 'Hello, I'm Susan,' and, 'I'm Bobby,' we all did that. I don't recall interacting with her a lot. I don't remember Jane being real accessible to me. I don't remember her being like Joanie at all. She just seemed like a very quiet, reserved person. She did her job.

"I don't' remember her being standoffish, but I kind of had the feeling that Jane was a little frightened. I don't know how much television she had done. This is dealing with a period piece and an hour show, and again, you're dropped down in a group of new people. When you're on a series forty years with the same group, when you drop down into another show, it's a little bit different. I just felt her being kind of like the mother she was on that show [*Father Knows Best*] — very reserved, kind of quiet — that may be just who she is."[280]

# *End Note*
# *The cancellation of* Here Come the Brides

Several reasons were given for the cancellation of *Brides*. To a number of fans, the show's more serious tone and move to a different time slot worked against the program; to professional critics, the show hurt itself from the beginning with what they saw as an unsustainable premise. As usual, the people who made *Here Come the Brides* knew the real answer. "It was a political decision," says leading lady Bridget Hanley. "Because we had been pretty well assured by [ABC's head] Elton Rule that we would have a third season."[287] "It went off the air because the guy who came out to run Screen Gems wanted his stuff in, and he wasn't interested in that," adds Robert Brown. "He was more of a *biggety, biggety, bang, bang, bang*. He wanted to put his own stuff in."[288]

"The potential was there," states story editor William Blinn. "Screen Gems wanted to appease the network, and the network thought that action-adventure was the wave of the future. Ratings were relatively good, and the audience didn't want it to disappear, but the network felt, I'm told, that they wanted to go get another action-adventure. *Brides* wasn't it, and they were gonna go find one."[289]

The one they found was *The Young Rebels* with Rick Ely, Lou Gossett, Alex Henteloff, and Bridget Hanley's friend, Hilarie Thompson. "The head of the studio had changed," explains Hanley. "Lenny Goldberg [Leonard Goldberg, of Spelling/Goldberg] was in, and Jackie Cooper was gone. The show that they brought in went out for a Bobby Sherman (Ely), and a young Bridget Hanley (Thompson), playing pretty much the Candyesque role, but softer, I think, not as harsh, because, listen, the new boss wanted his stuff. It only lasted for six months! And it breaks my heart, because there were protestations on street corners all over the United States about *Brides*. Had it been in the days of *Cagney and Lacey*, we might have been picked up by another network, but had it been in the days of *Cagney and Lacey*, we may never have gotten on the air."

The show's cancellation so upset Hanley that "I wandered for two weeks in my backyard, in my robe," she remembers. "We were not even called!"[290] Robert Brown was much more philosophical about the series being dropped. "When it was over, I said, 'Well, that was pleasant,' but some of the people were sobbing," recalls Brown. "The actors, they really…it became their family. Bridget was depressed. Oh, yes. Oh, the joy she had playing the roles there, but the new guy at the network — he didn't create that. If Jackie Cooper had stayed on, it would have been on. We had terrific ratings. When it was announced it was going off, the uproar from the country was enormous. They heard from lots and lots of people. It was really tough — we didn't expect it. The audience appreciation for it was high, and the sponsorship was good."[291]

Once Bridget Hanley got over the shock of *Brides'* cancellation, she moved on to other things. But she never lost her fondness for the show, and, at one point returned to the former set. "I visited the backlot that's now Warner Brothers," she says. "There's nothing left, some of it still looked the same, but none of our stuff is there. I didn't see the church. They sold off a huge, huge block — that's where I shot a lot of *The Flying Nuns*. It's all a big shopping center now. They used a lot of the berm and the lagoon and the ranch."[292]

That was years later. But despite its short run, based on the publicity *Here Come the Brides* continued to receive during its' Summer 1970 repeats, it was obvious that the series wasn't likely to fade from viewer memory anytime soon.

April 10, 1970: A Far Cry from Yesterday" vs. *The CBS Friday Night Movie: Advance to the Rear* starring Glenn Ford, Stella Stevens, Melvyn Douglas, Jim Backus and *Brides'* Joan Blondell as "Easy" Jenny; *The Name of the Game*, "The Other Kind of Spy" starring Tony Franciosa as Jeff Dillon and guest-starring Leslie Nielsen, Joseph Campanella, Ed Begley, and *HCTB* guest Jeanette Nolan, NBC.

April 17, 1970: The Wealthiest Man in Seattle" vs. *The CBS Friday Night Movie: The Third Day* starring George Peppard, Elizabeth Ashley, and Roddy McDowall; *The Name of the Game*, "Lady on the Rocks," starring Gene Barry as Glenn Howard and guest-starring Janice Rule, Nigel Davenport, Laurence Naismith, and James Robertson Justice, NBC.

April 18, 1970 – *TV Guide* Crossword – Vol. 18, No. 16, Issue #890 – 2 Down – Child actor on *Here Come the Brides* (2 words).

April 24, 1970: His Sister's Keeper" vs. *The CBS Friday Night Movie: The Angel Wore Red* starring Ava Gardner, Dirk Bogarde, Joseph Cotten, and Vittorio De Sica; *The Name of the Game–*"Chains of Command" starring Robert Stack as Dan Farrell and guest-starring Pernell Roberts, Sidney Blackmer, Dorothy Lamour and *HCTB* guests Jay C. Flippen and Steve Ihnat, NBC.

April 25, 1970 – *TV Guide* Crossword – Vol. 18, No. 17, Issue #891 – 2 Down – (2 words) – Answer: Eric Chase.

May 1970: 25 Faves Reveal Things That Are Better Together" *Tiger Beat;* Bobby Sherman article in *Tiger Beat;* Bobby Sherman article in *Flip Teen;* Joan Blondell article in *TV Radio Mirror;* "My Brother Bobby," Part 2 – *Tiger Beat;* "You've Come a Long Way, Bobby" *TV and Inside Movie;* Bobby Sherman, Bridget Hanley, Robert Brown article in *Teen Screen;* Bridget Hanley – *Teen Screen, Teen Life;* Bridget Hanley: You Can Be an Actress," Part 4 – *Tiger Beat.*

May 1, 1970: The Soldier" vs. *The CBS Friday Night Movie: Tarzan and the Valley of Gold* starring Mike Henry, Nancy Kovack, David Opatoshu, and Manuel Padilla, Jr.; *The Name of the Game*, "Blind Man's Bluff," starring Tony Franciosa as Jeff Dillon, and guest-starring Jack Klugman, Broderick Crawford, and Coleen Gray, NBC.

May 8, 1970 – *Brides* pre-empted by ABC News Special, *With These Hands* (saluting the American craftsman).

May 9, 1970 – *TV Guide* Crossword – Vol. 18, No. 19, Issue #893 – 30 Down – *Here* _____ *Brides* (2 words)

May 15, 1970: The Fetching of Jenny" vs. *The CBS Friday Night Movie: Come Fly With Me* starring Dolores Hart, Hugh O'Brian, Pamela Tiffin, Karl Malden, and Lois Nettleton; *The Name of the Game*, "The Prisoner Within," starring Tony Franciosa as Jeff Dillon, and guest-starring Steve Forrest, Ron Hayes, and Richard Van Vleet, NBC.

May 16, 1970 – *TV Guide* Vol. 18, No. 20, Issue # 894 – *Brides* referenced on page 19 in article, "I am totally feminine," by Dick Hobson,
about stunt women; "TV Teletype: Hollywood"
Joseph Finnigan reports that Bobby Sherman will make guest appearances on the summer series, *Johnny Cash Presents the Everly Brothers* and
that Mark Lenard is going to Tokyo to star in the motion picture, *Noon
Sunday; TV Guide* Crossword – 30 Down (2 words) – Answer: Come
The.

May 22, 1970: Hosanna's Way" vs. *The CBS Friday Night Movie: Hold On,*
starring Herman's Hermits and Shelley Fabares; *The Name of the Game,*
"The Civilized Men," starring Robert Stack as Dan Farrell and guest-
starring Jack Kelly, Rod Cameron, and Jill St. John, NBC.

May 23, 1970 – *TV Guide* Crossword – Vol. 18, No. 21, Issue #895 –
37 Across – Molly on *Here Come the Brides,* 8 Down – *Here Come the
Brides* setting.

May 29, 1970: The Legend of Big Foot" vs. *The CBS Friday Night Movie:
The Visit,* starring Ingrid Bergman, Anthony Quinn and Irina Demick;
*The Name of the Game,* "High Card," starring Gene Barry as Glenn
Howard and guest-starring Barry Sullivan, Gene Raymond, and Mar-
tine Beswick, NBC.

May 30, 1970 – *TV Guide* Crossword Answers– Vol. 18, No. 22, Issue
#896 – 37 Across – Answer-Patti, 8 Down – Seattle; new Crossword –
37 Down – Jeremy on *Here Come the Brides.*

Summer 1970 – Bridget Hanley – *Tiger Beat.*

June 1970: Brides Canceled"
*FaVE!;* "Bobby Sherman Takes You Home," Part 1 – *Flip Teen;* "Joan
Blondell: The Fan Letters I Answer First"
*Movieland and TV Time; Modern Movies* – Robert Brown presenting
Emmy to Barbara Bain for *Mission: Impossible;* "My Brother Bobby," Part
3 – *Tiger Beat;* Bobby Sherman article in *16 SPEC;* Susan Tolsky article
in *TV Radio Show;* Robert Brown article in *Tiger Beat;* Robert Brown
in *Modern Movies;* Bridget Hanley: You Can Be an Actress," Part 5 –
*Tiger Beat;* Bridget Hanley – *Movieland and TV Time, Modern Movies,
FaVE!*

June 5, 1970: The Road to the Cradle" vs. *The CBS Friday Night Movie:
My Blood Runs Cold* starring Troy Donahue and Joey Heatherton; *The
Name of the Game,* "The Power," starring Robert Stack as Dan Farrell

and guest-starring William Conrad, John Ireland, and Broderick Crawford, NBC.

June 6, 1970 – *TV Guide* Crossword Answer – Vol. 18, No. 23, Issue #897, 37 Down – Answer: Bobby.

June 12, 1970: Land Grant" vs. *The CBS Friday Night Movie: The Alphabet Murders* starring Tony Randall, Robert Morley, Anita Ekberg, and Maurice Denham; *The Name of the Game*, "Laurie Marie," starring Tony Franciosa as Jeff Dillon and guest-starring Peter Mark Richman, Antoinette Bower, John Kerr, Barry Atwater, and Carla Borelli, NBC.
It is announced in *TV Guide* that Joan Blondell has been nominated for an Emmy for Best Actress in Drama Series – *Here Come the Brides*.

June 13, 1970 – *TV Guide* Crossword – Vol. 18, No. 24, Issue #898 – 36 Down – Lady on *Here Come the Brides*.

June 19, 1970: A Bride for Obie Brown" vs. *The CBS Friday Night Movie: Mister Buddwing* starring James Garner, Jean Simmons, and Suzanne Pleshette; *The Name of the Game*, "The Perfect Image," starring Gene Barry as Glenn Howard and guest-starring Hal Holbrook, Clu Gulager, Diana Hyland, and *HCTB* guest Edward Asner, NBC.

June 20, 1970 – *TV Guide* Crossword – Vol. 18, No. 25, Issue #899 – 36 Down – Answer: Lottie; new crossword – 27 Down – Molly on *Here Come the Brides*.

June 26, 1970: Lorenzo Bush" vs. *The CBS Friday Night Movie: The Roman Spring of Mrs. Stone* starring Vivien Leigh, Warren Beatty, Lotte Lenya, and Jill St. John; *The Name of the Game*, "Goodbye, Harry," starring Gene Barry as Glenn Howard and guest-starring Darren McGavin, James Whitmore, Strother Martin, Jan Sterling, and Marsha Hunt, NBC.

June 27, 1970 – *TV Guide* Crossword answer – Vol. 18, No. 26, Issue #900 – 27 Down – Answer: Patti.

July 1970: Bobby As We Know Him"
*Tiger Beat;* "Bobby Sherman Takes You Home," Part 2 – *Flip Teen;* "Bridget's Mail Bag"
*16 Magazine;* "My Brother Bobby," Part 4 – *Tiger Beat;* "A Last Look Back with Bobby and Bridget"
*FaVE!;* Bobby Sherman article in *16 Magazine;* David Soul: Get It Together"
*16 Magazine;* David and Karen – *Tiger Beat;* David Soul article in *TV*

*Picture Life;* Bridget Hanley – *Tiger Beat, Teen Life, Movie TV Photo Stars;* Bridget Hanley: You Can Be an Actress," Part 6 – *Tiger Beat, FaVE!,* Bridget's Mail Bag – *16 Magazine.*

July 3, 1970: To Break the Bank of Tacoma" vs. *The CBS Friday Night Movie: Ten Little Indians* starring Hugh O'Brian, Shirley Eaton, and Fabian; *The Name of the Game,* "The Brass Ring," starring Robert Stack as Dan Farrell and guest-starring Van Johnson, Celeste Holm, Tim O'Connor, Jack Carter, and Herbert Anderson, NBC.

Week of July 4-10, 1970 – Bobby Sherman guests on *Upbeat* variety show.

July 10, 1970: The She-Bear" vs. *The CBS Friday Night Movie: Hawaii Five-O* (pilot film) starring Jack Lord, Nancy Kwan, Leslie Nielsen, Khigh Dhiegh and *HCTB* guest Lew Ayres; *The Name of the Game,* "Island of Gold and Precious Stones," starring Tony Franciosa as Jeff Dillon and guest-starring Lee Meriwether, Hazel Court, Yvonne De Carlo, *HCTB* guest Henry Jones, and as themselves: Edward Everett Horton, Rudy Vallee, and Estelle Winwood, NBC.

July 11, 1970 – *TV Guide* – Vol. 18., No. 28., Issue #902 – TV Teletype: Hollywood – Joseph Finnigan reports that *Brides'* Robert Brown will be guest-starring in the 1970-71 season on *Bewitched*, while Henry Beckman will be appearing on *Nancy.*

July 17, 1970: Debt of Honor" vs. *The CBS Friday Night Movie: Having a Wild Weekend* starring The Dave Clark Five; *The Name of the Game,* "The Garden," starring Robert Stack as Dan Farrell and guest-starring Richard Kiley, Anne Francis, and *HCTB* guests Michael Ansara and Brenda Scott, NBC.

July 18, 1970 – WJCL, Channel 22 (Savannah, Georgia), begins broadcasting on this day, or August 18, 1970.

July 24, 1970: How Dry We Are" vs. *The CBS Friday Night Movie: Double Trouble* starring Elvis Presley and Annette Day; *The Name of the Game*-"Tarot" starring Gene Barry as Glenn Howard and guest-starring Jose Ferrer, William Shatner, Lee Grant, Bethel Leslie, and David Carradine, NBC.

July 31, 1970: Candy and the Kid" vs. *The CBS Friday Night Movie: The Third Day* (see April 17, 1970); *The Name of the Game,* "The King of Denmark," starring Tony Franciosa as Jeff Dillon and guest-starring

Joseph Cotten, Margaret Leighton, Noel Harrison, Norma Crane, and Louise Latham, NBC.

August 1970 – David Soul tidbits in *Movie TV Pinups;* two David Soul tidbits in *FaVE!;* "Stars' Favorite Colors"
*Tiger Beat;* "Your Brides Farewell Yearbook"
*Flip Teen;* "My Brother Bobby," Part 5 – *Tiger Beat;* Two Bobby Sherman articles in *16 Magazine;* Bobby Sherman article in *Movie TV Pinups;* Bobby Sherman article in *Teen Pin-Ups;* Two Bobby Sherman articles in *FaVE!;* Bobby Sherman article in *Flip Teen;* Susan Tolsky: Stars' Favorite Colors"
*Tiger Beat;* "David Soul – Get It Together"
*16 SPEC;* Bridget Hanley – Movie TV Pinups; Bridget Hanley: You Can Be an Actress,"
Part 7 – *Tiger Beat.*

ABC affiliate WAPT-TV, Channel 16 (Jackson, Mississippi), signs on this month.

August 7, 1970: Two Worlds" vs. *The CBS Friday Night Movie: Tarzan and the Valley of Gold* (see May 1, 1970); *The Name of the Game,* "The Skin Game," starring Robert Stack as Dan Farrell and guest-starring Suzanne Pleshette, Charles Drake, Hari Rhodes, and Rossano Brazzi, NBC; also WDHN-TV, Channel 18, in Dothan, Alabama, signs on as an affiliate of ABC-TV.

August 14, 1970: To the Victor" vs. *The CBS Friday Night Movie: Nine Hours to Rama* starring Horst Bucholz, Jose Ferrer, Diane Baker, and Robert Morley; Pro-Football – Baltimore Colts meet Kansas City Chiefs, NBC.

August 18, 1970 (see July 18, 1970).

August 21, 1970: The Soldier" vs. *The CBS Friday Night Movie: Hold On* (see May 22, 1970); *The Name of the Game,* "Man of the People," starring Gene Barry as Glenn Howard and guest-starring Vera Miles, Fernando Lamas, Robert Alda, Jackie Coogan, and Patricia Medina, NBC.

August 22, 1970 – *TV Guide* – Vol. 18., No. 34, Issue #908 – TV Teletype: Hollywood – Joseph Finnigan reports that *Brides'* Bridget Hanley will be guest-starring on next season's *The Odd Couple.*

August 28, 1970 – *Brides* pre-empted by pro-football – New York Giants vs. Pittsburgh Steelers in pre-season game.

August 29, 1970 – *TV Guide* – Vol. 18., No. 35, Issue #909 – TV Tele-type: Hollywood – Joseph Finnigan reports that *Brides'* Bobby Sherman will be guest-starring on next season's *Bracken's World*.

Week of August 29-September 4, 1970 – Bobby Sherman guests on musical special, *Now Explosion,* a twenty-eight hour special telethon of Top 40 Hits.

September 1970: What It's Like to Tour with Bobby Sherman!" *Flip Teen;* Bridget Hanley: Three Lucky Contest Winners" *Tiger Beat;* Bridget Hanley – *Teen Life;* Bridget Hanley: You Can Be an Actress," Part 8 – *Tiger Beat.*

September 4, 1970: A Wild Colonial Boy" vs. *The CBS Friday Night Movie: Five Weeks in a Balloon* starring Red Buttons, Fabian, Barbara Eden, and Sir Cedric Hardwicke; *The Name of the Game,* "Jenny Wilde is Drowning," starring Tony Franciosa as Jeff Dillon and guest-starring Pamela Franklin, Frank Gorshin, Gavin MacLeod, and Ann Prentiss, NBC.

Week of September 5-11, 1970 – *Now Explosion* – ten-hour special starring Bobby Sherman et al.

September 18, 1970 – *Here Come the Brides'* final telecast: The Last Winter" vs. *The CBS Friday Night Movie: Casino Royale* starring David Niven, Deborah Kerr, Peter Sellers, Ursula Andress, Orson Welles, Woody Allen and Barbara Bouchet; *The Name of the Game,* "So Long, Baby and Amen," starring Robert Stack as Dan Farrell and guest-star-ring Julie Harris, Sal Mineo, Laurie Prange, James Gregory, and Harold J. Stone, NBC.

October 1970 – Bridget Hanley: You Can Be an Actress," Part 9 – *Tiger Beat.*

November 1970 – *Screen Scene* announces that *Here Come The Brides* is now in syndication

---

1. *TV Guide*, Vol. 15, No. 52, Dec 30, 1967, Issue #770
2. *TV Guide*, Vol. 16, No. 9, March 2, 1968, Issue #779
3. *TV Guide*, Vol. 16. No. 11, March 16, 1968, Issue #781
4. *TV Guide*, Vol. 16, No. 34, August 24, 1968, Issue #804
5. Dave Kaufman – *The Only Complete Guide to TV 69*, pg. 29, New Nighttime Series, *Here Come the Brides,* Wednesday, ABC, Signet, ©1968, Darien House, Inc.

*Episode #1: "Here Come the Brides"*
6. Brown – 2007
7. Hanley – 2007
8. Tolsky – 2007
9. Carlson – 2007
10. Hoag – 2007

*Episode #2: "A Crying Need"*
11. *TV Guide* – Vol. 16, No. 39 – September 28, 1968, Issue #809
12. George – 2000
13. Claver – 2007
14. Blinn – 2007
15. Blinn – 2007
16. Hanley – 2007
17. Tolsky – 2007
18. Claver – 2007
19. Hanley – 2007
20. Blinn – 2007
21. Hanley – 2008
22. Tolsky – 2007
23. Metcalfe – 2007

*Episode #3: "And Jason Makes Five"*
24. Blinn – 2007
25. Claver – 2007
26. Brown – 2007
27. Hanley – 2007
28. Metcalfe – 2007
29. Arthur Gardner – telephone interview – 2007

*Episode #4: "Man of the Family"*
30. Blinn – 2007
31. Henry Beckman to *Brides* fan Sharon – Message #2620 – Mon Sep 6, 1999 5:27 pm
32. Hanley – 2007
33. Blinn – 2007
34. Hanley – 2007
35. Ibid – 2007
36. Colley – 2007
37. Tompkins – 2007
38. Ibid

*Episode #5: "A Hard Card to Play"*
39. Blinn – 2007
40. Hanley – 2007
41. Ibid

*Episode #6: "Letter of the Law"*
42. Brown – 2007
43. Blinn – 2007
44. Hanley – 2007

*Episode #7: "Lovers and Wanderers"*
45. Blinn – 2007
46. Hoag – 2007
47. Balduzzi – 2007
48. Metcalfe – 2007
49. Hoag – 2007

*Episode #8: "A Jew Named Sullivan"*
50. Claver – 2007
51. Ibid
52. Blinn – 2007
53. Brown – 2007
54. Hanley – 2008
55. Tolsky – 2007
56. Ibid
57. William Windom – telephone interview – 2001
58. Michel Ciment, *Kazan on Kazan*, The Viking Press: "New York (1974), page 152.
59. Claver – 2007
60. Brown – 2007
61. Hanley – 2008
62. Tolsky – 2008
63. Hoag – 2007
64. Hanley – 2007
65. Claver – 2007
66. Blinn – 2007
67. Tolsky – 2007
68. Arthur Gardner – telephone interview – 2007
69. Hanley – 2008

*Episode #9: "The Stand-Off"*
70. Colley – 2007
71. Ibid
72. Ibid
73. Ibid
74. Ibid
75. Ibid
76. Hanley – 2007
77. Hoag – 2007
78. Review – *Here Come the Brides* – *TV Guide* – Vol. 16, No. 52, December 28, 1968, Issue #822

*Episode #10: "A Man and His Magic"*
79. Blinn – 2007
80. Hanley – 2008
81. Tolsky – 2007
82. Hanley – 2008
83. Balduzzi – 2007
84. Peter Mark Richman – telephone interview – 2002
85. Butler – 2003

*Episode #11: "A Christmas Place"*
86. Blinn – 2007

87. Hanley – 2008
88. Claver – 2007
89. Hanley – 2008
90. Tolsky – 2007
91. Lodge – 2007
92. Hanley – 2008

*Episode #12: "After a Dream Comes Mourning"*
93. Blinn – 2007
94. Silbersher – 2008
95. Ibid

*Episode #14: "The Firemaker"*
96. Robert de Roos: "I Sound Like a Fathead – Monte Markham Explains His Approach to Acting" *TV Guide* – Vol. 15, No. 52, December 30, 1967 – Issue #770, pg. 13.
97. Hanley – 2008
98. Tolsky – 2007
99. Blinn – 2007
100  Hanley – 2008
101. Tolsky – 2007
102. Hoag – 2007
103. Lodge – 2007

*Episode #15: "Wives for Wakando"*
104. Blinn – 2007
105. Hanley – 2008
106. Tolsky – 2007
107. Joan Crosby: "Ansara Would Play Indian Again" *The Indianapolis Star-TV Week* – March 21, 1971
108. Hanley – 2008
109. Ibid
110. Tolsky – 2007

*Episode #16: "A Kiss Just for So"*
111. Blinn – 2007
112. Forest – 2007
113. Hanley – 2008
114. Tolsky – 2007
115. Forest – 2007
116. Hanley – 2008
117. Lodge – 2007

*Episode #17: "Democracy Inaction"*
118. Blinn – 2007
119. Hoag – 2007
120. Hanley – 2008

*Episode #18: "One Good Lie Deserves Another"*
121. Blinn – 2007
122. Hanley – 2008

*Episode #19: "One to a Customer"*
123. Blinn – 2007

124. Hanley – 2008
125. Balduzzi – 2007

*Episode #20: "A Dream that Glitters"*
126. Hanley – 2008

*Episode #21: "The Crimpers"*
127. Hanley – 2008

*Episode #22: "Mr. and Mrs. J. Bolt"*
128. Blinn – 2007
129. Hanley – 2008

*Episode #23: "A Man's Errand"*
130. Hanley – 2008

*Episode #24: "Loggerheads"*
131. Blinn – 2007
132. Tolsky – 2007
133. Hanley – 2008
134. Ibid

*Episode #25: "Marriage: "Chinese Style"*
135. Blinn – 2007
136. Hanley – 2008
137. Lodge – 2007

*Episode #26: "The Deadly Trade"*
138. Blinn – 2007
139. Hanley – 2008
140. R.G. Armstrong – 2001
141. Hanley – 2008
142. Ibid

*The Second Season – Prologue – A Change in Direction*
143. Lenard – Fan Club newsletter – February 1969
144. Brown – 2007
145. Blinn – 2007
146. Ibid
147. Hanley – 2008
148. Brown – 2007
149. Hanley – 2007
150. George – 2004
151. Blinn – 2007
152. Brown – 2007
153. Blinn – 2007
154. George – 2004

*Episode #27: "A Far Cry from Yesterday"*
155. Blinn – 2007
156. Eric Chase – interview by telephone – 2008
157. Claver – 2007
158. Chase – interview – 2008

*Episode #28: "The Wealthiest Man in Seattle"*
159. Blinn – 2007
160. Balduzzi – 2007
161. Blinn – 2007

*Episode #29: "The Soldier"*
162. Chase – 2008
163. Hanley – 2008
164. Blinn – 2007
165. Biheller – 2008
166. Lodge – 2007

*Episode #30: "Next Week, East Lynne"*
167. Blinn – 2007
168. Brown – 2007
169. Lodge – 2007
170. Silo – 2007
171. Susan Silo – 2007
172. Hanley – 2008
173. Tolsky – 2007
174. Hanley – 2008
175. Silo – 2007
176. Tolsky – 2007

*Episode #31: "A Wild Colonial Boy"*
177. Blinn – 2007
178. Lodge – 2007
179. Brown – 2007
180. Hanley – 2008

*Episode #32: "Hosanna's Way"*
181. Blinn – 2007
182. Claver – 2007
183. Blinn – 2007
184. Hanley – 2008
185. Chase – 2008
186. Lodge – 2007
187. Cass – 2007
188. Gardner – 2007
189. Kessler – 2007

*Episode #33: "The Road to the Cradle"*
190. Cass – 2007
191. Blinn – 2007
192. Hanley – 2008
193. Blinn – 2007
194. Gardner – 2007

*Episode #34: "The Legend of Big Foot"*
195. Blinn – 2007
196. Chase – 2008

*Episode #35: "Land Grant"*
197. Blinn – 2007
198. Antonio – 2008
199. Hoag – 2007
200. Brody – by e-mail – December 19, 2007
201. Lodge – 2007
202. Cass – 2007
203. Brody – December 19, 2007
204. Antonio – 2008
205. Claver – 2007
206. Hanley – 2008
207. Valente – 2007
208. Hoag – 2007
209. Lodge – 2007
210. Cass – 2007
211. Kessler – 2007
212. Brody – 2007
213. Blinn – 2007
214. Valente – 2007

*Episode #36: "The Eyes of London Bob"*
215. Blinn – 2007
216. Lodge – 2007
217. Forest – 2007

*Episode #37: "The Fetching of Jenny"*
218. Blinn – 2007
219. Hanley – 2008
220. Ibid
221. Bruce Lansbury – telephone interview – 2007

*Episode #38: "His Sister's Keeper"*
222. Blinn – 2007
223. Lodge – 2007
224. Cass – 2007

*Episode #39: "Lorenzo Bush"*
225. Blinn – 2007
226. Tolsky – 2007
227. Hanley – 2007
228. Chase – 2008
229. Blinn – 2007
230. Ibid

*Episode #40: "A Bride for Obie Brown"*
231. Blinn – 2007
232. Cass – 2007
233. Hanley – 2008
234. Tolsky – 2007
235. Chase – 2008
236. Hanley – 2008
237. Blinn – 2007

*Episode #41: "To Break the Bank of Tacoma"*
238. Blinn – 2007
239. Hanley -2008

*Episode #42: "Debt of Honor"*
240. Blinn – 2007
241. Hanley – 2008
242. Ibid
243. Ibid

*Episode #43: "The She-Bear"*
244. Blinn – 2007
245. Hanley – 2008
246. Lodge – 2007

*Episode #44: "Another Game in Town"*
247. Blinn – 2007
248. Brody – 2007

*Episode #45: "Candy and the Kid"*
249. Blinn – 2007
250. Hanley – 2008

*Episode #46: "Two Worlds"*
251. Blinn – 2007
252. Antonio – 2008
253. Carlson – 2007
254. Hanley – 2008
255. Tolsky – 2007

*Episode #47: "To the Victor"*
256. Blinn – 2007
257. Brody – 2007
258. Antonio – 2008
259. Brody – 2007

*Episode #48: "How Dry We Are"*
260. Blinn – 2007
261. Tolsky – 2007

*Episode #49: "Bolt of Kilmaron"*
262. Blinn – 2007
263. Dorothy C. Fontana – by e-mail – February 18, 2008
264. Hanley – 2008
265. Biheller – 2008
266. Fontana – February 18, 2008

*Episode #50: "Absalom"*
267. Hanley – 2008
268. Chase – 2008

*Episode #51: "The Last Winter"*
269. Blinn – 2007

*Episode #52: "Two Women"*

270. George – 2003
271. Lodge – 2007
272. Beckman – Message #3640 -Fri Oct 29, 1999 11:06 am
273. Hanley – 2008
274. Blinn – 2007
275. George – 2003
276. Butler – 2004
277. George – 2002
278. Butler – 2003
279. Hanley – 2008
280. Tolsky – 2007
281. George – 2003
282. Claver – 2007
283. Hanley – 2008
284. Tolsky – 2007
285. Valente – 2007
286. Lodge – 2007

*End note – The cancellation of Here Come the Brides*

287. Hanley – 2008
288. Brown – 2007
289. Blinn – 2007
290. Hanley – 2008
291. Brown – 2007
292. Hanley – 2008

"I got to a place where I realized every time I would see a woman standing by with her hand up to her mouth while some guys were fighting over something, I would think, Oh. Yeah. Okay. Sure. We're just gonna stand there with our little hands up to our mouth going, 'Oooo, Ooooo.' I could never stand by with my hand to my mouth. I'd have to pull someone apart."[1]

*Here Come The Brides* guest star Lynda Day George

# Chapter 17

# *The Legacy of*
# Here Come the Brides

After two seasons of General Candy Pruitt and her friends, the likelihood of seeing weak female characters on television was becoming more and more remote. In fact, on September 20, 1970, (the day *Here Come the Brides* began airing repeats on Los Angeles, California, independent station KCOP (Channel 13) at 6 p.m., ABC-TV premiered the Revolutionary War-period, secret-agent series *The Young Rebels*. Playing the female lead in the series was Bridget Hanley's good friend, Hilarie Thompson; Thompson portrayed secret-agent Elizabeth Coates.

Even more significantly, of the eighteen new series to premiere on ABC, CBS, and NBC in the 1970-71 season, there were thirteen to feature a regular female character. Eight of these series were on ABC. Of the other five, both *The Mary Tyler Moore Show* (Mary Tyler Moore as Mary Richards) and *Nancy* (Renne Jarrett as Nancy Smith), gave top billing to a young woman. Both series had already debuted before ABC launched its premiere week on Sunday, September 20; *Nancy* began on Thursday, September 17 on NBC; *The Mary Tyler Moore Show* on Saturday, September 19 on CBS. CBS had also introduced *The Storefront Lawyers* — co-starring Sheila Larken as lawyer Deborah Sullivan on Wednesday, September 16, and *The Interns* — Sandra Smith as Dr. Lydia Thorpe, Elaine Giftos as Bobbe Marsh, on Friday, September 18. *The Interns* was executive produced by *Here Come the Brides'* Bob Claver; *Brides'* William Blinn was the story consultant on that series. Also premiering on September 18 on CBS was the Andy Griffith series, *Headmaster*, with Claudette Nevins as Griffith's wife Margaret Thompson. Margaret was an English teacher at the school where her husband, Andy Thompson (Griffith) was headmaster; co-starring in the program was (future *Eight is Enough* regular) Lani O'Grady as Judy.

One day after ABC premiered *The Young Rebels*, the network introduced two Aaron Spelling series, *The Silent Force* and *The Young Lawyers*. Featuring veteran actor Lee J. Cobb, *The Young Lawyers* co-starred black actress Judy Pace as Pat Walters, one of two young lawyers (the other was Zalman King as Aaron Silverman) who operate a neighborhood law office in Boston. The office provides free legal assistance to clients unable to afford a lawyer. Less idealistic was Spelling's *The Silent Force* starring Ed Nelson, Lynda Day (George), and Percy Rodriguez as three undercover government agents battling organized crime in America. The half-hour series was sold to ABC with an hour-long pilot which spent a good bit of time examining the background of team member Amelia Cole (George) and her reasons for joining the Force. George was the favorite of the series' late creator Luther Davis. Davis showed very

*Left to right: Ed Nelson, Percy Rodriguez, and Lynda Day George preparing some sort of sabotage against the Organization in the ahead-of-its time, ABC-TV secret-agent drama,* The Silent Force.

little interest in exploring the backgrounds of Amelia's four male associates (also in the pilot were Norman Alden and Richard Van Vleet).

A few weeks later, Aaron Spelling introduced another dramatic series. Entitled *The Most Deadly Game*, it co-starred Yvette Mimieux as college-trained criminologist Vanessa Smith. Working with former military intelligence officer Jonathan Croft (George Maharis), and Mr. Arcane (Ralph Bellamy) Vanessa tackled only the most unusual murder cases. Originally slated for Mimieux's role was *The Farmer's Daughter* star Inger Stevens. Perhaps Stevens' unexpected death was the reason *The Most Deadly Game* did not premiere until Saturday, October 10.

With the exception of Tuesday night, where the only new Tuesday series were NBC's variety entry, *The Don Knotts Show*, and the later *The Most Deadly Game*, starting on September 20, 1970 and continuing up through September 25th, for every night of the week, ABC-TV introduced to its audience a television series where a young woman played an important part. On Wednesday, September 23, black actress Ena Hartmann began a co-starring role as Santa Luisa, California, police department secretary Katy Grant on the Burt Reynolds series, *Dan August*. The following day, Tracy Reed (who would go on to play the role of Carol Broadhurst in the 1970-77 *NBC Mystery Movie* entry, *McCloud*) co-starred as Corie Bratter in a black version of *Barefoot in the Park*. That same evening, African-American actress Chelsea Brown played Tag, and June Harding played Ann on the Vince Edwards drama, *Matt Lincoln*.

The next day, Friday, September 25, *Here Come the Brides* executive producer Bob Claver launched a show which would prove to be an even bigger hit than *Brides* — 1970-74's *The Partridge Family*. Starring veteran actress and musical lead Shirley Jones as Shirley Partridge, the leader of the family, *The Partridge Family* also featured younger actresses Susan Dey (third-billed) as Laurie Partridge, and Suzanne Crough as Tracy Partridge.

One would be hard pressed to imagine a previous TV season where actresses of such a wide variety were playing such interesting and diverse regular series parts. Not too surprisingly, once the trend of actresses headlining their own series got underway, there was no turning back. For example, the following season (1971-72), motion picture star Shirley MacLaine debuted as globe-trotting reporter-photographer Shirley Logan in the situation comedy, *Shirley's World*. This series took the situation comedy concept to a new level — *Shirley's World* was filmed on location in England, Scotland, Hong Kong, Tokyo, etc. 1971-72 was also the season when Susan Saint James, whose Peggy Maxwell had acted as editorial assistant to all three male leads on the 1968-71 NBC anthology, *The Name of the Game*, began a long-running role as Sally McMillan on *The NBC Mystery Movie* entry, *McMillan and Wife*. Then there was Marlyn Mason in the interesting role of Nikki Bell on the James Franciscus series, *Longstreet*. And ABC's *Owen Marshall, Counselor at Law*, which co-starred future television director Jennifer Darling. In this same season, *Here Come the Brides'* Henry Beckman took fourth billing after Sandy Duncan, Valerie Armstrong, and Kathleen Freeman on Duncan's situation comedy, *Funny Face*. There was also an up-and-coming actress by the name of Donna Mills who co-starred with Larry Hagman in the situation comedy,

*The Good Life.* Mills was but a short time away from playing the very dramatic role of a tough policewoman in the Aaron Spelling TV-movie, *The Bait. The Bait* was based on the novel of the same title by real-life policewoman Dorothy Uhnak.

In the 1972-73 season, Sandy Duncan returned in *The Sandy Duncan Show,* Samantha Eggar played Anna in the series, *Anna and the King,* and Beatrice Arthur was *Maude.* Then there was *The Julie Andrews Hour, Search* with *Here Come the Brides* guest Angel Tompkins as technical specialist Gloria Harding, *Cool Million* with Adele Mara as James Farentino's superior, and Meredith Baxter as Bridget in the comedy, *Bridget Loves Bernie.* On maternity leave during *Mission: Impossible's* seventh season, Lynda Day George's temporary absence from the series was explained with the information that her character, Casey, was on temporary assignment in Europe. Casey nonetheless managed to remain a member of the team, contributing masks and so forth while carrying on with her European assignments. *Ironside* leading lady Barbara Anderson temporarily filled in for George in the role of ex-con turned IMF agent Mimi Davis.

The following season (1973-74), the season featuring Blythe Danner as lady lawyer Amanda Banner in the comedy *Adam's Rib,* the-two-or-more-women-leads concept kicked off with veteran actresses Helen Hayes and Mildred Natwick's *NBC Wednesday Mystery Movie* entry, *The Snoop Sisters.*

The following season, *Little House on the Prairie* (based on the *Little House* novels by Laura Ingalls Wilder) had one man (Michael Landon) with a family of four women: Karen Grassle as his wife, Caroline, Melissa Sue Anderson as his eldest daughter Mary, Melissa Gilbert as future novelist Laura Ingalls Wilder, and Lindsay/Sidney Greenbush as Carrie, the baby of the family. In this same season, three actresses headlined and portrayed the title detective characters of their respective series. Most successful of the three programs was Angie Dickinson's *Police Woman* with Dickinson as Sgt. Suzanne "Pepper" Anderson. Pepper was an undercover cop for the criminal conspiracy department of the LAPD. In *Get Christie Love,* black actress Teresa Graves also played an undercover officer. Graves' Detective Christie Love worked for the LAPD's Special Investigations Division. Despite this series'basis on a Dorothy Uhnak novel, it only lasted a season, as did *The NBC Sunday Mystery Movie* entry, *Amy Prentiss.* The excellent Jessica Walter played the title character. Amy was the Chief of Detectives of the San Francisco Police Department.

Though the next season continued to expand roles for women — Robert Brown's friend, Anne Meara, played the title character in the legal drama, *Kate McShane;* Julie Gregg was producer Maggie Spencer in *Mobile One;* it was in the following season: 1976-77, when things really took off for young actresses. In addition to two female superhero series: Lindsay Wagner as *The Bionic Woman,* Lynda Carter as *Wonder Woman,* there was the female buddy sitcom, *Laverne and Shirley.* Penny Marshall and Cindy Williams played the title characters.

But the program that really did it, the show which firmly established the female buddy series was the ABC hit, *Charlie's Angels,* with Kate Jackson, Farrah Fawcett-Majors and Jaclyn Smith. By the time *Angels* ended its five-season run, audiences had been treated to Priscilla Barnes and Debra Clinger as traveling reporters Rebecca

Tomkins and Amy Waddell on the 1978 adventure/drama, *The American Girls*, Denise Du Barry as Head Nurse Samantha Green on the second season of Robert Conrad's WWII adventure, *Baa Baa Black Sheep/Black Sheep Squadron* (playing Sam's fellow nurses were Kathy McCullem, Brianne Leary, and Nancy Conrad), Pat Klous, Connie Sellecca, and Kathryn Witt as stewardesses Marcy Bowers, Lisa Benton, and Pam Bellagio on the 1978 adventure, *Flying High*. There was also Pamela Sue Martin as teenage detective Nancy Drew on *The Hardy Boys/Nancy Drew Mysteries*, Anne Lockhart (June's daughter) as the fighter pilot Sheba on *Battlestar Galactica* and Erin Gray as Col. Wilma Deering: commander of the Earth's defenses in the science-fiction adventure, *Buck Rogers in the 25th Century*.

These, and the many other positive female characters seen in the TV-movies, TV-miniseries, and television series episodes of the 1970s, would have made Bridget Hanley's General Candy Pruitt proud.

"They're just more fun, and lovely, and we just have a great time. Those that can — come to see all of my plays at Theater West. They're just…they reached out. I think they're largely responsible for the DVD."

*Here Come The Brides* leading lady Bridget Hanley talking about the series' fans

Postscript

# Bridget Hanley, Robert Brown, and the Here Come the Brides Fans

According to its leading lady Bridget Hanley, the fan base for *Here Come the Brides* began during the series' original run. Recalls Hanley: "A lot of it happened…it started with a young woman in Texas who wanted to do a fan club. It was called 'Bridget's Boosters,' and I have big buttons with me on it. It (the button) said, 'I am a Bridget Booster.' She did newsletters and sent out mail to fans, then she started a 'Bridget's Boosters' club. I think I still tried to keep up with my share of it when Brownyn was born. That was in '71, but it just got to be more than I could handle, really.

"Then there was a young woman who came onboard who lived in Canada," continues the actress. "She started another kind of club. She put together our twentieth reunion. Then two other women — they kind of came to our attention when I…we met with them in one of the apartment buildings near Warner Brothers where I was staying. I had sold my house after Swack passed away. Then I was getting ready to move in the house I'm in now. We met with them, showed them all of our memorabilia and everything, and they got busy doing websites. I think the one was busy doing Susan [Tolsky] and the other was doing me. Then of course there's the gang there is now. [Hanley is referring to the fans in the Internet-based group.] They are just fabulous. They do this party every year. They go someplace — they go to New Bedford, they went to Seattle one year, and I arranged it so I would be there, too. We got to see each other in my hometown of Edmonds, and I did the underground Seattle tour with them. They were largely responsible for saving the cabin. The fans helped save my grandparents' log cabin in my little hometown of Edmonds. They have just been amazing — they have just been forever there. They're a wonderful gang. Every time we do something at the theater, they come and we try to go out and yak. It's really been — been many really loving relationships."

During the Seattle gathering, Hanley and the fans watched numerous *Brides* episodes. "I went to watch some of the episodes with them, snuggling under blankets and eating popcorn," she laughs. "It was fun. Then they would ask questions, and I would say, 'Well, no, no, this is my take on that,' and they love that, you know. It just amazes me that there are so many theories and everything. I love the fact that they spend so much time, you know. I have a stack of scripts that they've written, some of them are pretty damn good. It's just fascinating to me that they all get into it so much — it's just wild."

"Get into it" is a very good way to describe the types of conversations and analyses that characterize the discussions one can regularly find on the *Here Come the Brides* ever growing Yahoo group. The *Brides* ladies (most of the fans are women) definitely know their stuff. For example, there was the discussion about the staircase at Lottie's (suggesting a second floor) not being reflected in the exterior false front of the saloon (This problem was corrected during the second season) and the discussion about the furniture in the Bolt cabin changing time and again. This caused one fan to point out that she did not notice such things until years later when she could watch the episodes again and again. This same fan pointed out that the people making *Brides* probably never imagined there would come a day when viewers could watch the same series and same episodes over and over.

Then there was the fan who pointed out (very correctly) that two-hour pilots were not made back in the late '60s (unless the studio was Universal, and the network was NBC.) This same fan also explained to the other members that ninety-nine percent of all pilots didn't even make it to the air. The reason? It was just too expensive.

Another very helpful fan explained the mystery as to why viewers never heard the lyrics to the series theme, "Seattle." According to this individual, the instrumental-only version of the opening theme was replaced by the vocal version (by the New Establishment) midway through the first season. When *Brides* later went into syndication, Screen Gems replaced the vocal version with an instrumental-only version for all episodes. The lyrics can be heard on one 2nd season episode that the studio somehow overlooked when syndicating the show. The lyrics can also be heard on the CD, *Television's Greatest Hits – In Living Color #5.*

*Here Come the Brides* being mentioned on *Nightline* and more than one episode of *Mystery Science Theatre 3000* made for other conversational threads; then there was the anecdote about Bridget Hanley playing the seamstress who took down the deceased Scrooge's bed curtains in the theatrical production of *A Christmas Carol* and, on another occasion, the point that in real Seattle history, there'd been a story about Seattle's first bank having a safe without a back. (In "Next Week, East Lynne," the safe in Ben Perkins' general store has no back.) The safe in Seattle history was owned by one Dexter Horton. Horton's daughter later claimed that "the safe with no back" story was a joke.

The fan who provided the above tidbit also told the group why Washington state cable station KONG-TV (which had been airing reruns of *Brides*) was taking the series off the air. The station's program director explained to this individual that they had purchased *Brides* to run each episode three times. This turning out to be an expensive practice, the station was dropping *HCTB* in favor of newer series. Newer shows, the program director explained to the fan, could be aired much more cheaply.

A particularly interesting bit of information came through a post when a fan, who'd met Bobby Sherman and other members of the cast, talked about the cars driven by the *Brides* stars during the years the series was made. In addition to Sherman's midnight blue Rolls Royce, Bridget Hanley drove a gray Thunderbird, Robert Brown had a two-seater red Mercedes, and Henry Beckman drove a classic "Woody"-type station wagon.

Through these friendly and knowledgeable *Brides* fans, this writer has learned that *Here Come the Brides'* name in Portuguese was "The Fiancées Had Arrived." But when the program was aired in Brazil (where Portuguese is one of the languages spoken!) it was under the title, "The Adventurers." *Brides* fans also point out that the show has aired in France and Australia.

Even more fascinating was the revelation from one group member that after she and her friends watched the show, they would discuss it the next day at school, perform scenes from the episode, and try to fill in missing scenes. This fan remembered that even the creative writing assignments she and the other students received at school seemed to have *Brides* themes.

In 1998, thirty years after the premiere of *Brides*, the fans had their first "Get Together," or "GT." The GT is a planned event where *Brides* fans from numerous parts of the country agree to meet in a certain city. The first GT was in Los Angeles, the second in Seattle (this one was attended by Henry Beckman and his son, Stuart), the third was in New Bedford, Massachusetts (the actual city was Milford, but it was close to New Bedford.) Once again, Henry and Stuart Beckman attended, as did one of Mark Lenard's daughters. This GT was preceded by a totally unplanned GT in January 2000 at the Hollywood Collector's Show. Attending this GT were Bridget Hanley, Susan Tolsky, Mitzi Hoag, Henry Beckman, Eric Chase, and Patti Cohoon. By then, *Brides* fans had formed their online group — that group began in 1999.

Not long after the Massachusetts GT, there was a small GT in Edmonds, Washington, for Bridget Hanley's "Save the Cabin" effort. As noted previously, the effort was successful. In 2001, the GT took place in San Francisco, in 2002, Cleveland or Cincinnati, in 2003, Seattle, in 2004, Vermont, in 2005, Williamsburg, Virginia. The most recent GT — celebrating the series' fortieth anniversary — was held in Los Angeles, California. That way, the fans could visit filming locales and such.

Despite *Here Come the Brides* entering its fortieth anniversary, the series fan base continues to grow. Marvels Bridget Hanley: "I can't tell you how many letters I still get, and I'm sure everybody does, saying, with special emphasis, how it helped them grow up, how it helped them have confidence. I get so much fan mail and also the e-mails, and things, of people telling me how it affected their childhood. Most people seem to really, really love it. And have very, very fond memories of it…They really liked it."

With the release of *Brides* first season on DVD, Hanley began getting even more mail. "Now I'm getting a lot of e-mails and fan mail and stuff saying how much it means to see it again," she says. "It recalls a really lovely part of their life, or part of their family life, that they all watched it together."

One fan letter really touched Hanley. "It was an amazing story," remembers the actress. "She [the fan] would think of Candy Pruitt when things were rough, [and ask herself] 'What would Candy do?' I mean, it makes me so proud to have been able, not for myself, to be able to play a character like that — that would have that kind of effect."

As noted earlier, when Bridget Hanley and her fellow castmates were doing *Brides*, they approached their work with great enthusiasm. "We just loved the show and we thought it was…for all of us, it was just a very precious magical time," says the actress. "And, to know it affected children when they were growing up and also that they still remember it, and they're all going out and buying the DVD — it's just fabulous. And they're showing it to their kids, and their kids are getting hooked — it's just wonderful."[2]

Adds series star Robert Brown, "It was a family show, where everybody could sit down and find something in it. And I'm still getting mail, wonderful, touching letters from people that talk about what it was like when they were growing up, and how this show was like a family for them that they didn't have. If it was still around, we would not have kids dressed with tattoos, and plugs in their mouths and tongue, and baggy pants and shaving their heads, and gangs and fights and shooting."

Later inspiring professional historical fiction writer Charlotte Fox to pen the novel, *Spirit of the Northwest*, (the book updated the *Brides* characters to some thirty years later, and at one time, there was a possibility *Brides* director E.W. Swackhamer might put it on the screen!), forty years after its original run, *Here Come the Brides* continues to attract new fans. Why is probably best summed up by the show's star Robert Brown: "They [the writers/producers] created a terrific show!"[3]

*Bridget Hanley as 'Candy Pruitt' and Bobby Sherman as 'Jeremy Bolt'.* PHOTO
COURTESY BRIDGET HANLEY

# On The Air

U.S. Stations broadcasting *Here Come The Brides* during it's original network run (including Bermuda and U.S. Virgin Islands). Almost 170 stations aired the program.

WDHN-TV, Channel 18 – Dothan, Alabama *(signed on August 7, 1970)*
WKAB-TV, Channel 32 – Montgomery, Alabama
KIMO-TV, Channel 13 – Anchorage, Alaska
KFAR, Channel 2 – Fairbanks, Alaska *(secondary ABC affiliate)*
KINY, Channel 8 – Juneau, Alaska
KGUN-TV, Channel 9 – Tucson, Arizona
KAIT-TV, Channel 8 – Jonesboro, Arkansas
KATV, Channel 7 – Little Rock, Arkansas
KABC-TV, Channel 7 – Los Angeles, California
KPLM-TV, Channel 3 – Palm Springs, California *(signed on in November, 1968)*
KRCR-TV, Channel 7 – Redding-Chico, California
KOVR, Channel 13 – Sacramento, California
XETV, Channel 6 – San Diego, California
KGO-TV, Channel 7 – San Francisco, California
KEYT-TV, Channel 3 – Santa Barbara, California
KRDO-TV, Channel 13 – Colorado Springs, Colorado
WNHC-TV, Channel 8 – New Haven/Hartford, Connecticut
WMAL-TV, Channel 7 – Washington, D.C.
WLBW-TV, Channel 10 – Miami/Fort Lauderdale, Florida *(renamed WPLG-TV on March 16, 1970; WLBW from 1964-70; formerly WPST)*
WFTV, Channel 9 – Orlando, Florida
WEAR-TV, Channel 3 – Pensacola, Florida
WQXI-TV, Channel 11 – Atlanta, Georgia *(formerly WAII-TV, renamed WQXI in 1968)*
WJBF-TV, Channel 6 – Augusta, Georgia *(secondary ABC affiliate until December 24, 1968)*
WTVM-TV, Channel 9 – Columbus, Georgia *(secondary ABC affiliate)*

WJCL-TV, Channel 22 – Savannah Georgia *(began broadcasting on August 18, or July 18, 1970)*
KHVH-TV, Channel 4 – Honolulu, Hawaii
KBOI-TV, Channel 2 – Boise, Idaho *(CBS, NBC, ABC)*
KID-TV, Channel 3 – Idaho Falls, Idaho *(CBS, ABC)*
WAND-TV, Channel 17 – Decatur/Springfield, Urbana/Champaign, Illinois
WLS-TV, Channel 7 – Chicago, Illinois *(was WBKB until 1968)*
WSIL-TV, Channel 3 – Harrisburg/Marion/Carbondale, Illinois *(sister station KPOB, Channel 15 covers Poplar Bluff, Missouri, and surrounding areas)*
WQAD-TV, Channel 8 – Moline, Illinois
WRAU-TV, Channel 19 – Peoria-Bloomington, Illinois *(formerly WIRL-TV)*
WREX-TV, Channel 13 – Rockford, Illinois
WTVW-TV, Channel 7 – Evansville, Indiana
WPTA, Channel 21 – Fort Wayne, Indiana
WAND-TV, Channel 17 – Indianapolis, Indiana
WLWI, Channel 13 – Indianapolis, Indiana
KCRG-TV, Channel 9 – Cedar Rapids, Iowa
WOI-TV, Channel 5 – Des Moines-Ames, Iowa
KCAU-TV, Channel 9 – Sioux City, Iowa
KAKE-TV, Channel 10 – Wichita, Kansas
KUPK-TV, Channel 13 – Dodge City, Kansas
WLTV, Channel 13 – Bowling Green, Kentucky
WBLG-TV, Channel 62 – Lexington, Kentucky
WLKY-TV, Channel 32 – Louisville, Kentucky
WBRZ-TV, Channel 2 – Baton Rouge, Louisiana *(secondary ABC affiliate)*
WAFB-TV, Channel 9 – Baton Rouge, Louisiana *(secondary ABC affiliate)*
KATC-TV, Channel 3 – Lafayette, Louisiana
KTBS-TV, Channel 3 – Shreveport, Louisiana
WEMT-TV, Channel 7 – Bangor, Maine
WMTW-TV, Channel 8 – Portland/Auburn/Augusta, Maine
WJZ-TV, Channel 13 – Baltimore, Maryland
WNAC-TV, Channel 7 – Boston, Massachusetts
WHYN-TV, Channel 40 – Springfield/Holyoke, Massachusetts
WXYZ-TV, Channel 7 – Detroit, Michigan
WJMN-TV, Channel 3 – Escanaba/Marquette, Michigan
WJRT-TV, Channel 12 – Flint, Michigan
WZZM-TV, Channel 13- Grand Rapids, Michigan
WDIO-TV, Channel 10 – Duluth, Minnesota; Superior, Wisconsin
WIRT-TV, Channel 13 – Hibbing, Minnesota
KMSP-TV, Channel 9 – Minneapolis/St. Paul, Minnesota
KMMT-TV, Channel 6 – Austin/Albert Lea/Rochester, Minnesota; Mason City, Iowa
WABG-TV, Channel 6 – Greenwood/Greenville, Mississippi
WAPT-TV, Channel 16 – Jackson, Mississippi *(signed on August 1970)*

WTOK-TV, Channel 11 – Meridian, Mississippi *(CBS; secondary ABC affiliate)*
WKDH-TV, Channel 45- Tupelo, Columbus, West Point, Mississippi
WLOX-TV, Channel 13 – Biloxi/Gulfport/Pascagoula, Mississippi
KODE-TV, Channel 12 – Joplin, Missouri
KMBC-TV, Channel 9 – Kansas City, Missouri; Kansas City, Kansas
KTVO-TV, Channel 3 – Kirksville, Missouri; Ottumwa, Iowa
KMTC-TV, Channel 27 – Springfield, Missouri
KQTV, Channel 2 – St. Joseph, Missouri *(was KFEQ-TV until 1969)*
KDNL-TV, St. Louis, Missouri *(secondary ABC and NBC affiliate from 1969 until 1980s, signed on June 8, 1969)*
KFBB-TV, Channel 5 – Great Falls, Montana *(NBC affiliate/ABC secondary affiliate)*
KHOL-TV, Channel 13 – Kearney/Hastings, Grand Island, Nebraska.
KHPL-TV, Channel 6 – Kearney/Hastings, Grand Island, Nebraska.
KHQL-TV, Channel 8 – Albion, Nebraska
KHTL-TV, Channel 4 – Superior, Nebraska
KETV, Channel 7 – Omaha, Nebraska
KDUH, Channel 4 – Scottsbluff, Nebraska *(CBS affiliate, secondary ABC affiliate)*
KSHO-TV, Channel 13 – Las Vegas, Nevada
KOLO-TV, Channel 8 – Reno, Carson City, Nevada *(primarily a CBS affiliate, but carried ABC programs)*
WMUR-TV, Channel 9 – Manchester, New Hampshire
KOAT-TV, Channel 7 – Albuquerque, Santa Fe, New Mexico
KAVE-TV, Channel 6 – Carlsbad, New Mexico
WBJA-TV, Channel 34 – Binghamton, New York
WKBW-TV, Channel 7 – Buffalo, New York
WENY-TV, Channel 36 – Elmira, New York *(founded November 19, 1969)*
WABC-TV, Channel 7 – New York, New York
WORK-TV, Channel 13 – Rochester, New York
WNYS-TV, Channel 9 – Syracuse, New York
WUTR-TV, Channel 20 – Utica, New York *(founded February 28, 1970)*
WLOS-TV, Channel 13 – Asheville, North Carolina; Greenville, Spartanburg, Anderson, South Carolina
WCCB-TV, Channel 18 – Charlotte, North Carolina
WRAL-TV, Channel 5 – Raleigh, Durham, Fayetteville, North Carolina
WNBE-TV, Channel 12 – New Bern, Greenville, Washington, North Carolina *(becomes WCTI-TV in 1970)*
WWAY-TV, Channel 3 – Wilmington, North Carolina
KTHI-TV, Channel 11 – Fargo, North Dakota
WKRC-TV, Channel 12 – Cincinnati, Ohio
WEWS-TV, Channel 5 – Cleveland, Ohio
WTVN-TV, Channel 6 – Columbus, Ohio
WKEF-TV, Channel 22 – Dayton, Ohio
WDHO-TV, Channel 24 – Toledo, Ohio *(becomes full-time ABC affiliate in 1970)*

WSPD-TV, Channel 13 – Toledo, Ohio *(secondary ABC affiliate)*
WTOL-TV, Channel 11 – Toledo, Ohio *(secondary ABC affiliate until 1970)*
WYTV, Channel 33 – Youngstown, Ohio
KSWO-TV, Channel 7 – Lawton, Oklahoma; Wichita Falls, Texas
KOCO-TV, Channel 5 – Oklahoma City, Oklahoma
KTUL, Channel 8 – Tulsa, Oklahoma
KEZI-TV, Channel 9 – Eugene, Oregon
KOBI, Channel 5 – Medford, Oregon *(secondary ABC affiliate)*
KMED-TV, Channel 10 – Medford, Oregon *(secondary ABC affiliate)*
KATU, Channel 2 – Portland, Oregon
WJET-TV, Channel 24 – Erie, Pennsylvania
WTPA-TV, Channel 27 – Harrisburg, Pennsylvania
WFIL-TV, Channel 6 – Philadelphia, Pennsylvania
WTAE-TV, Channel 4 – Pittsburgh, Pennsylvania
WNEP-TV, Channel 16 – Scranton/Wilkes-Barre, Pennsylvania
WUSN-TV, Channel 2 – Charleston, South Carolina
WOLO-TV, Channel 25 – Columbia, South Carolina
WBTW-TV, Channel 13 – Florence, Myrtle Beach, South Carolina *(secondary ABC affiliate)*
KOTA-TV, Channel 3 – Rapid City, South Dakota *(joint primary affiliate of ABC and CBS)*
KORN-TV, Channel 5 – Mitchell, South Dakota
WTVC, Channel 9 – Chattanooga, Tennessee
WBBJ-TV, Channel 7 – Jackson, Tennessee
WKPT-TV, Channel 19 – Kingsport/Johnson City, Tennessee; Bristol, Tennessee/Virginia *(founded August 20, 1969)*
WCYB-TV, Channel 5 – Bristol Virginia-Tennessee; Kingsport/Johnson City, Tennessee *(secondary ABC affiliate until August 20, 1969 when WKPT-TV becomes full-time ABC affiliate)*
WJHL-TV, Channel 11 – Johnson City/Kingsport, Tennessee; Bristol, Tennessee-Virginia *(secondary ABC affiliate until August 20, 1969)*
WTVK, Channel 26 – Knoxville, Tennessee
WHBQ-TV, Channel 13 – Memphis, Tennessee
WSIX-TV, Channel 8 – Nashville, Tennessee
KPAR-TV, Channel 12 – Sweetwater, Abilene, Texas *(secondary ABC affiliate)*
KVII-TV, Channel 7 – Amarillo, Texas
KBMT, Channel 12 – Beaumont, Port Arthur, Texas
KIII-TV, Channel 3 – Corpus Christi, Texas
KXIX-TV, Channel 19 – Victoria, Texas *(satellite station of KIII-TV, founded November 21, 1969)*
WFAA-TV, Channel 8 – Dallas, Fort Worth, Texas
KELP-TV, Channel 13 – El Paso, Texas
KTRK-TV, Channel 13 – Houston, Texas

KSEL-TV, Channel 28 – Lubbock, Texas *(founded November 12, 1968, started carrying ABC programs, then became full-time ABC affiliate in 1969)*

KLBK, Channel 13 – Lubbock, Texas *(secondary ABC affiliate)*

KCBD, Channel 11 – Lubbock, Texas *(secondary ABC affiliate)*

KLTV, Channel 7 – Tyler, Longview, Jacksonville, Texas *(secondary ABC affiliate)*

KTRE-TV, Channel 9 – Lufkin, Nacogdoches, Texas *(secondary ABC affiliate)*

KVKM-TV, Channel 9 – Midland, Odessa, Texas

KBST-TV, Channel 4 – Big Spring, Texas

KONO-TV, Channel 12 – San Antonio, Texas *(becomes KSAT-TV in 1969)*

KGBT-TV, Channel 4 – Harlingen, Brownsville, McAllen, Texas *(secondary ABC affiliate)*

KCPX-TV, Channel 4 – Salt Lake City, Utah

WVNY, Channel 22 – Burlington, Vermont; Plattsburgh, New York *(founded 1968)*

WSVA, Channel 3 – Harrisonburg, Virginia

WVEC-TV, Channel 13 – Hampton Norfolk, Virginia

WLVA-TV, Channel 13 – Lynchburg/Roanoke, Virginia

WXEX-TV, Channel 8 – Petersburg/Richmond, Virginia

KREM-TV, Channel 2 – Spokane, Washington

KOMO-TV, Channel 4 – Seattle, Washington

WHTN-TV, Channel 13 – Huntington, Charleston, West Virginia

WAOW-TV, Channel 9 – Wausau, Wisconsin

WKOW-TV, Channel 27 – Madison, Wisconsin

WLUK-TV, Channel 11 – Green Bay, Wisconsin

WXOW-TV, Channel 19 – La Crosse, Wisconsin *(founded March 7, 1970; satellite sister of Madison station WKOW, Channel 27)*

WITI, Channel 6 – Milwaukee, Wisconsin

KTWO-TV, Channel 2 – Casper, Wyoming *(secondary ABC affiliate)*

KFBC-TV, Channel 5 – Cheyenne, Wyoming *(secondary ABC affiliate)*

ZFB-TV, Channel 7 – Hamilton, Bermuda

WSVI, Channel 8 – Christiansted, U.S. Virgin Islands

1. George – 2002
2. Hanley – 2008
3. Brown – 2007

# Index

# *About the Author*

Jonathan Etter's great enthusiasm for television shows of the 1960s and '70s started at age eight, thanks to the removal of a cyst from a bone in his right leg. Recuperation from the surgery lasted close to a year, severely limiting Jon's physical activities. To help him pass the time, his parents bought him a twelve-inch, black-and-white TV set. By the time he was back on his feet, Jon had become a die-hard fan of such '60s series as *Star Trek, Lost in Space,* and *Jonny Quest.* By the time he graduated from high school, he was already taking notes and keeping records on his favorite shows and performers. During his college years, Jon put in many twelve-hour days in the campus library, poring through reference book after reference book, totally immersing himself in the career or biography of whatever performer or production he was then studying. In 1983 he graduated from Wright State University with a B.A. in history.

Jon's hard work paid off when he became the film historian for the Dayton Victory Theatre's Summer Film Festival from 1985-87. A contributor to *TV Land Moguls: the 60s,* in 2003, Jon published *Quinn Martin, Producer* (his detailed account of Quinn Martin Productions) with McFarland Publishers, Inc.; that critically acclaimed book is now in its second printing. He has also written television series histories and talent profiles for such publications as *Filmfax, Big Reel, The TV Collector,* and *Movie Collector's World.* Now at work on a series history of George Peppard's *Banacek* and a multi-volume authorized biography of TV star Lynda Day George, Jonathan Etter makes his home in Dayton, Ohio. *Gangway, Lord (The) Here Come the Brides Book* is his first book for BearManor Media.

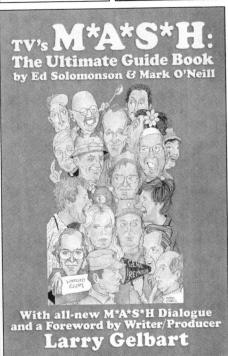
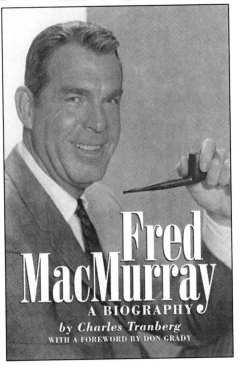

LaVergne, TN USA
22 December 2009
167866LV00003B/4/P